ABNORMAL PSYCHOLOGY

Clinical Perspectives on Psychological Disorders

NINTH EDITION

SUSAN KRAUSS WHITBOURNE

University of Massachusetts Boston

McGraw Hill Education

ABNORMAL PSYCHOLOGY: CLINICAL PERSPECTIVES ON PSYCHOLOGICAL DISORDERS, NINTH EDITION

2 3 4 5 6 7 8 9   LWI   21 20

ISBN   978-1-260-50019-6 (bound edition)
MHID   1-260-50019-5 (bound edition)

ISBN   978-1-260-07668-4 (loose-leaf edition)
MHID   1-260-07668-7 (loose-leaf edition)

Portfolio Manager: *Ryan Treat*
Product Development Manager: *Dawn Groundwater*
Senior Marketing Manager: *AJ Laferrera*
Lead Content Project Manager: *Jodi Banowetz, Sandy Wille*
Content Project Manager: *Ryan Warczynski, Sandra Schnee*
Senior Buyer: *Sandy Ludovissy*
Senior Designer: *Matt Backhaus*
Content Licensing Specialists: *Traci Vaske*
Cover Image: *©martin-dm/E+/Getty Images*
Compositor: *Lumina Datamatics, Inc.*

Library of Congress Cataloging-in-Publication Data

Names: Whitbourne, Susan Krauss, author.
Title: Abnormal psychology : clinical perspectives on psychological
   disorders / Susan Krauss Whitbourne, University of Massachusetts Boston.
Description: Ninth edition. | New York, NY : MHE, [2020] | Includes
   bibliographical references and indexes.
Identifiers: LCCN 2018048679 | ISBN 9781260500196 (alk. paper)
Subjects: LCSH: Psychology, Pathological. | Mental illness.
Classification: LCC RC454 .H334 2020 | DDC 616.89—dc23

LC record available at https://lccn.loc.gov/2018048679

To my wonderful, and growing, family: Richard, Stacey, Jenny, Taylor, Erik, Teddy, and Scarlett

ABOUT THE AUTHOR

©Noah Berg

Susan Krauss Whitbourne is professor emerita of Psychological and Brain Sciences at the University of Massachusetts Amherst, and adjunct professor of Gerontology at University of Massachusetts Boston. She has taught large undergraduate classes in addition to teaching and supervising doctoral students in developmental and clinical psychology. Her clinical experience has covered both inpatient and outpatient settings. Professor Whitbourne is a Fellow of the American Psychological Association.

Professor Whitbourne received her PhD from Columbia University and has a Diplomate in Geropsychology from the American Board of Professional Psychology. She taught at the State University of New York at Geneseo and the University of Rochester prior to moving to the University of Massachusetts Amherst, where she received the university's Distinguished Teaching Award, the Outstanding Advising Award, and the College of Arts and Sciences Outstanding Teacher Award. In 2001, she received the Psi Chi Eastern Region Faculty Advisor Award, and in 2002, the Florence Denmark Psi Chi National Advisor Award. In 2003, she received both the APA Division 20 and Gerontological Society of America Mentoring Awards. In 2018, she was recognized as a Psi Chi Distinguished Member.

As the departmental honors coordinator from 1990–2010, Professor Whitbourne was also the Psi Chi faculty advisor from 1990 through 2017, and the director of the Office of National Scholarship Advisement in the Commonwealth Honors College from 1999 through 2017. The author of 18 books and over 170 journal articles and book chapters, Professor Whitbourne is regarded as an expert on personality development in middle and late life. She is immediate past president of the Eastern Psychological Association and past chair of the Behavioral and Social Sciences Section of the Gerontological Society of America and was a member of the APA Board of Educational Affairs. She serves as APA Council Representative to Division 20 (Adult Development and Aging), having also served as Division 20 president. She is a fellow of APA's Divisions 20, 1 (General Psychology), 2 (Teaching of Psychology), 9 (Society for the Psychological Study of Social Issues), 12 (Clinical Psychology), and 35 (Society for the Psychology of Women). In 2018, Professor Whitbourne was nominated for president-elect of APA. She is also a member of the Board of Directors of the Massachusetts Psychological Association, where she also chairs the Nominations and Governance Committee.

Professor Whitbourne served as an item writer for the Educational Testing Service, was a member of APA's High School Curriculum National Standards Advisory Panel, wrote the APA High School Curriculum Guidelines for Life-Span Developmental Psychology, and serves as an item writer for the Examination for Professional Practice of Psychology. Her 2010 book, *The Search for Fulfillment,* was nominated for an APA William James Award. In 2011, she was recognized with a Presidential Citation from APA. In addition to her academic writing, she writes a highly popular blog on *Psychology Today* entitled "Fulfillment at Any Age" and has appeared on numerous media outlets, including *NBC Dateline* and *Today Show, AM Canada,* and CNN.

ABOUT THE CONTRIBUTOR

Jennifer L. O'Brien is a staff psychologist at the Massachusetts Institute of Technology's Mental Health and Counseling Service, providing psychotherapy to undergraduate and graduate students who present with a broad range of psychological concerns. In addition to her clinical role at MIT, Dr. O'Brien supervises clinical psychology trainees and serves on the MIT Medical Gender & Sexuality care team. Dr. O'Brien specializes in treating mood and anxiety disorders and has expertise in working with the LGBTQ+ population.

Dr. O'Brien received her PhD in clinical psychology from American University in Washington, D.C. Her dissertation, "Empathic Accuracy and Compassion Fatigue in Therapist Trainees," is published in *Professional Psychology: Research and Practice.* She completed her predoctoral internship at the Durham VA Medical Center in Durham, NC, and postdoctoral fellowship at the VA Boston Healthcare System, where she worked with military veterans and received extensive training in providing evidence-based treatments for depression, anxiety, PTSD, and substance abuse.

In addition to her clinical expertise, Dr. O'Brien has published manuscripts on topics such as gender and aging, and has served as editor on peer-reviewed journals. Dr. O'Brien previously contributed to the seventh and eighth editions of *Abnormal Psychology: Clinical Perspectives on Psychological Disorders.*

Courtesy of Jennifer O'Brien

BRIEF CONTENTS

CONTENTS

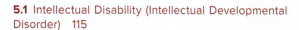

CHAPTER 9
Dissociative and Somatic Symptom Disorders   224

CHAPTER 10
Feeding and Eating Disorders; Elimination Disorders; Sleep-Wake Disorders; and Disruptive, Impulse-Control, and Conduct Disorders   246

CHAPTER 11

Paraphilic Disorders, Sexual Dysfunctions, and Gender Dysphoria   268

CHAPTER 12

Substance-Related and Addictive Disorders   294

CHAPTER 15
Ethical and Legal Issues   374

 McGraw-Hill Education Psychology's APA Documentation Style Guide

With its case-based approach, *Abnormal Psychology: Clinical Perspectives on Psychological Disorders* helps students understand the human side of psychological disorders. The Ninth Edition ties concepts together with an integrated, personalized learning program, providing students the insight they need to study smarter and improve performance.

A Personalized Experience that Leads to Improved Learning and Results

How many students think they know everything about abnormal psychology but struggle on the first exam? Students study more effectively with Connect and SmartBook.

• SmartBook helps students study more efficiently by highlighting what to focus on in the chapter, asking review questions, and directing them to resources until they understand.

• Connect's assignments help students contextualize what they've learned through application, so they can better understand the material and think critically.

• SmartBook creates a personalized study path customized to individual student needs.

• Connect reports deliver information regarding performance, study behavior, and effort so instructors can quickly identify students who are having issues or focus on material that the class hasn't mastered.

New to this edition, SmartBook is now optimized for mobile and tablet and is accessible for students with disabilities. Content-wise, it has been enhanced with improved learning objectives that are measurable and observable to improve student outcomes. SmartBook personalizes learning to individual student needs, continually adapting to pinpoint knowledge gaps and focus learning on topics that need the most attention. Study time is more productive and, as a result, students are better prepared for class and coursework. For instructors, SmartBook tracks student progress and provides insights that can help guide teaching strategies.

SMARTBOOK®

Experience the Power of Data

Abnormal Psychology: Clinical Perspectives on Psychological Disorders harnesses the power of data to improve the instructor and student experiences.

Better Data, Smarter Revision, Improved Results

For this new edition, data were analyzed to identify the concepts students found to be the most difficult, allowing for expansion upon the discussion, practice, and assessment of challenging topics. The revision process for a new edition used to begin with gathering information from instructors about what they would change and what they would keep. Experts in the field were asked to provide comments that pointed out new material to add and dated material to review. Using all these reviews, authors would revise the material. But now, a new tool has revolutionized that model.

McGraw-Hill Education authors now have access to student performance data to analyze and to inform their revisions. These data are anonymously collected from the many students who use SmartBook, the adaptive learning system that provides students with individualized assessment of their own progress. Because virtually every text paragraph is tied to several questions that students answer while using SmartBook, the specific concepts with which students are having the most difficulty are easily pinpointed through empirical data in the form of a "heat map" report.

Powerful Reporting

Whether a class is face-to-face, hybrid, or entirely online, McGraw-Hill Connect provides the tools needed to reduce the amount of time and energy instructors spend administering their courses. Easy-to-use course management tools allow instructors to spend less time administering and more time teaching, while reports allow students to monitor their progress and optimize their study time.

• The **At-Risk Student Report** provides instructors with one-click access to a dashboard that identifies students who are at risk of dropping out of the course due to low engagement levels.

• The **Category Analysis Report** details student performance relative to specific learning objectives and goals, including APA learning goals and outcomes and levels of Bloom's taxonomy.

• **Connect Insight** is a one-of-a-kind visual analytics dashboard—now available for both instructors and students—that provides at-a-glance information regarding student performance.

• The **SmartBook Reports** allow instructors and students to easily monitor progress and pinpoint areas of weakness, giving each student a personalized study plan to achieve success.

Informing and Engaging

McGraw-Hill Connect offers several ways to actively engage students. McGraw-Hill Education Connect is a digital assignment and assessment platform that strengthens the link between faculty, students, and course work. Connect for Abnormal Psychology includes assignable and assessable videos, quizzes, exercises, and Interactivities, all associated with learning objectives for *Abnormal Psychology: Clinical Perspectives on Psychological Disorders,* Ninth Edition.

New to the Ninth Edition, **Power of Process** guides students through the process of critical reading and analysis. Faculty can select or upload content, such as journal articles, and assign guiding questions to move students toward higher-level thinking and analysis.

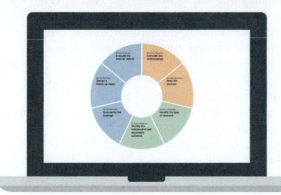

Power of Process for

PSYCHOLOGY

Through the connection of psychology to students' own lives, concepts become more relevant and understandable. **NewsFlash** exercises tie current news stories to key psychological principles and learning objectives. After interacting with a contemporary news story, students are assessed on their ability to make the link between real life and research findings. Topics include brain chemistry and depression, eating disorders in boys, and criticisms of the *DSM-5.*

Thinking Critically About Abnormal Psychology

Updated with *DSM-5* content, **Faces of Abnormal Psychology** connects students to real people living with psychological disorders. Through its unique video program, Faces of

Abnormal Psychology helps students gain a deeper understanding of psychological disorders and provides an opportunity for critical thinking.

Interactive Case Studies help students understand the complexities of psychological disorders. Co-developed with psychologists and students, these immersive cases bring the intricacies of clinical psychology to life in an accessible, gamelike format. Each case is presented from the point of view of a licensed psychologist, a social worker, or a psychiatrist. Students observe sessions with clients and are asked to identify major differentiating characteristics associated with each of the psychological disorders presented. Interactive Case Studies are assignable and assessable through McGraw-Hill Education's Connect.

SUPPORTING INSTRUCTORS WITH TECHNOLOGY

With McGraw-Hill Education, you can develop and tailor the course you want to teach.

McGraw-Hill Campus (www.mhcampus.com) provides faculty with true single sign-on access to all of McGraw-Hill's course content, digital tools, and other high-quality learning resources from any learning management system. McGraw-Hill Campus includes access to McGraw-Hill's entire content library, including eBooks, assessment tools, presentation slides, and multimedia content, among other resources, providing faculty open, unlimited access to prepare for class, create tests/quizzes, develop lecture material, integrate interactive content, and more.

With **Tegrity,** you can capture lessons and lectures in a searchable format and use them in traditional, hybrid, "flipped classes," and online courses. With Tegrity's personalized learning features, you can make study time efficient. Its ability to affordably scale brings this benefit to every student on campus. Patented search technology and real-time learning management system (LMS) integrations make Tegrity the market-leading solution and service.

With McGraw-Hill Education's **Create,** faculty can easily rearrange chapters, combine material from other content sources, and quickly upload content you have written, such as your course syllabus or teaching notes, using McGraw-Hill Education's **Create.** Find the content you need by searching through thousands of leading McGraw-Hill Education textbooks. Arrange your book to fit your teaching style. Create even allows you to personalize your book's appearance by selecting the cover and adding your name, school, and course information. Order a Create book, and you will receive a complimentary print review copy in three to five business days or a complimentary electronic review copy via email in about an hour. Experience how McGraw-Hill Education empowers you to teach your students your way. **http://create.mheducation.com**

Trusted Service and Support

McGraw-Hill Education's Connect offers comprehensive service, support, and training throughout every phase of your implementation. If you're looking for some guidance on how to use Connect, or want to learn tips and tricks from super users, you can find tutorials as you work. Our Digital Faculty Consultants and Student Ambassadors offer insight into how to achieve the results you want with Connect.

Integration with Your Learning Management System

McGraw-Hill integrates your digital products from McGraw-Hill Education with your school LMS for quick and easy access to best-in-class content and learning tools. Build an effective digital course, enroll students with ease, and discover how powerful digital teaching can be.

Available with Connect, integration is a pairing between an institution's learning management system (LMS) and Connect at the assignment level. It shares assignment information, grades, and calendar items from Connect into the LMS automatically, creating an easy to manage course for instructors and simple navigation for students. Our assignment-level integration is available with **Blackboard Learn, Canvas by Instructure,** and **Brightspace by D2L,** giving you access to registration, attendance, assignments, grades, and course resources in real time, in one location.

Instructor Supplements

Instructor's Manual The instructor's manual provides a wide variety of tools and resources for presenting the course, including learning objectives and ideas for lectures and discussions.

Test Bank By increasing the rigor of the test bank development process, McGraw-Hill Education has raised the bar for student assessment. A coordinated team of subject-matter experts methodically vetted each question and set of possible answers for accuracy, clarity, effectiveness, and accessibility; each question has been annotated for level of difficulty, Bloom's taxonomy, APA learning outcomes, and corresponding coverage in the text. Organized by chapter, the questions are designed to test factual, conceptual, and applied understanding. All test questions are available within TestGen™ software and as Word documents.

PowerPoint Presentations The PowerPoint presentations, available in both dynamic, lecture-ready and accessible, WCAG-compliant versions, highlight the key points of the chapter and include supporting visuals. All of the slides can be modified to meet individual needs.

Image Gallery The Image Gallery features the complete set of downloadable figures and tables from the text. These can be easily embedded by instructors into their own PowerPoint slides.

Clinical Perspectives on Psychological Disorders

The subtitle, *Clinical Perspectives on Psychological Disorders*, reflects the emphasis on the experience of clients and clinicians in their efforts to facilitate each individual's maximum functioning. Each chapter begins with an actual case study that typifies the disorders in that chapter, then returns to the case study at the end with the outcome of a prescribed treatment on the basis of the best available evidence. Throughout the chapter, the author translates the symptoms of each disorder into terms that capture the core essence of the disorder. The philosophy is that students should be able to appreciate the fundamental nature of each disorder without necessarily having to memorize all of its diagnostic criteria. In that way, students can gain a basic understanding that will serve them well regardless of their ultimate professional goals.

In this Ninth Edition, the author refreshes many of the cases to reflect stronger ethnic, international, gender, sexual orientation, and age diversity. In particular, the mini cases in each chapter are based on cases intended to reflect the importance of cultural variations that psychologists see in their private offices, clinics, hospitals, and counseling centers.

Above all, the study of abnormal psychology is the study of profoundly human experiences. To this end, the author has developed a biographical feature entitled "Real Stories." You will read narratives from the actual experiences of celebrities, sports figures, politicians, authors, musicians, and artists ranging from Ludwig van Beethoven to Herschel Walker. Each story is written to provide insight into the particular disorder covered within the chapter. By reading these fascinating biographical pieces, you will come away with a more in-depth personal perspective to use in understanding the nature of the disorder.

The author has developed this text using a scientist-practitioner framework. In other words, you will read about research informed by clinical practice. The author presents research on theories and treatments for each of the disorders based on the principles of evidence-based practice. This means that the approaches are tested through extensive research informed by clinical practice. Many researchers in the field of abnormal psychology also treat clients in their own private offices, hospitals, or group practices. As a result, they approach their work in the lab with the knowledge that their findings can ultimately provide real help to real people.

CHAPTER-BY-CHAPTER CHANGES

This edition reflects the most recent revision to the *Diagnostic and Statistical Manual of Mental Disorders (DSM)* published by the American Psychiatric Association in 2013 and known as *DSM-5*. The *DSM-5* was written following a lengthy process of revising the previous edition, the *DSM-IV-TR*, involving hundreds of researchers contributing to task forces intended to investigate each of the major categories of disorders.

Though replaced, the *DSM-IV-TR* still remains relevant, if only as a contrast to the *DSM-5*. Each chapter has a section entitled "What's in the *DSM-5*" that highlights the critical changes introduced in 2013 and shows why they matter. Because so much of our current understanding of research on psychological disorders used earlier editions of the *DSM* for diagnostic purposes, students will still encounter findings based on its diagnostic system. It generally takes several years for research to catch up with new diagnostic terminology, both because of the amount of time required for articles to reach publication stage, and also because of the dearth of available research instruments based on the new diagnostic criteria. From the student's point of view, the conceptual frameworks that inform the way we think about psychological disorders are most important.

Adding to this complexity is the fact that an entirely different classification system, the *International Classification of Diseases (ICD)*, is used by countries outside the United States and Canada, as well as by governmental insurance agencies in the United States. We will discuss the *ICD* when relevant, particularly as it relates to international comparisons.

The heat-map-directed revisions in this new edition are reflected primarily in Chapters 3, 5, 14, and 15. Other content changes include the following:

CHAPTER 1

- Reorganized presentation of themes throughout history to distinguish how each theme evolved over time.
- Added section on open-access journals and associated difficulties in relying on sources that did not receive extensive peer review.
- Updated examples of research designs and approaches in abnormal psychology.

CHAPTER 2

- Added further discussion on "client" vs. "patient" terminology.

- Expanded section on "Cultural Concepts of Distress" and updated the accompanying Table 3.
- Added new research on evidence-based practice in psychology.

CHAPTER 3

- Updated information on the SCID for *DSM-5*.
- Provided updated descriptions of personality assessment methods.
- Added section on Cultural Formulation Interview.
- Revised and updated section on neuropsychological assessment.

CHAPTER 4

- Updated and expanded treatment of genetic theories.
- Expanded the theoretical background and case regarding Core Conflictual Relationship Theme.
- Revised definitions of positive and negative reinforcement with new examples.
- Updated description of cognitive perspective.
- Added section on acceptance-based perspective.

CHAPTER 5

- Revised and updated section on intellectual disability.
- Updated section on treatment of autism spectrum disorder.
- Provided updated information and research on learning and communication disorders.
- Condensed information in Table 2.
- Added section on "Project Search."
- Updated information on ADHD, including ADHD in adults.
- Added new research on motor disorders.

CHAPTER 6

- Provided updated statistics on schizophrenia, including health care costs.
- Updated section on the course of schizophrenia.
- Reorganized biological perspectives section and updated research evidence in support of genetic contributions.

- Updated information about CBT for treatment of psychotic disorders.

CHAPTER 7

- Provided extensive updates of prevalence statistics.
- Expanded section on health problems for individuals with bipolar disorder.
- Added new information about biological contributors to mood disorders.
- Updated research on psychotherapy vs. medication effectiveness.
- Provided updates from recent data on suicide rates in the United States.

CHAPTER 8

- Updated prevalence statistics.
- Added new information about virtual reality exposure therapy.
- Provided new information about the role of personality traits in agoraphobia and panic disorder.
- Added new information comparing younger and older adults in generalized anxiety disorder.
- Included ACT treatment for anxiety disorders.
- Added new evidence in favor of CBT for obsessive compulsive disorder.
- Added research on PTSD in female combat veterans.
- Included new treatment guidelines published by APA for treatment of PTSD.
- Added new studies on couples therapy and post-traumatic growth in PTSD.

CHAPTER 9

- Added new section on treatment of dissociative identity disorder.
- Incorporated new research on brain imaging studies for individuals with motor conversion disorder.
- Updated research on malingering along with information on structured malingering assessment.
- Added new studies on ACT as treatment for illness anxiety disorder.
- Expanded treatment of workplace stress and health.

- Included new research on psychoeducation in behavioral medicine.

CHAPTER 10

- Provided new research on the relationship between altered brain activity and eating disorders.
- Added information about ACT as treatment for eating disorders.
- Summarized new research on treatment of childhood elimination disorders.
- Added information about the role of wearable technology in treatment of sleep disorders.
- Included new information about social competence therapy in treatment of oppositional defiant disorder.
- Updated treatment of intermittent explosive disorder with CBT.
- Added new longitudinal research on conduct disorder.
- Updated section on treatment of kleptomania with CBT.

CHAPTER 11

- Clarified terminology in section on definitions of paraphilic disorders.
- Added new perspectives on fetishistic disorder based on updated studies.
- Updated information about frotteuristic disorder.
- Provided new survey data on sexual sadism and sexual masochism disorders.
- Added new information about treatment of paraphilic disorders based on biological approaches.
- Incorporated new studies on the use of sexual diaries in treatment of women with sexual dysfunctions.
- Summarized research on body image and sexual dysfunction in women.
- Added section on CBT in treating couples with sexual dysfunctions.
- Clarified terms and theories in gender dysphoria.
- Summarized new APA Guidelines for Transgender and Gender Nonconforming People.

CHAPTER 12

- Updated statistics on use of alcohol and illicit substances based on new SAMHSA data.

- Clarified relationship between socialization and alcohol use disorders.

- Included updated discussion of marijuana based on changes in federal and state legislation on legality.

- Added new studies on prevalence of caffeine-related conditions.

- Updated information about e-cigarettes.

- Evaluated new research on biological treatments for substance-related disorders.

- Added new research on gambling disorder in older adult women.

- Provided new evidence on the pathways model of gambling disorder and related treatment.

CHAPTER 13

- Provided streamlined definitions of neurocognitive disorders and their symptoms.

- Expanded discussion of delirium and revised Table 2 to provide more accessible information.

- Updated prevalence statistics on Alzheimer's disease and clarified distinction between "dementia" and neurocognitive disorder."

- Evaluated new treatments for Alzheimer's disease.

- Revised section on neurocognitive disorder with Lewy bodies.

- Updated statistics on traumatic brain injury.

- Added new information about chronic traumatic encephalography (CTE).

CHAPTER 14

- Revised and simplified presentation of alternative personality disorder diagnostic system in *DSM-5*.

- Developed more concise approach to theories and treatments of antisocial personality disorder, along with updated research.

- Provided new information about treatment of antisocial personality disorder.

- Added information about attachment style in dependent personality disorder.

CHAPTER 15

- Ensured that all guidelines are compliant with APA updates and revisions.

- Added information about "duty to warn or otherwise protect."

- Added new section on ruling by Massachusetts Supreme Judicial Court based on MIT lawsuit regarding suicide prevention in college students.

- Updated information based on landmark forensic cases and the current status of the offenders.

Acknowledgments

The following instructors were instrumental in the development of the text, offering their feedback and advice as reviewers:

David Alfano, *Community College of Rhode Island*

Bryan Cochran, *University of Montana*

Julie A. Deisinger, *Saint Xavier University*

Angela Fournier, *Bemidji State University*

Richard Helms, *Central Piedmont Community College*

Heather Jennings, *Mercer County Community College*

Joan Brandt Jensen, *Central Piedmont Community College*

Cynthia Kalodner, *Towson University*

Patricia Kemerer, *Ivy Tech Community College*

Barbara Kennedy, *Brevard Community College-Palm Bay*

Joseph Lowman, *University of North Carolina-Chapel Hill*

Don Lucas, *Northwest Vista College*

James A. Markusic, *Missouri State University*

Mark McKellop, *Juniata College*

Maura Mitrushina, *California State University-Northridge*

John Norland, *Blackhawk Technical College*

Karen Clay Rhines, *Northampton Community College*

Ty Schepis, *Texas State University*

William R. Scott, *Liberty University*

Dr. Wayne S. Stein, *Brevard Community College*

Marla Sturm, *Montgomery County Community College*

Terry S. Trepper, *Purdue University-Calumet*

Naomi Wagner, *San Jose State University*

Nevada Winrow, *Baltimore City Community College*

It has been particularly satisfying to work on this edition with my daughter, Jennifer L. O'Brien, PhD, who served as my research assistant and author of all the Case Reports and Real Stories in the text. A psychologist at the Massachusetts Institute of Technology (MIT) Medical Mental Health and Counseling Services, Jenny received her PhD in 2015 from American University and completed a predoctoral internship at the Durham V.A. Hospital and a postdoctoral internship at the Boston V.A. Hospital. Her wide range of experiences with both veterans and university students from all over the world gives her a unique perspective and set of insights that inform the entire book.

Finally, a great book can't come together without a great publishing team. I'd like to thank the editorial team, all of whom worked with me through various stages of the publishing process. Ryan Treat was terrific in getting the revision off the ground, and I appreciate his enthusiasm and support. Dawn Groundwater has also been wonderful, and her long-term commitment to the book means a great deal to me. I would also like to thank my Content Project Manager Ryan Warczynski, whose patience and diligence helped ensure my vision was carried out effectively. I also wish to thank Sandy Wille, who has been wonderful in serving as Production Project Manager throughout previous editions and who is now back on the team. Kelly Heinrichs, the Program Manager, has ensured that all of the aspects of this revision have gone smoothly. Kristine Janssens, who helped me select photos for this revision, has shown terrific resourcefulness in dealing with the many issues involved in providing excellent photos to illustrate key points. Traci Vaske, Content Licensing Specialist, has been invaluable in assisting me in the complex process of acquiring permissions. Finally, I wish to give heartfelt thanks to Elisa Adams, Product Developer, not only for her vigilance in making sure that this revision reads as well as it can, but also for her friendly encouragement throughout the entire process. In this Ninth Edition, I feel very grateful to be part of the McGraw-Hill family, whose commitment to student success is truly remarkable.

A Letter from the Author

I am very glad that you are choosing to read my textbook. The topic of abnormal psychology has never been more fascinating or relevant. We constantly hear media reports of celebrities having meltdowns for which they receive quickie diagnoses that may or may not be accurate. Given all this misinformation in the mind of the public, I feel that it's important for you to be educated in the science and practice of abnormal psychology. At the same time, psychological science grabs almost as many headlines in all forms of news media. It seems that everyone is eager to learn about the latest findings, ranging from the neuroscience of behavior to the effectiveness of the newest treatment methods. Advances in brain-scanning methods and studies of psychotherapy effectiveness are greatly increasing our understanding of how to help treat and prevent psychological disorders.

Particularly fascinating to me was covering the changes made in the *DSM-5*. Each revision of the *DSM* brings with it controversies and challenges, and the *DSM-5* was no exception. Despite challenges in the new ways that the *DSM-5* defines and categorizes psychological disorders, it is perhaps more than any earlier edition based on strong research. Scientists and practitioners will continue to debate the best ways to interpret this research. We all will benefit from these dialogues.

The profession of clinical psychology is also undergoing rapid changes. With changes in health care policy, it is very likely that more professionals, from psychologists to mental health counselors, will be employed in providing behavioral interventions. By taking this first step toward your education now, you will be preparing yourself for a career that is increasingly being recognized as vital to helping individuals of all ages and all walks of life to achieve their greatest fulfillment.

I hope you find this text as engaging to read as I found it to write. Please feel free to e-mail me at swhitbo@psych.umass.edu with your questions and reactions to the material. As a long-time user of McGraw-Hill's Connect in my own abnormal psychology class, I can also vouch for its effectiveness in helping you achieve mastery of the content of abnormal psychology. I am also available to answer any questions you have, from an instructor's point of view, about how best to incorporate this book's digital media into your own teaching.

Thank you again for choosing to read this book!

Best,
Susan

Overview to Understanding Abnormal Behavior

Learning Objectives

1.1 Distinguish between behavior that is unusual but normal and behavior that is unusual and abnormal.

1.2 Describe how explanations of abnormal behavior have changed through time.

1.3 Identify the strengths and weaknesses of research methods.

1.4 Describe types of research studies.

©cybrain/Shutterstock

Case Report: Rebecca Hasbrouck

Demographic information: 18-year-old single Caucasian heterosexual female

Presenting problem: Rebecca self-referred to the university counseling center. She is a college freshman, living away from home for the first time. Following the first week of classes, Rebecca reports that she is having trouble falling and staying asleep, has difficulty concentrating in her classes, and often feels irritable. She reports she is frustrated by the difficulties of her coursework and worries that her grades are beginning to suffer. She also relays that she is having trouble making friends at school and that she has been feeling lonely because she has no close friends here with whom she can talk openly. Rebecca is very close to her boyfriend of 3 years, though they are attending college in different cities.

Rebecca was tearful throughout our first session, stating that, for the first time in her life, she feels overwhelmed by feelings of hopelessness. She reports that although the first week at school felt like "torture," she is slowly growing accustomed to her new lifestyle, despite her struggles with missing her family and boyfriend, as well as her friends from high school.

Relevant past history: Rebecca has no prior history of depressive episodes or other mental health concerns, and she reports no known family history of psychological disorders. She shared that sometimes her mother tends to get "really stressed out," though she has never received professional mental health treatment.

Symptoms: Depressed mood, difficulty falling asleep (insomnia), difficulty concentrating on schoolwork. She described feelings of hopelessness but denies any thoughts of suicide or self-harm.

Case formulation: Although it appeared at first as though Rebecca was suffering from a major depressive episode, she did not meet the diagnostic criteria. While the age of onset for depression tends to be around Rebecca's age, given her lack of a family history of depression and that her symptoms were occurring in response to a major stressor, the clinician determined that Rebecca was suffering from adjustment disorder with depressed mood.

Treatment plan: The counselor will refer Rebecca for weekly psychotherapy. Therapy should focus on improving her mood, and also should allow her a supportive space to discuss her feelings surrounding the major changes that have been occurring in her life.

Sarah Tobin, PhD
Clinician

Rebecca Hasbrouck's case report summarizes the pertinent features that a clinician would include when first seeing a client after an initial evaluation. Each chapter of this book begins with a case report for a client whose characteristics are related to the chapter's topic. A fictitious clinician, Dr. Sarah Tobin, who supervises a clinical setting that offers a variety of services, writes the case reports. In some instances, she provides the services, and in others, she supervises the work of another psychologist. For each case, she provides a diagnosis using the official manual adopted by the profession, known as the *Diagnostic and Statistical Manual of Mental Disorders, Fifth Edition (DSM-5)* (American Psychiatric Association, 2013).

At the end of this chapter, after you have developed a better understanding of the client's disorder, we will return to Dr. Tobin's description of the treatment results and expected future outcomes for the client. We also include Dr. Tobin's personal reflections on the case to help you gain insight into the clinician's experience in working with psychologically disordered individuals.

The field of abnormal psychology is filled with countless fascinating stories of people who suffer from psychological disorders. In this chapter, we will try to give you some sense of the reality that psychological disturbance is certain to touch everyone, to some extent, at some point in life. As you progress through this course, you will almost certainly develop a sense of the challenges people associate with psychological problems. You will find yourself drawn into the many ways that mental health problems affect the lives of individuals, their families, and society. In addition to becoming more personally familiar with the emotional aspects of abnormal psychology, you will learn about the scientific and theoretical basis for understanding and treating the people who suffer from psychological disorders.

1.1 What Is Abnormal Behavior?

It's possible that you know someone very much like Rebecca, who is suffering from more than the average degree of adjustment difficulties in college. Would you consider her psychologically disturbed? Would you consider giving her a diagnosis? What if she showed up at your door looking as if she were ready to harm herself?

At what point do you draw the line between someone who has a psychological disorder and someone who, like Rebecca, has an adjustment disorder? Is it even necessary to give Rebecca any diagnosis at all? Questions about normality and abnormality such as these are basic to advancing our understanding of psychological disorders.

Perhaps you yourself are, or have been, unusually depressed, fearful, or anxious. If not you, possibly someone you know has struggled with a psychological disorder or its symptoms. It may be that your father struggles with alcoholism, your mother has been hospitalized for severe depression, your sister has an eating disorder, or your brother has an irrational fear. If you have not encountered a psychological disorder within your immediate family, you have very likely encountered one in your extended family and circle of friends. You may not have known the formal psychiatric diagnosis for the problem, and you may not have understood its nature or cause, but you knew that something was wrong and recognized the need for professional help.

Until they are forced to face such problems, most people believe that "bad things" happen only to other people. You may think that other people have car accidents, succumb to cancer, or, in the psychological realm, become dependent on opioids. We hope that reading this textbook will help you go beyond this "other people" syndrome. Psychological disorders are part of the human experience, directly or indirectly touching the life of every person. However, they don't have to destroy those lives. As you read about these disorders and the people who suffer them, you will find that these problems can be treated, if not prevented.

This young woman's apparent despair may be the symptoms of a psychological disorder.

©wavebreakmedia/Shutterstock

1.2 The Social Impact of Psychological Disorders

Psychological disorders affect both the individual and the other people in the individual's social world. Put yourself in the following situation. You receive an urgent text from the mother of your best friend, Jeremy. You call her and find out he's been admitted to a behavioral health unit of the local hospital and wants to see you. According to Jeremy's mother, only you can understand what he is going through. The news comes out of the blue and is puzzling and distressing. You had no idea Jeremy had any psychological problems. You ponder what you will say to him when you see him. Jeremy is your closest friend, but now you wonder how your relationship will change. How much can you ask him about what he's going through? How is it that you never saw it coming? Unsure about what to do when you get there, you wonder what kind of shape he'll be in and whether he'll even be able to communicate with you. What will it be like to see him in this setting? What will he expect of you, and what will this mean for the future of your friendship?

Now imagine the same scenario, but instead you receive news that Jeremy was just admitted to the emergency room of a general hospital with acute appendicitis. You know exactly how to respond when you go to see him. You will ask him how he feels, what exactly is wrong with him, and when he will be well again. Even though you might not like hospitals very much, at least you have a pretty good idea about what hospital patients are like. The appendectomy won't seem like anything special, and you would probably not even consider whether you could be friends with Jeremy again after he is discharged. He'll be as good as new in a few weeks, and your relationship with him will resume unchanged.

Now that you've compared these two scenarios, consider the fact that people with psychological disorders frequently face situations such as Jeremy's in which even the people who care about them aren't sure how to respond to their symptoms. Furthermore, even after their symptoms are under control, individuals like Jeremy continue to experience profound and long-lasting emotional and social effects as they attempt to resume their former lives. Their disorder itself may also bring about anguish and personal suffering. Like Rebecca in our opening example, they must cope with feelings of loneliness and sadness.

The families of individuals with psychological disorders face significant stress when their relatives must be hospitalized.

©Ghislain & Marie David de Lossy/Getty Images

stigma
A negative label that causes certain people to be regarded as different, defective, and set apart from mainstream members of society.

Psychological disorders are almost inevitably associated with **stigma**, a negative label that causes certain people to be regarded as different, defective, and set apart from mainstream members of society. This stigma exists even in today's society, despite greater awareness of the prevalence of mental health issues. Social attitudes toward people with psychological disorders range from discomfort to outright prejudice. Language, humor, and stereotypes portray psychological disorders in a negative light, and many people fear that those who have these disorders are violent and dangerous.

There seems to be something about a psychological disorder that makes people want to distance themselves from it as much as possible. The result is social discrimination, which serves only to complicate the lives of the afflicted even more. Making matters worse, people experiencing symptoms of a psychological disorder may not avail themselves of the help they could receive from treatment because they too have incorporated stigmatized views of mental illness (Clement et al., 2015). Some individuals are able to resist the stigma of psychological disorders due to their ability, for example, to define their identity separate from their disorder and to reject the labels other people apply to them (Firmin et al., 2017).

In the chapters that follow, you will read about a wide range of disorders affecting mood, anxiety, substance use, sexuality, and thought disturbance. Case descriptions will give you a glimpse into the feelings and experiences of real people who have these disorders, and you may find that some of them seem similar to you or to people you know. As you read about the disorders, put yourself in the place of the people who have these conditions. Consider how they feel and how they would like people to treat them. We hope you will realize that our discussion is not about the disorders but about the people who have them.

1.3 Defining Abnormality

There is a range of behaviors people consider normal. Where do you draw the line? Decide which of the following actions you regard as abnormal.

- Feeling jinxed when your "lucky" seat in an exam is already occupied when you get to class
- Being unable to sleep, eat, study, or talk to anyone else for days after your boyfriend says, "It's over between us"
- Breaking into a cold sweat at the thought of being trapped in an elevator
- Swearing, throwing pillows, and pounding fists on the wall in the middle of an argument with a roommate
- Refusing to eat solid food for days at a time in order to stay thin
- Engaging in a thorough hand-washing after coming home from a bike ride
- Protesting the rising cost of college by joining a picket line outside the campus administration building
- Being convinced that people are constantly being critical of everything you do
- Drinking a six-pack of beer a day in order to be "sociable" with friends
- Playing videogames for hours at a time, avoiding other study and work obligations

If you're like most people, you probably found it surprisingly difficult to decide which of these behaviors are normal and which are abnormal. So many are part of everyday life. You can see now why mental health professionals struggle to find an appropriate definition of abnormality. Yet criteria need to exist so they can provide appropriate treatment in their work with clients.

Looking back at this list of behaviors, think now about how you would rate each if you applied the five criteria for a psychological disorder that mental health professionals use. In reality, no one would diagnose a psychological disorder on the basis of a single behavior, but using these criteria can at least give you some insight into the process that clinicians use when deciding whether a given client has a disorder or not.

The first criterion for a psychological disorder is **clinical significance**, meaning the behavior includes a measurable degree of impairment that a clinician can observe. People who feel jinxed about not having a lucky seat available for an exam would fit this criterion only if they could not concentrate on the exam at all unless they sat in that seat and this happened for every exam they take.

clinical significance
The criterion for a psychological disorder in which the behavior being evaluated includes a measurable degree of impairment that the clinician can observe.

Second, to be considered evidence of a psychological disorder, a behavior must reflect a dysfunction in a psychological, biological, or developmental process. Concretely, this means that even if researchers do not know the cause of that dysfunction, they assume that it can one day be discovered.

The third criterion for abnormality is that the behavior must be associated with significant distress or disability in important realms of life. This may sound similar to clinical significance, but what distinguishes distress or disability is that it applies to the way the individual feels or behaves, beyond a measurable effect the clinician can observe. The individual either feels negatively affected by the behavior ("distress") or suffers negative consequences in life as a result ("disability"). People may enjoy playing videogames to a point, but if they exclude their other obligations, this will negatively affect their lives. They may also feel distressed but unable to stop themselves from engaging in the behavior.

Fourth, the individual's behavior cannot simply be socially deviant as defined in terms of religion, politics, or sexuality. The person who refuses to eat meat for ideological reasons would not be considered to have a psychological disorder by this standard. However, if that person restricts all food intake to the point that his or her health is in jeopardy, then that individual may meet one of the other criteria for abnormality, such as clinical significance and/or the distress-disability dimension.

The fifth and final criterion for a psychological disorder is that it reflects a dysfunction within the individual. A psychological disorder cannot reflect a difference in political beliefs between citizens and their governments. Campus protesters who want to keep college costs down could not, according to this criterion, be considered psychologically disordered, although they may be putting themselves at other kinds of risk if they never attend a single class or are arrested for trespassing on university property.

This woman is distressed over her inability to fall asleep, but does this mean she has a psychological disorder?
©tab62/Shutterstock

What's in the *DSM-5*

Definition of a Mental Disorder

Compare what you think constitutes abnormal behavior with the five criteria for a mental disorder used by clinicians to arrive at diagnoses of their clients. These criteria are at the core of the *Diagnostic and Statistical Manual, Fifth Edition* (*DSM-5*). To constitute a disorder, the symptoms must be clinically significant in that the behaviors under consideration are not passing symptoms or minor difficulties. *DSM-5* refers to the behaviors as reflecting dysfunction in psychological, biological, or developmental processes, supporting the view of mental disorders as reflecting biopsychosocial influences. Furthermore, the disorders must occur outside the norm of what is socially accepted and expected for people experiencing particular life stresses. *DSM-5* also specifies that the disorder must have "clinical utility," meaning that, for example, the diagnoses help guide clinicians in making decisions about treatment. During the process of writing the *DSM-5,* the authors cautioned against either adding or subtracting diagnoses from the previous manual without taking into account potential benefits and risks. For example, they realized that adding a new diagnosis might lead to labeling as abnormal a behavior previously considered normal. The advantage of having the new diagnosis must outweigh the harm of categorizing a "normal" person as having a "disorder." Similarly, deleting a diagnosis for a disorder that requires treatment (and hence insurance coverage) might leave individuals who still require that treatment vulnerable to withholding of care or excess payments for treatment. With these cautions in mind, the *DSM-5* authors also recommend that the criteria alone are not sufficient for making legal judgments or eligibility for insurance compensation. These judgments would require additional information beyond the scope of the diagnostic criteria alone.

As you can see, deciding which behaviors are normal and which are not is a difficult proposition. Furthermore, when it comes to making an actual diagnosis to assign to a client, the mental health professional must also weigh the merits of using a diagnostic label against the disadvantages. The merits are that the individual will receive treatment (and be able to receive insurance reimbursement), but a possible disadvantage is that the individual will be labeled with a psychological disorder that becomes part of his or her health records. At a later point in life, that diagnosis may make it difficult for the individual to qualify for certain jobs.

Fortunately, mental health professionals have these criteria to guide them, with extensive manuals that allow them to feel reasonably confident they are assigning diagnoses when appropriate. These five criteria, and the specific diagnoses for the many forms of psychological disorders that can affect people, form the core content of this course.

1.4 What Causes Abnormal Behavior?

For the moment, we will leave behind the question of whether behavior is abnormal or normal while we look at the potential factors that can lead individuals to experience a psychological disorder. As you will learn, we can best conceptualize abnormal behavior from multiple vantage points. From the **biopsychosocial perspective**, we see abnormal behavior as reflecting a combination of biological, psychological, and sociocultural factors as these evolve during the individual's growth and development over time.

biopsychosocial perspective
A model in which the interaction of biological, psychological, and sociocultural factors is seen as influencing the development of the individual over time.

Biological Contributions

We start with the biological part of the equation. The factors within the body that can contribute to abnormal behavior include genetic abnormalities that, alone or in combination with the environment, influence the individual's psychological functioning. Biological contributions can also include physical changes that occur as part of normal aging, illnesses an individual develops, and injuries or harm caused to the body.

The most relevant genetic influences for our purposes are inherited factors that alter the functioning of the nervous system. However, psychological disorders can also be produced by environmental influences alone if these affect the brain or related organs of the body. For example, people with thyroid disturbances may experience wide fluctuations in mood. Brain injury resulting from a head trauma can result in altered thoughts, memory loss, and changes in mood.

Within the biopsychosocial perspective, we see social factors interacting with biological and psychological contributions, in that environmental influences such as exposure to toxic substances or stressful living conditions can also lead individuals to experience psychological disorders. Environmental deprivation caused by poverty, malnutrition, or social injustice can also place individuals at risk for psychological disorders by causing adverse physiological outcomes.

Psychological Contributions

The idea that psychological disorders have psychological contributions is probably not one that you believe requires a great deal of explanation. Within the biopsychosocial perspective, however, psychological causes are not viewed in isolation. They are seen as part of a larger constellation of factors influenced by physiological alterations interacting with exposure to a certain environment.

Psychological contributions can include the result of particular experiences within the individual's life. For example, individuals may find themselves repeating distressing behaviors that are instilled through learning experiences. They may also express emotional instability as the result of feeling that their parents or caretakers could not be relied on to watch over them.

Although there are no purely psychological causes in the biopsychosocial perspective, we can think of those that reflect learning, life experiences, or exposure to key situations in life as reflecting predominantly psychological influences. These can also include difficulty coping with stress, illogical fears, susceptibility to uncontrollable emotions, and a host of other dysfunctional thoughts, feelings, and behaviors that lead individuals to meet the criteria for psychological disorder.

Sociocultural Contributions

The **sociocultural perspective** looks at the various circles of influence on the individual, ranging from close friends and family to the institutions and policies of a country or the world as a whole. These influences interact in important ways with biological processes and with the psychological contributions that occur through exposure to particular experiences.

sociocultural perspective
The theoretical perspective that emphasizes the ways that individuals are influenced by people, social institutions, and social forces in the world around them.

One important and unique sociocultural contribution to psychological disorders is discrimination, whether based on social class, income, race and ethnicity, nationality, sexual orientation, or gender. Discrimination not only limits people's ability to experience psychological well-being; it can also have direct effects on physical health and development. For example, it has long been known that people from lower economic income and status brackets are more likely to have psychological disorders due to the constant strain of being discriminated against as well as the lack of access to education and health resources they experience.

And, as we pointed out earlier, people diagnosed with a psychological disorder are likely to be stigmatized as a result of their symptoms and diagnostic label. The stress of carrying the stigma of mental illness increases the emotional burden for these individuals and their loved ones. Because it may prevent them from seeking badly needed help, it also perpetuates a cycle in which many people in need become increasingly at risk and hence develop more serious symptoms.

The stigma of psychological disorders seems to vary by ethnicity and race. For example, European American adolescents and their caregivers are twice as likely as members of minority groups to define problems in mental health terms or to seek help for such problems (Roberts, Alegría, Roberts, & Chen, 2005). Variations in the willingness to acknowledge mental health issues also occurs across age and gender lines, with younger individuals and women more open to the experience of symptoms and therefore more willing to participate in therapy and other psychological interventions.

The existence of multiple forms of discrimination also means that individuals must cope not only with their symptoms and the stigma of their symptoms, but also with the negative attitudes toward their socially defined group. Clinicians working with individuals from discriminated-against groups are increasingly learning the importance of considering these factors in both diagnosis and treatment. We will learn later in the book about the specific guidelines that mental health experts are developing to help ensure that clinicians receive adequate training in translating theory into practice.

The Biopsychosocial Perspective

Table 1 summarizes the three categories of causes of psychological disorders just discussed. As you have seen, disturbances in any of these areas of human functioning can contribute to the development of a psychological disorder. Although this breakdown

TABLE 1 **Causes of Abnormal Behavior**

Biological	Genetic inheritance
	Physiological changes
	Exposure to toxic substances
Psychological	Past learning experiences
	Maladaptive thought patterns
	Difficulties coping with stress
Sociocultural	Social policies
	Discrimination
	Stigma

is helpful, keep in mind the many possible interactions among the three sets of influences.

As you will see when reading about the conditions in this textbook, the degree of influence of each of these variables differs among disorders. For some disorders, such as schizophrenia, biology seems to play a particularly dominant role. For other disorders, such as stress reactions, psychological factors predominate. Conditions such as post-traumatic stress disorder as a result of, for example, experiences under a terrorist regime have a primarily sociocultural cause.

The biopsychosocial perspective also incorporates a developmental viewpoint. This means we must understand how these three sets of influences change over the course of an individual's life. Some circumstances endanger the individual more at certain times than at others. Young children may be especially vulnerable to such factors as inadequate nutrition, harsh parental criticism, and neglect. Protective factors, on the other hand, such as loving caregivers, adequate health care, and early life successes, can reduce an individual's likelihood of developing a disorder. These early risk-protective factors become part of the individual's susceptibility to developing a disorder, and they remain influential throughout life.

Later in life, risk factors change in their specific form and potential severity. Individuals who experience physical health problems due to a lifetime of poor dietary habits may be more likely to develop psychological symptoms related to altered cardiovascular functioning. On the other hand, if they have developed an extensive social support network, this can somewhat offset the risk presented by their poor physical health.

At all ages, the biological, psychological, and sociocultural factors continue to interact and affect the individual's mental health and well-being as well as the expression of a particular psychological disorder (Whitbourne & Meeks, 2011). We can use the biopsychosocial framework to develop an understanding of the causes of abnormality and, just as importantly, the basis for treatment.

spiritual explanations
Explanations that regard psychological disorders as the product of possession by evil or demonic spirits.

humanitarian explanations
Explanations that regard psychological disorders as the result of cruelty, stress, or poor living conditions.

scientific explanations
Explanations that regard psychological disorders as the result of causes that we can objectively measure, such as biological alterations, faulty learning processes, or emotional stressors.

1.5 Prominent Themes in Abnormal Psychology Throughout History

The greatest thinkers of the world, from ancient times to the present, have attempted to explain the varieties of human behavior that we now regard as evidence for a psychological disorder. Throughout history, three prominent themes seem to recur: the spiritual, the humanitarian, and the scientific. **Spiritual explanations** regard abnormal behavior as the product of possession by evil or demonic spirits. **Humanitarian explanations** view psychological disorders as the result of cruelty, stress, or poor living conditions. **Scientific explanations** look for causes we can objectively measure, such as biological alterations, faulty learning processes, or emotional stressors.

The Greeks sought advice from oracles, wise advisors who made pronouncements from the gods.

©ullstein bild Dtl./Getty Images

Hieronymus Bosch's *Removal of the Stone of Folly* depicted a medieval "doctor" cutting out the presumed source of madness from a patient's skull. The prevailing belief was that spiritual possession was the cause of psychological disorder.

©PAINTING/Alamy Stock Photo

We will follow the trajectories of each of these perspectives throughout history. As you will see, each has had its period of major influence, but in some ways the issues are the same today as in ancient times in that the actual causes of psychological disturbance remain unknown. The scientific approach will undoubtedly provide the key to discovering what causes psychological disorders, but it will nevertheless be important for mental health professionals to follow the principles of the humanitarian approach. Spiritual explanations may never completely disappear from the horizon, but the idea that psychological disorders can be understood will certainly provide the best prospects for turning that understanding into treatment.

Spiritual Approach

We begin with the oldest approach to psychological disorders, dating back to prehistoric times. Archaeological evidence from about 8000 B.C.E. suggests that the spiritual explanation of psychological was then the most widely accepted. Skulls discovered in caves inhabited by prehistoric peoples showed signs of **trephining** in which holes were cut into the bone.

This evidence suggests an attempt to release "evil spirits" from the person's head (Maher & Maher, 1985). Archaeologists have found trephined skulls from many countries and cultures, ranging from the Far and Middle East to Britain and South America (Gross, 1999). Trephining continued to be practiced throughout history and even into modern times, but its use during ancient times seems to be specifically associated with beliefs in evil spirits.

A second manifestation of belief in spiritual possession as the cause of psychological disorders is the ritual of **exorcism**. In this practice, a shaman, priest, or person entrusted with the task (such as a "medicine man") carries out rituals that put the individual under extreme physical and mental duress in an effort to drive out devils.

During the Middle Ages, people used a variety of magical rituals and exorcism to "cure" people with psychological disorders, but this treatment also took the form of casting these individuals as sinners, witches, or personifications of the devil. Accordingly, they were severely punished. The view of afflicted individuals as possessed by evil spirits is apparent in the 1486 book *Malleus Maleficarum*, in which two German Dominican monks justified

trephining

The process of cutting a hole in the skull to allow so-called "evil spirits" to escape.

exorcism

A ritual believed to cure psychological disturbance by ritually driving away evil spirits.

In this modern-day reenactment of a trial for witchcraft, a woman is tortured for her supposed crimes.
©Tom Wagner/Alamy Stock Photo

their punishment of "witches." Depicting them as heretics and devils whom the Church had to destroy in the interests of preserving Christianity, the book's authors recommended "treatments" such as deportation, torture, and burning at the stake.

From the 1500s to the late 1600s, the majority of individuals accused of witchcraft were women. The burning and hanging of witches by the Puritans in the United States eventually ended after the infamous Salem witchcraft trials (1692–1693), when townspeople began to doubt the authenticity of the charges against these women.

Although the spiritual approach is no longer the prevalent explanation for psychological disorders in Western culture, there are still pockets of believers who feel people with these disorders require spiritual "cleansing." Across other cultures, those who enact the role of exorcists continue to practice, reflecting what are longstanding cultural and religious beliefs.

Humanitarian Approach

The humanitarian approach to psychological disorders developed in part as a reaction against the spiritual approach and its associated punishment of people with psychological disorders. Starting in the Middle Ages, poorhouses and monasteries in Europe became established as shelters to house these individuals, who often were ostracized by their families.

Although shelters could not offer treatment, they initially provided some protection. Unfortunately, however, they increasingly became overcrowded and conditions grew intolerable. Rather than providing protection, ironically, they then became places of neglect, abuse, and maltreatment. A widespread belief that psychologically disturbed people lacked ordinary sensory capabilities led to such practices as not providing them with heat, clean living conditions, or appropriate food. During the sixteenth and seventeenth centuries, views about medicine were generally primitive. Thus, like treatments for physical illness, the treatment of people with psychological disorders included bleeding, forced vomiting, and purging.

By the end of the eighteenth century, throughout hospitals in France, Scotland, and England, a few courageous people began to recognize the inhumanity of the conditions in the poorhouses and monasteries housing those with psychological disorders. They initiated sweeping reforms in an attempt to reverse these harsh practices. The idea of **moral treatment** took hold—the belief that people could develop self-control over their behaviors if they had a quiet and restful environment. Institutions following this model used restraints only if absolutely necessary, and even in those cases the patient's comfort came first.

moral treatment
The belief that people could develop self-control over their behaviors if they had a quiet and restful environment.

Yet again, however, conditions in the asylums originally formed to protect patients began to worsen in the early 1800s due to overcrowding and the increasing use of physical punishment as a means of control. In 1841, Boston schoolteacher Dorothea Dix (1802–1887) took up the cause of reform. Horrified by the overcrowding and appalling conditions in the asylums, Dix appealed to the Massachusetts legislature for more state-funded public hospitals to provide humane treatment for mental patients. From Massachusetts, she then spread her message throughout North America and Europe.

Over the next 100 years, governments built scores of state hospitals throughout the United States following the humanitarian model originally advocated by Dix. Once again, however, it was only a matter of time before the hospitals became overcrowded and understaffed. It simply was not possible to cure people by providing them with the well-intentioned but ineffective interventions proposed by moral treatment. However, the humanitarian goals that Dix advocated had a lasting influence on the mental health system. Her work was carried forward into the twentieth century by advocates of the **mental hygiene** movement, whose goal is helping individuals maintain mental health and prevent the development of psychological disorders.

Public outrage over the worsening situation in mental hospitals finally led to a more widespread realization that mental health services required dramatic changes. The federal government took emphatic action in 1963 with the passage of groundbreaking legislation. The Mental Retardation Facilities and Community Mental Health Center Construction Act of that year initiated a series of changes that would affect mental health services for decades to come. Legislators began to promote policies designed to move people out of institutions and into less restrictive programs in the community, such as vocational rehabilitation facilities, day hospitals, and psychiatric clinics. After their discharge from the hospital, people entered **halfway houses**—which are community treatment facilities designed for deinstitutionalized clients leaving a hospital who are not ready for independent living. This legislation paved the way for the **deinstitutionalization movement**—which was the release of hundreds of thousands of patients from mental hospitals starting in the 1960s. The legislation was intended to pave the way for improvement of community treatment as an alternative to institutional care.

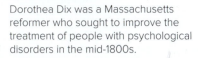

Dorothea Dix was a Massachusetts reformer who sought to improve the treatment of people with psychological disorders in the mid-1800s.

Source: Library of Congress, Prints & Photographs Division, Reproduction number LC-USZ62-9797 (b&w film copy neg.)

mental hygiene
The focus within psychiatry on helping individuals maintain mental health and prevent the development of psychological disorders.

halfway house
A community treatment facility designed for deinstitutionalized clients leaving a hospital who are not yet ready for independent living.

deinstitutionalization movement
The release of hundreds of thousands of patients from mental hospitals starting in the 1960s.

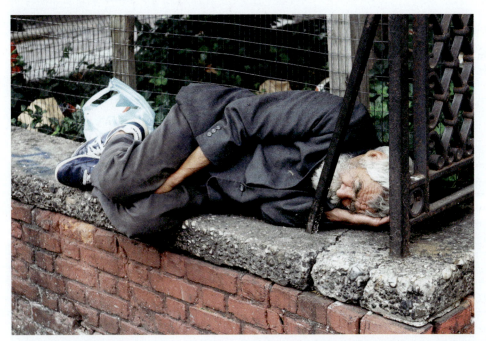

Although deinstitutionalization was designed to enhance the quality of life for people who had been held for years in public psychiatric hospitals, many individuals left institutions only to find a life of poverty and neglect on the outside.

©Gary He/McGraw-Hill Education

Also making deinstitutionalization possible was the development, in the 1950s, of pharmacological treatments that could successfully control the symptoms of psychological disorders for the first time. Now patients could receive treatments that would allow them to live on their own outside psychiatric hospitals for extended periods of time. By the mid-1970s, state mental hospitals that once overflowed with patients were practically deserted. Hundreds of thousands of institutionally confined people were freed to begin living with greater dignity and autonomy.

Unfortunately, the deinstitutionalization movement did not completely fulfill the dreams of its originators. Rather than eliminating inhumane treatment, it created another set of woes. Many of the promises and programs hailed as alternatives to institutionalization ultimately failed to materialize because of inadequate planning and insufficient funds. Patients were shuttled back and forth between hospitals, halfway houses, and shabby boarding homes, never gaining a sense of stability or respect. Although the intention behind releasing patients from psychiatric hospitals was to free people who had been deprived of basic human rights, the result may not have been as liberating as many had hoped. All too often, those who would have been in psychiatric hospitals in the past now must move through a circuit of shelters, rehabilitation programs, jails, and prisons. A disturbing number spend long periods of time as homeless and marginalized members of society.

Advocates of the humanitarian approach today suggest new forms of compassionate treatment for people who suffer from psychological disorders. They encourage mental health consumers to take an active role in choosing their treatment. Various advocacy groups have worked tirelessly to change the way the public views mentally ill people and the way society deals with them in all settings. These groups include the National Alliance for the Mentally Ill (NAMI), the Mental Health Association, the Center to Address Discrimination and Stigma, and the Eliminate the Barriers Initiative.

The U.S. federal government has become involved in antistigma programs as part of efforts to improve the delivery of mental health services through the President's New Freedom Commission (Hogan, 2003). At the end of 2017, progress toward these goals was reported by the U.S. Department of Health and Human Services (Table 2).

TABLE 2 Healthy People 2020 Goals

In 2015, the U.S. federal government took stock of the progress made toward each of these 2020 Healthy People Goals for Mental Health and Mental Disorders. Below are the goals along with the estimated progress in 2017 as reported by the Centers for Disease Control and Prevention.

Goal	Progress
Reduce suicide rate	−7%, moved away from target
Reduce suicide attempts, grades 9–12	−19%, moved away from target
Provide mental health services, homeless persons 18+ years with mental health problems	−33%, moved away from target
Reduce disordered eating behaviors, grades 9–12	0%
Increase primary care facilities providing mental health treatment onsite or by referral	200%, met target
Provide screening admissions for mental health problems in juvenile residential facilities	60%; moved toward target
Track consumer satisfaction with mental health services by state	0%
Ensure that state mental health plans address mental health care for older adults	12%; moved toward target

SOURCE: http://www.healthypeople.gov/2010/data/midcourse/html/tables/pq/PQ-18.htm

Scientific Approach

We now return to ancient times when, surprisingly, the early Greek philosophers took a scientific approach to understanding psychological disorders. Hippocrates (ca. 460-377 B.C.E.), considered the founder of modern medicine, believed that four important bodily fluids influenced physical and mental health, leading to four personality dispositions. To treat a psychological disorder would require ridding the body of the appropriate excess fluid. Although he was incorrect, Hippocrates was far ahead of his time in putting forth the notion that mental health reflected factors within the body rather than possession by evil spirits.

Several hundred years later, the Roman physician Claudius Galen (130-200 C.E.) developed a system of medical knowledge based on anatomical studies. This approach also helped to advance the position that diseases had their source in abnormal bodily functioning.

The scientific approach to psychological disorder receded for hundreds of years in favor of explanations rooted in the spiritual perspective, until Dr. Benjamin Rush (1745-1813), the founder of American psychiatry, rekindled interest. In 1783, Rush joined the medical staff of Pennsylvania Hospital. Appalled by the poor treatment of psychologically disturbed patients there, Rush advocated for improvements such as placing patients in their own wards, giving them occupational therapy, and prohibiting hospital visits by curiosity seekers looking for entertainment.

Dr. Benjamin Rush, founder of American psychiatry, was an ardent reformer who promoted the scientific study of psychological disorders.

Source: Library of Congress, Prints & Photographs Division, Reproduction number LC-DIG-pga-06328 (digital file from original item)

Reflecting the prevailing methods of the times, though, Rush also supported the use of bloodletting and purging in the treatment of psychological disorders, as well as the so-called tranquilizer chair, intended to reduce blood flow to the brain by binding the patient's head and limbs. Rush also recommended submerging patients in cold shower baths and frightening them with death threats. He thought that by inducing fear, he could counteract their sometimes violent behavior (Deutsch, 1949).

The next major advance occurred in 1844, when a group of 13 mental hospital administrators formed the Association of Medical Superintendents of American Institutions for the Insane. (This organization eventually changed its name to the American Psychiatric Association.) One year after its founding, in 1845, German psychiatrist Wilhelm Griesinger published *The Pathology and Therapy of Mental Disorders*, which proposed that "neuropathologies" were the cause of psychological disorders. Further advances occurred when German psychiatrist Emil Kraepelin (1856-1926) promoted a classification system much like that applied to medical diagnoses. He proposed that disorders could be identified by their patterns of symptoms. Ultimately, this work provided the scientific basis for current diagnostic systems.

While these advances in medical science and psychiatry were taking place, the early roots of a psychological approach to abnormality began to emerge in the early 1800s, when European physicians experimented with hypnosis for therapeutic purposes. Eventually, these efforts led to the groundbreaking work of Viennese neurologist Sigmund Freud (1856-1939), who in the early 1900s developed psychoanalysis, a theory and system of practice that relied heavily on the concepts of the unconscious mind, inhibited sexual impulses, and early development.

Throughout the twentieth century, psychologists continued to develop models based on observations of the behavior of laboratory animals. The work of Russian physiologist Ivan Pavlov (1849-1936), known for his discovery of classical conditioning, became the basis for the behaviorist movement begun in the United States by John B. Watson (1878-1958). B. F. Skinner (1904-1990) formulated a systematic approach to operant conditioning, specifying the types and nature of reinforcement and its use as a way to modify behavior. In the twentieth century, these models continued to evolve into the social learning theory of Albert Bandura (1925-), the cognitive model of Aaron Beck (1921-), and the rational-emotive therapy approach of Albert Ellis (1913-2007).

Positive psychology emphasizes personal growth through meditation and other alternate routes to self-discovery.

©Ben + Marcos Welsh/AGE Fotostock

positive psychology
Perspective that emphasizes the potential for growth and change throughout life.

scientific method
The process of testing ideas about the nature of psychological phenomena without bias before accepting these ideas as adequate explanations.

Most recently, the field of abnormal psychology is benefiting from the **positive psychology** movement, which emphasizes the potential for growth and change throughout life. The movement views psychological disorders as difficulties that inhibit the individual's ability to achieve highly subjective well-being and feelings of fulfillment. In addition, the positive psychology movement emphasizes prevention rather than intervention. Although its goals are similar to those of the humanitarian approach, the positive psychology movement has a strong base in empirical research and as a result is gaining wide support in the field.

These newer models, along with integrative models that take a biopsychosocial approach, are leading to promising empirical (evidence-based) ways to understand the causes of psychological disorder. Although not all may prove useful, they will help ensure that our application of the scientific perspective results in treatments that are both humane and effective.

1.6 Research Methods in Abnormal Psychology

As you've just learned, the scientific approach led to significant advances in the understanding and treatment of abnormal behavior. The essence of the **scientific method** is objectivity: the process of testing ideas about the nature of psychological phenomena without bias before accepting these ideas as adequate explanations.

The scientific method relies on a progression of steps, from posing questions of interest to sharing the results with the scientific community. Throughout their application of the scientific method, researchers maintain the objectivity that is the hallmark of the scientific approach. This means they do not let their personal biases interfere with the collection of data or the interpretation of findings. They remain open to alternate explanations that could account for their findings. Toward this end, researchers are now making their data available in open-access repositories that allow other scientists to examine their procedures, analyses, and conclusions.

Although the scientific method is based on objectivity, this does not mean scientists have no personal interest in what they are studying. In fact, many researchers pursue knowledge in areas that relate to their own lives, particularly in the field of abnormal psychology. They may have relatives afflicted with certain disorders, or they may have developed this interest through their clinical work. Regardless of what motivated them to study a particular topic, researchers in abnormal psychology must maintain their distance and be able to look at their findings without bias.

In posing questions of interest, psychological researchers may wonder whether a particular kind of experience led to an individual's symptoms, or they may speculate about the role of particular biological factors. Clinical psychologists are also interested in finding out whether a certain treatment will effectively manage the symptoms of a disorder. In either case, the ideal approach is to progress through the scientific method's steps, in which the researcher proposes a hypothesis, conducts a study, collects the data, and performs empirical analyses of the data. When this phase has been completed, researchers communicate results by publishing them in scientific journals, ideally after obtaining peer review to ensure the study's validity.

1.7 Experimental Design

In this approach to scientific research, an investigator sets up a test of a hypothesis to determine whether one variable or factor influences a second variable. The experimental method is the only approach that can test cause and effect because it allows investigators to change variable A to see how this affects variable B. For example, the investigator may wish to determine whether a particular form of therapy reduces anxiety levels in people seeking treatment. The investigator then provides some people with therapy and other people with no therapy. In this case, therapy is the **independent variable**, which is the variable whose level is adjusted or controlled by the experimenter. The "experimental" group receives the treatment, and the "control" group receives no treatment. The level of anxiety people report serves as the **dependent variable**, which is the variable whose value is the outcome of the experimenter's manipulation of the independent variable. The investigator may hope that the anxiety levels of the participants decrease more in the experimental than the control group if they are both compared before and after treatment, but cannot determine what those levels of anxiety will actually be. Depending on the nature of the particular study, there may be more than one experimental group. For example, an investigator may want to compare two different treatments against each other, evaluating both in comparison to a third control group. In that case, the independent variable takes on three values: treatment one, treatment two, and no treatment.

The gold standard for research in clinical psychology is the **randomized controlled trial (RCT)**, an experimental method in which participants are randomly assigned to intervention groups. The key to this method is the use of randomization, which minimizes the chances that bias can enter into the decision about which participants receive which treatment. Because this is such a powerful design, RCT is the foundation for **evidence-based treatment**, in which clients receive interventions based on the findings of controlled clinical studies.

Ideally, in a RCT, before conducting the study the investigators define a single primary outcome (that is, a specific dependent variable). They may also define secondary outcomes, but at the outset they need to be clear about their primary focus, such as levels of anxiety in the previous example. Otherwise, they may make the mistake of picking and choosing the results they report in a way that distorts the findings. Imagine if a researcher found no effect of a clinical treatment for anxiety on anxiety but instead found that it alleviated depression in the participants. This may be of interest, but because it was not predicted based on the study's underlying theory, it has no sound rationale and could have been due to chance factors.

To ensure that RCT-based studies conform to acceptable standards, researchers are increasingly being required to enter their work in a public trial registry before they begin. If they do not, their research will not be eligible for publication in any of the most prestigious research journals, which reports only findings that are reviewed by other experts in the field. Unfortunately, the implementation of these standards is falling behind; as reported in 2015, in the area of health psychology and behavioral medicine, about half the eligible published studies had been registered and only 21 percent reported primary outcomes (Riehm, Azar, & Thombs, 2015). Perhaps consumers should check how well a given study adheres to these guidelines before seeking a new intervention based on its results.

Consumers should also be wary of findings published in open-access journals that do not implement rigorous peer review. Researchers pay an often sizable fee to publish their findings in these journals, making them more open to skeptical reading than is true for articles that appear in journals sponsored by scientific associations or well-established editorial boards. Some of these journals are now called "predatory," because they literally prey on researchers, offering to publish their work but requiring high submission fees (Das & Chatterjee, 2017). You should also be critical of findings you read about in the news or in daily online digests, because these too may also fall short of peer-reviewed scrutiny.

Keep in mind, too, that well-controlled research in clinical psychology includes a **placebo condition** in which participants receive a treatment similar to the experimental treatment but lacking the key feature of the treatment of interest. Unlike the control group, the group receiving the placebo will be exposed to a set of conditions that mimic those associated with the treatment itself. If the study is evaluating the effectiveness of medication, the placebo will have inert ingredients. In studies on therapy effectiveness, a placebo group may involve participants meeting with experimenters who do not administer the actual intervention. When participants are randomly assigned to placebo versus treatment group, the design is referred to as a **placebo-controlled randomized clinical trial**.

independent variable
The variable whose level is adjusted or controlled by the experimenter.

dependent variable
The variable whose value is the outcome of the experimenter's manipulation of the independent variable.

randomized controlled trial (RCT)
Experimental method in which participants are randomly assigned to intervention groups.

evidence-based treatment
Treatment in which clients receive interventions based on the findings of controlled clinical studies.

placebo condition
Condition in an experiment in which participants receive a treatment similar to the experimental treatment, but lacking the key feature of the treatment of interest.

placebo-controlled randomized clinical trial
Experimental method in which participants are randomly assigned to a placebo versus treatment group.

In studies evaluating effectiveness of therapy, scientists must design the placebo in a way that mimics but is not the same as the actual therapy. Ideally, researchers would want the placebo participants to receive treatments of the same frequency and duration as the experimental group participants who are receiving psychotherapy. In studies with medication, a completely inert placebo may not be sufficient to establish true experimental control. In an "active placebo" condition, researchers build the experimental medication's side effects into the placebo. If they know that a medication produces dry mouth, difficulty swallowing, or upset stomach, then the placebo must also mimic these side effects, or participants will know are receiving placebos.

Expectations about the experiment's outcome can affect both the investigator and the participant. These so-called "demand characteristics" can compromise the conclusions about the intervention's true effectiveness. Obviously, the investigator should be as unbiased as possible, but there still may be subtle ways that he or she communicates cues that affect the participant's response. The participant may also have a personal agenda in trying to prove or disprove the study's supposed true intent. The best way to eliminate demand characteristics is to use a **double-blind** method, an experimental procedure in which neither the person giving the treatment nor the person receiving the treatment knows whether the participant is in the experimental or control group. To accomplish this, the investigator hires a research assistant or investigator who is not familiar with the study's purpose to run participants through the conditions.

The problem with the experimental method in the field of abnormal psychology is that many variables of greatest interest to psychologists are factors the investigator cannot control; hence, they are not truly "independent." For example, depression can never be a dependent variable because the investigator cannot manipulate it. A researcher interested in the effects of aging cannot make one group older than the other by randomly assigning people to the groups. Studies that investigate differences among groups not created by random assignment are known as "quasi-experimental." In such an experiment we can compare older and younger groups, for instance, but we cannot say that aging caused any differences we observe between them.

1.8 Correlational Design

Studies based on a **correlational design** test relationships between variables that researchers cannot experimentally manipulate. In a positive correlation, as the scores on one variable increase, so do the scores on the other. In a negative correlation, as scores on one variable increase, scores on the other decrease. For example, because one aspect of depression is that it causes a disturbance in normal sleep patterns, you would expect scores on a measure of depression to be positively correlated with scores on a measure of sleep disturbances. If the measure of sleep used in this study were the number of hours asleep, we could predict that the relationship would be negative. It is also possible that there is no correlation between two variables. In other words, two variables show no systematic relationship with each other. For example, depression is unrelated to the individual's height, and there would be no reason to expect the two variables to actually be correlated.

The statistic used in correlational studies is a number, expressed in decimals, between +1 and −1. Positive numbers (e.g., +.43) represent positive correlations, meaning that, as scores on one variable increase, scores on the second variable increase as well. Negative numbers (e.g., −.43) represent inverse relationships, so that as one variable increases, the other decreases to a similar extent. The number itself must be presented along with an indication of its statistical significance, meaning that based on the number of participants in the research (among other factors), the relationship has a low probability of occurring due to chance.

Regardless of the size or significance of a correlation, the key feature of studies using this method is that they cannot establish cause and effect. Just knowing that there is a correlation between two variables does not tell you whether one variable causes the other. The correlation simply tells you that the two variables are associated with each other in a particular way. Sleep disturbance might cause a higher score on a measure of depression, just as

double-blind
An experimental procedure in which neither the person giving the treatment nor the person receiving the treatment knows whether the participant is in the experimental or control group.

correlational design
Study in which researchers test the relationships between variables that they cannot experimentally manipulate.

Being Sane in Insane Places

In the early 1970s, psychologist David Rosenhan embarked upon a groundbreaking study that was to shatter people's assumptions about the difference between "sane" and "insane." Motivated by what Rosenhan regarded as a psychiatric diagnostic system that led to the hospitalization of people inappropriately diagnosed as having schizophrenia, he and his co-workers decided to conduct their own experiment to put the system to the test. See whether you think their experiment proved the point.

Eight people with no psychiatric history of symptoms of any kind, employed in a variety of professional occupations, checked themselves into psychiatric hospitals complaining about hearing voices that said, "Empty," "Hollow," and "Thud." These were symptoms that psychiatric literature never reported. In every other way, the "pseudopatients" provided factual information about themselves except their names and places of employment. Each was admitted to his or her respective hospital; once admitted, they showed no further signs of experiencing these symptoms. However, the hospital staff never questioned their need to be hospitalized; quite the contrary, their behavior on the hospital wards, now completely "normal," was taken as further evidence of their need for continued hospitalization. Despite the efforts of the pseudopatients to convince the staff that there was nothing wrong with them, it took from 7 to 52 days for all to be discharged. Upon their release, they received the diagnosis of "schizophrenia in remission" (meaning that for the moment they no longer would have a diagnosis of schizophrenia).

There was profound reaction to the Rosenhan study in the psychiatric community. If it was so easy to institutionalize nonpatients, wasn't there something wrong with the diagnostic system? How about the tendency to label people as "schizophrenic" when there was nothing wrong with them, and to hang on to the label even when they no longer showed any symptoms? The pseudopatients also reported that they felt dehumanized by the staff and failed to receive any active treatment. Once on the outside, they could report to the world at large about the failure of psychiatric hospitals to provide appropriate treatment. True patients would not have received so much sympathetic press, and therefore this study's findings could have a much broader impact on attitudes toward institutionalization.

Now, you be the judge. Do you think it was unethical for Rosenhan to devise such a study? The mental health professionals at the hospitals had no idea they were the actual subjects of a study. They had responded to what seemed to them to be serious psychological symptoms exhibited by individuals voluntarily seeking admission. At the point of discharge, the fact that the doctors labeled the pseudopatients as in remission implied that they were symptom-free, but there was no reason for the staff to doubt the truth of their symptoms. On the other hand, had the staff known they were in a study, they might have reacted very differently, and as a result, the study would not have had an impact.

How about the quality of this study from a scientific point of view? There was no control condition, so it was not truly an experiment. Moreover, the study did not take objective measures of the staffs' behavior, nor were there direct outcome measures that the researchers could statistically analyze.

Q: *You be the judge:* With all its flaws, was Rosenhan's study worthwhile? Did the ends justify the means?

a high degree of depression might cause more disturbed sleep patterns. Or, a third variable that you have not measured could account for the correlation between the two variables that you have studied. Both depression and sleep disturbance could be due to an underlying process that alters the body's hormones, such as an undetected medical condition, which causes both physiological and psychological disturbances.

Investigators who use correlational methods in their research must always be on guard for the potential existence of unmeasured variables influencing the observed results.

However, increasingly sophisticated statistical modeling procedures are making it possible to go beyond simply linking two variables to see whether they are correlated. A researcher can use such methods to assess the relative contributions of variables like self-esteem, gender, sleep patterns, and social class in predicting depression scores.

1.9 Types of Research Studies

Now that we've reviewed the basic analytical procedures, let's take a look at how investigators gather the data they use for analysis. Depending on the question under investigation, the resources available to the investigator, and the types of participants the investigator wants to study, the data gathering method may take one or more of several forms. Table 3 summarizes these methods.

Survey

survey
A research tool used to gather information from a sample of people considered representative of a particular population, in which participants are asked to answer questions about the topic of concern.

Investigators use a **survey** to gather information from a sample of people representative of a particular population. Typically, an investigator uses a survey to gather data that will be analyzed through correlational statistics. In a survey, investigators design sets of questions to tap into these variables, using questions to be answered with rating scales ("agree" to "disagree"), open-ended answers, or multiple choice. For example, a researcher may conduct a survey to determine whether age is correlated with subjective well-being, controlling for the influence of health. In this case, the researcher may hypothesize that subjective well-being is higher in older adults, but only after taking into account the role of health. The survey questions provide responses that can be translated into variables and subjected to statistical analysis.

Researchers also use surveys to gather statistics about the frequency of psychological symptoms. For example, the Substance Abuse and Mental Health Services Administration of the U.S. government (SAMHSA) conducts yearly surveys to establish the frequency of use of illegal substances within the population. The World Health Organization (WHO) conducts surveys comparing the frequency of psychological disorders by country. By asking approximately the same questions on each occasion, it is possible for these agencies, and users of the data set, to track changes in health and health-related behaviors over time.

TABLE 3 Research Methods in Abnormal Psychology

Type of Method	Purpose	Example
Survey	Obtain population data	Researchers working for a government agency attempt to determine disease prevalence through questionnaires administered over the telephone.
Laboratory study	Collect data under controlled conditions	An experiment is conducted to compare reaction times to neutral and fear-provoking stimuli.
Case study	An individual or a small group of individuals is studied intensively	A therapist describes the cases of members of a family who share the same unusual disorder.
Single case experimental design	The same person serves as subject in experimental and control conditions	Researchers report on the frequency of a client's behavior while the client is given attention (experimental treatment) and ignored (control condition) for aggressive outbursts in a psychiatric ward.
Behavioral genetics	Attempt to identify genetic patterns in inheritance of particular behaviors	Genetic researchers compare the DNA of people with and without symptoms of particular psychological disorders.

Some of the most important survey data we will rely on in this book come from large-scale epidemiological studies. This is how we know how many people are likely to develop a disorder and who is at risk. The type of data we use for these purposes falls into two categories: (1) number of new cases and (2) number of cases that have ever existed. Both are calculated for the population as a whole and for particular segments of the population by sex, age group, geographic region, or social class, for example.

The **incidence** of a disorder is the frequency of *new* cases within a given time period. Respondents providing incidence data state whether they now have a disorder they have never had before and are experiencing for the first time. Incidence information can cover any time interval; epidemiologists tend to report it in terms of 1 month, 6 months, and 1 year. Investigators use incidence data when they are interested in determining how quickly a disorder is spreading. For example, during an epidemic, health researchers need to know how to plan for controlling the disease, and incidence data are most pertinent to this question.

incidence
The frequency of new cases within a given time period.

The **prevalence** of a disorder refers to the number of people who have *ever* had the disorder over a specified period of time. To collect prevalence data, investigators ask respondents to state whether, during this period of time, they experienced the symptoms of the disorder. The time period of reference can be the day of the survey, in which case we call it "point prevalence." There is also "1-month prevalence," which refers to the 30 days preceding the study, and "lifetime prevalence," which refers to the entire life of the respondent. For example, researchers may ask respondents whether they smoked cigarettes at any time during the past month (1-month prevalence) or whether they ever used cigarettes in their lifetime (lifetime prevalence). Typically, lifetime prevalence is higher than 1-month or point prevalence because the question captures all past experiences of a disorder or a symptom.

prevalence
The number of people who have ever had a disorder at a given time or over a specified period.

Laboratory Studies

Researchers carry out most experiments in psychological laboratories in which participants provide data under controlled conditions. For example, investigators may show participants stimuli on computer screens and ask them to respond based on what the stimuli call for, such as the presence of a certain word or letter, or an arrow facing left or right that would have to be identified as such. The collected data might include speed of reaction or memory for different types of stimuli. Laboratory studies may also compare brain scan recordings taken while participants were responding under differing conditions or instructions (such as to press a button when they see an "A" but not a "C"). Another type of laboratory study may observe people in small-group settings while investigators study their interactions to a given instruction or prompt, such as to discuss a controversial issue or resolve a disagreement.

Although laboratories are ideal for conducting such experiments, they may also be appropriate settings for self-report data in which participants respond to questionnaires, especially if the researcher is seeking to collect those responses in a fixed period of time or under conditions offering a minimum of distractions. The laboratory may also be a desirable setting for investigators to ask respondents to complete self-report instruments via computer, allowing the investigator to collect data in a systematic and uniform fashion across respondents.

The Case Study

Many classic studies in early abnormal psychology used the **case study** method, in which the researcher or clinician intensively interviews, observes, and tests an individual or small group of individuals. For example, Freud based much of his theory on reports of his own patients, trying to trace the relationship between their recalled experiences, the development of their symptoms, and ultimately their progress in therapy.

case study
An intensive study of a single person described in detail.

In current research, investigators carry out a case study for a number of reasons. It affords the researcher the opportunity to report on rare cases or to chronicle the way a disorder evolved over time in a closely studied individual. For example, a clinical psychologist may write a report in a published journal about how she provided treatment to a client with a rare type of fear.

REAL STORIES

Vincent van Gogh: Psychosis

Vincent van Gogh, a Dutch-born Postimpressionist painter, lived most of his life in poverty and poor physical and mental health. After his death, the fame and popularity of his work grew immensely. His now instantly recognizable paintings sell for tens of millions of dollars, while during his lifetime he was supported mainly by his brother Theo, who sent him art supplies and money for living expenses. Van Gogh struggled with mental illness for much of his life, spending one year in an asylum before the last year of his life, when he committed suicide in 1890 at the age of 37.

Though the specific nature of van Gogh's mental illness is unknown, his 600 or so letters to Theo offer some insight into his experiences. Published in 1937, *Dear Theo: The Autobiography of Vincent van Gogh* provides an unfiltered glimpse into all aspects of his life including art, love, and his psychological difficulties. Van Gogh never received a formal diagnosis, and to this day many psychologists argue over the disorder from which he may have been suffering. They have suggested as many as 30 possible diagnoses, ranging from schizophrenia and bipolar disorder to syphilis and alcoholism. Constant poor nutrition, excessive consumption of absinthe, and a tendency to work to the point of exhaustion undoubtedly contributed to and worsened any psychological issues van Gogh experienced.

Van Gogh's romantic life was marked by a series of failed relationships, and he never had children. In 1881, when he proposed marriage to Kee Vos-Stricker, a widow with a child, she and her parents turned him down because he was having difficulty supporting himself financially and would not have been able to support the family. In response to this rejection, van Gogh held his hand over a lamp flame, demanding that Vos-Stricker's father allow him to see the woman he loved, an event he was later unable to recall entirely. Unfortunately for van Gogh, his affections were never reciprocated. His longest known romantic relationship lasted one year, during which he lived with a prostitute and her two children.

Van Gogh first learned to draw in middle school. He failed the entrance exam for theology school in Amsterdam, and he later failed missionary school. In 1880 he decided to devote his life to painting. After attending art school in Brussels, van Gogh moved around the Netherlands and fine-tuned his craft, often living in poverty and squalid conditions. He spent some time living with his parents but never stayed with them long, due to his tumultuous relationship with his father. By 1885, he had begun to gain recognition as an artist and had completed his first major work, *The Potato Eaters*. The following year he moved to Paris, where he lived with his brother and began to immerse himself in the thriving art world of the city. Due to his poor living conditions, van Gogh's health began to deteriorate, so he moved to the countryside in the south of France. There he spent two months living with and working alongside his good friend and fellow painter Paul Gauguin. Their artistic differences led to frequent disagreements that slowly eroded their amiable companionship. In *Dear Theo*, Johanna van Gogh, Vincent's sister-in-law, writes about the notorious incident that took place on December 23, 1888. Van Gogh, "in a state of terrible excitement and high fever, had cut off a piece of his own ear, and had brought it as a gift to a woman in a brothel. There had been a violent scene; Roulin, the postman, managed to get him home, but the police intervened, found Vincent bleeding and unconscious in bed, and sent him to the hospital."

After the incident, van Gogh was committed to an asylum in Saint-Remy de Provence, France, for about one year. While in the hospital, he often reflected on the state of his mental health in letters to his brother:

"These last three months do seem so strange to me. There have been moods of indescribable mental anguish, sometimes moments when the veil of time and of inevitable circumstance seemed for the twinkling of an eye to be parted. After all, you are certainly right, damn well right; even making allowance for hope, the thing is to accept the probably disastrous reality. I am hoping to throw myself once again wholly into my work, which has got behindhand."

While hospitalized and working on recovering from his "attacks," van Gogh

Vincent van Gogh's *Starry Night over the Rhone*, painted in 1888, one year before his death.
©SuperStock/Getty Images

spent most of his time working feverishly on painting, often finding inspiration in the scenery surrounding the asylum. For van Gogh, painting was a welcome relief that he hoped would cure his illness. Of his experiences with mental illness, he wrote, "I am beginning to consider madness as a disease like any other, and accept the thing as such; whereas during the crises themselves I thought that everything I imagined was real." It is clear from many of his letters that he had been experiencing hallucinations and perhaps delusions–two

hallmark symptoms of psychological disorders involving psychosis, such as schizophrenia.

After his release from the asylum, van Gogh participated in art shows in Brussels and Paris. Though he remained artistically productive, his depression deepened until, on July 29, 1890, he walked into a field and shot himself in the chest with a revolver, dying two days later. Van Gogh's last words, according to his brother who had rushed to his deathbed, were, "The sadness will last forever."

In his lifetime, Vincent van Gogh sold only one painting. In 1990, one hundred years after his death, his *Portrait of Dr. Gachet* sold for $82.5 million, making it one of the most expensive paintings ever sold. His priceless work graces galleries around the globe and has an invaluable influence in the art world. Had his story taken place now, with many different options for psychological treatment of psychotic symptoms and depression, his life might not have been cut so tragically short.

The in-depth nature of the case study is also a potential disadvantage in that it does not rely on the types of experimental control or sample size that would make it a useful addition to the literature. Investigators using case studies must therefore be extremely precise in their methods and, as much as possible, take an objective and unbiased approach. They are likely to seek publication in a journal that specializes in the case study approach rather than one that relies on large sample or experimental data.

Case studies may, however, be presented in a way that represents the best of both worlds. In **qualitative research**, researchers use rigorous methods to code the data and summarize information in a way that reflects an objectively applied set of standards. For example, a researcher may interview several families and then summarize their responses in categories that are clearly described and reflect agreement among independent raters.

qualitative research
A method of analyzing data in which researchers use rigorous methods to code the data and summarize information in a way that reflects an objectively applied set of standards.

Single Case Experimental Design

In a **single case experimental design (SCED)**, the same person serves as the subject in both the experimental and the control conditions. Particularly useful for studies of treatment effectiveness, a single-subject design typically alternates between the baseline condition ("A") and the intervention ("B"). Another term for SCEDs is *ABAB designs*, reflecting the alternation between conditions A and B. Figure 1 shows an example of an SCED studying self-injurious behavior.

In cases where withholding the treatment in the "B" phase would present an ethical problem because the researcher would be eliminating an effective treatment, the variation known as multiple baseline method is substituted. Here the researcher alternates between treatment and withdrawal of treatment across different subjects, for different behaviors, or in different settings. For example, in treating a suicidal client, an investigator may first target suicidal thoughts, and second, target suicidal behaviors. The power of the design lies in showing that the behaviors change only when the researcher introduces specific treatments directed at altering those specific behaviors (Rizvi & Nock, 2008).

single case experimental design (SCED)
Design in which the same person serves as the subject in both the experimental and control conditions.

Research in Behavioral Genetics

The goal of research in **behavioral genetics** is to identify the role of hereditary factors in psychological disorders. This area of research is becoming increasingly important in the field as investigators attempt to understand the biological component of biopsychosocial contributions to psychopathology.

Behavioral geneticists typically begin their investigation into a disorder's genetic inheritance after they find evidence that the disorder shows a distinct pattern of family inheritance. This part of the process requires that researchers obtain complete family histories from people whom they can identify as having symptoms of the disorder. The investigators then calculate the **concordance rate**, or agreement ratio, between people diagnosed as having the disorder and their relatives. For example, a researcher may observe that 6 of a sample of

behavioral genetics
Research area focused on identifying the role of hereditary factors in psychological disorders.

concordance rate
Agreement ratios between people diagnosed as having a particular disorder and their relatives.

FIGURE 1 ABAB Design

In an ABAB design, researchers observe behaviors in the "A" phase, institute treatment in the "B" phase, and then repeat the process. In this hypothetical study, suicide ideation seems to improve with treatment in the top set of graphs but shows no effect of treatment in the bottom set of graphs.

SOURCE: Rizvi, S. L., & Nock, M. K. (2008). Single-case experimental designs for the evaluation of treatments for self-injurious and suicidal behaviors. *Suicide and Life-Threatening Behavior, 38,* 498–510.

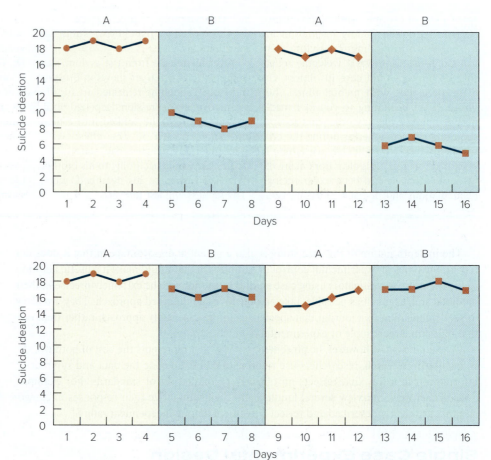

10 twin pairs have the same diagnosed psychological disorder. This would mean that, among this sample, there is a concordance rate of .60 (6 of 10).

We would expect an inherited disorder to have the highest concordance between monozygotic, or identical, twins because their genes are exactly the same. Next higher should be siblings and dizygotic, or fraternal, twins, because they come from the same parents. Lower and lower family concordance rates should be observed among relatives who are further and further removed from each other.

An intriguing variation on twin studies is research comparing the concordance rates between monozygotic twins reared in the same household and monozygotic twins reared by two different sets of parents. If twins reared apart are as likely to share a particular disorder as those reared together, this suggests that genetics played a stronger role in the development of the disorder than the environment.

Adoption studies along similar lines also contribute valuable information about a disorder's genetic basis. In one type of adoption study, researchers establish the rates of a disorder in children whose biological parents have diagnosed psychological disorders, but whose adoptive parents do not. If the children have the same disorder as their biological parents, this suggests that genetic factors play a stronger role than the environment. In a second type of adoption study, referred to as **cross-fostering**, researchers examine the frequency of the disorder in children whose biological parents had no disorder, but whose adoptive parents do. If the children and their adoptive parents share the disorder, this suggests that environmental factors contribute significantly to the disorder's development.

Twin and adoption studies enable researchers to draw inferences about the relative contributions of biology and family environment to the development of psychological disorders. However, they have important weaknesses and therefore cannot be conclusive. In an adoption study, unmeasured characteristics of the adoptive parents may influence the development of the disorder in the children. The most significant threat to the usefulness of twin studies is the

cross-fostering

A type of adoption study in which researchers examine the frequency of the disorder in children whose biological parents had no disorder, but whose adoptive parents do.

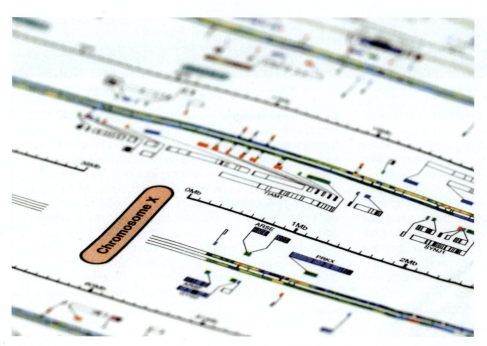

Gene mapping is revolutionizing the way that scientists understand and treat psychological disorders.
©Martin Shields/Alamy Stock Photo

fact that the majority of monozygotic twins do not share the same amniotic sac during prenatal development (Mukherjee et al., 2009). They may not even share 100 percent of the same DNA (Ollikainen et al., 2010). Therefore they are not truly identical. Similarly, in adoption studies, there may be reasons that children are adopted away from their biological parents that play an unmeasured role in influencing the development of a particular disorder.

More precise methods of behavioral genetics take advantage of new methods of genetic testing. In **gene mapping**, researchers examine variations in chromosomes and connect them to performance on psychological tests or diagnosis of specific disorders. **Molecular genetics** studies how genes translate hereditary information into the instructions the genes give for the manufacturing of proteins in the cell.

These newer methods in the study of abnormal psychology are providing a rapidly expanding literature to help us understand how hereditary information translates into behavior disorders. They have led to widespread advances in our understanding of autism, schizophrenia, and various anxiety disorders, for example (Hoffman & State, 2010). It is hoped that this field will give researchers insight into the biological causes, and ultimately the treatment, of many of the most serious and troubling psychological disorders that until now have eluded our grasp.

gene mapping
The approach used by biological researchers in which they examine variations in chromosomes and connect them to performance on psychological tests or diagnosis of specific disorders.

molecular genetics
The study of how genes translate hereditary information.

Bringing It All Together: Clinical Perspectives

As you come to the close of this chapter, you should have an appreciation of the issues central to your understanding of abnormal psychology. You should have a sense, too, of how complex is the definition of abnormality, and you will find yourself returning to this issue as you read about many of the disorders in the chapters that follow. We will elaborate on the historical perspective in subsequent chapters as we look at theories of and treatments for specific disorders. Developments in the field of abnormal psychology are emerging at an unbelievable pace thanks to the efforts of researchers applying the techniques described here. You will learn more about some of these research methods in the context of discussions regarding specific disorders. You will also develop an understanding of how clinicians, such as Dr. Sarah Tobin, study the range of psychological disorders that affect people throughout the life span. We will give particular attention to explaining how disorders develop and how clinicians can best treat them. Our discussion of the impact of psychological disorders on the individual forms a central theme for this book, as we return time and again to consider the human experience of psychological disorders.

An intern saw Rebecca at the counseling center once a week for 12 consecutive weeks. During the first few sessions Rebecca was often tearful, especially when talking about her boyfriend and how lonely she was feeling. In therapy, she and the intern worked on identifying her emotions and finding coping skills for dealing with stress. Eventually, Rebecca's feelings of sadness lifted as she became accustomed to her life on campus and was able to make a few close friends. Because she was feeling better, her sleeping also improved, which helped her to concentrate in class more easily, allowing her to perform better and thus feel more confident in herself as a student.

Dr. Tobin's reflections: It was clear to me in our initial session that Rebecca was a young woman who was having a particularly difficult time dealing with ordinary adjustment issues in adapting to college. She was overwhelmed by the many new experiences confronting her as well, and she seemed particularly unable to cope with being on her own and being separated from her support network including her family and boyfriend. Her high academic standards added to her stress, and because she didn't have social support, she was unable to talk about the difficulties she was having, which surely perpetuated her problems. I am glad she sought help early, before her difficulties became exacerbated, and that she responded so well to treatment.

SUMMARY

- Questions about normality and abnormality are basic to our understanding of psychological disorders. These disorders can affect us in very personal ways.

- Social attitudes toward people with psychological disorders range from discomfort to prejudice. Language, humor, and stereotypes all portray psychological disorders in a negative light. Stereotypes then result in social discrimination, which only serves to complicate the lives of the affected even more.

- The mental health community currently uses five diagnostic criteria to measure abnormality: (1) clinical significance, (2) dysfunction in psychological, biological, or developmental processes, (3) significant distress or disability, (4) behavior that cannot be defined as deviant in terms of sociopolitical conflicts, and (5) behavior that must reflect dysfunction in the individual. Although these five criteria can serve as the basis for defining abnormality, interactions among them often occur.

- Causes of abnormality incorporate biological, psychological, and sociocultural factors. Scientists use the term *biopsychosocial* to refer to the interaction among these factors and their role in the development of an individual's symptoms.

- The three prominent themes in explanations of psychological disorders that recur throughout history are spiritual, humanitarian, and scientific explanations. Spiritual explanations regard abnormal behavior as the product of possession by evil or demonic spirits. Humanitarian explanations view psychological disorders as the result of cruelty, stress, or poor living conditions. Scientific explanations look for causes that we can objectively measure, such as biological alterations, faulty learning processes, or emotional stressors.

- Researchers use various methods to study the causes and treatment of psychological disorders. These all rely on the scientific method, which is a progression of steps from posing questions of interest to sharing the results with the scientific community. Two research designs are experimental design, which tests a hypothesis by constructing a manipulation of a key variable interest, and correlational design, which tests relationships between variables that researchers cannot experimentally manipulate.

- Types of research studies include surveys, laboratory studies, and case studies. Surveys enable researchers to estimate the incidence and prevalence of psychological disorders. In a laboratory, participants are exposed to conditions based on the nature of the experimental manipulation. Case studies enable the researcher to intensively study one individual. A case study can also be a single-case experimental design, in which the researcher studies one person at a time in both the experimental and control conditions, in alternating phases.

- Investigations in the field of behavioral genetics attempt to determine the extent to which people inherit psychological disorders. Different types of studies enable researchers to draw inferences about the relative contributions of biology and family environment to the development of psychological disorders.

KEY TERMS

Behavioral genetics
Biopsychosocial perspective
Case study
Clinical significance
Concordance rate
Correlational design
Cross-fostering
Deinstitutionalization movement
Dependent variable
Double-blind
Evidence-based treatment
Exorcism

Gene mapping
Halfway house
Humanitarian explanations
Incidence
Independent variable
Mental hygiene
Molecular genetics
Moral treatment
Placebo condition
Placebo-controlled randomized
  clinical trial
Positive psychology

Prevalence
Qualitative research
Randomized controlled trial (RCT)
Scientific explanations
Scientific method
Single case experimental design
  (SCED)
Sociocultural perspective
Spiritual explanations
Stigma
Survey
Trephining

Diagnosis and Treatment

Learning Objectives

2.1 Describe the experiences of the client and the clinician.

2.2 Assess the strengths and weaknesses of the *DSM* approach to psychological disorders.

2.3 Identify the *International Classification of Diseases (ICD)*.

2.4 Explain the steps of the diagnostic process.

2.5 Describe treatment planning and goals.

2.6 Explain the course and outcome of treatment.

©Anton Samsonov/123RF

Case Report: Pedro Padilla

Demographic information: 28-year-old single heterosexual Latino male

Presenting problem: Pedro's girlfriend, Natalia, referred Pedro to an outpatient mental health clinic in the community. He is in his second year as a defense attorney at a small law firm. Natalia reported that about 6 months ago, Pedro's parents began divorce proceedings, at which point she noticed some changes in his behavior. Although his job had always been challenging, Pedro was a hard worker who devoted himself to his studies throughout his academic career and had been just as motivated at his current job. Since the divorce, however, Natalia reported that Pedro had been sleeping only a few hours a night and was having trouble keeping up with his caseload at work. It had gotten so bad that the firm considered firing him.

When he was seen at the outpatient clinic, Pedro reported that the past 6 months had been very difficult for him. Although he stated he had always been a "worrier," he couldn't get his parents' divorce off his mind, and it was interfering with his ability to focus and perform well at his job. He described most of the worried thoughts as fears that his parents' divorce would destroy their lives as well as his. He stated he worried that somehow their divorce was his fault, and that once the thought entered his mind, it would play on repeatedly like a broken record. He also explained that Natalia had threatened to break up with him if he didn't "get it together," about which he was also spending a great deal of time worrying. He stated that he constantly worried that he had ruined her life and that this thought was also very repetitive.

Pedro was noticeably anxious and irritable throughout the session, especially when talking about his parents or about Natalia. Early in the session, he expressed that he had been feeling very tense all day and that his stomach was "in knots." Throughout the session, his legs and hands were fidgety, and he stood up and sat down in his chair several times. He stated that since starting his new job, he had become very short-tempered with people and often felt "wired" and tense, and as a result had a difficult time concentrating on his work and sleeping soundly. He explained that he couldn't remember the last time he felt calm or didn't worry about anything for an entire day. He also stated that he could barely think about anything other than his parents' divorce and his relationship problems with Natalia, even if he tried to get his mind off it. He reported that prior to learning of his parents' divorce, he was mainly "obsessive" about his work, which he noted was similar to how he was as an undergraduate and in law school. He expressed that he was usually afraid he would make an error, and would spend more time worrying about failing than actually doing his work. As a result, he said, he often had little time for friends or romantic relationships because he would feel guilty if he were engaging in pleasurable activities rather than focusing on his work. A serious relationship of 4 years ended after his ex-girlfriend grew tired of what she had called his "obsession" with working and his neglect of their relationship. Currently, faced with losing his job and another important relationship, Pedro stated that he realizes for the first time that his anxiety might be interfering with his life.

Relevant history: Pedro reported that his mother had a history of panic attacks and his father had taken antianxiety medication, though he was unable to recall any further details of his family history. He stated that since he could remember he had "always" felt anxious and often worried about things more than other people. He remembered a particular instance in high school when he barely slept for 2 weeks because he was preparing for an argument for his school's debate team. Pedro stated he has never had any psychotherapy or taken any psychiatric medication. He reported that although his worrying often makes him feel "down," he has never felt severely depressed and has no history of suicidal ideation.

Symptoms: Over a period of approximately 6 months, Pedro had increased difficulty sleeping through the night, restlessness, difficulty concentrating, irritability. He said he found it difficult to control the worry and he spent most of his time worrying about either his parents' divorce, work, or his relationship with Natalia.

Case formulation: Pedro meets all the required *DSM-5* criteria for generalized anxiety disorder (GAD). He had been displaying excessive worry for more days than not for at least the past 6 months, was unable to control his

worry, and presented four of the six main symptoms associated with GAD. Additionally, Pedro's worry was not related to fears of having a panic attack (as in panic disorder), or about being in social or public situations (as in social anxiety disorder). His anxiety was causing him significant problems at work and in his relationship with Natalia. Finally, Pedro's anxiety was not the result of substance use.

Treatment plan: Pedro's treatment plan will involve a combination of two approaches. First, he will be referred to a psychiatrist for antianxiety medication to ease the physical symptoms of his anxiety. Cognitive behavioral psychotherapy will also be recommended, as this has been shown to be the most effective current therapeutic modality for treating GAD.

Sarah Tobin, PhD
Clinician

Pedro's life was thrown into havoc by the worsening of his anxiety symptoms, putting him at risk of losing his job and his relationship. Dr. Tobin's treatment plan suggests a set of steps to address Pedro's immediate symptoms and ultimately to bring him longer-term relief. In this chapter, you will learn about how clinicians proceed through the steps of diagnosis and treatment planning. In order to help you understand these steps, we will introduce you to the fundamental concepts that guide these key processes.

2.1 Psychological Disorder: Experiences of Client and Clinician

Professionals working in the field of mental health come from a wide range of backgrounds. The work of mental health professionals is directed toward both examining the causes of abnormal behavior and understanding the complex issues involved in the therapeutic process. In this chapter, we focus on treatment, beginning by introducing you to the relevant players, "client" and "clinician."

The Client

client
A person seeking psychological treatment.

patient
In the medical model, a person who receives treatment.

People working in the area of abnormal psychology refer to individuals seeking psychological intervention alternately as **client** and **patient**. In this book, we prefer to use the term *client*, to refer to the person seeking psychological treatment. This definition reflects the view that the people in treatment collaborate with those who treat them. Some psychologicals prefer the term *patient*, which is a term based in the medical model to refer to a person who receives treatment. Psychologists working in health care settings may find it more appropriate to use the term *patient*, to be consistent with the terminology used by other health care professionals. Typically, clinicians adapt their terminology to refer to those in treatment to the standards of the setting in which they work.

Whatever terminology you use to refer to people in treatment, it is important to be sensitive to the language you use to refer to those with a given disorder. We highly recommend that you refer to people as "clients" (or "patients") who *have* a certain disorder, and not refer to them by the name of their disorder. In other words, if you call someone a "schizophrenic" you equate the person with the disorder. People are more than the sum of their disorders, nor are all individuals with a given disorder exactly the same. By using your language carefully, you communicate greater respect for the total person.

The Clinician

In this book, we refer to the person providing treatment as the **clinician**. There are many types of clinicians who approach clinical work in a variety of ways, based on their training and orientation. **Psychologists** are licensed health care professionals offering psychological services. **Psychiatrists** are physicians (MDs) who receive specialized advanced training in diagnosing and treating people with psychological disorders. **Clinical psychologists** are mental health professionals with training in the behavioral sciences who provide direct service to clients. As of 2017, psychologists have prescribing privileges in Iowa, Idaho, Illinois, New Mexico, and Louisiana, as well as in the Public Health Service, the Indian Health Service, the U.S. military, and Guam. Psychologists with prescribing privileges are required to obtain specialized training that goes beyond the clinical coursework they complete as part of their education to be psychologists.

A trusting, positive relationship between therapist and client is crucial to a good therapeutic outcome.
©Tetra Images/Getty Images

There are three types of doctorates in psychology. The doctor of philosophy (PhD) is typically awarded for completing graduate training in a research-based program. In order to be able to practice, people who get their PhDs in clinical psychology must also complete an internship and at least 1 year of supervised postdoctoral training. The doctor of psychology (PsyD) is the degree that professional schools of psychology award and typically involves less training in research. Individuals with a PsyD also must complete an internship in order to practice. Counseling psychologists, with either a doctorate in education (EdD) or a PhD, also serve as clinicians. In order to qualify for a license to practice, doctoral-level clinicians must pass an examination.

Professionals with master's degrees also provide psychological services. These include social workers, master's-level counselors, marriage and family therapists, nurse clinicians, and school psychologists. The mental health field also includes a large group of individuals who do not have graduate-level training but serve a critical role in the functioning and administration of the mental health system. Included in this group are occupational therapists, recreational therapists, and counselors who work in institutions, agencies, schools, and homes. Clinicians within each specialty must train according to the standards of their discipline and maintain credentials, such as licenses, required by their state, province, or country in order to provide mental health services.

clinician
The person providing treatment.

psychologist
Licensed health care professional offering psychological services.

psychiatrist
Person with a degree in medicine (MD) who receives specialized advanced training in diagnosing and treating people with psychological disorders.

clinical psychologist
A mental health professional with training in the behavioral sciences who provides direct service to clients.

2.2 The Diagnostic Process

In order to treat psychological disorders, clinicians must first be able to diagnose them. The diagnostic process requires that clinicians use a systematic approach to classifying the disorders they see in their clients. A diagnostic manual serves to provide consistent diagnoses across people based on the presence or absence of a set of specific symptoms. Without an accurate diagnostic manual, it is impossible for the clinician to decide on the best treatment path for a given client. Researchers use standard forms of diagnostic manuals to provide investigators with consistent terminologies to use when reporting their findings. These may be the same manuals as those used by clinicians, or they may be research-based criteria accepted within the profession as providing terminology that can be translated into clinical use.

The diagnostic process requires that clinicians conduct an assessment in a sensitive and thorough manner.

©Wavebreak Media Ltd/1v23RF

reliability
When used with regard to diagnosis, the degree to which clinicians provide diagnoses consistently across individuals who have a particular set of symptoms.

validity
The extent to which a test, diagnosis, or rating accurately and distinctly characterizes a person's psychological status.

Diagnostic and Statistical Manual of Mental Disorders (DSM)
A book published by the American Psychiatric Association that contains standard terms and definitions of psychological disorders.

A diagnostic manual's ability to do its job hinges upon its meeting two sets of criteria. The first is **reliability**, meaning, when used with regard to diagnosis, the degree to which clinicians provide diagnoses consistently across individuals who have a particular set of symptoms. Clinicians rating similar clients need to be consistent, and different clinicians also need to be able to arrive at diagnoses that agree with each other. A manual would not be very useful if the symptom of sad mood led one clinician to assign one diagnosis and another to adopt a completely different one. Second, a diagnostic manual must have **validity**, which is the extent to which a test, diagnosis, or rating accurately and distinctly characterizes a person's psychological status.

Current diagnostic manuals are based on the medical model in that they serve as a resource for clinicians to match the client's symptoms with a standard label applicable to anyone with the same symptoms. Such labels then make it possible for clinicians to decide on a treatment that is most likely to treat those symptoms. Although this seems like a reasonable set of steps, some in the mental health community believe the advantages of being able to provide a diagnosis are outweighed by the costs. A diagnosis requires that an individual's behavior can be classified as either normal or abnormal rather than being graded on a continuum. It becomes all too easy for mental health providers to equate the individual with the disease, which, as we discussed earlier, fails to consider the person as an individual. This puts the individual at greater risk of being stigmatized than if no diagnosis at all were assigned.

Despite these criticisms, mental health professionals still must rely on diagnostic systems, if for no other reason than to allow their clients to receive treatment in hospitals and reimbursement from health care providers. Insurance companies utilize the diagnostic codes to determine payment schedules for both in-hospital and outpatient care. For our purposes, it is worthwhile to be alert to the criticisms of these diagnostic systems, particularly because they serve as a reminder that it is the person, not the disease, that should be at the center of the clinician's focus.

Diagnostic and Statistical Manual (DSM-5)

Clinicians use the standard terms and definitions contained in the *Diagnostic and Statistical Manual of Mental Disorders (DSM)* published by the American Psychiatric Association. We have organized this text according to the most recent version, which is the *DSM-5,* or fifth edition (American Psychiatric Association, 2013). The prior edition, the *DSM-IV-TR,* organized diagnoses using five separate axes. It defined an **axis** as a category of information regarding one dimension of an individual's functioning. The **multiaxial system** was a multidimensional classification and diagnostic system in previous *DSM*s summarizing relevant information about an individual's physical and psychological functioning. Now, *DSM-5* contains a "Section III," which includes assessment measures and diagnoses not considered well established enough to be part of the main system. These diagnoses may become incorporated into the next edition of *DSM-5* or a *"DSM-5.1,"* should clinical and research data support their inclusion.

Reflecting the increasing reliance of mental health professionals on online tools and mobile applications, the *DSM-5* is available for use on Apple and Android devices. In this form, the text behind the diagnoses is more difficult to read, but it is far easier for clinicians to scroll through categories of disorders and symptoms than in the paper version of the manual.

In whatever form clinicians use it, *DSM-5* is divided into 22 chapters that each include sets of related disorders. The chapters are organized so that the closer disorders appear sequentially in the text, the more closely related they are believed to be. Furthermore, because psychological and biological diseases often relate to each other, a number of diagnoses in *DSM-5* have embedded within them a medical diagnosis such as a neurological disease that produces cognitive symptoms. You can read examples of disorders in each category in Table 1.

axis
A class of information in previous *DSM*s regarding one dimension of an individual's functioning.

multiaxial system
A multidimensional classification and diagnostic system in previous *DSM*s summarizing relevant information about an individual's physical and psychological functioning.

TABLE 1 Disorders in *DSM-5*

Category	Description	Examples of Diagnoses
Neurodevelopmental disorders	Disorders that usually develop during the earlier years of life, primarily involving abnormal development and maturation	Autism spectrum disorder Specific learning disorder Attention-deficit hyperactivity disorder
Schizophrenia spectrum and other psychotic disorders	Disorders involving symptoms of distortion in perception of reality and impairment in thinking, behavior, affect, and motivation	Schizophrenia Brief psychotic disorder
Bipolar and related disorders	Disorders involving elevated mood	Bipolar disorder Cyclothymic disorder
Depressive disorders	Disorders involving sad mood	Major depressive disorder Persistent depressive disorder
Anxiety disorders	Disorders involving the experience of intense anxiety, worry, fear, or apprehension	Panic disorder Agoraphobia Specific phobia Social anxiety disorder
Obsessive-compulsive and related disorders	Disorders involving obsessions and compulsions	Obsessive-compulsive disorder Body dysmorphic disorder Hoarding disorder
Trauma and stressor-related disorders	Responses to traumatic events	Post-traumatic stress disorder Acute stress disorder Adjustment disorder
Dissociative disorders	Disorders in which the normal integration of consciousness, memory, sense of self, or perception is disrupted	Dissociative identity disorder Dissociative amnesia
Somatic symptom disorders	Disorders involving recurring complaints of physical symptoms that may or may not be associated with a medical condition	Illness anxiety disorder Functional neurological symptom disorder
Feeding and eating disorders	Disorders characterized by severe disturbances in eating behavior	Anorexia nervosa Bulimia nervosa Binge eating disorder

Elimination disorders	Disorders involving bladder and bowel disturbances	Enuresis (bladder) Encopresis (bowel)
Sleep-wake disorders	Disorders involving disturbed sleep patterns	Insomnia disorder Narcolepsy
Sexual dysfunctions	Disorders involving disturbance in the expression or experience of sexuality	Erectile disorder Female orgasmic disorder Premature ejaculation
Gender dysphoria	Mismatch between biological sex and gender identity	Gender dysphoria
Disruptive, impulse-control, and conduct disorders	Disorders characterized by repeated expression of impulsive or disruptive behaviors	Kleptomania Intermittent explosive disorder Conduct disorder
Substance-related and addictive disorders	Disorders related to the use of substances	Substance use disorders Substance-induced disorders
Neurocognitive disorders	Disorders involving impairments in thought processes caused by substances or medical conditions	Mild neurocognitive disorder Major neurocognitive disorder
Personality disorders	Disorders in an individual's personality	Borderline personality disorder Antisocial personality disorder Narcissistic personality disorder
Paraphilic disorders	Disorder in which a paraphilia causes distress and impairment	Pedophilic disorder Fetishistic disorder Transvestic disorder
Other mental disorders	Conditions or problems for which a person may seek professional help	Other specified mental disorder due to another medical condition
Medication-induced movement disorders and other adverse effects of medication	Disturbances that can be traced to use of medication	Tardive dyskinesia Medication-induced postural tremor
Other conditions that may be a focus of clinical attention	Conditions or problems for which a person may seek medical help	Problems related to abuse or neglect Occupational problem

SOURCE: From the *Diagnostic and Statistical Manual of Mental Disorders,* Fifth Edition. 2013 American Psychiatric Association.

International Classification of Diseases (ICD)
The diagnostic system of the World Health Organization (WHO).

Most mental health professionals outside the United States and Canada do not use the *DSM-5* but instead base their diagnoses on the World Health Organization's (WHO) diagnostic system, the **International Classification of Diseases (ICD)**. WHO developed the *ICD* as a tool to use for the purposes of comparing disease rates among the 110 member nations of WHO, providing assurance that countries employ the same terminology for the sake of consistency. As such, the *ICD* includes health conditions, not just those involving psychological disorders. The tenth edition *(ICD-10)* is currently in use; it is undergoing a major revision, which will be the *ICD-11*, due to be published in 2018 (World Health Organization, 2018). Although there are differences in specific areas, the two systems share more than 90 percent of diagnostic categories (Demazeux, 2013).

Additional Diagnostic Information

As part of the diagnostic process, clinicians may wish to add information about the medical status of their clients. If illnesses that are primarily medical are not specified in *DSM-5,* clinicians may use the standard *ICD* diagnoses for the conditions. By specifying these illnesses, clinicians transmit information that has important therapeutic implications. For example, many medications aimed at treating certain medical conditions have side effects that can alter a client's cognitive status, mood, or levels of alertness. In addition, knowing about a client's medical condition can provide the clinician with insights about the individual's psychological symptoms. It would be useful to know that a middle-aged man appearing in treatment for a depressive disorder for the first time had a heart attack 6 months ago. The heart attack may have constituted a risk factor for the development of depression, particularly in a person with no previous psychiatric history.

In providing a total diagnostic picture of the client's psychological disorder, clinicians may also decide it is important to specify particular sources of life stress that are affecting the individual's psychological status. In these cases, clinicians can use a set of codes in the *ICD* that indicate the presence of psychosocial and environmental problems known as **Z codes**. We have selected several examples of *ICD-10* Z codes in Table 2. These may be important because they can affect the diagnosis, treatment, or outcome of a client's psychological disorder. A person first showing signs of an anxiety disorder shortly after becoming unemployed presents a very different diagnostic picture than someone whose current life circumstances are stable and have no apparent impact on the individual's psychological symptoms.

What's in the *DSM-5*

Changes in the *DSM-5* Structure

All editions of the *DSM* have generated considerable controversy, and the fifth edition seems to be no exception. The need for a diagnostic manual meeting criteria of reliability and validity forms the heart of controversy regarding the *DSM-5*. In its current form, it reflects the collective wisdom of clinicians and researchers who believed they were providing criteria that would result in the consistent application of diagnoses (reliability) of disorders that individuals actually experience (validity). Although criticized on both counts, the *DSM-5* was written in such a way as to maximize its scientific and clinical merits. Much of what you will read about in this book regarding *DSM-5* controversies revolves around validity, but there are also challenges to its reliability. The challenge for the authors of any diagnostic system is to settle on agreed-upon categories of symptoms and translate them into terms that anyone who is trained in the system can apply.

The most significant changes concern the multiaxial system—the categorization of disorders along five separate axes. The *DSM-5* task force decided to eliminate the *DSM-IV-TR* multiaxial system and instead follow the system in use by the World Health Organization's *International Classification of Diseases (ICD)*. Axis I of the *DSM-IV-TR* contained major "syndromes," or illness clusters. Axis II contained diagnoses of personality disorders and what was then called mental retardation. Axis III was used to note the client's medical conditions. Axis IV rated the client's psychosocial stresses, and Axis V rated the client's overall level of functioning. The task forces also considered using a dimensional model in which disorders are viewed along a continuum instead of the categorical model represented by *DSM-IV-TR*. However, in the end, they chose not to do so. The current organization begins with neurodevelopmental disorders and then proceeds through "internalizing" disorders (characterized by anxiety, depressive, and somatic symptoms) to "externalizing" disorders (characterized by impulsive, disruptive conduct and substance-use symptoms). The hope is that eventually there will be new research allowing future diagnostic manuals to be based on underlying causes rather than symptoms alone.

Z codes
Codes in the *ICD* that indicate the presence of psychosocial and environmental problems.

TABLE 2 Examples from Z Codes in *ICD-10* (CDC, 2018)

Problem	Examples
Problems related to education and literacy	Underachievement in school
Problems related to employment and unemployment	Change of job Sexual harassment on the job Military deployment status
Problems related to housing and economic circumstances	Homelessness Extreme poverty Low income
Problems related to social environment	Acculturation difficulty
Other problems related to primary support group, including family circumstances	Problems in relationship with spouse Disappearance and death of family member Alcoholism and drug addiction in family
Problems related to certain psychosocial circumstances	Unwanted pregnancy

For the most part, environmental stressors are events that are inherently negative in nature, such as the death of a family member, an accident, or a high-pressure job. However, we might consider positive life events, such as a job promotion, as stressors. A person who receives a major job promotion may encounter psychological difficulties due to his or her increased responsibilities and demands with the new position. The clinician's job is to evaluate the impact of the stressful event or situation on the client's current symptoms.

Clinicians also may want to include their overall judgment of a client's psychological, social, and occupational functioning. An instrument known as the WHO Disability Assessment Schedule (WHODAS) is included as a section of the *DSM-5* so clinicians can provide such a rating. An example of a question from the WHODAS the clinician might ask is, "In the past 30 days, how much difficulty have you had in concentrating on doing something for 10 minutes?" The client indicates whether the difficult is None, Mild, Moderate, or Severe. Other questions ask about the client's difficulty in taking care of household duties, engaging in community activities, and performing activities such as washing and getting dressed.

Cultural Concepts of Distress

Within particular cultures are idiosyncratic patterns of symptoms, many of which have no direct counterpart to a specific diagnosis. Up through the *DSM-IV-TR,* a set of conditions were defined as **culture-bound syndromes** to refer to behavior patterns that exist only within particular cultures. For example, in Malaysia, a culture-bound syndrome known as amok was used to refer to an extreme reaction to an insult, consisting of brooding followed by a highly aggressive outburst. In *DSM-5*, the concept of culture-bound syndromes was expanded to the more general **cultural concepts of distress**, which are the ways that individuals in specific cultural groups experience, understand, and communicate their suffering, behavioral problems, or troubling thoughts and emotions. The three main categories of the cultural concepts of distress include the cultural syndromes, idioms of distress, and explanations. We define and illustrate each of these key concepts in Table 3.

culture-bound syndromes
Recurrent patterns of abnormal behavior or experience that are limited to specific societies or cultural areas.

cultural concepts of distress
Ways that individuals in specific cultural groups experience, understand, and communicate their suffering, behavioral problems, or troubling thoughts and emotions.

TABLE 3 **Cultural Concepts of Distress in *DSM-5***

Component of Cultural Concept of Distress	Problem	Examples
Cultural syndromes	Clusters of symptoms and attributions that tend to occur among individuals in specific groups who share the same culture	*Ataque de nervios*, a syndrome among people of Latino descent reflected in such symptoms as intense emotional upset, aggressive behaviors, and fainting episodes.
Cultural idioms of distress	Ways of expressing distress in a particular culture or group	*Kungfungisisa*, meaning "thinking too much" among the Shona of Zimbabwe, referring to depression, anxiety, and physical symptoms.
Cultural explanations or perceived causes	How people in the culture label or attribute causes to symptoms, illness, or distress	*Dhat syndrome*, the belief among South Asians that semen loss causes diverse symptoms in young men such as fatigue, anxiety, weight loss, and depressive mood.

SOURCE: From the *Diagnostic and Statistical Manual of Mental Disorders,* Fifth Edition. 2013 American Psychiatric Association.

As you can see, the *DSM-5* looks at cultural factors in the broadest sense, taking into account that factors other than nationality or ethnicity need to be considered in order for the clinician to get a full understanding of each client. These factors include race, religion, immigration status, and relationships with family and community as potential sources of not only symptoms but also support.

2.3 Steps in the Diagnostic Process

Throughout the diagnostic process, the clinician uses all relevant information to arrive at a label that best seems to capture the client's disorder. This information includes the results of any tests given to the client, material gathered from interviews, and knowledge about the client's personal history.

Diagnostic Procedures

The key to the diagnostic process is for the clinician to gain as clear a description as possible of a client's symptoms, both those the client reports and those the clinician observes. Dr. Tobin, when hearing Pedro describe himself as "anxious," assumes that he *may* have an anxiety disorder. However, clients do not always label their internal states accurately. Therefore, the clinician also must attend carefully to the client's behavior, emotional expression, and apparent state of mind. The client may express anxiety, but his behavior may suggest that instead he is experiencing a mood disorder. Dr. Tobin would therefore keep open the possibility that mood disturbances, rather than or in addition to anxiety, are involved in Pedro's diagnosis. Additionally, Dr. Tobin would need to take into account possible cultural factors that are impinging on Pedro's symptoms and understanding of his symptoms.

At the outset of the diagnostic process, clinicians listen to clients describe the experience of their symptoms in their own words. This initial stage leads into the more systematic approach to diagnosis, which allows clinicians to arrive at a provisional understanding of the client's symptoms. As you will learn in the chapter "Assessment," a variety of assessment tools give the clinician a framework for determining the extent to which these symptoms coincide with the diagnostic criteria of a given disorder. The clinician must determine the exact nature of a client's symptoms, the length of time the client has experienced these symptoms, and any other behaviors, thoughts, or feelings that may represent important symptoms that the client may not report. In the process, the clinician also obtains information about the client's personal and family history as well as cultural background and identity. By asking questions in this manner, the clinician begins to formulate the **principal diagnosis**—namely, the disorder most closely aligned with the primary reason the individual is seeking professional help.

principal diagnosis
The disorder most closely aligned with the primary reason the individual is seeking professional help.

For many clients, the symptoms they experience suggest that there is more than one principal diagnosis. In these cases, we use the term **comorbidity**, meaning literally two (or more) disorders that co-occur. Diagnoses involving comorbidity are remarkably common. The National Comorbidity Study (NCS) and its Replication (NCS-R) was an international collaboration carried out over two successive phases intended to document the extent to which psychiatric diagnoses co-occur in the general population. The most common comorbidities are occurrences of substance use with other psychiatric disorders. For example, among people with physical disabilities, substance use disorder was found to be linked to disorders reflecting exposure to traumatic events (Anderson, Ziedonis, & Najavits, 2014).

comorbidity
Two (or more) disorders that co-occur within the same individual.

Differential diagnosis, the process of systematically ruling out alternative diagnoses, is a crucial step in the diagnostic process. The clinician conducts a differential diagnosis by comparing the client's symptoms to those associated with similar disorders until other possibilities can be eliminated. This is important primarily so that the clinician can be sure to embark on the appropriate treatment. The clinician must also rule out medical diagnoses that could produce symptoms similar to those of a psychological disorder.

differential diagnosis
The process of systematically ruling out alternative diagnoses.

In Pedro's case, the predominant symptom is anxiety, which would suggest that he should receive the diagnosis of an anxiety disorder. Dr. Tobin must then determine which anxiety disorder most closely fits Pedro's symptoms. At the same time, she needs to consider whether Pedro suffers from a medical disorder that could produce similar symptoms. It is also possible that Pedro's symptoms represent adjustment difficulties related to the divorce of his parents or the stress he encounters at work. Add to these the possibilities that he has a disorder related to substance use. Dr. Tobin's initial diagnosis must be tested against these possibilities before she can proceed to provide Pedro with the type of care most likely to help alleviate his symptoms.

The diagnostic process can take anywhere from a few hours to weeks depending on the complexity of the client's presenting symptoms. The client and clinician need not wait until the diagnostic process is complete to begin doing therapeutic work, particularly if the client is in crisis. The course of therapy would then be adjusted as the diagnosis can become more firmly established.

Case Formulation

Once the clinician makes a formal diagnosis, he or she is still left with a formidable challenge—to piece together a picture of how the disorder evolved. With the diagnosis, the clinician can assign a label to the client's symptoms. Although informative and necessary for treatment, this label does not tell the client's full story.

case formulation
A clinician's analysis of the client's development and the factors that might have influenced his or her current psychological status.

To gain a full appreciation of the client's disorder, the clinician develops a **case formulation**, an analysis of the client's development and the factors that might have influenced his or her current psychological status. The case formulation transforms the diagnosis from a label and set of diagnostic code numbers to a more elaborated piece of descriptive information about the client's personal history. With this descriptive information, the clinician can more confidently design a treatment plan that is attentive to the client's symptoms, unique past experiences, and future potential for growth.

The cornerstone of a thorough case formulation is an understanding of the client from a biopsychosocial perspective that also takes into account the client's developmental history. Additionally, clinicians seek to incorporate the cultural formulation, family history, and any other relevant background or socially relevant information about the client.

In her work with Pedro, Dr. Tobin starts to flesh out the details of her case formulation as she gets to know him better in the initial therapy phases. Her case formulation will expand to include Pedro's family history, focusing on the divorce of his parents, as well as the possible causes of his perfectionism and concern over his academic performance. She will try to understand why he feels so overwhelmed at work and gain a perspective on why his relationship with Natalia has been so problematic. Finally, she will need to investigate the possible role of his mother's panic attacks and how they relate to Pedro's experience of anxiety symptoms. To aid in differential diagnosis, Dr. Tobin will also evaluate Pedro's pattern of substance use as well as any possible medical conditions that she did not detect during the initial assessment phase. As we will see below, Dr. Tobin will also want to include information based on her cultural formulation of Pedro's case.

Cultural Formulation

cultural formulation
A tool that includes the clinician's assessment of the client's degree of identification with the culture of origin, the culture's beliefs about psychological disorders, the ways in which the culture interprets particular events, and the cultural supports available to the client.

Making a diagnosis involves taking multiple factors from the client's life into account that include the client's sociocultural context. A **cultural formulation** includes the clinician's assessment of the client's degree of identification with his or her culture of origin, the culture's beliefs about psychological disorders, the ways in which people in the culture interpret particular events, and the cultural supports available to the client.

We might expect cultural norms and beliefs to have a stronger impact on clients who strongly identify with their culture of origin. The client's familiarity with and preference for using a certain language is one obvious indicator of cultural identification. A culture's approach to understanding the causes of behavior may influence clients who strongly identify with their culture. Exposure to these belief systems may, in turn, influence the expression of a client's symptoms.

Even if a client's symptoms do not specifically represent a culture-bound syndrome, clinicians must consider the individual's cultural background as a framework for interpreting

Symptoms of psychological disorders often vary based on the person's cultural background.
©wavebreakmedia/Shutterstock

these symptoms. For example, members of a given culture attach significant meanings to particular events. As stated earlier, the condition known as *amok* may occur in certain cultures in response to an insult. In certain Asian cultures, an insult may provoke the condition known as *amok*. Without taking this background into account, the clinician may very well draw the wrong conclusions, assuming that the symptoms reflect a disturbance within the individual when they in fact reflect the playing out of a culturally influenced scenario.

In Pedro's case, although he is a product of middle-class white background, it is possible that cultural factors are influencing his extreme preoccupation with his academic performance. Perhaps his family placed pressure on him to succeed due to their own incorporation of belief in the importance of upward mobility. They may have pressured him heavily to do well in school, and as a result, he felt that his self-worth as an individual depended on his grades. As an adult, he is unable to shake himself from this overly harsh and perfectionistic set of values.

Clinicians should look within the client's cultural background not only for diagnostic purposes but also as a way of determining what cultural supports may be available to them. Clients from cultures that incorporate extended family networks and religious connections can provide emotional resources to help individuals cope with stressful life events.

As you can appreciate, then, cultural formulations are important to understanding psychological disorders from a biopsychosocial perspective. The fact that psychological disorders vary from one society to another supports the claim of the sociocultural perspective that cultural factors play a role in influencing the expression of abnormal behavior.

2.4 Planning the Treatment

Clinicians typically follow up the diagnostic phase by setting up a **treatment plan**, the outline for how therapy should take place. In the treatment plan, the clinician describes the treatment goals, treatment site, modality of treatment, and theoretical approach. The decisions the clinician makes while putting the treatment plan together reflect what he or she knows at the time about the client's needs and the available resources; however, clinicians often revise the treatment plan once they see how the proposed intervention methods are actually working.

treatment plan
The outline for how therapy should take place.

Goals of Treatment

The first step in treatment planning is for the clinician to establish treatment goals, ranging from those that have immediate consequence to those of a more long-term nature. Ideally, treatment goals reflect what the clinician knows about both the disorder and the recommended therapy, and the particular needs and concerns of the individual client.

The immediate goal of treating clients in crisis is to ensure that their symptoms are managed, particularly if they are at risk to themselves or others. Pedro, for example, needs psychiatric treatment in order to bring his anxiety symptoms under control. The clinician may need to hospitalize a client who is severely depressed and suicidal. The treatment plan may include this immediate goal only until the clinician gains a broader understanding of the client's situation.

Short-term goals are aimed at alleviating the client's symptoms by addressing problematic behavior, thinking, or emotions. The plan at this point includes establishing a working relationship between the clinician and client, as well as setting up specific objectives for therapeutic change. Another short-term goal might be to stabilize a client taking medications, a process that could take several weeks or longer if the first round of treatment is unsuccessful. In Pedro's case, Dr. Tobin will need to ensure that the medications he is receiving are in fact helping to alleviate his anxiety. She will also need to work with the psychiatrist on the case to monitor any adverse side effects. Her short-term goals with Pedro will also include beginning to examine the nature of his anxiety and how he can start to manage his symptoms using psychological interventions.

Long-term goals include more fundamental and deeply rooted alterations in the client's psychological health. These are the ultimate aims of therapeutic change. Ideally, the long-term goals for any client are to achieve recovery, or at least to learn to cope with the symptoms of the disorder. Depending on the nature of the client's disorder, available supports, and life stressors, these long-term goals can take some time to accomplish. Dr. Tobin's long-term goals with Pedro are to take him off the medication. At the same time, she would plan to help him gain an understanding of the causes of his symptoms and, in the process, reduce their severity if not eliminate them altogether.

In many cases, clinicians carry out treatment goals in a sequential manner. The clinician first deals with the crisis, then handles problems in the near future, and finally addresses issues that require extensive work in the months ahead. Many clients, however, experience a cyclical unfolding of stages. New sets of immediate crises or short-term goals may arise in the course of treatment; or there may be a redefinition of long-term goals as the course of treatment progresses. It is perhaps more helpful to think of the three stages not as consecutive stages per se, but as implying different levels of treatment focus.

Treatment Site

Clinicians juggle a number of issues when recommending which treatment site will best serve the client. Treatment sites vary in the degree to which they provide a controlled environment and in the nature of the services that clients can receive. Clients who are in crisis or are at risk of harming themselves or others need to be in controlled environments. However, there are many other considerations including cost and insurance coverage, the need for additional medical care, availability of community support, and the projected length of treatment. Depending on the symptoms and the availability of these supports, clinicians recommend client treatment in outpatient settings, schools, or the workplace.

Psychiatric Hospitals In a psychiatric hospital, a client receives medical interventions and intensive forms of psychotherapy.

At this crisis center, telephone counselors are available 24 hours a day.

©PeopleImages/E+/Getty Images

These settings are most appropriate for clients at risk of harming themselves or others and who seem incapable of self-care. In some cases, clinicians may involuntarily hospitalize clients through a court order until they can bring the symptoms under control (we will discuss this in more detail in the chapter "Ethical and Legal Issues").

Specialized Inpatient Treatment Centers

Clients may need intensive supervision but not actual hospital care. For these individuals, specialized inpatient treatment centers provide both supportive services and round-the-clock monitoring. These sites include recovery treatment centers for adults seeking to overcome substance addiction. Clinicians may also recommend this treatment site to children who need constant monitoring due to severe behavioral disturbances.

Outpatient Treatment

By far the most common treatment site is a private therapist's outpatient clinic or office. **Community mental health centers (CMHCs)** are outpatient clinics that provide psychological services on a sliding fee scale for individuals who live within a certain geographic area. Professionals in private practice offer individual or group sessions. Some prepaid health insurance plans cover the cost of such visits, either to a private practitioner or to a clinician working in a health maintenance organization (HMO). Agencies supported partially or completely by public funds may also offer outpatient treatment. Dr. Tobin will see Pedro in outpatient treatment because his symptoms are not sufficiently severe to justify hospitalization.

Clients receiving outpatient services will, by necessity, receive more limited care than what they would encounter in a hospital, in terms of both the time involved and the nature of the contact between client and clinician. Consequently, clinicians may advise that their clients receive additional services, including vocational counseling, in-home services, or the support of a self-help organization, such as Alcoholics Anonymous.

community mental health center (CMHC)
Outpatient clinic that provides psychological services on a sliding fee scale for individuals who live within a certain geographic area.

Halfway Houses and Day Treatment Programs

Clients with serious psychological disorders who are able to live in the community may require the additional support of facilities that are intended to serve the needs of this specific population. These facilities may be connected with a hospital, a public agency, or a private corporation.

Community treatment centers provide much-needed care to individuals with a wide range of psychological disorders.

©James Shaffer/PhotoEdit

Guidance counselors are often the first professionals to whom troubled students turn for professional assistance.

©Yellow Dog Productions/Getty Images

day treatment program
A structured program in a community treatment facility that provides activities similar to those provided in a psychiatric hospital.

modality
Form in which the clinician offers psychotherapy.

individual psychotherapy
Psychological treatment in which the therapist works on a one-to-one basis with the client.

family therapy
Psychological treatment in which the therapist works with several or all members of the family.

group therapy
Psychological treatment in which the therapist facilitates discussion among several clients who talk together about their problems.

Halfway houses are designed for clients who have been discharged from psychiatric facilities but who are not yet ready for independent living. A halfway house provides a living context with other deinstitutionalized people, and it is staffed by professionals who work with clients in developing the skills they need to become employed and to set up independent living situations. **Day treatment programs** are designed for formerly hospitalized clients, as well as for clients who do not need hospitalization but do need a structured program during the day, similar to what a hospital provides.

Other Treatment Sites Clinicians may recommend that their clients receive treatment in the places where they work or go to school. School psychologists are trained to work with children and teenagers who require further assessment or behavioral interventions. In the workplace, employee assistance programs (EAPs) provide employees with a confidential setting in which they can seek individual help in the form of counseling, assistance with substance abuse, and family treatment. These resources may prove important for clinicians who wish to provide their clients with as many resources over the long term as possible.

Modality of Treatment

The **modality**, or form in which the clinician offers psychotherapy, is another crucial component of the treatment plan. Clinicians recommend one or more modalities depending on the nature of the client's symptoms and whether or not other people in the client's life should be involved.

Clients receive treatment on a one-to-one basis in **individual psychotherapy**. In couples therapy, both partners in a relationship, and in **family therapy**, several or all family members, are involved in treatment. In family therapy, family members may identify one person as the "patient." The therapist, however, views the whole family system as the target of the treatment. **Group therapy** is a psychological treatment in which the therapist facilitates

Milieu therapy involves many clients participating within a community setting.

©John Moore/Getty Images

discussion among several clients who talk together about their problems. In this way, clients have the opportunity to share their difficulties with others, receive feedback, develop trust, and improve their interpersonal skills.

A clinician may recommend any or all of these modalities in any setting. Specific to psychiatric hospitals is **milieu therapy**, which is based on the premise that the milieu, or environment, is a major component of the treatment. Ideally, the milieu is organized in a way that allows clients to receive consistent therapeutic and constructive reactions from all who live and work there. In addition to traditional psychotherapy, clients participate in other therapeutic endeavors through group or peer counseling, occupational therapy, and recreational therapy.

milieu therapy
A treatment approach, used in an inpatient psychiatric facility, in which all facets of the milieu, or environment, are components of the treatment.

You Be the Judge

Psychologists as Prescribers

In 2002, New Mexico became the first state to approve prescription privileges for psychologists. Louisiana followed shortly thereafter (2004), as did Illinois (2014), Iowa (2016), and Idaho (2017). These landmark pieces of legislation are paving the way for other states to take similar action. However, the move remains controversial. In 2010, the Oregon legislature passed a bill (SB 1046) granting prescriptive authority to psychologists, but Governor Ted Kulongoski vetoed the bill, in response to pressure from various lobbying groups, including psychiatrists.

There are several arguments against the granting of prescription privileges to psychologists. Unlike psychiatrists, psychologists do not receive medical training and therefore do not have the undergraduate premedical training or the years of medical school, internship, and residency that physicians receive. Philosophically, research-oriented psychologists argue that the granting of prescription privileges will refocus the profession away from science but instead emphasize the role of psychologists as practitioners. Psychologists should not be in the business, they argue, of handing out medication. A second argument against prescription privileges concerns the role of medication in psychological treatment. From this perspective, psychologists should be focused on psychotherapy. The long-term benefits of psychotherapy, these critics argue, are equal to if not greater than the long-term benefits of medication for the majority of disorders including major depression, anxiety disorders, and other nonpsychotic disorders. In the exceptional cases of serious mental illness, such as schizophrenia and bipolar disorder, psychologists can work as a team with psychiatrists to maintain their clients on long-term medication regimens.

The arguments in favor of prescription privileges are also compelling. If psychologists have the power to prescribe medications, they can do a better job than psychiatrists do integrating medication into psychotherapy. From the client's point of view, there is greater continuity of care, in that the individual does not need to see more than one mental health practitioner. Psychologists in favor of prescription privileges also point to the fact that specialized training is required for a clinical psychologist to be able to prescribe medications aimed at psychological disorders. Therefore, the psychologists who do prescribe have an equal knowledge base as do physicians. A second argument in favor of prescription privileges is that there are other nondoctoral-level health professionals with this legal power including psychiatric nurse practitioners and psychiatric nurse specialists, among others, although the exact nature of their privileges varies across states.

The American Psychological Association's Practice Directorate continues to lobby in favor of more widespread acceptance of prescription privileges across the United States. As the Oregon case demonstrates, however, this legislation is likely to face a rocky road in other states.

Q: *You be the judge:* Does having prescription privileges reduce the scientific status of psychology as a profession? Would you prefer that the psychologist you might see for treatment can also incorporate medications into your treatment?

Determining the Best Approach to Treatment

Whatever treatment modality a clinician recommends, it must be based on the choice of the most appropriate theoretical perspective or combination of perspectives. Many clinicians are trained according to a particular set of assumptions about the origins of psychological disorders and the best methods of treating these disorders. Often, this theoretical orientation forms the basis for the clinician's treatment decisions. However, just as frequently, clinicians adapt their theoretical orientation to fit the client's needs.

evidence-based practice in psychology
Clinical decision making that integrates the best available research evidence and clinical expertise in the context of the cultural background, preferences, and characteristics of clients.

After decades of debate regarding which treatments are most effective, and for whom, psychologists adopted the principles of **evidence-based practice in psychology**—clinical decision making that integrates the best available research evidence and clinical expertise in the context of the cultural background, preferences, and characteristics of clients (American Psychological Association Presidential Task Force on Evidence-Based Practice, 2006). Increasingly, training in evidence-based practice forms the basis for curricula in graduate programs and postdoctoral continuing education (Bearman, Wadkins, Bailin, & Doctoroff. 2015).

As you read in this book about various disorders and the most effective treatments, keep in mind that clinicians need to abide by the findings of empirically based research. However, evidence-based practice also implies that clinicians should base their treatments on state-of-the-art research findings that they adapt to the particular features of the client, taking into account the client's background, needs, and prior experiences.

2.5 The Course of Treatment

The way treatment proceeds is a function of the joint efforts of the clinician and client working together toward an improvement in the client's state of mental health and well-being. Each individual has a part to play in determining the outcome of the case, as does the unique interaction of their personalities, abilities, expectations, and backgrounds.

The Clinician's Role in Treatment

Above and beyond whatever treatment techniques a clinician uses, the quality of the relationship between the client and clinician is a crucial determinant of therapy's outcome. A good clinician does more than objectively administer treatment to a client. The best clinicians infuse a deep personal interest, concern, and respect for the client into the therapeutic relationship.

Dr. Tobin will work with Pedro in the initial weeks of therapy to establish this solid basis for their further work together. As treatment proceeds, she will continue to evaluate the effectiveness of her intervention and make adjustments accordingly.

The Client's Role in Treatment

In optimal situations, psychotherapy is a joint enterprise in which the client plays an active role. It is largely up to the client to describe and identify the nature of his or her disorder, to articulate his or her personal reactions as treatment progresses, and to initiate and follow through on changes as they emerge over time.

Throughout treatment, the client's attitudes toward therapy and the therapist are an important part of the contribution the client makes to the therapeutic relationship. There is a special quality to the help the client is requesting; it requires revealing potentially painful, embarrassing, and personal material that the client is not accustomed to sharing with a professional. For some clients, then, part of the work in treatment is learning to be more comfortable discussing their symptoms with a therapist or other mental health professional.

Social attitudes toward psychological disorders based on their cultural backgrounds can also affect how readily clients engage in treatment. The client may come from a culture in which it is taboo to admit to being sad or anxious. The client's family may communicate the idea that people should not need to rely on therapists to get better. They may think there's something wrong with them because they are in need of help. Although attitudes toward therapy are becoming more accepting in current Western culture, there is still a degree of potential shame or embarrassment that clients must confront. To someone who is already troubled by severe problems in living, the added anxiety caused by worrying about what it means to seek psychotherapy can be further inhibiting.

With so many potential forces driving the individual away from seeking therapy, the initial step is sometimes the hardest to take. Thus, the therapeutic relationship requires the client to be willing to work with the clinician in a partnership and to be prepared to endure the pain and embarrassment involved in making personal revelations. Moreover, it also requires a willingness to break old patterns and to try new ways of viewing the self and relating to others.

REAL STORIES

Daniel Johnston: Bipolar Disorder

Daniel Johnston, born January 22, 1961, is an American singer-songwriter well known for his unique musical talent as well as his lifelong struggle with bipolar disorder. The 2005 documentary *The Devil and Daniel Johnston* depicts his incredible story from childhood in West Virginia to the present day. Though Johnston has had an extraordinary musical career, his tumultuous journey with mental illness is not unlike that of many other individuals who suffer from severely debilitating psychological disorders. Through his music, Johnston expresses both the soaring, sometimes delusional manias and the dark, unbearable depths of depression he has faced throughout his life.

As his mother Mabel recalls, Daniel, the youngest of five children, "was different. . . . I noticed that from the start." As a teenager, inspired mostly by comic books, he took on countless artistic endeavors including drawing and making playful movies about his life at home. His creativity helped him gain attention from friends and classmates, but it also endlessly frustrated his highly religious and traditional parents, who would rather he spent his time attending church, working, and helping out around the house. Johnston's passion for creating has remained with him his entire life. In the words of Johnston's best friend, David Thornberry, "He exudes art . . . he can't stop making art."

As with many individuals with severe mood disorders, Johnston's behavior began to change for the worse after he left home for college. His family was used to his acting differently than his peers, but in college Johnston started to become confused and disoriented. A visit to the family physician resulted in a diagnosis of manic depression (bipolar disorder). Unable to continue with the challenges he faced at school, he returned home and enrolled in a small arts college in nearby Ohio. In art school, Johnston met and subsequently fell in love with his classmate Laurie. Though they never had a romantic relationship and she went on to marry another man, Johnston's unrequited love for her has been one of his most powerful creative muses and also caused his first major depressive episode. It was at this point, his mother recalls, that he began to play the piano and write songs.

Johnston was having trouble in his courses at art school, so his family once again took him out of school. This time they sent him to live with his older brother in Houston, in hopes that he could start building a productive life. Johnston worked part-time at a local amusement park and began recording music in his brother's garage. After his brother grew frustrated that Johnston was not finding stable work, he sent him to live with his sister, Margie. One morning, Margie noticed that Johnston had not come home the night before. His family did not hear from Johnston for months; when they did, they learned that he had spontaneously purchased a moped and joined a traveling carnival. When the carnival stopped in Austin, Texas, Johnston was assaulted on the fair grounds and fled to a local church for help. He was able to

Daniel Johnston's songs provide a glimpse into his struggles with mental illness.

©Gary Wolstenholme/Getty Images

find housing in Austin and began taking his homemade tape-recorded albums to local musicians and newspapers. One of the local musicians he met was Kathy McCarthy. The two briefly dated, and after meeting him, Kathy remembers, "It was undeniable after one or two weeks that something was dreadfully wrong with him."

In one scene of *The Devil and Daniel Johnston*, he reads a detailed account of the characteristics of an individual with his condition, stating, "There you have it. I'm a manic depressive with grand delusions." The majority of his delusions were paranoid and religious in nature, perhaps the result of his highly religious upbringing. Although Johnston was well aware of his illness, at the time he was doing little to manage it. In Austin, Johnston began to smoke marijuana and regularly experimented with LSD, causing several bizarre and sometimes violent episodes. Simultaneously, his music career began to blossom as he gained recognition as well as notoriety for his music and his often-bizarre live performances.

In 1986, a Christmas gathering with his siblings soon turned into a horrifying event. Johnston began preaching to his family about Satan and attacked his brother, breaking his rib. Frightened by his behavior and unsure of what to do, his siblings drove him to a nearby bus station. Soon after, the police discovered Johnston at the University of Austin, splashing in the middle of a pond and again preaching about Satan. It was at this point that his friends and family began to realize that, as one friend put it, "He was a really sick person." While his music had been a way for him to filter the demons in his mind, Johnston's illness was beginning to wreak havoc on his life, and drastic measures were necessary to ensure he did no further harm to others or to himself. Doctors prescribed Johnston the antipsychotic medication Haldol, and he spent the entire year of 1987 in bed (what he called his "lost year"). Although he was stabilized, Johnston found himself unable to write any music during this period. Indeed, throughout his life and like many individuals with bipolar disorder, Johnston often struggled with medication compliance. He felt that he was better at creating and performing when his mind was allowed to run free rather than when confined to the numbness he felt while on medication.

Because he often went off his medication, Johnston experienced a 5-year whirlwind of breakdowns that cycled between delusional mania and clinical depression, resulting in numerous hospitalizations that lasted months at a time. When he first went off his medication, Johnston's behavior and mood were normal for up to a few days until he took a sudden and unexpected turn for the bizarre. In one particular instance, Johnston had stopped taking his medication before playing to a large auditorium for a music festival in Austin, Texas. The appearance was one of the most acclaimed performances of his career. Shortly afterwards, however, when he and his father boarded the two-person plane to take them home to West Virginia, Johnston seized the controls from his father, sending their plane crashing toward the ground. Luckily, Johnston's father was able to regain control of the plane in time, and they survived after landing on a treetop. Johnston's father now recalls that at the time Johnston believed he was Casper (from the children's cartoon about the friendly ghost), and that taking over the plane was a heroic act.

Since that dark period of his life, Johnston has been stable in large part because of his supportive network of family and friends. He lives with his parents in Waller, Texas, and continues to write music and tour around the world. Many regard him as one of the most brilliant singer-songwriters in U.S. history. His heartbreaking battle with mental illness has been a destructive yet inspiring force in his work that blurs the line between artistic creativity and mental illness.

2.6 The Outcome of Treatment

remission
Situation in which the individual's symptoms no longer interfere with his or her behavior and are below those required for a *DSM* diagnosis.

In the best of all possible worlds, the treatment works. The client remains in treatment until the treatment has run its course; then he or she shows improvement and maintains this improved level of functioning. **Remission** is said to occur when the individual's symptoms no longer interfere with his or her behavior and are below those required for a *DSM* diagnosis (Wagner et al., 2017). Although this is obviously the most desirable outcome, the road to remission is often not so smooth, and either the client does not attain the treatment plan goals or unanticipated problems arise.

Change is very difficult, and many clients have become so accustomed to living with their symptoms that the effort necessary to solve the problem seems overwhelming. Clinicians find it particularly frustrating when they encounter these negative attitudes or when clients do not seem willing to follow through on their expressed desire to change. At times, clinicians also face frustration over practical constraints. They may recommend a treatment that they are confident can succeed but that would exceed available insurance reimbursement or would otherwise not be feasible given the client's current living situation. In other cases, people in the client's life refuse to support the client throughout the treatment, even though they play central roles.

Over time, those in the mental health field learn that they are limited in how effective they can be in changing the lives of people who go to them for help. However, as you will learn in this book, therapy is effective, and the majority of treatments do result in significant improvement.

Pedro was prescribed antianxiety medication through the psychiatrist at the mental health clinic. Within 4 weeks, he reported that he was able to sleep through the night and was feeling less restless. His psychotherapy focused on relaxation techniques such as deep breathing as well as cognitive techniques such as labeling and challenging his worrying, and coming up with various ways to cope with stress rather than worrying excessively. Therapy was also helpful for Pedro to discuss and sort through his feelings about his parents' divorce, and to understand how his anxiety affected his romantic relationships.

Dr. Tobin's reflections: Typical of many individuals with GAD, Pedro has always felt like a constant "worrier," but this anxiety was recently aggravated by a stressful event: his parents' divorce. Additionally, his lack of sleep was likely contributing to his difficulty with the concentration necessary for keeping up with the standards of work required by his career. Since he had been doing well at work up until this point, Pedro may not have felt that his anxiety was a problem. His anxiety may have also gone

unnoticed due to the intense pressure and sacrifice that all individuals face who work in Pedro's career area. It was clear, however, that Pedro worried about many issues to a greater degree than others in his situation. At the time he presented for treatment, it was clear that his inability to control his worry over his parents and his girlfriend was causing major problems in his work and social life. Not only that, but his past anxiety had caused problems that he did not recognize at the time. For many people who suffer from GAD, the longer it goes untreated, the worse it may get. Fortunately for Pedro, his girlfriend recognized that he was struggling and was able to obtain help for his overwhelming anxiety. I am pleased with the progress of therapy so far and hope that, given his many strengths, Pedro will be able to manage his symptoms through the psychological methods over which he is gaining mastery. Pedro has the potential to be a successful lawyer, and given his strong relationship with Natalia, I am hopeful that he will be able to turn his life around with only a slight chance of reexperiencing these symptoms.

SUMMARY

- The field of abnormal psychology goes beyond the academic concern of studying behavior. It encompasses the large range of human issues involved when a client and a clinician work together to help the client resolve psychological difficulties.

- People working in the area of abnormal psychology use both *client* and *patient* to refer to those who use psychological services. Our preference is to use the term *client,* reflecting the view that clinical interventions are a collaborative endeavor.

- The person providing the treatment is the clinician. There are many types of clinicians who approach clinical work in a variety of ways based on training and orientation. These include psychiatrists, clinical psychologists, social workers, counselors, therapists, and nurses. The field also includes those who do not have graduate-level training. These include occupational therapists, recreational therapists, and counselors who work in institutions, agencies, schools, and homes.

- Clinicians and researchers use the *Diagnostic and Statistical Manual of Mental Disorders, Fifth Edition* (*DSM-5*), which contains descriptions of all psychological disorders. In recent editions, authors of the *DSM* have strived to meet the criterion of reliability so that a clinician can consistently apply a diagnosis to anyone showing a particular set of symptoms. At the same time, researchers have worked to ensure the

validity of the classification system so that the various diagnoses represent real and distinct clinical phenomena.

- The *DSM-5* presents diagnoses organized into 22 chapters. The classification system is descriptive rather than explanatory, and it is categorical rather than dimensional.

- The diagnostic process involves using all relevant information to arrive at a label that characterizes a client's disorder. Key to diagnosis is gaining as clear a description as possible of a client's symptoms, both those that the client reports and those that the clinician observes. Differential diagnosis, the ruling out of alternative diagnoses, is a crucial step in the diagnostic process.

- To gain full appreciation of the client's disorder, the clinician develops a case formulation: analysis of the client's development and the factors that might have influenced his or her current psychological status.

- A cultural formulation accounts for the client's cultural background in making diagnoses.

- Culture-bound syndromes are behavior patterns that we find only within particular cultures.

- Clinicians typically follow up the diagnostic phase by setting up a treatment plan, the outline for how therapy should take place. The first step in a treatment plan is for the clinician to establish treatment goals, ranging from immediate to long term.

- Treatment sites vary in the degree to which they provide a controlled environment and in the nature of the services that clients receive. These include psychiatric hospitals, specialized inpatient treatment centers, and outpatient treatment ranging from a private therapist's outpatient clinic or office to a community-based mental health center. Other treatment sites include halfway houses, day treatment programs, places of work, and schools.
- Modality, or the form in which one offers psychotherapy, is also a crucial component of the treatment plan. It can be individual, family, group, or milieu therapy. Whatever treatment or modality a clinician recommends, it must be based on the choice of the most appropriate theoretical or combination of perspectives.
- In optimal situations, psychotherapy is a joint enterprise in which clients play an active role. In the best of all possible worlds, the client remains in treatment until the treatment runs its course, and the client shows improvement and maintains the improved level of functioning. Although not always successful, therapy is usually effective, and the majority of treatments do result in significant improvement.

KEY TERMS

Axis

Case formulation

Client

Clinical psychologist

Clinician

Community mental health center (CMHC)

Comorbidity

Cultural concepts of distress

Cultural formulation

Culture-bound syndromes

Day treatment program

Diagnostic and Statistical Manual of Mental Disorders (DSM)

Differential diagnosis

Evidence-based practice in psychology

Family therapy

Group therapy

Individual psychotherapy

International Classification of Diseases (ICD)

Milieu therapy

Modality

Multiaxial system

Patient

Principal diagnosis

Psychiatrist

Psychologist

Reliability

Remission

Treatment plan

Validity

Z codes

Assessment

Learning Objectives

3.1 Define key concepts of assessment.

3.2 Describe clinical interviews.

3.3 Identify mental status examination.

3.4 Explain intelligence testing.

3.5 Describe personality testing.

3.6 Recognize behavioral assessment.

3.7 Identify multicultural assessment.

3.8 Explain neuropsychological assessment.

3.9 Describe neuroimaging.

©otnaydur/123RF

Case Report: Ben Robsham

Demographic information: 22-year-old single heterosexual Caucasian male

Reason for referral: Ben's supervisor referred him for an assessment at his employer's employee assistance program following an incident in which Ben hit his head while operating a subway train. When driving aboveground, Ben reported that the brakes jammed as he was coming to an intersection where pedestrians were crossing. Using the emergency brake, Ben was able to stop the train, but the abrupt halt caused him to hit his head on the glass window and temporarily lose consciousness. He is unable to recall what happened directly after he hit his head. Ben took a 2-week leave of absence after the incident and avoided going to work for an additional 2 weeks. When his supervisor called him, Ben stated, "I can't leave my house. They'll come and get me."

Relevant history: Ben has no history of psychiatric treatment. He stated that he has never experienced depression or anxiety, and that he typically feels "just fine," which has made the recent changes in his psychological state all the more disturbing to him. Ben reported that he has never used drugs and only occasionally drinks when he is in a social environment. Additionally, Ben reported that his maternal grandfather and uncle had both been diagnosed with schizophrenia. Finally, Ben reported having no remarkable past or current medical history.

Case formulation: Because Ben's symptoms emerged following the incident, Ben will be referred for neuropsychological testing to rule out possible traumatic brain injury.

Diagnosis: Rule out mild neurocognitive disorder due to traumatic brain injury with behavioral disturbance.

Treatment plan: After an initial intake interview at the employee assistance program, Ben was referred for further psychological evaluation and psychiatric consultation to Dr. Antwan Washington, a neuropsychologist. The tests administered by Dr. Washington are in Table 1.

Sarah Tobin, PhD
Referring Clinician

TABLE 1 Tests Administered to Ben

Clinical Interview

Wechsler Adult Intelligence Scale, Fourth Edition (WAIS-IV)

Trail-Making Test, Parts A and B

Clock Drawing Test

Paced Auditory Serial Addition Test (PASAT)

Boston Naming Test, Second Edition (BNT)

Wechsler Memory Scale (WMS)

Minnesota Multiphasic Personality Inventory-2 (MMPI-2)

3.1 Characteristics of Psychological Assessments

psychological assessment
A broad range of measurement techniques, all of which involve having people provide scorable information about their psychological functioning.

A **psychological assessment** is a broad range of measurement techniques, all of which involve having people provide scorable information about their psychological functioning. You will see as we discuss Ben's case that a comprehensive assessment proved valuable in helping to understand the nature of his symptoms and potential directions for treatment.

Although the basic principles are the same across assessment methods, there are several types of assessments that vary according to the purpose toward which clinicians will use them. A diagnostic assessment provides a diagnosis, or at least a tentative diagnosis, of an individual's psychological disorder. Forensic assessments are used in the context of criminal cases where legal determinations are made on the basis of the psychologist's findings. In employment settings, an assessment provides information that an employer can use to evaluate whether a job applicant is suited for a position. Other assessments are conducted to evaluate whether an individual has suffered brain damage due to an accident or disease. Whatever the exact purpose of the assessment, the psychologist who conducts it is required to be objective, thorough, and knowledgeable about the most appropriate tools.

In Ben's case, the clinician must evaluate the potential contribution of the injury itself as well as the appearance of symptoms unrelated to the train incident. Dr. Tobin provided an initial evaluation, and as a result of this assessment, she decided to refer Ben to a specialist in the area of traumatic brain injury.

The tests that clinicians use in the assessment process must be held to high standards of consistency and accuracy. To be reliable, the test should produce the same results regardless of when it is given, and the individual should answer items within the same subscale of a test in reasonably similar fashion. The validity of a test reflects the extent to which a test measures what it is designed to measure. An intelligence test should measure intelligence, not personality. Before using a given test, clinicians should be aware of its reliability and validity, information that is readily available in the published literature about the instrument.

standardization
A psychometric criterion that clearly specifies a test's instructions for administration and scoring.

A test will be reliable and valid only to the extent that it is administered and scored similarly from person to person. In other words, it should meet the criterion of **standardization**, meaning that the test has clear instructions for administration and scoring. Each individual receiving the test should receive it in the same manner, and the test needs to be scored in the same manner for everyone according to the same predefined criteria. Furthermore, a given score on the test should have a clear meaning that differentiates it from another score; similarly, the same score should have the same meaning regardless of who receives that score. Ideally, the test's designers have a substantial enough database so that clinicians can make such determinations with confidence.

Barnum effect
The tendency for clinicians to unintentionally make generic and vague statements about their clients that do not specifically characterize the client.

In addition to ensuring a test's reliability and validity, clinicians should take into account its applicability to test-takers from a diversity of backgrounds. Test publishers design their measures for use by individuals from a range of ability levels, first languages, cultural backgrounds, and age. For example, clinicians may need to adapt assessment instruments for use by older adults who may require larger print, slower timing, or special writing instruments for those who have arthritis (Edelstein, Martin, & McKee, 2000). Even so, clinicians need to ensure that they are using the most appropriate instrument for a given client. It would not be appropriate to use a test standardized for young adults on an older adult population unless the test's equivalence across age groups has been firmly established.

When interpreting test results, clinicians can fall into a common trap known as the **Barnum effect**. Named after legendary circus owner P. T. Barnum (who supposedly said, "There's a sucker born

A patient completes a visuospatial task as part of a neuropsychological assessment.

©Will & Deni McIntyre/Science Source

every minute"), this is the tendency for clinicians unintentionally to make generic and vague statements about their clients that do not specifically characterize the client. The client will believe this statement because it's so general that it cannot be proven false.

Here's an example of a Barnum-effect statement: "Julia is often shy around other people, but at times she can be very outgoing. When presented with a challenge, she can often perform very well, but she occasionally becomes nervous and intimidated." These two sentences *could* apply to Julia, but they could also apply to most other people. Therefore, they don't say anything special about Julia. Furthermore, most people would find it difficult to disagree with this feedback. Julia "can" be this way, or she "occasionally" becomes nervous. Anyone "can" be one way at some point in time, and almost everyone becomes nervous from time to time.

You are most likely to encounter the Barnum effect when reading your horoscope or a fortune cookie. These are written generically because the message literally does need to be able to apply to anyone. They are relatively harmless, unless you decide to make a huge investment because your horoscope tells you it's your lucky day. In a clinical situation, the problem is that such statements are not particularly insightful or revealing and do not help inform the assessment process. Although clinicians are trained to avoid this trap, it can be tempting to believe one of these "can" statements about a given client.

These and other shortcomings can be averted when clinicians follow the principles of **evidence-based assessment**. Like evidence-based practice, assessment tied to a well-established knowledge base meets the criteria of (1) relying on research findings and scientifically viable theories, (2) using psychometrically strong measures, and (3) empirically evaluating the assessment process (Hunsley & Mash, 2007). By following these guidelines, clinicians ensure that they will evaluate their clients using the most current and appropriate materials available.

Consider the case of a seasoned clinician who remains attached to the assessment methods she learned about in graduate school 20 or 30 years ago and no longer evaluates them critically. Although they might still be appropriate for the purposes of her work, she should be on the lookout for newer procedures that rely on up-to-date technology or research. According to the third criterion, she should also develop evaluation methods to determine whether her assessments are continuing to provide useful information about her clients or whether another, more recently developed method would work better.

evidence-based assessment
Assessment characterized by the clinician's (1) relying on research findings and scientifically viable theories, (2) using psychometrically strong measures, and (3) empirically evaluating the assessment process.

3.2 Clinical Interview

Clinicians typically begin their assessment with the **clinical interview**, a series of questions that they administer in face-to-face interaction with the client. The answers to these questions provide important background information, allow clients to describe their symptoms in their own words, and enable clinicians to make observations of their clients to help guide decisions about the next steps, which may include further testing.

The least formal version of the clinical interview is the **unstructured interview**, which consists of a series of open-ended questions regarding the client's symptoms, health status, family background, life history, and reasons for seeking help. In addition to noting the answers to these questions, the clinician also observes the client's level of comfort, apparent mood, extraneous comments, and any other behaviors that might inform the clinician in understanding the client's psychological state. By noting the client's bodily movements, eye gaze, and facial expression, for example, the clinician can gain an understanding of whether the client is experiencing feelings of anxiety, difficulties in attending, an unwillingness to cooperate, or unusual worries about the testing process itself. The clinician may also use cues from the client's appearance that give further indication of the client's symptoms. A person with an unusually disheveled appearance may be experiencing cognitive symptoms that interfere with the ability to care for personal hygiene. Other cues given by individuals' clothing and overall appearance may also suggest their attitudes, values, and interests.

clinical interview
A series of questions that clinicians administer in face-to-face interaction with the client.

unstructured interview
A series of open-ended questions aimed at determining the client's reasons for being in treatment, symptoms, health status, family background, and life history.

TABLE 2 Areas Covered in a Clinical Interview

Topic	Purpose
Age and gender	Obtain basic demographic information.
Reason for referral	Hear client's reason for seeking treatment, in his or her own words.
Education and work history	Obtain socioeconomic status and determine whether client is still working.
Current social situation	Find out whether client is currently in a relationship and how much social support is potentially available.
Physical and mental health history	Determine whether client has any medical illnesses and whether there has been a recent change in health.
	Find out about history of present problem including past diagnoses and treatments and whether treatment was helpful or not.
Drug/alcohol use and current medication	Ascertain whether client is using psychoactive drugs (including alcohol and caffeine). Obtain list of prescriptions to avoid potential interactions with any psychotropic medications.
Family history	Find out whether client's family has medical and psychological disorders, particularly any relevant to client's current symptoms.
Behavioral observations	Note behaviors, including nonverbal behaviors, which indicate whether client is experiencing anxiety or altered mood. Also note whether client seems to be experiencing difficulties in attention or compliance. Attempt to determine client's mental status. Compare client's appearance with stated age. Determine whether client is oriented to time, place, and person. Observe any unusual motor behaviors.

The typical clinical interview covers the areas outlined in Table 2. Because the clinical interview allows for more freedom of administration than a test with preset questions and response categories, the clinician can vary the order of questions and the exact wording he or she uses to obtain this information. The main objective is for the clinician to obtain the information, even if the questions used to gather it differ slightly from client to client.

A clinical interview may last as long as 30 to 45 minutes. Because the client is providing highly personal information, the clinician attempts to draw the client out with questioning that is respectful, but also matter of fact. Unlike an ordinary conversation, the clinical interview has the purpose of obtaining material that will be used in assessment and treatment. It is important for the clinician, in this regard, to keep the questioning focused on the client rather than on mutual sharing of information.

In Ben's case, the clinical interview provided Dr. Tobin with key information about his history including his education, vocational background, and relationship history. She determined that, prior to the incident, he enjoyed engaging with others, so his current isolation is a change from his previous pattern of social functioning. His general appearance was slightly disheveled in that his clothes were wrinkled and he was unshaven. It is difficult to know exactly what this might mean without knowing how Ben was prior to the incident, so Dr. Tobin may make note of these features but reserve judgment on their meaning.

Following Dr. Tobin's interview with Ben, Dr. Washington conducted his own, more detailed, clinical interview with Ben. Upon further questioning about his symptoms, Ben stated that he has difficulty concentrating, and that his main symptom is the occurrence of "very strange thoughts" that have been quite troubling to him. Specifically, he stated that he feels too afraid to leave his apartment because he believes that the police will apprehend and arrest him as punishment for "what [he] did." Although there were no fatalities, Ben worries that others blame him for killing passengers and if he returned to work the passengers would turn on him, thus resulting in his apprehension. He states that he spends several hours a day worrying about the consequences of the incident and sometimes hears accusatory voices blaming him for hurting people and telling him that he is a "monster." He reported that he has heard these voices only a few times in the past 4 weeks.

Though Ben reports that he feels distressed about his recent psychological problems, he stated that he had no thoughts of hurting or killing himself. He also stated that he has been unable to get a full night's sleep since the incident. At times he is unable to fall asleep, and when he does, frequent nightmares about the incident awaken him, and he feels that those he believes he killed are "haunting" him.

Ben stated that although he was worried about what he had been experiencing recently, he had been too embarrassed to tell anyone, worrying that he was "going crazy." Since he had not spent time with friends or family and had not been to work, the people in his life were unaware of the extent of his psychological problems following the incident. Ben took a leave of absence for the first 2 weeks following the incident and has since been calling in sick daily. When the suggestion of psychological testing came up, Ben reports that he was hoping it might help reveal the nature of his troubling symptoms.

As you can see from Ben's case, the clinical interview becomes a key step in the diagnostic process because of the information it provides regarding the client's current symptoms, history, and availability of social support. In addition, it had the added benefit for Dr. Washington to allow him to establish a rapport with Ben that would be necessary as the assessment progressed.

Unlike the clinical interview, the **structured interview** provides a series of assessment questions, with a predetermined wording and order. A structured interview can either provide a diagnosis on which to further base treatment or classify the client's symptoms into a *DSM* disorder.

A clinical interview designed specifically to assess *DSM-5* symptoms is the **Structured Clinical Interview for *DSM-5* Disorders-CV (SCID-5-CV)**. The SCID-5-CV is structured in that it guides the clinician along each step of the way through the *DSM-5* diagnostic process. The clinician reads the interview questions provided along with each corresponding *DSM-5* criterion. This makes it possible for the clinician to rate each symptom as either present or absent. There is some flexibility in the SCID-5-CV in that the clinician can follow up with questions pertaining to specific symptoms that clients say they are experiencing. For example, if a client states that she has symptoms of anxiety, the interviewer would follow up with questions about these symptoms but otherwise would "skip out" or move on to the next area of the interview. As the authors note, it would not make sense to ask questions about an area if the individual never experienced the symptoms at all (Shankman et al., 2017). The SCID-5-CV takes 45 to 90 minutes to administer, depending on the complexity of the client's symptoms.

An advantage of this type of interview is a systematic approach that is less subject to variations among clinicians than an unstructured interview. Furthermore, anyone with the proper training in the instrument can administer the SCID-5-CV, not only licensed mental health professionals as is true for interviews that require more clinical judgment. This has practical value in that clients can receive initial screening prior to their beginning a course of therapy. Furthermore, there are other versions of the SCID-5-CV that can be used for research purposes or to assess specific disorders, such as personality disorders. The availability of these alternate versions means that researchers using the SCID-5 version designed for their purpose have a greater chance of publishing results that transfer across particular samples, because they were all assessed with the same instrument.

3.3 Mental Status Examination

A clinician uses a **mental status examination** to assess a client's current state of mind. The mental status examination is a method of objectively assessing a client's behavior and functioning in a number of spheres, with particular attention to the symptoms associated with psychological disturbance. In conducting a mental status examination, the clinician assesses a number of features of the client including appearance, attitudes, behavior, mood and affect, speech, thought processes, content of thought, perception, cognition, insight, and judgment. The outcome of the mental status examination is a comprehensive description of how the client looks, thinks, feels, and behaves.

structured interview
A standardized series of assessment questions, with a predetermined wording and order.

Structured Clinical Interview for *DSM-5* Disorders (SCID-5)
A structured clinical interview developed to assess *DSM-5* symptoms.

mental status examination
A method of objectively assessing a client's behavior and functioning in a number of spheres, with particular attention to the symptoms associated with psychological disturbance.

The **Mini-Mental State Examination (MMSE)** is a structured tool that clinicians use as a brief screening device to assess neurocognitive disorders. The clinician administers a set of short memory tasks and compares the client's scores to established norms. If the client scores below a certain cutoff, the clinician then continues on to administer tests that can more precisely evaluate the nature and potential cause of this low score.

In Ben's case, Dr. Washington noted that Ben was not experiencing an altered mental state at the time of the interview. He arrived on time and was alert and fully aware of his surroundings. His speech was normal in tone, rhythm, volume, and rate; in other words, he spoke to Dr. Washington without any apparent disability to converse. Ben also showed no deficits in his ability to understand Dr. Washington, and he was able to understand the instructions for each of the tests that he went on to complete. His affect was appropriate, meaning that his apparent emotional state matched that expected in the situation, though he made a few self-deprecating jokes when he became frustrated during the administration of a test he found difficult. In general, though, throughout testing he cooperated with the examiner and appeared motivated and interested in the tests themselves. Dr. Washington then proceeded directly to the next phase of testing.

3.4 Intelligence Testing

Intelligence tests are intended to serve a variety of functions, including overall cognitive evaluation, diagnosis of learning disabilities, determination of giftedness or intellectual disability, and prediction of future academic achievement. Clinicians may use intelligence tests in the diagnosis of neurological and psychiatric disorders as a component of a more comprehensive assessment procedure. Human resource departments often use intelligence tests in personnel selection to evaluate the potential for employees to perform in specific conditions. Of course, intelligence tests are also administered in educational settings, particularly when decisions must be made about grade or classroom placement.

For clinicians, intelligence testing makes it possible to obtain standardized scores that permit them to evaluate the cognitive strengths and weaknesses of their clients rather than simply to assign a score. The most commonly used intelligence tests in clinical settings are administered on a one-to-one basis, providing a comprehensive view of the client's abilities to perform a range of perceptual, memory, reasoning, and timed tasks.

©Media for Medical SARL/Alamy Stock Photo

Stanford-Binet Intelligence Test

First developed in the early 1900s by Alfred Binet, the Stanford-Binet is now in its fifth edition, known as the Stanford-Binet 5 (SB5). Children taking this test receive a **deviation intelligence (IQ)** score, calculated by converting their raw scores to standardized scores that reflect where a child stands in relationship to others of similar age and gender. The average deviation IQ score is set at 100 with a standard deviation of 15. If a child receives an SB5 IQ score of 115, this means the child stands at or above the IQ of 84 percent of the population.

In addition to yielding an overall IQ score, the SB5 yields scores on measures of scales labeled Fluid Reasoning, Knowledge, Quantitative Reasoning, Visuospatial Reasoning, and Working Memory (Table 3). These scales are intended to provide greater understanding of the child's cognitive strengths and weaknesses not necessarily conveyed in an overall IQ score.

deviation intelligence (IQ)
An index of intelligence derived from comparing the individual's score on an intelligence test with the mean score for that individual's reference group.

Wechsler Intelligence Scales

The first comprehensive individual test that researchers specifically designed to measure adult intelligence was the **Wechsler Adult Intelligence Scale (WAIS)**. Originally developed as the Wechsler-Bellevue test by David Wechsler in 1939, the WAIS, first published in 1955, is now in its fourth edition (WAIS-IV) (Wechsler, 2008). Researchers subsequently developed parallel tests for children based on the same format as the adult scales. Those currently in use are the Wechsler Intelligence Scale for Children–Fourth Edition (WISC-IV) (Wechsler, 2003) and the Wechsler Preschool and Primary Scale of Intelligence–Third Edition (WPPSI-III) (Wechsler, 2002).

Wechsler originally sought to develop a tool for use in clinical settings that could provide an adjunct to diagnoses of psychopathology. He also believed that it was important to include tests using words and tests that rely on pictures or actions. Originally he labeled these two categories "Verbal" and "Performance." For many years, clinicians reported the WAIS scores in terms of these two categories of subtests; however, over time it became increasingly evident that these two categorical scores did not adequately capture the full complexity of intellectual functioning. Thus, the WAIS-IV was published in 2008 to replace the WAIS-III, adding new tests and providing a completely revamped scoring system.

Wechsler Adult Intelligence Scale (WAIS)
The first comprehensive individual test that researchers specifically designed to measure adult intelligence.

TABLE 3 Types of Abilities Assessed by the Stanford-Binet 5 (SB5)

Scale	Definition	Example
Fluid Reasoning	Ability to solve novel problems	Sort picture chips into groups of three
Knowledge	Accumulated fund of general information	Show how to perform a given action
Quantitative Reasoning	Ability to solve problems with numbers or numerical concepts	Count a set of items
Visuospatial Reasoning	Ability to analyze spatial relationships and geometric concepts	Assemble puzzle-like forms
Working Memory	Ability to store, transform, and retrieve information in short-term memory	Recall a sequence of taps

SOURCE: Roid, G. H., & Barram, R. A. (2004). *Essentials of Stanford-Binet Intelligence Scales (SB5) assessment.* Hoboken, NJ: Wiley.

TABLE 4 **Scales on the Wechsler Adult Intelligence Scale-IV (WAIS-IV)**

Scale	Tests	Type of Item
Verbal Comprehension	Vocabulary	Define the word *barrel*.
	Information	How many minutes are there in an hour?
	Comprehension	Why do plants need water?
	Similarities	How are an elephant and a cat alike?
Perceptual Reasoning	Matrix reasoning	Choose which pattern logically follows after a set of patterns.
	Visual puzzles	Indicate which pictures of shapes go together in a drawing of a puzzle.
	Block design	Arrange a set of blocks so that they reproduce a design.
	Picture completion	State what is missing in a picture of a common object.
Working Memory	Digit span forward	Recall a series of digits in forward order.
	Digit span backward	Recall a series of digits in backward order.
	Letter-number sequencing	Recall a set of digits from smallest to largest.
		Recall a set of mixed letters and numbers from largest to smallest.
Processing Speed	Symbol search	Copy numbers that match symbols into appropriate boxes.
	Coding	

Researchers have proceeded to examine this most recent version of the WAIS to determine its validity as well as its ability to provide accurate intelligence test scores across a range of countries, ages, and diagnoses of test-takers.

The WAIS-IV, like its predecessors and the SB5, can produce an overall IQ score based on an age-normed mean of 100 and standard deviation of 15. The full scale IQ is typically not as useful for clinical purposes as are scores on the indexes of Verbal Comprehension, Perceptual Reasoning, Working Memory, and Processing Speed scales (Table 4). The four index scale scores allow clinicians to examine in depth the client's cognitive functioning along these key dimensions.

A helpful way to think of scores from the WAIS-IV is in terms of a triangle (Figure 1). At the top is the Full Scale IQ (FSIQ), which reflects general cognitive functioning and, as mentioned earlier, provides the least amount of specificity. Beneath the FSIQ score at the top of the pyramid are the four index scores. Verbal Comprehension Index (VCI) assesses acquired knowledge and verbal reasoning skills. Perceptual Reasoning Index (PRI) measures visuospatial and fluid reasoning. Working Memory Index (WMI) measures the capacity to hold and process information in memory. Processing Speed Index (PSI) measures the ability to process nonverbal information quickly. Beyond interpreting the index scores, clinicians propose hypotheses about individuals' performance based on an interpretation of clinical clusters, which are comprised of various combinations of individual index scores.

Because the WAIS-IV is given on an individual basis, clinicians have ample opportunities to observe the test-taker's behavior during the test, possibly gaining valuable diagnostic information to complement the test scores. In fact, the instructions for the WAIS-IV scoring include suggestions for the examiner to include behavioral observations such as the individual's native language fluency; physical appearance; problems with vision, hearing, or motor behavior; difficulties with attention and concentration; motivation for testing; and any unusual behaviors that the test-taker shows.

Table 5 shows Ben's performance on the WAIS-IV. Ben's FSIQ was 115, indicating that he has an above-average level of performance (higher than 84 percent of the population). If you look across the entire pattern of his scores, however, you'll notice that Ben demonstrated high variability among the index scores that make up the FSIQ. This type of variability suggests a wide range to Ben's cognitive abilities. The clinician found it noteworthy that Ben's

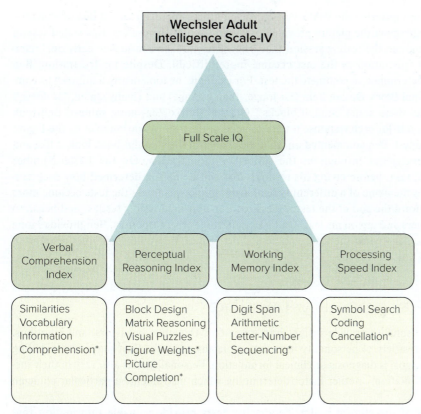

FIGURE 1 Structure of the WAIS-IV

*Supplemental subtest

TABLE 5 Ben's WAIS-IV Scores

Full Scale:	115		
Verbal Comprehension Index	132		
Perceptual Reasoning Index	107		
Working Memory Index	111		
Processing Speed Index	97		
Individual Subtests:			
Vocabulary:	15	Picture Completion:	12
Similarities:	17	Coding:	7
Arithmetic:	13	Block Design:	10
Digit Span:	11	Matrix Reasoning:	14
Information:	14	Symbol Search:	12
Comprehension:	18	Figure Weights:	13
Letter-Number Seq.:	10	Visual Puzzles:	10
		Cancellation:	12

Processing Speed cluster score was low (higher than only 40 percent of the population), suggesting that Ben struggles with the perception of visual patterns and stimuli, particularly when speed is a factor. The appearance of this low test score where he should have performed well given his job suggests possible injury to the areas of his brain involved in processing of spatial information.

While administering the WAIS-IV, Dr. Washington carefully recorded Ben's behaviors, further fleshing out the picture provided by the test scores themselves. Ben stated several times throughout the testing session that "they give you fake confidence early on," referring to his frustration as the test became more difficult. Despite his frustration, Ben remained determined to complete the test. For example, he took nearly 6 minutes to complete the final Block Design item (far longer than average) and finally stated, "It doesn't make sense—there aren't enough blocks." On the Matrix Reasoning subtest, Ben took nearly 1 minute for each response toward the end of the task. While completing the Figure Weights subtest, Ben commented on what the shapes in the stimulus book looked like and made several jokes throughout the subtest administration. On the Letter-Number Sequencing task, before giving his response to each item, Ben described how each correlated with the name of a different type of army ship or plane. As the tests became more difficult toward the end of the testing session, Ben appeared visibly restless and began to tap his fingers and tap on his legs. On tasks requiring verbal responses, Ben provided long elaborations, and when the test required a short answer, he would sometimes respond in a sing-song voice.

3.5 Personality Testing

Tests of personality provide insight into a person's thoughts, behaviors, and emotions. There are a variety of personality tests that clinicians adapt for their purposes, including whether the goal is diagnosis or clinical formulation. Personality tests also vary in their theoretical orientation, another factor determining which instruments a particular clinician might use.

Outside of the clinical realm, personality tests provide valuable information that researchers use to test predictions related to their own particular area of investigation. The scores from these tests are not used for diagnostic purposes, but to examine correlations among related theoretical variables. For example, researchers might examine whether scores on a personality test measuring self-esteem are related to scores on a measure of optimism.

Self-Report Tests

self-report clinical inventory
A psychological test with standardized questions having fixed response categories that the test-taker completes independently, self-reporting the extent to which the responses are accurate characterizations.

A **self-report clinical inventory** contains standardized questions with fixed response categories that the test-taker completes independently either in paper-and-pencil or online format. In a self-report inventory, test-takers rate the extent to which the items apply to them on a fixed scale of, for example, 7 = strongly agree to 1 = strongly disagree.

Easily scored by computer, self-report clinical inventories are objective in the sense that the scoring does not require any form of decision or judgment on the part of the examiner. Using predetermined criteria to interpret the scores, computers can even produce brief explanatory reports. However, clinicians need to balance the advantages of the ease of administration and objectivity of these tests against the possibility that the reports they produce are subject to the Barnum effect, because they are written in a somewhat generic manner. Because computer programs rely on linking specific response patterns to specific summary statements or phrases, they run the risk of being overly vague and not tailored to the particular test-taker's idiosyncrasies.

Nevertheless, a major advantage of self-report inventories is that they are relatively easy to administer and score. Consequently, large numbers of people can take them in an efficient manner. Moreover, clinicians can take advantage of the wealth of information about the validity and reliability of the better-known self-report inventories when interpreting the scores of their own clients.

Minnesota Multiphasic Personality Inventory (MMPI)
Self-report personality inventory containing 567 true-false items, all in the form of statements that describe the individual's thoughts, behaviors, feelings, and attitudes.

The most widely used self-report inventory used in clinical settings is the **Minnesota Multiphasic Personality Inventory (MMPI)**, originally published in 1943. The current version of the test is the 1989 revision known as the MMPI-2 (Table 6). There are 567 true-false items on the MMPI-2, all in the form of statements that describe the individual's

TABLE 6 **Clinical and Validity Scales of the MMPI-2, with Adapted Items**

Scale	Scale Name	Type of Content	Adapted Item
Clinical scales			
1	**Hypochondriasis**	Bodily preoccupations and concerns, fear of illness and disease.	I have a hard time with nausea and vomiting.
2	**Depression**	Unhappiness and feelings of low personal worth.	I wish I were as happy as others appear to be.
3	**Hysteria**	Denial of psychological problems and over-reactions to stressful situations, various bodily complaints.	Frequently my head seems to hurt everywhere.
4	**Psychopathic deviate**	Antisocial tendencies and delinquency.	I was occasionally sent to the principal's office for bad behavior.
5	**Masculinity-femininity**	Adoption of stereotypic sex-role behaviors and attitudes.	I like reading romantic tales (female item).
6	**Paranoia**	Feelings of persecution and suspiciousness of others.	I would have been a lot more successful had others not been vindictive toward me.
7	**Psychasthenia**	Uncontrollable urges to think and act; unreasonable fears.	Sometimes I think thoughts too awful to discuss.
8	**Schizophrenia**	Disturbances of thinking, mood, and behavior.	I have had some rather bizarre experiences.
9	**Hypomania**	Elevated mood, accelerated speech and motor activity.	I become excited at least once a week.
10	**Social introversion**	Tendency to withdraw from social situations.	I usually do not speak first. I wait for others to speak to me.
Validity scales (composed of items from clinical scales)			
L	**Lie scale**	Unrealistically positive self-representation	
K	**Correction**	Similar to L scale—more sophisticated indication of tendency toward positive self-presentation	
F	**Infrequency**	Presenting oneself in an unrealistically negative light	

SOURCE: *MMPI®-2 (Minnesota Multiphasic Personality Inventory®-2) Manual for Administration, Scoring, and Interpretation.* Regents of the University of Minnesota.

thoughts, behaviors, feelings, and attitudes. The developers of the MMPI sought to provide scores on 10 "clinical scales" corresponding to major diagnostic categories such as schizophrenia, depression, and anxiety. The text developers built an additional three "validity" scales into the test to guard against people trying to feign either exceptional psychological health or illness.

In the decades after its publication, researchers and clinicians became aware of limitations in MMPI-2 clinical scale scores. These scores did not correspond to the original clinical categories, meaning that the test's administrators could not interpret them as evidence of specific diagnoses (a high "Schizophrenia" scale score did not imply that the individual

TABLE 7 **Restructured Clinical (RC) Scales of the MMPI-2-RF®**

Scale	Scale Name	Type of Content
RCd	Demoralization	General unhappiness and dissatisfaction
RC1	Somatic Complaints	Diffuse physical health complaints
RC2	Low Positive Emotions	Lack of positive emotional responsiveness
RC3	Cynicism	Non-self-referential beliefs expressing distrust of others
RC4	Antisocial Behavior	Rule breaking and irresponsible behavior
RC6	Ideas of Persecution	Belief that others pose a threat to the self
RC7	Dysfunctional Negative Emotions	Maladaptive anxiety, anger, and irritability
RC8	Aberrant Experiences	Unusual thoughts or perceptions
RC9	Hypomanic Activation	Over-activation, aggression, impulsivity, and grandiosity

Restructured Clinical Scales listing. Excerpted from the *MMPI-2-RF ® Manual for Administration, Scoring, and Interpretation* by Yossef S. Ben-Porath and Auke Tellegen. Copyright ©2008, 2011 by the Regents of the University of Minnesota. Reproduced by permission of the University of Minnesota Press. All rights reserved. "Minnesota Multiphasic Personality Inventory-2-RF®" and "MMPI-2-RF®" are trademarks owned by the Regents of the University of Minnesota.

had a diagnosis of schizophrenia). Consequently, MMPI-2 users incorporate the newer, restructured clinical scales (or RCs). In fact, the newest version of the MMPI is the MMPI-2-RF, published in 2008 (Table 7). The MMPI-2-RF is based entirely on the restructured scales. Containing only 338 items, this latest version of the MMPI-2 also provides scores for "higher order" factors that indicate a client's overall emotional, cognitive, and behavioral functioning.

The Personality Assessment Inventory (PAI) (Morey, 1991, 2007) is a self-report clinical instrument that offers an alternative to the MMPI, differing in item content and scaling. The PAI consists of 344 items organized into 11 clinical scales (e.g., Anxiety, Depression, Somatic Complaints), 5 treatment scales (e.g., Aggression, Suicidal Ideation), 2 interpersonal scales (Dominance and Warmth), and 4 validity scales that assess the tendency to distort one's responses. One advantage of the PAI is that clinicians can use it with clients who may not have the language or reading skills to complete the MMPI-2. A second advantage is that, unlike those of the MMPI, its validity scale scores are independent of the actual content scales.

The SCL-90-R (Derogatis, 1994) measures the test-taker's current experiencing of 90 physical and psychological symptoms. There are nine overall symptom scales, such as Depression, Anxiety, and Hostility. Additionally, the SCL-90-R produces an overall global severity index and the number and intensity of the individual's symptoms. Unlike measures that have no defined target period, the SCL-90-R focuses on the client's current status. Because it is sensitive to the client's state, the SCL-90-R can be administered on multiple occasions, making it well suited for use by clinicians who wish to track the progress of their clients throughout the course of treatment.

Less oriented toward clinical use is the NEO Personality Inventory (Revised) (NEO-PI-R) (Costa & McCrae, 1992), a 240-item questionnaire that measures five personality dimensions, or sets of traits. The scales are designed so the test-taker can complete them as well as individuals who know the test-taker, such as spouses, partners, or relatives (Form R). People use the NEO-PI-R less in clinical settings than in personality research or in employee selection, although it can be of value in describing a client's "personality" as distinct from the client's symptoms. Various forms of the NEO-PI-R are available online, and researchers may use a briefer version consisting entirely of adjective rating scales.

Clinicians and researchers can also use specific self-report inventories designed to investigate a given disorder for which a general test may not be as relevant. There are literally hundreds of these developed for such purposes, including measures of individual diagnoses as well as measures that tap qualities related to such clinical traits as narcissism, psychopathy, and perfectionism. These inventories can also supplement more general assessment methods.

Returning to Ben, you can see his MMPI-2 scores in Figure 2. He has slightly elevated scores on the Paranoia scale and endorsed several critical items relating directly to psychosis such as "I have no enemies who really wish to harm me" (False), "I have strange and peculiar thoughts" (True), and "At times my thoughts have raced ahead faster than I could speak them" (True). According to his responses, he may have unusual thought content and may often feel suspicious that others are saying bad things about him. As a result, he may feel disconnected from reality. He may believe that his feelings and thoughts are controlled by others. His abnormal thought content was evidenced at times throughout the WAIS-IV administration in his unusual reactions to certain test items. His scores on the MMPI-2, however, indicate that he does not tend to be impulsive or take physical risks and generally follows rules and laws. These may be protective factors for Ben in that he may be able to maintain some control of his abnormal thoughts, which may differentiate him from those with diagnosable psychotic disorders.

From looking at Ben's scores, Dr. Washington concluded that his limited coping resources may be a more situational than long-standing problem. Further, his clinical profile suggests that he may be excessively sensitive and overly responsive to the opinions of others. He may overemphasize rationality and be moralistic and rigid in his attitudes and opinions. As a result, he may be argumentative and have a tendency to blame others and act suspicious, hostile, and guarded in relationships. This may account for his report of having few close friends at school and his preference for being alone in his dorm room.

Based on his scores on the MMPI-2, it appears that Ben has a traditional sense of masculinity and may have stereotypically masculine preferences in work, hobbies, and other activities. In the clinical interview, he reported having had no previous significant romantic relationships with women, which may be a result of his tendency to be guarded and hostile in his relationships with others. Ben's scores on the MMPI-2-R suggest that he does endorse aberrant experiences, but his score on persecution is within the normative range. He also received scores above the norm on somatic complaints.

Clinicians typically interpret the MMPI-2 scores in the context of other test scores. They also may use the content scales to flesh out the profiles provided by the basic 10 clinical scales of the MMPI-2. The Restructured MMPI-2 also provides a different perspective on a client's current psychological state, because the content scales provide a more descriptive summary of the client's symptoms. Dr. Washington noted that Ben's score was high on the Demoralization scale, suggesting that Ben felt discouraged and hopeless about his current life situation.

Projective Testing

A **projective test** is a technique in which the test-taker is presented with an ambiguous item or task and is asked to respond by providing his or her own meaning or perception. The underlying idea behind projective tests is that people cannot or perhaps will not provide accurate statements on self-report inventories. For example, clients may not wish to say outright that they are experiencing unusual symptoms or have qualities that could be construed in a negative light. On projective tests, clients may be less guarded about their responses because they do not know how the assessor will interpret their answers.

The most famous projective technique is the **Rorschach Inkblot Test**, named after Swiss psychiatrist Hermann Rorschach, who developed the method in 1911. To administer the test, the examiner shows the test-taker a set of 10 cards one by one (5 are black and white; 5 have color). The test-taker's job is to describe what the inkblot looks like. Although the method sounds simple enough, over the last century researchers and clinicians have continued to refine the scoring methods; now there is an elaborate interpretative system in place.

projective test
A technique in which the test-taker is presented with an ambiguous item or task and is asked to respond by providing his or her own meaning or perception.

Rorschach Inkblot Test
Projective assessment method in which individuals describe their perceptions of each of a set of symmetrical inkblots.

Ben's perception of this Rorschach-like inkblot was "An evil mask that's jumping out to get you. Also a seed, some kind of seed, which is dividing itself into two equal halves. It could be a sign of conception and yet it's dying. It's losing part of itself, falling apart, raging."
©Science Source

FIGURE 2 Ben's MMPI-2 Profile

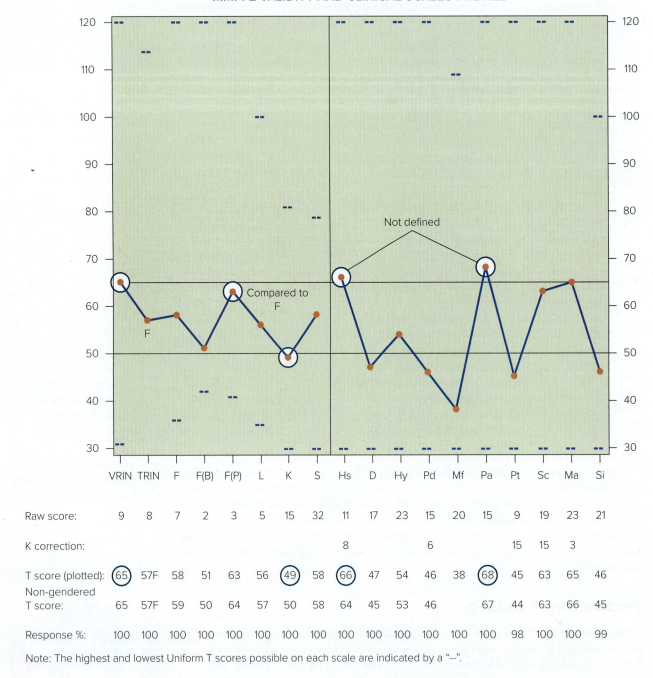

MMPI-2 VALIDITY AND CLINICAL SCALES PROFILE

	VRIN	TRIN	F	F(B)	F(P)	L	K	S	Hs	D	Hy	Pd	Mf	Pa	Pt	Sc	Ma	Si
Raw score:	9	8	7	2	3	5	15	32	11	17	23	15	20	15	9	19	23	21
K correction:									8			6			15	15	3	
T score (plotted):	65	57F	58	51	63	56	49	58	66	47	54	46	38	68	45	63	65	46
Non-gendered T score:	65	57F	59	50	64	57	50	58	64	45	53	46		67	44	63	66	45
Response %:	100	100	100	100	100	100	100	100	100	100	100	100	100	100	98	100	100	99

Note: The highest and lowest Uniform T scores possible on each scale are indicated by a "--".

Thematic Apperception Test (TAT)

A projective test in which individuals invent a story to explain what is happening in a set of ambiguous pictures.

The **Thematic Apperception Test (TAT)** presents test-takers with a very different task than the Rorschach. Test-takers look at black-and-white drawings that portray people in a variety of ambiguous situations such as standing in a dark hallway or sitting in a bedroom. The test-taker is asked simply to tell a story about what is happening in each scene, focusing on such details as what the characters in the picture are thinking and feeling. The TAT's original purpose was to evaluate motivational needs, such as the need for achievement or the need for power. Its use has expanded to clinical settings and, like the Rorschach, better scoring

FIGURE 2 Ben's MMPI-2 Profile (cont'd)

MMPI-2 RESTRUCTURED CLINICAL SCALES PROFILE

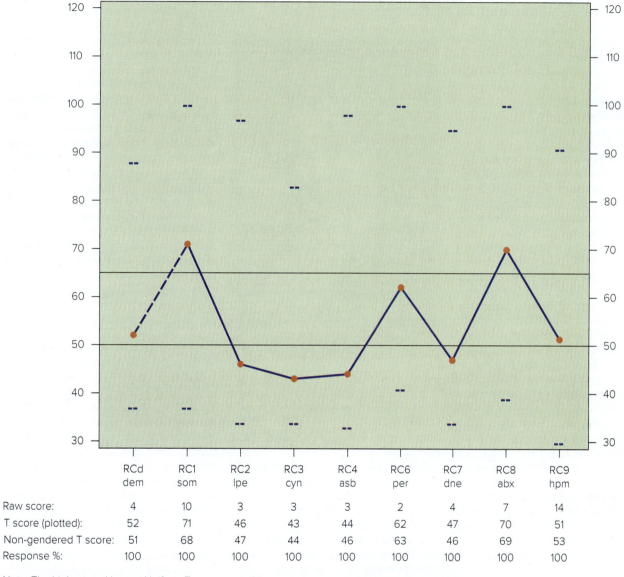

	RCd dem	RC1 som	RC2 lpe	RC3 cyn	RC4 asb	RC6 per	RC7 dne	RC8 abx	RC9 hpm
Raw score:	4	10	3	3	3	2	4	7	14
T score (plotted):	52	71	46	43	44	62	47	70	51
Non-gendered T score:	51	68	47	44	46	63	46	69	53
Response %:	100	100	100	100	100	100	100	100	100

Note: The highest and lowest Uniform T scores possible on each scale are indicated by a "--".

Legend		
dem = Demoralization	cyn = Cynicism	dne = Dysfunctional negative emotions
som = Somatic complaints	asb = Antisocial behavior	abx = Aberrant experiences
lpe = Low positive emotions	per = Ideas of persecution	hpm = Hypomanic Activation

systems are available to reduce the role of subjectivity in interpreting the stories that clients tell about the pictures (Jenkins, 2017).

Projective tests are most useful when combined with self-report inventories rather than when clinicians use them as the sole basis for diagnosing or evaluating a client. In Ben's case, Dr. Washington decided not to conduct projective testing until he completed the neuropsychological assessment. Clinicians typically do not administer these instruments as part of a standard battery, particularly if there is the potential that the client's symptoms are related to a trauma or injury.

REAL STORIES

Ludwig van Beethoven: Bipolar Disorder

The German composer Ludwig van Beethoven was one of the most brilliant musical composers of all time. His music captures the incredibly vast range of emotions he experienced throughout his lifetime–arguably a greater range than most people experience, because scholars believe he suffered from bipolar disorder. The book *The Key to Genius* chronicles stories from Beethoven's life based on letters from the composer and accounts by his friends who recall the emotionally chaotic and often volatile life he led. One friend quoted in the book said, "It seems unlikely that one could achieve works of emotional range and intensity comparable to those of Beethoven without such extraordinary emotional experiences."

Beethoven was raised by a father who often beat him and would reportedly lock him in the basement, and a mother whom he loved but who was more or less absent for much of the time he was growing up. When Beethoven was 17, his mother became ill and passed away, leaving behind three young sons and a husband who began abusing alcohol. Since their father was unable to care for his children, it fell to Beethoven to take care of his two younger brothers until they were grown.

At this point in his life, Beethoven had already published his first piano composition. At 22, he left his family to study with the renowned composer Franz Joseph Haydn in Vienna, Austria, where he remained for the rest of his life. Though most composers at the time worked on commission from churches, Beethoven was a freelance composer and quickly became a successful and respected name. This success protected him from a society that would have undoubtedly looked upon him in a negative light. Those close to Beethoven viewed him as an emotionally unstable man who was prone to periods of both intense irritability and paranoia, as well as lengthy periods of depression. His fiery temper often led to quarrels with landlords and servants, and he often moved residences as a result. His temper greatly affected his personal relationships, and he would often excommunicate friends only to later beg them for forgiveness, which they usually granted due to his generally good nature, aside

Ludwig van Beethoven is believed to have suffered from bipolar disorder.

SOURCE: Library of Congress, Prints & Photographs Division, Reproduction number LC-USZ62-29499 (b&w film copy neg.)

from his periods of agitation and melancholy.

Remarkably, although Beethoven suffered from hearing loss to the point that he became completely deaf for the last 10 years of his life, causing great anguish, he continued to compose and perform music until his death. As with many creative individuals with bipolar disorder, Beethoven's mania proved to be a strong creative force in his life. In contrast, his periods of depression were usually unproductive as he typically languished in solitude until the mood passed. He was often physically ill and dealt with asthma in the winters, which undoubtedly contributed to his persistent depression and high consumption of alcohol. In turn, his alcoholism led to many more physical problems. Unfortunately, substance abuse such as alcoholism is often a secondary problem for individuals suffering from bipolar disorder, in an attempt to control their distressing mood fluctuations.

Beethoven's episodes of mania allowed not only heightened periods of creativity but also opportunities to temporarily overcome any physical conditions he suffered, even in the later years of his life when he

was afflicted with a multitude of painful medical problems. As one doctor noted, "Often, with rare endurance, he worked at his compositions on a wooded hillside and his work done, still aglow with reflection, he would not infrequently run about for hours in the most inhospitable surroundings, denying every change of temperature, and often during the heaviest snowfalls."

Beethoven never married and had no children of his own, though he was known as a romantic who had many amorous pursuits. When his younger brother died, Beethoven took in his 9-year-old nephew, Karl, an arrangement that soon turned disastrous by all accounts. Beethoven was highly mistrustful of Karl's mother (he was often suspicious of the people in his life), and he took her to court over his nephew's custody. The custody dispute lasted for some time, and once Beethoven had gained guardianship of Karl, he was known to constantly harangue the boy and interfere with his life. Things became so hard on Karl that he attempted suicide and later decided to join the military, apparently in an effort to seek a more stable life than the one he had known with his uncle. It's not hard to imagine that it was difficult for Beethoven to take care of a young child when he often took very poor care of himself. His friends tell accounts in *The Key to Genius* about the composer's often complete lack of hygiene and self-care in his later years. He often appeared so disheveled that once he was imprisoned when he was mistaken for a burglar while walking around a neighborhood in Vienna; he was released only after a friend was able to identify him. Based on his appearance, the officers did not believe he was Beethoven.

Those close to Beethoven eventually came to tolerate his unusual, sometimes rapid shifts in mood and impulsive acts. Viennese society accepted his odd behavior due to his success and musical contributions. His unbounded creativity and love for music both benefited from his emotional experiences and helped him survive many trying periods of his life. Wrote one friend, "It may be that Beethoven survived as a creator because he was brave or because his love of music kept him going." However, his physical health was constantly compromised due in large part to the mania that caused him to push himself to the brink. When his illnesses became too much to bear, depression often would follow, and this constant cycle represents the struggles that those with bipolar disorder experience. In the end, Beethoven's passion for music was not enough to save him from cirrhosis of the liver caused by excessive alcohol consumption, and he died in 1827 at the age of 57. Though we remember him for his music, we can hear his emotional struggles within his creations. As one friend noted, "So much of Beethoven's life was spent in sickness and pain, weakness, and depression that it is remarkable that he accomplished anything at all. Given the pervasiveness of his misery, his work is all the more miraculous."

3.6 Behavioral Assessment

A **behavioral assessment** is a form of measurement based on objective recording of the individual's behavior. Unlike psychological tests, behavioral assessments record actions rather than responses to rating scales or questions. The **target behavior** is a behavior of interest or concern in an assessment, and is what the client and clinician wish to change. Behavioral assessments include descriptions of the antecedents (events that precede the behaviors) and consequences (the outcomes of those behaviors). For example, a child in a classroom may be unusually disruptive immediately following recess, but not immediately following lunch. The antecedent is recess, and the consequences are perhaps the teacher's attention or reactions of classmates to the child's disruptive behavior at play but not during a meal.

Clients often complete individual self-reports of behavioral patterns as part of a comprehensive psychological assessment.
©Zinkevych/Getty Images

When clinicians record behavior in its natural context, such as the classroom or the home, this is called *in vivo* **observation**. However, it is not always possible or practical to conduct an *in vivo* observation. The teacher or a teacher's aide may be too busy to record the behavior of one child. The alternative of having an outside observer record the child's behavior could create a distraction or influence the behavior the clinician wants to observe. In these cases, the classroom environment would be simulated and the behavior monitored in this controlled condition.

Analog observations allow for simulation of the behaviors under consideration to occur. They may take place in a setting or context such as a clinician's office or a laboratory specifically designed for observing the target behavior. A clinician assessing the disruptive child would need to arrange a situation as comparable as possible to the natural setting of the classroom for the analog observation to be valid.

Clients may also report on their own behavior rather than having someone observe them. A **behavioral self-report** is a method of behavioral assessment in which the individual provides information about the frequency of particular behaviors. This self-report also includes the antecedents and consequences of the behavior. **Self-monitoring** is a form of behavioral self-report in which the client keeps a record of the frequency of specified behaviors, such as the number of cigarettes smoked or calories consumed, or the number of times in a day that a particular unwanted thought comes to the client's mind. Clinicians may also obtain information from their clients using **behavioral interviewing** in which they ask questions about the target behavior's frequency, antecedents, and consequences. All these methods would be more appropriate when it is the adult seeking treatment rather than the child, as long as the adult is capable of monitoring his or her own behavior.

3.7 Multicultural Assessment

When psychologists conduct an assessment, they take into account the person's cultural, ethnic, and racial background by performing a **multicultural assessment**. To conduct this assessment, clinicians evaluating clients who speak English as a second language or not at all must ask a number of questions: Does the client understand the assessment process sufficiently to provide informed consent? Does the client understand the instructions for the

behavioral assessment
A form of measurement based on objective recording of the individual's behavior.

target behavior
A behavior of interest or concern in an assessment.

in vivo **observation**
Process of recording behavior in its natural context, such as the classroom or the home.

analog observations
Assessments that take place in a setting or context such as a clinician's office or a laboratory specifically designed for observing the target behavior.

behavioral self-report
A method of behavioral assessment in which the individual provides information about the frequency of particular behaviors.

self-monitoring
A self-report technique in which the client keeps a record of the frequency of specified behaviors.

It is important for psychologists to take multicultural considerations into account throughout each part of the assessment process.

©Eric Audras/Getty Images

behavioral interviewing
Assessment process in which clinicians ask questions about the target behavior's frequency, antecedents, and consequences.

multicultural assessment
Assessment process in which clinicians take into account the person's cultural, ethnic, and racial background.

Cultural Formulation Interview
A set of questions that assess the impact of culture on key aspects of the client's clinical presentation and care.

neuropsychological assessment
A performance-based method assessing cognitive functioning used to examine the cognitive consequences of brain damage, brain disease, and severe mental illness.

executive functioning
The ability to formulate goals, make plans, carry out those plans, and then complete the plans in an effective way.

instrument? Are there normative data for the client's ethnic group? Even if clients appear fairly fluent, they may not understand idiomatic phrases for which there are multiple meanings (Weiner & Greene, 2008).

To assess the contributions of these cultural concepts to the client's symptoms, clinicians can use the more formal mechanism in *DSM-5* based on cultural concepts of distress. The **Cultural Formulation Interview (CFI)** is a set of questions that assess the impact of culture on key aspects of the client's clinical presentation and care. The CFI assesses the client's cultural identity, the individual's cultural conceptualizations of distress, the way the client's culture defines vulnerability and resilience, and any cultural differences between the client and clinician. Questions on the CFI include, "For you, what are the most important aspects of your background or identity?" and "Why do you think this is happening to you?" Background or identity, in turn, refers to "the communities you belong to, the languages you speak, where you or your family are from, your race or ethnic background, your gender or sexual orientation, or your faith or religion" (American Psychiatric Association, 2013).

Publishers of psychological tests are continually reevaluating their instruments to ensure that clients from a range of diverse backgrounds can understand the items. At the same time, graduate trainees in clinical programs are trained to understand the cultural backgrounds of clients they assess, to evaluate assessment instruments from a critical perspective, and to recognize when to either conduct a culturally sensitive assessment or seek further consultation (Dana, 2002). Established clinicians, similarly, must seek continuing education to ensure that their assessments meet current multicultural assessment criteria (Edwards, Burkard, Adams, & Newcomb, 2017).

3.8 Neuropsychological Assessment

Neuropsychological assessment is a performance-based method assessing cognitive functioning used to examine the cognitive consequences of brain damage, brain disease, and severe mental illness. Scores on neuropsychological measures are used by clinicians to compare a client's responses on a particular test with normative data from individuals who are known to have certain types of injuries or disorders.

In a neuropsychological assessment, the clinician can choose from tests that measure attention and working (short-term) memory, processing speed, verbal reasoning and comprehension, visual reasoning, verbal memory, and visual memory. A number of tests evaluate what clinicians call **executive functioning**, the ability to formulate goals, make plans, carry out those plans, and then complete the plans in an effective way. There are a variety of available tests within each category. If the client appears to have suffered brain injury or dysfunction, the clinician will use neuropsychological testing to gain further insight into the exact nature of the damage.

There is no one set procedure for conducting a neuropsychological assessment because the purpose of the assessment is to tailor the tests for each client. Particular clinicians may have preferences for certain tests based on their own experiences and what they believe will be most effective in determining the nature of the client's strengths and weaknesses. The client's age is another factor that the clinician takes into account. Tests appropriate for older adults are generally not suitable for diagnosing a child or adolescent. Similarly, clinicians need to ensure the tests they use are suitable for people of a given cultural or linguistic background.

The key to understanding a neuropsychological test is that it is *psychological*, meaning that it does not employ brain scanning or physiological measures. To get an idea of what such tests might include, for example, there are tests that use scales from the WAIS-IV. Digit Span is used to assess verbal recall and auditory attention and Similarities to assess verbal abstraction abilities. Another widely used method, particularly for older adults, is the Trail

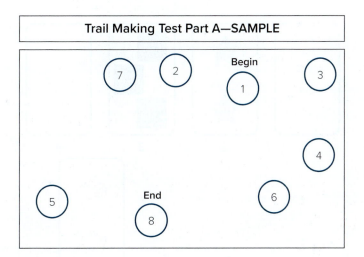

Trail Making Test Part A—SAMPLE

FIGURE 3 Trail Making Test

SOURCE: Adapted from Reitan, R. M. Validity of the Trail Making Test as an indicator of organic brain damage. *Perceptual and Motor Skills*, Vol. 8, 1958, 271–276.

Making Test (TMT), a simple test of executive functioning that can be administered via pencil and paper. Figure 3 shows a sample item from Trail Making Test Part A. In this example, the task you would be asked to complete is to draw a line connecting the numbers in order. Although this may seem simple enough, individuals with frontal lobe damage may find it challenging to track a sequence of numbers. The abilities tapped by the Trail Making Test include attention, scanning of visual stimuli, and number sequencing.

There are a large number of tests that measure visuospatial ability. One very simple one used in screening for neurocognitive impairment is the Clock Drawing Test (Sunderland et al., 1989). The examiner gives the individual being tested a sheet of paper with a large predrawn circle on it. The client's task is to draw the numbers around the circle to look like the face of an analog clock. Finally, the examiner asks the client to draw the hands of the clock to read "10 after 11." The clinician then rates the client's drawing according to number of errors. The most impaired clients are unable to reproduce a clock face at all, or they make mistakes in writing the numbers or placing them around the clock.

The Wisconsin Card Sorting Test (WCST) is used to assess executive functioning, in that it taps the client's ability to form higher-order abstract concepts. The client sees four cards, such as in the top row of Figure 4. The clinician deals one card at a time, and the client's job is to indicate which of the cards in the top row matches this card. There are 64 cards in the series. In the example shown here, the two red plus signs could match either Card 1 (color), Card 2 (number), or Card 4 (shape). The test-taker receives

What's in the *DSM-5*

Section 3 Assessment Measures

DSM-5's Section 3 contains a set of assessment measures that clinicians can use to enhance their decision-making process. These tools include a "cross-cutting" interview that reviews symptoms across all psychological disorders such as emotional distress, anger, and repetitive thoughts that either the client or someone close to the client can complete. This review of symptoms would allow clinicians to draw attention to symptoms that may not fit precisely into the categorically based diagnoses. Such questions could be incorporated into a mental status examination. One set of questions contains a brief survey of 13 domains for adults and 12 for children. The follow-up questions go into more depth in domains that seem to warrant further attention.

The *DSM-5* authors recognize that dimensional approaches are increasingly being supported by the literature due to the fact that categorical distinctions among disorders may, at times, seem arbitrary. In addition, there are disorders that combine features of two disorders. Many clients also have more than one disorder or diagnoses that do not fit easily into one category. Eventually, a dimensional approach could be combined with the *DSM*'s categorically based diagnoses. This approach would allow clinicians to indicate the severity of a client's disorder, making it possible to evaluate a client's progress during treatment.

In addition to these tools, Section 3 includes the WHODAS (as presented in the chapter "Diagnosis and Treatment" and a section providing clinicians with tools to perform a cultural formulation. This is a comprehensive semistructured interview that focuses on the client's experience and social context. The *DSM-5* authors emphasize that the interview should be conducted in a way that allows the client to report his or her subjective experiences. This is intended to reduce the chances that the clinician's stereotypes or preexisting biases will affect the diagnostic process.

The *DSM-5* authors hope that by providing these tools and techniques, they will not only improve the diagnostic process but also contribute to the research literature on the nature and causes of psychological disorders.

FIGURE 4 Sample Item from the Wisconsin Card Sorting Test

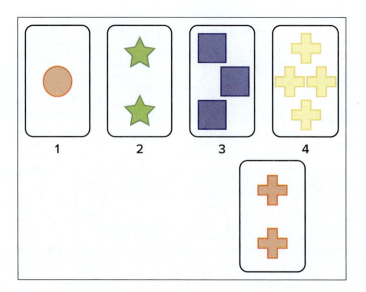

feedback about whether the choice was correct or not. On the next trial, this feedback would inform the client's choice of card. After several trials, the concept shifts and now the client must discover the new rule. The test was originally developed using physical cards, but now clinicians typically administer the test in its computerized format.

The WCST is a good test of executive functioning (Rabin, Barr, & Burton, 2005) that is sensitive to injury of the frontal lobes but also assesses damage in other cortical areas (Nagahama et al., 2005). Increasingly, data using brain scanning methods are being compared to WCST performance, providing an opportunity for researchers to expand their ability to interpret the scores the test provides (Lubeiro et al., 2017).

Neuropsychologists use the Boston Naming Test (BNT) to assess the word-retrieval abilities of children with learning disabilities and adults who have suffered brain damage. Each of the 60 items on the BNT contains a picture of an object, and the test-taker must retrieve its name. The BNT moves from simple items such as *bed*, *tree*, and *pencil* to difficult items at the end such as *palette* and *abacus*. Incorrect answers include the individual's failure to name the item, but also to give a related name (e.g., "mouth organ" for "harmonica") or to name only a part of the item. Because the test depends on the individual's fluency in English, the BNT would not be appropriate for individuals whose native language is not English.

The Paced Auditory Serial Addition Test (PASAT) assesses a client's auditory information processing speed, flexibility, and calculation ability. The client hears a recording of numbers between 1 and 9 every 3 seconds. The task is to add the number just heard with the number that preceded it. If the recording was "1-3-5-2-6-7," the correct response would be "4-8-7-8-13." In addition to its usage to assess traumatic brain injury, clinicians also use the PASAT extensively in assessing the functioning of individuals with multiple sclerosis (Tombaugh et al., 2006).

To assess the immediate aftermath of brain trauma, the clinician would give the Glasgow Coma Scale (GCS), which measures impairment of conscious level in response to defined stimuli. The GCS tests the individual's ability to open the eyes, to be oriented to his or her surroundings, and to obey commands. It is particularly useful for clinicians to give the GCS over a period of time following suspected trauma, to track progressive changes over time in the individual's level of consciousness. Because it is available in 32 languages, the GCS has the advantage of being highly useful in multicultural settings.

Other neuropsychological tests investigate a variety of memory functions. The Wechsler Memory Scale, Fourth Edition (WMS-IV) includes tests of working (short-term) and long-term

You Be the Judge

Psychologists in the Legal System

Psychologists working within the legal system are frequently called on to serve as expert witnesses, and their testimony often relies on psychological assessments. Unlike the therapeutic setting, the forensic setting does not necessarily involve a positive relationship. In fact, the psychologist may face a malpractice suit from the clients if they wish to seek revenge for an assessment that led to a conviction or unfavorable decision, as in custody cases.

Knapp and VandeCreek (2001) present an interesting case history of a psychologist involved in a custody case who wrote in his report that the father had "authoritarian tendencies and could benefit from participating in parenting classes" (pp. 244–245). However, the psychologist had not actually interviewed the father; he based this statement on what the children told him. As a result, the psychologist was reprimanded by his state licensing board.

Psychologists are also mandated by the APA Ethical Principles of Psychologists and Code of Conduct (also called the Ethics Code) to practice within their field of competence. If they have not received training in forensic psychology, they are required to seek consultation from an expert colleague. A second case example presented by Knapp and VandeCreek involved the testimony by a psychologist proficient in assessment, but not forensic assessment, who testified that on the basis of elevated scores on the MMPI-2 scales 6 and 9, the defendant was indeed "insane." However, legal insanity is not the same as being psychologically disordered, and therefore the psychologist's testimony was discredited in court.

Informed consent is another key ethical principle that applies not only to research but also to assessment and treatment. When a defendant with a psychological disorder is interviewed for a forensic assessment, the psychologist must take all possible precautions to let the defendant know about the limits of confidentiality in this context. In another example presented by Knapp and VandeCreek, a defendant was genuinely startled to hear the psychologist report on the interview, because the defendant had not understood the nature of the informed consent.

As a final example, consider the prohibition in the Ethics Code against dual relationships. Psychologists providing therapy should not be providing information that could be used by a lawyer in a legal case. The example cited by Knapp and VandeCreek was of a psychologist treating the children of a separated couple. The children stated that they preferred to live with their mother. The mother later requested that the psychologist write a letter to her attorney. In turn, the attorney asked the psychologist to "share your opinions as to where the children should live" (p. 250).

Q: *You be the judge:* As you can see, the APA Ethics Code clearly states the proper course of action in each case. The question for you to judge is not which course of action is proper, because this is clearly stated in the APA Ethics Code. Instead, consider the complexities psychologists face when interacting in the legal system. These examples are only a handful from the many possible scenarios that can ensue, placing psychologists in situations that require them to be entirely familiar with the principles that guide the profession.

memory for visual and verbal stimuli. Examiners can choose from among the WMS-IV sub-scales according to the areas they believe are most critical to evaluate in particular clients. For example, when testing an older adult, the examiner may use only the scales assessing Logical Memory (recall of a story), Verbal Paired Associates (ability to remember the second word in pairs of words), and Visual Reproduction (ability to draw a visual stimulus).

Computerized test batteries, which contain a range of tests adaptable to the possible brain damage in the client, provide the opportunity for **adaptive testing**, in which the client's responses to earlier questions determine the subsequent questions presented to him or her. For example, the Cambridge Neuropsychological Testing Automated Battery (CANTAB)

adaptive testing
Testing in which the client's responses to earlier questions determine the subsequent questions presented to him or her.

consists of 22 subtests that assess visual memory, working memory, executive function and planning, attention, verbal memory, and decision making and response control.

Before deciding whether to move to a computerized test, the clinician must weigh the advantages of ease of administration and scoring against the potential disadvantages that may exist for clients who are disadvantaged in their ability to use computers. Current cohorts of older adults may vary in their familiarity with technology, but as the fastest-growing segment of Internet users, this is likely to change in just a few years (Zygouris & Tsolaki, 2015). The benefits of the computerized battery need to be weighed against the costs if there is concern that the test-taker will be disadvantaged using this format.

Looking now at Ben's tests, Dr. Washington chose to administer tasks that would be sensitive to the type of injury that Ben might have sustained given his low WAIS-IV coding score, which suggested that Ben may have suffered brain damage that led to changes in his ability to focus his visual attention and perform quickly on a psychomotor speed task. Because Dr. Washington did not see Ben at the scene of the accident or in the ER, he could not administer the GCS.

Ben's completion time on Trail Making Test Part A was in the marginally impaired range. On the Clock Drawing Test, Ben received a score of 5 of a possible 10, erroneously crowding the numbers at one end of the clock. He received a score within the normal range on the PASAT, suggesting that the injury did not affect his auditory attentional functioning. On the WCST, Ben showed evidence of perseverative errors, meaning that he was unable to switch mental set in categorizing the cards according to different criteria. Ben's performance on the WMS-IV was within normal range, a finding consistent with his relatively high scores on the Verbal scales of the Wechsler, indicating that he had not suffered either short- or long-term memory loss.

3.9 Neuroimaging

neuroimaging

Assessment method that provides a picture of the brain's structures or level of activity and therefore is a useful tool for "looking" at the brain.

Neuroimaging provides a picture of the brain's structures or level of activity and therefore is a useful tool for "looking" at the brain. Psychologists use several types of neuroimaging methods, both in clinical work and research, that vary in the types of results they provide.

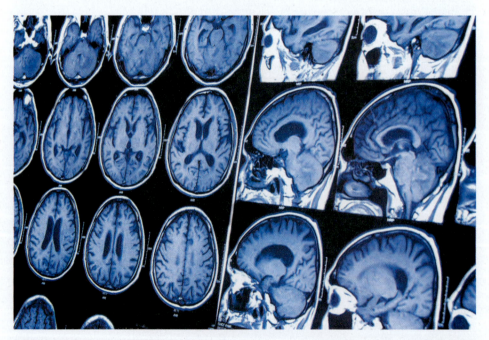

A CAT scan of a patient's brain helps neuropsychologists to find brain structure abnormalities that may be causing cognitive dysfunction.
©Tushchakorn Rushchatrabuntchasuk/123RF

The **electroencephalogram (EEG)** measures electrical activity in the brain. EEG activity reflects the extent to which an individual is alert, resting, sleeping, or dreaming. The EEG pattern also shows particular patterns of brain waves when an individual engages in particular mental tasks. Clinicians use EEGs to evaluate clients for conditions such as epilepsy, sleep disorders, and brain tumors.

Computed axial tomography (CAT or CT) scan uses a series of X-rays taken from various angles around the brain that are integrated by computer to produce a composite picture. CT scans of the brain provide a static image of the fluid-filled areas called the ventricles. The method is useful when clinicians are looking for structural damage to the brain because enlarged ventricles would signify loss of vital brain tissue.

Magnetic resonance imaging (MRI) uses radio waves rather than X-rays to construct a static picture of the living brain based on the water content of various tissues. To conduct an MRI of the brain, the individual is placed inside a capsule that contains a powerful electromagnet. Magnetic force causes the nuclei in hydrogen atoms to transmit electromagnetic energy (hence the term *magnetic resonance*). A computer produces a high-resolution picture of the scanned area based on activity recorded from thousands of angles. The picture from the MRI differentiates areas in the brain of white matter (nerve fibers) from gray matter (nerve cells) and is useful for diagnosing diseases that affect the nerve fibers that make up the white matter. However, because the MRI uses magnetism to detect brain activity, people who have metallic joints, pacemakers, or other permanent metallic implants cannot use this testing method.

A **positron emission tomography (PET) scan,** is a measure of brain activity in which a small amount of a radioactive compound is injected into an individual's bloodstream, following which a computer measures the various levels of radiation in different parts of the brain and yields a multicolored image.

In the variant known as **single photon emission computed tomography (SPECT) scan,** a longer and more detailed imaging analysis can be performed. In both methods, the compounds travel through the blood into the brain and emit positively charged electrons called positrons, which act very much like X-rays in a CT scan. The images, which represent the accumulation of the labeled compound, can show blood flow, oxygen or glucose metabolism, and concentrations of brain chemicals. Vibrant colors at the red end of the spectrum represent higher levels of activity, and colors at the blue-green-violet end of the spectrum represent lower levels of brain activity. **Proton magnetic resonance spectroscopy (MRS)** is another scanning method that measures metabolic activity of neurons and therefore may indicate areas of brain damage (Govind et al., 2010).

Functional magnetic resonance imaging (fMRI) provides a picture of how areas of the brain react to stimuli in real time, making it possible to precisely monitor the individual's response. Researchers are increasingly using fMRIs to understand the brain areas active in the processing of information. One major advantage of the fMRI is that it does not require injection of radioactive materials, like the PET or SPECT scan.

Researchers also use **diffusion tensor imaging (DTI),** a method to investigate abnormalities in the white matter of the brain. DTI scans show the activity of water molecules as they diffuse along the length of axons, making it possible to investigate abnormalities in neural pathways.

Keep in mind that brain scans can produce evidence of specific areas of damage, but they do not necessarily correspond to a specific loss of behavioral functioning (Meyers & Rohling, 2009). At present, then, they can be suggestive of brain damage or lowered neural activity, but their links to how people think, remember, plan, or perceive cannot be guaranteed. You may hear a brain scan described as showing an area that "lights up," but it is not always clear that higher or lower amounts of

electroencephalogram (EEG)
A measure of changes in the electrical activity of the brain.

computed axial tomography (CAT or CT) scan
A series of X-rays taken from various angles around the brain that are integrated by computer to produce a composite picture.

magnetic resonance imaging (MRI)
The use of radio waves rather than X-rays to construct a static picture of the living brain based on the water content of various tissues.

positron emission tomography (PET) scan
A measure of brain activity in which a small amount of radioactive compounds is injected into an individual's bloodstream, following which a computer measures the varying levels of radiation in different parts of the brain and yields a multicolored image.

single photon emission computed tomography (SPECT) scan
A variant of the PET scan that allows a longer and more detailed imaging analysis to be performed.

proton magnetic resonance spectroscopy (MRS)
A scanning method that measures metabolic activity of neurons and therefore may indicate areas of brain damage.

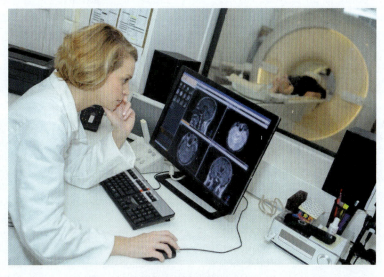

An fMRI is used to monitor changes in brain activity.
©ALPA PROD/Shutterstock

functional magnetic resonance imaging (fMRI)
Provides a picture of how areas of the brain react to stimuli in real time.

diffusion tensor imaging (DTI)
A method to investigate abnormalities in the white matter of the brain.

brain activity are directly translatable into their subjective equivalents in emotions such as fear, love, or anger.

Upon evaluating Ben through neuropsychological testing, Dr. Washington ordered a CT scan (de Guise et al., 2010), because Ben showed some signs of frontal lobe damage (personality changes, some perseveration on the WCST, and marginal errors on the TMT). However, it was necessary to rule out parietal lobe damage, which can also contribute to this performance pattern and to visual attentional deficits. The CT scan revealed that Ben had suffered a traumatic brain injury as a result of the incident, perhaps in the form of a brain hemorrhage.

3.10 Putting It All Together

As we have just shown in Ben's case, clinicians face a formidable task when attempting to develop a diagnosis from the evidence that they obtain through the assessment process. They must evaluate each client on an individual basis and determine which combination of tests is most appropriate to identify as closely as possible the nature and cause of that client's behavioral symptoms. In addition, clinicians performing assessments attempt to understand a client's adaptive skills, so that they can make recommendations to build on the client's existing abilities and help address treatment to maximize his or her functioning in everyday life.

Return to the Case: Ben Robsham

Given the potential cause of his symptoms, Dr. Washington recommended that Ben receive rehabilitation to strengthen his existing skills so that he can return to his previous employment. Ben will also receive supportive therapy and possibly vocational counseling if he continues to demonstrate deficits in visual and spatial processing speed, skills he clearly needs for his present job.

Dr. Tobin's reflections: It is somewhat reassuring to know that Ben's injury, though currently interfering with his ability to go to work, will most likely resolve on its own. A

neuropsychological assessment was clearly called for in this case; unfortunately, with increases in traumatic brain injuries in recent years, this type of assessment will be increasingly necessary. Ben's injury occurred at work, but many other young people are experiencing such injuries in areas of activity as diverse as playing hockey or football and fighting in war. With the development of more sophisticated neuroimaging and computerized testing, we will be better prepared to assess individuals like Ben in the future, as well as those clients we see whose disorders are primarily psychological in nature.

SUMMARY

- A psychological assessment is a procedure in which a clinician provides a formal evaluation of an individual's cognitive, personality, and psychosocial functioning. Clinicians conduct assessments under a variety of conditions. In many cases, clinicians use the assessment process to provide a diagnosis, or at least a tentative diagnosis, of an individual's psychological disorder.

- To be useful, clinicians must hold assessments to standards that ensure that they provide the most reproducible and accurate results. The reliability of a test indicates the consistency of the scores it produces. The test's validity reflects the extent to which a test measures what it is designed to measure.

- Clinicians should use the best assessment methods possible. Evidence-based assessment includes (1) relying on research findings and scientifically viable theories, (2) using psychometrically strong measures, and (3) empirically evaluating the assessment process.

- The clinical interview is a series of questions that clinicians administer in face-to-face interaction with the client. The answers clients provide to these questions provide important background information on clients, allow them to describe their symptoms, and enable clinicians to make observations of their clients that can guide decisions about the next steps, which may include further testing. The format can be structured or unstructured.

- A clinician uses a mental status examination to assess a client's current state of mind. The clinician assesses a number of features of the client including appearance, attitudes, behavior, mood and affect, speech, thought processes, content of thought, perception, cognition, insight, and judgment. The outcome of the mental status examination is a comprehensive description of how the client looks, thinks, feels, and behaves.

- Intelligence tests such as the Stanford-Binet Intelligence Test, but particularly the Wechsler scales, provide valuable information about an individual's cognitive functioning.

- Clinicians use tests of personality to understand a person's thoughts, behaviors, and emotions. There are two main forms of personality tests: self-report and projective. Tests include the Minnesota Multiphasic Personality Inventory (MMPI), the Personality Assessment Inventory (PAI), the SCL-90-R, the NEO Personality Inventory, and other specific self-report inventories designed to investigate specific disorders or research questions for which a general test may not be relevant.

- In projective tests, the examiner asks questions about an ambiguous stimulus. The most common are the Rorschach and the TAT. Behavioral assessments record actions rather than responses to rating scales or questions. The target behavior is what the client and clinician wish to change.

Behavioral assessments include descriptions of the events that precede or follow the behaviors. *In vivo* observation takes place when clinicians record behavior in its natural context, such as the classroom or the home. Analog observations take place in a setting or context such as a clinician's office or a laboratory specifically designed for observing the target behavior. In a behavioral self-report the client records the target behavior, including the antecedents and consequences of the behavior. Self-monitoring is a form of behavioral self-report in which the client keeps a record of the frequency of specified behaviors.

- When psychologists conduct a multicultural assessment, they must take into account the person's cultural, ethnic, and racial background.

- Neuropsychological assessment is the process of gathering information about a client's brain functioning on the basis of performance on psychological tests. Clinicians use neuropsychological assessment measures to attempt to determine the functional correlates of brain damage by comparing a client's performance on a particular test with normative data from individuals who are known to have certain types of injuries or disorders. There are a variety of tests to assess verbal recall and auditory attention. Neuroimaging includes EEG, CT scan, MRI, fMRI, PET scan, and DTI.

KEY TERMS

Adaptive testing

Analog observations

Barnum effect

Behavioral assessment

Behavioral interviewing

Behavioral self-report

Clinical interview

Computed axial tomography (CAT or CT) scan

Cultural Formulation Interview

Deviation intelligence (IQ)

Diffusion tensor imaging (DTI)

Electroencephalogram (EEG)

Evidence-based assessment

Executive functioning

Functional magnetic resonance imaging (fMRI)

In vivo observation

Magnetic resonance imaging (MRI)

Mental status examination

Mini-Mental State Examination (MMSE)

Minnesota Multiphasic Personality Inventory (MMPI)

Multicultural assessment

Neuroimaging

Neuropsychological assessment

Positron emission tomography (PET) scan

Projective test

Proton magnetic resonance spectroscopy (MRS)

Psychological assessment

Rorschach Inkblot Test

Self-monitoring

Self-report clinical inventory

Single photon emission computed tomography (SPECT) scan

Standardization

Structured Clinical Interview for *DSM-5* Disorders (SCID-5)

Structured interview

Target behavior

Thematic Apperception Test (TAT)

Unstructured interview

Wechsler Adult Intelligence Scale (WAIS)

Theoretical Perspectives

Learning Objectives

4.1 Assess theories of the biological perspective and identify treatments.

4.2 Describe trait theory.

4.3 Compare and contrast Freud's theory to post-Freudian psychodynamic views and identify treatments.

4.4 Assess theories of the behavioral perspective and identify treatments.

4.5 Assess theories of the cognitive perspective and identify treatments.

4.6 Assess theories of the humanistic perspective and identify treatments.

4.7 Assess theories of the sociocultural perspective and identify treatments.

4.8 Explain the biopsychosocial perspective.

©stockphoto-graf/Shutterstock

Case Report: Meera Krishnan

Demographic information: 26-year-old single heterosexual Indian American female

Presenting problem: Meera self-referred to my outpatient private practice upon the urging of a friend. For the past 3 weeks she reports feeling, in her words, "profoundly sad for no reason at all," lethargic, and preoccupied with feelings that she would be better off dead, though she states she has no specific plan or intent to commit suicide. She stated she oversleeps on most days, has decreased appetite on most days, resulting in weight loss of about 2–3 pounds, and tries to avoid any social contact. She further describes feeling that she has greatly let down her family and friends. As a result of these symptoms, Meera believes her work performance has suffered and notes that she has used all her sick days; she is on warning from her employer that her contract will be reviewed if she misses any more days of work.

Relevant history: A college graduate, Meera works as a biologist in a hospital research laboratory. She is the younger of two daughters and reports having a long-standing belief that her parents favor her older sister. She feels that her parents, who immigrated to the United States from India before Meera and her sister were born, disapprove of her current lifestyle in comparison to that of her sister, who married the son of family friends. Although Meera and her sister were once very close, they no longer maintain regular contact, and she rarely visits her parents, although they live in a neighboring town.

Meera reports that she rarely drinks alcohol and has never used illicit drugs. She has no medical conditions and reports that, in general, her health is very good. Prior to the onset of her current depressive episode, Meera reports that she exercised regularly by participating in a long-distance running club and enjoyed cooking with her friends and listening to music.

This is Meera's third depressive episode since her junior year of high school. Each episode has lasted approximately 2 months or slightly longer. She has not previously sought treatment.

Symptoms: For nearly every day of the last 3 weeks, Meera has been experiencing overwhelming feelings of sadness most of the day, not accounted for by bereavement, substance use, or a medical condition. Her symptoms include feelings of worthlessness, tearfulness, loss of interest, sleep disturbance (oversleeping), and loss of appetite. She has experienced recurrent thoughts about death and passive suicidal ideation, although she has never had any intent or plan to kill herself.

Case formulation: Because Meera has experienced two previous depressive episodes, each of which have been at least 2 months apart, and the symptoms of her current episode are interfering with her ability to carry out her normal daily functioning, she meets *DSM-5* criteria for major depressive disorder (MDD), recurrent.

Treatment plan: The principles of evidence-based practice suggest that the best treatment for Meera's depression is cognitive-behavioral therapy (CBT). Following the intake appointment, she will receive a complete psychological assessment. Given the severity of her symptoms, I will recommend a referral to a psychiatrist for consultation and medical evaluation to determine whether psychiatric medication could be beneficial.

Sarah Tobin, PhD

4.1 Theoretical Perspectives in Abnormal Psychology

theoretical perspective
An orientation to understanding the causes of human behavior and the treatment of psychological disorders.

Underlying **theoretical perspectives**, orientations to understanding the causes of human behavior and the treatment of psychological disorders, guide all research and clinical work in abnormal psychology. In this chapter, we will explore the major theoretical perspectives that form the foundation for the text. You will read in more detail about each perspective and how it applies to specific disorders within the chapters covering the major psychological disorders. To facilitate your understanding of these perspectives, we will use Meera's case as an example to show how clinicians working within each perspective would address her treatment. Although Meera's plan calls for treatment within the cognitive-behavioral perspective, her case has many facets that each of the major theories address and therefore warrants discussion.

4.2 Biological Perspective

biological perspective
A theoretical perspective in which it is assumed that disturbances in emotions, behavior, and cognitive processes are caused by abnormalities in the functioning of the body.

Psychologists working within the **biological perspective** believe that abnormalities in the body's functioning are responsible for the symptoms of psychological disorders. In particular, they maintain that we can trace the causes of psychological symptoms primarily to disturbances in the nervous system or other bodily systems that have an impact on the nervous system.

Theories

Biological approaches to abnormality focus on the roles of the nervous system and genetics. The ways in which these interact through life become important pieces of the biopsychosocial perspective.

neurotransmitter
A chemical substance released from a neuron into the synaptic cleft, where it drifts across the synapse and is absorbed by the receiving neuron.

Role of the Nervous System The transmission of information throughout the nervous system takes place at synapses, or points of communication between neurons. **Neurotransmitters** are chemical substances released from a neuron into the synaptic cleft, where they drift across the synapse and are absorbed by the receiving neuron. Neuroscientists assume that neurons that transmit and respond to the same neurotransmitters operate as pathways responsible for specific functions.

Table 1 shows the proposed role of several major neurotransmitters in psychological disorders. The "serotonin pathway" consists of neurons involved in regulating mood, among other functions. As you can see from the table, however, several neurotransmitters may be relevant to the same function. Conversely, some functions are served by more than one neurotransmitter. In other words, there is not a one-to-one mapping of functions and neurotransmitters, which greatly adds to the challenge of understanding how the nervous system works. Researchers hope that it may be possible for these links to be understood, and for practitioners to treat abnormalities in neurotransmitters that could alleviate psychological symptoms.

Alterations in brain structures that occur through injury or are present at birth may also play a role in psychological disorders. The role of structural abnormalities in the brain is getting greater attention with the availability of the increasingly sophisticated brain scanning methods that we described in the chapter "Assessment".

Role of Genetics

genes
The instructions for forming proteins contained within each of the body's cells.

Basics of Genetics **Genes** are the instructions for forming proteins contained within each of the body's cells. These instructions, in turn, determine how the cell performs. In the case of neurons, genes control the manufacturing of neurotransmitters, as well as the way the neurotransmitters behave in the synapse. Genes also determine, in part, how the brain's structures develop throughout life. Any factor that can alter the genetic code can also alter the way these structures perform.

TABLE 1 **Selected Neurotransmitters Involved in Psychological Disorders**

Neurotransmitter	Related Disorders
Norepinephrine	Depressive disorders Anxiety disorders (panic disorder)
Serotonin	Depressive disorders Anxiety disorders Schizophrenia Anorexia nervosa Substance use disorders
Gamma-aminobutyric acid (GABA)	Anxiety disorders Substance use disorders
Dopamine	Neurocognitive disorder due to Parkinson's disease Schizophrenia Eating disorders Substance use disorders
Acetylcholine	Neurocognitive disorder due to Alzheimer's disease
Opioid peptides	Substance use disorders

Inherited disorders result when the genes from each parent combine in such a way that the ordinary functioning of a cell is compromised. Genetic abnormalities can themselves produce the neurotransmitter and structural brain variations that can be tied to psychological disorders. The inheritance of particular combinations of genes, faulty copying when cells reproduce, or mutations that a person acquires over the course of life may all contribute to genetic alterations that have an effect on psychological functioning. These genetic abnormalities may also interact with damage caused by exposure to environmental agents such as toxins or injury. Increasingly, researchers are also becoming aware of the way exposure to harmful agents can actually alter the genetic code of an organism, a topic we shall return to shortly.

Your **genotype** is your genetic makeup, which contains the form of each gene you inherit, called an **allele**. Let's say that Allele A causes a protein to form that leads a neuron to form abnormally. Allele B causes the neuron to be entirely healthy. If you have inherited two genes containing Allele B, then you have zero chance of developing that disease. If, on the other hand, you have inherited two genes containing Allele A, you will almost certainly get the disease. If you inherit one Allele A and one Allele B, the situation becomes more complicated. Whether you get the disease depends on whether the disease is "dominant"; if so, you need only one affected allele to develop the disease, and Allele A's instructions to code the harmful protein will almost certainly prevail over those of Allele B (Figure 1, left). If the disease is "recessive," then Allele A alone cannot cause the harmful protein to form. In that case, however, if you have one Allele A and one Allele B, you are an unaffected carrier. Should you produce a child with another unaffected carrier, that child could receive the two Allele As and therefore develop the disorder (Figure 1, right).

The single-gene dominant-recessive inheritance model applies to a number of acquired characteristics, but psychological disorders typically involve a more complex set of processes. Instead, it is far more likely that psychological disorders reflect a **polygenic** model, a model of inheritance in which more than one gene participates in the process of

genotype
The genetic makeup of an organism.

allele
One of two or more different variations of a gene.

polygenic
A model of inheritance in which more than one gene participates in the process of determining a given characteristic.

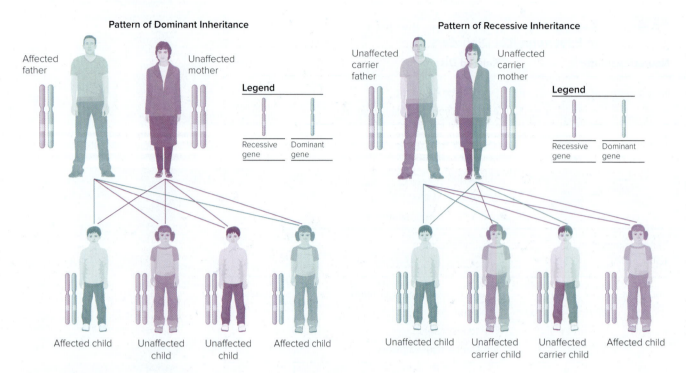

FIGURE 1 Pattern of Dominant-Recessive Trait Inheritance

When a genetic disease is dominant, a child who receives one copy of the affected allele will get the disease (left); when a genetic disease is recessive, only a child who receives two copies of the affected allele will get the disease (right).

SOURCE: NHGRI, www.genome.gov

phenotype
The expression of the genetic program in the individual's physical and psychological attributes.

epigenetics
The science that attempts to identify the ways that the environment influences genes to produce phenotypes.

endophenotypes
Biobehavioral abnormalities that are linked to genetic and neurobiological causes of psychological disorders.

determining a given characteristic.. There are other characteristics that reflect maternal linkages only, meaning they transmit only through the mother. These disorders occur with defects in the mitochondrial DNA, which is the DNA that controls protein formation in the cell's mitochondria (energy-producing structures).

To complicate matters further, not only are multiple genes implicated in the development of psychological disorders, but as we indicated earlier, the environment plays an important role in contributing to the way our behavior reflects our genetic inheritance. The **phenotype** is the expression of the genetic program in the individual's physical and psychological attributes. Some phenotypes are relatively close to their genotype. For example, your eye color does not reflect environmental influences. Complex organs such as the brain, however, often show a wide disparity between genotype and phenotype, because the environment to which people are exposed heavily influences brain development throughout life. Moreover, numerous genes participate in building the structures in the brain and influencing changes in them over time. The study of **epigenetics** attempts to identify the ways the environment influences genes to produce phenotypes.

Reflecting the complexity of the brain's structures and functions, leading researchers in schizophrenia (Gottesman & Shields, 1972, 1973) proposed the use of the term **endophenotypes** to characterize the contribution that genetic and environmental factors make to complex behaviors. An endophenotype is the biobehavioral abnormality linked to genetic and neurobiological causes of psychological disorders. Another way to think about the endophenotype is that it is an internal phenotype, not outwardly observable. In the case of schizophrenia, for example, several possible endophenotypes may underlie the disease's outwardly observed symptoms. These include abnormalities in memory, sensory processes, and particular types of nervous system cells. The assumption is that these unobservable characteristics, which are shaped by heredity and environmental influences, are responsible for the disease's behavioral expressions. The concept of endophenotypes was probably decades ahead of its time, because in the 1970s, researchers were limited in what they could study in terms of both genetics and the brain. With the development of sophisticated DNA testing and brain imaging methods, the concept gained renewed attention (Gottesman & Gould, 2003).

Genetics is becoming big business as DNA analyses made available through online companies make it possible for people to gain a view into their likelihood of developing a particular genetically based disease. People who send in their DNA samples may learn they have an elevated risk of developing blindness or even whether they are likely to consume less caffeine than the average person. Some of the findings these tests produce are rather trivial (such as whether you have dimples), but other results can help inform individuals' future health decisions.

Gene-Environment Interactions   The relationships between genetic and environmental influences fall into two categories: gene-environment correlations and interactions between genes and the environment (Lau & Eley, 2010). Gene-environment correlations exist when people with a certain genetic predisposition are distributed unequally in particular environments (Scarr & McCartney, 1983). Gene-environment correlations can come about in three ways. The first is through passive exposure. Children with certain genetic predispositions can be exposed to environments their parents create based on their genetic predispositions. For example, a child may have two athletically gifted parents who participate in sports. This child not only inherits the genes that help promote athletic ability but also grows up in a household in which the parents themselves engage in athletic activities. There is a good chance, furthermore, that the parents encourage the child to participate in sports based on their own personal interests.

The second gene-environment interaction occurs when parents treat children who have certain genetic predispositions in particular ways because their abilities bring out particular responses. Returning to the example of the budding athlete, the school coach may recruit the athletically gifted child for sports teams starting in early life, leading the child to become even more athletically skilled.

"Niche picking" is the third gene-environment correlation. The athletically gifted child may not wait to be recruited but instead seeks out opportunities to play sports from an early age. In this way, having selected an attractive niche, the child becomes even more skilled and advantaged as the years go by.

Turning now to genetically inherited disorders, any one or a combination of these three gene-environment correlations adds to whatever genetic predisposition a child inherits. On the one hand, a child born with a genetic tendency to develop a disorder may never express that inheritance if the child grows up under the right conditions. Alternatively, children with a genetic predisposition may be more likely to manifest the symptoms of the disorder if they are exposed to harsh or stressful environments that accentuate their risk.

MINI CASE

Biological Approaches to Treating Meera

A prescribing clinician (such as a psychiatrist or psychiatric nurse practitioner) who works within a biological perspective would treat Meera's depression with antidepressant medications, beginning, most likely, with selective serotonin reuptake inhibitors (SSRIs). Because these medications do not take effect for several weeks, the clinician would monitor Meera closely during this period to ensure she remains stable, meeting with her at least weekly to monitor her progress, learn of any side effects she is experiencing, and make adjustments as necessary, particularly after 4 to 6 weeks. Meera is not a suitable candidate for more radical interventions because, although she has suicidal thoughts, she does not have intent or plans and does not appear to be at significant risk. The clinician may also recommend that Meera attempt to resume her prior exercise routines to help augment the therapeutic effects of her medications.

Genetic predispositions may also interact with environmental influences when both alter the effect or expression of the other. In the case of major depressive disorder, for example, researchers have found that people with high genetic risk are more likely to show depressive symptoms when placed under high-stress conditions than are those with low genetic risk. Thus, the same stress has different effects on people with different genetic predispositions. Conversely, the genetic risk of people exposed to higher stress levels becomes higher than that of people who live in low-stress environments. In other words, a person may have a latent genetic predisposition or vulnerability that manifests itself only when that individual comes under environmental stress (Lau & Eley, 2010).

Researchers studying psychopathology have long been aware of the joint contributions genes and the environment make to the development of psychological disorders. The **diathesis-stress model** proposes that people are born with a diathesis (genetic predisposition) or acquire a vulnerability through exposure early in life to events such as traumas, diseases, birth complications, or harsh family environments (Zubin & Spring, 1977). This vulnerability then places these individuals at risk for lifelong effects in which they develop a psychological disorder as they grow older (Johnson et al., 2001).

With advances in genetic science, researchers are now much better able to understand the precise ways in which genes and environmental factors interact. The ordinary pathway for genetic transmission is that people inherit two copies of a gene, one from each parent, and both copies actively shape the individual's development. However, certain genes can be turned "on" or "off" through **epigenesis**, the process of inheriting alterations in gene regulation and expression. If the remaining working gene of the pair is deleted or severely mutated, then a person can develop an illness. The process of **DNA methylation** can turn off a gene when a chemical group, methyl, attaches itself to the gene (Figure 2). Epigenesis is a process that is not dependent on the DNA itself, so if methylation can be inhibited, the damage can be reversed.

Through the epigenetic processes of DNA methylation, maternal care, for example, can change gene expression. One study showed that during pregnancy, a mother's exposure to environmental toxins led to DNA methylation in her unborn child (Furness, Dekker, & Roberts, 2011). Studies on laboratory animals also show that stress can affect DNA in specific ways that alter brain development (Mychasiuk et al., 2011). Researchers believe that certain drugs the mother uses during pregnancy also cause DNA methylation, including nicotine, alcohol, and cocaine.

diathesis-stress model
The proposal that people are born with a predisposition (or "diathesis") that places them at risk for developing a psychological disorder if exposed to certain extremely stressful life experiences.

epigenesis
The process of inheriting alterations in gene regulation and expression.

DNA methylation
The process that can turn off a gene when a chemical group, methyl, attaches itself to the gene.

FIGURE 2 Epigenesis

The epigenome can mark DNA in two ways, both of which play a role in turning genes off or on. The first occurs when certain chemical tags, called methyl groups, attach to the backbone of a DNA molecule. The second occurs when a variety of chemical tags attach to the tails of histones, which are spool-like proteins that package DNA neatly into chromosomes. This action affects how tightly DNA is wound around the histones.

SOURCE: National Institute on Aging. (2010). 2009 progress report on Alzheimer's disease: U.S. Department of Health and Human Services.

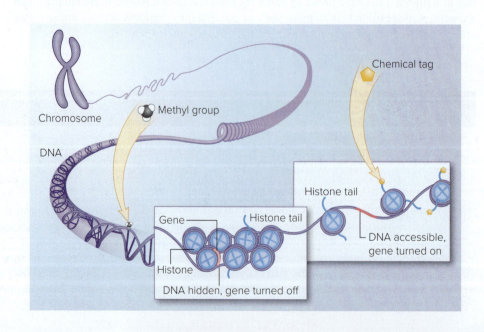

Conversely, on the treatment side, researchers are investigating the possibility that psychotropic medications can alter DNA methylation (e.g., Ovenden, McGregor, Emsley, & Warnich, 2018). People vary in their response to these medications, these studies are showing, due to the process of epigenesis. It might be possible to target the epigenome, the area affected by epigenesis, through medications that inhibit methylation from acting on specific neurotransmitters thought to be involved in schizophrenia, for example.

Research Methods in Genetics   To understand the contributions of genetics to psychological disorders, researchers use three methods: family inheritance studies, DNA linkage studies, and genomics combined with brain scan technology. The methods often complement each other as researchers attempt to tease apart the relationships that underlie the inheritance of complex traits.

In family inheritance studies, researchers compare the disorder rates across relatives who have varying degrees of genetic relatedness. The highest degree of genetic relatedness exists between identical or monozygotic (MZ) twins, who share 100 percent of their genotype. Dizygotic (DZ) or fraternal twins share, on average, 50 percent of their genomes, but both types of twins share the same familial environment. Therefore, although MZ-DZ twin comparisons are useful, they do not allow researchers to rule out the impact of the environment. Similarly, studies of parents and children are confounded by the fact that the parents create the environment in which their children are raised. In order to separate the potential impact of the environment in studies comparing MZ and DZ twins, researchers turned long ago to adoption studies in which different families raised MZ twins without having any contact, and therefore the twins experienced different environments.

For decades, family and twin studies were the only methods researchers had at their disposal to quantify the extent of genetic influences on psychological disorders. With the advent of genetic testing, however, researchers became able to examine specific genetic contributions to a variety of traits, including both physical and psychological disorders.

In a **genome-wide linkage study**, researchers study the families of people with specific psychological traits or disorders. The principle behind a linkage study is that characteristics near to each other on a particular gene are more likely to be inherited together. With refined genetic testing methods available, researchers can now carry this task out with far greater precision than was true in the past.

Even though linkage studies are useful, they have limitations primarily because they require the study of large numbers of family members and may produce only limited findings. In **genome-wide association studies (GWAS)**, researchers scan the entire genome of individuals who are not related to find the associated genetic variations with a particular disease. They are looking for a **single nucleotide polymorphism (SNP)** (pronounced "snip"), which is a small genetic variation that can occur in a person's DNA sequence. Four nucleotide letters—A, G, T, and C (adenine, guanine, thymine, and cytosine)—specify the genetic code. A SNP variation occurs when a single nucleotide, such as an A, replaces one of the other three. For example, a SNP is the alteration of the DNA segment CTAAGTA to CTAGGTA in which a "G" replaces the second "A" in the first snippet (Figure 3).

With high-tech genetic testing methods now more readily available, researchers have more powerful tools to find SNPs that occur with particular traits (or diseases) across large numbers of people. Although many SNPs do not have measurable effects, researchers believe that other SNPs may predispose people to disease and even influence their response to drug regimens.

Researchers studying the genetics of psychological disorders can combine linkage studies with brain imaging techniques. In this way, they can directly correlate the genetic variations they observe with the pictures they obtain of the brain's structures and functions.

genome-wide linkage study
Genetic method in which researchers study the families of people with specific psychological traits or disorders.

genome-wide association studies (GWAS)
Genetic method in which researchers scan the entire genome of individuals who are not related to find the associated genetic variations with a particular disease.

single nucleotide polymorphism (SNP)
A small genetic variation that can occur in a person's DNA sequence.

Treatment

Psychotropic medications are intended to reduce the individual's symptoms by altering the levels of neurotransmitters hypothesized to be involved in the disorder. In 1950, a French chemist, Paul Charpentier, synthesized chlorpromazine (Thorazine). This medication

FIGURE 3 SNP Detection

This figure shows how SNP variation occurs such as when two sequences of DNA differ only by a single nucleotide ("A" vs. "G").

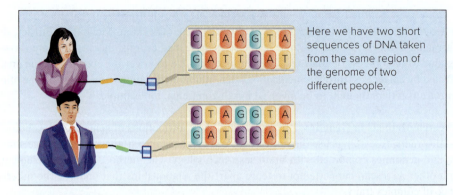

Here we have two short sequences of DNA taken from the same region of the genome of two different people.

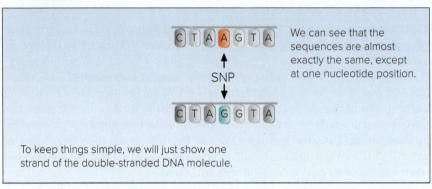

We can see that the sequences are almost exactly the same, except at one nucleotide position.

To keep things simple, we will just show one strand of the double-stranded DNA molecule.

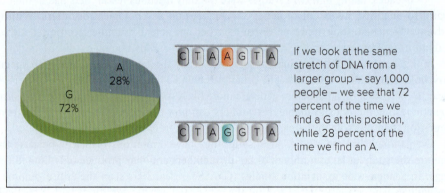

If we look at the same stretch of DNA from a larger group – say 1,000 people – we see that 72 percent of the time we find a G at this position, while 28 percent of the time we find an A.

gained widespread acceptance in the 1960s and led the way toward the development of a wider range of psychotropic agents.

Currently, the major categories of psychotropic agents are antipsychotics, antidepressants, mood stabilizers, anticonvulsants, antianxiety medications, and stimulants (Table 2). Antipsychotic medications are also called **neuroleptics** (derived from the Greek words meaning "to seize the nerve"). In addition to their sedating qualities, neuroleptics reduce the frequency and severity of the individual's psychotic symptoms.

Some medication categories that researchers developed to treat one disorder, such as antidepressants, also serve to treat other ones, such as anxiety disorders. That clinicians can use the same medications to treat different disorders suggests that abnormalities involving similar neurotransmitter actions may mediate these disorders.

Each of these medications can have serious side effects, leading clients experiencing adverse drug reactions to discontinue their use and try a different medication, perhaps from a different category. The Federal Drug Administration (2018) maintains a watch list of side effects associated with prescription medications. Individuals and their families can check their medications on this website or sign up for monthly updates.

The second major category of biological intervention, **psychosurgery**, is a treatment in which a neurosurgeon operates on brain regions thought to be responsible for the

neuroleptics
A term used to refer to antipsychotic medications.

psychosurgery
A form of brain surgery, the purpose of which is to reduce psychological disturbance.

TABLE 2 Major Psychotropic Medications

Used to Treat	Category
Schizophrenia spectrum and other psychotic disorders	Conventional or "typical" antipsychotic medications "Atypical" antipsychotic medications (also called "second generation")
Major depressive disorder	Selective serotonin reuptake inhibitors (SSRIs) Serotonin and norepinephrine reuptake inhibitors (SNRIs) Buproprion Tricyclics Tetracyclics Monoamine oxidase inhibitors (MAOIs)
Bipolar disorder	Anticonvulsants Mood stabilizers
Anxiety disorders	Benzodiazepines Buspirone SSRIs Beta blockers
Attention-deficit/hyperactivity disorder	Methylphenidate Amphetamine Dextroamphetamine Lisdexamfetamine Dimesylate

SOURCE: http://www.nimh.nih.gov/health/publications/mental-health-medications/complete-index.shtml

individual's disorder. The first modern use of psychosurgery was a prefrontal lobotomy, developed by Portuguese neurosurgeon Egas Moniz in 1935. The method severs the prefrontal lobes from the rest of the brain, a radical procedure that seemed to calm the behavior of a patient experiencing psychotic symptoms but that also created significant personality changes. The technique became widely practiced throughout the next two decades, and although Moniz received a Nobel Prize in 1949 for his work, the method is now discredited on scientific and humanitarian grounds (Dittrich, 2016).

Modern psychosurgery relies on targeted interventions designed to reduce symptoms in patients who have proven otherwise unresponsive to less radical treatment (Figure 4). Each type of psychosurgery targets a specific region of the brain that researchers believe is involved as a cause of symptoms. With higher levels of precision that reflect advances in surgical techniques, neurosurgeons can produce a lesion in a specific brain region to provide symptom relief.

For individuals with severe obsessive-compulsive or major depressive disorder, the lesions target the cortex, striatum, and thalamus. **Deep brain stimulation (DBS)**, also called *neuromodulation*, is another form of psychosurgery, in which a neurosurgeon implants a microelectrode that delivers a constant low electrical stimulation to a small region of the brain, powered by an implanted battery, a treatment also called *neuromodulation* (Shah et al., 2008).

Electroconvulsive therapy (ECT), involves the application of electric shock to the head for the purpose of inducing therapeutically beneficial seizures. Ugo Cerletti, an Italian neurologist seeking a treatment for epilepsy, developed this method in 1937, and it became used for psychiatric disorders because of its seemingly therapeutic side effects.

deep brain stimulation (DBS)
A treatment in which a neurosurgeon implants a microelectrode that delivers a constant low electrical stimulation to a small region of the brain, powered by an implanted battery; also called *neuromodulation*.

electroconvulsive therapy (ECT)
The application of electrical shock to the head for the purpose of inducing therapeutically beneficial seizures.

Psychiatric Neurosurgery
A handful of medical centers have been conducting several experimental brain surgeries as a last resort for severe obsessive-compulsive disorders that are beyond the range of standard treatment.

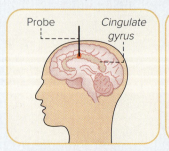
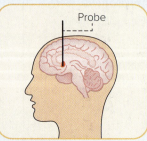
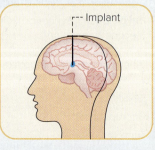
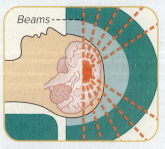

Cingulotomy
Probes are inserted into the brain to destroy a spot on the anterior cingulate gyrus, to disrupt a circuit that connects the emotional and conscious planning centers of the brain.

Capsulotomy
Probes are inserted deep into the brain and heated to destroy part of the anterior capsule, to disrupt a circuit thought to be overactive in people with severe OCD.

Deep brain stimulation
As an alternative to capsulotomy, an electrode is permanently implanted on one or both sides of the brain. A pacemaker-like device then delivers an adjustable current.

Gamma knife surgery
An MRI-like device focuses hundreds of small beams of radiation at a point within the brain, destroying small areas of tissue.

FIGURE 4 Forms of Psychosurgery for Treating Severe Obsessive-Compulsive Disorders That Are Beyond the Range of Standard Treatment

ECT became increasingly popular in the 1940s and 1950s, but, as the movie *One Flew over the Cuckoo's Nest* famously depicts, staff in psychiatric hospitals also misused it as a way to restrain violent patients.

Even though ECT had largely fallen into disuse by the mid-1970s, psychiatrists continued to use it to treat patients who did not respond to other measures. A comprehensive review of controlled studies using ECT for treatment of major depressive disorder showed that, in the short term, ECT was more effective than medications in producing rapid improvement of symptoms; however, there are long-term consequences, including memory impairment (UK ECT Review Group, 2003).

4.3 Trait Theory

personality trait
An enduring pattern of perceiving, relating to, and thinking about the environment and others.

Trait theory, as much about normal personality functioning as about psychological disorders, proposes that psychopathology develops when the individual has maladaptive **personality traits**, which are enduring patterns of perceiving, relating to, and thinking about the environment and others. In the chapter "Assessment," we mentioned briefly that some assessment methods focus on measuring these qualities of personality, which psychologists think of as stable, enduring dispositions that persist over time. For many personality trait theorists, these components of psychological functioning are more than long-standing qualities of personality and are actually genetically inherited.

It is easy for most people to relate to trait theory because it fits so closely with the use of the term *personality* in everyday life. When you think about how to describe the personality of someone you know, you will likely come up with a list of qualities that seem to fit the individual's typical way of behaving. These characteristics typically take the form of adjectives such as *friendly* or *calm*, or perhaps *anxious* and *shy*. Trait theories of personality propose that adjectives such as these capture the essence of the individual's psychological makeup. The fact that people use these adjectives in everyday life to describe themselves and others agrees with the basic principle of trait theory—namely, that personality is equivalent to a set of stable characteristic attributes.

Five Factor Model (or "Big Five")
Trait theory proposing that there are five basic dispositions in personality, each of which has 6 facets.

The predominant trait theory in the field of abnormal psychology is the **Five Factor Model**, also called the "Big Five" (Figure 5) (McCrae & Costa, 1987). According to this

Five Factor Model

		Low scorers	High scorers
1	Openness to experience	Conventional Down-to-earth Uncreative Uncurious	Original Imaginative Creative Curious
2	Conscientiousness	Negligent Lazy Disorganized Late	Conscientious Hard-working Well-organized Punctual
3	Extraversion	Loner Passive Quiet Reserved	Joiner Active Talkative Affectionate
4	Agreeableness	Critical Irritable Ruthless Suspicious	Lenient Good-natured Soft-hearted Trusting
5	Neuroticism	Calm Comfortable Even-tempered Unemotional	Worried Self-conscious Temperamental Emotional

FIGURE 5 Five Factor Model of Personality: Examples of qualities represented in each of the factors in the Five Factor Model.
SOURCE: http://dandebat.dk/eng-person3.htm

theory, each of the basic five dispositions has six facets, which leads to a total of 30 personality components. The Five Factor Model includes the personality traits of neuroticism, extraversion, openness to experience, agreeableness, and conscientiousness (conveniently, they spell out "OCEAN" or "CANOE"). A complete characterization of an individual on the five factors consists of providing scores or ratings on each facet.

According to trait theory, where people fall on the 30 facets strongly influences the shape of their lives. People high on personality traits representing riskiness (thrill seeking) are more likely to get hurt because their personalities lead them into situations that can land them in trouble. Similarly, people high on the traits that define the less

MINI CASE

Trait Theory Approaches to Treating Meera

Because trait theory does not have any direct clinical applications, there are no obvious ways in which a clinician would apply this perspective to Meera's depression. The information in Dr. Tobin's Case Report indicates that she was not diagnosed with a personality disorder. A clinician working with Meera from a trait theory approach could, however, order a more thorough assessment of Meera's personality traits that includes a personality trait-based measure to confirm these hypotheses and to determine whether she has a comorbid personality disorder. Even if she does not have a personality disorder, it is possible that Meera's personality trait profile would be

relevant to treatment. For example, she seems not to be overly introverted, because she interacts frequently with friends. Her depressive symptoms appear not to be overlaid on personality traits that include high neuroticism. She seems to enjoy activities that include creativity and exploration of the outdoors, indicating a normative personality for her age in openness to experience. Prior to her depressive episode, she was at least average in conscientiousness, as her successful work history indicated, and there is no evidence to suggest that she is unusually low in agreeableness. The clinician can share feedback about these results to increase Meera's insight into her personality traits, which could be useful in helping select the most effective strategies for reducing her depression.

What's in the *DSM-5*

Theoretical Approaches

Versions of the *DSM* prior to *DSM-III* were based almost entirely on clinical judgments framed within the psychodynamic model of abnormality. The *DSM* used terms such as *neurosis* and *psychosis*, which had meaning in the psychodynamic world, to differentiate disorder categories. For example, anxiety disorders fell into the category of neurosis because their primary symptoms included irrational fears and worries. It labeled schizophrenia a psychotic disorder because its primary symptoms include lack of contact with reality and other cognitive distortions. The *DSM-III* authors reconceptualized their approach along two major lines. First, they intended it to be atheoretical—meaning that there was no underlying theory, psychodynamic or otherwise. Second, they intended the diagnostic criteria to be ones that a variety of mental health professionals could reliably evaluate. The *DSM-III* task force therefore commissioned studies in which researchers could evaluate the reliability of the diagnostic criteria. Rather than use vague terminology (such as *neurosis*) that could be open to various interpretations, the *DSM-III* diagnostic spelled out criteria in exacting levels of detail. The *DSM-IV* and its later revision, the *DSM-IV-TR*, carried on this tradition of specifying diagnostic criteria in research-based, objective terms.

The *DSM-5* continues this empirical tradition and remains atheoretical. Critics now maintain that the authors should instead have developed a system that recognizes the known (to date) underpinnings of many of the disorders (Hyman, 2011). Rather than maintaining the distinct categorical system of past *DSM*s—grouping disorders that share common symptoms, risk factors, or neural abnormalities—they believe the *DSM-5* should have represented disorders on spectrums or in larger grouping systems. Although the *DSM-5* task force considered making this radical change, its members eventually decided to maintain the earlier categories, though with some alterations. The move away from categories and toward dimensions would have required not only a massive restructuring, but also retraining of clinicians who were trained on the earlier *DSM*s. These changes would also reinforce the medical model, because they would lead to a system more similar to the diagnosis of physical than psychological disorders.

Whether future *DSM*s move away from the present system will depend largely on developments in the field of psychopathology. Section III of the *DSM-5* contains a dimensional system that clinicians can use to supplement their formal diagnoses of the personality disorders. Diagnoses are now in groups or chapters according to their presumed underlying similarities or causes. Ultimately, the authors will make decisions on empirical grounds, which will maintain the intent of *DSM* to keep its atheoretical basis.

psychologically healthy end of each continuum may be more likely to experience negative life events because their personalities make them more vulnerable to life stresses. According to the Five Factor Model, although circumstances can change personality, it's more likely that personality molds circumstances.

However, according to research using highly sophisticated data analytic designs to follow people over time, people can change even their fundamental personality traits. Most of the research is based on samples whose scores fall within the normal range of functioning. For example, as people get older, they become less likely to act impulsively (Terracciano, McCrae, Brant, & Costa, 2005).

The main value of understanding personality trait theory is that it provides a perspective for examining personality disorders. Research based on the Five Factor Model became the basis for the current attempts to reformulate the personality disorders in the *DSM-5*. Although the Five Factor Model does not necessarily provide a framework for psychotherapy, it has proven valuable as a basis for personality assessment within the context of understanding an individual's characteristic behavior patterns (Bastiaansen, Rossi, Schotte, & De Fruyt, 2011).

4.4 Psychodynamic Perspective

psychodynamic perspective

The theoretical orientation in psychology that emphasizes unconscious determinants of behavior.

The **psychodynamic perspective** emphasizes unconscious determinants of behavior. Of all the psychological approaches, the psychodynamic gives greatest emphasis to the role of processes beneath the surface of awareness as influences on abnormality.

Freud's Theory

id

In psychoanalytic theory, the structure of personality hidden in the unconscious that contains instincts oriented toward fulfilling basic biological drives, including sexual and aggressive needs.

libido

An instinctual pressure that strives for gratification of sexual and aggressive desires.

Following up his interest in the origin of unusual symptoms in his clients, in the late 1800s Sigmund Freud began to explore the idea that it was possible to study and explain the causes, and symptoms, of psychological disorders. By the time of his death in 1939, Freud had articulated a vision for psychological disorder cause and treatment, with the basic tenet that most symptoms had roots buried deep within an individual's past.

According to Freud (1923), the mind has three structures: the id, the ego, and the superego. The **id** is the structure of personality hidden in the unconscious that contains instincts oriented toward fulfilling basic biological drives, including gratification of sexual and aggressive needs. The **libido** is the instinctual pressure that strives for gratification of sexual and aggressive desires.

Sigmund Freud believed an individual's dreams held vital information about innermost wishes and desires that could be understood through dream analysis.

©piskunov/Getty Images

The id follows the **pleasure principle**, a motivating force that seeks immediate and total gratification of sensual needs and desires. According to Freud, we can obtain pleasure only when we are able to reduce the tension of an unmet drive. The id, however, does not require tangible gratification of a need. Instead, it can use wish fulfillment to achieve its goals. Through wish fulfillment, the id conjures an image of whatever will satisfy the needs of the moment.

The center of conscious awareness in personality is the **ego**, the structure of personality that gives the individual the cognitive powers of judgment, memory, perception, and decision making. Freud (1911) described the ego as being governed by the **reality principle**, meaning it tries to deal with real-life constraints to achieve its goals. You may want to grab someone else's donut (id) but realize the best you can hope for is that the person will offer you a bite or two (ego). In contrast to the id's illogical primary process thinking, **secondary process thinking**—the use of logical analytic approaches to problem solving—characterizes the ego functions.

The third part of the equation in psychodynamic theory is the **superego**, which is the personality's seat of morality. The superego includes the conscience (sense of right and wrong) and the ego ideal, or aspirations. The superego would instruct you, for example, that to take someone else's donut constitutes theft and is therefore morally wrong.

In a healthy individual's personality, as described by Freud, the id achieves instinctual desires through the ego's ability to navigate in the external world within the confines the superego places on it. Psychodynamics, or the interplay among the structures of the mind, is thus the basis for both normal and pathological functioning.

Freud believed people were primarily sexual and aggressive in the content of their motives and therefore needed to be protected from knowing their own unconscious desires. They achieve this protection by using **defense mechanisms** (Table 3). According to Freud, everyone uses defense mechanisms on an ongoing basis to avoid recognizing the existence of their hidden desires. Defense mechanisms create problems when they prevent an individual from coming completely to terms with his or her true unconscious nature.

pleasure principle
In psychoanalytic theory, a motivating force that seeks immediate and total gratification of sensual needs and desires.

ego
In psychoanalytic theory, the structure of personality that gives the individual the mental powers of judgment, memory, perception, and decision making.

reality principle
In psychoanalyic theory, the motivational force that leads the individual to confront the constraints of the external world.

secondary process thinking
In psychoanalytic theory, the kind of thinking involved in logical and rational problem solving.

superego
In psychoanalytic theory, the structure of personality that includes the conscience and the ego ideal.

defense mechanisms
Tactics that keep unacceptable thoughts, instincts, and feelings out of conscious awareness and thus protect the ego against anxiety.

TABLE 3 **Categories and Examples of Defense Mechanisms**

Defense Mechanism	Definition
Displacement	Shifting unacceptable feelings or impulses from the target of those feelings to someone less threatening or to an object
Intellectualization	Resorting to excessive abstract thinking rather than focus on the upsetting aspects of response to issues that cause conflict or stress
Reaction formation	Transforming an unacceptable feeling or desire into its opposite in order to make it more acceptable
Repression	Unconsciously excluding disturbing wishes, thoughts, or experiences from awareness
Denial	Dealing with emotional conflict or stress by refusing to acknowledge a painful aspect of reality or experience that would be apparent to others
Projection	Attributing undesirable personal traits or feelings to someone else to protect one's ego from acknowledging distasteful personal attributes
Sublimation	Transferring an unacceptable impulse or desire into a socially appropriate activity or interest
Regression	Dealing with emotional conflict or stress by reverting to childish behaviors

psychosexual stages
According to psychoanalytic theory, the normal sequence of development through which each individual passes between infancy and adulthood.

The topic of development forms an important piece of Freud's theory. In 1905, Freud proposed that normal development occurs through a series of what he called **psychosexual stages**, and that children go through these stages in step with the development of their libido. At each stage, the libido becomes fixated on a particular "erogenous" or sexually excitable zone of the body. For example, the "anal retentive" personality is overly rigid, controlled, and perfectionist. According to Freud, an individual may regress to behavior appropriate to an earlier stage or may become stuck, or fixated, at a stage.

Freud believed the adult personality reflects the way in which the individual resolves the psychosexual stages in early life, though some reworking may occur at least up through middle adulthood. Freud also believed that the child's feelings toward the opposite-sex parent set the stage for later psychological adjustment. The outcome of what he called the **Oedipus complex** (named after a tragic character in ancient Greece) determined whether the individual had a healthy ego or would spend a life marred by anxiety and repressed, conflicted feelings associated with wanting to engage in what society deems taboo behavior (incest). In the course of ordinary development, children's desire for the opposite-sex parent eventually submerges beneath the surface of conscious awareness, thus posing no further threat to their sense of self-acceptance.

Oedipus complex
According to Freud, the child's feelings toward the opposite-sex parent peak in early childhood.

MINI CASE

Psychodynamic Approaches to Treating Meera

A clinician working with Meera from a psychodynamic perspective would assume that her difficulties stem from conflicts in early life. For example, the clinician would explore the resentment she feels toward her parents for favoring her sister, and her possible guilt over breaking away from the family when she established her own independent life. In treatment, the clinician would observe whether Meera reenacts her conflicted feelings about her parents in the relationship she establishes with the clinician. The Core Conflictual Relationship Theme (CCRT) approach would seem particularly appropriate for Meera, given the possible role of these difficult relationships in triggering her depressive disorder. Meera's depressive symptoms would warrant a time-limited approach focusing on her current episode, with the option for her to seek treatment in the future if her depression recurs.

Jung's archetype theory would explain that popular superheroes are outward representations of universal aspects of human personality.

©AF archive/Alamy Stock Photo

Post-Freudian Psychodynamic Views

Freud developed his theory in the context of his clinical practice, but he also encouraged like-minded neurologists and psychiatrists to work together to develop a new theory of the mind. Over a period of years, they spent many hours comparing notes about their clinical cases and trying to come to a joint understanding about normal and pathological functioning. Although they shared many of the same views when they began their discussions, several went on to develop their own unique brands of psychodynamic theory and now have their own schools of thought.

The most notable departure from Freud's school of thought came when Swiss psychiatrist Carl Jung (1875–1961) revamped the definition of the unconscious. According to Jung (1961), the unconscious is formed at its very root around a set of images common to all human experience, which he called **archetypes**. Jung believed that people respond to events in their daily lives on the basis of these archetypes, because they are part of our genetic makeup. For example, Jung asserted that archetypal characters (such as today's Batman and Superman) are popular because they activate the "hero" archetype. In addition, Jung believed that psychopathology resulted from an imbalance within related parts of the mind, especially when people fail to pay proper attention to their unconscious needs.

One group or category of post-Freudian theorists advocated for the study of **ego psychology**. These theorists believed that the ego, not the id, was the main driving force in personality.

Alfred Adler (1870–1937) focused on the "inferiority complex" as a cause of psychopathology. Neurotic individuals, he maintained, try to overcompensate for feelings of inferiority by constantly "striving for superiority." Karen Horney (1885–1952) proposed that neurotic individuals put up a false front to protect their very fragile true sense of self. Both Adler and Horney also emphasized social concerns and interpersonal relations in the development of personality. They saw close relationships with family and friends and an interest in the life of the community as gratifying in their own right, not because a sexual or an aggressive desire is indirectly satisfied in the process, as Freud might say.

Perhaps the only psychodynamic theorist to give attention to the whole of life, not just childhood, was Erik Erikson (1902–1994). Like Adler and Horney, Erikson gave greatest attention to the ego in development. Erikson believed the ego goes through a series of transformations throughout life in which new strengths or abilities can mature. According to his theory, each stage builds on the one that precedes it and, in turn,

archetypes
In Jung's theory, a set of images common to all human experience.

ego psychology
Theoretical perspective based on psychodynamic theory emphasizing the ego as the main force in personality.

According to Alfred Adler's theory, this person may be portraying himself negatively to others due to a sense of low self-worth and inferiority.

©BJI/Lane Oatey/Getty Images

This woman seems satisfied with her self-concept as a student, in accordance with Karen Horney's theory which proposes that the ego is the most important force in personality.
©JGI/Jamie Grill/Getty Images

influences all the stages that follow it. However, Erikson proposed that any stage could become a major focus at any age—identity issues can resurface at any point in adulthood, even after a person's identity has become relatively set. For example, a middle-aged woman who is laid off from her job may once again question her occupational identity as she seeks to find a new position for herself in the workforce.

Yet another group of psychodynamically oriented theorists focused on **object relations**, namely, the relationships people have with the others ("objects") in their lives. These theorists included John Bowlby (1907-1990), Melanie Klein (1882-1960), D. W. Winnicott (1896-1971), Heinz Kohut (1913-1981), and Margaret Mahler (1897-1995). Like the ego psychologists, the object relations theorists each have a particular model of therapy we associate with their theories. However, they all agree that early childhood relationships are at the root of abnormality.

Despite the differences among them, all theorists in the object relations perspective believed the individual's relationship with the caregiver (usually the mother) becomes an inner framework or model for all close adult relationships. Themes of your adult relationships, in other words, reflect themes from your early childhood and the way your caregivers (mother, father, other adults) treated you.

Putting their theory to the test, Canadian psychologist Mary Salter Ainsworth (1913-1999) and her associates (1978) studied differences among infants in **attachment style**, or the ways they related to a caregiver figure. The caregivers or adults to whom the individual is attached are referred to as the **attachment figures**. Ainsworth developed the "Strange Situation," an experimental setting in which researchers separated infants from and then reunited them with their mothers. Children who accepted the mother's leaving and then her return were regarded as securely attached. Those who either became frantic, on the one hand, or seemed distant and remote, at the other extreme, were considered insecurely attached.

Although attachment style was designed as a theory of child development, later researchers have adapted it to apply to adult romantic relationships. Most children develop secure attachment styles, and later in life they relate to their close romantic partners without undue anxiety about whether their partners will care about them. Those who are insecurely attached in childhood, however, may show a pattern of anxious attachment in adulthood in which they feel they cannot rely on their partner's love and support. Or they may show a dismissive or avoidant attachment style, in which they fear rejection from others and therefore try to protect themselves by remaining distant.

object relations
A psychodynamically oriented theory that focuses on the relationships people have with the others ("objects") in their lives.

attachment style
The way a person relates to a caregiver figure.

attachment figures
Caregivers or adults to whom the individual is attached.

Attachment theorists believe that a child transfers emotional bonding from the primary caregiver to an object, such as a teddy bear, and eventually from this object to people outside the family.

©Jiang Jin/Purestock/Superstock

An individual's attachment style may also influence the way he or she responds to psychotherapy. Across 19 separate studies of nearly 1,500 clients, researchers found that attachment security was positively related to therapy outcome. Individuals with a secure attachment style, these researchers showed, are better able to establish a positive working relationship with their therapists, which, in turn, predicts positive therapy outcomes (Levy, Ellison, Scott, & Bernecker, 2011). The therapeutic outcome can also be affected by interactions between the attachment styles of client and therapist (Steel, Macdonald, & Schroder, 2018). As you will see shortly, psychodynamic therapy specifically takes such client-therapist relationships into account.

Treatment

The main goal of traditional psychoanalytic treatment as developed by Freud was to bring repressed, unconscious material into conscious awareness. To accomplish this task, Freud developed the therapeutic method of **free association**, in which the client literally says whatever comes to mind during the treatment session. Freud believed that clients needed to work through their unconscious conflicts, bringing these gradually into conscious awareness by speaking them aloud. Eventually they could gain insight into the forces that produced their thoughts and words.

free association
A method used in psychoanalysis in which the client speaks freely, saying whatever comes to mind.

Current psychodynamic treatment is focused on helping clients explore aspects of the self that are "unconscious" in the sense that the client does not recognize them. Therapists focus in particular on the way clients reveal and influence these aspects of the self in their relationship with the therapist. The key elements of psychodynamic therapy delve into the client's emotional experiences, use of defense mechanisms, close relationships with others, past experiences, and exploration of fantasy life in dreams, daydreams, and fantasies (Shedler, 2010).

Psychodynamic therapists also use **transference** to help inform their treatment by analyzing the feelings their clients seem to have toward them. The idea behind this step is that clients regard their therapists in a way similar to the way they felt about their parents, because they see their therapists as important figures in their lives. In the context of therapy, these feelings can be examined and put to valuable use.

transference
The carrying over of feelings that clients have from their parents to their therapists.

Unlike the stereotyped portrayal you might see in movies or on television, clinicians need not conduct psychodynamic therapy on a couch, for years at a time, or in total silence.

behavioral perspective
A theoretical perspective in which it is assumed that abnormality is caused by faulty learning experiences.

classical conditioning
The process in the behavioral perspective that accounts for the learning of emotional, automatic responses.

aversive conditioning
Classical conditioning in which the individual associates a maladaptive response with a stimulus that could not itself cause harm.

operant conditioning
A learning process in which an individual acquires a response by learning to pair a behavior with its consequences.

reinforcement
In operant conditioning, the outcome that makes the individual more likely to repeat the behavior in the future.

However, given the impracticality of maintaining a long-term and intense form of treatment, psychotherapists began developing briefer and seemingly as effective forms of psychodynamic therapy. Instead of attempting to revamp a client's entire psychic structure, psychotherapists using these methods focus on a specific symptom or set of symptoms for which the client is seeking help. The number of sessions can vary but rarely exceeds 25. Unlike the case in traditional psychodynamic therapy, the therapist takes a relatively active approach in maintaining the focus of treatment on the client's presenting problem or issues immediately relevant to it (Lewis, Dennerstein, & Gibbs, 2008).

In one version of brief psychodynamic therapy, the clinician identifies the client's "Core Conflictual Relationship Theme" (CCRT). The clinician assesses the client's wishes, expected responses from others, and client responses either to the responses of others or to the wish itself. The client describes specific instances in relationships with others that allow the clinician to make the CCRT assessment. The clinician then works with the client in a supportive way to help him or her recognize and eventually work through these patterns (Jarry, 2010). For example, the therapist would induce individuals with obsessive-compulsive disorder to face the feared situation and use the aroused experiences to work on the underlying conflict (Leichsenring & Steinert, 2017).

Clearly, the psychodynamic perspective has come a long way from traditional Freudian psychoanalysis, although it maintains its focus on helping clients understand and overcome interpersonal issues from their past that continue to create challenges in their present lives.

4.5 Behavioral Perspective

According to the **behavioral perspective**, the individual acquires maladaptive behavior through learning. Consistent with its name, this perspective focuses on the individual's observable behavior, the factors that might precipitate it, and the consequences that maintain it over time.

Theories

The two main approaches within the behavioral perspective differ in focusing either on emotional, involuntary reactions such as fear, or on complex, voluntary actions such as engaging in an unwanted or undesirable habit.

Classical conditioning is the process in the behavioral perspective that accounts for the learning of emotional, automatic responses. As an extreme example, imagine someone tapped you hard on your knuckles whenever you reached for a piece of chocolate. If this continued, you would eventually come to dread that person, not to mention the scent or sight of chocolate. Much of the classical conditioning that behavioral clinicians attempt to help their clients overcome is this type of **aversive conditioning** in which the individual associates a maladaptive response with a stimulus that could not itself cause harm.

The learning of complex, voluntary behaviors occurs through **operant conditioning** in which an individual acquires a response by learning to pair a behavior with its consequences. The behavior's consequences are its **reinforcement**—the outcome that makes the individual more likely to repeat the behavior in the future. Reinforcement can take many forms. For example, through positive reinforcement, your friends may laugh when you express outrageous opinions, making you more likely to express those opinions in the future. You might also learn through negative reinforcement to take an over-the-counter sleep medication if you find that it helps alleviate your insomnia. This is considered negative reinforcement because the taking of the sleep medication (the behavior) increases because it removes the aversive state of being sleepless. Both negative and

Behavioral therapists often use a fear hierarchy to gradually expose individuals to their most feared situations, such as being trapped in a smoke-filled room with no escape.

©Michael Blann/Getty Images

You Be the Judge

Evidence-Based Practice

As we discussed in the chapter "Diagnosis and Treatment", APA adopted principles of evidence-based practice that provide guidelines for clinicians to follow in their provision of psychological treatment. In this chapter, you've learned about the wide range of theoretical models available to clinicians, ranging from psychosurgery at one extreme, to family therapy at another. Given the recommendation that psychologists provide the treatment best suited to the client's psychological disorder, the question is whether each clinician has the ability to provide treatment within each of these theoretical models. Is this a realistic expectation? Can we expect a clinician to be knowledgeable enough about each theoretical perspective to give clients the most effective interventions?

As research within clinical psychology and related fields continues to progress at an almost exponential rate, how can each clinician stay on top of all the latest developments well enough to be comfortable providing the most recent approaches to each client? According to the APA Ethical Guidelines, clinicians should work within their areas of expertise, and if they must extend outside this area, they should seek consultation from those who are knowledgeable in the area. Moreover, each state maintains strict licensing regulations to ensure that psychologists participate in continuing education. As a result, there are many safeguards to protect clients from outdated or inappropriate intervention methods.

Q: *You be the judge:* As a consumer of psychology, do you feel it is more important for potential clients to see a clinician whom they trust based on reputation, prior experience, or recommendations from other people, or should they instead find a specialist who, in the theoretical perspective, most closely adheres to evidence-based standards? Can a respected "generalist" provide care that is as high quality as another professional who is more narrowly trained? Ultimately, clients are protected against inadequate care by the standards that govern each profession (counseling, psychiatry, psychology, social work). However, it also benefits consumers to stay abreast of the latest developments so they can make the most informed choices possible.

positive reinforcement increase the frequency of the behaviors that precede them. In these examples, the behaviors that increase are speaking outrageous opinions and taking sleep medication.

According to the behavioral perspective, you don't have to directly experience reinforcement in order for it to modify your behavior. Psychologists who study **social learning theory** believe that people can learn by watching others. Thus, through **vicarious reinforcement** you

social learning theory
Perspective that focuses on understanding how people develop psychological disorders through their relationships with others and through observation of other people.

vicarious reinforcement
A form of learning in which a new behavior is acquired through the process of watching someone else receive reinforcement for the same behavior.

MINI CASE

Behavioral Approaches to Treating Meera

Following from the behavioral assumption that clients experiencing major depressive episodes have developed maladaptive responses, a behaviorally oriented clinician would give Meera the opportunity to learn new, adaptive behaviors. As you will learn in the chapter "Dissociative and Somatic Symptom Disorders", behavioral approaches to major depressive disorder have clients increase the frequency of positively reinforcing events (known as "behavioral activation"). Meera would keep a diary of her interactions with friends, participation in exercise, and other enjoyable activities, which she would then show to her therapist. To increase the frequency of these behaviors, Meera and her clinician would identify a set of desirable rewards to occur with their completion. For the intervention to be most effective, the clinician would need to ensure that Meera can realistically obtain her goals so she continues to experience success in achieving them.

acquire a new behavior through the process of watching someone else receive reinforcement for the same behavior.. You can also develop a perception of your own competence in various life situations, or **self-efficacy**, by watching the results of your own actions or those of other people with whom you identify. For example, you may wonder whether you have the ability to overcome your fear of public speaking, but if you see a fellow student give a successful presentation in class and feel you are not that different from this student, his or her success will build your feelings of self-efficacy, and you will do well when it's your turn to get up and speak.

self-efficacy

The individual's perception of competence in various life situations.

Treatment

Behavior therapists focus their therapeutic efforts on helping their clients unlearn maladaptive behaviors and replace them with healthy, adaptive behaviors. In **counterconditioning**, which is most closely related to classical conditioning, clients learn to pair a new response to a stimulus that formerly provoked the maladaptive response. The new response is, in fact, incompatible with the old (undesirable) response. For example, you cannot be physically anxious and relaxed at the same time. Through counterconditioning, as developed by physician Joseph Wolpe (1915–1997), clients learn to associate the response of relaxation with the stimulus that formerly caused them to feel anxious. Clinicians teach clients to relax through a series of progressive steps—for example, by first relaxing the head and neck muscles, then their hands and feet, and ultimately the rest of their bodies.

counterconditioning

The process of replacing an undesired response to a stimulus with an acceptable response.

Counterconditioning often occurs in gradual stages using the **systematic desensitization** method. The therapist breaks the maladaptive response into its smallest steps while pairing each step with relaxation, rather than exposing the client all at once to the feared stimulus. To assist in this process, the client may begin by providing the therapist with a hierarchy, or list, of situations associated with the feared stimulus. Starting with the least fearful situation in the hierarchy, the clinician asks the client to imagine that situation and practice progressive relaxation at the same time. After the client has established the connection between that image and relaxation, the clinician then moves up the hierarchy to the next level. Eventually, the client can confront the feared situation while at the same time feeling entirely relaxed. At any point, though, if the client suffers a setback, the clinician moves back down the hierarchy to help the client relearn to associate relaxation with the image at the previous

systematic desensitization

A variant of counterconditioning that involves presenting the client with progressively more anxiety-provoking images while in a relaxed state.

A behaviorally oriented psychologist would help a client overcome fear of flying by using such methods as breathing exercises, reducing physiological tensions, and overcoming automatic thoughts about the fear of flying.

©Bilderbox/INSADCO Photography/Alamy Stock Photo

FIGURE 6 Fear Hierarchy in Systematic Desensitization

lower level. Figure 6 shows an example of a fear hierarchy that a clinician might use in systematically desensitizing a person who fears spiders.

Based on principles of operant conditioning, **contingency management** is a form of behavioral therapy in which clinicians provide clients with positive reinforcement for performing desired behaviors. The client learns to connect the outcome of the behavior with the behavior itself, in order to establish a contingency or connection. The clinician works with the client to develop a list of positive reinforcements the client can receive only after performing the desired behavior. For example, if the client is trying to quit smoking, the clinician suggests a schedule in which the client can receive the designated reinforcement after going without a cigarette for a specific amount of time (such as permission to play video games). Gradually, the client extends the time period until he or she is able to cease smoking altogether. One contingency management form that residential settings use is the **token economy**, in which residents who perform desired activities earn tokens they can later exchange for tangible benefits (LePage et al., 2003).

Behavioral treatments can also invoke the principle of vicarious reinforcement, in which clinicians show live or recorded models of people receiving rewards for demonstrating the desired behaviors (Bandura, 1971). For example, the clinician may show a video of someone who is enjoying playing with a dog to a client who is afraid of dogs. The vicarious reinforcement in this situation is seeing the other person's enjoyment of playing with the dog. The therapist might also use **participant modeling**, a form of therapy in which the therapist first shows the client a desired behavior and then guides the client gradually through the behavioral change.

Clinicians working within the behavioral perspective often provide their clients with homework assignments. The clinician may ask the client to keep a detailed record of the behaviors he or she is trying to change, along with the situations in which the behaviors occur. The homework assignment might also include specific tasks the clinician asks the client to perform with instructions for observing the outcome of completing those tasks.

4.6 Cognitive Perspective

The **cognitive perspective** is the theoretical perspective in which it is assumed that abnormality is caused by maladaptive thought processes that result in dysfunctional behavior. Thus, psychologists working within the cognitive perspective focus on the way an individual's thoughts influence their emotions. One of the fundamental assumptions of the cognitive perspective is that having "rational," or logical, thoughts will help make it possible for people to develop and maintain their psychological health.

Theories

Consistent with its emphasis on thoughts, the cognitive perspective proposes that psychological disorders are the product of disturbed thoughts. By changing people's thoughts, cognitive psychologists believe they can also help clients develop more adaptive emotions.

Figure 7 illustrates the basic processes identified by the cognitive perspective as contributing to psychological disorders. The process originates with **dysfunctional attitudes**, negative beliefs about the self that are also deeply ingrained and difficult to articulate. People with psychological disorders experience **automatic thoughts**, the product of dysfunctional attitudes so deeply entrenched the individual is not even aware they exist. Dysfunctional attitudes influence the ways that people with psychological disorders interpret their experiences. As shown in Figure 7, a dysfunctional attitude about making a mistake can lead the

contingency management
A form of behavioral therapy in which clinicians provide clients with positive reinforcement for performing desired behaviors.

token economy
A form of contingency management in which a client who performs desired activities earns tokens that can later be exchanged for tangible benefits.

participant modeling
A form of therapy in which the therapist first shows the client a desired behavior and then guides the client through the behavioral change.

cognitive perspective
A theoretical perspective in which it is assumed that abnormality is caused by maladaptive thought processes that result in dysfunctional behavior.

dysfunctional attitudes
Negative beliefs about the self that are deeply ingrained.

automatic thoughts
Ideas that are the product of dysfunctional attitudes so deeply entrenched the individual is not even aware they exist.

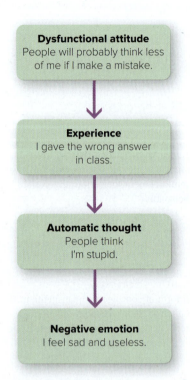

Dysfunctional attitude
People will probably think less of me if I make a mistake.

Experience
I gave the wrong answer in class.

Automatic thought
People think I'm stupid.

Negative emotion
I feel sad and useless.

FIGURE 7 The Relationship Among Dysfunctional Attitude, Experience, Automatic Thought, and Negative Emotion

SOURCE: Adapted from Beck, A. T., Bush, A. J., Shaw, B. F., & Emery, G. in *Cognitive Therapy of Depression.*

cognitive restructuring
One of the fundamental techniques of cognitive-behavioral therapy in which the clinician attempts to change the client's thoughts by questioning and challenging the client's dysfunctional attitudes and irrational beliefs.

cognitive-behavioral therapy (CBT)
Treatment method in which clinicians focus on changing both maladaptive thoughts and maladaptive behaviors.

individual to interpret the experience of giving the wrong answer in class as the basis for drawing the automatic (but incorrect) conclusion that people believe that he or she is "stupid."

Looking at Figure 7 again, you can see the chain leading from the automatic thought to the negative emotion. In the cognitive perspective, the flawed conclusion represented by the automatic thought produces the negative emotion of sadness (Ellis, 2005). Particularly problematic for people with psychological disorders, according to this perspective, are the unrealistic, extreme, and illogical ways in which they think about themselves and their behavior. Their irrational beliefs cause them to punish themselves because they fail to live up to the "musts" of being perfect. When they invariably fail, they can become so despondent that they give up on the idea of ever getting better, and should they enter treatment, they take an unduly pessimistic approach about whether they will improve.

Treatment

Therapists who adopt the cognitive perspective focus their attention on changing the dysfunctional attitudes that ultimately produce the negative emotions. The "cognitive" in this approach, then, means that thoughts become the target of treatment. One key method used by cognitively oriented therapists is **cognitive restructuring**, in which the clinician attempts to change the client's thoughts by questioning and challenging the client's dysfunctional attitudes and irrational beliefs. In this way, clients learn to reframe negative ideas into more positive ones.

In **cognitive-behavioral therapy (CBT)**, as the term implies, clinicians focus on changing both maladaptive thoughts and maladaptive behaviors. Clinicians incorporate behavioral techniques, such as homework and reinforcement, with cognitive methods that increase clients' awareness of their dysfunctional thoughts. Clients learn to recognize when their appraisals of situations are unrealistically contributing to their dysfunctional emotions. They can then try to identify situations, behavior, or people that help them counteract these emotions.

As an example, consider a client who believes she is incapable of being liked by anyone but her close family members and therefore feels alone and isolated. She feels so incapacitated that she turns down invitations for casual get-togethers with her co-workers. The clinician may assign the homework of accepting one of those invitations and then reporting back in therapy on how the event actually went, focusing on the client's feelings at the time. This report can then become the basis for another assignment, with perhaps a slightly wider group of acquaintances, until the client has enough "data" to challenge her belief that no one could possibly like her.

The central aim of CBT, then, is to give clients greater control over their dysfunctional behaviors, thoughts, and emotions. Through this approach, CBT seeks to empower clients to find more adaptive ways to respond to life's challenges—thus not only improving their current symptoms but decreasing the likelihood they will reoccur in the future.

MINI CASE

Cognitive Approach to Treating Meera

A clinician working within a cognitive perspective would treat Meera by helping her develop more adaptive thoughts. From a strictly cognitive point of view, the clinician would focus on Meera's beliefs that she has let down her family and friends and encourage her to challenge her conclusion, looking with her at the basis for her assumption about her family's feelings toward her.

Combining the cognitive and the behavioral approaches, the clinician would also ask Meera to keep a record of her behaviors, including her participation in positively rewarding activities. However, unlike the strict behaviorist, this clinician would also instruct Meera to keep a record of her dysfunctional thoughts, particularly those that exacerbate her negative emotions.

4.7 Humanistic Perspective

Psychologists who adhere to the **humanistic perspective** believe people are motivated to strive for self-fulfillment and meaning in life. The "human" in *humanistic* refers to the focus of this perspective on the qualities that make each individual unique. Unlike the behavioral perspective, which translates principles from animal research to the behavior of people, the humanistic perspective focuses specifically on the values, beliefs, and ability to reflect on our own experiences that separate humans from other species.

Theories

When they began to develop their theories in the 1960s, humanistic theorists and clinicians saw their ideas as a radical departure from the traditional focus of psychology, which minimized the role of free will and search for meaning in human experience. These humanists joined together to form a "third force" in psychology, with the intention of challenging psychoanalysis and behaviorism. Psychologists working within this tradition also saw human behavior in much more positive terms and viewed psychological disorders as the result of restricted growth potential.

The work of humanistic theorists was heavily influenced by existential psychology, a theoretical position that emphasizes the importance of fully appreciating each moment as it occurs (May, 1983). According to existential psychology, people who are tuned in to the world around them and experience life as fully as possible in each moment are the psychologically healthiest, and psychological disorders arise when people are unable to experience living in the moment. Thus we develop disorders due not to fundamental flaws in our biology or thoughts, but to restrictions modern society imposes on our ability to express our inner selves (Frankl, 1963; Laing, 1959). This focus on living in the moment is now seen in the mindfulness approach to treatment that emphasizes being aware of all that is going on around you while also gaining insight into your inner feelings (Shipherd & Salters-Pedneault, 2018).

The humanistic approach in clinical work is exemplified best by Carl Rogers's (1902–1987) **person-centered theory**, which focuses on each individual's uniqueness, the importance of allowing each individual to achieve maximum fulfillment of potential, and the individual's need to confront honestly the reality of his or her experiences in the world. In applying the person-centered theory to the therapy context, Rogers (1951) used the term **client-centered** to reflect his belief that people are innately good and that the potential for self-improvement lies within the individual rather than in the therapist or therapeutic techniques.

Rogers believed a well-adjusted person's self-image should be congruent with the person's experiences. In this state of congruence, a person is fully functioning—able to put his or her psychological resources to their maximal use. Conversely, a psychological disorder is the result of blocking the individual's potential for living to full capacity, resulting in a state of incongruence or mismatch between self-image and reality. Congruence is not a static state, however; to be fully functioning means the individual is constantly evolving and growing.

According to Rogers, psychological disorders have their origins in early life, when children are raised by parents who are harshly critical and demanding. Under such circumstances, children develop chronic anxiety about making mistakes that will cause their parents to disapprove of them even more. Rogers used the term *conditions of worth* to refer to the demands parents place upon

humanistic perspective
A theoretical view of personality and psychological disorder proposing that people are motivated to strive for self-fulfillment and meaning in life.

person-centered theory
The humanistic theory that focuses on the uniqueness of each individual, the importance of allowing each individual to achieve maximum fulfillment of potential, and the need for the individual to honestly confront the reality of his or her experiences in the world.

client-centered
An approach based on the belief held by Rogers that people are innately good and that the potential for self-improvement lies within the individual.

Many psychologists today believe that early childhood experiences with primary caregivers influence the way an individual behaves in interpersonal relationships throughout the life span.
©Yellow Dog Productions/Getty Images

Individuals who are self-actualized are able to achieve a sense of fulfillment by helping others because they have already met their own needs.
©Klaus Tiedge/Blend Images LLC

self-actualization
In humanistic theory, the maximum realization of the individual's potential for psychological growth.

children in which they communicate the message that in order to be loved, they have to meet these criteria. As adults, such children are constantly trying to meet the expectations of others instead of feeling that others will value them for their true selves, even with flaws.

Less focused on therapy but also highly influential in the humanistic movement, Abraham Maslow's (1962) humanistic model centers on the notion of **self-actualization**, the maximum realization of the individual's potential for psychological growth. According to Maslow, self-actualized people have accurate self-perceptions and are able to find rich sources of enjoyment and stimulation in their everyday activities. They are capable of peak experiences in which they feel a tremendous surge of inner happiness, as if they were totally in harmony with themselves and their world. But these individuals are not simply searching for sensual or spiritual pleasure. They also have a philosophy of life that is based on humanitarian and egalitarian values.

Maslow defined the hierarchy of needs, which proposes that people are best able to experience self-actualization when they have met their basic physical and psychological needs. We call needs that are lower on the hierarchy *deficit needs,* because they describe a state in which the individual seeks to obtain something that is lacking. An individual who is preoccupied with meeting deficit needs cannot achieve self-actualization. For example, people who are motivated solely to make money (a lower-order need) will not be able to move up the hierarchy to self-actualization until they set their materialistic motives aside. Self-actualization is not a final end-state but a process in which the individual seeks true self-expression.

Treatment

A theory rich with implications for treatment, person-centered theory now forms the foundation of much of contemporary therapy and counseling. The client-centered model of therapy proposed specific guidelines for therapists to follow in order to ensure that clients are able to achieve full self-realization. According to Rogers, clinicians should focus on the client's needs, not on preconceived clinician notions about what is best for the client. In fact, reflecting this emphasis on the inherent strengths of people seeking treatment, Rogers originated the use of the term *clients* because it implies a partnership between the helper and the person being helped. He preferred this to the illness-oriented term *patients.*

Rogers believed that a clinician's job is to help clients discover their inherent goodness and, in the process, to help each client achieve greater self-understanding. To counteract the problems caused by conditions of worth in childhood, Rogers recommended that therapists treat clients with **unconditional positive regard**, or total acceptance of what the client says, does, and feels. As clients begin to feel less self-critical, they become better able to tolerate the anxiety that comes with acknowledging their own weaknesses, because they no longer feel driven to see themselves as perfect. The clinicians try to be as compassionate as possible, and gradually the clients feel increasingly confident about revealing their true, inner selves because they know the clinician will not reject or label them as inadequate.

Contemporary humanistic and experiential therapists emphasize that therapists can be most effective if they are empathic, or able to see the world from the eyes of their clients, as much as possible. Therapists working within the client-centered model are trained in the techniques of reflection and clarification in order to express empathic understanding. In reflection, the therapist mirrors back what the client has just said, perhaps rephrasing it slightly, and makes every attempt to see the client's situation as it appears to him or her. These techniques allow clients to feel that the clinician is listening empathically and not judging them.

Rogers also suggested that clinicians should provide a model of genuineness and willingness to disclose their personal weaknesses and limitations. Clients then realize they don't have to put up a false front, trying to appear as something they are not. Ideally, the client will see that it is acceptable and healthy to be honest in confronting personal experiences, even if those experiences have less than favorable implications. For example, the Rogerian clinician might admit to having experiences similar to those the client describes, such as feeling anxious about speaking before a group. This is the kind of self-disclosure a Freudian psychoanalyst would never engage in, because it takes away from the therapist's status as a completely neutral party. To a Rogerian clinician, the sharing of personal experiences (within bounds) helps the client feel more accepted and understood.

Motivational interviewing (MI) is another client-centered technique that uses empathic understanding as a means of promoting behavioral change in clients (Magill et al., 2018). Here the clinician collaborates with the client to strengthen the client's motivation to make changes by asking questions that elicit the individual's own arguments for change. MI, like the client-centered approach in general, emphasizes the client's autonomy.

The humanistic perspective permeates much of contemporary psychology, particularly informing the mission of positive psychology, which emphasizes growth and fulfillment rather than psychopathology and disorder. Maslow's theory is perhaps most heavily employed within a vocational and educational framework, and the principles of person-centered therapy developed by Rogers now are an implicit component of the focus in psychotherapy on empathy and the therapeutic alliance. Mindfulness and motivational interviewing now receive widespread attention, giving clinicians additional and accessible tools to use with clients in a range of ages with a range of disorders.

unconditional positive regard
A method in client-centered therapy in which the clinician gives total acceptance of what the client says, does, and feels.

motivational interviewing (MI)
A technique that uses empathic understanding as a means of promoting behavioral change in clients.

MINI CASE

Humanistic Approaches to Treating Meera

In humanistic therapy, a clinician would work with Meera to establish a firm therapeutic alliance by empathically listening to her descriptions of her feelings. Consistent with Carl Rogers's emphasis on becoming more aware of our feelings, the clinician would encourage Meera to experience more fully her feelings about her rejection by her family and her sadness as a result of her disconnectedness from them. In this process, the clinician would help Meera identify her feelings and accept them without undue self-criticism. The clinician might also focus on Meera's feelings of low self-worth by exploring how she was influenced by the negative comparisons her parents made between she and her sister. The fact that they refused to accept Meera in the family unless she abided by their rules caused Meera to feel that people could not regard her as an individual on her own terms. To help increase authentic feelings of self-worth, the clinician would work with Meera to further her understanding of her own values and develop ways for her to build growth-enhancing experiences consistent with those values, rather than with those of her family.

4.8 Sociocultural Perspective

Theorists within the sociocultural perspective emphasize the ways that people, social institutions, and social forces influence individuals in the world around them. The sociocultural perspective reaches outside individuals to include factors that may contribute to their development of psychological disorders.

Theories

family perspective
A theoretical perspective in which it is assumed that abnormality is caused by disturbances in the pattern of interactions and relationships within the family.

social discrimination
Prejudicial treatment of a class of individuals, seen in the sociocultural perspective as a cause of psychological problems.

Proponents of the **family perspective** see psychological disorders as caused by disturbances in the patterns of interactions and relationships that exist within the family. These disturbed patterns of relationships may create the "identified patient"—namely, the individual in treatment whose difficulties reflect strains within the family.

Researchers within the sociocultural perspective also focus on **social discrimination** as a cause of psychological problems. Discrimination on the basis of gender, race, sexual orientation, religion, social class, and age, for example, can contribute to disorders in the realms of physical and mental health. Starting in the 1950s, researchers established the finding that psychological disorders are more commonly diagnosed among people in lower socioeconomic strata (Hollingshead & Redlich, 1958). This relationship may reflect the fact that people of lower social class experience economic hardships and have limited access to quality education, health care, and employment. Socioeconomic discrimination is further compounded by membership in groups identified as targets due to their race or ethnicity, sexual orientation, immigration status, or religion (to name a few). When people have limited opportunities or when they encounter oppression because of unalterable human characteristics, they are likely to experience inner turmoil, frustration, and stress, leading to the development of psychological symptoms.

Natural and human-caused disasters, political oppression, poverty, violence, and war are further contributors to psychological disorders, according to the sociocultural perspective. Since World War I, U.S. psychologists have conducted large-scale studies of the ways in which war negatively affects psychological functioning. People who are traumatized as a result of terrorist attacks, exposure to battle, persecution, or imprisonment are at risk of developing serious anxiety disorders. Similarly, fires and natural disasters such as earthquakes, tornadoes, and hurricanes leave psychological as well as physical destruction in their wake.

According to family systems theorists, dysfunction within the family dynamic may be a main source of an individual's psychological distress.

©rubberball/Getty Images

Treatment

How do clinicians intervene with people suffering from conditions that sociocultural factors cause or exacerbate? Clearly, it is not possible to change the world, but clinicians can play a crucial role in helping people come to grips with problems that have developed within a family system, the immediate environment, or extended society.

In the most immediate circle of the individual, namely the family, clinicians can intervene by encouraging all family members (however family is defined) to try new ways of relating to each other or thinking about their problems. The family therapist, sometimes working with a co-therapist, meets with as many family members as possible at one time. Rather than focusing on an individual's problems or concerns, family and couples therapists focus on the ways in which dysfunctional relational patterns maintain a particular problem or symptom. They also use a life-span perspective in which they consider the developmental issues, not only of each individual, but of the entire family or couple. Furthermore, family and couples therapists see the continuing relationships among the family members as potentially more healing than the relationship between clinicians and clients.

The particular techniques that clinicians use in family therapy depend greatly on the therapist's training and theoretical approach. An intergenerational family therapist might suggest drawing a diagram of all relatives in the recent past, in an effort to understand the history of family relationships and use this understanding to bring about change. A structural family therapist might suggest that a subset of the family members enact a disagreement as if they were characters in a play about the family. By doing so, the family members can step outside their current conflicts and see new ways of handling their recurring patterns of interaction. An experiential family therapist might work with the family members to develop insight into their relationships with each other by focusing on how they are feeling at the moment as they discuss their joint concerns.

In group therapy, people who share similar experiences share their stories with each other, aided by the facilitation of the therapist. According to Irvin Yalom (1931–), a founder of group therapy, clients can find relief and hope in the realization that their problems are not unique by hearing that others share their emotional experiences. In the group, they can also acquire valuable information and advice from people who share their concerns. Furthermore, in the process of giving to others, people generally find that they themselves derive benefit.

Clinicians use milieu therapy in treatment settings such as inpatient hospitals to promote positive functioning in clients by creating a therapeutic community. Community members participate in group activities, ranging from occupational therapy to training classes. Staff members encourage clients to work and spend time with other residents with the goal of increasing the positive bonds among them. Every staff person, whether a therapist, nurse, or paraprofessional, takes part in the overall mission of providing an environment that supports positive change and reinforces appropriate social behaviors. The underlying idea behind milieu therapy is that the pressure to conform to conventional social norms of behavior fosters more adaptive behavior on the part of individual clients. In addition, the normalizing effects of a supportive environment are intended to help the individual make a smoother and more effective transition to life outside the therapeutic community.

Although clinicians cannot reverse social discrimination, they can adopt a **multicultural approach** to therapy that relies on awareness, knowledge, and skills of the client's sociocultural context. In keeping with the principles of cultural formulations, therapy should be sensitive to the ways in which the client's cultural background interacts with his or her specific life experiences and family influences. Clinicians make a commitment to learning about the client's cultural, ethnic, and racial group and the way these factors play a role in assessment, diagnosis, and treatment. Multicultural skills include mastery of culture-specific therapy techniques that are responsive to a client's unique characteristics.

multicultural approach
Therapy that relies on awareness, knowledge, and skills of the client's sociocultural context.

MINI CASE

Sociocultural Approach to Treating Meera

A clinician working within the sociocultural perspective would incorporate Meera's specific family issues within the context of her cultural background. Not only have Meera's symptoms likely emerged from her own construction of her family's attitude toward her work and relationship decisions, but they also reflect her Indian cultural background, which tends to place heavy emphasis on family obligations. By choosing a path different from that of her sister, Meera has perhaps, in reality or in her own perception, violated her familial and larger cultural expectations. In therapy, Meera should be encouraged to reflect on and develop her own sense of identity within both her family and the larger cultural context as a first-generation American, and to acknowledge how that affects her family dynamics and relates to her depressive symptoms. The clinician might suggest that Meera be seen with her family, if possible, to work through these cultural and relational conflicts. Or the clinician could help Meera develop a way to communicate her observations with her family and work toward managing their expectations of her. This could help to rebuild the relationship in a way that takes into account both Meera's framework and the family's own beliefs. Through the sociocultural lens, reworking the relationship in this way could help reduce Meera's depressive symptoms by allowing her to be herself within the family without feeling she is constantly violating their expectations.

REAL STORIES

Sylvia Plath, Major Depressive Disorder

At the age of 30, U.S. poet Sylvia Plath succumbed to her lifelong battle with depression. On the night of February 11, 1963, with her two infant children asleep, Plath carefully placed towels in the cracks under the doors to her children's bedroom and her kitchen, turned on the gas in her oven, and laid her head inside. She had left milk and bread in the children's room with the window open to the chilly London night so their breakfast would be fresh for the morning.

Only days before, she had begun a course of antidepressants, and experts believe her suicide occurred at a dangerous time in the course of treatment with such medications, when the individual—still depressed—becomes simultaneously more active, leading to an increased risk for suicide attempts. *Bitter Fame: A Life of Sylvia Plath,* by Anne Stevenson, chronicles the life and writings of the notoriously tortured writer through her journal entries, personal letters, and interviews with those who were in her life. Born and raised around Boston,

Massachusetts, Plath began writing at the age of 7. Throughout her childhood and adolescence, she produced an impressive

Sylvia Plath in 1957.
©Bettmann/Getty Images

number of poems and short stories that gave rise to her ultimate dream of being a professional writer.

Plath's experiences served to inspire her until the final days of her life. Perhaps the most influential was the sudden death of her father shortly after her eighth birthday, a loss that fueled her innermost fears and desires and became an ever-present theme in her work. It also left her incredibly sensitive to depression following abandonment from others in her life, particularly romantic partners.

Plath grew up in the prototypical New England town of Wellesley, Massachusetts, and attended Smith College in Northampton, Massachusetts, on an academic scholarship. Although the transition to college was initially difficult for her, her intelligence and diligent work ethic earned her high grades and a prominent reputation at Smith. As she grew into young adulthood, she began to experience heightened moodiness and bouts of depression. At age 19, she attempted suicide by swallowing her mother's sleeping pills and hiding in a crawlspace in her house. It was 2 days before anyone discovered her in a dazed and semiconscious state. Following the attempt, Plath entered a nearby psychiatric hospital for a 4-month period, where she received electroconvulsive therapy (ECT). This marked a major turning point in her life and in her writing.

"Attributable to her ECT," Stevenson writes in *Bitter Fame*, "is the unseen menace that haunts nearly everything she wrote, her conviction that the world, however benign in appearance, conceals dangerous animosity, directed particularly toward herself." We can observe Plath's deeply introspective nature in the personal journals she faithfully kept throughout her life. They served as an important source of self-expression into which she poured her every thought and feeling, particularly in times of distress, offering us an intimate view of her darkest moments.

After her hospitalization, Plath returned to Smith, graduated summa cum laude in 1954, and went on to pursue graduate studies on a prestigious Fulbright scholarship in Cambridge, England. As she matured professionally while studying there, her romantic interests turned to a fellow poet whom she greatly admired, Ted Hughes. Upon meeting at a party, the two experienced an immediate attraction and, after a whirlwind romance, married in a secret ceremony in England. At the time, Plath was funded by a fellowship that she feared would be withdrawn should news of her marriage surface. Eventually their union became public, and the couple spent the first few months of their married life in Spain while Hughes was teaching.

In *Bitter Fame*, Stevenson describes how Plath's mood shifts became highly pronounced after the initial period of marital bliss faded. "Her moods seemed to soar and sink with alarming rapidity. Sylvia recorded in her journal her volatile and intense reactions to some unmentioned incident, possibly arising out of her husband's surprise at the rancor she displayed in a running tiff with the house owner, who wanted to raise the rent, or perhaps arising out of an evening when they had drinks with some English people who upset Sylvia. These moods, Ted found, were largely unaccountable: they began and ended like electric storms, and he came to learn simply to accept their occurrence."

The couple then moved to Plath's home state of Massachusetts, where she taught English courses at her alma mater, Smith College. Her initial excitement about the prestige of teaching at such a renowned institution quickly gave way to her anxiety about the amount of work it entailed, and particularly about the fact that it left no time for her to work on her own writing. She was further plagued by crippling periods of self-doubt that propelled her again into depression. She wrote, "Last night I felt . . . the sick, soul-annihilating flux of fear in my blood switching its current to defiant fight. I could not sleep, although tired, and lay feeling my nerves shaved to pain and the groaning inner voice: oh, you can't teach, can't do anything. Can't write, can't think. And I lay under the negative icy flood of denial, thinking that voice was all my own, a part of me, and it must somehow conquer me and leave me with my worst visions: having had the chance to battle it and win day by day, and having failed." Such thoughts of worthlessness are common to individuals suffering from major depression.

After a year of teaching, Plath and Hughes moved to Boston, where they became part of a closely knit community of poets and writers. At this point, Hughes had begun to gain considerable accolades for his writing, and the couple lived mainly off of his award money. This allowed Plath to spend the majority of her time developing her writing. When she was pregnant with the couple's first child, they moved to England, settling in an apartment in London and then in a home in the countryside prior to the birth of their second child.

Although by all accounts Hughes was a devoted husband and father, Plath was stricken by fears of his infidelity and often accused him of extramarital affairs. On one occasion, Hughes was late returning home from an interview with the BBC. Plath reacted by destroying a large portion of his writing materials, along with some of his most prized books. Eventually the two separated (although they never divorced), and after Hughes moved out of their home, Plath moved to a flat in London with their two children. Here, she experienced a surge of creative energy that produced many of her most famous poems. At this point she had completed her first and what was to be her only novel, *The Bell Jar*, a semi-autobiographical account of a young woman's journey through young adulthood, navigating the muddy waters of career, romance, and psychological distress. Much of the narrative of the book directly mirrors Plath's own experiences.

Her poetry, too, reflected her struggles as she continued to grapple with her deteriorating mental health. "As absorbed and intent as a cartographer," Stevenson writes in *Bitter Fame*, "Sylvia reported in her poems on the weather of her inner universe and delineated its two poles: 'stasis' and rage. At the depressed pole there was a turning in on herself, a longing for nonbeing. . . . It was as though she looked in a glass and a huge mirror image of her traumatized childhood self stared back."

Although she was experiencing a surge of creativity, Plath was falling into a deep depression. She began seeing a psychiatrist, who noted the severity of her condition. Unable to care for herself and her children, Plath stayed with friends while she tried to recuperate, too afraid to face another round of ECT in a psychiatric hospital. One day, she defiantly decided that she was ready to return to her flat with her children. Her friends, puzzled by her sudden determination, tried in vain to persuade her to stay in their care. The very evening she went home, finally away from watchful eyes, Plath ended her short but intense life.

In the years following her death, critics have come to regard Sylvia Plath as one of the most talented and influential poets of the twentieth century. Compiled by Ted Hughes, who went on to raise their two children with his second wife, *The Collected Poems*, a complete collection of the poems she wrote between adolescence and the end of her life, won the Pulitzer Prize in 1982.

4.9 Acceptance-Based Perspective

Also referred to as the "third-wave" movement in psychotherapy, the acceptance-based perspective follows in the footsteps of behavioral and cognitive theorists. Many of these treatments were developed during the 1970s and were influenced by traditional Eastern philosophy (Baer & Huss, 2008). They started to gain traction later in the 1990s, for instance when acceptance and commitment therapy was first established as a treatment approach, and are now widely used for a variety of psychological disorders.

Theories

acceptance-based approaches
A group of psychotherapy approaches that use behavioral strategies as well as cognitive framework to improve overall effectiveness.

Acceptance-based approaches are based upon the theoretical underpinnings of behavioral and cognitive therapies. These present-oriented approaches use behavioral strategies as well as the cognitive framework. They build on these traditional approaches by taking into account the context of the individual. The focus is on improving overall effectiveness in functioning, rather than on reduction of specific symptoms, as in CBT for instance (Hayes, 2016). These approaches have received a good deal of empirical support in the research literature (Kahl, Winter, & Schweiger, 2012), although ongoing research is still determining their effectiveness for treatment of specific psychological disorders.

mindfulness
A mental state achieved by intentionally bringing one's awareness to the present moment without judgment of internal or external observations.

Mindfulness is a mental state achieved by intentionally bringing one's awareness to the present moment without judgment of internal or external observations. Mindfulness training is a core behavioral component of many of the acceptance-based approaches and can be practiced in various forms. Researchers have found that mindfulness has many therapeutic benefits, both on its own and through incorporation into psychological treatment. It should be noted that mindfulness is often synonymous with meditation. Although mindfulness is the foundation of Buddhist meditation practice, it is possible to practice mindfulness outside of the context of meditation and using a variety of techniques. Whereas meditation often aims to focus awareness on a particular sensory experience, mindfulness aims to expand awareness more broadly. Furthermore, mindfulness does not emphasize spirituality in the way that many meditation practices do (Kabat-Zinn, 2003).

The basic goal of mindfulness practice is to cultivate awareness of current external and internal experiences without judgment. This is achieved through purposeful and intentional practice of the act of being mindful, with an emphasis on attending to one's observations openly (Brown & Ryan, 2003; Kabat-Zinn, 2003). Although judgments or appraisals are often valuable and necessary, when people make automatic assumptions about what is observed, there is a tendency to interpret those assumptions as facts. Mindfulness aims to increase psychological flexibility by expanding ones' awareness to other interpretations, versus getting stuck in negative belief cycles. Acceptance-based approaches posit that, in treatment of psychological suffering, it is crucial to address the ways that an individual is acting upon automatic interpretations about both external and internal experiences, in order to promote more effective ways of coping. What is inherent to this process is an acceptance of the experience as it is, whether positive or negative. In acceptance-based approaches, the aim is not to change the experience itself (as this is not possible), but to change one's relationship to the experience in a way that increases psychological flexibility and helps the individual to function more effectively and fluidly based on the demands of the situation.

Treatment

acceptance and commitment therapy (ACT)
A therapeutic approach that aims to indirectly reduce symptoms by focusing on improving psychological flexibility.

One of the more commonly known acceptance-based approaches used in psychotherapy currently is **acceptance and commitment therapy**, or ACT (Hayes, Strosahl, & Wilson, 1999). ACT is a behavior-based approach which looks more broadly at human suffering and aims to increase the individual's cognitive flexibility. The theoretical model of ACT looks at six main psychological processes that are thought to be correlated with psychopathology: experiential avoidance, cognitive fusion, dominance of the conceptualized past and future, limited self-knowledge, lack of values, and inaction/impulsivity. In ACT, therapists work with clients to explore each of these areas and how they influence the person's suffering, and then use various skills-based techniques and exercises to demonstrate how to work through each of these areas in which a person may be "stuck."

MINI CASE

Acceptance-Based Approach to Treating Meera

A clinician working from an acceptance-based perspective would target Meera's experience of depression in the context of her stressors by focusing less on the content of her stress and more on her relationship to her thoughts and feelings. For instance, it might be that Meera has tried to "fight off" her depression, which, through an acceptance-based lens, would likely serve to exacerbate her feelings and make them more difficult to live with. The clinician could teach Meera mindfulness skills to help her become more aware of how she experiences her emotions in her body, so that she is able to process her feelings more fully rather than trying to suppress or avoid thinking about them. Often, mindfulness skills are taught as coping tools to help manage particular times of distress. This could be very helpful for Meera, who has struggled with ongoing suicidal ideation. Her clinician could also use materials from the DBT module on Distress Tolerance to teach her additional skills for adapting to acute feelings of sadness or hopelessness. A clinician working from an ACT-based perspective would help Meera identify her values and develop ways for her to act more consistently with the areas in her life that are important in order to promote feelings of well-being and agency.

Dialectical behavior therapy, or DBT, is a skills-based approach developed by Marsha Linehan for the treatment of borderline personality disorder (Linehan, 1993). Since its inception, however, DBT has been used more broadly in therapy for treating a variety of psychological issues (Baer & Huss, 2008). Underlying DBT is the "biosocial theory," which hypothesizes that individuals who suffer from BPD or similarly struggle with regulating their emotions might be prone to these difficulties because of a combination of biological vulnerability and social environments that were either invalidating or ineffective in terms of teaching the individual how to cope with emotions. The term *dialectical* in DBT refers to what Linehan observed to be characteristic of individuals with BPD, whose experiences are often separated into opposite extremes. Thus, DBT focuses on teaching individuals to synthesize these extremes via acceptance and behavioral change.

In its most recent version, published in 2014, the DBT Skills Training Manual comprises four main modules: Mindfulness, Emotion Regulation, Interpersonal Effectiveness, and Distress Tolerance. In treatment these modules are covered step-by-step via structured worksheets and handouts that the therapist and client work through together (Linehan, 2014).

Mindfulness-based cognitive therapy (MBCT; Segal, Williams, & Teasdale, 2002) combines cognitive therapy with mindfulness skills to help patients who struggle with major depressive disorders by learning effective ways of managing their symptoms long term and preventing relapse of depressive episodes. The core of this is to teach clients "decentering" techniques which aim to take on a more acceptance-based stance of painful thoughts and feelings, versus trying to change the thoughts themselves as in typical cognitive therapy (Baer & Huss, 2008).

dialectical behavior therapy (DBT)
Treatment approach for people with borderline personality disorder that integrates supportive and cognitive-behavioral treatments to reduce the frequency of self-destructive acts and to improve the client's ability to handle disturbing emotions, such as anger and dependency.

Mindfulness-based cognitive therapy (MBCT)
Treatment that combines cognitive therapy with mindfulness skills.

4.10 Biopsychosocial Perspectives on Theories and Treatments: An Integrative Approach

Now that you have read about the major perspectives on abnormal behavior, you can probably see value in each of them. Certain facets of various theories may seem particularly useful and interesting. In fact, you may have a hard time deciding which approach is the "best." However, as we have said repeatedly, most clinicians select aspects of the various models, rather than adhering narrowly to a single one. In fact, in recent decades, there has been a dramatic shift away from narrow clinical approaches rooted in a single theoretical model. Increasingly, clinicians use approaches that are integrative or eclectic. The therapist views the needs of the client from multiple perspectives and develops a treatment plan that responds to these particular concerns.

Following a more comprehensive psychological assessment as her treatment plan indicated, the clinician determined that Meera would benefit the most from a cognitive-behavioral approach to psychotherapy in conjunction with medication. Meera followed up both these recommendations and saw a psychiatrist, who prescribed her an SSRI. She met with her psychiatrist once per week for the first month of her medication course and then once per month for a check-in. Meera also began seeing a therapist for weekly psychotherapy sessions. Using a cognitive-behavioral perspective, the beginning of the work with her therapist focused on strategies such as behavioral activation that would help her cope with the depressive symptoms that were interfering with her functioning. Once Meera's depression remitted, the therapy began to focus on her maladaptive thought patterns regarding her interpersonal relationships. With help from her therapist, Meera recognized that she had created unachievable standards for herself, which she thought her friends and family were expressing. Looking more carefully at her relationships, she discovered that she was imposing these expectations upon herself and that her friends and family accepted her for who she was.

Dr. Tobin's reflections: Given her response to treatment, Meera's depression appears to be a result of both a biological vulnerability and a maladaptive thought process that began to emerge as she grew into adulthood. Given that, it will be important for Meera to remain on the antidepressant medication to prevent future depressive episodes from occurring. Her therapist may also recommend that she stay in therapy, even after her initial symptoms have remitted, since it can take some time for her thought patterns to become more balanced and adaptive. The goal with therapy would be to ensure that she adapts to a more corrective way of coping with her environment and with stress. An additional area of focus in treatment will be exploring the impact of culture on Meera's development of beliefs around her place in her family. Through developing her own sense of identity, Meera can start to work on ways to resolve the tensions in her relationship with her family, which could help reduce the likelihood she may become symptomatic again in the future. Overall, Meera's strong commitment to recovery helped motivate her to receive the treatment that she needed, and as a result, her prognosis is quite positive.

SUMMARY

- Theoretical perspectives influence the ways in which clinicians and researchers interpret and organize their observations about behavior. In this chapter, we discussed seven major theoretical perspectives: biological, trait theory, psychodynamic, behavioral, cognitive, humanistic, and sociocultural. We concluded the discussion with a consideration of an integrative approach in which theorists and clinicians bring together aspects and techniques of more than one perspective.

- Within the biological perspective, clinicians view disturbances in emotions, behavior, and cognitive processes as caused by abnormalities in the body's functioning, such as brain and nervous system or endocrine system disorders. A person's genetic makeup can play an important role in precipitating certain disorders. In trying to assess the relative roles of nature and nurture, researchers have come to accept the notion of an interaction between genetic and environmental contributors to abnormality. Treatments that clinicians base on the biological model involve a range of somatic therapies, the most common of which is medication. More extreme somatic interventions include psychosurgery and electroconvulsive treatment (ECT).

- Trait theory proposes that abnormal behavior reflects maladaptive personality traits. The basic principle of trait theory is that personality is equivalent to a set of stable characteristics. In abnormal psychology, the predominant trait theory is the Five Factor Model, or "Big Five," which includes the personality traits of neuroticism, extraversion, openness to experience, agreeableness, and conscientiousness ("OCEAN" or "CANOE"). Although the Five Factor Model does not necessarily provide a framework for psychotherapy, it does provide a perspective for assessing for personality disorders.

- The psychodynamic perspective is a theoretical orientation that emphasizes unconscious determinants of behavior and is derived from Freud's psychoanalytic approach. We use the term *psychodynamics* to describe interaction among the id, the ego, and the superego. According to psychodynamic theorists, people use defense mechanisms to keep unacceptable thoughts, instincts, and feelings out of conscious awareness. Freud proposed that there is a normal sequence of development through a series of psychosexual stages.

- Post-Freudian theorists such as Jung, Adler, Horney, and Erikson departed from Freudian theory, contending that

Freud overemphasized sexual and aggressive instincts. Object relations theorists such as Klein, Winnicott, Kohut, and Mahler proposed that interpersonal relationships lie at the core of personality and that the unconscious mind contains images of the child's parents and of the child's relationships with them.

- Treatment within the psychodynamic perspective may incorporate techniques such as free association, dream analysis, transference, and resistance. Considerable debate about the tenets and techniques of the psychodynamic perspective continues to take place. Much of this debate focuses on the fact that psychodynamic concepts are difficult to study and measure and that some clinicians now regard Freudian notions as irrelevant in contemporary society. Newer approaches, based on object relations theory, have adapted the concept of infant attachment style to understanding the ways that adults relate to significant people in their lives.

- According to the behavioral perspective, faulty learning experiences cause abnormality. According to the cognitive-behavioral (sometimes called cognitive) perspective, maladaptive thought processes cause abnormality. Behaviorists contend that individuals acquire many emotional reactions through classical conditioning. Operant conditioning, with Skinner's emphasis on reinforcement, involves the learning of behaviors that are not automatic. Social learning theorists have studied the process of acquiring new responses by observing and imitating the behavior of others, which we call modeling. In interventions based on behavioral theory, clinicians focus on observable behaviors.

- Cognitive theories emphasize disturbed ways of thinking. Clinicians adhering to a cognitive perspective work with clients to change maladaptive thought patterns.

- Acceptance and commitment therapy, otherwise referred to as ACT, is an acceptance-based psychotherapeutic approach based on principles of cognitive-behavioral therapy (CBT). This type of treatment aims to reduce psychological suffering indirectly by increasing psychological flexibility by helping clients accept unwanted, difficult emotional experiences and modify behaviors to help increase time spent in valued activities.

- At the core of the humanistic perspective is the belief that human motivation is based on an inherent tendency to strive for self-fulfillment and meaning in life, notions that are rooted in existential psychology. Carl Rogers's person-centered theory focuses on the uniqueness of each individual, the importance of allowing the individual to achieve maximum fulfillment of potential, and the need for the individual to confront honestly the reality of his or her experiences in the world. Maslow's self-actualization theory focuses on the maximum realization of the individual's potential for psychological growth. In client-centered therapy, Rogers recommended that therapists treat clients with unconditional positive regard and empathy, while providing a model of genuineness and a willingness to self-disclose.

- Theorists within the sociocultural perspective emphasize the ways that people, social institutions, and social forces influence individuals. Proponents of the family perspective see the individual as an integral component of the pattern of interactions and relationships that exists within the family. Psychological disturbance can also arise as a result of discrimination that occurs with attributes such as gender, race, or age or of pressures associated with economic hardships. General social forces such as fluid and inconsistent values in a society, and destructive historical events such as political revolution, natural disaster, or nationwide depression also can adversely affect people. The nature of the group involved determines treatments within the sociocultural perspective. In family therapy, clinicians encourage family members to try new ways of relating to each other and thinking about their problems. In group therapy, people share their stories and experiences with others in similar situations. Milieu therapy provides a context in which the intervention is the environment, rather than the individual, usually consisting of staff and clients in a therapeutic community.

- In contemporary practice, most clinicians take an integrative approach, in which they select aspects of various models rather than adhering narrowly to a single one. Increasingly, clinicians use approaches that are integrative or eclectic.

KEY TERMS

Acceptance and commitment therapy (ACT)
Acceptance-based approaches
Allele
Archetypes
Attachment figure
Attachment style
Automatic thoughts
Aversive conditioning
Behavioral perspective
Biological perspective

Classical conditioning
Client-centered
Cognitive-behavioral therapy (CBT)
Cognitive perspective
Cognitive restructuring
Contingency management
Counterconditioning
Deep brain stimulation (DBS)
Defense mechanisms
Dialectical behavior therapy (DBT)
Diathesis-stress model

DNA methylation
Dysfunctional attitudes
Ego
Ego psychology
Electroconvulsive therapy (ECT)
Endophenotypes
Epigenesis
Epigenetics
Family perspective
Five Factor Model (or "Big Five")
Free association

Genes
Genome-wide association studies
  (GWAS)
Genome-wide linkage
  study
Genotype
Humanistic perspective
Id
Libido
Mindfulness
Motivational interviewing (MI)
Multicultural approach
Neuroleptics
Neurotransmitter

Object relations
Oedipus complex
Operant conditioning
Participant modeling
Personality trait
Person-centered theory
Phenotype
Pleasure principle
Polygenic
Psychodynamic perspective
Psychosexual stages
Psychosurgery
Reality principle
Reinforcement

Secondary process thinking
Self-actualization
Self-efficacy
Single nucleotide polymorphism
  (SNP)
Social discrimination
Social learning theory
Superego
Systematic desensitization
Theoretical perspective
Token economy
Transference
Unconditional positive regard
Vicarious reinforcement

Neurodevelopmental Disorders

Learning Objectives

5.1 Explain the characteristics and causes of intellectual disability.

5.2 Explain characteristics, theories, and treatment of autism spectrum disorder.

5.3 Differentiate among learning and communication, and communication disorders.

5.4 Explain characteristics, theories, and treatment of ADHD.

5.5 Describe motor disorders.

5.6 Analyze the biopsychosocial model of neurodevelopmental disorders.

©olegdudko/123RF

Case Report: Jason Newman

Demographic information: 8-year-old African American male

Presenting problem: Jason's third-grade teacher, Mrs. Brownstein, notes his increasingly hyperactive behavior and inability to pay attention in class from the first day of school. Because she does not wish to alarm his parents, she observes Jason's behavior over the first few weeks of the term to see whether settling into the classroom might decrease his rowdy behavior. However, Jason's behavior only deteriorates as the weeks go on, and Mrs. Brownstein decides to contact his parents, Pam and John Newman, and suggest a psychological evaluation for him. Though they had been advised by his earlier teachers to bring Jason to a psychologist, the Newmans' health insurance does not cover this expense, and they are unable to afford it on their own. However, it is becoming clear that treatment for Jason will be necessary in order for him to successfully complete his schooling. Mrs. Brownstein refers his parents to a local child psychologist with a private practice, Dr. Scott, who is able to work with the family on a sliding scale so that they can afford an evaluation.

Jason's mother, Pam, accompanies him to see Dr. Scott, who interviews her separately before seeing Jason. Pam explains that Jason has been a "very fidgety child" from infancy but that his disruptive and often inappropriate behavior in school has been getting notably worse over the past 3 years. Because he was their first child, Pam did not perceive that his apparent abundance of energy was abnormal. The couple also has a 4-year-old child, Nicholas, whose behavior as an infant was much calmer in comparison, further alerting them that something was different about Jason. Pam further explains that outside the classroom environment, Jason is usually more restless

than others in situations where he has to sustain attention for a long period of time. For instance, Pam notes that in church on Sundays, Jason typically starts to squirm in his seat after the first 5 minutes of the service. She remarks that this is quite embarrassing for her and her husband, who have difficulty getting Jason to sit still. As a result, they have stopped going to church altogether. She reports that it was often difficult to take care of Nicholas when he was an infant, because Jason would run into the nursery when Nicholas was being fed or changed and demand that Pam pay attention to him. On several occasions Jason grabbed the feeding bottle out of Pam's hand as she was feeding Nicholas.

Pam attempts to be very patient with Jason, but she reports that her husband, John, has more difficulty coping with their son's restless behavior. Pam describes instances in which Jason has been particularly "rowdy" in the home and has broken furniture and expensive items when he climbed on tabletops. She states that this has greatly strained the relationship between John and Jason and has been a source of tension between her and John as well, because they often disagree on how to discipline their son. Pam and John have tried, unsuccessfully, to implement a system of punishments and rewards based on his performance at school; however, this has only caused further frustration because they often disagree as to the appropriate amount of punishment.

Pam states that Jason's teachers have been describing the same patterns of behavior each year, though during this current school year his ability to pay attention has severely declined, perhaps, as Pam notes, because the material presented in the classroom is more complex and requires more attention and thought. During earlier years, the extent of Jason's inability to pay attention would manifest in his leaving classroom materials strewn about after he was finished, and he would never pick up after himself. Mrs. Brownstein has reported that during the current school year, when presented with difficult problems in the classroom, Jason bolts from his desk to another part of the room and begins playing with art supplies in the room even when she is giving a lesson. Pam is particularly concerned that Jason's behavior in school will continue to negatively affect the quality of his education throughout the years. Furthermore, it had been difficult for Jason to make friends at school, given his overly energetic demeanor and his propensity to be rude or impatient with other children. Pam states her fear that without good peer associations at school, Jason may become isolated and an object of ridicule to his schoolmates. She remarks that Jason and Nicholas do not get along very well either, because Jason tends to be bossy with his younger brother and is usually unwilling to play with him.

When Dr. Scott calls Jason into his office after the interview with Pam, he finds that Jason has gone out into the hallway and is running up and down the staircase that leads to the office. Pam retrieves Jason and brings him back into the office, then waits outside while Dr. Scott interviews Jason individually. Once seated in the office, Jason sits still for several minutes but becomes increasingly restless, climbing out of his seat and trying to leave the office several times throughout the interview. His responses to Dr. Scott's questions are tangential and difficult to comprehend, and he repeatedly gets out of his chair while talking. When asked why it is so difficult for him to sit still, Jason responds, "I'm just bored all the time. I can't help it!"

In order to observe Jason's ability to maintain attention on a task, Dr. Scott presents him with colored markers and asks him to draw a house. Jason begins to draw the shape of a house but soon gives up the task and runs over to one corner of the room where he sees toy building blocks and begins playing with them. When Dr. Scott asks Jason to return to the task, Jason angrily states, "No! No! No! No! No! They make me draw in school all the time! Where is my mommy?" At this point, Jason begins to cry. Being careful not to cause undue distress, Dr. Scott calls Pam back into the office, and Jason immediately settles down and begins to smile.

Relevant history: Pam reports having no birth complications during her pregnancy, and Jason has had no health problems during his development. There is no family history of childhood or attention-deficit disorders.

Case formulation: Based on his interview with Pam and his observation of Jason's behavior, Dr. Scott determines that Jason meets *DSM-5* diagnostic criteria for attention-deficit/hyperactivity disorder, hyperactive-impulsive type. His symptoms have been present for longer than 6 months and were present before the age of 7. He displays predominantly hyperactive-impulsive symptoms, and though he has some symptoms of inattention, they are too few to distinguish him as having combined presentation.

Treatment plan: Jason will be referred to his pediatrician for a medication consultation. He will also be referred for behavior therapy at a low-cost clinic in the area.

Sarah Tobin, PhD

neurodevelopmental disorders
Conditions that begin in childhood and have a major impact on social and cognitive functioning.

Conditions that begin in childhood and have a major impact on social and cognitive functioning are known as **neurodevelopmental disorders**. These disorders typically become evident early in children's development, often before they reach school age. The associated deficits include impairments in personal, social, academic, or occupational functioning. Some disorders have specifiers to indicate, for example, that the disorder is linked to a genetic abnormality or environmental factors affecting the individual during the prenatal period.

Because they strike so early, disorders that begin in childhood are particularly significant in affecting the lives of individuals with the disorders, their families, the schools, and society as a whole. Interventions targeting these disorders are particularly important because they can entirely reshape the direction of the individual's life. At the same time, however, clinicians, parents, and teachers struggle with the decision whether to apply diagnoses of a particular disorder to children who show behavioral disturbances. Once given a diagnosis, these children may be treated differently by others and experience effects that go beyond their initial symptoms. For example, is it right to give a psychiatric diagnosis to a boy who frequently loses his temper, argues with his parents, refuses to obey rules, acts in annoying ways, swears, and lies? How do these behaviors differ from those of the normal child going through phases such as the "terrible twos" or the rebellion of early adolescence? As you will learn, clinicians attempt to define these diagnoses as restrictively as possible to avoid confusing normal with abnormal development. Invariably, however, cases arise in which a clinician considers normal behavior as meeting the criteria for a psychological disorder.

Keep in mind that, by definition, neurodevelopmental disorders may show important changes over time. As individuals develop from childhood through adolescence and adulthood, they may experience maturational changes that alter the way their disorder manifests in particular behaviors. Fortunately, with appropriate interventions, clinicians can help children either learn to manage their symptoms or overcome the symptoms entirely.

5.1 Intellectual Disability (Intellectual Developmental Disorder)

The category of disorders marked by intellectual disability is used by clinicians to diagnose people who first began showing cognitive and adaptive deficits during childhood. The exact terminology used for these disorders varies across diagnostic systems, with the *ICD* using the term *intellectual developmental disorder*. The *DSM-IV-TR* used the term mental retardation to apply to this group of disorders, but the authors of the *DSM-5* preferred the term **intellectual disability**, in keeping with the American Association of Intellectual and Developmental Disabilities (AAIDD) recommendations, with the *ICD* term in parentheses. For the sake of brevity, we will refer to the disorder as intellectual disability, though technically the disorder should include "intellectual developmental disorder" as well.

To receive a diagnosis of intellectual disability, an individual must meet criteria that fall into three sets, with the first referring to deficits in the general intellectual abilities that an intelligence test might measure. These deficits include reasoning, problem solving, judgment, ability to learn from experience, and learning in an academic context. The cutoff for meeting this criterion is a measured intelligence of approximately 70 or below on a test considered appropriate for the individual's cultural and linguistic background.

The second set of criteria for a diagnosis of intellectual disability identifies impairments in adaptive functioning relative to a person's age and cultural group. These impairments occur in a variety of areas such as communicating, participating in social activities, and performing activities of daily living in an independent manner. People who show adaptive difficulties, for example, are unable to use money, cannot tell time, and relate inappropriately to others in social settings. As is true for measuring abilities with an intelligence test, clinicians should judge whether an individual's adaptive behavior is impaired using tests that are standardized, individualized, psychometrically sound, and culturally appropriate.

The third criterion is that age of onset must be under 18 years. It is most likely that individuals with this disorder would be brought to professional attention well before that age. Therefore, this criterion is not relevant for a first diagnosis in adulthood, unless for some reason the disability was missed when the individual was a child.

Having established the diagnosis of intellectual disability, the clinician must next rate the degree of severity. In past versions of the *DSM*, level of severity was based entirely on an individual's intelligence test performance. In *DSM-5,* the level of severity takes into account how well the individual is able to adapt in conceptual, social, and practical domains. Within each domain, clinicians rate their clients using four severity levels ranging from mild to profound. For example, in the conceptual domain, a mild level of severity would signify difficulties in learning academic skills, but the profound level would mean the individual is completely unable to think symbolically. Social skills similarly range from mild problems in emotional regulation to profound inability to engage in social interaction. Within the practical domain, the levels of severity range from the individual's needing support to carry out

intellectual disability (intellectual developmental disorder)
Diagnosis used to characterize individuals who have intellectual and adaptive deficits that first became evident when they were children.

MINI CASE

Intellectual Disability

Juanita is a 5-year-old Latina female with Down syndrome. Her mother was 43 when she and her husband decided to start their family. Because of her age, doctors advised Juanita's mother to have prenatal testing for any abnormalities in the chromosomal makeup of the developing fetus. Juanita's parents were shocked and distressed when they learned the test results. When Juanita was born, her parents knew what to expect in terms of the child's appearance, behavior, and possible medical problems, but fortunately she needed no special medical attention. Very early in Juanita's life, her parents

consulted with educational specialists, who recommended an enrichment program designed to maximize cognitive functioning. From age 6 months, Juanita attended a program each morning in which the staff made intensive efforts to facilitate her motor and intellectual development. Now that she is school age, Juanita will enter kindergarten at the local public school, where teachers will make efforts to bring her into the mainstream of education. Fortunately, Juanita lives in a school district where administrators recognize the importance of providing resources for pupils like Juanita so they will have the opportunity to learn and grow as normally as possible.

tasks such as shopping and money management to needing extensive training to perform even simple, everyday life tasks.

Compared to previous versions of the *DSM*, the combination of improved specificity in adaptive behavior criteria and inclusion of culturally sensitive tests can result in a more accurate basis for diagnosis and, ultimately, better treatment of individuals with intellectual developmental disorders.

Estimates show that approximately 1 percent of the world's population has intellectual disability, but the prevalence is higher in low-income countries (1.64 percent) than in countries classified as middle income (1.59 percent) or high income (1.54 percent). The highest prevalence occurs in urban slums or mixed rural-urban settings. Studies on children and adolescents also report higher prevalence rates than studies on adults. The costs to the economy associated with the care of these individuals can be burdensome, with lifetime estimates as high as $51.2 billion in the United States alone. Offsetting these costs are efforts to improve maternal and child health and interventions aimed at teaching adaptive skills to children with these disorders so they can live at higher functional levels (Maulik et al., 2011).

Causes of Intellectual Disability

Down syndrome
A form of intellectual disability caused most commonly when individuals inherit an extra copy of chromosome 21 and therefore have 47 chromosomes instead of the typical 46.

Genetic Abnormalities Abnormalities in the genes controlling prenatal development of the cortex are significant causes of intellectual disability. The three most important genetic causes are **Down syndrome**, phenylketonuria, and fragile X syndrome. Epigenetics also appears to play an important role in increasing an individual's risk of developing an intellectual disability (Iwase et al., 2017). The mother's lifestyle, diet, living conditions, and age can affect the expression of the genes she passes down to her child through mutations, deletions, or altered positions of genes on the chromosomes (Franklin & Mansuy, 2011). Although Down syndrome is associated with older maternal age, because the majority of women who give birth are under the age of 35 years old, there are more Down syndrome children born to younger mothers. Furthermore, because younger pregnant women are less likely to undergo genetic testing of their children, they may not actually learn that their child has Down syndrome until after the baby is born (Grinshpun-Cohen, Miron-Shatz, Ries-Levavi, & Pras, 2015).

The most common form of Down syndrome occurs when individuals inherit an extra copy of chromosome 21 and therefore have 47 chromosomes instead of the typical 46 (23 pairs). In this form of Down syndrome, called trisomy 21, the extra chromosome causes changes in the brain and a set of characteristic physical features. The symptoms of Down syndrome range from mild to severe and can vary from person to person. Down syndrome is in fact the most common cause of birth defects in humans. Estimates place the prevalence of Down syndrome at 11.1 per 10,000 live births in 2015, with about one-half the women who potentially would give birth to a child with Down syndrome voluntarily terminating the pregnancy (de Graaf et al., 2017).

The physical changes caused by the extra chromosome include a smaller-than-average head and neck with a flattened face, small ears, small mouth, upward-slanting eyes, excess skin at the nape of the neck, and white spots on the colored part of the eye. Additionally, individuals with Down syndrome are short in stature, and they never reach full adult height. The physical abnormalities include heart defects, eye cataracts, hearing loss, hip problems, digestive distress, sleep apnea, underactive thyroid, and teeth that appear later than normal and in locations that can lead to problems with chewing. Individuals with Down syndrome have a higher risk of developing Alzheimer's disease in middle age, suggesting a common underlying set of genetic mechanisms (Salehi, Ashford, & Mufson, 2016).

Behaviorally, in addition to lower IQ scores, individuals with Down syndrome are more likely to act impulsively, show poor judgment, be easily distractable, and become frustrated and angry over their limitations. The high levels of life stressors they face also make them vulnerable to developing major depressive disorder (Walton & Kerr, 2015).

Infants with **phenylketonuria (PKU)** are born missing an enzyme called phenylalanine hydroxase, which breaks down phenylalanine, an amino acid found in foods that contain protein. Shortly after birth, as phenylalanine builds up in the body, the infant can suffer irreversible damage. Untreated, PKU leads to developmental delays, a smaller than normal head size, hyperactivity, jerking arm and leg movements, seizures, skin rashes, and tremors. Fortunately, a simple blood test administered to all babies shortly after birth can diagnose PKU.

If they test positive, infants with PKU must then be placed on a diet low in phenylalanine, particularly early in life. This means they must avoid milk, eggs, and other common foods high in protein, as well as the artificial sweetener aspartame. To compensate, they are advised to eat foods high in fish oil, iron, and carnitine (a food additive that promotes energy production in the cell). There is no cure for PKU, so individuals with this disorder must maintain a strict diet throughout life. If they do not, they may develop attention-deficit/hyperactivity disorder. They may also show cognitive abnormalities on certain tasks even if they received proper care when they were first diagnosed (Banerjee, Grange, Steiner, & White, 2011).

In children born with **Tay-Sachs disease**, deficits in intellectual functioning occur due to a lack of hexosaminidase A, an enzyme that helps break down an otherwise toxic chemical in nervous tissue called ganglioside. The cause of Tay-Sachs disease is a defective gene on chromosome 15. For someone to develop the disease, both parents must have this genetic defect. If only one parent does, the child becomes a carrier and could transmit the disease to offspring if his or her partner also has the defective gene. The disease is most common among the Ashkenazi Jews, who are of Eastern European descent.

The symptoms of Tay-Sachs disease, in addition to developmental delays, include deafness, blindness, loss of muscle tone and motor skills, dementia, delayed reflexes, listlessness, paralysis, seizures, and slow growth. Although a milder form of Tay-Sachs disease can develop later in life, most individuals have the form that appears within the first 3 to 10 months after birth. The disease progresses rapidly, and most children with it do not live past the age of 4 or 5 years. There is no treatment for Tay-Sachs; however, prospective parents can receive genetic testing that may help prepare them for aspects of the disease before the child is born. Tay-Sachs screening may also be completed as part of premarital counseling, a situation

phenylketonuria (PKU)
Condition in which children are born missing an enzyme called phenylalanine hydroxase.

Tay-Sachs disease
An inherited disease that produces deficits in intellectual functioning due to a lack of hexosaminidase A, an enzyme that helps break down an otherwise toxic chemical in nervous tissue called ganglioside.

Children with Down syndrome suffer from a genetic abnormality that can lead to moderate to severe intellectual disability.
©Monkey Business Images/Getty Images

What's in the *DSM-5*

Neurodevelopmental Disorders

Many changes occurred in the organization of disorders of childhood when *DSM-5* was finalized. Perhaps the most significant was the relabeling of a large group of conditions with the term *neurodevelopmental*. Critics of *DSM-5* argue that this term presumes a theoretical model by attributing many of the disorders to biological causes that in the past clinicians viewed as reflecting multiple factors. Specifically, putting ADHD into this category suggests that the appropriate treatment would, in turn, focus on changing the individual's biology through medication.

The more generic category "specific learning disorder" replaced what had been separate disorders, such as mathematical skills disorder. The more generally accepted term *intellectual disability* replaced the term *mental retardation. Autistic spectrum disorder* replaced *autistic disorder*, and the term *Asperger's disorder* was completely eliminated. People who received the diagnosis of Asperger's disorder are now included in the autistic spectrum.

There were other major category shifts in the move to *DSM-5*. Separation anxiety disorder was included in disorders originating in childhood and is now included in the category of anxiety disorders. Oppositional defiant and conduct disorders moved to "disruptive, impulse control, and conduct disorders," a category we will discuss in the chapter "Personality Disorders". Pica, rumination disorder, and feeding disorder of infancy and early childhood moved to the category of "feeding and eating disorders."

By moving many of these childhood disorders to new or other existing categories, the *DSM-5* authors acknowledge the continuity of behavior from infancy through adulthood, a position consistent with life-span developmental principles. However, children may be more likely than they were in *DSM-IV-TR* to receive diagnoses that clinicians previously considered appropriate only for adults.

fragile X syndrome
A genetic disorder caused by a change in the gene FMRI.

that can create challenges for individuals who fear being stigmatized if they test positively (Rose et al., 2016).

The most common form of intellectual disability in males is **fragile X syndrome**, a genetic disorder caused by a change in the gene FMRI. A small part of the gene's code is repeated on a "fragile" area of the X chromosome, and the higher the number of repeats, the greater the deficit. Because males have only one X chromosome, this genetic defect is more likely to occur in this gender.

Boys with fragile X syndrome may appear normal for the most part, but they do show some physical abnormalities, including a large head circumference and subtle abnormalities of facial appearance such as a large forehead and long face, flat feet, large body size, and large testicles after they start puberty. Parents notice delays in achieving benchmarks such as crawling or walking, hyperactive or impulsive behavior, hand clapping or biting, speech and language delay, and a tendency to avoid eye contact. Females with this disorder may show no symptoms other than premature menopause or difficulty conceiving a child.

Clinicians also associate fragile X syndrome with hyperactivity and poor attention as well as other neurodevelopmental disorders, including autism spectrum disorder. These

In this 2013 photo, Ethan Fishman of Highland Park, then 20, hugs his mother Rebecca as they walk, to the office of Ethan's tutor in Winnetka, Illinois. Ethan suffers from fragile X syndrome, a genetic disorder.
©Chris Walker/Tribune News Service/Highland Park/IL/USA

behavioral disturbances, along with the expense of caring for children with this syndrome, can create stress in the family. A survey of more than a thousand families who had at least one child with fragile X syndrome revealed that over half experienced significant financial burden as a direct result of the disorder, and nearly 60 percent had to stop work or significantly change their work hours (Ouyang, Grosse, Raspa, & Bailey, 2010).

Environmental Hazards   Environmental hazards that mothers experience while pregnant are the second category of causes of intellectual disability. These hazards, called **teratogens**, include drugs or toxic chemicals and maternal malnutrition. Mothers may develop infections that alter the brain development of their unborn children, such as when they contract rubella (German measles) during the first 3 months of pregnancy. Infections, anoxia (oxygen deprivation) during birth, premature birth, and brain injury during delivery can also lead to brain damage and associated intellectual deficits in the child. Diseases, head injuries caused by accidents or child abuse, and exposure to toxic substances such as lead or carbon monoxide can also lead young children to suffer loss of intellectual capacity.

Environmental hazards may also take the form of substance use on the part of the mother during pregnancy. **Fetal alcohol syndrome (FAS)** is a condition associated with intellectual disability in a child whose mother consumed large amounts of alcohol on a regular basis while pregnant. Children with FAS develop specific facial abnormalities, slower than average growth patterns, and most importantly, nervous system delays that result in intellectual deficits. Children who have some exposure to alcohol prenatally may also develop a lesser form of FAS known as a **fetal alcohol spectrum disorder (FASD)**.

Because of the high risks associated with alcohol intake during pregnancy, medical guidelines err on the side of conservatism by recommending complete abstinence from alcohol during pregnancy. Occasional studies may suggest that some alcohol use will not hurt the developing child, but for many mothers, it is simply easier to refrain from alcohol use altogether.

Table 1 shows recommended diagnostic guidelines for FAS, based on the consensus of expert panels commissioned by the German government to arrive at criteria for a development-based diagnosis of full-blown fetal alcohol syndrome in children and adolescents.

Fetal alcohol syndrome causes children to be born with severe developmental and intellectual disabilities.
©Stuart Wong/KRT/Newscom

TABLE 1 Diagnosis of Fetal Alcohol Syndrome

Area of Functioning	Criteria
Growth abnormalities	Height, weight, or both at or below the 10th percentile (adjusted for age, sex, and race or ethnicity)
Facial abnormalities	Smooth ridge between nose and lip, thin edge around the lip, and small separation between upper and lower eyelids (based on racial norms)
Central nervous system abnormalities	Smaller head circumference and brain abnormalities visible on imaging Performance on functional measures substantially below that expected for an individual's age, schooling, or circumstances in areas such as speech, fine motor skills, attention, arithmetic skills, and social skills or behavior.
Maternal alcohol exposure	Confirmed prenatal alcohol exposure; if this information is not available, children who meet all three of the above criteria would be referred for further testing

SOURCE: Landgraf, M. N., Nothacker, M., Kopp, I. B., & Heinen, F. (2013). The diagnosis of fetal alcohol syndrome. *Deutsches Arzteblatt International, 110*(42), 703–710.

teratogens
Environmental hazards mothers experience while pregnant that affect the developing child.

fetal alcohol syndrome (FAS)
A condition associated with intellectual disability in a child whose mother consumed large amounts of alcohol on a regular basis while pregnant.

fetal alcohol spectrum disorder (FASD)
A lesser form of fetal alcohol syndrome developed in children who have some exposure to alcohol prenatally.

The cognitive deficits of children with FAS seem particularly pronounced in the area of executive functioning. Thus, such children find it difficult to perform tasks that require them to regulate their attentional control and perform mental manipulations (Kodituwakku, 2009). Although alcohol exposure affects the entire brain, children with FAS experience reduced brain volume and malformations of the corpus callosum, the tissue that connects the brain's two hemispheres (Lebel, Roussotte, & Sowell, 2011).

Epidemiologists estimate the prevalence of FAS at approximately 30 of every 1,000 children born per year in the United States (Centers for Disease Control and Prevention, 2015b). This means that among the approximately 4 million infants born in the United States each year, as many as 1,200 will have FAS, although these rates vary tremendously within particular subgroups of the population—economically disadvantaged groups, Native Americans, and other minorities have rates that are as high as 3 to 5 of every 1,000 births.

Children with FAS are at risk for a variety of negative outcomes as they mature, including dropping out of school, committing criminal acts, and developing diagnoses of other mental health problems including substance use disorders. Their adaptive abilities are challenged further by the tendency to engage in inappropriate sexual behavior, and they have difficulty living independently and staying employed (Bertrand et al., 2004).

Treatment of Intellectual Disability

People with intellectual disability can benefit from early intervention aimed at providing them with training in motor coordination, language use, and social skills. Educators can combine **mainstreaming**, which integrates these children into ordinary school classrooms, with special education that provides them with assistance geared to their particular needs.

mainstreaming
A governmental policy to integrate fully into society people with cognitive disabilities.

Moving outside the classroom and into daily life, individuals with intellectual disability experience limitations in their ability to carry out activities of daily living as well as their understanding of social situations. Therefore, treatment for these individuals often takes the form of behavioral or social interventions that train them to cope with such demands. Some of the services they can benefit from include coordinated care that integrates behavioral treatment, outreach, and multidisciplinary assessment. It may also be helpful to provide them with treatment of related conditions, including depression, anxiety disorder, bipolar disorder, or an autism spectrum disorder (Richings, Cook, & Roy, 2011).

Of course, to the extent that it is possible, prevention rather than treatment is preferable to reduce the risk of intellectual disabilities. In the case of FAS, education and counseling seem to have the greatest potential value. Unfortunately, there is limited evidence to show that such programs actually reduce alcohol consumption in pregnant women or, more importantly, produce beneficial effects on children (Stade et al., 2009).

Once they are born, children identified as having FAS can benefit from several protective factors that reduce the impact of their disorder on their later adaptation and development. Early diagnosis can help educators place children in appropriate classes and get them the social services that can help them and their families. Enrollment in special education focused specifically on their needs and learning styles can be particularly beneficial. They can also benefit from learning appropriate ways to control their anger or frustration so they do not become involved in youth violence (Centers for Disease Control and Prevention, 2011a).

Friendship training is one behavioral intervention that can help children with FAS learn how to interact appropriately with other children so they can make and keep friends. This type of training teaches a combination of social skills such as how to play with other children, arrange and handle play dates in the home, and work out or avoid conflicts (O'Connor et al., 2006). Cognitive interventions that focus on taking into account the specific executive function deficits of children with FAS can help improve their school performance. These methods include using concrete examples, repeating information, and breaking a problem down into parts (Kodituwakku & Kodituwakku, 2011). Parents also need to learn how to better manage their children's behaviors, which ultimately reduces their distress and therefore leads to a less stressful home environment.

Although psychological methods of intervention have traditionally been the primary focus for children with FAS, promising leads in the biological approach rely on neural stem cell implantation. Neural stem cells are undifferentiated cells that have the capacity to differentiate into neural cells that lack the defects of the cells already growing in the individual's nervous system. If these could be used in children with FAS, the process of neural development could be altered and normal cells could grow in place of those that were damaged by exposure to alcohol during fetal brain growth (Lippert, Gelineau, Napoli, & Borlongan, 2018).

5.2 Autism Spectrum Disorder

The neurodevelopmental disorder commonly called "autism" is titled **autism spectrum disorder** in *DSM-5* and involves impairments in the domains of social communication and the performance of restricted, repetitive behaviors. This disorder incorporates a range of serious disturbances in the ways that individuals interact with and communicate with others, as well as certain patterns of interests and activities they tend to have. The constellation of diagnostic criteria associated with this disorder can persist throughout life, but depending on severity, it is possible for individuals to improve over time, particularly if they receive appropriate help.

The *DSM-5* diagnosis of autism spectrum disorder replaces the *DSM-IV-TR* term *autistic disorder*, which in the old terminology was in a separate category from Asperger's disorder, childhood disintegrative disorder, and pervasive developmental disorder not otherwise specified. The current term provides a more reliable and valid distinction between children who clearly show typical development and those who demonstrate a range of deficits in communication and social behaviors. The term *autism spectrum disorder* reflects a consensus among the scientists writing the *DSM-5* that four disorders previously considered to be separate are a single condition with differing levels of severity that rest on a continuum.

To diagnose autism spectrum disorder, clinicians evaluate children along two core domains. The first includes disturbances in social relationships and communication. The second domain incorporates the individual's interests and behaviors. These interests occupy a narrow but intense range of hobbies or expertise. The behaviors exhibited by children with autism spectrum disorder are distinguished by extreme repetition and rigidity. Within each domain, clinicians specify one of three severity levels based on the amount of support required, ranging from some to substantial to very substantial.

In the area of communication, children with autism spectrum disorder may show developmental delays in the use of language. People with other disorders also show delayed language, so this quality is not unique to autism spectrum disorder. More typical of autism spectrum disorder are deficits in the social aspects of communication. Individuals with this

autism spectrum disorder
A neurodevelopmental disorder involving impairments in the domains of social communication and the performance of restricted, repetitive behaviors.

MINI CASE

Autism Spectrum Disorder

Jeong is a 6-year-old Chinese American male currently receiving treatment at a residential school for children with intellectual disabilities. As an infant, Jeong did not respond well to his parents' efforts to play with and hold him. His mother noticed that his whole body seemed to stiffen when she picked him up from his crib. No matter how much she tried, she could not entice Jeong to smile. When she tried to play games by tickling his toes or touching his nose, he averted his eyes and looked out the window. Not until Jeong was 18 months old did his mother first realize that his behavior reflected more than just a quiet temperament—that he was, in fact, developing abnormally. Jeong never did develop an attachment to people; instead, he clung to a small piece of wood he carried with him everywhere. His mother often found him rocking his body in a corner, clinging to his piece of wood. Jeong's language, though, finally indicated serious disturbance. At an age when most children start to put together short sentences, Jeong was still babbling incoherently. His babbling did not sound like that of a normal infant. He said the same syllable over and over again—usually the last syllable of something that had just been said to him—in a high-pitched, monotone voice. Perhaps the most bizarre feature of Jeong's speech was that he did not direct it to the listener. Jeong seemed to be communicating in a world of his own.

Hodan Hassan is shown at her Minneapolis home with her 6-year-old daughter Geni, who has autism spectrum disorder. Health officials struggling to contain a measles outbreak that hit Minneapolis's large Somali community hard met resistance from parents who feared the vaccine could give their children autism.

©Jim Mone/AP Images

echolalia
Repetition of the same sounds over and over.

disorder may avoid eye contact, and their facial expressions, gestures, and even posture may strike others as odd or unusual. For example, individuals with the disorder may find it difficult to understand the body language of others, and their own body language may strike others as odd and extremely awkward.

Unlike normally developing children, those with autism spectrum disorder do not seem to enjoy playing with others, sharing experiences, or engaging in the usual give-and-take of social interactions. In extreme cases, they may completely avoid social interactions, or at least not attempt to initiate interactions with other people. Imaginative play, an essential component of normal development, presents these children with particular challenges. They may be unable to engage in the type of imitative play patterns that characterize the ordinary social interactions of young children in which they copy each other as they share toys and play games.

Separate from the deficient communication and social patterns of people with autism spectrum disorder are disturbances in motor behavior in which they engage in restricted or repetitive behaviors, such as tapping their fingers incessantly or twisting their bodies around in unusual poses. The repetitive behaviors can also affect their speech, taking the form of **echolalia**, in which they repeat the same sounds over and over again. Repeating the same routines without permitting any changes may be another manifestation of their disorder. Although many children prefer certain routines, for children with autism spectrum disorder, any variation in such everyday activities as getting dressed or eating breakfast can become highly upsetting.

Particularly distressing to families are the disturbances that some individuals with autism spectrum disorder show in their altered sensitivity to sensory stimuli. They may seem almost impervious to pain, heat, or cold, and as a result they can easily place themselves at risk of significant injury. On the other hand, their sensory abnormalities may take the form of hypersensitivity to noise, light, or smell, leaving them unable to withstand normal atmospheric sights and sounds.

The unusual characteristics of autism spectrum disorder may change substantially as children move into their teenage years and beyond. In one large cross-sectional study comparing children, adolescents, and adults, the ability to interact with others was less impaired among the adolescents than among the adults, and the adults were less impaired in the area of repetitive, restricted behaviors (Seltzer et al., 2003).

One variant of autism spectrum disorder, called autistic savant syndrome, occurs when people possess an extraordinary skill such as the ability to perform extremely complicated numerical operations almost instantaneously. They may, for example, be able to name correctly and with certainty the day of the week on which a date thousands of years away will fall (Thioux, Stark, Klaiman, & Schultz, 2006). Autistic savant syndrome typically appears at an early age, when a young child with the disorder appears to have exceptional musical skills, artistic talent, or the ability to solve extremely challenging puzzles. It is possible that the tendency to focus intensely on the physical attributes of objects gives people this uncanny set of abilities. Their memory in areas outside their areas of expertise appears to be no better than that of people with autism spectrum disorder who do not have these special memory skills (Neumann et al., 2010).

Some children with autism spectrum disorder appear to develop normally for the first 2 years but, at some point before age 10, start to lose language and motor skills as well as other adaptive functions, including bowel and bladder control. This rare condition was formerly called childhood disintegrative disorder, but the diagnosis was eliminated from *DSM-5* and is now incorporated into autism spectrum disorder.

Autistic savants often excel in one specific skill, such as playing an entire song on the piano from memory after hearing it only one time.
©Boston Globe/Getty Images

In 2007, the Centers for Disease Control and Prevention reported an estimated prevalence rate in the United States of 0.66 percent or approximately 1 of every 150 children, which itself was a large increase from previously reported rates. Over subsequent years, however, the prevalence estimates have continued to increase, reaching, among people born in 2002, an estimated 1 in 68 living within 11 communities tracked throughout the United States (Centers for Disease Control and Prevention, 2015a). The reasons for this increase are not clear, though one set of Danish researchers attribute the rise, at least in their country, to changes in reporting practices (Hansen, Schendel, & Parner, 2015).

Part of the issue in estimating prevalence is that standards for diagnosis vary considerably across studies, as do the sources of information used for establishing a diagnosis. The question is whether children are actually interviewed or the researchers use clinical case summaries, in which the ratings are made from the child's records. To establish better diagnostic precision, researchers recommend using standardized instruments based on interview and observation of the child, rather than relying on case records (Wiggins et al., 2015).

Theories and Treatment of Autism Spectrum Disorder

Evidence pointing to patterns of familial inheritance supports the theory that autism spectrum disorder is biologically based. Researchers estimate the heritability of the disorder to be high, at approximately 90 percent, and associated with genetic abnormalities suspected to exist on chromosomes 7, 2, and 15.

Advances in brain-scanning techniques, coupled with a movement to share data among international researchers, are helping to clarify possible neurological abnormalities in people with autism spectrum disorder. Some evidence suggests altered brain activity during periods of wakefulness while the individual is at rest. This pattern may indicate a deficiency in the sharing of information between the two hemispheres of the brain. Such findings are promising, but, as the researchers involved are the first to admit, they do not necessarily explain the behavioral abnormalities associated with autism spectrum disorder (Rane et al., 2015).

Even as research on neurological abnormalities in individuals with autism spectrum disorder is advancing, the behavioral perspective remains the most realistic approach to treatment. Clinicians treating children with this disorder from a behavioral perspective base their methods

With early therapeutic intervention, children who are diagnosed with autism spectrum disorder can experience significant symptom improvement.

Courtesy of the Mary Black Foundation and Carroll Foster

on the early intervention programs devised by UCLA psychologist Ivar Lovaas in the late 1980s (Lovaas, 1987). In the original report on the program, Lovaas and his associates randomly assigned 38 children ages 3 to 4 diagnosed with autism spectrum disorder to two treatment groups. One group received intervention for at least 40 hours per week for 2 or more years. Children in the second group received treatment with the same intervention for less than 10 hours per week. Another group of children received treatment outside the Lovaas clinic. Using IQ scores as dependent variables, nearly half (9) the 19 children who received intensive treatment increased by over 20 points; by age 13, 8 of the children had maintained their IQ gains. By contrast, only 1 child in the less intensive treatment showed these IQ improvements. The Lovaas studies, as impressive as they were, received criticism from other researchers because the study never assessed the intervention's effects on social and communication skills.

The Lovaas treatment rests on principles of operant conditioning, practiced both by student therapists and by parents. The behavioral aspects of the intervention consisted of ignoring the child's aggressive and self-stimulatory behaviors, using time-outs when children were disruptive, and positively attending to the children only when they engaged in socially appropriate behavior, using shaping to increase the performance of the targeted behaviors. As a last resort, when children engaged in undesirable behavior, they were given a loud "no" or a slap on the thigh.

In the first year, the treatment focused on reducing self-stimulatory and aggressive behaviors, shaping the children to comply with simple verbal requests, using imitation learning, establishing the beginnings of play with toys, and extending the treatment into the family home. In the second year of the intervention, the children learned how to use language in an expressive and abstract manner. They also learned how to play interactively with their peers. In the third year, the children learned how to express emotions appropriately, completed academic tasks to prepare them for school, and engaged in observational learning in which they learned by watching other children learn. The clinicians attempted to place the children in mainstream classes rather than special education classes, with the idea that others would not then label them as "autistic" or "difficult." Children who did not recover received an additional 6 years of training. The others remained in contact with the project team for occasional consultation.

In the years following Lovaas's study, a number of researchers attempted to replicate his findings. Reviewing 14 of the best controlled of these studies, Makrygianni and Reed (2010) concluded that the weight of evidence supports the use of behavioral early-intervention projects. These programs are effective in improving the children's intellectual, linguistic, communication, and social abilities. The more intensive the program, and the longer it lasts, the stronger the impact on the children. However, intensive programs of 25 hours per week were sufficient to provide a beneficial effect, rather than the 40 hours per week of the Lovaas program. In addition, as we would expect, children who are younger and those who are higher functioning at the outset improve more through treatment. Programs are also more successful if they involve parents and use some combination of home- and clinic-based approaches (Leaf et al., 2017).

Children with autism spectrum disorder will show a decrease in disruptive and self-stimulatory behaviors if they receive reinforcement for appropriate behaviors, such as asking for help or feedback. Such reinforcement can make them less likely to engage in self-injurious or aggressive behaviors. In this type of treatment, clinicians find it more useful to focus on changing pivotal behaviors, with the secondary goal of bringing about improvements in other behaviors, rather than focusing on changing isolated behavioral disturbances. The therapist may also help a child develop new learning skills that will give him or her some experiences of success in problem solving. For example, the therapist might teach the child to break a large problem, such as getting dressed, into smaller tasks the child can accomplish. As a result the child feels less frustrated and is therefore less likely to regress to problem behaviors, such as rocking and head banging. Clinicians also focus on the need to motivate the child to communicate more effectively. The child will then be more ready to respond to social and environmental stimuli, which is the key to treatment (Koegel, Koegel, & McNerney, 2001). Over time, children in treatment will be more motivated to regulate and initiate behaviors on their own. Even simple changes can have this impact, such as having the child, rather than the clinician, choose the materials, toys, and activities for the intervention.

Another approach to intervention is to have peers rather than adults interact with the child. This situation approximates a more normal type of social environment, in which children typically serve a powerful role in modifying a peer's behavior. In contrast to interventions in which adults provide the reinforcement, peer-mediated interventions have the advantage of allowing children to carry on with their ordinary activities without adult interruption. The most effective engage younger boys whose older male siblings provide the intervention, use peer modeling, attempt to generalize across situations, and involve collaboration among family members and with school staff (Zhang & Wheeler, 2011).

Other behavioral strategies include self-control procedures, such as self-monitoring, relaxation training, and covert conditioning. Children can also learn to touch an icon of a "frowny" face to indicate their displeasure rather than act out aggressively when they are upset or unhappy (Martin, Drasgow, Halle, & Brucker, 2005). Token economies are another behavioral intervention that may produce value for some children (Fiske et al., 2015).

Reinforcement may also help advance additional clinical goals. As adults, individuals with autism spectrum disorder do not spontaneously choose to exercise. There is evidence supporting the use of reinforcers to help instill better exercise habits (LaLonde et al., 2014). Such an approach can benefit their health and may have the added plus of improving their overall well-being.

Taking advantage of new technologies, future treatments of children with autism spectrum disorder may be able to rely increasingly on such methods as virtual reality. In a 28-session virtual reality–based intervention lasting 14 weeks, researchers were able to demonstrate improved adaptation in some measures of social and emotional functioning among a community sample of children 6 to 12 years of age (Ip et al., 2018). This approach has been known for decades, but only relatively recently has virtual reality become more widely available.

Rett Syndrome

In **Rett syndrome**, the child develops normally early in life (up to age 4) and then begins to show neurological and cognitive impairments including deceleration of head growth and some of the symptoms of autism spectrum disorder. The syndrome occurs almost exclusively in females.

Rett syndrome
A condition in which the child develops normally early in life (up to age 4) and then begins to show neurological and cognitive impairments including deceleration of head growth and some of the symptoms of autism spectrum disorder.

The symptoms of Rett syndrome begin to appear after about 5 months of age.
©Megan Sorel Photography

Although not a separate diagnosis in *DSM-5*, Rett syndrome was a topic of clinical and research focus after its introduction in the *DSM-IV-TR*.

Clinicians who would have diagnosed children as having Rett syndrome prior to *DSM-5*'s elimination of this diagnosis now use the autism spectrum diagnosis. However, by specifying that the children have a known genetic or medical condition, they are able to indicate that the symptoms are related to Rett syndrome.

Researchers identified the gene for Rett syndrome in 1999. Mutations in this gene, which is named MECP2, lead to abnormalities in the production of a specific protein important in the normal functioning of neurons. There is hope that studies of the genes in mouse models will prove useful in the treatment of children with this disorder. Until then, one clinical trial of dextromethorphan (a type of cough medicine) showed encouraging results in reducing the neurological symptoms and improving language and behavioral symptoms of the disorder (Smith-Hicks et al., 2017).

High-Functioning Autism Spectrum Disorder, Formerly Called Asperger's Disorder

Asperger's disorder
A term once used to describe individuals with high-functioning autism spectrum disorder.

As we pointed out earlier, **Asperger's disorder** is not in the *DSM-5*. Its symptoms continue to define the high-functioning end of the autism spectrum, and therefore, although not part of the nomenclature, it is worth its own coverage here.

The term *Asperger's disorder* is named after Hans Asperger, a Viennese physician who, during World War II, described a group of boys who possessed rather good language and cognitive skills but had marked social problems because they acted like pompous "little professors" and were physically awkward. Indeed, high-functioning people on the autism spectrum have less severe and more focused impairments than their lower-functioning counterparts, perhaps showing their symptoms only after they reach preschool age. At that point, when most children develop social and interactive skills, these children have difficulty reading the social cues of others and taking turns talking, and they are unable to interpret language subtleties. Early in their lives, they tend to become preoccupied with a narrow set of interests about which they may talk extensively, not realizing that such one-sided conversations are not socially appropriate. However, they are more likely than children at the lower-functioning end of the autism spectrum to try to make friends.

REAL STORIES

Daniel Tammet: Autism Spectrum Disorder

In many ways, Daniel Tammet's developmental journey followed a path typical of most children's, although several aspects of his childhood set him apart from others. Tammet was 26 years old when he wrote his autobiography, *Born on a Blue Day*, which describes his experiences in vivid detail.

Born in 1979, Tammet was the first child of an English couple living in poverty who went on to have eight more children after him. As an infant, Tammet cried inconsolably except when eating or sleeping. The doctors believed it was simply a case of colic, and the crying was a phase that would quickly end. In the book, Tammet reflects on what he has come to understand about the early period in his life: "My parents tell me I was a loner, not mixing with the other children, and described by the supervisors as being absorbed in my own world. The contrast between my earliest years and that time must have been vivid for my parents, evolving as I did from a screaming, crying, head-banging baby to a quiet, self-absorbed, aloof toddler. With hindsight, they realize now that the change was not necessarily the sign of improvement they took it to be at the time. I became almost too good–too quiet and too undemanding."

When Tammet was a child, the scientific world knew little about developmental disorders, and his parents could not understand what their son was experiencing. In the book, he describes how they did their best to provide him with a normal childhood, possibly based on their own fears of what it meant to have a child with a developmental disorder. When friends or neighbors questioned his parents, they would say that Tammet was just sensitive or shy.

At the age of 4, Tammet began having seizures, and doctors eventually diagnosed him with temporal lobe epilepsy. The condition caused major problems with his sleeping, and he took medication for about 3 years until the seizures subsided. His doctors now believe that these seizures led to savant syndrome, a rare condition from which Tammet suffers. Tammet describes his synesthesia (a neurologically based condition in which sensory or cognitive pathway stimulation leads to automatic, involuntary experiences in a second sensory or cognitive

In *Born on a Blue Day,* Daniel Tammet describes his childhood experiences with autism spectrum disorder and savant syndrome, at a time when scientists knew very little about either condition.
©Photoshot/Getty Images

pathway) as causing a blurring of his senses and emotions when someone presents him with numbers or words. He writes, "The word *ladder,* for example, is blue and shiny, while *hoop* is a soft, white word."

Much like others with savant syndrome, Tammet also has a diagnosis of autism spectrum disorder, and throughout the book he describes having many experiences during his childhood that are consistent with the diagnosis. He recalls that as a child he took comfort in the daily routines at school and would become highly anxious should the routines be upset in any way. Many of his classmates teased him for his unusual quirks, such as uncontrollably flapping his arms. When he was feeling particularly anxious, he would bang his head against a wall, and he would run home to his parents' house when he felt overwhelmed during school. Looking back, Tammet wonders, "What must the other children have made of me? I don't know, because I have no memory of them at all. To me they were the background to my visual and tactile experiences."

Tammet had an especially difficult time connecting with other children at school. He describes spending most of his childhood in isolation, where he learned to comfort himself by making up games,

thinking about numbers, or fanatically collecting small items such as chestnuts and coins. Although his parents tried hard to get him to socialize outside the home with his siblings and other children, Tammet found it difficult to be away from home comforts. He made friends with children whom others regarded as outsiders in the classroom, but generally he preferred to keep to himself. As Tammet transitioned to high school, he continued to find it difficult to relate to others and maintained an almost obsessive interest in his studies, particularly history. He also struggled with some subjects, especially those that required interaction with others.

As his body was adjusting to adulthood, Tammet recalls feeling the typical rush of hormones and increased interest in relationships, although his social skills made peer relationships excessively awkward and hard to sustain. Making social interactions more difficult was Tammet's inability to understand his emotions and the catalysts that led to certain emotional reactions. As he recalls, "All I knew is that I wanted to be close to someone, and not understanding closeness as being primarily emotional, I would walk up to some of the other students in the playground and stand very close to them until I could feel the warmth of their body heat against my skin. I still had no concept of personal space, that what I was doing made other people feel uncomfortable around me." During adolescence, Tammet became unquestionably aware that he was attracted to other boys and even recalls having his first crush and making a subsequent disappointing attempt at dating.

After finishing high school, Tammet decided not to attend college and instead took a job with Voluntary Services Overseas, a charity focused on international development. As part of the work, he lived in Lithuania for a year and found the experience to be a crucial part of his development into adulthood. Of what he learned from his time in Lithuania he writes, "For one thing, I had learned a great deal about myself. I could see more clearly than ever before how my 'differences' affected my day-to-day life, especially my interactions with other people. I had eventually come to understand that friendship was a delicate, gradual process that mustn't be rushed or seized upon, but allowed and encouraged to take its course over time."

Tammet writes about struggling to find a job after returning home to England, due to his difficulties functioning not only in social settings, but also in job interviews that required him to think about abstract, theoretical situations. As Tammet explains, he does not easily adjust to novel situations. Eventually, he started an online program that teaches different languages, which has become successful over the years.

Around the time he returned from Lithuania, Tammet met the man who would become his life partner, Neil. They connected in an online chat group and exchanged e-mails for many months before finally meeting in person. Tammet explains that it was much easier for him to communicate electronically with Neil while they got to know each other, because it did not require complex social skills.

Through their relationship, Tammet writes that he has learned to be more open with others, and that Neil's support has been a source of immense strength that has helped him learn to cope with autism. Tammet's savant syndrome grants him the ability to see letters and numbers as colors and textures and has led to some remarkable lifetime achievements. For example, Tammet has taught himself to speak at least 10 languages, including Icelandic, which he learned in just 4 days for his part in a documentary film. In 2005, Tammet set the British and European records for reciting 22,514 digits of pi in just over 5 hours. Although he has gained considerable media attention for his extraordinary abilities, Tammet enjoys a quiet life, which he spends mostly at home where he takes pleasure in his daily routines. He has also found strength through attending church and especially enjoys the ritual aspect of it. From time to time he gives talks for the National Autistic Society and the National Society for Epilepsy, and he writes that he hopes to continue contributing to an understanding and acceptance of developmental disorders. Tammet has gone on to write another book, *Embracing the Wide Sky*, in addition to many other articles and public appearances.

SOURCE: Tammet, Daniel, 2007, *Born on a Blue Day: Inside the Extraordinary Mind of an Autistic Savant,* New York, NY: Free Press.

In one fascinating case described in the literature (Volkmar et al., 2000), an 11-year-old boy, Robert, had the verbal abilities of a 17-year-old but the social skills of a 3-year-old. Although Robert had remarkable knowledge of the stars, planets, and time, his exclusive intellectual devotion to these subjects kept him from acquiring other kinds of knowledge. Peers rejected him because of his one-sided and naïve overtures. His case highlights the complex nature of autism spectrum disorder for individuals at the high-functioning end of the continuum. In the early years of life, parents are more likely to view their child as especially gifted rather than as suffering from a serious impairment. As the children get older, their problems become more prominent, and it is then that parents and educators may seek to intervene.

Whether called Asperger's or not, the form of autism spectrum disorder that involves higher levels of functioning can be one with which individuals learn to cope and even thrive. Career planning in this regard is particularly important, taking into account people's strengths and the demands of potential employment positions (Mynatt, Gibbons, & Hughes, 2014). For example, if they have the aptitude, they would seem well-suited for careers in fields such as science and engineering in which their intensity can lead to success in research and development. In addition, as adults they may be able to gain considerable self-insight into their strengths and weaknesses as they also learn to acquire social skills.

5.3 Learning and Communication Disorders

Specific Learning Disorder

specific learning disorder
A delay or deficit in an academic skill that is evident when an individual's achievement and skills are substantially below what would be expected for others of comparable age, education, and level of intelligence.

Children who have a **specific learning disorder** experience a delay or deficit in their ability to acquire a basic academic skill. These difficulties become evident when their achievement and skills are substantially below the level of performance based on their age, education, and measured intelligence. Within this general category, clinicians also specify which academic domain the disorder affects and its level of severity (mild, moderate, or severe).

In the United States, researchers estimate that approximately 8 percent of children have a diagnosed learning disorder (Centers for Disease Control and Prevention, 2015b). The factors that appear to increase a child's risk of developing a learning disorder include a number of sociocultural factors: lower socioeconomic status, growing up in a two-parent stepfamily, being adopted, and being raised in the presence of a smoker. Other psychosocial family risk factors include having parents who experience more difficulty in parenting, fail to share ideas with children, and do not openly discuss disagreements in the home (Altarac & Saroha, 2007). These parenting difficulties may stem in part from the parents themselves having had a poorer reading history and feeling that their children are more anxious and depressed than parents of children with typical developmental trajectories (Bonifacci, Storti, Tobia, & Suardi, 2016).

Individuals with **specific learning disorder with impairment in mathematics** have difficulty with tasks and concepts relying on numbers and numerical reasoning; they may be unable to understand mathematical terms, symbols, or concepts. Some may have **dyscalculia**, a pattern of difficulties in number sense, ability to learn arithmetic facts, and calculations. A school-age child with this disorder may have problems completing homework. An adult may be unable to balance a checkbook because of difficulty performing addition and subtraction.

There are serious long-term consequences of having a specific learning disorder with impairment in mathematics. Apart from the impact on school performance, individuals with this disorder will face greater challenges in the job market and as adults may have lower income, higher risk of being sick, and even a higher risk of mortgage default (Kuhn, 2015).

In **specific learning disorder with impairment in written expression**, individuals have difficulty spelling, properly using grammatical or punctuation rules, and organizing paragraphs. Such challenges lead children to have serious problems in many academic subjects. For adults, the disorder of written expression can create numerous interpersonal and practical problems. Fewer job opportunities will be open to them, particularly if their symptoms place them in the severe level of functioning.

Individuals with **specific learning disorder with impairment in reading**, commonly called **dyslexia**, omit, distort, or substitute words when they read. Consequently, they read in a slow, halting fashion. Their disorder can cause children to fail to show adequate progress in a variety of school subjects. Like other individuals with specific learning disorders, as adults these individuals also experience lower educational attainment and occupational success (Smart et al., 2017).

The core features of these disorders seem to be deficits in the planning and programming of behavior, not difficulties in motor execution, motor control across brain hemispheres, or visual or visual perceptual disorders (Vaivre-Douret et al., 2011b). Practitioners believe the best way to identify children with learning disorders is the response to intervention (RTI) approach, which consists of evidence-based procedures that follow a series of steps. First, practitioners use screening criteria to identify at-risk children. Next, the children identified as being at risk receive a well-established intervention for a specific period of time. Those children who do not benefit from this intervention receive an even more intensive intervention. At this point, the children who do not benefit from the treatment are classified as having learning disorders. To aid in diagnosis, the children also undergo a comprehensive evaluation using information from multiple sources, including standardized tests (Büttner & Shamir, 2011).

For the majority of children with specific developmental disorders, schools are the primary intervention site. An interdisciplinary team consisting of various professionals—for example, a school psychologist, a special education teacher, the classroom teacher, a speech language therapist, and possibly a neurologist—design a treatment plan. Typically, children with these disorders require more structure, fewer distractions, and a presentation of new material that uses more than one sensory modality at a time. For example, the instructor may teach math concepts by using oral presentation combined with hands-on manipulation of objects. Teaching children through the use of heuristics can also be beneficial. In this method the child learns a general strategy for approaching any problem, not just the way to solve specific problems (Geary, 2011). Perhaps most important is building on the child's strengths, so he or she can feel a sense of accomplishment and increased self-esteem.

As adults, individuals with learning disorders can benefit from vocational rehabilitation programs designed specifically for their needs. Partnering with employers, such approaches identify areas in which new employees are in need of training while they learn the skills

specific learning disorder with impairment in mathematics
A learning disorder in which the individual has difficulty with tasks and concepts involving numbers and numerical reasoning.

dyscalculia
A pattern of difficulties in number sense, ability to learn arithmetic facts, and calculations.

specific learning disorder with impairment in written expression
A learning disorder in which the individual's writing is characterized by poor spelling, grammatical or punctuation errors, and disorganization of paragraphs.

specific learning disorder with impairment in reading (dyslexia)
A learning disorder in which the individual omits, distorts, or substitutes words when reading and reads in a slow, halting fashion.

This Project Search Team of Miami is a one-year School-To-Work Transition Program designed for students with disabilities who are in their last year of high school and are pursuing a special diploma.

©Jeff Greenberg/Getty Images

required for their particular jobs (see Table 2) (Müller & VanGilder, 2014). Rehabilitation can reduce the otherwise negative consequences associated with the long-term impact of learning disorders that emerge during the school years, allowing individuals to lead more fulfilling adult lives.

Training in Job Skills for Young Adults with Learning Disabilities　Project Search, a business-led transition program for high school students, is intended to provide on-the-job training for young adults. In one test of its effectiveness (Müller & VanGilder, 2014), the program successfully improved job readiness by focusing on both specific job skills and overall "soft skills" in the following areas:

TABLE 2

Job Skills Overall	Soft Skills
Copying	Work ethic
Organizing supplies	Self-esteem
Assembly/collating/labeling	Remaining on task
E-mailing	Meeting deadlines
Using Microsoft Word and Excel	Flexibility in handling change
Delivering	Interacting with supervisors and co-workers
Lifting	Calling in when sick or late
	Traveling to and from work
	Navigating the workplace

Communication Disorders

Communication disorders are conditions characterized by impairment in language, speech, and communication. Children with **language disorder** lack the ability to express themselves in ways appropriate to their age and developmental level. They use limited and faulty vocabulary and speak in short sentences with simplified grammatical structures, omitting critical words or phrases. They may also put words together in a peculiar order. A person with this disorder may, for example, always use the present tense, saying, "I have a good time yesterday" instead of "I had." Developmental delays may cause expressive language disorders, but similar symptoms can arise from a medical illness or head injury.

The expressive difficulties of some people are characterized not by their inability to understand or express language, but by difficulties specific to speech. A person with **speech sound disorder** substitutes, omits, or incorrectly articulates speech sounds. For example, a child may use a *t* sound for the letter *k*, saying "tiss" rather than "kiss." People often regard the mispronunciations of children as cute; however, these childhood speech patterns are likely to cause academic problems as the child grows older and is ridiculed by other children in school.

Children who experience **childhood-onset fluency disorder** or **stuttering** are unable to produce fluent speech. They may emit verbalizations such as sound repetitions and prolongations, broken words, the blocking out of sounds, word substitutions to avoid problematic words, and words expressed with an excess of tension. Although it is difficult to determine cause and effect, a team of Australian researchers demonstrated a strong negative correlation between stuttering severity and educational attainment. It is possible that this relationship reflects, at least in part, the long-term consequences faced by children whose speech problems create negative experiences in their early school years (O'Brian et al., 2011). However, over the long term, these individuals may better come to cope with their speech disorder and, by their sixties, feel less distressed by the impact it has on their lives (Freud et al., 2017).

Children who have **social** or **pragmatic communication disorder** have deficits in their ability to use verbal and nonverbal communication in relating to others. They have problems adjusting their behavior to the social context, such as by knowing how to greet people or interpret the way others greet them. In addition, they are unable to match their communication with the needs of the listener, such as by talking in different ways to children and adults. In a conversation, they have difficulties following the ordinary conventions of taking turns when speaking. Finally, they have trouble understanding implicit or ambiguous meanings such as expressions used in humor and metaphors. These deficits can make it difficult for individuals not only to communicate effectively, but also to perform on the job and participate in ordinary social interactions.

communication disorders
Neurodevelopmental disorders involving impairment in language, speech, and communication.

language disorder
A communication disorder characterized by having a limited and faulty vocabulary, speaking in short sentences with simplified grammatical structures, omitting critical words or phrases, and putting words together in peculiar order.

speech sound disorder
A communication disorder in which the individual substitutes, omits, or misarticulates speech sounds.

childhood-onset fluency disorder (stuttering)
A communication disorder that involves a disturbance in the normal fluency and patterning of speech characterized by such verbalizations as sound repetitions or prolongations, broken words, the blocking out of sounds, word substitutions to avoid problematic words, or words expressed with an excess of tension.

social (pragmatic) communication disorder
Disorder involving deficits in the ability to use verbal and nonverbal communication in relating to others.

5.4 Attention-Deficit/Hyperactivity Disorder (ADHD)

One of the most commonly recognized psychological disorders in popular media is **attention-deficit/hyperactivity disorder (ADHD)**, a neurodevelopmental disorder characterized by a persistent pattern of inattention and/or hyperactivity. In all likelihood, you have heard the term *ADHD* in its common sense. Like autism spectrum disorder, ADHD now has a broad meaning that many people use to describe a child or adult whose symptoms are readily apparent in a variety of social and educational settings. Sensitized to the disorder by media coverage of ADHD in both children and adults, parents, teachers, and friends may view children who disrupt the classroom or home environment as either having or being at risk for this disorder because they show signs of hyperarousal and distractibility. Keep in mind, however, that, like the names of all disorders in the *DSM-5*, the term *ADHD* should be used only in reference to people who meet a set of specific diagnostic criteria.

The first set of criteria for ADHD consists of disturbances in attention and includes at least six from a larger set of specific behaviors. These are failure to pay close attention to

attention-deficit/ hyperactivity disorder (ADHD)
A neurodevelopmental disorder involving a persistent pattern of inattention and/or hyperactivity.

details or the making of careless mistakes, difficulty staying focused on tasks at school or play, an apparent failure to listen when others are speaking, failure to follow through on projects, disorganized approaches to tasks, distractability, forgetfulness, a tendency to lose things, and reluctance to engage in tasks requiring sustained mental effort.

The second set of ADHD criteria is at least six behaviors involving hyperactivity that can be fidgeting, inability to sit in one place, restlessness, inability to engage in quiet activities, excessive talking or motor behavior, difficulty waiting for a turn when speaking or engaging in group activities, and frequent interruptions of other people.

Clinicians can also diagnose children with ADHD "combined type" who meet both sets of criteria for at least 6 months. They can diagnose the ADHD "predominantly inattentive type" if the child meets the criteria for inattentiveness but not hyperactivity-impulsivity for the past 6 months. Finally, clinicians can diagnose children as "predominantly hyperactive-impulsive" if they meet the second set of criteria but have not shown inattentiveness for the previous 6 months.

Researchers estimate the mean prevalence of ADHD around the world at 5.29 percent, but prevalence rates vary widely by country and region of the world (Figure 1) (Polanczyk et al., 2007). Despite these differences, it seems clear that prevalence is higher in males than in females, and higher in children than in adolescents.

Moving on to understanding the clinical picture of ADHD, it is clear that children who experience this disorder can face many challenges that persist into adulthood (Sayal et al., 2017). During the grade school years, ADHD places children at risk for receiving lower grades, as well as for showing repeated discipline problems that require placement in special education classes (Wilens, Faraone, & Biederman, 2004). As they reach early adulthood, children with ADHD are more likely to develop substance use disorders (Wilens et al., 2011).

Although researchers and clinicians once thought that ADHD symptoms subside by adolescence, increasing evidence shows that people with ADHD continue to experience symptoms during adolescence and adulthood. The picture does change; the hyperactivity so evident during preschool and early childhood years declines by adolescence. Even so, individuals continue to have difficulty maintaining attentional focus.

As children move into their adolescent years, if their ADHD is untreated they show a wide range of behavioral, academic, and interpersonal problems that create serious difficulties for them and challenges in their relationships with family, friends, and educators. They tend to be less mature than others their own age and more likely to engage in conflict with

FIGURE 1 Worldwide Prevalence of ADHD

SOURCE: Polanczyk et al, 2007, "The worldwide prevalence of ADHD: A systematic review and metaregression analysis," *American Journal of Psychiatry, 164*(6):942–948.

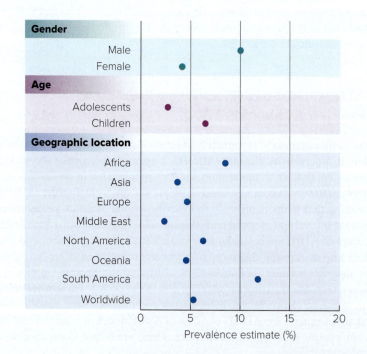

MINI CASE

Attention-Deficit/Hyperactivity Disorder

Zaman's mother has just had a conference with her son's teacher, who related that Zaman, a 7-year-old Iranian male, has been extremely restless and distractible in class. Every few minutes, he is up from his desk, exploring something on a bookshelf or looking out the window. When he is in his seat, he kicks his feet back and forth, drums his fingers on the table, shifts around, and generally keeps up a constant high level of movement. He may ask to go to the bathroom three times in an hour. He speaks very quickly, and his ideas are poorly organized. During recess, Zaman is aggressive and violates many of the playground rules. His mother corroborates the teacher's description of Zaman with similar stories about his behavior at home. Although Zaman is of normal intelligence, he is unable to sustain concentrated attention on any one activity for more than a few minutes.

---

their parents, they have strikingly poor social skills, and they engage in more high-risk activities such as substance abuse, unprotected sex, and reckless driving (Resnick, 2005).

Educators and clinicians are likely to miss a diagnosis of ADHD in girls, whose symptoms tend to be less overt than those of boys. In girls, ADHD may include symptoms such as unusual forgetfulness, disorganization, low self-esteem, and demoralization. Unlike boys, girls with ADHD tend to internalize their symptoms and become anxious, depressed, and socially withdrawn (Quinn, 2005). Girls who show these symptoms of ADHD may therefore be seen as having a depressive or anxiety disorder and might not receive appropriate treatment.

ADHD in Adults

Once regarded as a disorder restricted to childhood, ADHD is now seen as having the potential to continue into adulthood. Perhaps as many as 4 percent of U.S. adults meet the diagnostic criteria for this disorder, with nearly equal numbers of men and women having the condition (Kessler, Adler, et al., 2006). It is unlikely that ADHD shows up for the first time in people of adult age, but rather that it was improperly diagnosed earlier. This might be especially true for individuals who had inattentive but not disruptive symptoms as children.

The symptoms of ADHD appear in different forms in adults than in children. Whereas children may show greater evidence of restlessness and impulsivity, adult ADHD manifests as difficulties in maintaining attentional focus (Kessler et al., 2010). Reflecting abnormalities in executive functioning, people with adult ADHD are more likely to have trouble organizing tasks, make careless mistakes, lose things, and perform more poorly on tasks that require them to prioritize activities on the basis of importance.

In their daily lives, then, adults with ADHD have trouble devising routines, are haphazard in their management of time and money, and find it difficult to complete academic work or follow through on job tasks. Throughout adulthood, men in particular are at higher risk of having vehicular accidents and receiving moving vehicle citations (Cox, Cox, & Cox, 2011).

A small percentage of adults with ADHD are able to channel their excessive energy and restlessness into creative endeavors, such as entrepreneurial ventures (Weiss & Murray, 2003), although their inability to sustain attention and commitment to a project may limit the likelihood of their succeeding for any extended period of time.

Women with ADHD are less likely to show the high-risk behaviors seen in men. Instead, they are more likely to experience dysphoria, organization problems, impulsivity, and inattention, characteristics that are of particular concern if they interfere with consistent parenting (Quinn, 2005).

Typically, the symptoms of ADHD can lead adults with the disorder to have serious problems in relationships, whether the relationship is with an intimate partner, a co-worker, an

Children and adolescents who suffer from ADHD experience significant difficulties in keeping up with their schoolwork due to symptoms such as inattention and extreme restlessness. Many researchers believe that the disorder is influenced by environmental and sociocultural factors.

©Implementar Films/Alamy Stock Photo

acquaintance, or even a stranger (Barkley, 2017). Because they become easily bored, adults with ADHD seek excitement by starting arguments with the people close to them. They find it difficult to listen to others, they may hear only parts of a conversation, they are prone to interrupting, and they speak while others are trying to speak. Moody and high-strung, they irritate their intimate partners by their impulsivity, poor decision making, and inept money management. Other problems ensue in their relationships due to their disorganization, forgetfulness, chronic lateness, repeated misplacement of objects around the house, and overall lack of dependability (Robbins, 2005).

Even more serious are the possible effects of ADHD on the individual's tendency to engage in deviant or antisocial behavior (Barkley & Murphy, 2011). ADHD may also make people prone to developing substance use disorders as well as higher rates of cigarette smoking (Wilens, 2011).

Theories and Treatment of ADHD

The biological determinants of ADHD have been well established by family, twin, adoption, and molecular genetic studies. Researchers estimate ADHD heritability to be as high as 76 percent (Faraone et al., 2005), among the highest rates of all psychiatric disorders. Studies of individuals with ADHD have found evidence for the involvement of several genes related to dopamine, suggesting that deficits in reward patterns may contribute to the symptoms of this disorder (Volkow et al., 2009).

Researchers have also found structural brain abnormalities in people with ADHD, and they believe a network of interrelated brain areas is involved in the impairment of attentional-executive functions of these individuals. For example, the MRIs of children with ADHD in one recent study revealed that, on average, they had 9 percent less volume in the cortex and disruptions in circuits necessary for regulating motor control (Qiu et al., 2011).

Depending on comorbidity with other disorders, there may be subtypes of ADHD, such as mood or anxiety disorders, learning disabilities, and conduct or oppositional defiant disorder (Adler, Barkley, Wilens, & Ginsberg, 2006). Each of these subtypes may have a different pattern of family inheritance, risk factors, neurobiology, and responses to medications (Biederman, Mick, Faraone, & Burback, 2001).

Tying together biological abnormalities and behavioral problems in ADHD, Barkley's (1997) theory of ADHD proposes that the core impairment is inability to inhibit responses due to abnormalities in the prefrontal cortex and the way it communicates with other parts of the brain. This impairment of response inhibition manifests itself in four areas of the individual's functioning: (1) working memory; (2) internalization of self-directed speech; (3) self-regulation of affect, motivation, and level of arousal; and (4) reconstitution—the ability to break down observed behaviors into component parts that can recombine into new behaviors directed toward a goal. In addition, according to Barkley, children with ADHD fail to develop a future orientation and sense of the self across time.

Consider how each of these impairments is expressed in a child's behavior. Problems with working memory cause the child to have difficulty keeping track of time and remembering such things as deadlines and commitments. Having an impaired internalization of self-directed speech means that these children fail to keep their thoughts to themselves or engage in private self-questioning or self-guidance. Their impaired self-regulation of mood and motivation causes them to display all their emotions outwardly without censorship, while being unable to self-regulate their drive and motivation. Their impaired ability to reconstitute causes these children to be less able to solve problems, because they are unable to analyze behaviors and synthesize new behaviors.

Barkley's theory continues to receive support. Most recently, he has devised a scale to measure executive functioning in adults that assesses self-management with regard to time, self-organization and problem solving, self-discipline, self-motivation, and self-activation/concentration. Adults with ADHD show impairment not only on these ratings, but also on their scores related to measures of deviant behavior in daily life, including antisocial acts, a diversity of crimes, and traffic offenses committed while driving (Barkley & Murphy, 2011). Sample items from the adult executive functioning scale are shown in Table 3.

TABLE 3 Sample Items from the Adult ADHD Executive Functioning Rating Scale

Each item is rated on a 1–4 Likert scale (1 = Rarely or not at all; 2 = Sometimes; 3 = Often; 4 = Very Often).	
Scale	**Sample Items**
Self-Management to Time	Procrastinate or put off doing things until the last minute
	Late for work or scheduled appointments
Self-Organization and Problem-Solving	Often at a loss for words when I want to explain something to others
	Unable to "think on my feet" or respond as effectively as others to unexpected events
Self-Discipline	Make impulsive comments to others
	Trouble following the rules in a situation
Self-Motivation	Likely to take short cuts in my work and not do all that I am supposed to do
	Others tell me I am lazy or unmotivated
Self-Activation/ Concentration	Easily distracted by irrelevant thoughts when I must concentrate on something
	Have trouble staying alert or awake in boring situations

SOURCE: Gersten, R., Beckman, S., Clarke, B., Foegen, A., Marsh, L., Star, J. R., & Witzel, B. (2009). *Assisting students struggling with mathematics: Response to intervention (TRI) for elementary and middle schools (NCEE 2009–4060).* Washington, D.C.: National Center for Education Evaluation and Regional Assistance, Institute of Education Sciences, U.S. Department of Education.

Prescribing Psychiatric Medications to Children

Research on human participants of any age requires that investigators adhere strictly to the APA Ethical Principles of Psychologists and Code of Conduct. In the case of children, however, the issues shift considerably given that they are vulnerable populations. This means they may be at increased risk for abuse and exploitation. Consequently, for decades, researchers avoided conducting studies to test the efficacy of psychotherapeutic medications on children, to avoid exposing them to unnecessary harm during research trials. With no conclusive data about effectiveness, safety, or pharmacological action on which to base treatment recommendations, psychiatrists treated their pediatric patients using so-called "off-label" prescriptions that had not received U.S. Food and Drug Administration (FDA) approval.

The practice of prescribing off-label medications for disorders is widespread in the United States, but because of the problems of conducting research on children, these prescriptions are often targeted toward this population. The FDA has no authority to regulate the way in which physicians practice medicine, so doctors must make their own decisions about whether to prescribe an off-label medication to a child. In the process, they must balance the potential benefits with the risks of the medication. With few studies on the safety and efficacy of the medications, physicians rely on their own experience (Spetie & Arnold, 2007).

Children may therefore be at greater risk of side effects than other populations about whom extensive data exists. This situation was brought to light in a dramatic manner in 2003 when the FDA received reports showing an association between SSRI use in adolescents and a heightened risk of self-harm and suicidal thoughts. By 2007, these medications had received "black box" warnings from the FDA: warnings that appear on the package insert for certain prescription drugs to call attention to serious risks. These new warnings applied not only to children and adolescents, but also to young adults. Because the FDA did not have extensive data on the use of these medications for young people, its administrations used the information they had at their disposal to make this ruling. Considerably more information about these medications is now available, suggesting that antidepressants may, in fact, reduce suicide risks in this population over the course of continued treatment (Dudley, Goldney, & Hadzi-Pavlovic, 2010).

Q: *You be the judge:* Should researchers conduct more studies on psychotherapeutic medication with children? Do the risks of side effects that may occur during this research justify such investigations? Furthermore, if researchers discover that a medication has harmful side effects, how should prescribing health professionals weigh these against the possible benefits?

Although functional and structural abnormalities are found in the brains of people with ADHD, most researchers believe the disorder emerges from an interaction between genetic vulnerability and exposure to environmental stressors. These stressors include birth complications, acquired brain damage, exposure to toxic substances, infectious diseases, and even marital stress of parents (Martel et al., 2011). Children of parents who were diagnosed with ADHD as children also have a higher risk of developing the disorder, particularly if they live in families with lower educational and occupational attainment (Rowland et al., 2017). Children who experienced a major trauma in their lives also have higher ADHD prevalence rates (Schilpzand et al., 2017).

Individuals with ADHD who are treated from the biological perspective receive medications intended to control their symptoms. Although there are more than a dozen brand names under which such prescriptions are written, most medications are based on methylphenidate (Ritalin).

Over the past few decades, pharmaceutical companies have made significant advances in developing effective medications for ADHD, such that more recently produced medications, in extended-release formulations, are longer lasting. The first class of stimulant medications, which included methylphenidate, was effective for brief durations (3 to 5 hours) and required multiple well-timed doses throughout the day.

The extended-release formulations work in one of two ways: via back-loaded delivery systems that work later in the dosage interval, and through beaded 50-50 delivery systems that divide delivery up equally early and late. One advantage of long-acting medications is that they are less likely to be abused (Mao, Babcock, & Brams, 2011). The individual is also less likely to forget to take the medication because there is a longer time frame between doses.

Concerta is a back-loaded product: 22 percent of the dose is in the immediate release overcoat, and 78 percent is delivered approximately 4 hours after ingestion. Adderall XR is a 50-50 beaded delivery product and mimics the effect of taking two equal doses. The duration of action is 7 to 9 hours in adults (Dodson, 2005).

As an alternative to methylphenidate, antidepressant medications are sometimes prescribed for people with ADHD. These include bupropion (Wellbutrin SR), pemoline (Cylert), atomoxetine (Strattera), and imipramine (Tofranil). Clinicians use these medications to treat mild to moderate ADHD, with some effects starting to appear as soon as 2 to 3 days after beginning treatment. Clinicians typically use this group of medications for individuals with mild ADHD symptoms and coexisting symptoms (such as anxiety or depression), medical conditions that contraindicate stimulant use, tic disorder or Tourette's disorder (discussed later in this chapter), and drug abuse histories (Dodson, 2005). However, methylphenidate can be prescribed with either antidepressants or antipsychotics, given that individuals with ADHD may also have comorbidities that bring them to the attention of a psychiatrist (Hauck et al., 2017).

Parents are understandably concerned about the side effects that occur with stimulant use by their children requiring ADHD treatment. Some children on the medication have trouble sleeping and have a reduced appetite. More serious side effects occur when the child develops uncontrollable bodily twitches and verbalization. The child's growth may also be temporarily suppressed.

Critics contend that clinicians overprescribe stimulant medications for ADHD, using medication as the primary, and often only, intervention for dealing with behavior problems. Moreover, based on animal models, long-term use of stimulants such as Ritalin may provoke persistent neurobehavioral consequences that actually exacerbate ADHD symptoms (Marco et al., 2011).

In the nonpharmacological realm, a number of interventions are effective in reducing ADHD symptoms and helping individuals with this condition function better interpersonally and feel better about themselves. Murphy (2005) outlines a multipronged approach to psychosocial treatment. Although he focuses on the treatment of teens and adults with ADHD, we can apply some of the strategies to families of children with ADHD. The eight strategies are as follows:

1. **Psychoeducation**, or professionally delivered treatment that integrates psychotherapeutic with educational interventions, is the starting point, because the more people with ADHD know about their condition and how it affects them, the better they will be able to understand the impact of this disorder on their daily functioning and develop coping strategies. Psychoeducation instills hope and optimism as the individual frames the condition as treatable and begins to expect that life will become better once he or she begins making changes.

2. Psychological therapies, such as individual therapy, provide a context in which clinicians and their clients can set treatment goals, resolve conflicts, solve problems, manage life transitions, and treat coexisting problems such as depression and anxiety. Specific techniques, such as cognitive-behavioral strategies, can help clients change maladaptive behavior and thought patterns that interfere with daily functioning. Maladaptive thought patterns have commonly become entrenched as the result of recurrent negative messages from teachers, parents, and peers.

psychoeducation
Professionally delivered treatment that integrates psychotherapeutic with educational interventions.

3. Compensatory behavioral and self-management training provides the opportunity to build skills by incorporating more structure and routine into the person's life. Simple strategies can make day-to-day tasks and responsibilities more manageable. These include making to-do lists, using appointment books, keeping notepads in useful locations, and having multiple sets of keys.

4. Other psychological therapies, such as marital counseling, family therapy, career counseling, group therapy, and college planning also provide opportunities to assess the various ways in which ADHD symptoms affect life choices and the people with whom the individual is involved.

5. Coaching, a more recently developed intervention, consists of consulting with a professional who can assist the individual with ADHD to focus on the practical implementation of goals. In other words, the coach helps the person find ways to accomplish things through a pragmatic, behavioral, results-oriented approach.

6. Technology-based computer programs can help individuals with ADHD access tools and devices that assist them to communicate more effectively, write, spell, stay organized, remember information, stay on schedule, and keep track of time.

7. School and workplace accommodations can facilitate productivity and minimize distraction. Students and employees with ADHD usually work better in quiet, nondistracting environments. They are also more likely to succeed when they receive more frequent performance reviews to help shape their performance and establish priorities. Teachers and supervisors should restructure tasks in ways that capitalize on the person's strengths and talents.

8. Advocacy, particularly in the form of advocating for oneself, is especially important in attaining success. Although it is difficult for most people to disclose the disabling aspects of ADHD to others, they may find that explaining their condition improves the situation for everyone involved.

This multipronged approach is obviously most appropriate for teens and adults who can take more managerial responsibility for their lives. Clinicians, parents, and teachers treating children with ADHD can nevertheless adapt some of these strategies, which can also be combined with stimulants as part of an integrated intervention (Breggin & Barkley, 2005).

Implicit in the behavioral approach is the notion that the family must learn to use behavioral methods and directly involve themselves in helping their child reduce disruptive behaviors. Coordinating these efforts with comparable intervention by classroom teachers improves the odds for helping the child gain better self-control.

5.5 Motor Disorders

Developmental Coordination Disorder

developmental coordination disorder
A motor disorder characterized by marked impairment in the development of motor coordination.

The primary form of motor disorder is **developmental coordination disorder**. Children with this surprisingly common disorder experience marked impairment in their abilities to coordinate the movements of their hands and feet. Affecting as many as 6 percent of children, developmental coordination disorder can lead to problems in academic achievement and ability to engage in ordinary tasks of daily life (Nass & Ross, 2008). There may be subtypes of developmental coordination disorder, with one subtype limiting hand-eye coordination and the other causing visual-spatial difficulties (Vaivre-Douret et al., 2011). Children whose coordination disorder represents deficits in executive function, meaning they cannot gain control over their motor functions, represent another important subtype (Michel, Molitor, & Schneider, 2018).

In infancy and early childhood, children with developmental coordination disorder have trouble crawling, walking, and sitting. As they develop, their performance on other age-related tasks also is below average. They may be unable to tie their shoelaces, play ball,

This child suffers from a developmental coordination disorder, making it difficult for him to learn to put objects in order at a normative developmental rate.

©Nicholas Kamm/Getty Images

complete a puzzle, or even write legibly. Consequently, they may experience problems of low self-esteem. In addition, their lack of coordination may make them less able to participate in sports and exercise programs, leading them to become overweight.

Given the complexity of their symptoms, children with motor disorder seem to benefit from an integrated approach that identifies the needs of clients and their families in the early stages, when symptoms first begin to emerge. An integrated approach to assessment can then proceed in which children, families, and professionals share their perspectives on the child's symptoms and start to formulate therapeutic goals. Next, professionals, parents, and children plan how intervention will proceed, taking advantage of community resources. Here again, all must collaborate in setting goals for the child. They should base their planned interventions on evidence-supported treatments. Finally, the intervention team should develop strategies that will continue to support the children and their families as they transition to self-management within the home, school, and the community (Forsyth et al., 2008).

Tic Disorders

A **tic** is a rapid, recurring, and involuntary movement or vocalization. There are several kinds of tic disorders. Examples of motor tics are eye blinking, facial twitches, and shoulder shrugging. Vocal tics include coughing, grunting, snorting, coprolalia (the uttering of obscenities), and tongue clicking.

Tourette's disorder is perhaps the best known of the tic disorders, affecting approximately 1 percent of children, the majority of whom are male. People with this disorder experience a combination of chronic motor and vocal tics. Their disorder begins gradually, often with a single tic, such as eye blinking, which over time grows into more complex behaviors. The tics can include uncontrollable movements of the head and sometimes parts of the upper body. In some cases, individuals engage in complex bodily movements involving touching, squatting, twirling, or retracing steps. At the same time, they utter vocalizations that sound odd to others; for example, an individual may have a complex tic behavior in which he rolls his head around his neck while making sniffing and barking noises. In only a small percentage of cases do people with Tourette's disorder utter obscenities.

tic
A rapid, recurring, involuntary movement or vocalization.

Tourette's disorder
A disorder involving a combination of chronic motor and vocal tics.

This is not a passing condition but one that can be lifelong, with onset in childhood or adolescence. Individuals with this disorder also have other psychological symptoms, the most common of which are obsessive-compulsive symptoms, speech difficulties, and attentional problems. Deficits in brain inhibitory mechanisms in the prefrontal cortex may be involved in Tourette's disorder, a feature that is shared with obsessive-compulsive disorder and ADHD (Aliane et al., 2011). The condition may resolve itself by adulthood, as the brain structures that inhibit the tics mature.

Children with Tourette's can benefit from educational interventions that help bolster self-esteem and provide supportive counseling. However, if the tics are painful, self-injurious (such as scratching), and cause significant disability, clinicians need to intervene more systematically. Individuals with these symptoms can benefit from a form of cognitive-behavioral therapy that uses habit reversal. In this approach, the professional trains clients to monitor their tics and the sensations that precede them and then respond to them with a voluntary behavior that is physically incompatible with the tics.

Cognitive-behavioral treatment is the first line of treatment (Martino & Pringsheim, 2018), but if this proves to be ineffective, clinicians may place the individual on pharmacological therapy, which can include SSRIs, atypical antipsychotic agents, and, in extreme cases, deep brain stimulation (Budman et al., 2018).

Stereotypic Movement Disorder

stereotypic movement disorder
A disorder in which the individual engages in repetitive, seemingly driven nonfunctional behaviors.

Children with **stereotypic movement disorder** engage in repetitive, seemingly driven nonfunctional behaviors. These can include waving their hands, rocking their bodies, banging their heads, and biting and picking at their skin. As you can imagine, these behaviors can interfere with their normal functioning and cause them to injure themselves. It is important to distinguish stereotypic movement disorder from the developmentally normal repetitive movements estimated to occur in as many as 60 percent of children between the ages of 2 and 5 years old. Subgroups of children are particularly likely to engage in stereotyped motor disorders, including children who are blind and those who have developmental delays.

For children who are truly impaired, or who risk serious injury as a result of their behavior, behavior modification appears to be the most efficacious way to help them stop engaging in the behavior. Parents can be taught how to use behavior therapy in the home, an effective method particularly for children between the ages of 7 and 8 years old (Specht et al., 2017).

5.6 Neurodevelopmental Disorders: The Biopsychosocial Perspective

The disorders that we have covered in this chapter include a range of conditions that reflect, to differing degrees, combinations of biological, psychological, and sociocultural influences. Genetic influences on many of these disorders are clearly evident, but even so, interactions with social context play an important role. Moreover, because these disorders begin early in life, they have the potential to exert profound psychological effects on an individual. Family factors also play a critical role, given the importance of early childhood experiences as contributors to psychological outcomes.

Just as the disorders reflect multiple influences, so do treatments. In providing interventions to children, clinicians are becoming justifiably concerned about the use of medication. Treatment from the behavioral perspective seems to have a number of advantages, because children's symptoms may be particularly receptive to treatments that focus on principles of reinforcement.

The tremendous growth of interest within the past few decades in the conditions that can affect children means that considerably more information about causes and interventions is available than was true even a few years ago. Although interventions can be effective for people of any age, targeting children as soon as possible can help them achieve favorable outcomes that can influence their lives for decades to follow.

Jason was started on a stimulant medication, and both his parents and Mrs. Brownstein noted an improvement in his ability to pay attention and to sit still for longer periods of time. Though he continued to feel restless, Jason's behavioral work with a therapist at the clinic began to help decrease his disruptive behavior at school. The therapist also worked with Pam and John to create a consistent system of rewards and punishment for Jason's behavior. Together they realized that due to their differing opinions on how strict to be with Jason, Pam and John had been sending him diverging reinforcement messages. In order to facilitate an agreement on how to punish or reward Jason, Pam and John worked on creating a set system of reinforcement that they then shared with him, so that he was better informed about what to expect should he misbehave. After several months of medication and therapy, and with his parents' improved ability to discipline him, Jason became less hyperactive while in school, and his grades began to improve. He started getting along better with his classmates and joined a basketball league, which allowed him to make friends and channel his energy appropriately.

Dr. Tobin's reflections: It can be difficult to differentiate normal overactivity in young children from the more severe symptomatology indicative of ADHD. Dr. Scott made careful consideration of this when diagnosing Jason, based on Pam's description of his behavior over the years. It was clear that Jason's behavioral problems were severely interfering with his ability to lead a normal childhood and attain an education. Especially compared with his brother Nicholas, Jason was visibly struggling with symptoms that went beyond normative childhood behavior.

ADHD is typically diagnosed during the elementary school years, and though the disorder can last through adolescence, with appropriate treatment such as the kind Jason is receiving, the symptoms can begin to diminish toward adulthood. It can be a difficult ethical decision to place children on stimulant medication. In Jason's case, however, medication was important in helping decrease the hyperactive symptoms that were causing him problems at school and that would have made behavior therapy difficult to conduct. With continued therapy and behavioral strategies implemented by his parents, it is hoped that he will be able to discontinue medication in the near future.

SUMMARY

- Neurodevelopmental disorders include disorders that strike children early in life and appear to affect their behavioral functioning by creating brain abnormalities.

- Intellectual disability refers to intellectual and adaptive deficits that are first evident in childhood. Genetic abnormalities are a significant cause. The three most important genetic causes are Down syndrome, phenylketonuria, and fragile X syndrome. Another genetic disorder is Tay-Sachs disease.

- Environmental hazards during prenatal development are the second category of causes of intellectual disability. These hazards, called teratogens, include drugs and toxic chemicals, maternal malnutrition, and infections in the mother during critical phases of fetal development. Consumption of alcohol during pregnancy can lead to fetal alcohol syndrome (FAS).

- People with intellectual disability can benefit from early intervention aimed at providing them with training in motor coordination, language use, and social skills. Educators can combine mainstreaming, which integrates them into ordinary school classrooms, with special education that provides them with assistance geared to their particular needs.

- The *DSM-5* authors created the category of autism spectrum disorder to provide a more reliable and valid distinction

between children who clearly show typical development and those who demonstrate the range of deficits in communication and social behavior that *DSM-IV-TR* attempted to differentiate. The new spectrum format for this category underscores the commonalities between disorders previously considered discrete. Disorders listed separately in *DSM-IV-TR*, such as Asperger's, autism, Rett syndrome, childhood disintegrative disorder, and pervasive developmental disorder, are included in autism spectrum disorder in the *DSM-5*. Symptoms that formerly differentiated these disorders from one another now are indicated by diagnostic specifiers.

- Evidence pointing to patterns of familial inheritance supports the theory that autism spectrum disorder is biologically caused. Although it is evident that neurological differences exist between people with and without this autism spectrum disorder, the basis for these differences and their implications are not clear.

- The behavioral perspective is the most relevant to treatment, particularly interventions that rest on principles of operant conditioning practiced by student therapists and parents. Disruptive and self-stimulatory behaviors will decrease if children with autism spectrum disorder receive reinforcement for appropriate behaviors, such as asking for help or feedback. In such instances, they are less likely to engage in self-injurious or aggressive behaviors.

- The specific learning disorders include impairment in mathematics, written expression, reading, and communication. Communciation disorders include speech sound disorder, childhood-onset fluency disorder, and social communication disorder. For the majority of children with specific developmental disorders, schools are the primary intervention site.

- Attention-deficit/hyperactivity disorder (ADHD) is characterized by inattentiveness or hyperactivity and impulsivity. There are many theories about the cause of this disorder, but familial heritability rates may be as high as 76 percent. Although researchers have found fundamental and structural abnormalities in the brains of people with

ADHD, most agree that genetic vulnerability interacts with environmental exposure. Treatment takes a multipronged approach.

- Developmental coordination disorders are characterized by tics, recurring involuntary movements or vocalizations. This type of disorder includes Tourette's and stereotypic movement disorder.

- The disorders covered in this chapter include a range of conditions that reflect, to differing degrees, combinations of biological, psychological, and sociocultural influences. Genetic influences on the development of many of these disorders are clearly evident, but even so, interactions with social context play an important role. Moreover, because these disorders begin early in life, they have the potential to exert profound psychological effects on an individual.

KEY TERMS

Asperger's disorder
Attention-deficit/hyperactivity disorder (ADHD)
Autism spectrum disorder
Childhood-onset fluency disorder (stuttering)
Communication disorders
Developmental coordination disorder
Down syndrome
Dyscalculia
Echolalia
Fetal alcohol spectrum disorder (FASD)

Fetal alcohol syndrome (FAS)
Fragile X syndrome
Intellectual disability (intellectual developmental disorder)
Language disorder
Mainstreaming
Neurodevelopmental disorders
Phenylketonuria (PKU)
Psychoeducation
Rett syndrome
Social (pragmatic) communication disorder
Specific learning disorder

Specific learning disorder with impairment in mathematics
Specific learning disorder with impairment in reading (dyslexia)
Specific learning disorder with impairment in written expression
Speech sound disorder
Stereotypic movement disorder
Tay-Sachs disease
Teratogens
Tic
Tourette's disorder

Schizophrenia Spectrum and Other Psychotic Disorders

Learning Objectives

6.1 Identify the characteristics of schizophrenia.

6.2 Describe the key features of other psychotic disorders.

6.3 Explain the theories and treatments of schizophrenia.

6.4 Analyze the biopsychosocial model of schizophrenia.

©stillfx/123RF

Case Report: David Chen

Demographic information: 19-year-old single Chinese American male who identifies as queer

Presenting problem: David was evaluated at an inpatient psychiatric facility following his second psychotic episode within a 1-year period. He was brought to the hospital by his mother, Ann, who had noticed that David's behavior had become increasingly bizarre over the past year. David's mother was the main source of information during the interview, because David was a poor historian, meaning he was unable to give an accurate personal history.

David is a college sophomore attending a university in his hometown. Though he lived at home during his first year (Ann has raised him since getting a divorce when David was 5), he and his mother decided it would be beneficial for him to move into the dormitories to gain a sense of independence. Ann reported that David was doing well for the first 2 weeks of living in the dormitories. She and David typically spoke on the phone a few times per week, and he had been coming home for dinner on Sunday evenings.

One Sunday evening in mid-October, Ann reported that David failed to show up for dinner as he had been planning to. She called David's best friend Mark, who had not heard from him for a few days and was himself worried about David. Mark has known David since high school and lives in the same town. He noted to Ann that David didn't "quite seem to be himself lately," as he had been acting particularly aloof. Mark had been concerned that he hadn't heard from David, so he went to search for him in different parts of town where he knew David liked to spend time and eventually found him outside a coffee shop.

When Mark approached him, David stated that he wished to be referred to as "Joey." Mark noted that David appeared particularly unkempt, which was unusual because he normally took very good care of himself. Mark also noticed that David was smiling and laughing to himself. Mark assumed that he was doing so because he was in a particularly good mood, though David's tone became more serious when Mark offered to drive him back to his dorm room. David refused, stating, "I have a lot of writing to do. My poems are going to be published and they want me to write 20 more so they can publish a book of my poems." Writing had always been one of David's hobbies, and he and Mark often discussed their respective creative endeavors. Mark was alerted when he looked down at David's notebook, which was open in his lap while they were talking, and noticed only illegible scribbling. Mark also noticed that throughout their conversation, David's left arm repeatedly and seemingly involuntarily extended with a jerking motion every few minutes. Mark was unable to convince David to go back to campus with him, and he reluctantly left the coffee shop. After hearing these details Ann was shocked about her son's behavior, remarking that she had never seen David acting so oddly. Unsure what to do, Ann decided to wait until she heard from David.

David eventually returned to his dorm room and called Ann around 3 A.M., stating, "I can't stay here because there are no poets here. They need me there. Meeting, meeting, bus, poems. I need poems for a money to go to meet. A meeting. I have to get there. I have got there. I have to go there." He repeated this last part several times. Confused, Ann asked David what he meant, at which point David hung up the phone. After that, Ann reported, she didn't hear from him for about a week.

David was returned to Ann's house by the police, who had found him on campus causing a disturbance by yelling at some other students who were waiting for a bus nearby. Ann was unsure whether David had actually gone to New York or had been on campus the whole time. She was able to extract from him that he had not been attending his classes. She decided to write to David's professors and ask for an incomplete grade, since it was clear he was unable to successfully complete his classes in his current state.

David stayed with Ann for the next 3 weeks, during which time he continued to display bizarre behavior. Ann hoped he was going to recover at any moment, but it was becoming clear that he was not improving. When Ann returned home from work, she would find dirty laundry, dishes, pizza boxes, and cigarette ashes all around the house. Often David would stay in his room all day, coming out only to use the bathroom or eat a meal. When Ann did see him, she noticed that he appeared rather sad and withdrawn, barely speaking to her. Normally they had a very close relationship and enjoyed spending time together around the house. Though she worried about her son, she wasn't sure what she could do to help him. They decided it would be best for David to take the next semester off, since Ann didn't feel he would be able to focus enough on his school work and wanted to make sure he could handle the stress of going back to school.

By the end of the summer, Ann felt that David seemed to have made a great improvement—he was engaging more with her at home and was less messy, and the content of his speech was less bizarre. He did seem much more withdrawn in general than he once had been, engaging in minimal activities and rarely leaving the house. In the spring he was able to hold a part-time job at a gas station for a month before being fired for showing up late too many times. Otherwise, he mostly stayed in his room listening to music and writing. He spent time with Mark occasionally, though David often cancelled their plans, stating that he simply didn't feel like being around people. Ann took David to China to visit relatives for a few weeks, and she remembers his behavior there as normal for the most part.

David and Ann eventually decided that he should reenroll at the university to resume his degree in the fall, and at David's urging, he left home to live in the dorm again. Two weeks later, David once more disappeared. As before, Ann got a phone call from him one evening, during which he said he had been living in Manhattan.

She reported that David said he had owed his landlord some money for a new set of keys. Ann had been unaware that David even went to New York or that he was living there. David asked for her credit card information and said that if he didn't come up with the money the landlord was threatening violence against him. When Ann asked where he was exactly, David hung up the phone. She did not hear from him until he showed up at her house 3 days later, completely disheveled and visibly filthy. He told Ann that he was afraid his roommate was going to burn all his belongings. While he was telling the story, he was laughing and smiling. It appeared to Ann that David was once again acting bizarrely, and after the previous experience she knew that this time something had to be done, because she felt very worried about his safety. Unsure where to turn, Ann brought David to the closest emergency room. The doctors in the ER sent him to a nearby hospital, where he was admitted to the psychiatric inpatient unit.

Relevant history: David has no previous history of psychiatric treatment. His mother reported that he had experienced some mild depression earlier in his teenage years. She recalled that David had always been "somewhat different" from his peers, noting that he had only a few close friends throughout his childhood and adolescence.

In terms of family history, Ann reported that David's paternal grandfather had been diagnosed with schizophrenia, though there was no other known family history of mental illness.

Case formulation: It is clear from the presenting story that David had experienced two psychotic episodes over the past year. The first occurred after a major stressor—moving away from home for the first time. This change came around the developmental period when psychotic symptoms may begin to fully emerge, due to the high base rate of major life events that occur during this time. By Ann's report, David may have displayed some prodromal symptoms as an adolescent, which is typical in the case of individuals with schizophrenia.

David meets *DSM-5* diagnostic criteria for schizophrenia because he displayed delusions, disorganized speech, grossly disorganized behavior, and negative symptoms (constricted affective expression) for over 1 month. There were signs of the disturbance for at least 6 months, including more than 1 month of active symptoms, and a period of negative symptoms. Further, David's general level of functioning was greatly reduced following the first psychotic episode; he was unable to hold a job and remained withdrawn from his interpersonal relationships. Lastly, he was not taking any substances, nor did he have a medical condition that would contribute to his symptoms.

Treatment plan: David will be stabilized on antipsychotic medication while in the hospital, and his psychiatrists will aim to find a suitable maintenance dose for the point at which he is discharged to go home. He will be set up with an outpatient psychiatric facility to provide him medication and weekly psychotherapy. It is also recommended that David find a case manager to help him with vocational activities and to decide whether continuing to pursue a higher educational degree is a possibility, given his past vulnerabilities when enrolled in college.

Sarah Tobin, PhD

6.1 Schizophrenia

The broad category of **schizophrenia** includes a set of disorders in which individuals experience distorted perception of reality and impairment in thinking, behavior, affect, and motivation. Schizophrenia is a serious mental illness, given its potentially broad impact on an individual's ability to live a productive and fulfilling life. Although a significant number of people with schizophrenia eventually manage to live symptom-free lives, in some ways, all must adapt their lives to the reality of the illness. In economic terms, schizophrenia also exacts a heavy burden, with an estimated annual cost in health care alone of $12,000 to $20,000 per person per year in the United States, third only to heart disease and cancer (Chapel, Ritchey, Zhang, & Wang, 2017).

One important symptom of schizophrenia is the presence of a **delusion**, a deeply entrenched false belief not consistent with the client's intelligence or cultural background. For example, a delusion of persecution is the false belief that someone or something is out to harm you when in fact there is no basis for such a belief. More examples of delusions are described in Table 1.

A second major symptom of schizophrenia is **hallucinations**, which are false perceptions not corresponding to the objective stimuli present in the environment. People may suffer from hallucinations in several sensory modalities, including vision, hearing, smell, and touch. Individuals who experience both visual and auditory hallucinations appear to have more significant deficits than those who experience hallucinations in one sensory modality, who in turn are more significantly impaired than individuals with no hallucinations (Clark, Waters, Vatskalis, & Jablensky, 2017).

Associated with delusions or auditory hallucinations related to a theme of persecution may be **paranoia**, the irrational belief or perception that others wish to cause you harm. People who experience paranoia become unable to trust others, feeling convinced that they will be mistreated or even threatened with bodily injury.

Language that is incomprehensible and incoherent is referred to as **disorganized speech**. The thought process underlying this type of speech reflects **loosening of associations**—that is, a flow of thoughts that is vague, unfocused, and illogical. The speech of individuals with schizophrenia may contain **neologisms**, which are words not contained in language. Unlike words that eventually may become accepted words in a particular language (such as *google*), these words have highly idiosyncratic meanings that are used only by the individual.

Another characteristic symptom that people with schizophrenia may show is **inappropriate affect**, meaning that the person's emotional response does not match the social cues present in a situation or the content of what is being discussed. The individual may, for example, burst into laughter during a sad situation or when hearing someone express discontent or unhappiness. We saw this in the case of David, who was laughing and smiling while telling his mother that he believed his roommate was going to burn his belongings.

schizophrenia
A disorder with a range of symptoms involving disturbances in content of thought, form of thought, perception, affect, sense of self, motivation, behavior, and interpersonal functioning.

delusion
Deeply entrenched false belief not consistent with the client's intelligence or cultural background.

hallucination
A false perception not corresponding to the objective stimuli present in the environment.

paranoia
The irrational belief or perception that others wish to cause you harm.

disorganized speech
Language that is incomprehensible and incoherent.

loosening of associations
Flow of thoughts that is vague, unfocused, and illogical.

neologisms
Invented ("new") words.

inappropriate affect
The extent to which a person's emotional expressiveness fails to correspond either to the social cues present in a situation or to the content of what is being discussed.

TABLE 1 Types and Examples of Delusions

Grandeur

A grossly exaggerated conception of the individual's own importance. Such delusions range from beliefs that the person has an important role in society to the belief that the person is actually Christ, Napoleon, or Hitler.

Control

The feeling that one is being controlled by others, or even by machines or appliances. For example, a man may believe that his actions are being controlled by the radio, which is "forcing" him to perform certain actions against his will.

Reference

The belief that the behavior of others or certain objects or events are personally referring to oneself. For example, a woman believes that a soap opera is really telling the story of her life, or a man believes that the sale items at a local food market are targeted at his own particular dietary deficiencies.

Persecution

The belief that another person or persons are trying to inflict harm on the individual or on that individual's family or social group. For example, a woman feels that an organized group of politically liberal individuals is attempting to destroy the right-wing political organization to which she belongs.

Self-blame

Feelings of remorse without justification. A man holds himself responsible for a famine in Africa because of certain unkind or sinful actions that he believes he has committed.

Somatic

Inappropriate concerns about one's body, typically related to a disease. For example, without any justification, a woman believes she has brain cancer. Adding an even more bizarre note, she believes that ants have invaded her head and are eating away at her brain.

Infidelity

A false belief usually associated with pathological jealousy involving the notion that one's lover is being unfaithful. A man lashes out in violent rage at his wife, insisting that she is having an affair with the mailman because of her eagerness for the mail to arrive each day.

Thought broadcasting

The idea that one's thoughts are being broadcast to others. A man believes that everyone else in the room can hear what he is thinking, or possibly that his thoughts are actually being carried over the airwaves on television or radio.

Thought insertion

The belief that outside forces are inserting thoughts into one's mind. For example, a woman concludes that her thoughts are not her own, but that they are being placed there to control her or upset her.

active phase
A period in the course of schizophrenia in which psychotic symptoms are present.

positive symptoms
The symptoms of schizophrenia that represent exaggerations or distortions of normal thoughts, emotions, and behavior.

Table 2 contains the six criteria associated with a diagnosis of schizophrenia. The symptoms in Criterion A refer to the **active phase** of the disorder, that is, the period during which the individual's symptoms are most prominent. The symptoms the individual experiences during the active phase fall into two categories based on their nature. In the first category are **positive symptoms**, exaggerations or distortions of normal thoughts, emotions, and behavior. In Table 2, the disturbances numbered 1 through 4 under Criterion A fit into the category of positive symptoms.

The symptoms in Criterion A-5 are **negative symptoms**, which relate to functioning that is below the normal level of behavior or feeling. **Restricted affect** refers to a narrowing of the range of outward expressions of emotions. **Avolition** is a lack of initiative, either not wanting to take any action or lacking the energy and will to take action. **Asociality** refers to a lack of interest in social relationships, including an inability to empathize and form close relationships with others.

MINI CASE

Catatonia, Unspecified

Maria is a single 21-year-old Caucasian, heterosexual female. She is a junior in college who has been psychiatrically hospitalized for a month. The resident assistant in Maria's dormitory notified the campus police because she had grown increasingly concerned about Maria's deteriorating behavior over the course of the semester. When Maria returned to college in September, her roommate told others, including the resident assistant, that Maria's behavior seemed odd. For example, she had a habit of repeating other people's words, she stared listlessly out the window, and she ignored her personal hygiene. As the semester's end approached, Maria retreated more and more into her own world, until her behavior reached a point at which she was completely unresponsive to others. Eventually, her resident assistant had to call the police, because Maria had not been seen outside her room for about a week.

The police found Maria in a trancelike state, unable to respond to any of their questions or attempts to engage with her. She was sent to the hospital for a psychiatric evaluation and was admitted because she was deemed unable to take care of herself. In the hospital, Maria maintains rigid posturing of her body, while staring blankly most of the time. The staff members treating her are in a quandary about what intervention to use because of her hypersensitivity to most medications. At present, the clinicians are attempting to determine whether she has another medical condition or a psychological disorder, but because they cannot identify any, for the moment they have diagnosed her as having unspecified catatonia.

TABLE 2 Diagnostic Features of Schizophrenia

For an individual to be diagnosed with schizophrenia, he or she must meet all of the criteria listed in A–F.
A. Two (or more) of the following symptoms must be present for a significant portion of time during a 1-month period (although this can be less if the individual is successfully treated). At least one symptom must be from the first three categories. 1. Delusions 2. Hallucinations 3. Disorganized speech 4. Grossly abnormal psychomotor behavior 5. Negative symptoms such as restricted affect, avolition, and asociality
B. Occupational dysfunction
For a significant portion of the time since the onset of the disturbance, one or more major areas of functioning such as work, interpersonal relations, or self-care are markedly below the level achieved prior to the onset (or when the onset is in childhood or adolescence, the person fails to achieve expected level of interpersonal, academic, or occupational achievement).
C. Duration of at least 6 months
Continuous signs of the disturbance must persist for at least 6 months. During at least one of these six months, the person must show the active-phase symptoms from Criterion A (or less if the person was successfully treated). The six months may include periods during which the individual had symptoms leading up to (prodromal) or following (residual) an active phase. During these periods, the person must show only negative symptoms or two or more of the active-phase symptoms but in attenuated form.
D. No evidence of schizoaffective, depressive, or bipolar disorder
E. Symptoms are not due to substance use disorder or general medical condition
F. If there is a history of autism spectrum disorder or a communication disorder of childhood onset, the additional diagnosis of schizophrenia is made only if prominent delusions or hallucinations are also present for at least a month (or less if successfully treated).

negative symptoms
The symptoms of schizophrenia that involve functioning below the level of normal behavior.

restricted affect
Narrowing of the range of outward expressions of emotions.

avolition
A lack of initiative, either not wanting to take any action or lacking the energy and will to take action.

asociality
Lack of interest in social relationships.

MINI CASE

Schizophrenia, Continuous

Joshua is a single 43-year-old biracial heterosexual male. Most days, he stands near the steps of a local bank on a busy street corner, wearing a Red Sox baseball cap, a yellow T-shirt, worn-out hiking shorts, and orange sneakers. Rain or shine, day in and day out, Joshua maintains his post at the bank. Sometimes he converses with imaginary people. Sometimes he explodes in shrieks of laughter. Without provocation, he sobs miserably. Police and social workers keep taking him to shelters for the homeless, but Joshua manages to get back on the street before he can receive treatment. He has repeatedly insisted that these people have no right to keep bothering him.

Criterion B is consistent with other, general *DSM* criteria for psychological disorders, in that it stipulates that there must be significant impairment. The degree of impairment in schizophrenia, however, implies a particularly serious and far-reaching impact in the individual's life. Criterion C, indicating the period of disturbance, is also carefully delineated to ensure that individuals receive this diagnosis only if they show a substantial duration of symptoms.

Criteria D and E refer to other disorders that should not be present in people diagnosed with schizophrenia. It is particularly important for clinicians to rule out Criterion D, schizoaffective disorder, when making their diagnosis. We will discuss this disorder in more detail later in the chapter. Similarly, in the interests of differentiating schizophrenia from other disorders, Criterion F makes it clear that the symptoms of schizophrenia involving, for example, communication must not overlap with symptoms of an autism spectrum disorder.

catatonia
A condition in which the individual shows marked psychomotor disturbances.

Before publication of *DSM-5,* the diagnostic criteria for schizophrenia included five subtypes based on which symptoms were most prominent in the individual. These subtypes were labeled catatonic, disorganized, paranoid, undifferentiated, and residual. They were dropped from *DSM-5,* since researchers studying schizophrenia now believe they represent fine-grained distinctions not supported by empirical evidence. However, the terms may still be in use today by mental health professionals who believe they capture qualitatively important diagnostic entities.

Individuals with schizophrenia present with a wide range of symptoms. For example, they may maintain paranoid delusions that they are in danger.
©Roy McMahon/Media Bakery

Once a subtype of schizophrenia, a separate disorder is now known in *DSM-5* as **catatonia**, a condition in which the individual shows marked psychomotor disturbances. These disturbances may consist of decreased, excessive, or peculiar motor activity that is not in response to what is occurring in the individual's environment. For example, with no apparent provocation, the individual may hold odd, rigid poses for long periods of time as well as being unable to speak or move. Catatonia may be diagnosed in association with another psychological disorder, a medical condition, or a cause the clinician cannot identify.

Schizophrenia has a long and fascinating history. French physician Benedict Morel (1809–1873) first identified it as a disease, which he named *démence precoce* (brain dementia of the young). The next major point in schizophrenia's history is associated with the German psychiatrist Emil Kraepelin (1856–1926), who used Latin to refer to the condition, which then became known as *dementia praecox.* At the root of its symptoms, Kraepelin believed, was one underlying and progressively degenerating disease process that caused, in his terms, the "weakening" of mental processes.

In 1911, Swiss psychologist Eugen Bleuler (1857–1939) revised the concept of schizophrenia once again, to reflect his belief that the disorder was actually a set of diseases. He coined the term *schizophrenia* to signify that the underlying cause was a splitting ("schiz") among the functions of the mind. Unlike Kraepelin, Bleuler thought it was possible for people with schizophrenia to recover from the disorder.

Reflecting the importance of Bleuler's contributions, clinicians still refer to the fundamental features of the disorder he identified as Bleuler's "Four A's." Briefly, the four A's are:

1. *Association*—thought disorder, as might be evident through rambling and incoherent speech

2. *Affect*—disorder of the experience and expression of emotion

3. *Ambivalence*—inability to make or follow through on decisions

4. *Autism*—withdrawal from reality

Note that Bleuler did not intend for the "splitting" to be a splitting of personalities, as is often mistakenly thought (as in "split personality"). Instead, it is a discontinuity between the individual's experience of an emotion and the way the emotion is expressed.

In the decades following Bleuler's work, clinicians in Europe and the United States proposed further distinctions among forms of schizophrenia. One notable contributor to the debate was the German psychiatrist Kurt Schneider (1887–1967), who believed clinicians should diagnose schizophrenia only when an individual displays what he called **first-rank symptoms (FRS)**. These are the symptoms that are truly key, defining features of the disorder. They include audible thoughts (voices heard arguing), the experience of outside influences on the body, the belief that others are taking thoughts out of one's head, and diffuse or vague thoughts, delusions, and acts or behaviors seen as reflecting the influence of other people on the individual.

First-rank symptoms retain a special meaning even today (e.g., Crump et al., 2017). *DSM-III* and the *ICD-10* included them as an advance on the less precise set of criteria included in earlier diagnostic manuals. However, researchers disagree on whether FRS represent valid criteria, given that using them may lead clinicians to falsely diagnose as many as nearly one in five individuals (Soares-Weiser et al., 2015).

As debate continues on the FRS, researchers are also rethinking whether schizophrenia is best thought of as a spectrum rather than a single disease entity. The **schizophrenia**

What's in the *DSM-5*

Schizophrenia Subtypes and Dimensional Ratings

The *DSM-5* authors implemented major changes in their approach to diagnosing schizophrenia. As we mentioned at the beginning of the chapter, they eliminated the subtypes of schizophrenia. Instead, using a scale that is in Section 3 of the *DSM-5*, clinicians assign a diagnosis of schizophrenia to which they can add a rating of the individual's symptoms along a set of dimensions, as Table 3 shows.

By eliminating the subtypes of schizophrenia, the *DSM-5* authors sought to improve both the diagnostic reliability and the validity of the system. They also sought to establish a more quantifiable basis for research into the disorder's causes and for treatment planning. For example, a clinician evaluating the results of cognitive-behavioral therapy could use the ratings of hallucination and delusion severity to determine whether the intervention is reducing the specific symptoms toward which they are targeting treatment.

The *DSM-5* authors also decided to include cognitive impairment as a dimension in the Section 3 severity ratings, given the importance of cognitive deficits in current understandings of the individual's ability to carry out social and occupational activities and the tasks of everyday living. In this regard, a neuropsychological assessment can help to inform the diagnostic process (Reichenberg, 2010).

The current system in the *DSM-5* represents a step away from the old categorization system and toward the dimensional approach. Including severity ratings rather than subtypes in Section 3 makes it possible for clinicians and researchers to track individuals over time in a quantifiable fashion.

The *DSM-5* authors also considered eliminating schizoaffective disorder as a separate entity but decided not to. They believe clinicians will eventually diagnose schizophrenia as a spectrum disorder. This would mean that even diagnoses long in use in psychiatry would disappear, including schizophreniform disorder, schizoaffective disorder, and two of the personality disorders associated with schizophrenia-like symptoms, which you will read about in the chapter "Personality Disorders".

first-rank symptom (FRS)
Symptom that is truly defining, or key, in the diagnosis of schizophrenia.

schizophrenia spectrum
Range of disorders that reflect a similar underlying disease process as that involved in schizophrenia.

MINI CASE

Schizophrenia, Multiple Episodes, Currently in Full Remission

Esther is a single 36-year-old heterosexual Caucasian female. She lives with her mother, and for the past 10 years she has worked as a clerical assistant in an insurance company and no longer shows the delusions, disorganized speech, and lack of emotional expression that originally led to her two prior hospitalizations within a 2-year period. At the moment, she is able to hold her job and maintain a relationship with her mother and a few friends.

TABLE 3 Dimensions of Psychosis Symptom Severity in Section 3 of DSM-5

	0	1	2	3	4
Hallucinations	Not present	Equivocal (severity or duration not sufficient to be considered psychosis)	Present, but mild (little pressure to act upon voices, not very bothered by voices)	Present and moderate (some pressure to respond to voices, or is somewhat bothered by voices)	Present and severe (severe pressure to respond to voices, or is very bothered by voices)
Delusions	Not present	Equivocal (severity or duration not sufficient to be considered psychosis)	Present, but mild (delusions are not bizarre, or little pressure to act upon delusional beliefs, not very bothered by beliefs)	Present and moderate (some pressure to act upon beliefs, or is somewhat bothered by beliefs)	Present and severe (severe pressure to act upon beliefs, or is very bothered by beliefs)
Disorganized speech	Not present	Equivocal (severity or duration not sufficient to be considered disorganization)	Present, but mild (some difficulty following speech and/or occasional bizarre behavior)	Present and moderate (speech often difficult to follow and/or frequent bizarre behavior)	Present and severe (speech almost impossible to follow and/or behavior almost always bizarre)
Abnormal psychomotor behavior	Not present	Equivocal (severity or duration not sufficient to be considered abnormal psychomotor behavior)	Present, but mild (occasional abnormal motor behavior)	Present and moderate (frequent abnormal motor behavior)	Present and severe (abnormal motor behavior almost constant)
Negative symptoms (restricted emotional expression or avolition)	Not present	Equivocal decrease in facial expressivity, prosody, gestures, or self-initiated behavior	Present, but mild decrease in facial expressivity, prosody, gestures, or self-initiated behavior.	Present and moderate decrease in facial expressivity, prosody, gestures, or self-initiated behavior.	Present and severe decrease in facial expressivity, prosody, gestures, or self-initiated behavior.
Impaired cognition	Not present	Equivocal (cognitive function not clearly outside the range expected for age or SES, i.e., within 0.5 SD of mean)	Present, but mild (some reduction in cognitive function below expected for age and SES, 0.5–1 SD from mean)	Present and moderate (clear reduction in cognitive function below expected for age and SES, 1–2 SD from mean)	Present and severe (severe reduction in cognitive function below expected for age and SES, >2 SD from mean)
Depression	Not present	Equivocal (some depressed mood, but insufficient symptoms, duration, or severity to meet diagnostic criteria)	Present, but mild (meets criteria for major depression, with minimum number of symptoms, duration, and severity)	Present and moderate (meets criteria for major depression with somewhat more than the minimum number of symptoms, duration, and/or severity)	Present and severe (meets criteria for major depression with many more than the minimum number of symptoms and/ or severity)
Mania	Not present	Equivocal (some inflated or irritable mood, but insufficient symptoms, duration, or severity to meet diagnostic criteria)	Present, but mild (meets criteria for mania with minimum number of symptoms, duration, and severity)	Present and moderate (meets criteria for mania with somewhat more than the minimum number of symptoms, duration, and/or severity)	Present and severe (meets criteria for mania with many more than the minimum number of symptoms and/or severity)

Note: SD = standard deviation; SES = socioeconomic status

spectrum refers to a range of disorders that reflect a similar underlying disease process. To this end, a provisional section of the *DSM-5* (Section 3) includes a set of symptom severity ratings (see Table 3). Although not formal diagnostic categories, they can inform the assessment process as well as allowing clinicians to track changes in a client's symptoms across time and over the course of treatment.

Estimates from the United States place the lifetime prevalence of schizophrenia at 1 percent (National Institute of Mental Health, 2015). Men and women are equally likely to develop the disorder over the course of their lifetimes, although women typically do so later in life (Falkenburg & Tracy, 2014).

The prevalence of schizophrenia is relatively low compared to other psychological disorders, but a surprisingly high percentage of adults report experiencing minor psychotic symptoms. Reviewing a large number of studies on psychotic symptoms, one group of researchers estimate the lifetime prevalence as about 5 percent, and the prevalence at any one time as about 3 percent (van Os et al., 2009).

Course of Schizophrenia

The course of schizophrenia, as mentioned, was once thought to be lifelong. This situation began to change during the 1970s as researchers and clinicians developed a better diagnostic system and understanding of the nature of psychotic disorders. We now know that schizophrenia may take one of several courses. Even so, compared to other psychological disorders, both course and outcome are poorer for people with schizophrenia (Jobe & Harrow, 2010).

Researchers who follow people with schizophrenia for extended periods of time propose a long-term framework in which 25 to 35 percent show chronic psychotic symptoms. Some people with schizophrenia can even show complete recovery for the remainder of their lives; 40 percent show significant improvement if they receive current treatment during their

You Be the Judge

Schizophrenia Diagnosis

As we discussed in the chapter, the outcome of schizophrenia is not necessarily positive. Although many people do achieve recovery, particularly if they are treated early in the course of the disorder, people with schizophrenia nevertheless face substantial risks of relapse over the rest of their lives. Therefore, when a mental health professional delivers a diagnosis of schizophrenia, it is serious news that could lead the individual to experience great distress.

Practitioners thus face some ethical issues when working with people diagnosed with schizophrenia (Howe, 2008). Not only must they attempt to determine whether to provide a diagnosis of this serious disorder; they must also address specific questions relevant to the individual's particular symptoms. For example, the clinician may consider it more acceptable to inform clients with delusional disorder that they are receiving medication for anxiety, stress, or dysphoria rather than for delusions. To inform the client about the actual nature of his or her symptoms might interfere with the ability to form a therapeutic alliance, which could in turn interfere with the ultimate success of the treatment.

To overcome this obstacle, a clinician may decide to share a partial truth. Specifically, the clinician may reframe a client's symptoms as strengths. Rather than seeing a client's attachments to inanimate objects as a symptom, for example, the clinician may reframe the behavior as proving the client's exceptional capacity for caring.

A second ethical dilemma arises in balancing a client's desire to succeed in life with the reality that, due to the disorder, he or she may be unable to realize these ambitions. The stress of a competitive career, for example, might push the client over the edge into a relapse. Should the clinician try to protect the client from undertaking this venture, or respect the client's autonomy to make his or her own decisions?

As if these two challenges were not enough, consider the situation in which a clinician wishes to involve the client's family in treatment. As you will see later in the chapter, overinvolved and critical family members can exacerbate a client's symptoms. Should the clinician try to persuade the client to make the family part of the treatment, knowing this could improve the client's chances of recovery? Or would such persuasion be unethical, a violation of the client's autonomy?

Finally, given that people with a family history of schizophrenia have increased risk of developing the disorder, how much should clinicians warn high-risk adolescents or young adults? On the one hand, telling people who are asymptomatic that they may develop this serious illness could itself provoke an episode. On the other hand, not telling those at genetic risk about the possibility of their developing schizophrenia may mean they don't take preventive steps.

Howe (2008) suggests that mental health professionals can navigate these ethical dilemmas by using an "ethical sliding scale." In other words, they can make their ethical decisions by taking into account the client's ability to achieve insight, the strength of their own relationship with the client, and the nature and strength of the client's relationship with family. Although respecting the client's autonomy should be the primary guiding principle, clinicians should balance it against the client's decision-making abilities.

Q: *You be the judge:* Do you agree with the idea of using an ethical sliding scale?

acute phase. However, even when they are symptom-free, these individuals may still be impaired in their functioning and adjustment. Furthermore, people with schizophrenia are two to three times more likely to die than others in their age group, leading to a reduction in life expectancy of 15 to 20 years (Gatov, Rosella, Chiu, & Kurdyak, 2017). This higher mortality reflects, in part, the economic and social challenges these individuals face in their daily lives. The use of antipsychotic medications may improve mortality by reducing suicide rates, but alternatively may increase mortality due to negative effects on cardiovascular health (Vermeulen et al., 2017).

The factors that contribute to poorer prognosis among people with schizophrenia include deficits in cognitive functioning, a longer period of time without treatment, substance abuse, a poorer course of early development, higher vulnerability to anxiety, and negative life events. In addition, overinvolvement of family members in the individual's life, as we discuss later in the chapter, also predicts poorer outcome (Jobe & Harrow, 2010).

Single men seem to be at particularly high risk if they possess these additional characteristics (Gómez-de-Regil et al., 2010). Men also are more likely to experience negative symptoms, to have poorer social support networks, and to have poorer functioning over time than women (Willhite et al., 2008). Perhaps surprisingly, given better resources for treating affected individuals, the prognosis for individuals from developing (agricultural-based) countries is better than that for individuals from developed (industrial) nations (Hopper, Harrison, Janca, & Sartorius, 2007).

brief psychotic disorder
A diagnosis clinicians use when an individual develops symptoms of psychosis for more than a day but less than a month.

6.2 Brief Psychotic Disorder

As the term implies, **brief psychotic disorder** is a diagnosis that clinicians use when an individual develops symptoms of psychosis for more than a day but less than a month. The individual must experience one of four symptoms, which are delusions, hallucinations, disorganized speech, and grossly disorganized or catatonic behavior.

Clinicians assigning this particular diagnosis need to note the context in which individuals display the symptoms of this disorder. Has the client experienced a recent stressor, such as a natural disaster, the loss of a close relative, or an accident? Another possibility is that a woman develops this disorder soon after giving birth. Such circumstances might affect the clinician's decision-making process in making a diagnosis of brief psychotic disorder.

A brief psychotic episode can last anywhere between 1 day and 1 month.

©ljubaphoto/Getty Images

MINI CASE

Brief Psychotic Disorder, with Marked Stressors

Anthony is a 22-year-old Caucasian heterosexual male. He is a senior at a prestigious small college. His family has traditionally held high standards for Anthony, and his father had every expectation that his son would go on to study at Harvard Law School. Anthony often felt intensely pressured as he worked day and night to maintain a high grade-point average, while diligently preparing for the national examination for admission to law school. His social life became devoid of any meaningful contact. He even began skipping meals, because he did not want to take time away from studying. When Anthony received his scores on the law school admission exam, he was devastated, because he knew they were too low to allow him to get into any of the better law schools. He began crying uncontrollably, wandering around the dormitory hallways, screaming obscenities, and telling people there was a plot on the part of the college dean to keep him from getting into law school. After 2 days of this behavior, Anthony's resident advisor convinced him to go to the infirmary, where clinicians diagnosed and treated his condition. After a week of rest and medication, Anthony returned to normal functioning and was able to assess his academic situation more rationally.

MINI CASE

Schizophreniform Disorder, with Good Prognostic Features

When Deion, a married African American male, developed a psychological disorder, he was 26 years old and worked for a convenience store chain. Although family and friends always regarded Deion as unusual, he had not experienced psychotic symptoms. This all changed as he grew more and more disturbed over the course of several months. His mother thought that he was just "stressed out" because of his financial problems, but Deion did not seem concerned about such matters. He gradually developed paranoid delusions and became preoccupied with reading the Bible, though he did not actively practice any religion. What brought his disturbance to the attention of his supervisors was the fact that he had submitted an order to the district office for 6,000 loaves of bread. He had scribbled at the bottom of the order form, "Jesus will multiply the loaves." When his supervisors questioned this inappropriate order, Deion became enraged and insisted that they were plotting to prevent him from fighting world hunger. Paranoid themes and bizarre behaviors also surfaced in Deion's interactions with his wife and children. Following 2 months of increasingly disturbed behavior, Deion's boss urged him to see a psychiatrist. With rest and relatively low doses of antipsychotic medication, Deion returned to normal functioning after a few weeks.

6.3 Schizophreniform Disorder

People receive a diagnosis of **schizophreniform disorder** if they experience symptoms of schizophrenia for a period of 1 to 6 months. If symptoms persisted for longer than 6 months, the clinician conducts an evaluation to determine whether a diagnosis of schizophrenia is appropriate. Those clients who show a rapid development of symptoms (within a span of 4 weeks), seem confused or perplexed while in the peak of the episode, and have otherwise good social and personal functioning prior to the episode have a better chance of not developing schizophrenia. They are also likely to have a good prognosis if they do not show the negative symptoms of apathy, withdrawal, and asociality.

schizophreniform disorder
A disorder characterized by psychotic symptoms that are essentially the same as those found in schizophrenia, except for their duration; specifically, symptoms usually last from 1 to 6 months.

6.4 Schizoaffective Disorder

In **schizoaffective disorder**, individuals with depressive or bipolar disorder also experience delusions and/or hallucinations. However, the diagnosis can be made only if, during a 2-week period, clients have psychotic but not mood disorder symptoms. For most of the duration of their illness, they must have a major mood episode (depressive or manic) as well as symptoms of schizophrenia. In other words, they must have both a mood episode and a psychotic disorder, and at least 2 weeks during which delusions and/or hallucinations are the only symptoms they show.

schizoaffective disorder
A disorder involving the experience of a major depressive episode, a manic episode, or a mixed episode while also meeting the diagnostic criteria for schizophrenia.

MINI CASE

Schizoaffective Disorder, Bipolar Type

At the time of her admission to a psychiatric hospital, Hazel, a married Caucasian heterosexual woman originally from Canada, was a 52-year-old mother of three children. She had a 20-year history of schizophrenia-like symptoms, and she experienced periodic episodes of mania. Her schizophrenia-like symptoms included delusions, hallucinations, and thought disorder. These symptoms were fairly well controlled by antipsychotic medications, which she received by injection every 2 weeks. She was also treated with lithium to control her manic episodes; however, she often skipped her daily dose because she liked "feeling high." On several occasions following extended periods of abstinence from lithium, Hazel became manic. Accelerated speech and bodily activity, sleepless nights, and erratic behavior characterized these episodes. At the insistence of her husband and her therapist, Hazel would resume taking her lithium, and shortly thereafter her manic symptoms would subside, although her schizophrenia-like symptoms were still somewhat evident.

delusional disorder
Disorder in which the only symptoms are delusions that have lasted for at least 1 month.

erotomanic type of delusional disorder
Delusional disorder in which individuals falsely believe that another person is in love with them.

grandiose type of delusional disorder
An exaggerated view of oneself as possessing special and extremely favorable personal qualities and abilities.

jealous type of delusional disorder
Delusional disorder in which individuals falsely believe that their romantic partner is unfaithful to them.

persecutory type of delusional disorder
Delusional disorder in which individuals falsely believe that someone close to them is treating them in a malevolent manner.

somatic type of delusional disorder
Delusional disorder in which individuals falsely believe that they have a medical condition.

6.5 Delusional Disorders

People with **delusional disorders** have delusions that have lasted for at least 1 month as their only symptom. Furthermore, they must have no other symptoms of schizophrenia and must never have met the criteria for schizophrenia. In fact, these individuals can function very well and do not seem odd to others except when they talk about their particular delusion.

Based on which delusional theme is prominent, clinicians diagnose these individuals with one of five major types of disorder, or with mixed or unspecified types that include people who have no one prominent delusion. People with the **erotomanic type of delusional disorder** falsely believe that another person is in love with them. The target of their delusion is usually a person of higher status than they are. For example, a woman may be certain that a famous singer is in love with her and that he communicates secret love messages to her in his songs.

The conviction that they possess special and extremely favorable personal qualities and abilities characterizes people who have the **grandiose type of delusional disorder**. A man may believe that he is the Messiah waiting for a sign from heaven to begin his active ministry. In the **jealous type of delusional disorder**, individuals are certain their romantic partner is unfaithful to them. They may even construct a plan to entrap their partner to prove his or her infidelity. People with the **persecutory type of delusional disorder** believe that someone close to them is treating them in a malevolent manner. They may, for example, become convinced that their neighbors are deliberately poisoning their water. People with the **somatic type of delusional disorder** believe they have a medical condition causing an abnormal bodily reaction that does not actually exist.

The *DSM-IV* listed **shared psychotic disorder** as a separate diagnosis for use when one or more people develop a delusional system as a result of a close relationship with a psychotic person who is delusional. This case is more familiarly referred to as *folie à deux* (folly of two) when two people are involved. Occasionally, three or more people or the members of an entire family are affected.

MINI CASE

Delusional Disorder, Jealous Type

Paul is a 32-year-old heterosexual Hispanic American male who has recently experienced tremendous stress at his job of 5 years. Although he has avoided dwelling on his work problems, he has begun to develop irrational beliefs about his girlfriend, Elizabeth. Despite Elizabeth's repeated vows that she is consistently faithful in the relationship, Paul has become obsessed with the belief that she is sexually involved with another person. He is suspicious of everyone with whom Elizabeth interacts and questions her about every insignificant encounter. He searches her closet and drawers for mysterious items, looks for unexplained charges on credit card bills, listens in on Elizabeth's phone calls, and has contacted a private investigator to follow her. Paul is now insisting that they move to another state.

MINI CASE

Delusional Disorder, Persecutory Type

Julio is a 25-year-old Latino male who identifies as gay. Recently Julio met with his co-worker Ernesto in the company cafeteria of the accounting firm where they both work. After a brief and very casual conversation, Julio began to develop the belief that Ernesto was secretly trying to break into his workstation to plant faulty reports. Soon Julio became convinced that Ernesto was conspiring with three others in their unit to make it appear that he was incompetent. He requested a reassignment so his job would, in his opinion, no longer be jeopardized by the behavior of his co-workers.

Shared psychotic disorder now appears in the *DSM-5* in the section on other specified schizophrenia spectrum and other psychotic disorders, as "delusional symptoms in partner of individual with delusional disorder" (American Psychiatric Association, 2013, p. 122). Although rare, shared psychotic disorder is occasionally found in forensic cases, both criminal and civil (Parker, 2014).

6.6 Theories and Treatment of Schizophrenia

Schizophrenia reflects a complex interplay of biological, psychological, and sociocultural forces. As a result, researchers are well aware of the need to approach the disorder from an interactive perspective.

A key concept in understanding schizophrenia's causes is **vulnerability**, the idea that individuals have a biologically determined predisposition to developing schizophrenia but that the disorder develops only when certain environmental conditions are in place. As we look at each of the contributions to a vulnerability model, keep in mind that no single theory contains the entire explanation.

Biological Perspectives

Theories Biological explanations of schizophrenia have their origins in the writings of Emil Kraepelin, who thought of schizophrenia as a disease caused by degenerative processes in the brain. Although it was following from Kraepelin's work that scientists first became interested in possible brain abnormalities in people with schizophrenia, nineteenth-century technology was not up to the kind of research needed to identify those abnormalities. Contemporary neuroimaging methods are providing scientists with key data that is just now making such investigations possible.

People with a persecutory type of delusional disorder believe, incorrectly, that someone is plotting or planning against them.
©Noel Hendrickson/Getty Images

One of the earliest discoveries to emerge as a result of developments in neuroimaging methods was that individuals with schizophrenia have enlarged ventricles, the structures in the brain holding cerebrospinal fluid. This condition was accompanied by cortical atrophy, a wasting away of brain tissue, and is found primarily in two areas: the frontal and temporal lobes. Deterioration of the frontal lobes results in a diminished ability to plan as well as to exert control over intrusive thoughts and unwanted behaviors (Molina et al., 2005). Loss of tissue in the temporal lobes interferes with the processing of auditory information (van Haren et al., 2011). Altered activity in the frontal and temporal lobes of the brain in turn seems related both to negative symptoms and cognitive deficits (Abram et al., 2017). Decreased activity in the frontal lobe also has been shown to be linked to poorer social functioning (Watanabe, Urakami, Hongo, & Ohtsubo, 2015), reflecting the lack of inhibitory control that this area of the brain ordinarily provides in mature adults.

Figure 1 compares fMRI scans averaged across the brains of people with schizophrenia with those of normal controls on one type of social task in which participants tried to infer the intentions of fictional characters depicted in comic strips. As shown, participants with schizophrenia had decreased activation of areas of the frontal and temporal lobes involved in social judgments (Walter et al., 2009).

This reduced ability of the brain regions to communicate with each other seems particularly to affect working memory and the ability to control cognitive operations, by reducing links between the thalamus and the frontal lobe of the cortex (Wagner et al., 2015). It may also add to further changes in the frontal and temporal lobes.

As important as they may be, structural changes alone cannot entirely explain what happens to the brain to increase the individual's vulnerability to developing schizophrenia.

shared psychotic disorder
Delusional disorder in which one or more people develop a delusional system as a result of a close relationship with a psychotic person who is delusional.

vulnerability
The idea that individuals have a biologically determined predisposition to developing schizophrenia but that the disorder develops only when certain environmental conditions are in place.

FIGURE 1 fMRI
Scans Comparing
Health Controls with
Schizophrenia Patients

As is seen in comparing the
top and bottom rows, the
brains of patients with
schizophrenia show reduced
activation in the frontal and
temporal lobes involved in
social judgment.

SOURCE: Walter, H., et al. (2009)
Dysfunction of the social brain in
schizophrenia is modulated by
intention type: An fMRI study.
*Social Cognitive and Affective
Neuroscience, 4*(2): 166–176. Oxford
University.

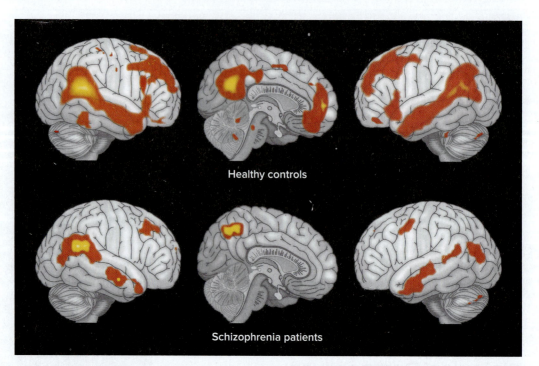

Healthy controls

Schizophrenia patients

**neurodevelopmental
hypothesis**
Theory proposing that schizophrenia
is a disorder of development that arises
during adolescence or early adulthood
due to alterations in the genetic
control of brain maturation.

Instead, researchers believe that additional clues to schizophrenia's causes exist in the neu-rotransmitters responsible for communicating information in the nervous system. An early candidate for such altered neurotransmitter functioning is dopamine. Alterations in dopa-mine receptors mean that they do not bind properly when dopamine is released from pre-synaptic neurons. Such alterations, in turn, lead to excess amounts of dopamine in the brain that contribute to schizophrenia's effects on cognition and goal-directed behavior (Vyas et al., 2017).

Gamma-aminobutyric acid (GABA), an inhibitory neurotransmitter, also appears to play a role in schizophrenia due to changes the disorder may produce in the N-methyl-D-aspartate (NMDA) receptors. Evidence supporting this idea is based on the fact that the drug ketamine reduces the activity of NMDA receptors. Studies using animal models sug-gest that dysfunctions in these receptors could contribute to abnormal neural oscillations (brain waves), which in turn could lead to difficulties in both sensory integration and cogni-tion (Michaels et al., 2018).

Research on patterns of family inheritance supports the idea that schizophrenia is, at least in part, a genetically caused disorder, with heritability estimates known to range from 60 to 70 percent (Tsuang, Stone, & Faraone, 1999). Having established this high heritability, researchers have since moved on to try to locate the specific genes involved and to under-stand the factors that increase the genetically vulnerable person's chances of actually developing the disorder. Particularly intriguing is the continued evidence connecting cogni-tive functioning to schizophrenia, with large-scale studies suggesting the overlap of multiple genes in both areas (Wang et al., 2018).

The search for genetic abnormalities in schizophrenia is made considerably more compli-cated by the fact that, over recent decades, researchers have identified abnormalities among at least 19 possible genes dispersed over as many as 10 chromosomes. Some of the func-tions served by these genes rely on the actions of dopamine and GABA, but other candi-dates include serotonin and glutamate. Researchers are also searching for abnormalities in the genetics of immune functioning among individuals with schizophrenia (Crisafulli et al., 2015). Such abnormalities might predate the apparent onset of the illness, reflecting neuro-developmental changes much earlier in life.

Indeed, according to the **neurodevelopmental hypothesis** (Andreasen, 2010), schizophre-nia is a disorder of development that arises during adolescence or early adulthood due to

REAL STORIES

Elyn Saks: Schizophrenia

In her memoir, *The Center Cannot Hold: My Journey Through Madness*, UCLA professor Elyn Saks tells the moving story of her lifelong struggle with schizophrenia. Her story provides a unique perspective on one of the most debilitating psychological disorders and a firsthand account of the experience of psychosis.

Saks begins the book by describing the first signs of her illness when she was a child growing up in an upper-middle-class family in Miami, Florida. These included idiosyncratic behaviors like organizing and lining up her possessions in her room, and frightening dissociative experiences when she was only 8 years old. Saks recalls feeling fearful of these experiences, partly because she was unable to express what was happening to her even though her family was otherwise supportive and caring.

Throughout her formative years, Saks continued to experience what she now recognizes as prodromal symptoms of schizophrenia. At the time her experiences caused her to feel paranoid around others, afraid they would find out her secret. She attended Vanderbilt University and at first greatly enjoyed her newfound independence. However, within the first 2 weeks of school, away from the protective clutches of her family and all the comforts that came with being taken care of, everything, as she puts it, "slowly began to unravel." Her inability to perform self-care activities such as bathing signaled the start of her illness, and Elyn had several brief psychotic episodes that resolved without intervention. In the book, she describes the insidious nature of her illness when it began to manifest itself.

After returning home from her freshman year of college, Saks continued to experience paranoia and occasional hallucinations. In addition to those symptoms, she was feeling depressed and lethargic. Her parents took her to see a psychiatrist, whose only insight into her condition was that she "needed help." Once Saks returned to Vanderbilt for her sophomore year, her symptoms subsided as she found comfort

Elyn Saks has enjoyed a successful law career despite suffering from schizophrenia.

©Damian Dovarganes/AP Images

in her studies and a close-knit group of friends. With strong social support, Saks was able to remain in a relatively stable condition for the rest of her time in college. However, that comfort quickly turned to fear as graduation approached and she felt the fragile structure that kept her content was about to be shaken.

Saks won a highly prestigious Marshall scholarship to study philosophy at Oxford University in England. She was terrified of living in a new country, so far away from everything she knew, and particularly of being away from her routine and friends at college. Indeed, after just a few weeks at Oxford, Saks's still unnamed illness again began to take hold, and her fear of her illness turned into suicidal ideation. At the urging of a friend, she saw a psychiatrist and admitted that she had thoughts of ending her life. She entered a day

treatment program at a psychiatric hospital, though she had no idea just how ill she was. Her perspective on her symptoms at the time was that they were simply a problem that needed to be solved and could be easily fixed, a view that grossly underestimated the complexity of her illness.

During her hospitalization, Saks received intensive psychotherapy and spent the rest of her time working on her studies. Her academic program did not require her to attend classes, so she was able to isolate herself in her apartment while she worked, which made it difficult for her to realize the extent of her psychological difficulties. She was not taking any medication at the time, and her ability to attain a firm grasp on reality slowly deteriorated. When she reported to her psychiatrist that her suicidal ideation had worsened, she was urged to become a full-time patient at the hospital, where she remained for 2 weeks. After beginning a course of psychotherapeutic medication, Saks eventually felt well enough to return to her studies, although she soon began deteriorate psychologically. She returned to the hospital, where she languished in psychosis and depression for several months. Once she was stabilized, her psychiatrist recommended that she enter psychoanalysis. Determined to complete her degree at Oxford, Saks continued her studies while seeing a psychoanalyst 5 days a week. Even after finishing her studies, which ended up taking 4 years instead of 2, Saks felt that her relationship with her analyst was helping her so much that she decided to stay in England to continue their work together for 2 more years.

In the book, Saks describes her experience of living with her illness during this time in her life. "Completely delusional, I still understood essential aspects of how the world worked. For example, I was getting my schoolwork done, and I vaguely understood the rule that in a social setting, even with the people I most trusted, I could not ramble on about my psychotic thoughts. To talk about killing children, or burning whole worlds, or being able to destroy cities with my mind was not part of polite conversation . . . At times, though, I was so psychotic that I could barely contain myself. The delusions expanded into full-blown hallucinations, in which I could clearly hear people whispering. I could hear my name being called when no one was physically around–in a corner of the library, or late at night, in my bedroom where I slept alone. Sometimes, the noise I heard was so overwhelming it drowned out almost all other sound."

After leaving England, Saks decided to attend law school at Yale University, where she continued to struggle with psychotic episodes that resulted in several lengthy hospitalizations, although she was eventually able to finish her degree. After working in a mental health law clinic, she had discovered a passion for helping psychiatric patients, fueled by her intimate understanding of the experience of being a psychiatric patient. Throughout her career she has worked toward creating a high legal standard of care for psychiatric patients in the United States.

Saks eventually took a position at the law school at UCLA, where she continues to work as a tenured faculty member. Over the years she has worked hard to keep her psychotic symptoms at bay with help from a combination of talk therapy, medication, and social support from her husband and close friends. Though Saks struggled for many years to accept the reality of her illness, she now accepts her diagnosis and all that it entails. At the end of the book, Saks writes that she feels grateful to be one of the lucky few able to successfully live with schizophrenia. She dispels the idea that she has had a better life because of schizophrenia but instead states that she has been able to live her life despite it.

Throughout her career, when discussing legal aspects of mental health treatment, she often noticed others stigmatizing those with mental illness, not believing they could lead normal lives or even be trusted to not be violent. When describing why she decided to write the book and "out" herself as mentally ill, she explains, "I want to bring hope to those who suffer from schizophrenia, and understanding to those who do not."

SOURCE: *The Center Cannot Hold: My Journey Through Madness* by Elyn Saks.

alterations in the genetic control of brain maturation. The genetic vulnerability some individuals inherit becomes evident if they are exposed to certain risks during early brain development. These risks can occur during the prenatal period in the form of viral infections, malnutrition, or exposure to toxins. Thus, schizophrenia may reflect not only abnormal genetic inheritance but also deficits associated with epigenetic processes. As their illness progresses over time, individuals may show continued deleterious changes through a process of neuroprogression, in which the effects of schizophrenia interact with brain changes caused by normal aging.

Somewhat related to the neurodevelopmental hypothesis is the idea that cognitive deficits of people with schizophrenia reflect a loss of **neuroplasticity**, adaptive changes in the brain in response to experience. According to this view, people with schizophrenia form too many associations when attempting to learn and remember new material, in contrast to the normal way people trim out or prune information they do not need to retain (McCullumsmith, 2015). The cognitive functioning of individuals with schizophrenia suffers because they essentially remember "too much," including information they never actually encountered, perhaps leading to the characteristic psychological symptoms of delusions and hallucinations.

neuroplasticity
Adaptive changes in the brain in response to experience.

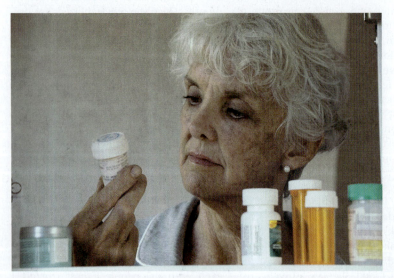

Neurodegenerative disorders in older adults can exacerbate negative changes if clients are unable to take the correct dosages of their medication.
©Ariel Skelley/Blend Images

Treatments The primary biological treatment for schizophrenia is antipsychotic medication, or neuroleptics. As we discussed in the chapter "Theoretical Perspectives", psychiatrists prescribe two categories of neuroleptics: the so-called typical or first-generation antipsychotics, and the atypical or second-generation antipsychotics.

Chlorpromazine (Thorazine) and haloperidol (Haldol) are two of the typical antipsychotic medications. They seem to reduce symptoms primarily by acting on the dopamine receptor system in areas of the brain associated with delusions, hallucinations, and other positive symptoms.

In addition to being highly sedating, causing a person to feel fatigued and listless, the typical antipsychotics also have serious undesirable consequences. These include **extrapyramidal symptoms (EPS)**, which are motor disorders like rigid muscles, tremors, shuffling movement, restlessness, and muscle spasms affecting posture. After several years, people being treated with the typical antipsychotics can also develop **tardive dyskinesia**, another motor disorder, which consists of involuntary movements of the mouth, arms, and trunk of the body.

The distressing side effects and failure of typical antipsychotics to treat negative symptoms of schizophrenia led psychiatric researchers several decades ago to embark on a search for alternatives that would both be more effective and have fewer motor symptoms. These are the medications we now refer to as atypical antipsychotics. Such medications operate against both serotonin and dopamine neurotransmitters and hence are also called serotonin-dopamine antagonists.

Despite hopes that the atypical antipsychotic medications would result in fewer side effects, one of the first, clozapine (Clozaril), soon turned out to have potentially lethal side effects by leading to agranulocytosis, a condition that affects the functioning of the white blood cells. Now, patients receive the atypical medications only under very controlled conditions, and only when other medications do not work. Instead, clinicians can prescribe one of a number of safer atypical antipsychotics, including risperidone (Risperdal), olanzapine (Zyprexa), and quetiapine (Seroquel).

Unfortunately, even medications in the newer group of atypical antipsychotics are not without potentially serious side effects. They can cause metabolic disturbances, particularly weight gain, increases in blood cholesterol, and greater insulin resistance, placing clients at greater risk of diabetes and cardiovascular disease (Ringen et al., 2014).

Because of the many complexities in the biological treatment of individuals with schizophrenia, researchers and clinicians increasingly recognize the need to take the individual's medical and psychiatric profile into account. For treatment-resistant clients, clozapine is the only approach that has empirical support. In other instances, clinicians may attempt to find either a combination of antipsychotics or a combination of antipsychotics and other classes of medications. The next question is how long to maintain a client on medications, balancing the value of continued treatment against the risk of relapse and possible health hazards that occur with their use over time (Kane & Correll, 2010).

extrapyramidal symptoms (EPS)
Motor disorders involving rigid muscles, tremors, shuffling movement, restlessness, and muscle spasms affecting posture.

tardive dyskinesia
Motor disorder that consists of involuntary movements of the mouth, arms, and trunk of the body.

Psychiatrists strive to find an appropriate regimen of medication in order to prevent individuals with psychotic disorders from experiencing highly disruptive psychotic symptoms.
©JGI/Getty Images

Psychological Perspectives

Theories Although evidence continues to accumulate regarding the role of genetics in schizophrenia, researchers nevertheless believe that psychological theories can provide important insights. Those who continue to explore the cognitive functions affected by schizophrenia are increasingly seeing these as potentially fundamental to understanding the disorder's central features.

The cognitive correlates of schizophrenia, as shown by the summary of neuropsychological performance in Figure 2, range from general intellectual ability to deficits in attention, declarative memory (long-term recall of information), and processing speed. Overall, estimates of the number of people with schizophrenia who are cognitively impaired vary from 55 to 70 or 80 percent (Reichenberg, 2010).

Keep in mind, however, that factors extraneous to the disease can also cause these abnormalities. Such factors include age, educational background, use of medication, and severity

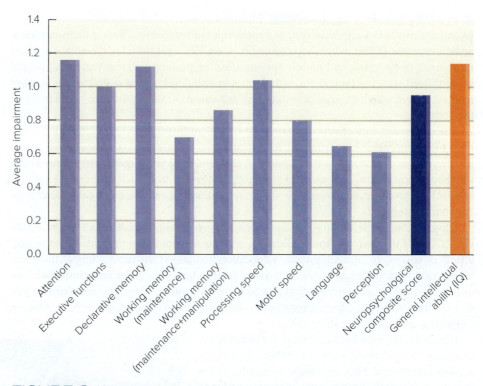

FIGURE 2 Neuropsychological Performance Profile of Schizophrenia (note, the dark blue and orange bars at the right indicate summary scores)

Reichenberg, A. (2010). The assessment of neuropsycholgical functioning in schizophrenia. *Dialogues in Clinical Neuroscience, 12*(3), 383–392. Les Laboratoires Servier, Neuilly-sur-Seine, France. Copyright © Les Laboratoires Servier 2010.

or length of illness. If they are not controlled for, the cognitive impairment thought to be associated with schizophrenia may be due to these extraneous factors and not to the disorder itself.

People who use cannabis (marijuana) also show an elevated risk of developing schizophrenia. Although researchers were long aware of the cannabis-schizophrenia link, they believed that people with schizophrenia used the drug to alleviate their symptoms. Long-term follow-up studies show instead, however, that people develop the disorder after continued use of cannabis. The relationship is specific to extent of marijuana use, with people who are heavier marijuana users prior to being diagnosed with schizophrenia placing themselves at higher risk of developing it (Kelley et al., 2016).

One significant psychological area studied in people with schizophrenia is social cognition, meaning the ability to accurately read the emotions of others. A deficit in social cognition is particularly problematic when individuals with schizophrenia are given the task of recognizing negative emotions such as fear, anger, and disgust, though they are better at identifying mild happiness in the facial expressions of others. Not surprisingly, the nonverbal communicative abilities of people with schizophrenia also appear to be impaired (Walther et al., 2015).

These impairments in cognitive functioning can set up a vicious cycle that leads to a worsening of the individual's situation. Problems in memory, planning, and processing speed, for example, interfere with the ability to hold mentally challenging jobs. The limitations people with schizophrenia have in social cognition and communication make it particularly difficult for them to work in people-oriented jobs. Unable to maintain consistent employment, they can slip into poverty, which further stresses their ability to lead a productive life. Living in high-poverty areas in turn places them at risk for engaging in substance abuse, which can contribute to the symptoms they experience as a result of their disorder.

Treatments   For many years, the most common psychological interventions for people with schizophrenia were behavioral treatments intended to lower the frequency of maladaptive behaviors that interfere with social adjustment and functioning. These interventions typically employed the token economy method of contingency management (see the chapter "Theoretical Perspectives") in which institutionalized individuals received rewards for acting in socially appropriate ways. The expectation was that, over time, the new behaviors would become habitual and the person would not depend on reinforcement in order to engage in that behavior.

However, the token economy as a form of intervention is no longer practical, given that most individuals with schizophrenia receive treatment in the community. In addition, there is little data on its effectiveness, and with clinicians focusing on evidence-based treatment, the profession cannot justify its use (Dickerson, Tenhula, & Green-Paden, 2005).

More promising is cognitive-behavioral therapy, an approach most effective when administered as an adjunct to pharmacological treatments (Wykes, Steel, Everitt, & Tarrier, 2008). Clinicians using **cognitive-behavioral therapy for psychosis (CBTp)** do not try to change clients' delusions or eliminate their hallucinations but instead try to reduce their distress and preoccupation with these symptoms. In addition, they attempt to teach their clients coping skills to improve their ability to live independently. They might assign their clients the homework of keeping a diary of their experiences of hearing voices or making a "reality check" of their delusional beliefs.

CBTp was initially developed in the United Kingdom, perhaps because service providers were more interested in finding nonmedical approaches to treating the symptoms of psychosis than is true in the United States. However, the method is gaining more widespread acceptance in the United States based on studies showing its effectiveness, particularly in conjunction with atypical antipsychotics (Li et al., 2015). CBTp can be administered in a milieu therapy format that would make access possible for a larger number of individuals in a variety of treatment settings (Riggs & Creed, 2017).

Researchers are also developing interventions to help address the cognitive deficits of individuals with schizophrenia, particularly those who suffer from primarily negative symptoms. Like those who seek physical fitness training, people with schizophrenia can receive individualized training, in this case cognitive training, that builds on their current level of functioning to restore or enhance their performance. Cognitive training is guided by findings from neuroscience showing that people with schizophrenia have deficits in memory and sensory processing.

In one promising approach, computers present individuals with a series of auditory training trials in which they must respond rapidly in order to receive a reward. To test the effectiveness of this method, researchers compare the effects of computer games and auditory training (Figure 3). Participants with schizophrenia who received auditory training improved in several areas of cognitive functioning known to be affected by the disorder. These results are also being replicated on laptops, making the method even more transportable to a variety of settings (Fisher et al., 2015). As they improve their memory and sensory skills, individuals with schizophrenia can then become better able to take advantage of other psychologically based interventions, including more successful participation in vocational rehabilitation programs.

Sociocultural Perspectives

Theories   In some of the earliest formulations of the causes of schizophrenia, psychological theorists proposed that disturbed patterns of communication in a child's family environment could precipitate the development of the disorder. In studies of modes of communication and behavior within families with a schizophrenic member, researchers attempted to document deviant patterns of communication and inappropriate ways that parents interacted with their children. Clinicians thought these disturbances in family relationships led to the development of defective emotional responsiveness and cognitive distortions fundamental to the psychological symptoms of schizophrenia.

cognitive-behavioral therapy for psychosis (CBTp) Method of treating symptoms of psychosis in which clinicians do not try to change clients' delusions or eliminate clients' hallucinations but instead try to reduce their distress and preoccupation with these symptoms.

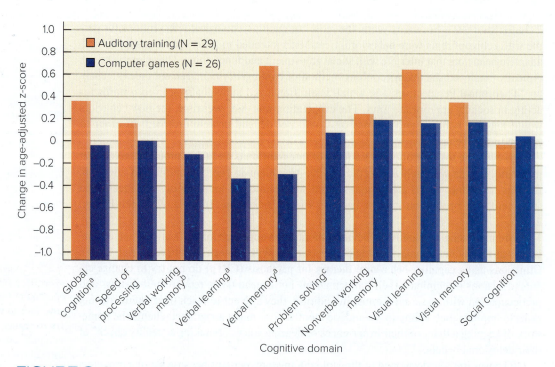

FIGURE 3 Change in Cognitive Performance in Patients with Schizophrenia After 50 Hours of Computerized Auditory Training

[a]Significant difference between groups (P < .01, repeated-measure ANOVA)
[b]Significant difference between groups (P < .05, repeated-measure ANOVA)
[c]Nonsignificant difference between groups (P = .10, repeated-measure ANOVA)

SOURCE: Fisher, M., Holland, C., Merzenich, M. M., & Vinogradov, S. (2009). Using neuroplasticity-based auditory training to improve verbal memory in schizophrenia. *The American Journal of Psychiatry, 166*, 805–811. doi:10.1176/appi.ajp.2009.08050757.

expressed emotion (EE)
Family interactions with the individual that reflect criticism, hostile feelings, and emotional overinvolvement or overconcern.

Contemporary researchers have approached the issue of the extent to which family communications contribute to the disorder by trying to predict outcome or recovery in adults hospitalized for schizophrenia. Instead of regarding a disturbed family as the cause of schizophrenia, they view it as a potential source of stress in the environment of the person trying to recover from a schizophrenic episode. The stress family members create is called **expressed emotion (EE)** and includes interactions with the individual that reflect criticism, hostile feelings, and emotional overinvolvement or overconcern.

Supporting the concept of EE as a source of stress, researchers find that people living in families high in EE are more likely to suffer a relapse, particularly if they are exposed to high levels of criticism (Marom et al., 2005). When in treatment, these individuals may also develop less trust in their therapists (von Polier et al., 2014).

EE may also affect the way that people with schizophrenia process social information. Researchers found higher activation in brain regions involved in self-reflection and sensitivity to social situations when exposing schizophrenic patients to speech that was high in EE compared to neutral speech (Rylands et al., 2011).

It goes without saying that research on EE could never employ an experimental design, and this has been a criticism of the research. Even EE critics, however, recognize that the presence of an individual with schizophrenia creates stress within the family, even if the individual is not living at home. The client's disorder can affect parents, siblings, and even grandparents, particularly when the symptoms first begin to emerge in the early adult years.

Moving beyond the family environment, researchers have also studied broader social factors, such as social class and income, in relationship to schizophrenia. In perhaps the first epidemiological study of mental illness in the United States, Hollingshead and Redlich (1958) observed that schizophrenia was far more prevalent in the lowest socioeconomic classes.

A number of researchers have since replicated the finding that more individuals with schizophrenia live in the poorer sections of urban areas. One possible interpretation of this finding is that people with schizophrenia experience **downward drift**, meaning that their disorder drives them into poverty, which interferes with their ability to work and earn a living. The other possibility is that the stress of living in isolation and poverty in urban areas contributes to the risk of developing schizophrenia (Hudson, 2012).

People born in a country other than the one in which they are currently living (those who have migrant status) also have higher rates of schizophrenia. The individuals most at risk for schizophrenia are those who migrate to lower-status jobs and urban areas, where they are more likely to suffer from exposure to environmental pollutants, stress, and overcrowding (McGrath, Saha, Chant, & Welham, 2008). However, as the number of ethnic minorities in a neighborhood increases, the rates of schizophrenia become lower, suggesting that these individuals benefit from less exposure to discrimination and more opportunities for social support in their immediate environments (Veling et al., 2007).

Other sociocultural risk factors for schizophrenia, or at least for symptoms of psychosis, include adversity suffered in childhood, such as parental loss or separation, abuse, and bullying. In adulthood, individuals more vulnerable to first or subsequent episodes of psychosis include people who have experienced severely stressful life events, including being a victim of assault (Stilo & Murray, 2010). Individuals with high genetic risk who are exposed to environmental stressors are more likely than others who experience mild psychotic symptoms to develop a full-blown disorder (van Os et al., 2009).

Recognizing that the causes of schizophrenia are multifaceted and develop over time, Stilo and Murray (2010) proposed a **developmental cascade hypothesis** that integrates genetic vulnerabilities, damage occurring in the prenatal and early childhood periods, adversity, and drug abuse as ultimately leading to changes in dopamine expressed in psychosis. In Figure 4, the specific genes affected by schizophrenia are shown as developmental genes, or those that play a role in brain development, and as neurotransmitter genes, which play a more direct role in neural activity.

downward drift
A progression observed in people with schizophrenia in which their disorder drives them into poverty, which interferes with their ability to work and earn a living.

developmental cascade hypothesis
A proposal for the cause of schizophrenia that integrates genetic vulnerabilities, damage occurring in the prenatal and early childhood periods, adversity, and drug abuse as causes of changes in dopamine expressed in psychosis.

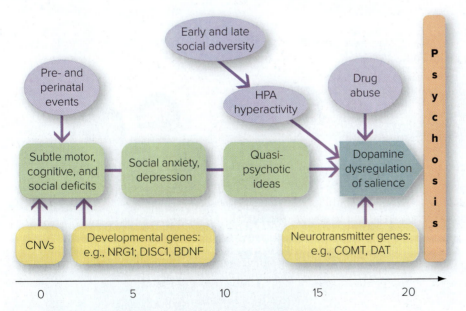

FIGURE 4 Developmental Cascade Toward Schizophrenia

As can be seen from this figure, developmental progression from birth to age 20 (as shown on the horizontal axis) can produce a cascade leading to the onset of schizophrenia.

Note: HPA stands for hypothalamic pituitary adrenal; CNV for copy number variation, a genetic defect. COMT and DAT are genes involved in neurotransmitters.

Modified from Stilo, S. A., & Murray, R. M. (2010). The epidemiology of schizophrenia: replacing dogma with knowledge. *Dialogue in Clinical Neuroscience, 12*(3), 305–315. Les Laboratoires Servier, Neuilly-sur-Seine, France. Copyright © Les Laboratoires Servier 2010.

assertive community treatment (ACT)
Treatment modality in which a team of professionals from psychiatry, psychology, nursing, and social work reach out to clients in their homes and workplaces.

Treatments The coordination of services is especially important in programs geared toward helping people with schizophrenia. One approach to integrating various services is **assertive community treatment (ACT)**, in which an interprofessional team representing psychiatry, psychology, nursing, and social work reaches out to clients in their homes and workplaces. ACT's focus is on engendering empowerment and self-determination in its "consumers," the term such teams use to refer to their clients. Typically, a team of about a dozen professionals work together to help approximately 100 consumers with issues such as complying with medical recommendations, managing their finances, obtaining adequate health care, and dealing with crises when they arise. This approach brings care to the clients, rather than waiting for them to come to a facility for help, a journey that may be too overwhelming for seriously impaired people.

Although approaches such as ACT are expensive, the benefits are impressive. Researchers have conducted dozens of studies on the effectiveness of ACT and have concluded that it has had significant positive impact in reducing hospitalizations, stabilizing housing in the community, and lowering overall treatment costs (Karow et al., 2012).

As effective as it can be, critics charge that ACT is not provided in a manner consistent with its goal of empowering consumers and instead is coercive and paternalistic. To address this charge, ACT researchers are investigating the possibility of combining ACT with another program, called illness management and recovery (IMR). In IMR, consumers receive training in effective ways to manage their illnesses and pursue their goals for recovery. Resting on the principle of self-determination, IMR assumes consumers should be given the resources they need to make informed choices. The program uses peers and clinicians to deliver structured, curriculum-based interventions. Although an initial investigation of ACT-IMR revealed that the providers experienced a number of difficulties in implementing the program, it appeared to reduce hospitalization rates. Moreover, even after funding for the study ran out, the teams continued to provide services (Salyers et al., 2010).

Assertive community treatment involves a highly skilled and collaborative team of psychiatrists, nurses, social workers, and other mental health care professionals.

6.7 Schizophrenia: The Biopsychosocial Perspective

Definitions and diagnostic approaches to schizophrenia are undergoing significant revisions, but throughout the past decade, researchers have gained a great deal of understanding about its many possible causes. Perhaps most exciting is the evolution of an integrated approach to theories that focus on underlying brain mechanisms as expressed in cognitive deficits. Treatment is moving beyond the provision of medication to greater use of evidence-based psychological interventions. Finally, researchers appear to be gaining greater appreciation of the role of sociocultural influences. Together, these advances are increasing the chances that individuals with these disorders will receive integrated care, maximizing their chances of recovery (Sungur et al., 2011).

Clinicians, also, increasingly understand schizophrenia from a life-span perspective. The needs and concerns of individuals with this disorder vary over the years of adulthood, and many recover. Thus, researchers and mental health practitioners are recognizing that part of their job is to provide ways to help people with long-term schizophrenia adapt to changes in both the aging process and the evolution of the disease. The idea that schizophrenia is a neurodevelopmental disorder highlights this important new focus and provides a basis for interventions that take into account individual changes over time.

Return to the Case: David Chen

David was eventually able to return to school part-time, living at home with Ann. Though he struggled with the change in his level of functioning, he was able to use therapy and case management to understand his limitations. The aim was to prevent future stressors from occurring and triggering psychotic episodes. It is difficult to completely avoid all symptoms of psychosis with a disorder as severe as schizophrenia. However, with the proper contingencies and social support, David will be better able to tolerate his symptoms and live a meaningful life.

Dr. Tobin's reflections: David's move into the dorms presented him with his first major life stressor. Although he had previously been living on campus at school, living with his mother after his first hospitalization seemed to have provided a feeling of safety that was shattered once he moved back to school. It was difficult, though, because David certainly wished he could attain independence successfully. Though he was not at his same level of functioning as before, David and Ann had assumed that whatever he had been going through was finished. Returning to the dormitories, however, proved too great a stressor and so David's symptoms resurfaced once again.

Luckily for David, Ann was able to take action to help him after it became clear that he was suffering from something very serious that neither of them had quite understood. With the disorder identified early on, entering a treatment program was beneficial in decreasing the likelihood that David's life will be complicated by the fallout from future psychotic episodes. However, prevention of future episodes is contingent upon his participation in therapy and his medication compliance.

SUMMARY

- Schizophrenia is a serious mental illness, given its potentially broad impact on an individual's ability to live a productive and fulfilling life. Although a significant number of people with schizophrenia eventually manage to live symptom-free lives, many must find ways to adapt their lives to the reality of the illness.

- There are six diagnostic criteria for schizophrenia (see Table 2). In addition to the diagnostic criteria for schizophrenia and related psychotic disorders, the *DSM-5* authors provide a set of severity rating criteria in several spheres of functioning. *DSM-5* authors conceptualize schizophrenia as a spectrum or set of related disorders characterized by dimensions.

- Using the *DSM-IV-TR*, clinicians could make subtype diagnoses to provide more information about the presenting symptoms. With *DSM-5,* these same subtypes (disorganized, paranoid, undifferentiated, and residual) have become specifiers. Specifiers serve the same purpose of providing more diagnostic information, without standing alone as discrete disorders. The exception to this change is catatonia, which has become its own disorder. This exception came about as a result of evidence that the symptoms of catatonia develop differently from the other specifiers.

- First identified as a disease in the 1800s by Benedict Morel, schizophrenia has been studied by physicians, psychiatrists, and psychologists theorizing its origin and identifying symptoms and categories. As the years unfold, researchers attempt to develop a more precise set of diagnostic criteria.

- Schizophrenia may take one of several courses. The course and outcome are poorer for people with schizophrenia than for people with other psychological disorders.

- Other disorders on the schizophrenia spectrum include brief psychotic disorder, schizophreniform disorder, schizoaffective disorder, and several specific types of delusional disorders including erotomanic type, grandiose type, jealous type, persecutory type, and somatic type.

- Theories accounting for the origin of schizophrenia have traditionally fallen into two categories: biological and psychological. The neurodevelopmental hypothesis states that schizophrenia is a disorder of development that arises during the years of adolescence or early adulthood due to alterations in the genetic control of brain maturation.

- The primary biological treatment for schizophrenia is antipsychotic medication, or neuroleptics. The two main categories of neuroleptics are the "typical" or "first generation" and "atypical" or "second generation" antipsychotics. The distressing side effects and failure of typical antipsychotics to treat negative symptoms of schizophrenia have led psychiatric researchers on a search for alternatives that would both be more effective and not cause tardive dyskinesia, a motor disorder that consists of involuntary movements of the mouth, arms, and trunk of the body. Because of the many complexities in the biological treatment of individuals with schizophrenia, researchers and clinicians increasingly recognize the need to take the individual's medical and psychiatric profile into account.

- From a psychological perspective, with increasing evidence suggesting specific genetic and neurophysiological abnormalities in the brains of people with schizophrenia, researchers are becoming increasingly interested in finding out more about the role of cognitive deficits in causing the disorder.

- For many years, the most common psychological interventions for people with schizophrenia were behavioral treatments, but this method is no longer practical given that most individuals with schizophrenia receive treatment in the community. In addition, there is little data on its effectiveness, and the profession cannot justify its use. More promising is cognitive-behavioral therapy when clinicians use it as an adjunct to pharmacological treatments. Clinicians using cognitive-behavioral therapy to treat individuals with symptoms of psychosis (CBTp) do not try to change their delusions or eliminate their hallucinations, but instead try to reduce their distress and preoccupation with these symptoms. Researchers are also developing interventions to help address the cognitive deficits of individuals with schizophrenia, particularly those who suffer from primarily negative symptoms.

- There have been many theories regarding schizophrenia from a sociocultural perspective. Contemporary researchers have approached the issue by trying to predict the outcome or recovery of adults hospitalized for schizophrenia. The index of expressed emotion (EE) provides a measure of the degree to which family members speak in ways that reflect criticisms, hostile feelings, and emotional overinvolvement or overconcern. Moving beyond the family environment, researchers have also studied broader social factors, such as social class and income, in relationship to schizophrenia. Other sociocultural risk factors for schizophrenia, or at least for symptoms of psychosis, include adversity in childhood such as parental loss or separation, abuse, and bullying.

- The coordination of services is especially important in programs geared toward helping people with schizophrenia.

- From a biopsychosocial perspective, an exciting development is the evolution of an integrated approach to theories that focus on underlying brain mechanisms as expressed in cognitive deficits. Treatment is moving beyond the provision of medication to greater use of evidence-based psychological interventions. Finally, researchers appear to be gaining greater appreciation of the role of sociocultural influences. Together, these advances are increasing the chances that individuals with these disorders will receive integrated care, maximizing their chances of recovery. Clinicians also increasingly understand schizophrenia from a life-span perspective. The idea that schizophrenia is a neurodevelopmental disorder highlights this important new focus and provides a basis for interventions that take into account individual changes over time.

KEY TERMS

Active phase

Asociality

Assertive community treatment (ACT)

Avolition

Brief psychotic disorder

Catatonia

Cognitive-behavioral therapy for psychosis (CBTp)

Delusion

Delusional disorder

Developmental cascade hypothesis

Disorganized speech

Downward drift

Erotomanic type of delusional disorder

Expressed emotion (EE)

Extrapyramidal symptoms (EPS)

First-rank symptom (FRS)

Grandiose type of delusional disorder

Hallucination

Inappropriate affect

Jealous type of delusional disorder

Loosening of associations

Negative symptoms

Neologisms

Neurodevelopmental hypothesis

Neuroplasticity

Paranoia

Persecutory type of delusional disorder

Positive symptoms

Restricted affect

Schizoaffective disorder

Schizophrenia

Schizophrenia spectrum

Schizophreniform disorder

Shared psychotic disorder

Somatic type of delusional disorder

Tardive dyskinesia

Vulnerability

Depressive and Bipolar Disorders

Learning Objectives

7.1 Explain the key features of major depressive disorder and persistent depressive disorder, including prevalence.

7.2 Compare and contrast bipolar I, bipolar II, and cyclothymic disorder.

7.3 Understand theories and treatments of depressive and bipolar disorders.

7.4 Discuss the relationships among age, gender, and suicide.

7.5 Analyze the biopsychosocial model of depressive and bipolar disorders.

©fotointeractiva/123RF

Case Report: Janice Butterfield

Demographic information: 47-year-old married heterosexual African American female

Presenting problem: Janice was referred for psychotherapy after a recent hospitalization following a suicide attempt. Janice reported that the precipitant to her suicide attempt was the loss of her job in a real estate company, where she had worked for 25 years. Although she realized her company had downsized due to the economy, she found herself feeling profoundly guilty for the negative impact her unemployment would have on her family. Janice reported she has been married for 27 years and has three daughters, one of whom lives at home. Another is in college, and her youngest will be attending college at the start of the next school year. Janice reported she had become increasingly overwhelmed by stress about her financial situation, because her family mainly relied on her income.

Along with feelings of guilt, Janice reported she had felt so depressed and down that she had spent many days in the past 2 weeks in bed and often found herself thinking of ending her life. She stopped taking the pain pills prescribed for her chronic backaches, "to save up if I needed them later." One evening when her husband was out, she attempted suicide by taking all her saved-up medications at once. Janice's husband returned to find her unresponsive and rushed her to the hospital just in time to save her life. She was hospitalized in an inpatient psychiatric unit and given medication until her suicidal thoughts and severe depression decreased enough so that the doctors deemed her no longer a threat to herself. She followed the referral given to her by the psychiatrists on the inpatient unit to attend weekly psychotherapy for follow-up. She had never been in therapy before.

During her first therapy session, Janice reported that she had thought about going to therapy many times before. She explained that her depressive episodes

usually lasted about 1 month, but sometimes as long as 3 months. During these episodes, she missed a few days of work but would manage to go about her normal routine, although with much difficulty. She described how, while she was at work, she would go out to her car to cry because it was too painful to be around others. "I just didn't want anything to do with life at those points," she recalled. Her depression would eventually improve on its own, and she would lose interest in getting treatment as a result. She reported that she had occasionally thought about suicide in the past when feeling depressed, but she had never before made and carried out a plan as she had during the most recent episode. Janice cited her family as her main reason for never taking her thoughts about suicide more seriously.

Janice went on to explain how these depressed moods always caught her off guard, because they would occur directly after long periods when she felt happy and energetic. She stated these moods usually started after she had made a large real estate sale and felt "invincible" afterwards. During these times, she described how she often needed very little sleep due to the seemingly endless amounts of energy she possessed, and she would begin to take on many new projects and clients at work—much more than would be expected of her. She also splurged on lavish clothing or jewelry, and during her last energetic period she had purchased new cars for herself and her husband. These expenditures were uncharacteristic for Janice; she described herself as usually being quite frugal.

Due to her constantly moving thoughts, Janice found it difficult to concentrate and was so distracted she was rarely able to finish anything she began to take on at work. She would feel disappointed that she had to give up some of her projects, and her joyful feelings would turn to irritability and anger. She reported that her

Case Report *continued*

husband usually experienced the brunt of her irritable mood, and this caused major problems in their marriage. Janice further reported that she felt like she ignored her family altogether due to her work habits when she was feeling particularly energetic. She remarked, "When I'm feeling that good, I can only think about myself and what feels good to me. I stop being a mother and a wife." Her extreme spending periods eroded her family's savings, which was especially a concern now that she had lost her job. She also felt incredibly guilty for not being able to pay for her daughters' college tuition. Janice had never talked directly with her husband or her children about her vast mood shifts. She worried that if she told her family about her personal difficulties, they would "see me as a weakling, instead of the head of the household."

Relevant history: Janice had never received psychiatric treatment or therapy in the past, though she reported she had experienced mood swings since she was 19. She estimated that she had severe mood episodes (either manic or depressive) about three to four times per year. When reflecting on the severity of her mood episodes, she stated that she felt her behaviors had been more "extreme" in more recent years than when she was younger. Janice reported that she noticed the patterns in her mood swings always began with an energetic period, directly followed by a depressive episode, and then a period of several months of stability. More recently, though, she noted that the periods of stability had only been lasting 1 or 2 months, and her mood episodes had been lasting longer.

Case formulation: Janice's initial diagnosis from the psychiatric unit was major depressive episode, and her current presentation also met this criteria. However, in the initial therapy session she reported also having a history of manic episodes that were followed by periods of depression, which she had not mentioned while she had been hospitalized. The symptoms of the manic episode she described caused significant financial problems for Janice, due to her excessive spending sprees. In combination with losing her job, these financial problems caused significant stress and may have contributed to the severity of her most recent depressive episode, which eventually led to a suicide attempt. Therefore, her diagnosis is bipolar I disorder, most recent episode depressed.

Treatment plan: It is recommended that Janice continue to attend weekly psychotherapy. In therapy, it will be necessary to make a suicide safety plan, given her history of suicidal ideation and recent suicide attempt. Therapy should initially focus on psychoeducation, symptom management, and mood monitoring. She will also be referred to an outpatient psychiatrist for medication reconciliation, given that psychotherapeutic medication is clinically recommended in the treatment of bipolar disorder.

Sarah Tobin, PhD

---

depressive disorder
A disorder characterized by periods in which, among other symptoms, an individual experiences an unusually intense sad mood.

dysphoria
An unusually elevated sad mood.

major depressive disorder
A disorder in which the individual experiences acute but time-limited episodes of depressive symptoms.

major depressive episode
A period in which the individual experiences intense psychological and physical symptoms accompanying feelings of overwhelming sadness (dysphoria).

People can experience day-to-day highs and lows, but when their disturbances of mood reach a point of clinical significance, they may be considered to have a depressive or bipolar disorder. In *DSM-5,* these two disorders (sometimes referred to as mood disorders) carry a set of criteria that allow clinicians to establish whether their clients show alterations in mood that significantly deviate from the individual's baseline or ordinary emotional state.

7.1 Depressive Disorders

A **depressive disorder** is characterized by periods in which, among other symptoms, an individual experiences an unusually intense sad mood. The disorder's essential element—this sad mood—is known as **dysphoria**.

Major Depressive Disorder

Major depressive disorder consists of acute but time-limited periods of depressive symptoms that are called **major depressive episodes** (see Table 1).

Major depressive disorder can be diagnosed with a range of other disorders including, for example, personality disorders, substance use disorders, and anxiety disorders. A number of

TABLE 1 Criteria for a Major Depressive Episode

For most of the time during a 2-week period, a person experiences at least five or more of the first nine symptoms in addition to the last two. He or she must experience a change from previous functioning, and at least one of the first two symptoms must be present. During this 2-week period, most of these symptoms must be present nearly every day.

- Depressed mood most of the day
- Markedly diminished interest or pleasure in all or most daily activities
- Significant unintended weight loss or unusual increase or decrease in appetite
- Insomnia or hypersomnia
- Psychomotor agitation or retardation observable by others
- Fatigue or loss of energy
- Feelings of worthlessness or excessive or inappropriate guilt
- Difficulty maintaining concentration or making decisions
- Recurrent thoughts of death or having suicidal thoughts, plans, or attempts
- The symptoms are not attributable to a medical condition or use of a substance
- The symptoms cause significant distress or impairment

conditions can mimic major depressive disorder, including those associated with disorders that we discussed in the chapter "Schizophrenia Spectrum and Other Psychotic Disorders," which include or are related to schizophrenia. These include schizophrenia, schizoaffective disorder, schizophreniform disorder, and delusional disorder. The clinician must rule out these specific disorders before assigning the diagnosis of major depressive disorder to the client.

Second only to lower back pain as a cause of years lived with disability around the world, major depressive disorder is also the 19th most common global disease (Vos et al., 2012). In the United States, the lifetime prevalence of major depressive disorder is 16.6 percent of the adult population (Kessler et al., 2012). The 1-year prevalence of a major depressive episode is estimated to be 6.7 percent of all adults in the United States, or 16.2 million individuals (National Institute of Mental Health, 2018). Figure 1 summarizes the 1-year prevalence of major depressive episodes along with variations by sex, age, and race/ethnicity.

As you can see from this figure, the highest 1-year prevalence of major depressive episode is found among individuals 18–25 years of age, and the numbers decrease after that to 4.8 percent at ages 50 and older. These generational differences may reflect a number of

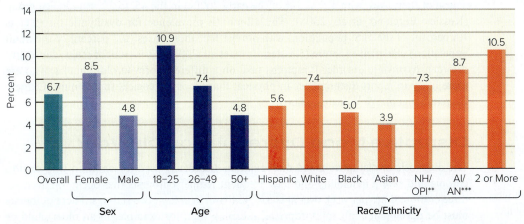

*All other groups are non-Hispanic or Latino; **NH/OPI = Native Hawaiian/Other Pacific Islander; ***AI/AN = American Indian/Alaskan Native

FIGURE 1 One-Year Prevalence of Major Depressive Episodes in the United States, 2016

SOURCE: https://www.nimh.nih.gov/health/statistics/major-depression.shtml

MINI CASE

Major Depressive Disorder, Recurrent Episode

Daryll is a 37-year-old married heterosexual African American male. His wife recently took him to a psychiatric facility for evaluation. Although Daryll has been functioning normally for the past several years, he suddenly became severely disturbed and depressed. At the time of admission, Daryll was agitated, dysphoric, and suicidal, even going as far as to purchase a gun to kill himself. He had lost his appetite and had developed insomnia during the preceding 3 weeks. As each day went by, he found himself feeling more and more exhausted, less able to think clearly or to concentrate, and uninterested in anyone or anything. He had become hypersensitive in his dealings with neighbors, co-workers, and family, insisting that others were being too critical of him. This was the second such episode in Daryll's history, the first having occurred 5 years earlier, following the loss of his job due to a massive layoff.

factors, including a tendency for younger adults to be more open about reporting their symptoms, and the lower survival rates into the later decades of people with major depressive disorder. Age differences in the nature of reported symptoms may also influence prevalence statistics, in that depressive symptoms may be reported as physical rather than psychological concerns in older adults (Schaakxs et al., 2017).

Persistent Depressive Disorder (Dysthymia)

persistent depressive disorder (dysthymia)
Chronic but less severe mood disturbance in which the individual does not experience a major depressive episode.

The mood disturbance occurring with major depressive disorder may take a chronic, enduring form. People with **persistent depressive disorder (dysthymia)** have, for at least 2 years (1 year for children and adolescents), a more limited set of the symptoms that occur with major depressive disorder, including sleep and appetite disturbances, low energy or fatigue, low self-esteem, difficulty with concentration and decision making, and feelings of hopelessness. However, people with persistent depressive disorder currently do not meet the criteria for a major depressive episode, which requires that the client meet five of the criteria in Table 1.

Despite the fact that people with persistent depressive disorder do not experience all the symptoms of a major depressive episode, they are never free of their symptoms for longer than 2 months. Moreover, they are likely to have other serious psychological disorders, including a heightened risk for developing major depressive disorder, personality disorder, and substance use disorder.

Approximately 2.5 percent of the adult population will develop dysthymic disorder in the course of their lives, with a peak (as of the early 2000s) in the 45- to 59-year-old age group (Kessler, Berglund, et al., 2005). The 12-month prevalence for dysthymic disorder is 1.5 percent of the U.S. population, with almost half these cases (0.8 percent of the adult population) classified as severe (Kessler, Chiu, et al., 2005). As is true for major depressive disorder, dysthymic disorder symptoms take on a different form in older adults, who are more likely to report disturbances in physical than in psychological functioning (Oxman, Barrett, Sengupta, & Williams, 2000).

Disruptive Mood Dysregulation Disorder

disruptive mood dysregulation disorder
A depressive disorder in children who exhibit chronic and severe irritability and have frequent temper outbursts.

The diagnosis of **disruptive mood dysregulation disorder** is used for children who exhibit chronic and severe irritability and have frequent temper outbursts that occur, on average, three or more times per week over at least 1 year and in at least two settings. These outbursts must be developmentally inappropriate, meaning that, for example, in an older child or young teen they take the form of the behavior of a much younger child.

Between outbursts, children with this disorder remain angry or at least extremely irritable. The criteria specify that the diagnosis should not be made for the first time for children whose first episode occurs when they are younger than 6 or older than 18. However, either by directly observing the child or from the child's history, the clinician must determine that

MINI CASE

Persistent Depressive Disorder (Dysthymia)

Kimiko is a single 34-year-old heterosexual Japanese American female. She currently works as a community college instructor, and for the past 3 years has had persistent feelings of depressed mood, inferiority, and pessimism. She realizes that, since her graduation from college, she has never felt really happy and that, in recent years, she has struggled with thoughts of

worthlessness and sad mood. Her appetite is low, and she struggles with insomnia. During waking hours, she lacks energy and finds it difficult to do her work. She often finds herself staring out the window of her office, consumed by thoughts of how inadequate she is. She fails to fulfill many of her responsibilities and has received consistently poor teacher evaluations for the past 3 years. Getting along with her colleagues has become increasingly difficult. Consequently, she spends most of her free time alone in her office.

the disorder had its onset before the age of 10. In other words, a teen of 13 must be reported by parents or teachers, for example, to have been subject to angry episodes prior to turning 10 years old.

The authors of *DSM-5* recognized a potential criticism of this disorder that might be characterized as pathologizing a child's "temper tantrums," but they believed it was important to have a disorder earmarked for children and teens who in the past would have been diagnosed with bipolar disorder. Follow-up data of children who show this pattern of extreme irritability and angry outbursts suggest that, rather than developing bipolar disorder, they are at risk of developing depressive and/or anxiety disorders when they reach adulthood.

Premenstrual Dysphoric Disorder

Women who experience depressed mood or changes in mood, irritability, dysphoria, and anxiety during the premenstrual phase that subside after the menstrual period begins for most of the cycles of the preceding year may be diagnosed with **premenstrual dysphoric disorder (PMDD)**. This disorder was in the Appendix (it was not a diagnosable condition) in *DSM-IV-TR*. By making this disorder part of the standard psychiatric nomenclature, the *DSM-5* authors believed that better diagnosis and treatment could result for women who experience its symptoms.

Critics argue that the PMDD diagnosis pathologizes the normal variations in mood that can occur over the course of a woman's monthly menstrual cycle. However, the counterargument is that the majority of women do not experience monthly mood alterations so severe that they would show such extreme symptoms. Including PMDD as a diagnosis allows those with these severe episodes of depression to receive treatment that might not otherwise be available to them.

premenstrual dysphoric disorder (PMDD)
Changes in mood, irritability, dysphoria, and anxiety that occur during the premenstrual phase of the monthly menstrual cycle and subside after the menstrual period begins for most of the cycles of the preceding year.

7.2 Disorders Involving Alterations in Mood

Two sets of disorders are characterized by alterations in mood that go beyond everyday variations in levels of sadness or happiness. These are bipolar disorder and cyclothymic disorder. **Bipolar disorder** includes an intense and disruptive experience of a **manic episode**. During a manic episode, the individual may experience unusually high levels of **euphoria**, which is the feeling state of an abnormally positive mood.

bipolar disorder
A mood disorder involving manic episodes–intense and disruptive experiences of heightened mood, possibly alternating with major depressive episodes.

manic episode
Acute but time-limited period of intense and unusual elation.

Bipolar Disorder

Clinicians diagnose people who have manic episodes with bipolar disorder, a term that has replaced "manic depression." An individual must experience a manic episode in order for a

euphoria
A feeling state that is more cheerful and elated than average, possibly even ecstatic.

REAL STORIES

Carrie Fisher: Bipolar Disorder

Carrie Fisher was a U.S. actress, screenwriter, novelist, and lecturer who appeared in over 40 films–most notably as Princess Leia Organa in the *Star Wars* trilogy. She wrote four novels, one of which, *Wishful Drinking*, was turned into a one-woman play performed in venues across the country. In the book, she chronicles her life–from her growing up in a Hollywood family, her rise to fame, and her struggles with drugs and alcohol to her battles with bipolar disorder. Fisher talks about her experiences with humor and honesty, revealing the reality of her mental illness.

Born in 1956 in Beverly Hills, California, Fisher was the daughter of actress Debbie Reynolds and singer Eddie Fisher. As the product of a Hollywood marriage, she seemed to have been destined to be a Hollywood star from the very beginning. When she was 2 years old, Fisher's father left her mother for Elizabeth Taylor, her mother's best friend. The media highly publicized this story, although in her book, Fisher states that she doesn't believe her childhood experiences had a major impact on any of the problems she encountered later in life.

Fisher first began acting at the age of 12, appearing in Las Vegas with her mother. She later dropped out of high school in order to perform with her mother on tour. In 1973, Fisher appeared with her mother in the Broadway musical *Irene*, and 2 years later, after attending drama school in London, she made her film debut in the 1975 film *Shampoo* with Warren Beatty. Two years after that, at 21, she instantly became an icon and an international celebrity for her role in the *Star Wars* trilogy. According to Fisher, it was at this point that she began to heavily abuse cocaine and alcohol, having already experimented with marijuana at the age of 13. Looking back on her drug abuse, Fisher recalls that she used drugs as a way to self-medicate her extreme mood episodes. She first received a diagnosis of manic depression (as it was called at the time) when she was 24 years old. Although she did not pursue any treatment at that point, she began to understand what was driving much of her heavy substance use. In the

book, she describes how she did not accept her diagnosis and even felt personally insulted by it. Rather than taking medication as recommended by her psychiatrist, she dropped out of treatment and impulsively moved from Los Angeles to New York, marrying singer Paul Simon shortly after.

Fisher and Simon were married from 1983 to 1984, though they dated on and off for a total of 12 years. In 1992, Fisher had a daughter, Billie, with her partner Bryan Lourd.

Despite her chronic battles with substance abuse and bipolar disorder, Fisher continued to appear in films and television shows throughout the 1980s. Her substance abuse led to a hospitalization in the mid-1980s, inspiring her first novel, *Postcards from the Edge*, a semi-autobiographical account of an actress suffering from substance abuse, published in 1987. The book became a successful movie for which she received critical acclaim.

Throughout the 1990s, Fisher continued to appear in films and became well known in Hollywood for her screenwriting talents. In 1997, she suffered a psychotic break after she sought medication to treat her chronic depression. She describes that experience in *Wishful Drinking*: "Now, anyone who has stayed awake for six days knows that there's every chance that they'll wind up psychotic. Anyway, I did, and part of how that manifested was that I thought everything on television was about me . . . I watched CNN, and at the time Versace had just been killed by that man Cunanin, and the police were frantically scouring the

Eastern seaboard for him. So, I was Cunanin, Versace, and the police. Now this is exhausting programming." She was hospitalized for 6 days and then spent 6 months receiving outpatient treatment.

After having accepted her diagnosis of bipolar disorder and finally come to terms with her need for treatment, Fisher set out to educate the public about the stigmatization of mental illness. In the years leading up to her death, she was an active voice in speaking out about the need for government funding for mental health treatment and for greater public acceptance of mental illness.

In *Wishful Drinking*, Fisher describes her experiences switching between mania and depression. "I have two moods. . . . One is Roy, rollicking Roy, the wild ride of a mood. And Pam, sediment Pam, who stands on the shore and sobs . . . sometimes the tide is in, sometimes it's out." Fisher also writes of some of the various

After struggling for many years with substance abuse and bipolar disorder, Carrie Fisher became an activist for the destigmatization of mental illness.

©Jason LaVeris/Getty Images

treatments for her illness that she has received, including electroconvulsive therapy (ECT).

She recalls her mix of emotions and reactions to receiving ECT, including fear, humiliation, and concern about dangerous side effects, particularly given the way the treatment had been portrayed in popular culture. However, she eventually decided that her symptoms were becoming far too severe and needed more intensive treatment.

"I'd been feeling overwhelmed and pretty defeated. I didn't necessarily feel like *dying*–but I'd been feeling a lot like not being alive. The second reason I decided to get ECT is that I was depressed. Profoundly depressed. Part of this could be attributed to my mood disorder, which was, no doubt, probably the source of the emotional intensity. That's what can take simple sadness and turn it into sadness squared." Fortunately for Fisher, ECT proved to be an effective treatment for combating her intense depressive episodes.

"At times," she writes at the end of *Wishful Drinking*, "being bipolar can be an all-consuming challenge, requiring a lot of stamina and even more courage, so if you're living with this illness and functioning at all, it's something to be proud of, not ashamed of."

Fisher passed away on December 27, 2016, at the age of 60. The cause of her death was confirmed to be cardiac arrest, though there were also traces of several drugs in her system. In *Wishful Drinking*, she writes what she hoped to be in her obituary one day: "I want it reported that I drowned in moonlight, strangled by my own bra."

SOURCE: *Wishful Drinking* by Carrie Fisher. Deliquesce Inc.

---

clinician to diagnose bipolar disorder, as Table 2 shows. The diagnosis does not require that the individual has ever experienced a major depressive episode.

The two major categories of bipolar disorder are bipolar I and bipolar II. A diagnosis of bipolar I disorder describes a clinical course in which the individual experiences one or more manic episodes with the possibility, although not the necessity, of experiencing one or more major depressive episodes. In contrast, a diagnosis of bipolar II disorder means the individual has had one or more major depressive episodes and at least one **hypomanic episode**. The criteria for a hypomanic episode are similar to those for a manic episode but require a shorter duration (4 days instead of 1 week).

Individuals who are in a manic, hypomanic, or major depressive episode may show features of the opposite pole but not to an extreme enough degree to meet the relevant diagnostic criteria for bipolar disorder. For example, people in a manic episode may also report feeling sad or empty, fatigued, or suicidal. *DSM-5* uses a specifier of "mixed features" to apply to cases in which an individual experiences episodes of mania or hypomania when depressive features are present, and to episodes of depression in the context of major depressive disorder or bipolar disorder when features of mania/hypomania are present. The "mixed" category accounts for individuals with bipolar disorder who may show features of both depression and mania/hypomania, either simultaneously or nearly simultaneously.

hypomanic episode
A period of elated mood not as long as a manic episode.

TABLE 2 Criteria for a Manic Episode

A distinct period of abnormally and persistently elevated, expansive, or irritable mood and abnormally and persistently increased activity or energy must last at least 1 week and the symptoms must be present most of the day, nearly every day (or for any duration if hospitalization is necessary).

During the period of mood disturbance and increased energy or activity, three (or more) of the following symptoms are present to a significant degree (four if the mood is only irritable) and represent a noticeable change from usual behavior:

- inflated self-esteem or grandiosity
- decreased need for sleep (the client feels rested after, say, only 3 hours of sleep)
- more talkative mood than usual or pressure to keep talking
- flight of ideas or subjective experience that thoughts are racing
- distractibility (attention is too easily drawn to unimportant or irrelevant external stimuli), as reported or observed
- increase in goal-directed activity (either socially, at work or school, or sexually) or psychomotor agitation
- excessive engagement in activities that have high potential for painful consequences (such as unrestrained buying sprees, sexual indiscretions, or foolish business investments)

This episode must represent a clearly observable change in functioning but not be severe enough to require hospitalization to prevent harm to self or others.

MINI CASE

Bipolar I Disorder, Current Episode Manic

Isabel is a single 38-year-old bisexual Hispanic American female. She works as a software engineer at a large tech company, where she has worked for about 10 years. For the past week, she has shown signs of uncharacteristically outlandish behavior, beginning with thoughts of quitting her job so that she could develop her own software company out of her apartment. Isabel went without sleep for 3 days, spending most of her time at her computer developing a business model for the company.

Within a few days, she took out nearly $1 million in loans, although she had few resources to finance even one of them. She visited several banks and other investors, each time making a scene with anyone who expressed skepticism about her plan. While at a bank, she became so upset when she was denied a loan that she angrily pushed over the banker's desk, and screamed at the top of her lungs that the bank was keeping her from her multimillion-dollar profit. The police were called, and Isabel was brought to an emergency room, from which she was transferred for intensive evaluation and treatment at a nearby psychiatric hospital.

Bipolar disorder has a lifetime prevalence rate of 3.9 percent in the U.S. population (Kessler, Berglund, et al., 2005) and a 12-month prevalence of 2.6 percent (Kessler, Chiu, et al., 2005). Of those diagnosed with bipolar disorder in a given year, nearly 83 percent (2.2 percent of the adult population) have cases classified as severe. At least half of all cases begin before a person reaches the age of 25 (Kessler, Chiu, et al., 2005). Approximately 60 percent of all individuals with bipolar disorder can live symptom-free if they receive adequate treatment (Perlis et al., 2006). This means a large percentage continue to experience symptoms. According to one estimate, over the course of a 5-year period, people with bipolar disorder feel that their mood is normal only about half the time (Pallaskorpi et al., 2015).

Of all psychological disorders, bipolar disorder is the most likely to occur in people who also have problems with substance abuse. People with both bipolar and substance use disorders have earlier onset of bipolar disorder, more frequent episodes, and higher risk of developing anxiety- and stress-related disorders, aggressive behavior, problems with the law, and risk of suicide (Swann, 2010).

People with bipolar disorder are also at risk of more severe chronic health problems than others their own age. They have higher rates of heart disease and diabetes (Silarova et al., 2015) and higher levels of cholesterol (Kessing, Vradi, McIntyre, & Andersen, 2015). These may be the reasons that, according to a comprehensive population study conducted in Denmark, bipolar disorder is associated with lower life expectancy across a variety of causes (Kessing et al., 2015). In addition to higher mortality due to illness, people with bipolar disorder also have elevated rates of suicide and other forms of violent death (Hayes et al., 2015). Their risks are similar in magnitude to those found in people with schizophrenia; the gap between their mortality and that of the general population has also widened in the past decade (Hayes et al., 2017).

As you can see in Figure 2, bipolar disorder can cause people to experience a range of moods. You can also see that there is a range from depressed mood to severe mania, with some overlap occurring at the boundaries.

Clinicians diagnose people as having **bipolar disorder, rapid cycling** if they have had four or more episodes within the previous year that meet the criteria for manic,

bipolar disorder, rapid cycling

A form of bipolar disorder involving four or more episodes within the previous year that meet the criteria for manic, hypomanic, or major depressive disorder.

FIGURE 2 Range of Moods Present in People with Bipolar Disorder

SOURCE: https://www.nimh.nih.gov/health/topics/bipolar-disorder/index.shtml

severe depression, moderate depression, and mild low mood

normal or balanced mood

hypomania and severe mania

MINI CASE

Cyclothymic Disorder

Larry is a divorced 60-year-old Caucasian heterosexual male who works as a bank cashier. For much of his adult life, co-workers, family, and friends have repeatedly told him he is very moody. He acknowledges that his mood never feels quite stable, although at times others tell him he seems more calm and pleasant than usual. Unfortunately, these intervals are quite brief, lasting for a few weeks and usually ending abruptly. Without warning, he may experience either a somewhat depressed mood or a period of elation.

During his depressive periods, Larry's confidence, energy, and motivation are very low. During his hypomanic periods, he willingly volunteers to extend his workday and to undertake unrealistic challenges at work. On weekends, he might decide to put in long shifts at a homeless shelter without getting any sleep. Larry disregards the urging of his family members to get professional help, insisting that it is his nature to be high-energy at times. He also states that he doesn't want some "shrink" to steal away the periods during which he feels on top of the world.

hypomanic, or major depressive disorder. In some individuals, the cycling may occur within 1 week or even 1 day. The factors that predict rapid cycling include earlier onset, higher depression scores, higher mania scores, and lower global assessment of functioning. A history of rapid cycling in the previous year and use of antidepressants also predict rapid cycling (Schneck et al., 2008). Medical conditions such as hypothyroidism, disturbances in sleep/wake cycles, and use of antidepressant medications can also contribute to the development of rapid cycling (Papadimitriou, Calabrese, Dikeos, & Christodoulou, 2005). Individuals who experience bipolar disorder, rapid cycling are at higher risk of suicide than others with bipolar disorder, and also of a longer duration of the disorder (Gigante et al., 2016).

Cyclothymic Disorder

Cyclothymic disorder is characterized by alternations between dysphoria and briefer, less intense, and less disruptive euphoric states called hypomanic episodes. People with this disorder have met the criteria for a hypomanic episode many times over a span of at least 2 years (1 year in children and adolescents) and also experience numerous periods of depressive symptoms but never meet the criteria for a major depressive episode. During their respective time frames, adults, children, or adolescents have never been without these symptoms for more than 2 months at a time.

cyclothymic disorder
A mood disorder with symptoms that are more chronic and less severe than those of bipolar disorder.

7.3 Theories and Treatment of Depressive and Bipolar Disorders

Biological Perspectives

Long aware of the tendency for mood disorders to occur more frequently among biologically related family members, researchers working within the biological perspective are attempting to pinpoint genetic contributors to these disorders. However, multiple genes interact with environmental risk factors in complex ways, with epigenetics playing a significant role (Walker et al., 2016).

Biological Theories Supporting the role of genetics, it has long been known that first-degree relatives of people with major depressive disorder are 15 to 25 percent more likely to have the disorder than are people who do not have this close biological relationship. Based on the existing literature, major depressive disorder has an estimated

Antidepressant medication is commonly prescribed to individuals who suffer from major depressive disorder.

heritability of 37 percent (Sullivan, Neale, & Kendler, 2000), with rates higher in women than men (approximately 40 percent for women vs. 30 percent for men) (Flint & Kendler, 2014). The age at onset of first major depressive episode also appears to have a genetic component (Ferentinos et al., 2015). Compared to major depressive disorder, bipolar disorder has an even stronger pattern of genetic inheritance, with an estimated heritability of 60 to as high as 85 percent (Berrettini & Lohoff, 2017).

Moving from genetics to the biochemical abnormalities, increasing evidence points to the role of altered serotonin and norepinephrine levels in causing the mood changes associated with major depressive disorder. However, not everyone with genetic predisposition shows these mood-changing alterations in neurotransmitter levels. If exposed as adults to life stressors and other environmental factors, the genetically predisposed can experience a series of changes in the neural pathways active in regulating mood. Contributing further to their chances of developing depression are abnormalities in brain-derived neurotrophic factor (BDNF), a protein that helps keep neurons alive and able to adapt and change in response to experience (Naoi, Maruyama, & Shamoto-Nagai, 2018).

These alterations in neurotransmitters can further influence the mood of individuals with major depressive disorder by causing activation within the brain's internally based attentional circuits. Rather than focus their attention outward, individuals with major depressive disorder become overly preoccupied with their thoughts and feelings (Kaiser, Andrews-Hanna, Wager, & Pizzagalli, 2015). Because areas within the brain's inner network responsible for emotional processing are also disrupted, this set of changes causes the depressed person to turn those thoughts and feelings in a negative direction (Guo et al., 2015).

Brain scan and neuropsychological testing of individuals with bipolar disorder suggest that they have difficulties in attention, memory, and executive function consistent with abnormalities in the prefrontal lobe (Abé et al., 2015). These changes may have their origins in altered genetics which, in turn, place individuals at risk when they are exposed to life stressors, particularly early in life (Pfaffenseller, Kapczinski, Gallitano, & Klamt, 2018).

Antidepressant Medications   At present, biological interventions for mood disorders target not the genetic abnormalities themselves but the effect of those abnormalities on neurotransmitters. Therefore, antidepressant medication is the most common form of biologically based treatment for people with major depressive disorder. Clinicians prescribe antidepressants from four major categories: selective serotonin reuptake inhibitors (SSRIs), serotonin and norepinephrine reuptake inhibitors (SNRIs), tricyclic antidepressants (TCAs), and monoamine oxidase inhibitors (MAOIs).

The choice of antidepressant depends primarily on the clinician's preference for a particular class of medications. Ultimately, the medications the individual receives may be selected by trial and error as the clinician attempts to identify which work best and produce the fewest side effects.

SSRIs block the uptake of serotonin, making more of this crucial neurotransmitter available to act at the receptor sites of receiving neurons. SSRIs include fluoxetine (Prozac), citalopram (Celexa), escitalopram (Lexapro), paroxetine (Paxil), and sertraline (Zoloft). Balancing their positive effects on mood are their side effects. The most commonly reported are nausea, agitation, and sexual dysfunction. A newer class of antidepressants are serotonin modulators (such as vortioxetine) that target the postsynaptic serotonin receptors rather than the reuptake of serotonin in the synapse. These medications were approved for use in the United States in 2013, and results are still coming in on whether they will prove to be as effective as, but with fewer side effects than, other classes of antidepressants (Nishimura et al., 2018).

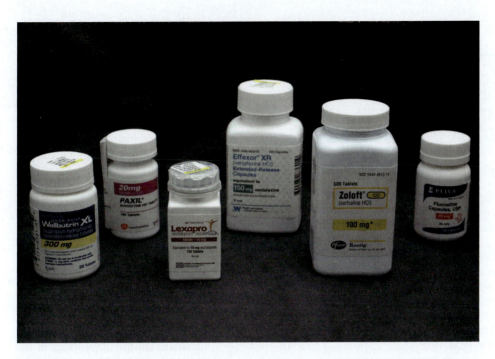

Psychotherapeutic medication offers relief to many individuals who suffer from mood disorders and is often used in combination with other modes of treatment, such as psychotherapy, to help patients manage their symptoms.

©Joe Raedle/Getty Images

SNRIs increase both norepinephrine and serotonin levels by blocking their reuptake. They include duloxetine (Cymbalta), venlafaxine (Effexor), and desvenlafaxine (Pristiq). These medications also carry with them a number of undesirable side effects including suicidal thoughts or attempts as well as allergic symptoms, gastrointestinal disturbances, weakness, nausea, vomiting, confusion, memory loss, irritability, and panic attacks, among others. Compared to SSRIs, the SNRIs show statistically significant effects in experimental studies, but clinically they seem to hold no advantages. If anything, SNRIs bring a higher risk of adverse reactions than SSRIs (Machado & Einarson, 2010).

TCAs, which derive their name from the fact that they have a three-ring chemical structure, include amitriptyline (Elavil, Endep), desipramine (Norpramin), imipramine (Tofranil), and nortriptyline (Aventyl, Pamelor). These medications are particularly effective in alleviating depression in people who have some of the more common biological symptoms, such as disturbed appetite and sleep. Although the exact process by which TCAs work remains unclear, we do know that they block the premature reuptake of biogenic amines back into the presynaptic neurons, thus increasing their excitatory effects on the postsynaptic neurons.

The antidepressant effects of MAOIs, such as phenelzine (Nardil) and tranylcypromine (Parnate), prolong the life of serotonin and norepinephrine in the synapse, thereby increasing their actions in the central nervous system. MAOIs are particularly effective in treating chronic depression in people who have not responded to other medications. However, they have serious side effects that can be life-threatening when people taking them are also on allergy medications or ingest foods or beverages such as beer, cheese, and chocolate, all of which are high in a substance called tyramine. As a result, clinicians do not prescribe MAOIs as commonly as other types of antidepressant medications.

Antidepressant medications take time to work, requiring 2 to 6 weeks to take effect. Once the depression has subsided, the clinician will urge the client to remain on the medication for 4 or 5 additional months, and much longer for people with a history of

What's in the *DSM-5*

Depressive and Bipolar Disorders

Modifications to the category of mood disorders in the *DSM-5* were intended to provide greater precision in the diagnosis by refining the criteria for major depressive episode, manic episode, and hypomanic episode. One of the major problems in the *DSM-IV-TR* was a failure to differentiate these episodes from a person's typical level of activity, sadness, or disturbance. In particular, the failure to distinguish bipolar disorder from attention-deficit/hyperactivity disorder might, in turn, have led to overdiagnosis of children and adolescents with bipolar disorder. Thus, the changes represent a slight but important improvement and will lead to greater specificity.

A highly controversial decision in the *DSM-5* was the addition of premenstrual dysphoric disorder (PMDD). As you have learned, this change was met with criticism for pathologizing normal experiences in women. Similarly, critics argue that disruptive mood dysregulation disorder pathologizes children's normal experience of temper tantrums. The rationale for proposing this new diagnosis, however, was that it would reduce the frequency of bipolar disorder diagnoses in children. Separating severe chronic irritability from bipolar disorder, the authors argued, means that children will not be misdiagnosed.

Finally, the *DSM-5* authors angered many critics when they decided to leave out the "bereavement exclusion" present in *DSM-IV-TR*. This change means that an individual who meets the criteria for a major depressive episode and who has lost a loved one in the past 2 months (which was the bereavement exclusion) can receive a psychiatric diagnosis. Thus, prior to the *DSM-5*, losing a loved one in the past 2 months excluded people from receiving this diagnosis. The argument in favor of making this change was that, in a vulnerable individual, bereavement could trigger a major depressive episode that would be appropriate to diagnose. Moreover, in a lengthy note of clarification, the *DSM-5* authors maintain that the grief associated with normal bereavement is different from the symptoms that occur in individuals who develop a true depressive disorder.

recurrent, severe depressive episodes. It is best for the clinician and client to work together to develop therapeutic programs that include regular visits early in treatment, expanded educational efforts that focus on the medications, and continued monitoring of treatment compliance.

Even though these medications can be effective, especially for certain clients, researchers are concerned that studies of antidepressants suffer from the "file drawer problem"—the fact that investigators are likely to file away, and not even submit for publication, studies that fail to establish significant benefits. In one analysis of 74 FDA-registered studies on antidepressants, 31 percent, accounting for 3,349 study participants, were not published. On the other hand, in the published studies, 94 percent of the medication trials reported positive findings. This bias toward publishing only positive results severely limits our ability to evaluate the efficacy of antidepressants because we are seeing only a slice of the actual data (Turner et al., 2008).

Adding further complications, some researchers have questioned whether people with less-than-severe depression might experience positive results because of the so-called placebo effect, in which they get better because they expect to get better (Kirsch et al., 2008).

Medication is certainly one route for the clinician to follow in treating individuals with major depressive disorder. However, increasing attention is being given to the possibility that psychotherapy can be equally effective (Farabaugh et al., 2015). Psychotherapy also carries fewer risks and adverse side effects than medication use. Over the long term, it could therefore be a better treatment route with more enduring effects than medication (Hollon, 2016). This is possible in part because, through therapy, individuals can work through some of their underlying issues and also learn skills for managing their symptoms that they can continue using on their own.

Bipolar Medications The traditional treatment for bipolar disorder is lithium carbonate, referred to as lithium, a naturally occurring salt found in small amounts in drinking water that, when used medically, replaces sodium in the body. Clinicians advise people who have frequent manic episodes (two or more a year) to remain on lithium continuously as a preventive measure. The drawback is that, even though lithium is a natural substance in the body, it can have side effects. These include mild central nervous system disturbances, gastrointestinal upsets, and more serious cardiac effects. As a consequence, people who experience manic episodes may be reluctant or even unwilling to take lithium continuously.

From the client's perspective, lithium can be seen to interfere with the euphoria that can accompany the beginnings of a manic episode. Consequently, people with this disorder who enjoy those pleasurable feelings may resist taking the medication. Unfortunately, by the time their euphoria escalates into a full-blown episode, it is often too late because their judgment has been clouded by their manic symptoms of grandiosity and elation. To help overcome this dilemma, clinicians may advise their clients to participate in lithium groups, in which members who use the medication on a regular basis provide support to each other and reinforce the importance of staying on the medication.

Because of the variable nature of bipolar disorder, other medications can be beneficial in treating symptoms apart from the mania itself. For example, people in a depressive episode may need to take an antidepressant medication in addition to the lithium for the duration of the episode. However, this can be problematic for a person who is prone to developing mania, because an antidepressant might provoke hypomania or mania. Those who have psychotic symptoms may benefit from taking antipsychotic medication such as clozapine (Li, Tang, Wang, & de Leon, 2015). People who experience rapid cycling present a challenge for clinicians because of the sudden changes that take place in their emotions and behavior.

Psychopharmacologists report that rapid cyclers, especially those for whom lithium has not been sufficient, seem to respond positively to prescriptions of anticonvulsant medication, such as carbamazepine (Tegretol) or valproate (Depakote), although these alone are not as effective as lithium (Kessing et al., 2011; Zivanovic, 2017).

Alternative Biologically Based Treatments   For some clients with mood disorders, medication is either ineffective or slow in alleviating symptoms that are severe and possibly life-threatening. Even with the best treatment, between 60 and 70 percent of individuals with major depressive disorder do not achieve symptom relief (Rush et al., 2006). A combination of genetic, physiological, and environmental factors govern the response to medication. Researchers hope to improve the efficacy of medications through **pharmacogenetics**, the use of genetic testing to identify who will improve with a particular medication, including antidepressants (Crisafulli et al., 2011) and lithium (McCarthy, Leckband, & Kelsoe, 2010).

Clinicians, at present, have several somatic alternatives to medication for treatment-resistant depression. As we discussed in the chapter "Theoretical Perspectives," one

pharmacogenetics
The use of genetic testing to identify who will and will not improve with a particular medication.

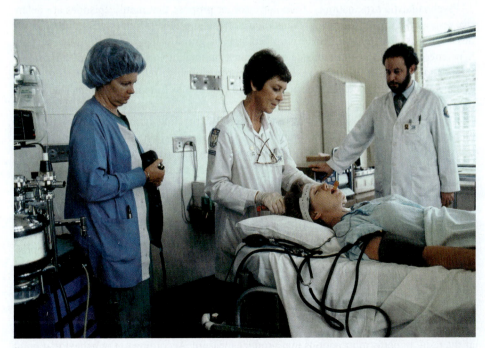

Once a risky and controversial procedure, electroconvulsive therapy is now a highly regulated and safe procedure available for individuals with severe depression who have not responded to other treatment options.

©WILL & DENI MCINTYRE/Getty Images

circadian rhythms
Biological clocks that set patterns of sleepfulness and wakefulness on approximately a 24-hour basis.

alternative is electroconvulsive therapy (ECT) (Lisanby, 2007). Clinicians and clients are not sure exactly how ECT works, but most current hypotheses center on ECT-induced changes in neurotransmitter receptors and in the body's natural opiates which, in turn, cause structural changes in the brain (Yrondi et al., 2018). As we discussed in the chapter "Theoretical Perspectives," deep brain stimulation (DBS) is another somatic treatment clinicians use to target major depressive disorder (as well as obsessive-compulsive disorder and movement disorders).

Based on the hypothesis that at least some mood disorders reflect a disruption in daily biological clocks known as **circadian rhythms**, researchers are proposing the use of treatments that "reset" the individual's bodily clock. Such treatments include light therapy, in which the individual is seated in front of a bright light for a period of time, such as 30 minutes in the morning. One distinct advantage of light therapy is that its side effects are minimal and almost entirely disappear after the dosage is reduced or treatment discontinued (Pail et al., 2011). Researchers also believe lithium may work on at least some individuals with bipolar disorder by resetting their circadian rhythms (McClung, 2007).

Psychological Perspectives

Psychodynamic Approaches

Early psychoanalytic theories based on the psychodynamic approach proposed that people with depressive disorders had suffered a loss early in their lives that affected them at a deep, intrapsychic level (Abraham, 1911/1968). It was attachment theory, however, that focused attention on people's feelings of security or insecurity arising from the way their caregivers reared them in childhood. Bowlby (1980) proposed that people with an insecure attachment style have a greater risk for developing a depressive disorder in adulthood. Following up on Bowlby's ideas, Bemporad (1985) proposed that insecurely attached children become preoccupied with the need to be loved by others. As adults, they form relationships in which they overvalue the support of their partners. When such relationships end, they become overwhelmed with feelings of inadequacy and loss.

Psychoanalytic explanations of bipolar disorder propose that manic episodes are defensive responses through which individuals stave off feelings of inadequacy, loss, and helplessness. Clients are thought to develop feelings of grandiosity and elation or become hyperenergetic as an unconscious defense against sinking into a state of gloom and despair. Supporting this interpretation, researchers report a positive relationship between use of denial and narcissistic defense mechanisms and the extent of manic symptoms (Sharma & Sinha, 2010).

Contemporary approaches to treatment within the psychodynamic perspective focus on helping individuals manage their symptoms rather than attempting to repair the core of the individual's disturbed attachment. These approaches consist of short (8- or 10-session), focused treatments. A review of eight studies comparing short-term psychodynamic therapy to other methods showed this method to be as least as effective as CBT in the treatment of major depressive disorder (Lewis, Dennerstein, & Gibbs, 2008).

Behavioral and Cognitive-Behavioral Approaches

One of the earliest behavioral formulations of theories of depression regards the symptoms of depression as resulting from lack of positive reinforcement (Lazarus, 1968; Skinner, 1953). According to this view, depressed people withdraw from life because they no longer have incentives to be active. Contemporary behaviorists base their approach on Lewinsohn's (1974) model. Lewinsohn maintained that depressed people have a low rate of what he termed "response contingent positive reinforcement behaviors," which increase in frequency as the result of performing actions that produce pleasure. According to the behaviorist point of view, the lack of positive reinforcement elicits the symptoms of low self-esteem, guilt, and pessimism.

In the method known as **behavioral activation** for depression, based on these behaviorist principles, the clinician helps the client identify activities associated with positive mood. The client keeps a record of the frequency of engaging in these rewarding activities and sets small weekly goals that gradually increase in frequency and duration. These activities are preferably consistent with the client's core values. Some clients may prefer to explore the arts, whereas others spend time in physical activity. Behavioral activation seems particularly well suited for clients who are not "psychologically minded," for group therapy, and for settings such as hospitals, nursing homes, and substance-abuse treatment centers (Sturmey, 2009).

Clinicians are increasingly integrating behavioral with cognitive approaches that focus on the role of dysfunctional thoughts as causes of, or at least contributors to, mood disorders. People with depressive disorders, according to the cognitive-behavioral perspective, think in repetitively negative ways that perpetuate their negative emotions. Beck (1967) defined these depressive thoughts as the **cognitive triad**—that is, a negative view of the self, the world, and the future.

These negative views lead depressed individuals, in turn, to experience a profound loss of self-esteem, convinced they will never have what they need to feel good about themselves. They assume they are worthless and helpless and that their efforts to improve their lives are doomed to fail. In the course of their daily experiences, the depressed, in this perspective, make faulty interpretations that keep alive the cycle of negative thoughts and emotions (Beck, Rush, Shaw, & Emery, 1979; Beck & Weishaar, 1989). Each of these faulty interpretations, or cognitive distortions, has its own unique qualities (see Table 3), but they share a failure to draw logical conclusions from the individual's experiences.

Behavioral therapy with clients who have depressive disorders follows the general principles that we outlined in the chapter "Theoretical Perspectives" in which clinicians help their clients develop more positively reinforcing experiences. In this approach, clinicians begin with a careful assessment of the frequency, quality, and range of activities and social interactions in their client's life, focusing on sources of positive and negative reinforcement. Based on this analysis, the clinicians work with their clients to institute changes in their environments while also teaching them social skills to improve the quality and number of their positive interactions. An important focus of the work

behavioral activation
Behavioral therapy for depression in which the clinician helps the client identify activities associated with positive mood.

cognitive triad
According to the cognitive theory of depression, the view that a depressed person's dysphoria results from a negative view of the self, the world, and the future.

TABLE 3 Examples of Cognitive Distortions

Type of Distortion	Definition	Example
Overgeneralizing	If it's true in one case, it applies to any case that is even slightly similar.	"I failed my first English exam, so I'm probably going to fail all of them."
Using selective abstraction	Taking seriously only events that represent failures, deprivation, loss, or frustration.	"Even though I won the election for the student senate, I'm not really popular because not everyone voted for me."
Taking excessive responsibility	Feeling responsible for all bad things that happen to you or to others to whom you are close.	"It's my fault that my friend didn't get the internship—I should've warned her about how hard the interview would be."
Assuming temporal causality	Assuming that if it has been true in the past, it's always going to be true.	"My last date was a wipeout, my next date will probably hate me too."
Making excessive self-references	Feeling at the center of everyone else's attention and assuming everyone can see your flaws and errors.	"When I tripped over the branch in the sidewalk, everyone could see how clumsy I am."
Catastrophizing	Always thinking the worst and being certain that it will happen.	"Because I failed my accounting exam, I will never make it in the business world."
Engaging in dichotomous thinking	Seeing everything as either one extreme or another rather than as mixed or in between.	"I can't stand people who are liars because I can never trust them."

SOURCE: Adapted from A. T. Beck, A. J. Rush, B. F. Shaw, & G. Emery in *Cognitive Therapy of Depression.*

done by behaviorally oriented clinicians is to encourage clients to increase their participation in activities they find inherently rewarding. These rewarding activities, in turn, can help boost the client's mood.

Behaviorally oriented clinicians also believe that education is an essential component of therapy. They regard individuals with depressive disorders as perpetuating their negative emotions by setting unrealistic goals, which they are then unable to achieve. To counteract these, clinicians working in the behavioral perspective assign homework exercises that encourage clients to make gradual behavioral changes, which will increase the probability that they can achieve their goals and thus feel rewarded.

Another technique used by the behavioral clinician combines behavioral contracting with self-reinforcement. For example, the clinician and client may agree that a client would benefit from the opportunity to socialize outside the home more often. Together, they would then set up a schedule of rewards in which they pair the social activity with something the client identifies as a desirable reward compatible with the goals of treatment (the clinician would not recommend that the client use the rewards of alcohol, drugs, or online gambling). Other methods the behaviorally oriented clinician would use include more extensive instruction, modeling, coaching, role playing, rehearsal, and perhaps working with the client in a real-world setting.

The focus of cognitive-behavioral therapy (CBT) is on helping clients try to change their dysfunctional thought processes that in turn will improve their mood. Like behaviorally oriented therapy, CBT requires an active collaboration between the client and the clinician. In contrast to behaviorally oriented therapy, however, CBT also focuses on the client's dysfunctional thoughts and how to modify them through cognitive restructuring. Mindfulness training, as an additional component of a cognitive-behavioral intervention, can help clients develop a greater sense of self-efficacy, an added boost to its positive effects on mood (Eisendrath et al., 2015). Another CBT technique known as mood monitoring can further help clients learn ways to track their mood over time and look for patterns in mood fluctuation. This is particularly helpful in the case of clients with bipolar disorder, who through the mood monitoring technique become more self-aware of when their symptoms might be worsening, so they can intervene using skills or other methods to avoid a full-blown manic or depressive episode.

Clinicians treating people with bipolar disorder customarily turn first to pharmacological interventions. However, psychological interventions can be beneficial in helping clients develop better coping strategies in an effort to minimize the likelihood of relapse. As we mentioned earlier, people who have experienced a manic episode may be tempted to forgo taking their medication because they wish to reexperience the exciting highs of a manic episode. If they can develop insight into the risks of noncompliance, however, and gain an improved understanding of medications such as lithium, they are more likely to adhere to the treatment program.

Psychoeducation is an especially important aspect of treating people with bipolar disorder to help them understand its nature, as well as the reasons medication is so important in controlling symptoms (Bond & Anderson, 2015). Moreover, CBT can also be an effective intervention for clients with bipolar disorder to help them cope with the periods in which their symptoms are beginning to emerge but are not yet full-blown (Driessen & Hollon, 2010). Rather than using one therapeutic approach, then, clinicians currently recommend the use of a combination of methods ranging from traditional psychotherapeutic medications to mindfulness training, and even nutritional supplements and hormone therapy. They are also now turning to cognitive remediation therapy, based on the findings in the literature of cognitive abnormalities in memory, inhibitory control, and attention (Dean et al., 2018).

Interpersonal Approaches   Developed as a brief intervention, **interpersonal therapy (IPT)** is a focused approach intended to last between 12 and 16 weeks. In IPT, clients are helped to manage the interpersonal stress associated with their depressive episodes, which themselves are seen as a function of genetic predisposition. Administered

interpersonal therapy (IPT)
A time-limited form of psychotherapy for treating people with major depressive disorder, based on the assumption that interpersonal stress induces an episode of depression in a person who is genetically vulnerable to this disorder.

according to a set of guidelines, interpersonal therapy provides clinicians with a clear model to follow so that treatment can proceed within the scheduled time frame. The IPT manual has the additional advantage of ensuring some consistency across therapists, making it possible to evaluate its effectiveness empirically.

Clinicians administer interpersonal therapy in three broad phases. In the first phase, the clinician assesses the magnitude and nature of the individual's depression using quantitative assessment measures and semistructured interviews. Depending on the type of depressive symptoms the individual shows, the therapist may consider combining treatment with antidepressant medications along with psychotherapy.

In the second phase, the therapist and the client collaborate on formulating a treatment plan that focuses on the primary problem. Typically, these problems are related to grief, interpersonal disputes, role transitions, and problems in interpersonal relationships stemming from inadequate social skills.

The therapist then carries out the treatment plan in the third phase, varying the methods according to the precise nature of the client's primary problem. The IPT approach encourages clinicians to combine such techniques as encouraging self-exploration, providing support, educating the client on the nature of depression, and offering feedback on the client's ineffective social skills. A primary focus of therapy is on the here and now, rather than on past childhood or developmental issues.

An interpersonal therapist carefully collaborates with each client to generate a unique treatment plan, based on the client's symptoms and particular areas of concern.
©sturti/Getty Images

For clients who cannot take antidepressant medications or for whom it is impractical to use medications, IPT is an especially valuable intervention in that nonmedical staff can administer it, or clients, with instruction, can learn it themselves (Weissman, 2007). A large-scale analysis of studies conducted over 30 years showed that interpersonal therapy was significantly more effective than cognitive-behavioral therapy or medications (Bowden, 2005).

Interpersonal and social rhythm therapy (IPSRT) (Frank, 2007) is a biopsychosocial approach to treating people with bipolar disorder that incorporates the concepts of stressful life events and disturbances in circadian rhythms (such as altered sleep/wake cycles, appetite, and energy level) into a focus on the individual's personal relationships. According to the IPSRT model, mood episodes are likely to emerge from medication nonadherence, stressful life events, and disruptions in social rhythms.

Clinicians who use IPSRT focus on educating clients about medication adherence, giving them a forum to explore their feelings about the disorder, and helping them develop insight about the ways in which the disorder has altered their lives. Clients learn to pay careful attention to the regularity of daily routines (including the timing of events and the stimulation that occurs with these events), and the extent to which life events, positive as well as negative, influence daily routines. The goal of IPSRT is to increase the stability of a client's social rhythms.

Reducing interpersonal stress for clients with bipolar disorder is important for several reasons. First, stressful life events heighten the arousal of the individual's autonomic nervous system and hence alter circadian rhythms. Helping clients cope with stress helps adjust these rhythms. Second, many life events, whether perceived as stressful or not, themselves cause changes in daily routines that in turn create more stress. Third, major life stressors affect a person's mood and also lead to significant changes in social

Interpersonal and social rhythm therapy incorporates biological approaches to treatment such as light therapy to regulate an individual's circadian rhythms.
©BSIP/Science Source

routines (Frank, 2007). As clients stabilize their social rhythms and routines while improving their interpersonal relationships, their stress levels decline accordingly. Researchers employing IPSRT support its use on an outpatient and inpatient basis (Swartz et al., 2011). However, in comparing IPT with IPSRT, a randomized clinical treatment study showed that the two were equally effective (Inder et al., 2015).

Looking across the results of virtually all published studies on interventions for mood disorders, Hollon and Ponniah (2010) concluded that cognitive-behavioral and behavioral therapy meet the criteria for evidence-based treatments, receiving strong support particularly for individuals with less severe or chronic depression. A review of randomized clinical trials comparing CBT with IPT shows both to be equally effective in treating major depressive disorder for at least 1 year post-treatment (Lemmens et al., 2015). Individuals with more severe depressive or bipolar disorders also benefit from cognitive-behavioral, interpersonal, and behaviorally oriented therapy above and beyond the effects of medication, and perhaps even instead of medication entirely, particularly over the long term (McHugh et al., 2013).

Sociocultural Perspectives

According to the sociocultural perspective, individuals develop depressive disorders in response to external life circumstances. These circumstances can be specific events such as sexual victimization, chronic stress such as poverty and single parenting, or episodic stress such as bereavement or job loss. Women are more likely to be exposed to these stressors than are men, a fact that may account, at least in part, for the higher frequency in the diagnosis of depressive disorders in women (Hammen, 2005).

However, acute and chronic stressors seem to play a differential role in predisposing an individual to experiencing depressive symptoms. Exposure to an acute stress such as the death of a loved one or an automobile accident could precipitate a major depressive episode. However, exposure to chronic strains from poor working conditions, health or interpersonal problems, or financial adversity can interact with genetic predisposition and personality to lead certain individuals to experience more persistent feelings of hopelessness. Moreover, once activated, an individual's feelings of depression and hopelessness can exacerbate the effects of exposure to stressful environments, which, in turn, can further increase the individual's feelings of chronic strain (Brown & Rosellini, 2011).

On the positive side, strong religious beliefs and spirituality may combine with the social support that membership in a religious community provides to lower an individual's chances of developing depression, even among those with high risk. Among the adult children of individuals with major depressive disorder, those with the strongest religious beliefs were less likely to experience a recurrence over a 10-year period (Miller et al., 2011).

7.4 Suicide

Although not a diagnosable disorder, suicidality is one potential diagnostic feature of a major depressive episode. The definition of suicide is "a fatal self-inflicted destructive act with explicit or inferred intent to die" (Goldsmith, Pellman, Kleinman, & Bunney, 2002, p. 27). Suicidal behavior runs along a continuum of thinking about ending one's life ("suicidal ideation"), to developing a plan, to undertaking nonfatal suicidal behavior ("suicide attempt"), to actually ending one's life ("suicide") (Centers for Disease Control and Prevention, 2011b).

The rate of completed suicide in the United States is far lower than the rates of other reported causes of death, amounting to slightly over 44 per 100,000 deaths in 2015 (Murphy et al., 2017). However, underreporting is likely, due to the difficulty of establishing cause of death as intentional rather than unintentional harm. The highest suicide rates by age are for people 45 to 54 years old (20.3 per 100,000). Individuals 85 and older have the next highest

FIGURE 3 Map of Suicide Rates

SOURCE: Age-standardized suicide rates (per 100,000 population), both sexes, 2012 World Health Organization.

rates (19.4) as well as the highest rates of suicide by discharge of firearms (13.7). Within the United States, white men are much more likely than are nonwhite men to commit suicide.

Around the world, there are approximately 1 million suicides each year, with a global mortality rate of 16 per 100,000. The highest global suicide rates are for males in Lithuania (61.3 per 100,000) and for females in South Korea (22.1 per 100,000), and the lowest rates (near 0) for several Latin American and Caribbean countries, Jordan, and Iran (see Figure 3).

Young adults are at highest risk of suicide in many countries outside the United States. In Europe and North America, depression and alcohol-use disorders are major psychological risk factors for suicide. In the United States, more than 90 percent of suicides occur in people with a psychological disorder (Goldsmith et al., 2002). In contrast, impulsiveness plays a higher role in the suicides of people from Asian countries (World Health Organization, 2011).

The biopsychosocial perspective is particularly appropriate for understanding why people commit suicide and in many ways parallels the understanding gleaned from an integrative framework for major depressive disorders. Biological theories emphasize the genetic and physiological contributions that also contribute to the causes of mood disorders. Psychological theories focus on distorted cognitive processes and extreme feelings of hopelessness that characterize suicide victims. From a sociocultural perspective, the variations between and within countries suggest contributions relating to an individual's religious beliefs and values and the degree to which the individual is exposed to life stresses.

The perspective of positive psychology provides a framework for understanding why individuals who are at high risk for the reasons above nevertheless do not commit suicide.

You Be the Judge

Do-Not-Resuscitate Orders for Suicidal Patients

The question whether physicians should assist patients in ending their own lives, a process known as physician-assisted suicide, came to public attention in the 1990s when Dr. Jack Kevorkian, a Michigan physician, began providing terminally ill patients with the means to end their lives through pharmacological injections. Kevorkian's very public involvement sprang from what he saw as a righteous campaign to alleviate people's suffering and allow them to "die with dignity." He was imprisoned for 8 years following the televised assisted suicide he performed on a man with amyotrophic lateral sclerosis (ALS), a terminal nervous system disease.

Medical professionals encourage (or sometimes require) patients, terminally ill or not, to direct them—in an "advance directive" or "living will"—by stating whether they wish to have artificial life support should they be unable to survive on their own. The advance directive often includes a DNR or "do not resuscitate" order in which the patient specifies that no heroic life-support measures should be taken to prolong life with, for example, life-support machines. Medical professionals respect the conditions of the DNR when they must make life-and-death decisions. In contrast, when individuals who have psychological disorders and wish to end their lives embark upon the same plans as a medical patient with a life-threatening illness, clinicians treat them to prevent them from committing suicide. The treatment may include involuntary hospitalization.

The obligation to respect end-of-life wishes may present an ethical conflict for mental health professionals when treating suicidal individuals who complete a DNR stating that they do not wish to be given life support. The question is whether having a serious psychological disorder that is incapacitating, resistant to treatment, and debilitating is any different from having a similarly untreatable and painful medical illness.

Q: *You be the judge:* Does the individual's right to autonomy, respected with a DNR, differ in this type of case (Cook, Pan, Silverman, & Soltys, 2010)?

The buffering hypothesis of suicidality (Johnson et al., 2011) describes resilience as a separate dimension from risk. You may be at risk of committing suicide, but if you are high on resilience, you are unlikely to do so. The statistically higher risk you may face due to living in a stressful environment may not translate into higher suicidality if you feel you can cope successfully with these circumstances.

The factors that seem to contribute to high resilience include the ability to make positive assessments of your life circumstances and to feel in control over these circumstances. Additional buffers to suicide risk are a number of psychosocial factors such as being able to solve problems, having high self-esteem, feeling supported by family and significant others, and being securely attached. People who do not believe suicide is an acceptable option to stress are also better able to overcome high risk. On the negative side, low resilience occurs with high levels of perfectionism and hopelessness (Hewitt, Caelian, Chen, & Flett, 2014). Having friends or family members who attempted suicide represents another risk factor (Mueller, Abrutyn, & Stockton, 2015).

Interventions based on the resilience model would not only address the individual's specific risk factors, then, but also assess and then strengthen the individual's feelings of personal control and perceived abilities to handle stress. CBT is one such intervention shown to be effective on reducing suicide attempts in populations such as adolescents (Ougrin et al., 2015) and members of the military with a history of suicide attempts (Rudd et al., 2015).

7.5 Depressive and Bipolar Disorders: The Biopsychosocial Perspective

The disorders we covered in this chapter span a range of phenomena, from chronic but distressing sad moods to rapidly vacillating alternations between mania and depression. Although these disorders clearly indicate disturbances in neurotransmitter functioning, they also reflect the influences of cognitive processes and sociocultural factors. Because individuals may experience the symptoms of depressive disorders for many years, clinicians are increasingly turning to nonpharmacological interventions, particularly for cases in which individuals have mild or moderate symptoms. The situation for clients with bipolar disorder is more complicated, because lifelong maintenance therapy on medication is more likely necessary. Nevertheless, these individuals can benefit from psychological interventions to help keep their symptoms monitored and under control.

Even individuals whose mood disorder symptoms reflect a heavy influence of biology, however, should have access to a range of therapeutic services. With the development of evidence-based approaches, which integrate interventions across the individual's multiple domains of functioning, the chances are good that people with these disorders will increasingly have the ability to obtain treatment that allows them to regulate their moods and lead more fulfilling lives.

Return to the Case: Janice Butterfield

After several weeks in therapy, Janice's depression had started to show improvement. Once her depression remitted, however, she discontinued taking her medication. As she discussed in her initial therapy session, Janice found it important to appear strong to her family and associated psychological problems with weakness. Despite her concerns about admitting her psychological struggles, Janice continued to come to her weekly psychotherapy, and the sessions focused on her feelings about her diagnosis and the importance of taking her medication to prevent future mood swings, though she felt stable at the time. Reminded of examples of the past consequences of her mood swings, however, Janice was slowly able to better understand that the impact on her family would be far worse should she continue to go through mood cycles than if she worked at maintaining stability.

Dr. Tobin's reflections: Though it is a natural reaction to feel down when faced with a challenge such as losing a job and having to find a way to support your family, Janice's response went beyond the typical depression most people feel, and she met diagnostic criteria for major depressive episodes. Janice's description of her past depressive episodes was also consistent with this diagnosis. It was also revealed that Janice experienced manic episodes in the past that had not only greatly affected her life but had put her family at great financial risk. Unfortunately, it wasn't until Janice had attempted suicide that she finally sought the help she needed. It is not unusual for individuals with bipolar disorder to be noncompliant with medication, because they go through long periods of feeling "normal" or being at their baseline. This was especially true of Janice, who had gone her entire life without seeking treatment and had difficulty understanding the need to take medication when she was not feeling depressed or manic.

Janice described experiencing a worsening of her mood episodes over time. This is typical for individuals with bipolar disorder who go without treatment for many years. Though she has been hesitant to talk about her problems with her family, it will be important to include them in her treatment because they can help Janice understand when her mood may start to shift. Individuals with bipolar disorder may struggle to be aware of these changes in mood. Over time, it will be important for Janice to continue to explore her concerns about the stigma of mental health treatment, given that this had been a major barrier to her reaching out for help in the past.

SUMMARY

- Depressive and bipolar disorders reflect a disturbance in a person's emotional state or mood. People can experience this disturbance in the form of extreme depression, excessive elation, or a combination of these emotional states. An episode is a time-limited period during which specific intense symptoms of a disorder are evident.

- Major depressive disorder is characterized by acute but time-limited episodes of depressive symptoms, such as feelings of extreme dejection, a loss of interest in previously pleasurable aspects of life, bodily symptoms, and disturbances in eating and sleeping behavior. Individuals with major depressive disorder also have cognitive symptoms, such as a negative self-view, feelings of guilt, inability to concentrate, and indecisiveness. Depressive episodes can be melancholic or seasonal. Persistent depressive disorder consists of depression that is not as deep or intense as that experienced in major depressive disorder but has a longer-lasting course. People with persistent depressive disorder have, for at least 2 years, depressive symptoms such as low energy, low self-esteem, poor concentration, decision-making difficulty, feelings of hopelessness, and disturbances of appetite and sleep. Disruptive mood dysregulation disorder consists of chronic and severe irritability, and premenstrual dysphoric disorder occurs in women prior to their monthly menstrual periods.

- Bipolar disorder is characterized by an intense and highly disruptive experience of extreme elation, or euphoria, called a manic episode, which manifests in abnormally heightened levels of thinking, behavior, and emotionality that cause significant impairment. Bipolar episodes in which both mania and depression are displayed can be labeled with specifiers to indicate mixed symptoms. Cyclothymic disorder consists of a vacillation between dysphoria and briefer, less intense, and less disruptive states called hypomanic episodes.

- Clinicians have explained depressive and bipolar disorders in terms of biological, psychological, and sociocultural approaches. The most compelling evidence supporting a biological model relies on the role of genetics; it has been well established that these disorders run in families. Biological theories focus on neurotransmitter and hormonal functioning.

Psychological theories have moved from early psychoanalytic approaches to more contemporary viewpoints that emphasize the behavioral, cognitive, and interpersonal aspects of mood disturbance. The behavioral viewpoint assumes that depression is the result of a reduction in positive reinforcements, deficient social skills, or the disruption caused by stressful life experiences. According to the cognitive perspective, depressed people react to stressful experiences by activating a set of thoughts called the cognitive triad: negative views of the self, the world, and the future. Cognitive distortions are errors people make in the way they draw conclusions from their experiences, applying illogical rules such as arbitrary inferences and overgeneralizing. Interpersonal theory posits a model of understanding depressive and bipolar disorders that emphasizes disturbed social functioning.

- Clinicians also base depressive and bipolar disorder treatments on biological, psychological, and sociocultural perspectives. Antidepressant medication is the most common form of somatic treatment for people who are depressed, and lithium carbonate is the most widely used medication for people who have bipolar disorder. In cases of incapacitating depression and some extreme cases of acute mania, the clinician may recommend electroconvulsive therapy. The psychological interventions most effective for treating people with depressive and bipolar disorders are those rooted in the behavioral and cognitive approaches. Sociocultural and interpersonal interventions focus on the treatment of mood symptoms within the context of an interpersonal system, such as an intimate relationship.

- Although no formal diagnostic category specifically applies to people who commit suicide, many suicidal people have depressive or bipolar disorders, and some suffer from other serious psychological disorders. Clinicians explain the dramatic act of suicide from biological, psychological, and sociocultural perspectives. The treatment of suicidal clients varies considerably, depending on the context, intent, and lethality. Most intervention approaches incorporate support and direct therapy.

KEY TERMS

Behavioral activation

Bipolar disorder

Bipolar disorder, rapid cycling

Circadian rhythms

Cognitive triad

Cyclothymic disorder

Depressive disorder

Disruptive mood dysregulation disorder

Dysphoria

Euphoria

Hypomanic episode

Interpersonal therapy (IPT)

Major depressive disorder

Major depressive episode

Manic episode

Persistent depressive disorder (dysthymia)

Pharmacogenetics

Premenstrual dysphoric disorder (PMDD)

Anxiety, Obsessive-Compulsive, and Trauma- and Stressor-Related Disorders

Learning Objectives

8.1 Distinguish between a normal fear response and an anxiety disorder.

8.2 Describe separation anxiety disorder.

8.3 Describe theories and treatments of specific phobias.

8.4 Describe theories and treatments of social anxiety disorder.

8.5 Contrast panic disorder with agoraphobia.

8.6 Describe generalized anxiety disorder.

8.7 Contrast obsessive-compulsive disorder with body dysmorphic disorder and hoarding.

8.8 Identify the trauma- and stress-related disorders.

8.9 Explain the biopsychosocial perspective on anxiety, obsessive-compulsive, and trauma- and stressor-related disorders.

©evymmnt/Shutterstock

Case Report: Barbara Wilder

Demographic information: 30-year-old single Caucasian heterosexual female

Presenting problem: At age 18, Barbara enlisted in the Army to help pay for college. Shortly after she graduated with a bachelor's degree in business, the United States declared war on Iraq and Barbara was sent on her first tour of duty, which lasted 18 months. She returned for three more tours before she was injured so severely in a military police raid that her lower left leg required amputation and she was forced to discontinue her service with the military.

While Barbara was receiving medical treatment at the Veterans Affairs (VA) Medical Center, her doctors noticed that she seemed constantly "on edge." When asked to provide details about her leg injury, she would grow anxious and withdrawn. She stated that she had difficulty sleeping because of frequent nightmares. Suspecting that she could be suffering from post-traumatic stress disorder (PTSD), the VA physicians referred her to the PTSD specialty clinic. Barbara reported that she had indeed been suffering a great deal of psychological stress since returning from her final tour of duty. She described her time in Iraq as incredibly dangerous and stressful. She worked on the military police unit and was in charge of guarding prisoners of war. Her station was often attacked, and gunfire fights were a frequent occurrence. Barbara also witnessed numerous incidents in which civilians and fellow soldiers were injured and killed.

Although she was under constant threat of injury or death while in Iraq and witnessed many grotesque scenes, Barbara stated that for the first three tours she was generally able to stay focused on her work without being unduly fearful. Over time and with repeated long tours of duty, however, she found it increasingly difficult not to be affected by the events around her. At the start of what was to be her last tour of duty, Barbara recalled that she felt as if she were starting to "mentally break down." When she was injured in the raid, she was certain she had been killed and remained in a state of shock for nearly 12 hours. Once she regained consciousness, Barbara recalled, she "just lost it" and began screaming at the medical staff around her. She now remembers very little of that day, but she recalls the feeling of total fear that overcame her and that remains with her to the present time.

In addition to the emotional difficulties she faced when she came home from the war, Barbara also was required to readjust to life in her community and to no longer living the life of a soldier. This adjustment was difficult not only because she had been away from her friends and family for so long, but also because she felt overwhelming distress associated with combat memories. Nevertheless, Barbara was coping well with her injury—undergoing physical therapy at the VA and getting used to life as an amputee. However, there was no denying that she was a different person than she had been before her time as a soldier, due to both her injury and the horrifying experiences she had survived during her time in Iraq.

Barbara originally planned to return to school to receive a degree in business administration when her contract with the military expired. However, since returning to the United States 6 months ago, she has given up on this plan. She rarely leaves the house where she resides with her parents. For the first 2 months after her return stateside, she drank alcohol excessively on a daily basis. She eventually noticed that drinking only seemed to make her anxiety worse, and so she stopped altogether. Though she stated she never talks about her experiences in Iraq, at least once every day

Barbara is haunted by disturbing, vivid flashbacks to violent images she witnessed while in the war. These visions also come to her in nightmares. She remarked that she must have replayed the image of seeing her leg blown up thousands of times in her mind. She reported feeling as if she were in a state of constant anxiety and that she was particularly sensitive to loud, unexpected noises. As a result, Barbara reported she was often irritable and jumpy around other people, growing angry quite easily. She expressed fears that she would never be able to make anything of her life, and that she barely felt motivated to make strides toward independence. Once social and outgoing, she no longer has any desire to see her friends and mostly ignores her parents. She described being emotionally "numb" and very detached from her feelings—a great departure from her usual temperament.

Relevant history: Barbara reported that she had always been "somewhat anxious," but that she never experienced this anxiety as an interference with her daily functioning. She described herself before her military enlistment as a normal, outgoing person who was mostly content with her life. She reported no history of mental illness in her immediate family.

Symptoms: Barbara reported that since her return from Iraq, she has frequently experienced a number of distressing symptoms that have significantly interfered with her life. These include difficulty sleeping, nightmares, flashbacks, restlessness, feelings of detachment from others, diminished interest, emotional "numbness," avoidance of talking about the trauma,

hypervigilance, increased anger, and irritability for the past 6 months.

Case formulation: Barbara's symptoms over the past 6 months meet the required *DSM-5* criteria for post-traumatic stress disorder: intrusive recollection, avoidance/numbing, hyperarousal, duration (at least 1 month), and interference with functioning. During her three tours of duty in Iraq, she was repeatedly exposed to dangerous or life-threatening situations and witnessed many gruesome events as a soldier. Though she was initially able to cope with these experiences, over time her resolve was shaken and she began to respond to her surroundings with fear and horror, especially pertaining to the incident in which she lost part of her left leg. Despite drinking heavily for a period of weeks, she has been abstinent for several months and did not meet enough criteria for a *DSM-5* diagnosis of alcohol use disorder.

Treatment plan: After the psychological assessment determined that Barbara was suffering from PTSD, she was referred for weekly individual psychotherapy as well as a weekly PTSD therapy group at the VA. Psychotherapy for PTSD often consists of some exposure to the trauma via talking and/or writing about it in detail. Some treatments include reflecting on the ways in which trauma has affected the individual's general beliefs about trust and safety. The purpose of group therapy is to provide social support for those suffering from the disorder and to work on coping skills training. Group therapy can sometimes be utilized in place of individual therapy.

Sarah Tobin, PhD

---

anxiety disorders
Disorders characterized by excessive fear and anxiety, and related disturbances in behavior.

anxiety
A future-oriented and global response, involving both cognitive and emotional components, in which an individual is inordinately apprehensive, tense, and uneasy about the prospect of something terrible happening.

fear
The emotional response to real or perceived imminent threat.

8.1 Anxiety Disorders

The central defining feature of **anxiety disorders** is the experience of a chronic and intense feeling of **anxiety** in which people feel a sense of dread about what might happen to them in the future. The anxiety experienced by people with anxiety disorders causes them to have great difficulty functioning on a day-to-day basis. This feeling goes beyond the typical worries people have from time to time about performing their everyday activities at work or home, or in their interactions with other people.

People with anxiety disorders also experience **fear**, which is the emotional response to real or perceived imminent threat. Again, like the experience of anxiety, the sense of fear that people with these disorders have goes beyond ordinary or even rational concern over the possible dangers of the situations in which they find themselves.

People with anxiety disorders go to great lengths to avoid situations that provoke the emotional responses of anxiety and fear. When they are unable to do so, they will have difficulty performing jobs, enjoying leisure pursuits, or engaging in social activities with friends and families.

Across all categories, anxiety disorders have a lifetime prevalence rate in the United States of 28.8 percent and an overall 12-month prevalence of 18.1 percent. Of all 12-month prevalence cases, nearly 23 percent are classified as severe. The percent of people reporting lifetime prevalence across all anxiety disorders peaks between the ages of 30 and 44, with a sharp dropoff to 15.3 percent among people 60 years and older (Kessler, Chiu, et al., 2005). The annual prevalence rate averages at 19.3 percent, with a drop from the high at ages 30–44 to 9 percent at ages 60 and older (Figure 1). The average age of onset across all anxiety disorders is 21.3 years of age, with ranges from 15 years and younger to up to 39 years, depending on the nature of the disorder (de Lijster et al., 2017).

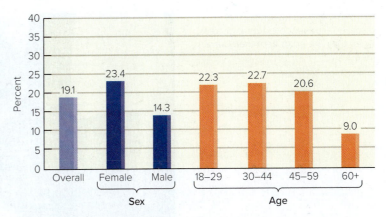

FIGURE 1 Past-Year Prevalence of Any Anxiety Disorder among U.S. Adults (2001–2003)

SOURCE: https://www.nimh.nih.gov/health/statistics/any-anxiety-disorder.shtml

Separation Anxiety Disorder

Individuals with **separation anxiety disorder** have intense and inappropriate anxiety about leaving home or being left by their attachment figures, the people close to them in their lives. Children with this disorder may cling so closely to a parent they will not let the parent out of their sight. Adults who meet the criteria for this disorder have intense anxiety about being separated from the person to whom they are most emotionally attached.

Prior to the *DSM-5,* the condition of separation anxiety disorder was considered specific to children. However, recognizing that there are a significant number of adult-onset cases, *DSM-5* lifted the disorder's age restriction to make it diagnosis applicable to adults as well as children. Although the key features of the disorder can vary according to the individual's age, always included is being excessively distressed when separated from the home or the attachment figure or even at the thought of such separation occurring.

Part of the anxiety people with the disorder experience is worry about harm befalling their attachment figure, such as him or her being kidnapped, a fear that can become extreme and irrational. This worry leads them to try to avoid spending any time apart or away from home, interfering with their ability to work or go to school. They need to sleep near their attachment figures and may have nightmares about separation. The prospect of separation may lead them to develop physical complaints such as headaches, stomachaches, or even nausea and vomiting.

Worldwide, epidemiologists estimate that 5.3 percent of individuals experience separation anxiety disorder at some point in life, with 43.1 percent of those developing the symptoms in adulthood. Regardless of when the symptoms first become evident, people with this disorder were more likely to have suffered adversities during their childhood or traumatic events at some point in their lives. Females are more likely than males to experience separation anxiety disorder. People who develop this disorder are at greater risk of subsequently developing other anxiety disorders and depressive disorder ("internalizing" disorders) as well as ADHD and conduct disorder (Silove et al., 2015).

Theories and Treatment of Separation Anxiety Disorder

Although twin studies supported the role of genetic contributions to this disorder, a novel children-of-twins study conducted by Swedish researchers suggested that anxiety is passed down from parents to children through environmental, rather than genetic, mechanisms. In other words, children with anxious parents learn to develop anxiety through modeling (Eley et al., 2015).

Sociocultural factors also play a role in predisposing certain individuals to developing separation anxiety disorder. The symptoms of the disorder seem to be more severe in countries that promote an individualistic, independent culture than in those with a more collectivist set of cultural norms (Eley et al., 2015). Remaining with attachment figures may seem

separation anxiety disorder
A childhood disorder characterized by intense and inappropriate anxiety, lasting at least 4 weeks, concerning separation from home or caregivers.

Children with separation anxiety disorder experience extreme distress when they are apart from their primary caregivers.

©Design Pics/Kelly Redinger

more acceptable in collectivist cultures, so the behavior of individuals with separation anxiety disorder may not appear so out of the ordinary.

As mentioned, trauma may play a role in the development of separation anxiety disorder. In the aftermath of the September 11 terrorist attacks in 2001, nearly 13 percent of New York City schoolchildren had a probable diagnosis of separation anxiety disorder (Hoven et al., 2005). It is possible that temperamental differences rooted in biology cause some children to experience heightened reactivity in these kinds of situations.

At present, the treatment literature does not include studies of adults, given that the condition was considered specific to childhood until *DSM-5*'s publication. For children, both behavioral and cognitive-behavioral therapies (CBT) seem to have the greatest promise. Behavioral techniques include systematic desensitization, prolonged exposure, and modeling. Contingency management and self-management are also useful in teaching the child to react more positively and competently to a fear-provoking situation.

Researchers investigating the effectiveness of this approach have developed a form of CBT that clinicians can administer in an intensive and time-limited manner, so children do not have to commit to weeks or months of therapy. In one version, girls with separation anxiety disorder attended a 1-week camp where they received intensive CBT in a group setting (Santucci et al., 2009). The treatment included working with parents and their children in a combination of psychoeducation, cognitive restructuring, and relaxation training. Craft activities without the parents present took place at regularly scheduled times. At the end of the week, the children and their parents attended an awards ceremony. At that time, parents were also given training for follow-up during the weeks subsequent to camp. Relapse prevention training was also built into the final day's activities to ensure that, should a bout of separation anxiety reoccur, parents and children did not revert completely to their pretreatment behavior.

Selective Mutism

selective mutism
A disorder originating in childhood in which the individual consciously refuses to talk.

Refusing to talk in specific situations is the core feature of **selective mutism**. Children with this disorder are capable of using normal language, but they become almost completely silent under certain circumstances, most commonly the classroom. This is a relatively rare disorder, with estimates of its prevalence ranging from a low of 0.2 percent to a high of 2 percent and beginning between the ages of 3 and 6 years; frequency is equal among boys and girls (Kearney & Vecchio, 2007). Anxiety may be at the root of selective mutism given that children most typically show this behavior in school rather than at home (Shriver, Segool, & Gortmaker, 2011).

Children with selective mutism seem to respond well to behavioral therapy. The clinician devises a hierarchy of desired responses, beginning by rewarding the child for making any utterances and then progressing through words and sentences, perhaps moving from the home to the clinic and eventually to the school. Another behavioral approach uses contingency management, in which children receive rewards if they engage in the desired behavior of speaking. Contingency management seems particularly well suited for use in the home by parents. Of the two methods, shaping plus exposure therapy seems to be more effective, but contingency management in the home can nevertheless serve as an important adjunct (Vecchio & Kearney, 2009).

CBT is another method that produces improvement in children with selective mutism. An investigation of CBT's effectiveness among children age 3 to 9 years showed high rates of improvement for children younger than 5 (78 percent) and less improvement for children 6 and older. The treatment, which was adapted for school settings, progressed through six levels, from speaking to the therapist with the parent present to ultimately speaking to other children with neither the therapist nor the parent present. Parents and teachers were instructed to use "defocused communication," in which they minimize the direct pressure placed on the child to speak (Oerbeck, Stein, Pripp, & Kristensen, 2015). CBT can have lasting benefits, as indicated in a follow-up showing the gains in these children persisting 5 years post-treatment (Oerbeck et al., 2018).

Specific Phobias

A **phobia** is an irrational fear associated with a particular object or situation. It is common to have some fear of or at least a desire to avoid such objects as spiders or situations with enclosed spaces or heights. In a **specific phobia**, however, the fear or anxiety is so intense that it becomes incapacitating. People with specific phobia go to great lengths to avoid the feared object or situation. If they can't get away, they endure the situation but only with marked anxiety and discomfort. Like all anxiety disorders, a specific phobia induces significant distress. Moreover, it is not a fleeting condition but must be present for at least 6 months to justify a diagnosis.

Almost any object or situation, from the act of driving to syringes, can form the target of a phobia. Trivia games might ask you to define terms that refer to unusual phobias such as coulrophobia (fear of clowns).

However endless the list of possible specific phobias may be, they fall into four major categories: insects and animals, the natural environment (storms or fires), blood-injection-injury (seeing blood, having an invasive medical procedure), and engaging in activities in particular situations (riding an escalator, flying). A fifth category includes a variety of miscellaneous stimuli or situations such as fear of vomiting.

Overall, the lifetime prevalence for specific phobia in the United States is 12.5 percent (Kessler, Chiu, et al., 2005). The highest lifetime prevalence rates are for fear of natural situations, particularly heights, and are estimated to be between 3.1 and 5.3 percent. Animal phobia ranges in prevalence from 3.3 to 7 percent. That these are the two most common forms of specific phobia is indicated by the fact that among people with any form of specific phobia, 50 percent have a fear of animals or a fear of heights (LeBeau et al., 2010). A comparison of lifetime prevalence rates among 22 countries shows similar rates of 12.5 percent in the United States, Colombia, and Brazil, with the lowest rates in China (2.6 percent). Animal phobias are the most prevalent overall (3.8%), followed by fear of medical procedures (3.0%), then still water and weather events (2.3%). Worldwide, specific phobias were less prevalent in adults 60 and older than in younger people, and in males than in females (Wardenaar et al., 2017).

phobia
An irrational fear associated with a particular object or situation.

specific phobia
An irrational and unabating fear of a particular object, activity, or situation.

Theories and Treatment of Specific Phobias   As you have just seen, there are many types of specific phobias, ranging from the common to the relatively obscure. However, the fact that they are grouped together suggests an underlying theme or element at the root of their cause and, potentially, their treatment.

A common phobia is an excessive fear of spiders.
©Design Pics/Yuri Arcurs

Within the biological perspective, researchers believe the anxiety associated with specific phobias may relate to abnormalities in the anterior insular cortex (Rosso et al., 2010). This area of the brain lies between the temporal and frontal lobes and is associated with emotion and self-awareness. The amygdala, which moderates the fear response, also seems to play a role in specific phobias, particularly those acquired through learning in which people associate a given stimulus with the emotion of fear (Garcia, 2017).

Treatment of specific phobias following from the biological perspective focuses on symptom management. Clinicians operating from this perspective prescribe medications, primarily benzodiazepines, but only if their clients do not respond to other treatments (Kimmel, Roy-Byrne, & Cowley, 2015). Unlike other forms of anxiety disorder, specific phobias are more circumscribed in nature and the situations are generally more easily avoided. Thus, clinicians would prescribe medications only when the specific phobia interferes with the individual's ability to carry out ordinary activities to such a degree that he or she cannot function on a daily basis.

The behavioral approach to specific phobias emphasizes the conditioning that occurs when the individual learns to associate unpleasant physical sensations with a certain kind of stimulus or situation. Behaviorists assume there may be some adaptive value to having such reactions, because the situations may truly be ones we should fear, such as poisonous snakes. The symptoms become maladaptive, according to this view, as individuals begin to generalize an appropriate fear reaction to all stimuli in that category, including harmless ones.

There may also be developmental aspects to specific phobias. Very young children tend to fear objects or situations they can see; as they get older, feared objects become more abstract in nature (such as "the bogeyman") (Davis & Ollendick, 2011). Further, older children may view the objects and situations they fear as more catastrophic than younger children with the same phobias do (Ollendick et al., 2017). At the other end of the age spectrum, older adults with specific phobias may not report symptoms but instead misattribute their anxiety to a physical condition (Coelho et al., 2010).

According to the cognitive-behavioral view, individuals with specific phobias have overactive alarm systems for danger, and they perceive things as dangerous because they misinterpret harmless stimuli. For example, the mistaken perception of an object or a situation as uncontrollable, unpredictable, dangerous, or disgusting is correlated with feelings of vulnerability. These attributions might explain the common phobia of spiders, an insect about which people have many misconceptions and apprehensions. In blood-injection-injury phobia, in contrast, disgust and fear of contamination play a prominent role (de Jong & Peters, 2007). People with phobias also tend to overestimate the likelihood of a dangerous outcome after becoming exposed to the feared stimulus (de Jong & Merckelbach, 2000).

All behavioral techniques rely on positive reinforcement as the mechanism for achieving symptom relief. However, clinicians' specific approaches to providing this reinforcement differ.

In exposure therapy, positive reinforcement is used to lead clients to substitute adaptive responses (relaxation) for maladaptive ones (fear or anxiety). The four methods of exposure

MINI CASE

Specific Phobia, Natural Environment

Aarman is a married 32-year-old heterosexual Indian American male seeking treatment for his irrational fear of thunderstorms. He has had this phobia since age 4, and throughout life he has developed various strategies for coping with his fear. Whenever possible, he avoids going outside when a storm is forecast. Not only will he stay within a building, but he will ensure that he is in a room with no windows and no electrical appliances. As his job as a lawyer has grown in responsibility, Aarman has found that he can no longer afford to take time off because of his fear, which he knows is irrational.

TABLE 1 **Methods of Exposure Used in Behavioral Therapy of Phobias**

	Graduated Exposure	Immediate Full Exposure
Imagery	Systematic desensitization	Imaginal flooding
Live	Graded *in vivo*	*In vivo* flooding

therapy vary in the way this basic procedure is carried out (see Table 1). Systematic desensitization presents the client with progressively more anxiety-provoking images while at the same time the client is being trained to relax. The idea is that the client cannot feel both anxious and relaxed at the same time, and that over the course of treatment, anxiety will be completely replaced with relaxation.

In the behavioral technique called **flooding**, clients are totally immersed in the feared situation, where they feel the anxiety with full force. *In vivo* **flooding** exposes the client to the actual feared situation, such as the top floor of a tall building for a client who fears heights. Another variant of flooding is **imaginal flooding**, in which the clinician exposes the client virtually to the feared situation.

In vivo flooding is probably the most stressful of any of the treatments described and therefore has a high dropout rate (Choy, Fyer, & Lipsitz, 2007). An alternative is the **graded *in vivo*** method in which clients initially confront situations that cause only minor anxiety and then gradually progress toward those that cause greater anxiety. Often the therapist tries to be encouraging and to model the desired nonanxious response. In treating a client who has a fear of enclosed spaces, the therapist could go with the client into smaller and smaller rooms. Seeing the therapist showing no signs of fear could lead the client to model the therapist's response. The therapist could also offer praise to further reinforce the new response the client is learning. As illustrated in Table 1, behavioral treatments vary according to the nature of the client's exposure to the phobic stimulus (live or imaginal) and the degree of intensity with which the stimulus is confronted (immediate full exposure or exposure in graduated steps).

The most recently tested variant of exposure therapy uses **virtual reality exposure therapy (VRET)**, in which clients become immersed in computer-generated environments that resemble the situations they fear. Safer than *in vivo* therapy for obvious reasons and more realistic than imaginal methods, VRET would seem to be an ideal way to provide clients with experiences that can allow them to unlearn their fears. A meta-analysis conducted on clinical trials using VRET to treat people with fear of heights or fear of spiders showed effects on phobic behaviors comparable to those seen with behavior therapy (Morina, Ijntema, Meyerbröker, & Emmelkamp, 2015). It is quite likely that VRET will become increasingly used to treat specific phobias given the rapid growth in the availability of this form of technology.

Cognitive-behavioral treatment for specific phobia focuses on helping the client learn more adaptive ways of thinking about previously threatening situations and objects by challenging their irrational beliefs about the feared stimuli. For example, a therapist may show a young man with an elevator phobia that the disastrous consequences he believes will result from riding in an elevator are unrealistic and exaggerated. The client can also learn the technique of "talking to himself" while in this situation, telling himself that his fears are ridiculous, that nothing bad will really happen, and that he will soon reach his destination.

Social Anxiety Disorder

The primary feature of **social anxiety disorder** is a fear of becoming humiliated or embarrassed in front of other people. Extending beyond the ordinary concerns people may have about looking foolish or making a mistake during a performance, this disorder makes people anxious even at the prospect of eating or drinking in front of others. Thus, the fear is not

flooding
A behavioral technique in which the client is immersed in the sensation of anxiety by being exposed to the feared situation in its entirety.

***in vivo* flooding**
A behavioral technique in which the client is immersed in the actual feared situation.

imaginal flooding
A behavioral technique in which the client is immersed through imagination into the feared situation.

graded *in vivo*
A procedure in which clients gradually expose themselves to increasingly challenging anxiety-provoking situations.

virtual reality exposure therapy (VRET)
A method of exposure therapy that uses virtual reality, in which clients become immersed in computer-generated environments that resemble the situations they fear.

social anxiety disorder
An anxiety disorder characterized by marked, or intense, fear or anxiety in social situations in which the individual may be scrutinized by others.

What's in the *DSM-5*

Definition and Categorization of Anxiety Disorders

The *DSM-5* unveiled major changes in the definition and categorization of anxiety disorders. Agoraphobia became a separate disorder, much as it is now in the *ICD-10*. In addition, social phobia in *DSM-IV-TR* was renamed social anxiety disorder. The change reflects the fact that social anxiety disorder is not a phobia in the sense of representing fear of other people, although "social phobia" still appears in parentheses. Obsessive-compulsive disorder (OCD) is categorized with body dysmorphic disorder, hoarding disorder, trichotillomania (excessive hair pulling), and skin picking. Acute and post-traumatic stress disorders moved into their own category of "Trauma and Stressor-Related Disorders." Finally, several disorders formerly in the group that originated in childhood (a designation now dropped) were moved into the anxiety disorder grouping.

of other people (it is not a phobia), but rather of what other people may think of the individual. In *DSM-IV-TR*, the disorder was referred to as social phobia; it was renamed in *DSM-5* with "social phobia" in parentheses.

Second only to specific phobia in prevalence as an anxiety disorder, social anxiety disorder has a lifetime prevalence of 12.1 percent in the United States. Of the 6.8 percent who develop this disorder over a 12-month period, nearly 30 percent have cases classified as severe (Kessler, Berglund, et al., 2005).

Theories and Treatment of Social Anxiety Disorder The biological underpinnings of social anxiety disorder may, some researchers believe, be related to partly heritable mechanisms (Stein & Gelernter, 2014). The intense anxiety experienced by an individual with social anxiety disorder, from this perspective, is essentially a form of intense shyness combined with the personality trait of neuroticism. These qualities in turn either cause or are caused by alterations in areas of the brain responsible for attention. Individuals with social anxiety disorder, according to this view, become excessively self-focused and therefore exaggerate the extent to which others look critically upon them.

Of the possible medications that can be used to treat social anxiety disorder, the selective serotonin or norepinephrine reuptake inhibitors (SSRIs and SNRIs) are regarded as having the greatest effectiveness. Other medications that may work as well have considerable drawbacks. Benzodiazepines have significant potential for abuse; moreover, they may actually interfere with treatment that includes psychological methods such as exposure to feared situations. MAOIs, which can also effectively manage social anxiety symptoms, have potentially dangerous side effects (Jorstad-Stein & Heimberg, 2009).

Among psychological approaches, the cognitive-behavioral perspective regards people with social anxiety disorder as unable to gain a realistic view of how others really perceive them. As in other forms of cognitive-behavioral therapy, the clinician working from this perspective attempts to reframe the client's thoughts in combination with real or imagined exposure.

Related to the cognitive-behavioral approach is the view of social anxiety disorder as reflecting a core fear of interacting with new people in new situations. Rather than viewing the various symptoms of the disorder as having independent origins, researchers working within this network model believe the specific fears (such as being unable to look new

MINI CASE

Social Anxiety Disorder, Performance Only Type

Theo is a single 19-year-old Caucasian bisexual male. He is a sophomore in college and reports that he is terrified at the prospect of speaking in class. His anxiety is so intense that he enrolls only in very large lecture classes, where he sits in the back of the room, slouching in his chair to make himself as invisible as possible. On occasion, one of his professors randomly calls on students to answer certain questions. When this occurs, Theo begins to sweat and tremble. Sometimes he rushes from the classroom and frantically runs back to his dormitory for a few hours and tries to calm himself down.

people in the eye or to take a test in front of others) may all be inter-related via a central connection to that core fear of strangers. Following this approach, therapy would attempt to treat the core set of fears, which would then have a cascade effect on the more peripheral symptoms (Heeren & McNally, 2018).

Nevertheless, treatment of social anxiety disorder can be particularly challenging, because clients may tend to isolate themselves socially and therefore have fewer opportunities to expose themselves to challenging situations in the course of their daily lives. Their impaired social skills may then lead them to experience negative reactions from others, thus confirming their fears. Unfortunately, researchers attempting to use VRET find virtual scenarios less effective than in the treatment of specific phobias. Although virtual exposure may evoke similar responses as *in vivo* exposure to social situations, when it comes to reenacting those social situations in therapy, individuals need to be exposed to an actual audience (Owens & Beidel, 2015).

For clients who do not respond to psychotherapy or medication, there are promising signs about the benefits of alternate methods, including motivational interviewing, acceptance and commitment therapy, and mindfulness/meditation. Their common element, also present in CBT, is the practice of stepping back from situations to identify and challenge automatic thoughts (Kocovski et al., 2015).

Panic Disorder and Agoraphobia

In *DSM-IV-TR*, agoraphobia was not considered a diagnosis separate from panic disorder. The *DSM-5*, consistent with emerging research and the *ICD*, now separates the two disorders, although the two diagnoses may both be assigned if the individual meets the criteria for both. We present them in one section because the majority of research on theories and treatment was conducted on the basis of the *DSM-IV-TR* diagnostic categorization.

Social anxiety disorder causes distress by preventing an individual from engaging in social activities he or she would normally enjoy.
©Comstock/age fotostock

Panic Disorder People with **panic disorder** experience periods of intense physical discomfort known as **panic attacks**. During a panic attack, the individual feels overwhelmed by a range of highly unpleasant physical sensations. These can include respiratory distress (shortness of breath, hyperventilation, feeling of choking), autonomic disturbances (sweating, stomach distress, shaking or trembling, heart palpitations), and sensory abnormalities (dizziness, numbness, or tingling). During a panic attack, people may also feel that they are "going crazy" or losing control. *DSM-5* includes specifiers for panic attacks, indicating the nature of the symptoms the individual experiences, such as palpitations, sweating, trembling, chest pain, nausea, chills, fear of "going crazy," and fear of dying. Of these symptoms, palpitations ("heart pounding") and dizziness are the most commonly reported (Craske et al., 2010).

Having an occasional panic attack is not enough to justify a diagnosis of panic disorder. To meet the diagnostic criteria, the panic attacks have to occur on a repeated basis and be accompanied by fear of having another. People with this disorder also might engage in avoidance behaviors, staying away from situations in which another panic attack might occur.

Agoraphobia In **agoraphobia**, the individual feels intense fear or anxiety triggered by real or anticipated exposure to situations such as using public transportation, being in an enclosed space such as a theater or an open space such as a parking lot, and being outside the home alone. People with agoraphobia are fearful not of the situations themselves but of

panic disorder
An anxiety disorder in which an individual has panic attacks on a recurrent basis or has constant apprehension and worry about the possibility of recurring attacks.

panic attack
A period of intense fear and physical discomfort accompanied by the feeling that one is being overwhelmed and is about to lose control.

agoraphobia
Intense anxiety triggered by the real or anticipated exposure to situations in which individuals may be unable to get help should they become incapacitated.

the possibility that they can't get help or escape if they have panic-like symptoms or other embarrassing or incapacitating symptoms when in those situations. Their fear or anxiety is out of proportion to the actual danger they might face. If they cannot avoid the situation, they become highly anxious and fearful, and to cope, they might require the presence of a companion. As in other psychological disorders, these symptoms must persist over time (in this case, at least 6 months), cause considerable distress, and not be due to another psychological or medical disorder.

Panic attacks are somewhat common in that they are estimated to occur in 20 percent or more of adults; panic disorder has a much lower lifetime prevalence of between 3 and 5 percent. Across a variety of studies, settings, and diagnostic criteria, approximately 25 percent of people who have *DSM-5* panic disorder with the agoraphobia syndrome would meet diagnostic criteria for agoraphobia alone (Wittchen et al., 2010).

Theories and Treatment of Panic Disorder and Agoraphobia

anxiety sensitivity theory
The belief that panic disorder is caused in part by the tendency to interpret cognitive and somatic manifestations of stress and anxiety in a catastrophic manner.

Researchers studying biological contributions to panic disorder focus on norepinephrine, the neurotransmitter that helps prepare the body to react to stressful situations. Higher levels of norepinephrine can make the individual more likely to experience fear, anxiety, and panic. Serotonin may also play a role in increasing a person's likelihood of developing panic disorder, as deficits in serotonin are linked to anxiety (Kalk, Nutt, & Lingford-Hughes, 2011). Furthermore, according to **anxiety sensitivity theory**, people who develop panic disorder have heightened responsiveness to the presence of carbon dioxide in the blood. Hence, they are more likely to panic due to the sensation that they are suffocating (Pérez Benítez et al., 2009).

The most effective antianxiety medications for panic disorder and agoraphobia are benzodiazepines, which increase the availability of the inhibitory neurotransmitter GABA. However, because benzodiazepines can lead clients to become dependent on them or to abuse them, clinicians may prefer to prescribe SSRIs or SNRIs (Pollack & Simon, 2009).

conditioned fear reactions
Acquired associations between an internal or external cue and feelings of intense anxiety.

From a classical conditioning perspective, panic disorder results from **conditioned fear reactions** in which the individual associates bodily sensations such as difficulty breathing with memories of the last panic attack, causing a full-blown panic attack to develop. The cognitive-behavioral model proposes that people with panic disorder, upon feeling the unpleasant sensations of the panic attack begin (loss of breath), believe it is unpredictable and uncontrollable and that they will not be able to stop it (White, Brown, Somers, & Barlow, 2006).

Adding to their desire to avoid the unpleasant emotions associated with these experiences, people with panic disorder and agoraphobia may also have personality traits that exacerbate their symptoms, including high levels of neuroticism and low levels of extraversion (Zugliani, Martin-Santos, Nardi, & Friere, 2017). Their tendency to ruminate, to prefer not to experience strong emotions, and to keep to themselves may serve to maintain their symptoms above and beyond whatever was their prior exposure to anxiety-provoking situations (Spinhoven, van Hemert, & Penninx, 2017).

MINI CASE

Panic Disorder and Agoraphobia

Frieda is a single 31-year-old heterosexual Latina female. She is a former delivery driver who sought treatment because of recurrent panic attacks that have led her to become fearful of driving. She has become so frightened of the prospect of having an attack on the job that she has asked for medical leave. Although initially she would leave the house when accompanied by her mother, she now is unable to go out under any circumstances, and her family is concerned that she will become a total recluse.

In relaxation therapy, patients learn a variety of techniques that focus on breathing and relaxation in order to overcome the physiological symptoms of anxiety.

©PhotoAlto/John Dowland/Getty Images

Relaxation training is one behavioral technique used to help clients gain control over the bodily reactions that occur in panic attacks. After training, the client should be able to relax the entire body when confronting a feared situation. Another approach focuses on breathing. The client is instructed to hyperventilate intentionally and then to begin slow breathing, a response that is incompatible with hyperventilation. Following this training, the client can begin the slow breathing at the first signs of hyperventilation. In addition to changing the response itself, this method allows clients to feel that they can exert voluntary control over the development of a panic attack. In the method known as **panic-control therapy (PCT)**, the therapist combines breathing retraining, psychoeducation, and cognitive restructuring to help individuals recognize and ultimately control the bodily cues associated with panic attacks (Hofmann, Rief, & Spiegel, 2010).

relaxation training
A behavioral technique used in the treatment of anxiety disorders that involves progressive and systematic patterns of muscle tensing and relaxing.

panic-control therapy (PCT)
Treatment that consists of cognitive restructuring, exposure to bodily cues associated with panic attacks, and breathing retraining.

Generalized Anxiety Disorder

The key feature of **generalized anxiety disorder** is that, unlike the disorders you have learned about so far, it does not have a particular focus. People with generalized anxiety disorder feel anxious for much of the time, even though they may not be able to say exactly why they feel this way. In addition, they worry a great deal, apprehensively expecting the worst to happen to them. Their symptoms span a range of physical and psychological experiences including general restlessness, sleep disturbances, feelings of fatigue, irritability, muscle tension, and trouble concentrating, to the point where their mind goes blank. There is no particular situation they can identify as lying at the root of their anxiety, and they find it difficult to control their worrying.

There are differences between older and younger adults in the nature of generalized anxiety disorder. Older individuals worry more about their own health and family well-being, and young adults worry more about their own future and the health of other people. Older adults also show more sleep disturbances, are less likely to seek

generalized anxiety disorder
An anxiety disorder characterized by anxiety and worry that is not associated with a particular object, situation, or event but seems to be a constant feature of a person's day-to-day existence.

MINI CASE

Generalized Anxiety Disorder

Jin is a 32-year-old heterosexual Korean female and the single mother of two children. She is seeking professional help for her longstanding feelings of anxiety. Despite the fact that her personal and financial life is relatively stable, she worries most of the time that she will develop financial problems, that her children will become ill, and that the political situation in the country will make life for her and her children more difficult.

Although she tries to dismiss these concerns as excessive, she finds it virtually impossible to control her worrying. Most of the time, she feels uncomfortable and tense, and sometimes her tension becomes so extreme that she begins to tremble and sweat. She finds it difficult to sleep at night. During the day she is restless, keyed up, and tense. She has consulted a variety of medical specialists, each of whom has been unable to diagnose a physical problem.

reassurance, and show higher rates and severity of depression accompanying their anxiety (Altunoz et al., 2018).

Generalized anxiety disorder has a lifetime prevalence of 5.7 percent. Over a 12-month period, the prevalence is reported to be 3.1 percent; of these cases, 32 percent are classified as severe (Kessler, Berglund, et al., 2005).

Theories and Treatment of Generalized Anxiety Disorder

Biologically based theories of generalized anxiety disorder focus on disturbances in GABA, serotonergic, and noradrenergic systems (Nutt & Malizia, 2001). Support for the notion that there is a biological component to generalized anxiety disorder is the finding of an overlap in genetic vulnerability with the personality trait of neuroticism (see the chapter "Assessment"). In other words, people who are prone to developing this disorder have inherited an underlying neurotic personality style (Hettema, Prescott, & Kendler, 2004).

Cognitive-behavioral therapy builds on the assumption that the anxiety people with this disorder experience results from cognitive distortions in their interpretation of the minor inconveniences of life (Borkovec & Ruscio, 2001). Clinicians using this approach attempt to break the cycle of negative thoughts and worries by helping clients learn how to recognize anxious thoughts, to seek more rational alternatives to worrying, and to take action to test these alternatives. Once the cycle of worry has been broken, the individual can develop a sense of control over the worrying behavior and become better able to manage and reduce anxious thoughts when they threaten to become overwhelming.

Another compounding factor in generalized anxiety disorder may be the individual's inability to tolerate uncertainty or ambiguity. The outcomes of many common situations in life are indeed ambiguous. People with this disorder seek to reduce uncertainty by trying to know exactly what will happen when, without taking into account the fact that it is not always possible to know the outcome of every situation. Cognitive-behavioral therapy can be of benefit in helping individuals with the disorder come to accept such ambiguities (Bomyea et al., 2015).

Cognitive-behavioral therapy is therefore considered the method of choice in treating individuals with generalized anxiety disorder, particularly because it avoids the potentially negative side effects of antianxiety medications. Researchers are continuing to explore variations in the basic cognitive-behavioral approach to give individuals a broader set of options. Acceptance and commitment therapy (ACT) is thought to have similar mechanisms to CBT and is gaining evidence as a stand-alone treatment for various anxiety disorders (Arch et al., 2012).

8.2 Obsessive-Compulsive and Related Disorders

An **obsession** is a recurrent and persistent thought, urge, or image that the individual experiences as intrusive and unwanted. Individuals try to ignore or suppress the obsession or to neutralize it by engaging in some other thought or action. The thought or action the person uses to try to neutralize the obsession is known as a **compulsion**, a repetitive behavior or mental act the person feels driven to carry out according to rigid rules. Compulsions need not, however, be paired with obsessions.

In **obsessive-compulsive disorder (OCD)**, individuals experience either obsessions or compulsions to such an extent that they find it difficult to conduct their daily activities. As part of the disorder, they may experience significant distress or impairment in their ability to work and have a satisfying family or social life.

The most common compulsions experienced by people with OCD are repeated behaviors such as washing and cleaning, counting items, putting items in order, checking, or requesting assurance. These compulsions may also take the form of mental rituals, such as counting up to a certain number every time the individual has an unwanted thought. Some individuals with OCD experience tics, which are uncontrollable motor movements such as twitches, vocalizations, and facial grimaces.

In general, there appear to be four major dimensions of the symptoms of OCD. These are the needs for symmetry, order, and cleanliness and the saving of apparently useless items (Mataix-Cols, Rosario-Campos, & Leckman, 2005). Table 2 lists items from the Yale–Brown Obsessive-Compulsive Symptom Checklist, an instrument commonly used for assessing individuals with OCD.

Rated as one of the top 10 debilitating disorders by the World Health Organization (Veale & Roberts, 2014), OCD has a lifetime prevalence in the United States estimated at 1.6 percent. The 12-month prevalence is slightly lower, 1 percent; of these, about half are classified as severe (Kessler, Berglund, et al., 2005). Many more individuals seek help for OCD-like symptoms than are diagnosed with the disorder (Leckman et al., 2010).

Theories and Treatment of Obsessive-Compulsive Disorder

Given the prominent role in OCD of motor movements such as cleaning and ordering, the biological basis for the disorder has long been thought to originate in abnormalities in the basal ganglia, which are subcortical areas of the brain active in motor control. Further contributing to the motor symptoms was thought to be failure of the prefrontal cortex to inhibit unwanted thoughts, images, or urges. Brain scan evidence now supports these explanations, showing heightened levels of activity in the brain's motor control centers of the basal ganglia and frontal lobes (Cocchi et al., 2012).

The most effective biological treatment for OCD is clomipramine (a tricyclic antidepressant) or an SSRI such as fluoxetine or sertraline (Kellner, 2010). In extreme cases in which no other treatments provide symptom relief, people with OCD may be treated

obsession
An unwanted thought, word, phrase, or image that persistently and repeatedly comes into a person's mind and causes distress.

compulsion
A repetitive and seemingly purposeful behavior performed in response to uncontrollable urges or according to a ritualistic or stereotyped set of rules.

obsessive-compulsive disorder (OCD)
An anxiety disorder characterized by recurrent obsessions or compulsions that are inordinately time-consuming or that cause significant distress or impairment.

MINI CASE

Obsessive-Compulsive Disorder, with Poor Insight

Cesar is a 16-year-old Mexican American male high school student. He was referred for treatment by one of his teachers, who became disturbed by Cesar's irrational concern about the danger posed by an electrical outlet at the front of the classroom. Cesar pleaded daily with the teacher to have the outlet disconnected to prevent someone from accidentally getting electrocuted while walking by it. The teacher told Cesar his concerns were unfounded, but he remained so distressed that he felt driven, when entering and leaving the classroom, to shine a flashlight into the outlet to make sure a loose wire was not exposed. During class time, he could think of nothing else but the outlet.

TABLE 2 Sample Items from the Yale–Brown Obsessive-Compulsive Symptom Checklist

Scale	Sample items
Aggressive obsessions	Fear might harm self Fear of blurting out obscenities Fear will be responsible for something else terrible happening (e.g., fire, burglary)
Contamination obsessions	Concerns or disgust with bodily waste or secretions (e.g., urine, feces, saliva) Bothered by sticky substances or residues
Sexual obsessions	Forbidden or perverse sexual thoughts, images, or impulses Sexual behavior toward others (aggressive)
Hoarding/saving obsessions	Distinguish from hobbies and concern with objects of monetary or sentimental value
Religious obsessions	Concerned with sacrilege and blasphemy Excess concern with right/wrong, morality
Obsession with need for symmetry or exactness	Accompanied by magical thinking (e.g., concerned that another will have an accident unless things are in the right place)
Miscellaneous obsessions	Fear of saying certain things Lucky/unlucky numbers Colors with special significance Superstitious fears
Somatic obsessions	Concern with illness or disease Excessive concern with body part or aspect of appearance (e.g., dysmorphophobia)
Cleaning/washing compulsions	Excessive or ritualized hand-washing Excessive or ritualized showering, bathing, toothbrushing, grooming, or toilet routine
Checking compulsions	Checking locks, stove, appliances, etc. Checking that nothing terrible did not/will not harm self Checking that did not make mistake completing a task
Repeating rituals	Rereading or rewriting Need to repeat routine activities (e.g., in/out door, up/down from chair)
Counting compulsions	(Check for presence)
Ordering/arranging compulsions	(Check for presence)
Hoarding/collecting compulsions	Distinguish from hobbies and concern with objects of monetary or sentimental value (e.g., carefully reads junk mail, sorts through garbage)
Miscellaneous compulsions	Excessive list making Need to tell, ask, or confess Need to touch, tap, or rub Rituals involving blinking or staring

SOURCE: Adapted from W. K. Goodman, L. H. Price, S. A. Rasmussen, C. Mazure, P. Delgado, G. R. Heninger, and D. S. Charney (1989a), "The Yale-Brown Obsessive-Compulsive Scale II. Validity" in *Archives of General Psychiatry, 46,* 1012–1016.

with psychosurgery. For example, deep-brain stimulation to areas active in motor control can help relieve symptoms by reducing the activity of the prefrontal cortex, which in turn may help reduce the frequency of obsessive-compulsive thoughts (Le Jeune et al., 2010).

The cognitive-behavioral perspective on OCD proposes that maladaptive thought patterns contribute to the development and maintenance of OCD symptoms. Individuals with OCD may be primed to overreact to anxiety-producing events in their environment. Such priming may place OCD in a spectrum of so-called internalizing disorders that include other anxiety and mood disorders invoking a similar pattern of startle reactivity (Vaidyanathan, Patrick, & Cuthbert, 2009). For people with OCD, these experiences become transformed to disturbing images, which they then try to suppress or counteract by engaging in compulsive rituals. Complicating their symptoms are beliefs in the danger and meaning of their thoughts, or their "metacognitions," which lead people with OCD to worry, ruminate, and feel they must monitor their every thought (Solem et al., 2009). Additionally, people with OCD may be high in the personality trait of perfectionism, a component of neuroticism, that can be thought of as a cognitive vulnerability unique to this disorder (Naragon-Gainey & Watson, 2018).

Some people with obsessive-compulsive disorder worry incessantly about germs and dirt and feel irresistible urges to clean and sanitize.

©baona/Getty Images

Cognitive-behavioral therapy is currently regarded as the most effective treatment for OCD (Öst, Havnen, Hansen, & Kvale, 2015). However, a large analysis of studies meeting the criteria for relational-cultural therapy (RCT) showed greater effects for OCD than for other anxiety disorders. In addition to reducing target symptoms, cognitive-behavioral therapy had beneficial effects on the individual's everyday quality of life (Carpenter et al., 2018).

Body Dysmorphic Disorder

People with **body dysmorphic disorder (BDD)** are preoccupied with the idea that a part of their body is ugly or defective. Their preoccupation goes far beyond the ordinary dissatisfaction many people feel about the size and shape of their body or appearance of a particular body part. People with BDD may check themselves constantly, groom themselves to an excessive degree, or constantly seek reassurance from others about how they look. They don't necessarily see themselves as fat or excessively heavy, both of which are common concerns in Western cultures, but they may believe that their body build is too small or not muscular enough.

body dysmorphic disorder
A disorder in which individuals are preoccupied with the idea that a part of their body is ugly or defective.

The *DSM-5* reclassified BDD from its prior placement in the anxiety disorders to its current inclusion with obsessive-compulsive and related disorders. The main change was to include repetitive behaviors, such as checking the mirror or seeking reassurance, as part of the criteria, changes that seem to have improved diagnostic accuracy (Schieber, Kollei, de Zwaan, & Martin, 2015). Table 3 illustrates these types of repetitive behaviors, which include items from the Body Dysmorphic Disorder version of the Yale–Brown Obsessive-Compulsive Disorder Scale (BDD-YBOCS) (Phillips, Menard, Fay, & Pagano, 2005).

As many as 87 percent of women are dissatisfied with some aspect of their body's appearance (Mond et al., 2013). Overall, however, at any one point in time, the prevalence of BDD is a much lower 2.5 percent of women and 2.2 percent of men. The most common areas that concern people with BDD differ by gender, with men more likely to be concerned with their body build and thinning hair, and women with their weight and hip size.

BDD is frequently accompanied by major depressive disorder, social anxiety disorder, obsessive-compulsive disorder, and eating disorders. Clients' distress clearly can become intense. Completed suicides are 45 times more common among people with this disorder than in the general U.S. population (Phillips et al., 2005).

REAL STORIES

Howie Mandel: Obsessive-Compulsive Disorder

In his autobiography *Here's the Deal: Don't Touch Me*, Canadian comedian, actor, and television personality Howie Mandel tells a candid account of how he rose to fame while suffering from obsessive-compulsive disorder (OCD). In the book, Mandel uses a humorous perspective to describe his often painful experiences. His passion for comedy and connecting with audiences help him through difficult periods, and his honest and frank approach to discussing his illness in the public eye makes his story remarkable.

In addition to OCD, Mandel was diagnosed with ADHD as an adult, and in the book he recounts the ways in which he remembers being affected by both diagnoses during his childhood. He grew up in Toronto, Ontario, and he recalls having a great deal of difficulty in school, often getting into trouble for pulling pranks or using inappropriate and impulsive behavior in the classroom. He writes about one particularly upsetting incident while he was a child, in which sand flies had laid eggs under his skin. Rather than undergoing an expensive medical procedure, his mother elected to remove the eggs herself by placing Mandel in a hot bath and scrubbing his skin until the eggs came out.

Mandel explains, "I can't even begin to tell you what this did to me psychologically. To this day, when I think about it, I can see the image of my skin bubbling. It feels as if there are organisms trying to make their way under my skin, and I'm taken back to those icky, creepy crawling monsters that need to be burned away. This is the feeling that recurs each and every time my OCD is triggered by the thought of germs on my body." Mandel reveals that the main content of his obsessions revolves around fears of dirt and contamination, which he attributes in part to what he describes as his family's obsessive attention to cleanliness from early on. For example, he writes that his grandmother would clean and wax even the outside of her house.

©s_bukley/Shutterstock

Mandel was never diagnosed with either OCD or ADHD as a child and did not receive any treatment until he was an adult. He was expelled from high school due to his behavioral issues and spent the next several years living with his parents while working as a carpet salesman. When he decided to try stand-up comedy in a popular comedy club in Toronto, he finally felt he had found a way to channel his quirky and eccentric sense of humor and find relief from obsessive thoughts and worries about germs and contamination: "My entire life is about distracting myself from horrible thoughts that constantly creep into my head. If I'm not doing something productive, I will find something to distract me. These distractions come upon me impulsively. Many people seek relief from their demons through food, alcohol, or drugs. My drug of choice is humor." As it turned out, he also discovered he was a talented and gifted performer.

It wasn't long before Mandel's high energy and sometimes bizarre stage show started to gain acclaim, and he soon moved to Los Angeles to embark on an acting career, joining the cast of the popular television show *St. Elsewhere* for six seasons. During this time he continued to work in comedy and secured several film roles. He was later given his own animated comedy series, *Bobby's World*, which ran for eight seasons. He then hosted a talk show for one season and became the host of a television game show, *Deal or No Deal*. While filming these shows, he was stricken with the difficult prospect of shaking hands with guests and contestants, which would act as a trigger for obsessive worries about contamination that stayed with him the entire day. Mandel tried several strategies to cope with his concerns about shaking hands with guests, including using "vats" of antibiotic lotion, scrubbing with surgical-grade soap before and after each taping, and "fist bumping" rather than shaking hands. He eventually decided to stop shaking hands with guests altogether.

Throughout the book, Mandel describes how his wife Terry, whom he met in high school, and their three children provided extra support throughout his struggles with OCD.

In 2006, Mandel went public with his diagnosis of OCD during a live airing of Howard Stern's radio show. He later publicly revealed his ADHD diagnosis and has gone on to promote awareness of the disorder, particularly adult ADHD. Most recently, he joined the celebrity cast of the popular television show *America's Got Talent*.

Despite his enormous success in the entertainment industry, Mandel continues to deal with symptoms of OCD. Though he once feared that being open about his diagnosis would be a career-ending move, in his book he writes that it in fact has brought him closer to his fans. With his characteristic humor and remarkable self-awareness, Howie Mandel's story demonstrates how someone can live and achieve success even with a severe psychological disorder.

You Be the Judge

Psychosurgery

As we discussed in the chapter "Theoretical Perspectives," psychosurgery is increasingly being used to give clinicians a tool for controlling the symptoms of obsessive-compulsive disorder. However, to what extent is surgical intervention justifiable to control the occurrence of psychological symptoms? This surgery is not reversible.

The debate over psychosurgery goes back to the mid-twentieth century when physician Walter Freeman traveled around the country, performing approximately 18,000 psychosurgeries in which he severed psychiatric patients' frontal lobes from the rest of their brains to control their unmanageable behaviors. Will future generations look upon psychosurgery and similar interventions as excessively punitive and even barbaric? On the other hand, with symptoms that are so severe and disabling, is any method that can control them valid even if imperfect?

Gillett (2011) raised these issues regarding the use of current forms of psychosurgery. By altering the individual's brain through such radical techniques, psychiatrists are tampering with a complex system of interactions that make up the individual's personality. Just because they "work" and no other methods are currently available, does this justify making permanent changes to the individual's brain? The victims of the leukotomies performed by Freeman "improved" in that their behavior became more docile, but they were forever changed.

Q: *You be the judge:* Is it appropriate to transform the person using permanent methods whose basis for effectiveness cannot be scientifically established? As Gillett (2011) concludes, "burn, heat, poke, freeze, shock, cut, stimulate or otherwise shake (but not stir) the brain and you will affect the psyche" (p. 43).

TABLE 3 Body Dysmorphic Disorder Modification of the Yale–Brown Obsessive-Compulsive Scale (BDD-YBOCS)

This modification of the Yale–Brown Obsessive-Compulsive Scale uses the following criteria to determine the severity of the client's symptoms regarding the presumed body defect or defects:

1. Time occupied by thoughts about body defect
2. Interference due to thoughts about body defect
3. Distress associated with thoughts about body defect
4. Resistance against thoughts about body defect
5. Degree of control over thoughts about body defect
6. Time spent in activities related to body defect such as mirror checking, grooming, excessive exercise, camouflaging, picking at skin, asking others about defect
7. Interference due to activities related to body defect
8. Distress associated with activities related to body defect
9. Resistance against compulsions
10. Degree of control over compulsive behavior
11. Insight into the nature of excessive concern over defect
12. Avoidance of activities due to concern over defect

SOURCE: http://www.veale.co.uk/wp-content/uploads/2010/11/BDD-YBOCS-Adult.pdf

Individuals with body dysmorphic disorder often feel that their appearance is much more flawed than what others actually see.
©Glow Images/Media Bakery

BDD has cross-cultural aspects. In Japan, the belief that physical appearance is offensive to others is called *shubo-kyufo*, a subtype of *taijin kyofusho* or "fear of interpersonal relations." The syndrome *koro* or *suoyang* ("disappearance of the penis" in Chinese) includes other BDD symptoms as well (Fang & Hofmann, 2010).

Treatment of BDD from a biological perspective includes medications, particularly SSRIs, that can reduce the associated symptoms of depression and anxiety as well as the more obsessive symptoms of distress, bodily preoccupations, and compulsions. Once on SSRIs, people with BDD can experience improved quality of life and overall functioning and perhaps gain insight into their disorder (Bjornsson, Didie, & Phillips, 2010).

From a psychosocial perspective, people with BDD may have experienced being teased about their appearance or made to feel sensitive in some other way during a time when their identities were in a critical period of formation. Once they start to believe that their bodily appearance is defective or deviates from the ideal to which they aspire, they become preoccupied with this belief, setting off a series of dysfunctional thoughts and repetitive behaviors. For example, they may look at an ordinary feature of their appearance, such as their waist size, and see only their "too large" waist when they view themselves. Their selective attention to this body part is accompanied by the belief that no one could possibly like them, which in turn can lead them to avoid social situations and engage in rituals such as looking in the mirror and frequently studying their waist.

Clinicians treating clients with BDD from a cognitive-behavioral perspective focus on helping them to understand that appearance is only one aspect of their total identity, while at the same time challenging them to question their assumptions that their appearance is, in

MINI CASE

Body Dysmorphic Disorder, with Poor Insight

Lydia is a divorced 63-year-old Caucasian female whose local surgeon referred her to the mental health clinic. For the past 8 years, Lydia has visited plastic surgeons across the country to find one who will perform surgery to reduce the size of her hands, which she perceives as "too fat." Until she has this surgery, she will not leave her house without wearing gloves. The plastic surgeon concurs with Lydia's family members and friends that Lydia's perception of her hands is distorted and that plastic surgery would be inappropriate and irresponsible.

fact, defective. The clinician may also help these individuals realize that other people looking at them may not even be thinking about their appearance at all, or if so, not critically (Fang & Wilhelm, 2015).

In one hands-on cognitive technique, clinicians encourage clients to look at themselves in a mirror and change their negative thoughts about what they see (Wilhelm et al., 2010). Interpersonal therapy can also help people with BDD develop improved strategies for dealing with the distress they feel in their relationships with others, as well as addressing their low self-esteem and depressed mood (Bjornsson et al., 2010).

Hoarding Disorder

In the compulsion known as **hoarding**, people have persistent difficulties discarding or parting with their possessions, even if they are not of much value. These difficulties include any form of discarding, including putting items into the garbage. People with hoarding disorder believe these items have utility or aesthetic or sentimental value, but in reality they often consist of old newspapers, bags, or leftover food.

When faced with the prospect of discarding the items, these individuals become distressed, while their homes can become unlivable due to the clutter that accumulates over the years. The rooms fill up with a mixture of objects that actually are of value and items that ordinarily would be thrown away, such as old magazines. Unlike ordinary collectors, who organize their items in a systematic way, people with hoarding disorder accumulate items without any form of organization.

Because the disorder became a diagnosis on its own in *DSM-5*, the only prevalence data available are the estimates the authors cite, from 2 to 6 percent of adults. A substantial percentage of adults with hoarding disorder also have comorbid depressive symptoms (Hall, Tolin, Frost, & Steketee, 2013). Older adults who develop hoarding disorder are likely to become physically and cognitively impaired, experiencing significant effects on their daily functioning (Ayers, Najmi, Mayes, & Dozier, 2015).

Treatment of hoarding disorder that follows a biopsychosocial approach appears to be the most effective. Biological treatments have traditionally included SSRIs, but researchers believe the disorder may also have a neurocognitive component that would warrant treatment through addressing cognitive function. For example, people with hoarding disorder may have a form of ADHD in which they lack the ability to focus their attention on specific details (Tolin, 2011). Hoarding disorder is also becoming understood from a developmental perspective as reflecting attachment difficulties and growing up in a household that lacked warmth (Kyrios et al., 2017).

Home visits in which the therapist uses cognitive-behavioral methods seem to hold the most promise, particularly in encouraging clients to discard their hoarded items (Tolin, Frost, Steketee, & Muroff, 2015). Practical assistance from movers or professional organizers may also be useful in supplementing medications and cognitive-behavioral treatment. Friends, family members, and local officials may also be consulted to assist in clearing the individual's living space.

hoarding
A compulsion in which people have persistent difficulties discarding things, even if they have little value.

Trichotillomania (Hair-Pulling Disorder)

A diagnosis of **trichotillomania (hair-pulling disorder)** is given to individuals who pull out their hair in response to an increasing sense of tension or urge. After they pull their hair, they feel temporary relief, pleasure, or gratification. People with trichotillomania are upset by their uncontrollable behavior and may find that their social, occupational, or other areas of functioning are impaired because of the disorder. They feel unable to stop the behavior, even when it results in bald patches and lost eyebrows, eyelashes, armpit hair, and pubic hair. As they get older, they increase the number of bodily sites from which they pull hair (Flessner et al., 2009).

People with this disorder experience significant impairment in areas of life ranging from sexual intimacy to social activities, medical examinations, and haircuts. They can also develop skin infections, scalp pain or bleeding, and carpal tunnel syndrome. Psychologically, they may suffer low self-esteem, shame and embarrassment, depressed mood, irritability, and argumentativeness. Their impairments appear early in life and continue through to middle and late adulthood (Duke, Keeley, Geffken, & Storch, 2010). Those who also eat the hair they pull can develop hairballs (Grant & Odlaug, 2008), which settle in their gastrointestinal tract and cause abdominal pain, nausea and vomiting, weakness, and weight loss.

Diagnosable trichotillomania is relatively rare, with an estimated current prevalence rate of 0.6 percent. However, trichotillomania may be underreported because people with this disorder are secretive about the behavior and tend to engage in hair pulling only when alone (Duke et al., 2009).

In *DSM-IV-TR* trichotillomania was included in the category of impulse-control disorders, but in *DSM-5* it moved to the category that includes obsessive-compulsive and related disorders. In addition, the name changed to hair pulling, which the *DSM-5* authors concur is a better description of the disorder than "mania."

There may be two types of hair pulling. In the "focused" type, which may account for one-quarter of cases, the individual is aware of having the urge to pull and may develop compulsive behaviors or rituals to avoid doing so. In "automatic" hair pulling, the individual is engaged in another task or is absorbed in thought while pulling hair. Individuals who fall into the automatic category experience pronounced stress and anxiety. For people in the focused category, depression and disability are likely to occur along with stress and anxiety (Duke et al., 2010).

Genetics seems to play an important role in trichotillomania, with an estimate of 80 percent heritability of the disorder (Novak, Keuthen, Stewart, & Pauls, 2009). Abnormalities in a gene on chromosome 1 known as SLTRK1 may play a role in the disorder; this gene is also linked to Tourette's disorder (Abelson et al., 2005). Researchers have also identified abnormalities in SAPAP3, a gene related to glutamate, which in turn is implicated in obsessive-compulsive disorder (Zuchner et al., 2009). The neurotransmitters serotonin, dopamine, and glutamate are, in turn, thought to play a role in the development of trichotillomania (Duke et al., 2009). Brain imaging studies of individuals with trichotillomania suggest that they may also have abnormalities in brain regions active in attentional control, memory, and the ability to suppress automatic motor reactions (Slikboer et al., 2018).

Taking account of these abnormalities in neurotransmitter and brain functioning, the regulation model of trichotillomania suggests that individuals with this

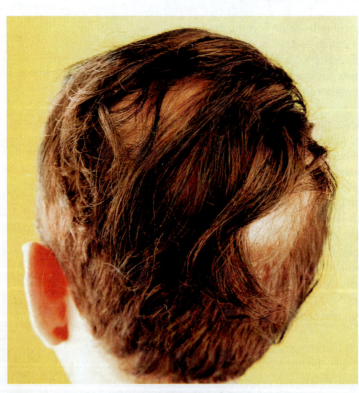

This man, like many who suffer from trichotillomania, has marked hair loss as a result of frequent and uncontrollable urges to pull his hair out.

MINI CASE

Trichotillomania (Hair-Pulling Disorder)

Audra is a 15-year-old Caucasian female. For most of her childhood and adolescence, she lived a fairly isolated existence with no close friends. Although she never discussed her unhappiness with anyone, she often felt depressed and hopeless. As a young child, Audra lay in bed on many nights secretly tugging at her hair. Over time, this behavior increased to the point at which she plucked the hair, strand by strand, from her scalp.

Typically, she pulled out a hair, examined it, bit it, and either threw it away or swallowed it. Because her hair was thick and curly, her hair loss was not initially evident, and Audra kept her hair carefully combed to conceal the bald spots. One of her teachers noticed that she was pulling her hair in class, however, and in looking more closely, she saw the bald patches on Audra's head. She referred Audra to the school psychologist, who called Audra's mother and recommended professional help.

disorder seek an optimal state of emotional arousal, providing them with greater stimulation when they are understimulated and calming them when they are overstimulated. At the same time, hair pulling may bring them from a negative to a positive affective state. Using the Trichotillomania Symptoms Questionnaire (see Table 4), researchers conducting an online survey found that individuals who engaged in hair pulling experienced more difficulty controlling their emotions than those who did not. There were subgroups in the sample, which varied in whether the subjects were more likely to experience boredom or anxiety and tension, and in the overall intensity of emotions they felt that seemed to drive them toward hair pulling. The researchers suggested that these subgroups on the questionnaire seemed to correspond to the automatic and focused subtypes of the disorder (Shusterman, Feld, Baer, & Keuthen, 2009).

Pharmacological treatments for trichotillomania include antidepressants, atypical antipsychotics, lithium, and naltrexone. Of these, naltrexone seems to have shown the most promising results. However, the results of controlled studies are not compelling and do not seem to justify the use of medications when weighed against the side effects, which can include obesity, diabetes, neurotoxicity, delirium, encephalopathy, tremors, and hyperthyroidism, among others (Duke et al., 2010).

The behavioral treatment of habit reversal training (HRT) is regarded as the most effective approach to treating trichotillomania. Not only does this method prevent the side effects of medication, but it is more successful in reducing the symptoms of hair pulling (Duke et al., 2010); however, for treatment-resistant individuals, a combination of medication and HRT may be required (Franklin, Zagrabbe, & Benavides, 2011).

In HRT, the individual learns a new response to compete with the habit of hair pulling, such as fist clenching. The key feature is that the new response is incompatible with the

TABLE 4 Trichotillomania Symptoms Questionnaire

1. Do you currently pull your hair out?
2. At any point in your life, including now, have you had periods of uncontrollable hair-pulling?
3. Do you (or did you in the past) experience urges to pull your hair out?
4. Do you (or did you in the past) try to resist pulling your hair out?
5. Do you (or did you in the past) feel relief when pulling your hair out?
6. Do you (or did you in the past) wish that the urge to pull your hair out would go away?
7. Have you been diagnosed with trichotillomania by a professional?
8. Do you, or did you in the past, feel shame, secrecy, or distress about your hair-pulling?

SOURCE: Shusterman et al., 2009

undesirable habit. When it was first developed several decades ago, HRT was given for only one session. Since that time, clinicians have extended the length of treatment and added several cognitive components, including self-monitoring and cognitive restructuring. For example, clients may learn to challenge their cognitive distortions such as their perfectionistic beliefs. Dialectical behavior therapy (DBT) may add to these methods a combination of mindfulness training, in which clients learn to identify the cues that trigger their hair pulling, and imagery training, in which they visualize themselves in a tranquil state (Snorrason, Berlin, & Lee, 2015).

Combining acceptance and commitment therapy (ACT) with HRT is also shown to produce relief from hair-pulling symptoms. Cognitive-behavioral therapy can help in treating children and adolescents with trichotillomania, with very little alteration from the basic protocol used for adults. In one study, 77 percent of those who received treatment remained symptom-free after 6 months (Tolin et al., 2007). An advantage of ACT for this disorder is that it can be administered along with cognitive-behavioral treatment in a group format with results as effective as those obtained with individual therapy (Haaland et al., 2017).

Although trichotillomania can be a highly disabling condition, there is promise in the range of therapies based on behavior therapy, cognitive-behavior therapy, and the newer approaches that help individuals identify and cope with the feelings associated with the behavior. Newer therapies are also including psychoeducation to provide clients with the opportunity to gain insight into their disorder.

Excoriation (Skin-Picking) Disorder

excoriation (skin-picking) disorder
Recurrent picking at one's own skin.

In a new diagnosis in *DSM-5,* individuals are regarded as having **excoriation (skin-picking) disorder** if they repeatedly pick at their own skin, perhaps as much as several hours a day. The skin picking may be of healthy skin, skin with mild irregularities (such as moles), pimples, calluses, or scabs. People with this disorder pick at these bodily areas either with their own fingernails or with instruments such as tweezers. When they are not picking their skin, they think about picking it and try to resist their urges to do so. They may attempt to cover the evidence of their skin picking with clothing or bandages, and they feel ashamed of and embarrassed about their behavior.

Because this is a new diagnosis, epidemiological data are limited, but *DSM-5* estimates the prevalence as at least 1.4 percent of adults, three-quarters of whom are female. Researchers believe skin picking is valid as a distinct diagnosis from trichotillomania (Lochner, Grant, Odlaug, & Stein, 2012). However, the two disorders share causes and effective treatment approaches (Snorrason, Belleau, & Woods, 2012). For some individuals with excoriation disorder, high levels of impulsivity also appear to play an important role (Oliveira, Leppink, Derbyshire, & Grant, 2015).

8.3 Trauma- and Stressor-Related Disorders

Individuals who are exposed to trauma or a stressful event may be at risk for developing a psychological disorder. The category of trauma- and stressor-related disorders have as a diagnostic criterion the condition of an actual event that acts as a precipitant. *DSM-5* includes disorders in this group that were originally in their own category within the anxiety disorders. The *DSM-5* also places into this category a set of disorders in childhood that can be traced to exposure to stress or trauma.

reactive attachment disorder
A disorder involving a severe disturbance in the ability to relate to others in which the individual is unresponsive to people, is apathetic, and prefers to be alone rather than to interact with friends or family.

Reactive Attachment Disorder and Disinhibited Social Engagement Disorder

In this first of the trauma- and stressor-related disorders we find **reactive attachment disorder (RAD)**, a diagnosis given to children who literally "react against" attachment to others. Their symptoms include becoming withdrawn and inhibited. They tend not to show positive affect, but they also lack the ability to control their emotions. Unlike normal children, when they become distressed, they do not seek comfort from adults.

The diagnosis of **disinhibited social engagement disorder** describes an opposite situation in which a child with a history of trauma engages in culturally inappropriate, overly familiar behavior with people who are relative strangers.

These disorders are placed among the trauma- and stressor-related disorders because they are found in children who have experienced an abuse pattern of social neglect, repeated changes of primary caregivers, or rearing in institutions with high child-to-caregiver ratios. Consequently, such children are significantly impaired in their ability to interact with other children and adults.

Researchers conducting a longitudinal study of previously institutionalized Romanian children found they developed as indiscriminately social/disinhibited during early infancy as a result of poor caregiving. Their disorders did not improve, even when the quality of their care did (see Figure 2).

Children with reactive attachment disorder have also received poorer caregiving and are more likely to have insecure attachment styles as they grow older (Gleason et al., 2011). These effects can persist for years, lingering until at least the age of 12 (Humphreys, Nelson, Fox, & Zeanah, 2017).

There are underlying similarities in the origins of the two disorders. Nevertheless, research supports the distinction between them and hence their conceptualization by *DSM-5* as separate dimensions of psychopathology in childhood (Lehmann et al., 2015).

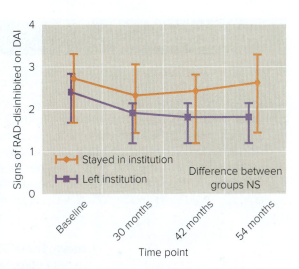

FIGURE 2 Signs of Indiscriminately Social/ Disinhibited Reactive Attachment Disorder Across Time Points by Placement Status at 54 Months

SOURCE: Gleason et al., 2011

Acute Stress Disorder and Post-Traumatic Stress Disorder

A **trauma** is said to occur when an individual is exposed, either once or repeatedly, to circumstances that are harmful or life threatening and that have lasting adverse effects on the individual's functioning and mental health. When people are exposed to the threat of death, or to actual or threatened serious injury, or sexual violation, they risk developing **acute stress disorder**. Being exposed to the death of others, or to any of these events, real or threatened, to others can also lead to the development of this disorder. For example, first responders to the scene of an accident or police officers who are regularly exposed to the details of child abuse cases may also experience this disorder.

The symptoms of acute stress disorder fall into four categories: intrusion of distressing reminders of the event, dissociative symptoms such as feeling numb or detached from others, avoidance of situations that might serve as reminders of the event, and hyperarousal including sleep disturbances or irritability. The symptoms may persist for a few days to a month after the traumatic event.

The events that can cause acute stress disorder may lead to the longer-lasting disorder known as **post-traumatic stress disorder (PTSD)**. If the individual experiences acute stress disorder symptoms for more than a month, the clinician assigns the PTSD diagnosis. The intrusions, dissociation, and avoidance seen in acute stress disorder are also present in PTSD. Symptoms also include loss of memory of the event, excessive self-blame, distancing from others, and inability to experience positive emotions.

The diagnosis of PTSD has a long history. The Vietnam War was perhaps the most publicized war to produce psychological casualties, but reports of psychological dysfunction following exposure to combat emerged after the Civil War. In World Wars I and II, the condition was referred to with such terms as *shell shock*, *traumatic neurosis*, *combat stress*, and *combat fatigue*. Survivors of European concentration camps in the 1930s and 1940s also were reported to suffer long-term psychological effects, including chronic depression,

disinhibited social engagement disorder
Diagnosis given to children who engage in culturally inappropriate, overly familiar behavior with people who are relative strangers.

trauma
A condition that results from circumstances experienced by an individual as harmful or life threatening and that has lasting adverse effects on the individual's functioning and mental health.

acute stress disorder
An anxiety disorder that develops after a traumatic event, and lasts for up to 1 month with symptoms such as depersonalization, numbing, dissociative amnesia, intense anxiety, hypervigilance, and impairment of everyday functioning.

post-traumatic stress disorder (PTSD)
An anxiety disorder in which the individual experiences several distressing symptoms for more than a month following a traumatic event, such as a reexperiencing of the traumatic event, an avoidance of reminders of the trauma, a numbing of general responsiveness, and increased arousal.

MINI CASE

Acute Stress Disorder

Brendan is a married 40-year-old Caucasian heterosexual male. He had no prior history of mental health concerns until 2 weeks ago when he survived a wildfire that destroyed his apartment and many buildings in his neighborhood. Since the fire Brendan has been tormented by graphic images of waking to see his room filled with smoke. Although he was treated and released within several hours from the emergency room, he described himself as feeling in a daze, emotionally unresponsive to the concerns of his friends and family, and seemingly numb. He continued to experience these symptoms for several weeks, after which they gradually subsided.

anxiety, and difficulties in interpersonal relationships due to guilt over having survived when so many others were killed.

The lifetime prevalence of PTSD is 6.8 percent, with a yearly prevalence of 3.5 percent. Of those who develop PTSD within a given year, 37 percent experience severe symptoms (Kessler, Berglund, et al., 2005). Among U.S. Army soldiers returning from Afghanistan, 6.2 percent met the PTSD diagnostic criteria, and more than double that rate, 12.9 percent, was seen among soldiers returning from Iraq (Hoge et al., 2004). With the surges of combat in these two war zones, the number of soldiers developing mental health problems, particularly PTSD, has continued to climb. It is estimated that nearly 17 percent of Iraq War veterans meet the screening criteria for this disorder (Hoge et al., 2007).

Although PTSD is often studied among male combat veterans, researchers are beginning to examine the phenomenon in women exposed to trauma during their military service. A traumatic experience more likely to affect women than men is sexual assault. Women exposed to combat-related trauma and sexual assault show a cumulatively higher risk of developing both PTSD and substance use disorders (Yalch, Hebenstreit, & Maguen, 2018).

The symptoms of PTSD and related disorders, such as depression, can persist for many years. For example, survivors of the North Sea oil rig disaster in 1980 continued to experience symptoms of PTSD along with anxiety disorders (not including PTSD), depressive disorders, and substance use disorders that were significantly higher than those of a matched comparison group (Figure 3) (Boe, Holgersen, & Holen, 2011). Furthermore, individuals who were previously exposed to trauma are more likely to experience thoughts of suicide after exposure to a second traumatic event such as a natural disaster (Brown et al., 2018).

Theories and Treatment of Post-Traumatic Stress Disorder

A traumatic experience is an external event that impinges on the individual and hence does not have biological "causality." However, researchers propose that traumatic experiences have their impact in part because they do lead to changes in the brain that make certain regions primed or hypersensitive to possible danger in the future. Individuals with PTSD experience alterations in the hippocampus, the structure in the brain responsible for consolidating short-term memory. As a result, these individuals become unable to distinguish relatively harmless situations (such as fireworks) from the ones in which real trauma occurred (such as combat). They continue to reexperience the event

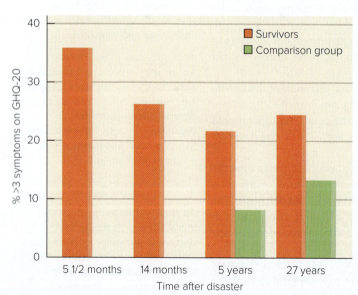

FIGURE 3 Percent of Long-Term Survivors of the North Sea Disaster Still Experiencing Symptoms After 27 Years

MINI CASE

Post-Traumatic Stress Disorder

Steve is a single 35-year-old biracial heterosexual male. For the past 10 years, he has suffered from flashbacks in which he relives the horrors of his 9-month-long deployment as a marine in Afghanistan. These flashbacks occur unexpectedly in the middle of the day, and Steve is thrown back into the emotional reality of his war experiences. These flashbacks, and the nightmares from which he often suffers, have become a constant source of torment. Steve has found that alcohol provides the only escape from these visions and from the distress he feels. Often, he ruminates about how he should have done more to prevent the deaths of his fellow soldiers, and he feels that his friends should have survived rather than he.

with heightened arousal and therefore avoid situations that resemble those in which they were traumatized (Hayes et al., 2011).

SSRI antidepressants are the only FDA-approved medications for people with PTSD. However, the response rates of patients with PTSD to these medications are rarely more than 60 percent, and fewer than 20 to 30 percent achieve full remission of their symptoms. Research does not support the use of benzodiazepines in treatment of PTSD, although these medications may relieve insomnia or anxiety (Berger et al., 2009). Although researchers believed the antipsychotic medication risperidone might benefit individuals with PTSD, findings from a large-scale study of nearly 300 veterans did not provide empirical support for its use in reducing symptoms (Krystal et al., 2011).

From a psychological perspective, people with PTSD have a biased information-processing style that, due to the trauma they experienced, causes their attention to be highly attuned toward potentially threatening cues. Therefore they are more likely to feel that they are in danger, and also are more likely to avoid situations they perceive as potentially

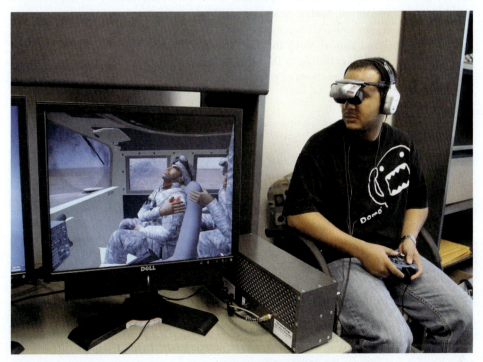

A military veteran suffering from PTSD uses virtual reality technology to expose himself to anxiety-provoking imagery as part of his treatment at a VA hospital.

©Orlando Sentinel/Getty Images

threatening (Huppert, Foa, McNally, & Cahill, 2009). Personality and coping style also predict responses to trauma, including high levels of neuroticism and extreme sensitivity to internal cues of anxiety (Naragon-Gainey & Watson, 2018).

Barbara, whose case opened the chapter, seems to have been an exception in this regard; she did not appear to be high on neuroticism, negative, or a victim of childhood abuse. Her prolonged exposure to severe combat along with the loss of her leg seemed to account for her development of the disorder.

Generally considered the most effective psychological treatment for PTSD, cognitive-behavioral therapy combines some type of exposure (*in vivo* or imaginal) with relaxation and cognitive restructuring. Specific trauma-focused psychotherapy that focuses on memory of the traumatic event or its meaning is gaining support as a first-line treatment (Lee et al., 2016). Trauma-focused therapy produces longer-lasting results without the side effects associated with psychotropic interventions. The American Psychological Association's Clinical Practice Guidelines for the Treatment of PTSD in Adults (2017) also strongly recommended cognitive-behavioral and exposure therapy and, if medication is indicated, the use of SSRIs but not antipsychotics.

trauma informed care
An approach to treatment that acknowledges the role that trauma can have on the mental health of individuals.

Because trauma is so often a component of other disorders, including substance use disorders, the U.S. government's Substance Abuse and Mental Health Services Administration (SAMHSA) has compiled a treatment manual for clinicians working in behavioral health (SAMHSA, 2014). This manual is based on the principles of **trauma informed care**, a model that promotes trauma awareness and understanding to professionals treating individuals with a history of trauma. The idea of resilience is central to this philosophy of treatment, helping individuals foster their own inner strengths as they develop a greater sense of competence. Furthermore, according to the principles of trauma informed care, clinicians must avoid retraumatizing clients who already have histories of trauma.

Couples therapy is another method that can prove beneficial in reducing symptoms as well as reducing distress both in the individual and in the individual's partner (Sautter et al., 2015). Such an approach can help lower reintegration stress in both partners, improving their communication and expression of intimacy and reducing the number of disagreements about parenting (D'Aniello, Marek, & Moore, 2017).

post-traumatic growth
The personal growth that can occur following exposure to a traumatic experience.

An alternative view to PTSD comes from the field of positive psychology, which proposes that people can grow through the experience of trauma, a phenomenon known as **post-traumatic growth**. According to this approach, trauma can allow clients to cope by developing positive interpretations of their experiences (Achterhof et al., 2018).

8.4 Anxiety, Obsessive-Compulsive, and Trauma- and Stressor-Related Disorders: The Biopsychosocial Perspective

The disorders we covered in this chapter span a broad spectrum of problems, ranging from specific and seemingly idiosyncratic responses to diffuse and undifferentiated feelings of dread. There are differences among the disorders in symptoms and causes, but there do seem to be important similarities in that they all involve regions of the brain active in responding to fearful or threatening situations. Perhaps what determines whether an individual with a propensity toward developing an anxiety disorder does so are the combined effects of genetics, brain functioning, life experiences, and social context. Across these disorders, there also appear to be similarities in treatment approach, with cognitive-behavioral methods showing perhaps the greatest effectiveness.

Barbara's therapist decided not to use pharmacological interventions but instead to begin treatment with cognitive processing therapy, a cognitive-behavioral therapy specifically aimed at reducing symptoms of PTSD. In therapy, Barbara learned to challenge the thoughts that she was still in danger much of the time. Through the use of imaginal flooding, she became accustomed to discussing her experiences in Iraq without provoking fear or anxiety by relearning to associate her memories of the war with relaxation.

In addition to individual therapy, Barbara's therapist suggested that she participate in group therapy. In these sessions, Barbara met with seven other Iraq War veterans for 90 minutes a week for 10 weeks. She was able to talk about her traumatic memories as well as provide support to other veterans as they discussed their experiences. By interacting with veterans she could relate to, she relearned how to interact with others socially, which decreased her feelings of irritability and anger around other people in her life.

Within 1 month of beginning her treatment at the VA, Barbara began to experience some relief from her PTSD symptoms, though she continued to have occasional nightmares. Using the coping skills she learned in therapy, Barbara was able to recover from the flashbacks and began to participate in life once again. She made a full physical recovery after receiving a prosthetic leg. Within 2 months,

her emotional numbing, irritability, and anxious symptoms completely subsided. Barbara often remarked to her therapist that she felt that she was "herself" again. Several months later, she took a part-time job in an electronics store and enrolled in a part-time MBA program at a nearby community college. She moved into her own apartment a few towns away from her parents' home and began to reconnect with old friends who still lived close by. Barbara continues to come to the VA for individual therapy every week, and though the events she experienced in Iraq still haunt her, she has learned to live with the memories and has begun to adjust to civilian life.

Dr. Tobin's reflections: It was clear upon her initial presentation that Barbara was presenting with classic symptoms of PTSD. Fortunately she was able to utilize the resources available for her to get help and provide relief from her suffering. Early intervention for those with PTSD is critical in preventing the prolonging of symptoms throughout the life span, and Barbara was able to put her life back together as a result of addressing her PTSD through treatment early on. For many veterans of wars fought in earlier eras (such as Vietnam), the needed resources were not available when they returned home from war. These veterans currently make up a large population of the Veterans Affairs system, though the rates of PTSD continue to increase for soldiers fighting in the wars in Iraq and Afghanistan.

SUMMARY

- Anxiety disorders are characterized by the experience of physiological arousal, apprehension or feelings of dread, hypervigilance, avoidance, and sometimes a specific fear or phobia.

- Separation anxiety disorder is characterized by intense and inappropriate anxiety about being separated from home or caregivers. Many infants go through a developmental phase in which they become anxious and agitated when they are separated from their caregivers. In separation anxiety disorder, these emotions continue far longer than is age appropriate. Even the prospect of separation causes extreme anxiety. Although there appears to be a strong genetic component to separation anxiety disorder, environmental factors also contribute. Cognitive-behavioral techniques may be most effective. Another disorder appearing in childhood and thought to center on anxiety is selective mutism, in which

a child refuses to speak in specific situations, such as the classroom. Behaviorist methods using shaping and exposure seem particularly well suited to treating children with selective mutism.

- Specific phobias are irrational fears of particular objects or situations. Cognitive behaviorists assert that previous learning experiences and a cycle of negative, maladaptive thoughts cause specific phobias. Treatments recommended by the behavioral and cognitive-behavioral approaches include flooding, systematic desensitization, imagery, *in vivo* exposure, and virtual reality exposure therapy (VRET) as well as procedures aimed at changing the individual's maladaptive thoughts, such as cognitive restructuring and thought stopping. Treatment based on the biological perspective involves medication.

- Social anxiety disorder is a fear of being observed by others while acting in a way that will be humiliating or embarrassing. Cognitive-behavioral approaches to social anxiety disorder regard the disorder as due to an unrealistic fear of criticism, which causes people with the disorder to lose the ability to concentrate on their performance, instead shifting their attention to how anxious they feel, which then causes them to make mistakes and, therefore, to become more fearful. Behavioral methods that provide *in vivo* exposure, along with cognitive restructuring and social skills training, seem to be the most effective in helping people with social anxiety disorder. Medication is the treatment recommended within the biological perspective for severe cases of this disorder.

- Panic disorder is characterized by frequent and recurrent panic attacks—intense sensations of fear and physical discomfort. This disorder is often comorbid with agoraphobia, a disorder new to the *DSM-5*. Agoraphobia presents with intense anxiety around the thought or experience of being in a public place. In particular, the fear of being trapped or unable to escape from a public place is common. Biological and cognitive-behavioral perspectives have been particularly useful for understanding and treating this disorder. Some experts explain panic disorder as an acquired "fear of fear," in which the individual becomes hypersensitive to early signs of a panic attack, and the fear of a full-blown attack leads the individual to become unduly apprehensive and avoidant of another attack. Treatment based on the cognitive-behavioral perspective involves methods such as relaxation training and panic-control therapy. Medications can also help alleviate symptoms, with the most commonly prescribed being antianxiety and antidepressant medications.

- People who are diagnosed as having generalized anxiety disorder have a number of unrealistic worries that spread to various spheres of life. The cognitive-behavioral approach to generalized anxiety disorder emphasizes the unrealistic nature of these worries and regards the disorder as a vicious cycle that feeds on itself. Cognitive-behavioral treatment approaches recommend breaking the negative cycle of worry by teaching individuals techniques that allow them to feel they control the worrying. Biological treatment emphasizes the use of medication.

- In obsessive-compulsive disorder, individuals develop obsessions, or thoughts they cannot rid themselves of, and compulsions, which are irresistible, repetitive behaviors. A cognitive-behavioral understanding of obsessive-compulsive disorder regards the symptoms as the product of a learned association between anxiety and the thoughts or acts, which can temporarily produce relief from anxiety. A growing body of evidence supports a biological explanation of the disorder, with the most current research suggesting that it is associated with an excess of serotonin. Treatment with medications, such as clomipramine, seems to be effective, although cognitive-behavioral methods involving exposure and thought stopping are quite effective as well. Body dysmorphic disorder involves preoccupation with the idea that a part of the body is ugly or defective. Other disorders related to OCD include hoarding disorder, trichotillomania, and excoriation disorder.

- Individuals who are exposed to trauma or stressors may develop one of a set of disorders. *DSM-5* includes in this group disorders that were originally in the category of traumatic and stressor-related anxiety disorders, including post-traumatic stress disorder and acute stress disorder along with the childhood disorders reactive attachment disorder and disinhibited social engagement disorder. This set of disorders include, as a diagnostic criterion, the condition that there is an actual event that precipitates the symptoms. Children with reactive attachment disorder have severe disturbances in the way they relate to others and are emotionally withdrawn and inhibited. In contrast, children with disinhibited social engagement disorder engage in culturally inappropriate, overly familiar behavior with people who are relative strangers. Both of these disorders are found in children who have experienced social neglect through repeated changes of primary caregivers or being reared in institutions with high child-to-caregiver ratios. Research indicates that children with these disorders continue to have problems even if their circumstances improve.

- In post-traumatic stress disorder, the individual is unable to recover from the anxiety associated with a traumatic life event, such as tragedy or disaster, an accident, or participation in combat. The aftereffects of the traumatic event include flashbacks, nightmares, and intrusive thoughts that alternate with the individual's attempts to deny that the event ever took place. Some people experience a briefer but troubling response to a traumatic event; this condition, called acute stress disorder, lasts from 2 days to 4 weeks and involves the kinds of symptoms that people with PTSD experience over a much longer period of time. Cognitive-behavioral approaches regard PTSD as the result of negative and maladaptive thoughts about one's role in causing the traumatic events to happen, feelings of ineffectiveness and isolation from others, and a pessimistic outlook on life as a result of the experience. Treatment may involve teaching people with PTSD new coping skills, so that they can more effectively manage stress and reestablish social ties with others who can provide ongoing support.

KEY TERMS

Acute stress disorder

Agoraphobia

Anxiety

Anxiety disorders

Anxiety sensitivity theory

Body dysmorphic disorder

Compulsion

Conditioned fear reactions

Disinhibited social engagement disorder

Excoriation (skin-picking) disorder

Fear

Flooding

Generalized anxiety disorder

Graded *in vivo*

Hoarding

Imaginal flooding

In vivo flooding

Obsession

Obsessive-compulsive disorder (OCD)

Panic attack

Panic-control therapy (PCT)

Panic disorder

Phobia

Post-traumatic growth

Post-traumatic stress disorder (PTSD)

Reactive attachment disorder

Relaxation training

Selective mutism

Separation anxiety disorder

Social anxiety disorder

Specific phobia

Trauma

Trauma informed care

Trichotillomania (hair-pulling disorder)

Virtual reality exposure therapy (VRET)

Dissociative and Somatic Symptom Disorders

Learning Objectives

9.1 Specify the symptoms of dissociative disorders.

9.2 Identify symptoms and treatments of somatic symptom disorders.

9.3 Recognize psychological factors affecting other medical conditions.

9.4 Explain the biopsychosocial perspective for dissociative and somatic symptom disorders.

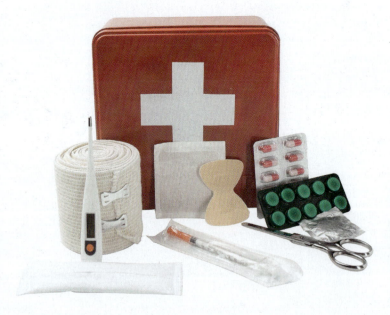

©LightFieldStudios/Getty Images

Case Report: Rose Marston

Demographic information: 37-year-old heterosexual Caucasian female

Presenting problem: Rose was referred for a psychological evaluation by her physician, Dr. Stewart, who became concerned that Rose may have been suffering from symptoms of a psychological disorder. For the past year, Rose had made weekly appointments with Dr. Stewart as well as other health practitioners due to her concern that she was suffering from a severe physical condition. Dr. Stewart diagnosed Rose with early-onset lactose intolerance. However, this did not seem to correspond with the intense and frequent stomach pains Rose complained of, which persisted even after she cut dairy out of her diet.

During the psychological evaluation, Rose reported she was dissatisfied with Dr. Stewart's conclusions, and she consulted with alternative health care practitioners such as homeopathic physicians and even a Reiki master. She admitted she had been hoping that one of the practitioners would discover she suffered from a diagnosable medical condition, and many had even suggested she receive a psychological evaluation, which she refused. She finally agreed to Dr. Stewart's recommendation after much persistence from him.

Rose reported she had recently lost her job after calling in sick nearly every day over the past 3 months. She stated she felt it was more important to spend her time consulting health care practitioners, and she also preferred not to leave her house for fear of exacerbating her symptoms. She stated she was distressed about the amount of time she had spent worrying about her stomach pain, but she also was overwhelmed by feelings of guilt if she did not direct her activities toward trying to identify the cause of her physical symptoms. Rose said her symptoms originated as mild stomach irritation, and that over the past year they had escalated to the point where her stomach was causing her constant and severe pain. She reported having tried a multitude of remedies, all unsuccessful.

During the evaluation, Rose stated that she felt "devastated" about how her worry over her physical symptoms had interfered with her life but believed she had to focus on finding a diagnosis. Her boyfriend of 2 years had recently ended their relationship, and she admitted she had distanced herself from him since her concerns about her physical symptoms began. She found, in addition, that her concern about these symptoms overshadowed any thoughts about the relationship.

The clinician conducting the evaluation asked Rose to describe any recent major stressors in her life, and she reported she had lost her favorite uncle to cancer in the previous year. When describing this loss, Rose immediately became tearful and admitted she felt she had never mourned her uncle and instead pushed away her feelings about his death most of the time.

Following the evaluation, the clinician contacted Dr. Stewart to consult about her case, which Rose had consented to by signing a release of information. Dr. Stewart told the clinician he believed Rose's physical symptoms seemed to be indicative of late-onset lactose intolerance, but that she had refused to accept this diagnosis. Her symptoms may have worsened as a result of her failure to get the proper treatment. Dr. Stewart also remarked that Rose seemed to have been acting very differently since the death of her uncle.

Relevant history: Rose had previously seen a psychiatrist for depression in her late twenties. Her depressive symptoms began after she graduated from college and varied in severity until she endured an episode so intense she contemplated suicide. She had received a course of antidepressants that had been effective. At the time of the evaluation, Rose had not been on any psychiatric medications for approximately 5 years because she felt the previous course had been effective enough for her to discontinue.

Case formulation: Rose meets criteria for somatic symptom disorder, moderate to severe, with predominant pain. This diagnosis is based on her heightened anxiety, which is excessive, in response to her physical symptoms, to the point where her life has been significantly disrupted (loss of her job and her romantic relationship). Her concerns about her symptoms are both persistent (lasting longer than 6 months) and disproportionate to their actual severity. She has devoted an objectively excessive amount of time and energy to her

physical symptoms and has refused to accept a relatively mild diagnosis of lactose intolerance. The onset of Rose's symptoms may originate from distress caused by the death of her uncle, due to her report that she engaged in avoidance of processing her reaction.

Treatment plan: Following the evaluation and consultation with Dr. Stewart, the clinician referred Rose to a therapist specializing in cognitive-behavioral treatment for somatic disorders. In this evidence-based approach, Rose's therapist should focus on evaluating her excessive concerns about her physical condition with cognitive restructuring, and behavioral strategies to increase her engagement with recommendations from Dr. Stewart to improve her physical symptoms.

Sarah Tobin, PhD

9.1 Dissociative Disorders

The human mind seems almost endlessly capable of dissociating, or separating attentional focus. You can think intensively about a problem while jogging, perhaps not even realizing that you ran a mile without being aware of your surroundings. In dissociative disorders, this separation of a person's mental functions occurs to a far more extreme degree than what many people experience in daily life.

Dissociative disorders raise intriguing questions about the ways in which people's sense of self evolves over time, and the way memory and sense of reality can become fragmented and distinct within the same individual. In contrast, somatic symptom disorders, discussed later in this chapter, raise equally fascinating questions about mind-body relationships.

Major Forms of Dissociative Disorders

dissociative identity disorder (DID)
A dissociative disorder in which an individual develops more than one self or personality.

We generally take for granted the idea that each individual has one personality and one sense of identity. However, in **dissociative identity disorder (DID)**, separate personalities and identities can develop within the same individual. The separate personalities seem to have their own unique characteristic ways of perceiving, thinking, and relating to others. By definition, people with DID have at least two distinct identities and, when inhabiting the identity of one, are not aware that they also inhabit the other. As a result, their experiences lack continuity. They have large gaps in important memories about themselves and their lives, often memories of a traumatic nature such as being victimized or abused.

dissociative amnesia
An inability to remember important personal details and experiences; usually associated with traumatic or very stressful events.

People with **dissociative amnesia** are unable to remember information about an event or set of events in their lives. This type of memory loss is different from the everyday slips that cause us to misplace objects or forget people's names. People with dissociative amnesia forget a specific event in their lives, most likely one of a traumatic or stressful nature. Their amnesia may even invoke a **fugue** state, an episode of amnesia that leaves them unable to recall some or all of their past and identity, along with either bewildered wandering or travel that seems focused on a particular purpose.

fugue
An episode of amnesia involving inability to recall some or all of one's past and the loss of identity, with either bewildered wandering or travel that seems focused on a particular purpose.

MINI CASE

Dissociative Identity Disorder

Maya is a 26-year-old Latina heterosexual woman. She is single, lives with two roommates, and works as a store clerk at a department store. She rarely leaves her apartment except to go to work and to see her family who live close by. She is known at work for being rather quiet and shy, even around customers. As a teenager, she was in an intimate relationship for about 2 years with a middle-aged man who was physically and emotionally abusive toward her. Although others often remind her of this troubled relationship, Maya claims to remember very little about that time and has no recollection of the physical abuse she endured. Currently, she says she is totally uninterested in pursuing any romantic relationships. Those to whom Maya is closest know different versions of her personality or "alters" that go by different names and behave in ways that are totally incongruous with Maya's personality. Whereas Maya is quiet and reserved, her main alter "Rita" is flamboyant, outgoing, and hypersexual. A second alter, "Joe," occasionally emerges from Maya's apartment dressed in men's clothing and speaking in deep tones. Maya's alters are oblivious to the details of her life.

Your ordinary perception of who you are includes knowing that you live within your own body. **Depersonalization** is the condition in which people feel their identities have become detached from their bodies. They may have experiences of unreality, of being an outside observer, and of emotional or physical numbing. **Derealization** is a condition in which people feel a sense of unreality or detachment from their surroundings. **Depersonalization/ derealization disorder** is a condition in which people have the experience of depersonalization, derealization, or both.

depersonalization
Condition in which people feel detached from their own body.

derealization
Condition in which people feel a sense of unreality or detachment from their surroundings.

depersonalization/ derealization disorder
A dissociative disorder in which the individual experiences recurrent and persistent episodes of depersonalization, derealization, or both.

Theories and Treatment of Dissociative Disorders

In normal development, people integrate the perceptions and memories they have of themselves and their experiences. You can remember many of the events from your past, which give you a sense of continuity over time. In a dissociative disorder, the individual loses this continuity, trying to block out or separate from conscious awareness events that caused extreme psychological, if not physical, pain.

Individuals with dissociative identity disorder have learned to cope with extremely stressful life circumstances by creating "alter" personalities that unconsciously control their thinking and behavior when they are experiencing stress.

©Ingram Publishing/Newscom

REAL STORIES

Herschel Walker: Dissociative Identity Disorder

Herschel Walker is perhaps one of the most successful professional U.S. football players of all time. He received the prestigious Heisman Trophy in his junior year of college at the University of Georgia and went on to play 11 seasons with the National Football League. Although he is famous for his talents on the field, the difficulties he endured in childhood nearly prevented him from attaining any of the achievements he has accrued over the years.

Herschel was able to overcome the challenges in his life and go on to reach immense success as a professional athlete by developing alternate personalities as a younger boy. By using those alternate personalities to cope with stressful situations, however, he eventually lost the ability to have control over when his "alters" took over his regular self, and in 2001 he was diagnosed with dissociative identity disorder (DID). In his autobiography, *Breaking Free: My Life with Dissociative Identity Disorder*, Herschel reveals the challenges he faced and continues to face in his personal life due to his struggle with DID, though his case is mild compared with those of some others afflicted with the same disorder. For example, his alters do not have names or speak differently or dress differently. In fact, he states most people wouldn't even notice when he was in an altered state. He would transform his personality in the moment.

Herschel was born in 1962 in Wrightsville, Georgia, one of seven children of blue-collar parents. As a child, he struggled with a weight problem and a severe stutter that rendered him almost unable to speak to others for fear of ridicule and embarrassment. He recalls being teased and bullied every day at school by his peers. He was so tortured by his speech impediment that he was often afraid to speak up in class, even though he was a diligent student who enjoyed learning. Although Herschel describes his family as loving and supportive, he found it difficult to reach out to them for emotional support. He also suffered from a debilitating fear of being in the dark as a result of frightening visions and nightmares that would come to him when he tried to go to sleep. To find relief from the anxiety, he would retreat into a fantasy world in which he felt safe and protected

Football legend Herschel Walker wrote a book, *Breaking Free: My Life with Dissociative Identity Disorder*, in which he relates that he cannot remember the season he won the Heisman Trophy, let alone the day of the ceremony.

©John Amis/AP Images

from any harm that his fears could cause him. Herschel told no one about these difficulties and instead developed various personalities in his mind to cope with them. These personalities took on characteristics Herschel thought he lacked in order to deal with the constant embarrassment and emotional torture.

In *Breaking Free*, Herschel describes how this coping system changed him. "When the choice I made to deal with the pain worked, I used it again when a similar kind of threatening situation occurred. Through repetition, the habit of having an alter take over became a routine, and the brain is a marvelously efficient machine that likes to take any process we are engaged in–from driving a car to walking to insulating ourselves against hurtful negative comments–from the conscious to the subconscious level. That is what DID did for me, and why as I was growing up, I didn't consciously realize I was doing it."

In high school, Herschel worked hard academically, earning top honors at his school. He also began to work hard athletically, running several miles a day and joining his school's football and track teams. He lost the weight that had been causing him ridicule from his peers and eventually

overcame his speech impediment. He excelled in both track and football, although it was his strength and prowess on the football field that gained him the most attention from college recruiters. After receiving many offers, Herschel decided to attend the University of Georgia, helping his school earn a National Championship in his junior year. The same year he received the prestigious Heisman Trophy. Instead of going on to finish his senior year at college, he joined a new professional football league that rivaled the NFL, the United States Football League. He also married his college sweetheart.

Herschel played with the league for two seasons before it dissolved. He was then drafted by the Dallas Cowboys and went on to play for four different teams throughout his 11-season NFL career. All the while, Herschel's DID helped him cope with the many challenges–both physical and emotional–that came along with his career. Whenever he was faced with stress or pain, "my alters functioned as a kind of community supporting me. . . . I never wanted to experience the kind of lows that I had known as a kid," he writes in *Breaking Free*, "so I became a kind of emotional bulldozer–a machine, a powerful force, something you turn the key on, fire up the ignition, throw into gear. The machine goes, almost always forward, leveling the highs and lows of the terrain it crosses into a smooth, flat, featureless plane."

However, the alters were not always positive ways of helping Herschel cope. They often kept his emotions at arm's length, preventing him from being close to teammates and loved ones—especially his wife. He was often unable to recall episodes from his life when his alters had come into play. It wasn't until his marriage and his life in general began to fall apart that he realized he needed help. Although his marriage was never able to recover, Herschel began to put his life in order after seeking help in 2001 from a psychologist friend, Dr. Jerry Mungadze at the Dissociative and Trauma Related Disorders Unit at Cedars Hospital in DeSoto, Texas. Herschel was diagnosed with DID and began intensive therapeutic treatment, which helped him identify and gain control over his alters, making a cohesive whole self out of the separate personalities he had been maintaining for most of his life.

Herschel has since started a career in mixed martial arts and recently appeared on a season of *Celebrity Apprentice* with Donald Trump. He lives in Dallas, Texas, and often gives motivational speeches to others who have been diagnosed with DID. In *Breaking Free*, he writes, "I hope my legacy will be more than what I have achieved on the football field and on the track. I would rather be remembered for opening my heart and sharing my experience with DID so that others can understand this condition."

Clinicians face a daunting task in both diagnosing and treating an individual's dissociative symptoms. In the first place, they must determine whether the condition is real or fabricated. People may deliberately feign a dissociative disorder to gain attention or avoid punishment. However, they may unwittingly develop one of these disorders if they have come under the influence of popular treatment of such a disorder in movies such as *Shelter* or television shows such as *The United States of Tara*. As a result of the potential fabrication of dissociative disorder by people who appear to have its symptoms, DID remains one of the most controversial of psychological disorders (Lilienfeld & Lynn, 2015).

In true cases of a dissociative disorder, when the symptoms do not appear feigned, the current consensus is that the dissociation is a response to early emotional or physical trauma (Vissia et al., 2016). One large psychiatric outpatient study demonstrated that people with dissociative symptoms in fact had high prevalence rates of both physical and sexual abuse in childhood (Foote et al., 2006). However, many people without a dissociative disorder have been subjected to traumatic events early in life that they do remember (Kihlstrom, 2005). Along similar lines, traumatic experiences in childhood can lead to other types of disorders. The question remains why some individuals exposed to trauma develop a dissociative disorder, but others do not.

MINI CASE

Dissociative Amnesia with Dissociative Fugue

Troy is a 39-year-old heterosexual Caucasian man. He entered the mental health crisis center in a daze, tears streaming down his face, and wearing only a T-shirt despite the frigid temperatures outside. "I have no idea where I live or who I am! Will somebody please help me?" The crisis team asked Troy to search his pockets for an ID or other identifying information, but the only thing he had on him was a picture of a little blonde-haired girl. Troy appeared exhausted and was taken to a bed, where he promptly fell asleep. The crisis team called the local police to find out whether there was a report of a missing child. As it turned out, the little girl in the photograph was Troy's daughter. She had been hit by a car in a shopping center parking lot. Although she had suffered a broken leg, the child was resting comfortably in a hospital pediatrics ward. Her father, however, had disappeared. Troy had apparently been wandering around the hospital for several hours, leaving his wallet and cell phone with the hospital social worker in the emergency room. When he awoke, he was able to recall who he was and the circumstances of the accident, but he remembered nothing of what had happened since.

Dissociative Identity Disorder

The possibility that an individual may not be responsible for actions committed while multiple personalities are in control of the person's behavior leads to fascinating legal questions. Theoretically, of course, it's possible for one alter to commit a crime while the other alters, or even the host, remain unaware. Obviously, however, convicting one alter means the host (along with all the other alters) is also put in prison. At another level, however, this question relates to the legal definition of insanity. Is a person with dissociative identity disorder able to control his or her own mind if part of the mind has split off and is acting independently?

There are three possible approaches to defending a client who legitimately has this diagnosis. In the "alter-in-control" approach, the defendant claims that an alter personality was in control at the time of the offense. In the "each-alter" approach, the prosecution must decide whether each personality met the insanity standard. In the "host-alter" approach, the issue is whether the host personality meets the insanity standard.

Dissociative identity disorder has rarely been successful as a legal defense after a public outcry following the ruling in 1974 that serial rapist Billy Milligan was insane due to lack of an integrated personality (*State v. Milligan,* 1978). Since that time, cases have had a variety of outcomes, ranging from the judgment that multiple personalities do not preclude criminal responsibility (*State v. Darnall,* 1980) to the ruling that alter personalities are not an excuse for inability to distinguish right from wrong (*State v. Jones,* 1998). The courts threw out two more recent cases in Washington State (*State v. Greene,* 1998) and West Virginia (*State v. Lockhart,* 2000) on the grounds that scientific evidence and/or adequate reliability standards do not exist in the diagnosis of the disorder (Farrell, 2010). The key issue for forensic psychologists and psychiatrists is identifying the difference between malingering and the actual disorder (Farrell, 2011).

Tools are now available for expert clinicians to use in aiding accurate diagnosis. The Structured Clinical Interview for *DSM–IV* Dissociative Disorders—Revised (SCID-D-R) (Steinberg, 1994; see Table 1), which the profession has rigorously standardized,

TABLE 1 **Items from the SCID-D-R**

Scale	Items
Amnesia	Have you ever felt as if there were large gaps in your memory?
Depersonalization	Have you ever felt that you were watching yourself from a point outside of your body, as if you were seeing yourself from a distance (or watching a movie of yourself)?
	Have you ever felt as if a part of your body or your whole being was foreign to you?
	Have you ever felt as if you were two different people, one going through the motions of life and the other part observing quietly?
Derealization	Have you ever felt as if familiar surroundings or people you knew seemed unfamiliar or unreal?
	Have you ever felt puzzled as to what is real and what's unreal in your surroundings?
	Have you ever felt as if your surroundings or other people were fading away?
Identity confusion	Have you ever felt as if there was a struggle going on inside of you?
	Have you ever felt confused as to who you are?
Identity alteration	Have you ever acted as if you were a completely different person?
	Have you ever been told by others that you seem like a different person?
	Have you ever found things in your possession (for instance, shoes) that belong to you, but you could not remember how you got them?

SOURCE: Steinberg, M. (1994). *Structured clinical interview for DSM-IV dissociative disorders—Revised (SCID-D-R).* Washington, DC: American Psychiatric Association.

includes a careful structuring, presentation, and scoring of questions. The professionals who developed and conducted research on this instrument emphasize that only experienced clinicians and evaluators who understand dissociative diagnosis and treatment issues must administer and score it.

The *DSM-5* considers the diagnosis of dissociative identity disorder to be valid. The precedents created by rulings that the diagnosis is not admissible due to failure to meet scientific standards may in time be overturned. Nevertheless, the diagnosis is challenging at best and potentially easy to feign, particularly if a clinician inadvertently plants the idea of using it as a defense.

Q: *You be the judge:* Should dissociative identity disorder be considered admissible in criminal cases? Why or why not?

Assuming that people with dissociative disorders are reacting to trauma by developing dissociative symptoms, the treatment goal becomes primarily one of integrating the disparate parts of self, memory, and time within the person's consciousness. Treatment guidelines for dissociative identity disorder emphasize best practices such as establishing and maintaining a strong therapeutic alliance, not playing favorites with any of the alters, and, from a positive psychology perspective, helping clients see themselves and their worlds in a more favorable manner by restoring their shattered assumptions (Ducharme, 2017).

As a specific technique, cognitive-behavioral therapy is well suited to helping clients with dissociative identity disorder develop a coherent sense of themselves and their experiences. To help clients view themselves more favorably, clinicians can stimulate them to question long-held core assumptions about themselves that are contributing to their symptoms. For example, they may believe they are responsible for their abuse, or that it is wrong for them to show anger toward their abusers, or that they can't cope with their painful memories. By confronting and then changing these cognitions, clients can gain a sense of control that will allow them to incorporate those memories into their sense of self.

Clinicians should also attend to the comorbidity of a dissociative disorder with other symptoms, including post-traumatic stress disorder (Tsai, Armour, Southwick, & Pietrzak, 2015). Treatment of dissociative disorders often addresses not only these disorders themselves but also associated disorders of mood, anxiety, and post-traumatic stress.

MINI CASE

Depersonalization/Derealization Disorder

Robert is a 49-year-old heterosexual African American male. He entered the psychiatrist's office in a state of extreme agitation, almost panic. He described the terrifying nature of his "nervous attacks," which began several years ago but had now reached catastrophic proportions. During these "attacks," Robert feels as though he is floating in the air, above his body, watching everything he does but feeling totally disconnected from his actions. He reports that he feels as if his body is a machine controlled by outside forces: "I look at my hands and feet and wonder what makes them move." However, Robert's thoughts are not delusions. He is aware that his altered perceptions are not normal. The only relief he experiences from his symptoms comes when he strikes himself with a heavy object until the pain finally penetrates his consciousness. His fear of seriously harming himself adds to his main worry that he is losing his mind.

Individuals with somatic symptom disorder suffer from physical ailments beyond those explained by a medical condition.

©Terry Vine/Getty Images

somatic symptoms
Symptoms involving physical problems and/or concerns about medical symptoms.

somatic symptom disorder
A disorder involving physical symptoms that may or may not be accounted for a medical condition and accompanied by maladaptive thoughts, feelings, and behaviors.

9.2 Somatic Symptom and Related Disorders

In the group of disorders in which **somatic symptoms** are prominent, people experience physical problems and/or concerns about medical symptoms. The term *somatic* comes from the Greek word *soma*, meaning "body." Somatic symptom disorders are psychological in nature, because although people with these disorders may or may not have a diagnosed medical condition, they seek treatment for their physical symptoms and associated distressing behaviors, thoughts, and feelings. These disorders have an intriguing history; among them were the antecedents of cases central to Freud's recognition of the role of the unconscious mind in personality.

Somatic Symptom Disorder

People with **somatic symptom disorder** have physical symptoms that may or may not be accounted for by a medical condition; they also have maladaptive thoughts, feelings, and behaviors. These symptoms disrupt their everyday lives. People with this disorder think to a disproportionate degree about the seriousness of their symptoms, feel extremely anxious about them, and spend a great deal of time and energy on the symptoms or their concerns about their health. Although it may appear that people with this diagnosis are intentionally manufacturing symptoms, they actually are not consciously attuned to the ways in which they express these psychological problems physically.

The somatic symptoms individuals experience may include pain as the primary focus. A diagnosable medical condition may exist, but it cannot account for the amount and nature of the pain clients report. There are also clients with pain disorder for whom no diagnosable medical condition exists.

Somatic symptom disorder is relatively rare, but it is present with higher than expected frequency among patients seeking treatment for chronic pain (Reme, Tangen, Moe, & Eriksen, 2011). In one study, over half the patients referred to cardiologists for heart palpitations or chest pain were found, upon physical examination, not to have heart disease (Jonsbu et al., 2009). In a small number of cases, individuals with somatic symptom

MINI CASE

Somatic Symptom Disorder, with Predominant Pain

Helen, a 34-year-old married Caucasian bisexual woman, is seeking treatment because her physician said there was nothing more he could do for her. When asked about her physical problems, Helen recited a litany of complaints, including frequent episodes when she could not remember what had happened to her and other times when her vision was so blurred that she could not read the words on a printed page. Helen enjoys cooking and doing things around the house, but she becomes easily fatigued and short of breath for no apparent reason. She often is unable to eat the elaborate meals she prepares, because she becomes nauseated and is prone to vomit any food with even a touch of spice. According to Helen's husband, she has lost all interest in sexual intimacy, and they have intercourse only about once every few months, usually at his insistence. Helen complains of painful cramps during her menstrual periods and at other times says she feels that her "insides are on fire." Because of additional pain in her back, legs, and chest, Helen wants to stay in bed for much of the day. She lives in a large, old Victorian house, from which she ventures only infrequently "because I need to be able to lie down when my legs ache."

disorder do suffer from a diagnosable medical condition, but their complaints and impairment levels are far in excess of those health professionals would customarily associate with the condition.

Further complicating the picture in the diagnosis and treatment of somatic symptom disorder is the fact that often people with this disorder also have other psychological disorders, including major depressive disorder, panic disorder, and agoraphobia. Researchers are also attempting to rule out the role of diagnosable medical conditions that may be associated with somatic symptom disorder and its comorbid anxiety and depressive disorders (Newby et al., 2017).

Illness Anxiety Disorder

People with **illness anxiety disorder** fear or mistakenly believe that normal bodily reactions represent the symptoms of a serious illness. They easily become alarmed about their health and seek unnecessary medical tests and procedures to rule out or treat their exaggerated or imagined illnesses. Their worry is not about the symptoms themselves but about the possibility that they have a serious disease. They also are preoccupied with their mistaken beliefs about the seriousness of their symptoms. They may turn to nonmedical abuse of prescription drugs, which in turn can expose them to harmful side effects as well as to dependence on the medications themselves (Jeffers et al., 2015).

illness anxiety disorder
A somatic symptom disorder characterized by the misinterpretation of normal bodily functions as signs of serious illness.

Conversion Disorder (Functional Neurological Symptom Disorder)

The essential feature of **conversion disorder (functional neurological symptom disorder)** is that the individual experiences a change in a bodily function that is not due to an underlying medical condition. The forms the disorder can take range from movement abnormalities such as paralysis or difficulty walking to sensory abnormalities such as inability to hear or see.

The term *conversion* in the name of this disorder refers to the transformation of psychological conflict to physical symptoms presumed to underlie the disorder. The term *functional neurological symptom disorder* in parentheses represents an alternate way of referring to the disorder that some clinicians may prefer. In some ways it is more descriptive than "conversion," which has historic roots in Freudian psychoanalysis in which the assumption was made that psychological conflicts "convert" or transfer into what look like neurological symptoms, such as paralysis. *Functional* in this context refers to abnormal functioning of the central nervous system. It is somewhat awkward to use the complete form of the disorder's name, so we will refer here to "conversion disorder" with the understanding that its formal title includes the parenthetical addition.

conversion disorder (functional neurological symptom disorder)
A somatic symptom disorder involving the translation of unacceptable drives or troubling conflicts into physical symptoms.

MINI CASE

Illness Anxiety Disorder, Care-Seeking Type

Hannah is a 48-year-old heterosexual Japanese American woman. She is a mother of two children, both of whom have recently moved away from home. Within the past year, her menstrual periods have become much heavier and more irregular. Seeking an explanation, Hannah began to spend days reading everything she could find on uterine cancer. Although medical books specified menstrual disturbance as a common feature of menopause, one newspaper article mentioned the possibility of uterine cancer. Hannah immediately made an appointment with her gynecologist, who tested her and concluded that her symptoms were almost certainly due to menopause. Convinced that her physician was trying to protect her from knowing "the awful truth," Hannah visited one gynecologist after another in search of someone who would properly diagnose what she was certain was a fatal illness. She decided to give up her job as a restaurant hostess. First, she was concerned that long hours of standing at the cash register would aggravate her medical condition. Second, she felt she could not be tied down by a job that was interfering with her medical appointments.

MINI CASE

Conversion Disorder, with Sensory Loss

Brian is a 24-year-old Caucasian man who identifies as gay. He is pursuing a PhD in engineering and constantly feels stressed by his rigorous academic workload. He has always thought of himself as a person to whom weird things happen and has commonly made more of situations than was warranted. Driving on a snowy night, he accidentally hit an elderly man who was walking on the side of the road, causing the man a near-fatal injury. In the months that followed, Brian became caught up in lengthy legal proceedings, which distracted him from his work and caused him tremendous emotional stress. On awakening one Monday morning, he found himself staggering around, unable to see anything other than the shadows of objects in the room. At first he thought he was just having a hard time waking up. As the morning progressed, however, he realized that he was losing his vision. He waited 2 days before going to the emergency clinic on campus. When he did go, he was oddly unconcerned about what seemed like such a serious physical condition.

Clients with conversion disorder may show a wide range of physical ailments, including "pseudoseizures" (not real seizures, but appearing as such), disorders of movement, paralysis, weakness, disturbances of speech, blindness and other sensory disorders, and cognitive impairment. The symptoms can be so severe that they make it impossible for clients to perform their work duties. Over half are bedridden or require assistive devices. Even though virtually all clients with conversion disorder do not have a medical diagnosis, clinicians must nevertheless rule out medical diagnoses before assigning the diagnosis (Rosebush & Mazurek, 2011).

Conversion disorder is a rare phenomenon, affecting 1 to 3 percent of those whom clinicians refer for mental health care. The disorder, which often runs in families, generally appears between ages 10 and 35 and is more frequently observed in women and people with less education. Perhaps as many as half of individuals with conversion disorder also suffer from a dissociative disorder (Sar et al., 2004). In fact, the *ICD-10* classifies conversion disorders as a form of dissociative disorder.

A large review of brain imaging studies on patients with motor conversion disorder (movement abnormalities) identified alterations in areas of the frontal and prefrontal regions active in planning and executing movements, as well as altered activities in brain regions responsible for emotion (Boeckle, Liegl, Jank, & Pieh, 2016). Individuals with this form of conversion disorder may, then, be unaware of what their bodies are doing and therefore unable to control their actions.

Conditions Related to Somatic Symptom Disorders

malingering
The fabrication of physical or psychological symptoms for some ulterior motive.

Malingering consists of deliberately feigning the symptoms of physical illness or psychological disorder for an ulterior motive such as receiving disability or insurance benefits. Though a diagnosis in *DSM-IV-TR*, malingering is not one in *DSM-5*. It nevertheless remains a concern when diagnoses must be made in a forensic, occupational, or military setting and the possibility that clients are feigning symptoms must at least be ruled out.

primary gain
The relief from anxiety or responsibility due to the development of physical or psychological symptoms.

Clinicians assume that clients engage in malingering in order to get a direct benefit, such as paid time off from work, insurance payments, or some other tangible reward. Some of these situations can yield what we call **primary gain**—namely the direct benefits of occupying the sick role. Structured malingering assessments are becoming more widely used, both to improve the evaluation of suspected malingerers and to protect the practitioners who are faced with making the determination (Weiss & Van Dell, 2017).

factitious disorder imposed on self
A disorder in which people fake symptoms or disorders not for the purpose of any particular gain but because of an inner need to maintain a sick role.

In **factitious disorder imposed on self**, people show a pattern of falsifying symptoms that are either physical, psychological, or a combination of the two. The individual falsifies these symptoms not to achieve economic gain but for the purpose of adopting the sick role. In extreme cases, known informally as instances of Munchausen's syndrome, the individual's entire existence becomes consumed with the pursuit of medical care. The individual may also feign the illness of someone else in cases of **factitious disorder imposed on another** or Munchausen's syndrome by proxy. Interestingly, one epidemiological study of individuals with factitious disorder as a diagnosis showed the most frequent occupations to be those in the health professions (Caselli et al., 2017).

Unlike people with conversion disorder, people with factitious disorder are consciously producing their symptoms, but their motives are internally rather than externally driven. They may be motivated by **secondary gain**, which is the sympathy and attention they receive from other people when they are ill. They know they are producing their symptoms, but they don't know why. People with conversion disorder, in other words, believe they are ill and rightfully assume the sick role. People who are malingering know that they are not ill, and therefore, any rewards they receive from sickness are illegally obtained (Kanaan & Wessely, 2010).

Theories and Treatment of Somatic Symptom and Related Disorders

Early psychodynamic theorists were the first to attempt to understand and treat this group of disorders from what they regarded as a scientific perspective. Lacking sophisticated diagnostic tools and basing their work on the concept of unconscious conflict, they referred to conversion disorder as "hysteria" (meaning, literally, "wandering uterus"). They could not find a physiological basis for the symptoms, which tended to disappear after the individual received treatment through hypnosis or psychoanalysis, reinforcing the notion that the symptoms were psychologically based.

In keeping with Freud's general formulation of hysteria, clinicians working from a psychodynamic approach today aim to identify and bring into conscious awareness the underlying conflicts that we associate with the individual's symptoms. Through this process, the client gains insight and self-awareness and becomes able to express emotion directly, rather than through physical manifestation.

From the cognitive-behavioral perspective, the dissociative, somatic symptom, and related disorders are viewed in terms of the thoughts linked to their physical symptoms. The underlying model is based on the premise that people with these disorders are subject to cognitive distortions that lead them to misinterpret normal bodily sensations.

factitious disorder imposed on another
A condition in which a person induces physical symptoms in another person who is under that person's care.

secondary gain
The sympathy and attention that a sick person receives from other people.

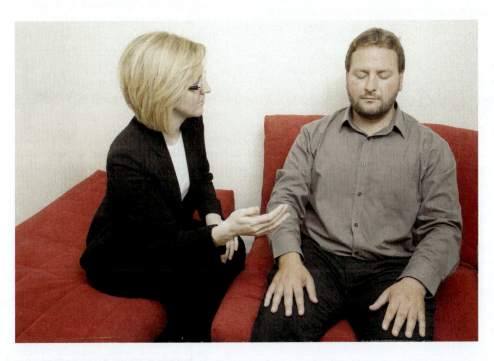

Hypnotherapy can be effective in helping individuals to recount memories that are too troubling to consciously recall.
©PaulaConnelly/Getty Images

Medical settings can be a source of significant anxiety for some individuals.

©Hero Images/Getty Images

Once they start to exaggerate the importance of their symptoms, they become even more sensitized to internal bodily cues, which in turn leads them to conclude that they are truly ill (Witthoft & Hiller, 2010).

What's in the *DSM-5*

Somatic Symptom and Related Disorders

The *DSM-5* brought a number of significant changes to the entire category of what we now call somatic symptom disorders. The authors of the *DSM-5* acknowledge that the terminology for what were called somatoform disorders in *DSM-IV-TR* was potentially confusing. They also recognize that somatic symptom disorders, psychological factors affecting other medical conditions, and factitious disorders all include the presence of physical symptoms and/or concern about medical illness. Furthermore, they recognize that the mind and body interact, so clinicians cannot separate physical symptoms from their psychological basis, nor vice versa. Further complicating the prior system, according to the *DSM-5* authors, was the fact that it is never entirely possible to determine that a psychological symptom has no physical basis.

The term *illness anxiety disorder* replaced *hypochondriasis*. Clinicians will give those individuals who have no physical symptoms but are highly anxious this diagnosis, specifying whether it includes care-seeking.

Conversion disorder now has "functional neurological disorder" in parentheses following the diagnosis, indicating that the individual shows abnormal nervous system functioning. However, to receive the diagnosis, the person must have symptoms that cannot be explained by a nervous system disease. Individuals will need to have a full neurological examination before health care professionals conclude that their symptoms have no neurological basis.

Other than improving the terminology, the *DSM-5* authors hope their revisions will lead to improved data collection on this group of disorders. Inconsistencies in the diagnostic criteria, combined with the main theoretical focus shifting from the psychodynamic to the cognitive-behavioral, have produced a situation in which there are not yet solid epidemiological data on a group of disorders whose prevalence we can now more accurately estimate.

In applying cognitive-behavioral therapy to clients with somatic symptom and related disorders, clinicians help their clients gain a more realistic appraisal of their body's reactions. For example, in one study, clients who had no cardiac illness but complained of palpitations or chest pain were exposed to exercise on a treadmill while being taught to interpret their raised heartbeat not as a sign of disease but as a normal reaction to exertion (Jonsbu et al., 2011).

Hypnotherapy and medication are two additional approaches that clinicians use specifically for treating conversion disorder. In hypnotherapy, the therapist instructs the hypnotized client to move the paralyzed limb. The therapist then makes the posthypnotic suggestion to enable the client to sustain the movement after the therapist brings him or her out of the hypnotic trance. SSRIs are the medication clinicians generally use in treating conversion disorder, but there are almost no well-controlled investigations of their effectiveness (Rosebush & Mazurek, 2011).

Cognitive-behavioral therapy for individuals with illness anxiety disorder focuses on their high levels of **health anxiety**, or undue concern about physical symptoms and illness. In therapy, individuals learn to restructure their maladaptive beliefs about their physical symptoms and gain more realistic interpretations of their body's reactions. However, in severe cases, where clients either do not want to enter or stay in individual therapy, group therapy using principles of ACT may provide an effective alternative (Eilenberg et al., 2016).

health anxiety
Undue concern about physical symptoms and illness.

9.3 Psychological Factors Affecting Other Medical Conditions

So far we have looked at disorders in which individuals are experiencing physical symptoms that do not have a physiological cause. The diagnostic category called **psychological factors affecting other medical conditions** includes conditions in which a client's physical illness is adversely affected by one or more psychological states. These can include depression, stress, denial of a diagnosis, or engaging in poor or even dangerous health-related behaviors.

In Table 2 we outline several examples of medical conditions that can be affected by psychological factors. Specifying the interaction of psychological factors with medical conditions provides health professionals with a clearer understanding of how the two interact. Once this interaction has been identified, the clinician can address the issues and work to help the client's medical condition improve.

psychological factors affecting other medical conditions
Disorder in which clients have a medical disease or symptom that appears to be exacerbated by psychological or behavioral factors.

Relevant Concepts for Understanding Psychological Factors Affecting Other Medical Conditions

Mental disorders, stress, emotional states, personality traits, and poor coping skills are psychological factors that can affect an individual's physical health and well-being. This category of disorders acknowledges the complex interactions through which psychological and physical conditions can affect each other.

Stress and Coping

Within psychology, the term **stress** refers to the unpleasant emotional reaction experienced when a person perceives an event to be threatening. This emotional reaction may include heightened physiological arousal, reflecting increased reactivity of the sympathetic nervous system. A **stressful life event** is a stressor that disrupts the individual's life. A person's efforts to reduce stress is called **coping**. It is when coping is unsuccessful, and the stress does not subside, that the individual may seek clinical attention for medical or psychological

stress
The unpleasant emotional reaction that a person has when an event is perceived as threatening.

stressful life event
An event that disrupts the individual's life.

coping
The process through which people reduce stress.

MINI CASE

Psychological Factors Affecting Other Medical Conditions

Michael is a 41-year-old biracial heterosexual male. He currently works as a manager of a large discount chain store, a position to which he has worked his way up over the past few years. Despite his success, Michael struggles with an agitated depression, which causes him to feel impatient and irritable most of the time. He recognizes that his emotional problems relate to long-standing issues with his parents, and he resents the fact that he chronically suffers from an inner tension that has always been part of his personality. The youngest in a family of four children, Michael perceived that throughout his childhood he had to do "twice as much" as his siblings to gain his parents' attention and affection. Now, as an adult, he is caught up in a drive toward success that literally makes him physically sick. He has intense headaches and stomachaches on most days, yet he is reluctant to seek medical help because he doesn't want to take time away from work.

TABLE 2 **Psychological Factors Affecting Other Medical Conditions**

Medical Condition	Possible Psychological Factor
Hypertension (high blood pressure)	Chronic occupational stress increasing the risk of high blood pressure.
Asthma	Anxiety exacerbating the individual's respiratory symptoms.
Cancer	Denying the need for surgical interventions.
Diabetes	Being unwilling to alter lifestyle to monitor glucose levels or reduce intake.
Chronic tension headache	Continuing family-related stresses that contribute to worsening of symptoms.
Cardiovascular disease	Refusing to visit a cardiac specialist for evaluation despite chest discomfort.

problems that have developed as a consequence of the constant physiological arousal caused by the experience of chronic negative emotions.

What types of events qualify as stressors? The most common way to describe stressors is through stressful life event rating scales, which are intended to quantify the degree to which individuals were exposed to experiences that could threaten their health. One of the best known of these is the Social Readjustment Rating Scale (SRRS) (Holmes & Rahe, 1967), which assesses life stress in terms of life change units (LCUs). In developing the LCU index, researchers calculated how strongly each type of event was associated with physical illness. The rationale behind this measure is that the more an event causes you to adjust your life circumstances, the more deleterious it is to your health.

The College Undergraduate Stress Scale (CUSS) (Renner & Mackin, 1998) is a good example of a stressful life events scale. Unlike the SRRS, which is used with adults of all ages, the CUSS assesses the kinds of stressors most familiar to traditional-age college students (90 percent of the people in the sample were under age 22). The most stressful event in the CUSS is rape, which has an LCU score of 100. Talking in front of class has a score of 72, however, which is also relatively high. Getting straight As has a moderately high score of 51. The least stressful event on the CUSS is attending an athletic event (LCU score = 20).

Life events scales have merit because they are relatively easy to complete and present a set of objective criteria against which we can compare people. However, it is not always easy to quantify stress. You and your best friend may each experience the same potentially stressful event, such as being late for class, but you may be far more perturbed by this situation than your friend. Your day will thus be far less pleasant than your friend's, and if you are repeatedly late, you might be at risk for a stress-related illness.

The cognitive model of stress places greater emphasis on the way you interpret events than on whether you experienced a given event. Like the cognitive approach in general, the cognitive model of stress proposes that the appraisal of an event as stressful determines whether it will have a negative impact on your emotional state. Not only do people differ in the way they interpret events, the circumstances surrounding the event also affect them. If your friend's professor doesn't take class attendance but yours does, this would help explain why you feel more stressed about being late than your friend.

As this example shows, stress is in the eye of the beholder. Even a relatively minor event can lead you to experience stress if you interpret it negatively. The cognitive model assumes, furthermore, that these "little" events can have a big impact, especially when they build up in a short period of time. Events called **hassles** can have significant effects on health when there are enough of them and you interpret them negatively. If you are not only late for class but get into an argument with your friend, stub your toe, spill your coffee, and miss your bus home, you will have as many potentially stress-causing events in one afternoon as someone experiencing a "bigger" life event such as going out on a first date.

hassle
A relatively minor event that can cause stress.

This woman's anger-control problems make it difficult for her to deal with everyday situations in a rational, calm manner.
©Fancy/SuperStock

On the positive side, you can balance your hassles with what researchers call **uplifts**, which are events on a small scale that boost your feelings of well-being. Perhaps you open up your Facebook page and find a pleasant greeting from a former high school acquaintance. The smile this greeting brings to your face can help make up for some of the stress of the hassles you just experienced. Uplifts are especially important within the positive psychology movement, which views them as contributing to people's feelings of day-to-day happiness.

It's wonderful when life sends a few uplifts your way, but when it doesn't, you need to find other ways to reduce stress through coping if you are to maintain your mental health. The two basic ways of coping are **problem-focused coping** and **emotion-focused coping** (Lazarus & Folkman, 1984). In problem-focused coping, you attempt to reduce stress by acting to change whatever it is that makes the situation stressful. If you're constantly late for class because the bus is overcrowded and tends to arrive 5 or 10 minutes after it's supposed to, then you can cope by getting an earlier bus, even if it means you have to wake up 10 minutes ahead of schedule. In contrast, in emotion-focused coping, you don't change the situation but instead change the way you feel about it. Maybe your professor doesn't care if you're a little bit late, so you needn't be so hard on yourself. Avoidance is another emotion-focused strategy. This coping method is similar to the defense mechanism of denial. Rather than think about a stressful experience, you just put it out of your mind.

Which is the better of the two ways of coping? The answer is, it depends. People cope with some situations more effectively through problem-focused coping. In changeable situations, you are most likely better off if you use problem-focused coping. If you're stressed because your grades are in a slump, rather than not think about the problem, you would be well advised to try to change the situation by studying harder. If you're stressed because you lost your cell phone and you truly cannot find it, then you may be better off by using emotion-focused coping such as telling yourself you needed a newer model anyhow (and taking some problem-focused steps as well, such as closing down that lost phone).

As people get older, they are able to use coping strategies that more effectively alleviate their stress, perhaps because they are better able to tolerate the mixed emotions that come with experiencing life's highs and lows (Schneider & Stone, 2015). In comparing samples of community-dwelling older adults and college undergraduates, for example, Segal, Hook, and Coolidge (2001) found that younger adults received higher scores on the dysfunctional coping strategies of focusing on and venting emotions, mentally disengaging, and using alcohol and drugs. Older adults, in contrast, were more likely to use impulse control and turn to their religion as coping strategies. It may in fact be their better use of coping strategies that accounts for the

uplifts
Events that boost your feelings of well-being.

problem-focused coping
Coping in which the individual takes action to reduce stress by changing whatever it is about the situation that makes it stressful.

emotion-focused coping
A type of coping in which a person does not change anything about the situation itself but instead tries to improve feelings about the situation.

Drinking alcohol to cope with stress is a maladaptive coping strategy, as it can cause further problems for the stressed individuals, particularly if they drink to excess.

©Stockbyte/Getty Images

resilience older adults show in the face of the stresses associated with caregiving for an ill spouse or other relative (Fortinsky, Tennen, & Steffens, 2013).

Personality also plays a role in affecting how much stress individuals experience as a result of exposure to potential stressors. In general, people with high levels of optimism are more resilient to stress. As you can probably recall from your own experience, the first year of college is associated with a great deal of stress, both academically and socially. Using measures of optimism and exposure to stressors, researchers found that both independently predicted the levels of subjective well-being undergraduates reported during their transition to the new academic environment (Yovita & Asih, 2018).

Sociocultural factors also play a role in causing and aggravating an individual's level of stress. For example, living in a harsh social environment that threatens a person's safety, interferes with the establishment of social relationships, and includes high levels of conflict, abuse, and violence is a condition related to lower socioeconomic status. Chronic exposure to the stresses of such an environment can lead to a number of changes in hormones that ultimately have deleterious effects on cardiovascular health, interacting with an individual's genetic and physiological risk. Both cardiovascular health and immune system functioning seem to be sensitive to the degree of stress a person experiences as a function of being lower in socioeconomic status. The limbic system, which mediates a person's responses to stress, appears to play a large role in accounting for these connections between social class and health (McEwen & Gianaros, 2010).

Ample evidence supports the role of stress in a variety of medical conditions through its interaction with immune status and function (Schneiderman, Ironson, & Siegel, 2005). A stressful event can initiate a set of reactions within the body that lowers its resistance to disease. These reactions can also aggravate the symptoms of a chronic, stress-related physical disorder. Personality also interacts with stress in influencing health. Studies of workplace stress show that people high in the tendency to overcommit themselves tend to put more effort into their job than is rewarded and, in turn, have poorer cardiovascular health (Eddy, Wertheim, Kingsley, & Wright, 2017).

Emotional Expression

Coping with stress by controlling your negative emotions is one way to reduce your levels of perceived stress. However, there are times when expressing your emotions, even if they are negative, can improve your physical and mental well-being. In one classic study, researchers instructed a group of first-year college students to write about the experience of coming to college, a highly stressful one, as noted above. A control group wrote about superficial topics. Those who wrote about coming to college reported being more homesick than the control subjects. Even though they experienced more negative emotions, however, they made fewer visits to physicians and, by the end of the year, were doing as well as or better than the control subjects in terms of grade point average and the experience of positive moods. The researchers concluded that confronting feelings and thoughts about a stressful experience can have long-lasting positive effects, even though the initial impact of such a confrontation may be disruptive (Pennebaker, Colder, & Sharp, 1990).

Pennebaker and his colleagues have expanded their findings to a variety of populations. In a meta-analysis of 146 randomized studies, disclosure had a positive and significant effect for people with a wide range of emotional concerns (Frattaroli, 2006). More recently, researchers have even identified positive mental health effects of writing on social media sites, including blogging (Ko & Kuo, 2009).

Keep in mind, however, that although the person expressing these feelings may feel better, the person who listens to the retelling of a sad or difficult story may suffer negative

Conditions at work that create stress can have significant mental health consequences, such as workplace bullying.
©SpeedKingz/Shutterstock

emotional consequences (Kellas, Horstman, Willer, & Carr, 2015). This is one of the reasons individuals who work in the helping professions may experience burnout, otherwise known as "compassion fatigue" (West, 2015).

Personality Style

One of the most thoroughly researched connections between personality and health is the **type A behavior pattern**, a set of behaviors that include being hard-driving, competitive, impatient, cynical, suspicious of and hostile toward others, and easily irritated (Table 3).

    People with a type A behavior pattern experience high levels of emotional arousal that keep their blood pressure and sympathetic nervous system on overdrive, placing them at risk for developing heart disease and at greater risk for heart attacks and stroke. Not only are they at high risk because their bodies are placed under stress, but their hard-driving and competitive lifestyles often include high-risk behaviors including smoking, drinking alcohol to excess, and failing to exercise (Mainous et al., 2010).

type A behavior pattern
Set of behaviors that include being hard driving, competitive, impatient, cynical, suspicious of and hostile toward others, and easily irritated.

TABLE 3 Are You Type A?

The Jenkins Activity Survey assesses the degree to which a person has a coronary-prone personality and behavior pattern. People with high scores, referred to as Type A, tend to be competitive, impatient, restless, aggressive, and pressured by time and responsibilities. In the items below, you can see which responses would reflect these characteristics.
Do you have trouble finding time to get your hair cut or styled?
Has your spouse or friend ever told you that you eat too fast?
How often do you actually "put words in the person's mouth" in order to speed things up?
Would people you know well agree that you tend to get irritated easily?
How often do you find yourself hurrying to get to places even when there is plenty of time?
At work, do you ever keep two jobs moving forward at the same time by shifting back and forth rapidly from one to the other?

From C. D. Jenkins, S. J. Zyzanski, and R. H. Rosenman, *The Jenkins Activity Survey.* Copyright © 1965, 1966, 1969, 1979 by The Psychological Corporation. Used by permission of the author.

Stressful life events, such as moving away to college, can be damaging to physical health if the individual has difficulty coping with stress he or she may be experiencing.

©Sam Edwards/Ojo Images/AGE Fotostock

type D personality

A personality type seen in those who experience emotions that include anxiety, irritation, and depressed mood.

behavioral medicine

An interdisciplinary approach to medical conditions affected by psychological factors that is rooted in learning theory.

Another significant personality risk factor for heart disease occurs among people who experience strong depressive affect but keep their feelings hidden—the so-called **type D personality**. Unlike the "A" in type A, which is not an acronym, the "D" in type D stands for "distressed." Type D personalities experience emotions that include anxiety, irritation, and depressed mood. These individuals are at increased risk for heart disease due to their tendency to experience negative emotions while inhibiting the expression of these emotions when they are in social situations. In addition to being at higher risk of becoming ill or dying from heart disease, these individuals have reduced quality of daily life and benefit less from medical treatments. Psychologists think the link between personality and heart disease for these people is due in part to an impaired immune response to stress (Denollet & Pedersen, 2011).

Applications to Behavioral Medicine

Because psychological factors that contribute to a medical condition have such a wide range, clinicians must conduct a careful assessment of the way each particular client's health is affected by behavior. The field of **behavioral medicine** applies the growing field in the health sciences regarding mind-body relationships to helping improve people's physical health by addressing the psychological factors of stress, emotions, behavior patterns, and personality. In addition, clinicians working in behavioral medicine often team up with psychologists and other mental health professionals to help clients learn and maintain behaviors that will maximize their physical functioning. By improving patients' compliance with medical treatment, clinicians can help them achieve better health and avoid further complications (Wilson, 2015).

Psychoeducation is an important component of behavioral medicine. Clients need to understand how their behavior influences the development or worsening of the symptoms of chronic illness. Then the clinician can work with them to develop specific ways to improve their health habits. For example, diet control and exercise are key to preventing and reducing the serious complications of cardiovascular disease. Time spent outdoors, even if not in active exercise, can also reduce stress levels (Beyer, Szabo, Hoormann, & Stolley, 2018). The clinician can teach clients ways to build these new health habits into their daily regimens and train people with sleep disorders to improve their sleep habits. People can manage chronic pain, which contributes to depressive symptoms, through strategies such as biofeedback.

Behavioral medicine is also moving increasingly toward interventions the profession once considered alternative, including mindfulness training, relaxation, and meditation. In these approaches, clinicians teach clients to monitor their internal bodily states (such as heart rate and breathing), as well as their perceptions, affective states, thoughts, and imagery, without judging. By observing their bodily reactions in this objective fashion, clients gain a more differentiated understanding of which aspects of their experiences illness affects and which it does not. Thus they can gain self-control over their body's reactions and see their ailments as having natural roles, not as impeding their ability to enjoy life in general (Carmody, Reed, Kristeller, & Merriam, 2008).

For example, people with a type A behavior pattern can benefit from training aimed at improving awareness of their reactions to stress, methods of coping with stressful situations, and behavioral interventions intended to improve their compliance with medical advice aimed at reducing their cardiovascular risk. Particularly important is a sense of mastery—namely, the belief that you have the ability to cope with or control the problems you encounter in life. People who feel they are in greater control over their life circumstances have a reduced risk of developing cardiovascular and related health problems (Roepke & Grant, 2011).

Increasingly, clinicians are finding that efforts to improve people's health by addressing only their medical needs do not have the long-term desired effects unless the clinicians also incorporate these psychological issues into treatment.

9.4 Dissociative and Somatic Symptom Disorders: The Biopsychosocial Perspective

Although distinct, the disorders we've covered in this chapter all reveal the complex interactions between mind and body and call for distinctions between "real" and "fake" psychological symptoms. They also all raise questions about the nature of the self. We've also examined the role of stress in psychological disorders and its relationship to medical illnesses and physical symptoms.

Biology clearly plays a role in making some individuals more vulnerable to psychological disorders, and particularly these disorders. A person may have a known or undiagnosed physical condition that certain stressors particularly affect, which then trigger the symptoms for a somatic symptom or related disorder. However, whatever the role of biology, cognitive-behavioral explanations provide useful approaches for treatment. Even people whose medical condition is clearly documented, as in chronic pain disorder, can benefit from learning how to reframe their thoughts about their disorder, if not also their actual health-related behaviors. At the same time, we are learning more about how stress affects physical functioning, including the impact of social discrimination on chronic conditions such as heart disease and diabetes.

It is quite likely that the mind-body connections underlying these disorders will come under even closer scrutiny as work on *DSM-5* evolves. The historical connections between these and the so-called "neurotic" disorders that seemed to affect many of Freud's patients will fade. Nevertheless, dissociative and somatic symptom disorders will maintain their fascination, if not their names.

Return to the Case: Rose Marston

Rose underwent 16 weekly individual therapy sessions, focusing on specific CBT techniques such as psychoeducation, cognitive restructuring techniques, exposure and response prevention, perceptual retraining exercises, and self-monitoring techniques in which she recorded the number of minutes spent thinking about her symptoms every day. These exercises focused on teaching Rose to look at her body in a more holistic, objective way and take the focus away from her stomach. During each session, Rose and her therapist discussed what happened during the previous week, reviewed "homework," and set an agenda for the session. Using this highly structured approach, Rose began to feel relief from her symptoms after the first few weeks of treatment. In addition, she began to treat her lactose intolerance through a combination of diet control and over-the-counter medication. By the end of the 16 weeks, Rose's pain was gone, and she had reconciled with her boyfriend, recognizing the strain put on their relationship by her constant concerns over her stomach pain. Her depression had also lifted, and she and her clinician agreed that taking an antidepressant would not be necessary. Rose continued to visit her clinician once per month for check-in visits, to review her progress and assess for recurrence of symptoms.

Dr. Tobin's reflections: Rose's apparent sensitivity to her rather mild physical symptoms likely contributed to her previous depression. Though that had been temporarily treated with antidepressants, it was clear that her concerns continued until the concomitant stressors of breaking with her boyfriend and losing her job led to an exacerbation of symptoms. It was helpful in Rose's case that she was highly motivated for treatment, which contributed to her positive outcome. Although individuals with somatic symptom disorder may be uncomfortable disclosing the extent of their symptoms and thoughts about them, Rose's motivation allowed her to reveal her thoughts and beliefs about her stomach discomfort. This information allowed her clinician to successfully tailor treatment to her specific concerns. Although Rose will require constant monitoring of her lactose intake, fortunately she will be able to keep her physical symptoms under control, which will ameliorate the source of her psychological preoccupation and distress.

SUMMARY

- This chapter covered three sets of conditions: dissociative disorders, somatic symptom disorders, and psychological factors affecting other medical conditions. In each of these sets of conditions, the body expresses psychological conflict and stress in an unusual fashion.

- Dissociative disorders occur when the human mind seems capable of dissociating, or separating, mental functions. Major forms of dissociative disorders include dissociative identity disorder (DID), dissociative amnesia, depersonalization, derealization, and depersonalization/derealization disorder.

- Among mental health professionals, the general viewpoint regarding dissociative disorders is that some type of traumatic event leads people with these disorders to experience a splitting apart of their conscious experiences, sense of self, or feelings of continuity over time. Clinicians, nevertheless, face a daunting task both in diagnosing and treating an individual's dissociative symptoms.

- Somatic symptom and related disorders are a group of conditions in which an individual's major symptoms involve what the individual experiences as physical problems and/or concerns about medical illness. Illness anxiety disorder involves mistaken fears about normal bodily reactions.

- The essential feature of conversion disorder (functional neurological symptom disorder) is that the individual experiences a change in a bodily function not due to an underlying medical condition. The term *conversion* refers to the presumed transformation of psychological conflict to physical symptoms. The difference between somatic symptom disorder and conversion disorder is that the former involves multiple and recurrent bodily symptoms rather than a single physical complaint.

- Conditions related to somatic symptom disorders include malingering, the deliberate feigning of symptoms of physical illness or psychological disorder for an ulterior motive such as receiving disability or insurance benefits; and factitious disorder,

where people show a pattern of falsifying symptoms that are either physical, psychological, or a combination of the two.

- The diagnostic category called psychological factors affecting other medical conditions includes conditions in which a client's physical illness is adversely affected by one or more psychological states such as depression, stress, denial of a diagnosis, or engaging in poor or even dangerous health-related behaviors.

- Mental disorders, stress, emotional states, personality traits, and poor coping skills are just some of the psychological factors that can affect an individual's medical conditions. This category of disorders acknowledges the complex interactions through which psychological and physical conditions can affect each other.

- Coping can help regulate the emotion of anxiety and hence reduce stress. However, there are times when expressing emotions can improve both physical and mental well-being. Actively confronting the emotions that arise from an upsetting or traumatic event can have long-term health benefits.

- Because psychological factors that contribute to a medical condition have such a wide range, clinicians must conduct a careful assessment of how each particular client's health is affected by behavior. The field of behavioral medicine applies the growing body of scientific evidence regarding mind-body relationships to helping improve people's physical health by addressing its relationships to the psychological factors of stress, emotions, behavior patterns, and personality.

- Biology clearly plays a role in making some individuals more vulnerable to psychological disorders, and particularly so in these disorders. A person may have a known or undiagnosed physical condition that may be affected by certain stressful life events, which then trigger the symptoms for a somatic symptom disorder. However, whatever the role of biology, cognitive-behavioral explanations provide useful approaches for treatment.

KEY TERMS

Behavioral medicine

Conversion disorder (functional neurological symptom disorder)

Coping

Depersonalization

Depersonalization/derealization disorder

Derealization

Dissociative amnesia

Dissociative identity disorder (DID)

Emotion-focused coping

Factitious disorder imposed on another

Factitious disorder imposed on self

Fugue

Hassle

Health anxiety

Illness anxiety disorder

Malingering

Primary gain

Problem-focused coping

Psychological factors affecting other medical conditions

Secondary gain

Somatic symptom disorder

Somatic symptoms

Stress

Stressful life event

Type A behavior pattern

Type D personality

Uplifts

Feeding and Eating Disorders; Elimination Disorders; Sleep-Wake Disorders; and Disruptive, Impulse-Control, and Conduct Disorders

Learning Objectives

10.1 Identify characteristics, theories, and treatments of eating disorders.

10.2 Understand symptoms and theories of elimination disorders.

10.3 Recognize indicators of sleep-wake disorders.

10.4 Differentiate among disruptive, impulse-control, and conduct disorders.

10.5 Analyze the biopsychosocial model for eating, elimination, sleep-wake, and impulse-control disorders.

©horvathta/Shutterstock

Case Report: Rosa Nomirez

Demographic information: 25-year-old married heterosexual Latina female

Presenting problem: Rosa self-referred to a community mental health center due to concerns about feeling depressed. During the initial intake evaluation, Rosa stated that she had been feeling down and depressed for several months, and since her depression had not improved on its own, she had decided to seek treatment. She stated this was not an easy decision for her, because she usually was able to handle difficult emotions on her own. Rosa also reported that those close to her were worried about her health and had been urging her for some time to seek treatment, although that she couldn't understand why they were concerned.

The clinician noted that Rosa appeared severely underweight and frail. Rosa said she was feeling depressed, mainly because, as she described it, "I feel like a fat monster all the time." She estimated that these feelings originated while she was pregnant with her daughter, now 2 years old. She stopped working after giving birth in order to focus on raising her daughter, while her husband provided for the family. Rosa said she had had a difficult time returning to her normal weight after giving birth, and that she believed she still appeared pregnant: "All I can see in the mirror is my stomach and how enormous it makes me look all over." She reported that she did not know her current weight and was afraid to weigh herself for fear that she was continuing to gain weight. She exclaimed, "I feel so ashamed that I am so fat still. I feel like I'll never look normal again."

Rosa reported that she followed a diet consisting of about 300 to 400 calories per day, and that she had been "working her way down" in terms of daily caloric consumption ever since her concerns about her weight began. At that time, Rosa had searched online for diet tips and discovered an online community devoted to supporting women who wanted to lose weight and stay thin. These "pro-ana" (slang for pro-anorexia) sites, as she described them, offered her support from other users, as well as helpful tips not only for restricting her caloric intake but also for hiding it from others, whose concern she saw as bothersome and interfering with her goals of losing weight. Rosa had been visiting the sites daily for about 6 months. Her husband discovered them on their computer and, recognizing the danger they posed, pleaded with Rosa to stop using them. She said she didn't understand why, because maintaining a low body weight was so important to her and the thought of gaining weight caused her intense feelings of anxiety.

Although she said she rarely felt interested in sex and had not gotten her menstrual period for about 4 months, Rosa explained that she and her husband had been trying to have another child for about 6 months. The clinician asked about any other physiological changes she might have noticed. Rosa said she felt tired much of the time, but beyond that, she denied any difficulties. "I usually just think about my daughter and about staying thin. There isn't really time to worry about much else." She said further that while out in public, she often compared her body to those of others. This had become a source of overwhelming anxiety, so she typically preferred to stay home to avoid feeling "judged for being fat."

According to Rosa, her family had been "constantly bothering" her about her weight. "They just don't understand how I feel. They try to force me to eat and it just makes me feel so uncomfortable and depressed. It feels like they are mocking me because they know how disgusting I am, so I usually just avoid spending time with them now." Her parents had emigrated from Colombia when Rosa was an infant, and since then several other relatives had moved close by. Although Rosa described the family as close-knit, she explained that it was difficult for her older relatives to understand the differences between Colombian and U.S. culture, which she felt exerted pressure to be thin and attractive. "It's just not that way where they are from, and so they don't know what it's like for me."

Relevant history: Rosa reported that as a teenager she occasionally had episodes of bingeing and purging by vomiting, although she found the effects of the purging aversive. She explained that she has been concerned about her body weight "for as long as I can remember," and that she generally tries to maintain a low body weight. However, her restrictive eating behaviors became more severe following the birth of her daughter. She denied a family history of eating disorders.

Case formulation: Rosa meets diagnostic criteria for anorexia nervosa, binge-eating/purging type. Criterion A states the individual must maintain a body weight significantly lower than what is expected for age and height. With permission, the clinician obtained Rosa's weight from her most recent physician visit and found that it was less than 85 percent of her expected weight— significantly lower than the minimal expectation for a

woman her age. Rosa also meets Criterion B because she has been intensely fearful of gaining weight, even though she is of lower-than-average body weight. She meets Criterion C because she fails to recognize the seriousness of her low body weight.

Although Rosa reported often feeling depressed, the clinician determined that it appears that her symptoms of depression are directly related to her heightened concern about her weight. Therefore, the clinician will not give her an additional diagnosis of depression. It is clear that Rosa's concern about her weight has alienated her from those to whom she is closest, namely her husband and her immediate family.

Treatment plan: Rosa was resistant to the clinician's advice that she should receive treatment for her anorexia. With her permission, the clinician reached out to Rosa's husband and family, who agreed that treatment was crucial for her. After discussing the matter with her husband, Rosa agreed to present for an initial consultation at a day treatment program that specializes in eating disorders. After the evaluation there, Rosa decided that pursuing treatment would be the best decision for her family and would help reduce her feelings of depression. She agreed to sign a contract to participate in the treatment program for at least 2 months.

Sarah Tobin, PhD

The disorders we cover in this chapter include eating disorders, elimination disorders, and a range of disorders in which individuals exhibit a lack of control over their impulses. Eating disorders are characterized by difficulties individuals have regarding food and control over their eating, dieting, or elimination of food. Elimination disorders specifically affect primarily children or adolescents who are having difficulty controlling the biological functions of urination and defecation, generally due to psychological disturbances. People with sleep-wake disorders lack control over biological processes that often have a relationship to psychological functions. Finally, the impulse-control disorders reflect disturbances in the individual's ability to regulate one or more of a range of behaviors related to particular desires, interests, and the expression of emotions.

eating disorders
Diagnosis for people who experience persistent disturbances of eating or eating-related behavior that result in the person's altering the consumption or absorption of food.

10.1 Eating Disorders

People who have **eating disorders** experience persistent disturbances of eating or eating-related behavior that change the way they eat or retain their food. These disorders go beyond dieting or occasional overeating, significantly impairing the individual's physical and psychosocial functioning.

Characteristics of Anorexia Nervosa

Clinicians diagnose an individual as having **anorexia nervosa (AN)** when he or she shows three basic types of symptoms: severely restricted eating, which leads to an abnormally low body weight; intense and unrealistic fear of getting fat or gaining weight; and disturbed self-perception of body shape or weight. In other words, people with AN restrict their food intake, become preoccupied with gaining weight, and feel that they are already overweight even though they may be seriously underweight.

DSM-IV-TR used "intense fear" of gaining weight as a criterion for AN, but *DSM-5* replaced this subjective assessment with behavior ("persistent behavior that interferes with weight gain"). Within the AN category, clinicians can differentiate between their clients who restrict their intake and those who alternate between the extremes of restriction and uncontrollable eating.

In addition to the psychological consequences of AN, the depletion of nutrients in people who merit the diagnosis leads them to develop a series of serious health changes that can, in the extreme, become life threatening. Constant undereating causes cardiac and respiratory problems, thinning bones, changes in gastrointestinal functioning, and loss of energy. Not only does their appearance change in terms of becoming abnormally thin and gaunt, but they can also suffer hair loss, and their nails become weak and brittle. Changes in their hormones caused by constant food deprivation can also lead them to become infertile. Their sexual functioning becomes disturbed (Gonidakis, Kravvariti, & Varsou, 2015).

The higher risk of mortality in people with AN has been firmly established. The longer individuals have the disorder, the greater their risk (Franko et al., 2013). Although the majority of deaths from AN occur in young adults, a Norwegian study found that 43 percent of AN-related deaths occurred in women age 65 and older (Reas et al., 2005). Women with AN die not only from the complications of their disorder but from suicide, particularly if they have comorbid depression and the form of the disorder in which they alternate overeating with severe food restriction (Forcano et al., 2011).

Individuals with anorexia nervosa experience distress associated with feeling "fat" despite having a low body weight.

©Ted Foxx/Alamy Stock Photo

anorexia nervosa (AN)
An eating disorder characterized by severely restricted eating, an intense fear of gaining weight, and distorted body perception.

MINI CASE

Anorexia Nervosa Restricting Type

Blake is an 18-year-old bisexual Caucasian male in his first year of college. Growing up, Blake was usually low-average in weight, but in his first few months of college he began to lose significant amounts of weight. His parents first noticed that he looked underweight when he came home for Thanksgiving break, but when they asked him about it, he denied that he had been trying to lose weight intentionally. He told his parents that he sometimes forgot to eat meals in the dining common because he was so busy with school, but he assured them he would try to eat regular meals more often. It turned out that Blake was indeed obsessed with dieting and exercise and had been keeping very careful food diaries and exercising daily since high school, but he did not tell anyone. Since coming to college, he felt he was able to restrict his eating more without his parents noticing. By the end of his first year, he had gone down from 130 to 95 lbs, though he assured his family that he felt "fine."

REAL STORIES

Portia de Rossi: Anorexia Nervosa and Bulimia Nervosa

Born in Australia as Amanda Lee Rogers, actress Portia de Rossi has come a long way since she began her professional career at the age of 12 as a fashion model. That was the time, as she recalls in her memoir *Unbearable Lightness: A Story of Loss and Gain,* when she began to focus obsessively on her weight. In the book, she writes that from the time she embarked on a modeling career as a very young girl, "I'd never known a day where my weight wasn't the determining factor for my self-esteem. My weight was my mood, and the more effort I put into starving myself to get it to an acceptable level, the more satisfaction I would feel as the restriction and the denial built into an incredible sense of accomplishment."

After her father unexpectedly passed away when she was 9 years old, Portia and her older brother were raised by their mother. Although her mother supported her quest for perfection and helped her in her rise to fame, Portia does not blame her for creating pressure to lose weight, writing that "it has always felt internal." She describes this internal drive as a "drill sergeant of a voice" she developed, which ordered her to keep pushing herself to lose weight and to keep a strict record of her food intake and exercise.

Portia remembers getting "ready" for photo shoots as a teenager, which consisted of losing weight in a short amount of time. With her mother's help, she would restrict her diet severely or not eat at all in the days leading up to the shoots. As she recalls, "Me losing weight before a job was like an athlete training for a competition." Before long, Portia's intense focus on dieting before photo shoots became a constant presence in her life. After unsuccessfully trying diet pills to maintain her weight, she followed the example her fellow models set and began bingeing and purging. She writes that this seemed like the best solution at the time, given that she loved to reward herself after each modeling job by bingeing on junk food, an act that provided emotional nourishment to counteract her negative feelings about herself. However, this pattern became increasingly destructive as she started to schedule more frequent modeling jobs and

had less time between them to get "back on track," or to compensate from any weight gained during a period of bingeing.

After a few years of modeling, Portia discovered her love of acting. At first she loved it because she was able to escape from herself for a while. After a few high-profile appearances in Australian films, Portia moved to Los Angeles, where she eventually had her big break. At age 25, she joined the cast of the popular television series *Ally McBeal*, playing Nelle Porter, the gutsy and outspoken new member of the law firm the show portrayed. One of the first things she did when she landed the job was to purchase a treadmill to put in her dressing room, as she had seen her cast mates do, so she could work out during her lunch breaks.

Although she was proud of her accomplishment, joining the show marked a new chapter in Portia's life in which she began to experience immense pressure to be thin, along with the pressure she felt from herself to blend into the Hollywood crowd. In addition, Portia was faced with the realization that she was homosexual. She became plagued by fear that the public would find out about her sexuality, marring her image as a Hollywood star. As she hid this part of herself, she continued to struggle with her weight throughout her tenure at *Ally McBeal*.

Portia remembers that though she enjoyed her work on the show's set, intense feelings of insecurity continued to plague her. Ironically, the hallmark of the character she played was the confidence she exuded, and Portia struggled to maintain this image on the show. Compounding her suffering was the fact that she did not share her feelings with anyone, and she remembers driving home from the set every day and crying to herself for hours.

When she started on *Ally McBeal*, Portia was bingeing and purging frequently. However, as is common in the case of those with bulimia, this did not achieve her desired body weight, and she felt undeserving of her success. One incident on the set of a commercial she was to shoot for a beauty campaign catapulted her into what would eventually become anorexia. Portia was mortified when she

Portia de Rossi
©AF archive/Alamy Stock Photo

was unable to fit into any of the suits that the stylists provided for her. She recalls feeling crushed when the stylists announced that she was a size 8.

After this incident, Portia began seeing a nutritionist, who provided her with a list of healthy foods to eat and required her to fill out a daily food diary. The nutritionist, Suzanne, also taught her to measure her food portions with a scale to achieve successful weight loss. Portia was excited to have some direction for her dieting, although she soon took the nutritionist's recommendations to an unhealthy extreme. "Suzanne had set my calorie intake for optimum weight loss at 1,400 calories a day. I reset it to 1,000. Problem solved." This daily calorie count began to dwindle as Portia continued to lose weight. Her weight loss never left her feeling satisfied, and she constantly lowered her goal weight. She began exercising frequently throughout the day, including on her drive to see Suzanne when she would pull over so she could go for a jog because sitting in the car for a prolonged period of time made her feel anxious. Although she was faithfully seeing the nutritionist, she concealed her extreme food restriction, creating a fake food diary that mimicked what her food intake should have been.

As her weight plummeted, Portia was encouraged by the positive media attention she was receiving, including magazine covers and constant paparazzi coverage. Her friends' and family's reaction, however, was much different. While visiting Portia in Los Angeles, her best friend commented that she appeared too thin. Portia recalls her reaction to this statement. "That's funny: too thin. Just this morning on the set I had to clench my buttocks as I walked through the law office on a full-length lens because if I walked normally the part where my hips meet my thighs bulged out rhythmically with each step: left fat bulge, right fat bulge, left fat bulge, and cue dialogue, 'You wanted to see me?' Too thin." This highlights the extreme and unrealistic standards Portia placed on her appearance, and that also drove her to the depths of anorexia.

Portia's weight continued to plunge, thanks to a combination of severe calorie restriction (down to a few hundred calories per day) and extreme amounts of exercise. She utilized several tricks, such as keeping her apartment at 60 degrees so her body would burn more calories and not using toothpaste in order to avoid "accidentally" ingesting excess calories.

She had also stopped menstruating. Portia's weight loss did not go unnoticed by the media, although she didn't understand why there was cause for concern. As she writes, "Some of them said that I was anorexic. It wasn't true. At 100 pounds I was way too heavy to be anorexic."

With the distorted mindset typical in those suffering from anorexia nervosa, Portia continued on her path to weight loss until she was down to a frightening 82 pounds. At the time, she was shooting her first major Hollywood film as a leading actress in *Who Is Cletis Tout?* She ran into major physical difficulties while making the film, which required her to perform in many action shots. Due to her dietary restriction and low body weight, her joints ached to the point where she could barely move without extreme agony. She eventually collapsed while shooting a particularly challenging scene and received immediate medical attention. The results of her medical tests indicated that she had osteoporosis, cirrhosis of the liver, and lupus. For the first time, Portia was forced to confront the reality of her obsession with weight loss. She had nearly starved herself to death, and so began her long and difficult journey toward recovery.

In the book, Portia equates anorexia to her first love. "We met and were instantly attracted to each other. We spent every moment of the day together . . . losing anorexia was painful–like losing your sense of purpose. I no longer knew what to do without it to consider. . . . Without anorexia, I had nothing. Without it, I was nothing. I wasn't even a failure; I simply felt like I didn't exist." As she began to eat more and gain weight, she struggled once again with bulimia due to her feelings of guilt over eating foods that she had restricted for over a year. Her treatment regimen included seeing a therapist and taking hormone replacement pills and antidepressants to help reduce her obsession with food. In 10 months, Portia gained 80 pounds. As she slowly recovered, she also came to terms with her sexuality. From living with a girlfriend, she learned how to eat what she wanted rather than constantly restricting her cravings, which she recognized as leading to obsessive dieting behaviors. By the time she started dating her now wife, Ellen DeGeneres, in 2004, Portia had fully recovered from anorexia. She now enjoys a healthy and active lifestyle, free of the constraints of her eating disorder. "I never wanted to think about food and weight ever again," she writes. "For me, that's the definition of recovered."

At the heart of the experience of AN is a core disturbance in the individual's body image. People with AN believe their bodies are larger than they really are, which, in turn, they believe makes them unattractive. Women with the restrictive form of AN appear not to value thinness so much as to be repelled by the idea of being overweight (Cserjési et al., 2010).

The lifetime prevalence of AN is 0.9 percent for women and 0.3 percent for men. In addition, people with anorexia nervosa have higher rates of mood, anxiety, impulse-control, and substance use disorders. The majority of individuals who develop anorexia nervosa between their early teenage years and their early twenties have the disorder for just under 2 years (Hudson, Hiripi, Pope, & Kessler, 2007).

Characteristics of Bulimia Nervosa

People with the eating disorder **bulimia nervosa** engage in **binge eating**, during which they rapidly eat an inordinately excessive amount of food, perhaps amounting to several thousand calories in a sitting. During these episodes, they experience a lack of control, which makes them feel they cannot stop eating or regulate how much they eat. Following the binge, they then engage in **purging**, during which they try to rid themselves of their excess caloric consumption by engaging in self-induced vomiting, taking laxatives or diuretics, and fasting or exercising excessively. For a bulimia nervosa diagnosis, these episodes must not occur exclusively during episodes of anorexia nervosa.

Formerly, clinicians assigning a diagnosis of bulimia nervosa distinguished between subtypes called "purging" and "nonpurging." In *DSM-IV-TR*, people diagnosed with the purging type would induce vomiting, administer an enema, or take laxatives or diuretics. Those who received the nonpurging diagnosis were seen as trying to compensate for what they ate by

bulimia nervosa
An eating disorder involving alternation between the extremes of eating large amounts of food in a short time, and then compensating for the added calories either by vomiting or other extreme actions to avoid gaining weight.

binge eating
The ingestion of large amounts of food during a short period of time, even after reaching a point of feeling full, and a lack of control over what or how much is eaten.

purging
Eliminating food through unnatural methods, such as vomiting or the excessive use of laxatives.

Bulimia Nervosa

Elena is a 26-year-old single heterosexual Russian American woman. She has struggled with her weight and body image since her early teenage years, when she was a competitive ballroom dancer. Her parents were very watchful of her eating habits during her adolescence and kept her on a very strict diet. Over time, Elena started sneaking junk food to her room late at night and then forcing herself to vomit. Since then, she has started to binge and purge nearly daily, which has led to a number of physical problems over the years, though her weight has remained about the same.

fasting or engaging in excessive exercise. The *DSM-5* authors found evidence that this was not a valid distinction and removed the subtypes (van Hoeken et al., 2009).

Like those who have AN, people with bulimia nervosa develop a number of medical problems. The most serious occur with purging. For example, ipecac syrup, the medication that people use to induce vomiting, has severe toxic effects when taken regularly and in large doses. People who induce vomiting frequently also suffer from dental decay because the regurgitated material is highly acidic. The laxatives, diuretics, and diet pills that people with bulimia use can also have toxic effects. Other health problems stem from behaviors they use to try to lose weight, such as giving themselves frequent enemas, regurgitating and then rechewing their food, and spending too much time in saunas. Related to being in a state of constant dehydration, the bulimic individual runs the risk of permanent gastrointestinal damage, fluid retention in the hands and feet, and heart muscle destruction or heart valve collapse.

The lifetime prevalence of bulimia nervosa is 1.5 percent among women and 0.5 percent among men. Researchers estimate the prevalence of bulimia nervosa at any one time at 1.3 percent among college women, but binge eating (8.5 percent), fasting (8.1 percent), and excessive exercise (14.9 percent) are far more common. The majority of college women (59.7 percent) have concerns about their weight or body shape. These estimates remained relatively stable over the 15-year period from 1990 to 2004 (Crowther et al., 2008).

Disordered eating patterns in college tend to improve over time but do not disappear completely. A 20-year follow-up of a sample of college men and women showed that 75 percent no longer had symptoms in early midlife; however, 4.5 percent still had a clinically significant eating disorder (Keel, Gravener, Joiner, & Haedt, 2010). The nature of the eating disorder may also change over time. In a study of middle-aged and older adult women seeking help with eating disorders, bulimia nervosa was less prevalent than in younger samples, but other forms of disordered eating continued to persist (Elran-Barak et al., 2015).

Although bulimia nervosa receives more attention among and is more prevalent in women, men also experience the disorder. An online survey of over 6,500 members of a health maintenance organization revealed that substantial percentages of men engaged in periods of uncontrolled eating (20 percent), binge eating at least once a week (8 percent), fasting (4 percent), laxative use (3 percent), exercise (6 percent), and body checking (9 percent). Women were more likely than men to show almost all these behaviors, but there were no significant sex differences in the use of laxatives and exercise to avoid weight gain after a period of binge eating (Striegel-Moore et al., 2009).

A binge is a loss of control when eating that allows the consumption of a large amount of (usually unhealthy) food in a short amount of time. Individuals with bulimia nervosa will purge following a binge, in order to avoid gaining weight from the binge.

©Digital Vision/Getty Images

Binge-Eating Disorder

Binge-eating disorder is a new diagnosis added to *DSM-5* that covers individuals who lack control over their eating and engage in binges at least twice a week for 6 months. For binge-eating disorder to be diagnosed, the binges must occur with the intake of large amounts of food, go past the point of feeling full or hungry, occur while the person is alone, and be followed by self-disgust or guilt. Because the binge eating does not occur in association with compensatory behaviors, it is possible that individuals with this disorder gain a significant amount of weight.

binge-eating disorder
An eating disorder in which individuals lack control over their eating and engage in binges for at least twice a week for 6 months.

Theories and Treatment of Eating Disorders

Eating disorders reflect a complex set of interactions among an individual's experiences with eating, body image, and exposure to sociocultural influences. The attitudes people develop throughout life toward food, eating, and body size can all play a role in influencing the risk of developing an eating disorder.

Researchers working within the biological perspective are increasingly focusing on altered brain activity in individuals with eating disorders. In one innovative study, women with AN and women who had recovered from AN were compared on their fMRI responses to food-related cues with healthy controls after a night of fasting. Even those who were no longer symptomatic still showed lowered activation in the food reward centers and higher activation of inhibitory control areas of the brain, suggesting that the disorder creates lingering effects in the ways that individuals process food-related cues (Sanders et al., 2015). Further research supports the effect of AN in altered brain activity in areas responsible for processing emotions, body-related stimuli, and self-perception (Esposito, Cieri, di Giannantonio, & Tartaro, 2018).

From the biological perspective, binge-eating disorder is understood as a form of addiction, in that individuals with this disorder engage in repetitive behaviors that persist despite the negative consequences. Because of its efficacy in treatment and the similarity of the disorder to other addictive disorders, researchers propose that lower levels of serotonin could be operating in this case. The fact that people with binge-eating disorder also experience mood and anxiety disorders further supports the role of serotonin. Researchers investigating altered serotonin activity in the brains of individuals with binge-eating disorder have indeed found evidence of its role. Compared to both healthy controls and people with gambling disorder, people with binge-eating disorder had effectively lower serotonin in brain regions active in addictive behaviors (Majuri et al., 2017).

Clinicians working from the biological perspective base their treatment of people with eating disorders on administering psychotropic medications, particularly SSRIs. However, despite their continued use, these are no longer considered advisable from an evidence-based perspective (Garner et al., 2016).

Psychological perspectives are now considered the treatment of choice for eating disorders. These approaches focus on the core psychological components of disturbances in body image (Figure 1). The cognitive-affective component of body image includes evaluation of one's own appearance (satisfaction or dissatisfaction) and the importance of weight and shape for an individual's self-esteem. The perceptual component of body image includes the way individuals mentally represent their bodies. Individuals with eating disorders typically overestimate their own body size. The behavioral component includes body checking, such as frequent weighing or measuring body parts, and avoidance, which is the wearing of baggy clothing or avoiding of social situations that expose the individual's body to viewing by others (Ahrberg, Trojca, Nasrawi, & Vocks, 2011).

The primary aim of treatment, according to the model in Figure 1, is identifying and changing the individual's maladaptive assumptions about his or her body shape and weight. In addition, clinicians attempt to reduce the frequency of such maladaptive behaviors as body checking and avoidance (Hrabosky, 2011).

In cognitive-behavioral therapy, clinicians first attempt to change selective biases in people with eating disorders that lead them to focus on the parts of their bodies they

FIGURE 1 Components of Body Image

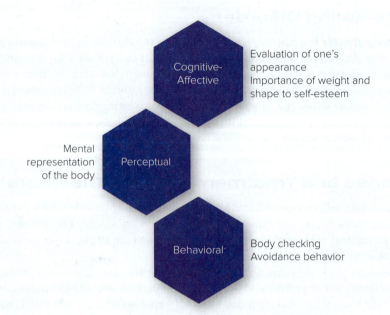

dislike. Second, by using exposure therapy in which clients view their own bodies ("mirror confrontation"), clinicians attempt to reduce the negative emotions they ordinarily experience. Behavioral interventions focus on reducing the frequency of body checking. Third, clinicians can address size overestimation by helping clients view their bodies more holistically in front of a mirror, by teaching them mindfulness techniques to reduce their negative cognitions and affect about their bodies, and by giving them psychoeducation about the ways their beliefs reinforce their negative body image (Delinsky, 2011).

Although ACT, mindfulness, and other third-wave therapies are being explored as treatments for eating disorders, they are not yet considered to have sufficient empirical support to justify their use instead of cognitive-behavioral therapy. However, interpersonal therapy is an empirically supported method that could be used as an alternative to cognitive-behavioral therapy for individuals with binge-eating disorder (Linardon et al., 2017).

Within the sociocultural perspective, clinicians use interventions incorporating a family component for clients with eating disorders who are still in their teens and who have had symptoms for only a brief time (Ciao, Accurso, Fitzsimmons-Craft, & Le Grange, 2015). Family-based therapies appear to be particularly effective in reducing depressive symptoms among adolescents with bulimia nervosa (Valenzuela, Lock, Le Grange, & Bohon, 2018).

Avoidant/Restrictive Food Intake Disorder

avoidant/restrictive food intake disorder
A disorder in which individuals avoid eating out of concern about aversive consequences or restrict intake of food with specific sensory characteristics.

In **avoidant/restrictive food intake disorder**, individuals show an apparent lack of interest in eating or food. They do so because they are concerned about the aversive consequences. In addition, they may avoid food based on its sensory characteristics (color, smell, texture, temperature, or taste). People may develop this disorder as the result of a conditioned negative response to having an aversive experience while eating, such as choking.

Previously included as a feeding disorder of infancy or early childhood in the *DSM-IV-TR* and regarded as an extreme version of "picky eating" (Menzel, 2018), this diagnosis is now applicable to individuals of any age who do not have another eating disorder or concurrent medical condition, or who are following culturally prescribed eating restrictions. As a result of their disorder, they lose a significant amount of weight (or fail to achieve expected weight gain), show a significant nutritional deficiency, become dependent on feeding through a stomach tube or oral nutritional supplements, and show marked interference with their psychosocial functioning.

Young adults seem particularly prone to this disorder, with one study estimating that 25 percent of college-age women and 20 percent of college-age men engage in significant restricted eating (Quick & Byrd-Bredbenner, 2012). Social norms may reinforce this behavior, because certain peer networks appear prone to setting expectations of restricted eating habits (Howland, Hunger, & Mann, 2012).

Eating Disorders Associated with Childhood

The authors of *DSM-5* moved the *DSM-IV-TR* eating disorders of infancy and childhood to the overall category of eating disorders in adolescents and adults. Researchers in the field hoped that reclassifying these disorders would allow them to evaluate more systematically the incidence, etiology, and treatment effectiveness of these disorders, and this appears to have been the case (Dahlgren, Wisting, & Rø, 2017).

Children with **pica** eat inedible substances, such as paint, string, hair, animal droppings, and paper. This is a serious disorder because even one incident can cause the child to experience significant medical consequences due to lead poisoning or injury to the gastrointestinal tract. Pica is the most serious cause of self-injury to occur in people with intellectual developmental disabilities. Clinicians treating pica must not only use a behavioral treatment strategy to reduce the individual's injurious behaviors, but also institute prevention by ridding the home of potentially dangerous substances (Williams et al., 2009). In one study, the parents of children who ate holiday decorations were trained to reinforce the children for playing with toys instead (Mitteer, Romani, Greer, & Fisher, 2015).

In **rumination disorder**, the infant or child regurgitates and rechews food after swallowing it. Researchers investigating rumination disorder (when it was included, with feeding disorder, as a disorder of childhood) identified five common disturbances in these children: (1) delayed or absent development of feeding and eating skills; (2) difficulty managing or tolerating food or drink; (3) reluctance to eat food based on taste, texture, and other sensory factors; (4) lack of appetite or interest in food; and (5) the use of feeding behaviors to comfort, self-soothe, or self-stimulate.

Not surprisingly, 25 to 45 percent of developmentally normal children have some type of problem with food and feeding, but 80 percent of those who are intellectually disabled do. Because of the many variations in the way clinicians report these disturbances, epidemiologists lack exact estimates of their prevalence. Further complicating the clinical picture is the fact that many factors can contribute to eating problems in children, ranging from a choking

---

What's in the *DSM-5*

Reclassifying Eating, Elimination, Sleep-Wake, and Disruptive, Impulse-Control, and Conduct Disorders

DSM-5 reflects a number of changes across categories of the disorders we present in this chapter. In addition, diagnoses were added and removed to be consistent with emerging research in these important psychological disorders.

With regard to eating disorders, the most significant change in *DSM-5* was to move all the eating disorders into a new category called "Feeding and Eating Disorders" that also includes feeding disorders of childhood. Another major change by the *DSM-5* authors was to eliminate the two subtypes of bulimia nervosa (with and without purging).

A new category called "Binge-Eating Disorder," which was in the appendix of *DSM-IV-TR*, was added to eating disorders based on a comprehensive literature review (Wonderlich et al., 2009) that showed there was sufficient validity to the diagnosis to justify its inclusion. The *DSM-5* authors decided to include binge-eating disorder to reduce the number of diagnoses given for eating disorder "not otherwise specified."

The feeding disorders pica and rumination disorder, formerly in the *DSM-IV-TR* section of disorders of childhood, were moved into the same category as eating disorders. Elimination disorders became its own chapter.

Sleep-wake disorders received a major overhaul, as the *DSM-5* authors worked to develop a classification system that would be in greater conformity with the system used by sleep specialists. The *DSM-5* work group on sleep disorders took a "lumping versus splitting" approach that was to put related disorders into a single category and separate disorders that warranted their own distinct diagnoses.

Finally, in the area of disruptive, impulse-control, and conduct disorders, the *DSM-5* authors moved disorders that were in the section on childhood into one chapter that also includes disorders of adulthood in which individuals have problems in regulating their emotions and/or behaviors. As you can see in this chapter, these disorders cut across the divisions in *DSM-IV-TR* in which impulse-control and childhood antisocial-like disorders were treated separately. The authors believe these disorders are linked by dysfunctions in regulation and therefore conceptually and practically belong together.

---

pica
A condition in which a person eats inedible substances, such as dirt or feces; commonly associated with intellectual developmental disabilities.

rumination disorder
An eating disorder in which the infant or child regurgitates food after it has been swallowed and then either spits it out or reswallows it.

experience to gastrointestinal abnormalities (Bryant-Waugh, Markham, Kreipe, & Walsh, 2010). However, the percent of children who meet the diagnosis for a feeding-related disorder remains relatively small (Eddy et al., 2015).

10.2 Elimination Disorders

elimination disorders
Disorders characterized by age-inappropriate incontinence, beginning in childhood.

enuresis
An elimination disorder in which the child is incontinent of urine and urinates in clothes or in bed after the age when the child is expected to be continent.

encopresis
An elimination disorder in which the child is incontinent of feces and has bowel movements either in clothes or in another inappropriate place.

Elimination disorders are characterized by age-inappropriate incontinence and are generally diagnosed in childhood. Individuals with **enuresis** wet the bed or urinate in their clothing after they have reached the age of 5 years, at which point it is expected that they should be completely toilet trained. To receive this diagnosis, the child must show symptoms of enuresis for three consecutive months. In **encopresis**, a child who is at least 4 years old repeatedly has bowel movements either in his or her clothes or in another inappropriate place.

Despite the expectation that children by the age of 4 or 5 should be completely toilet-trained, perhaps as many as 20 to 25 percent of 4-year-old children still wet the bed, and 30 percent of children 3 years old still soil (von Gontard, 2011). By the age of 5, enuresis affects approximately 5 to 10 percent of the population, but prevalence decreases over time to about 1 percent in individuals 15 years and older. Boys are more likely than girls to experience this condition (Brown, Pope, & Brown, 2011), and over the past 15 years, there has been a trend for children to be diagnosed at younger ages (Kushnir, Kushnir, & Sadeh, 2013).

There are subtypes of enuresis based on the time of day the child inappropriately passes urine (daytime only, night only, or both). The subtypes of encopresis distinguish between children who have constipation and then become incontinent due to overflow of feces, and those who do not have constipation and overflow. Researchers believe these distinctions are important because they can differentiate which children do and do not have a medical condition that underlies their symptoms (von Gontard, 2011).

Evidence-based treatment for childhood elimination disorders focuses on biobehavioral methods to establish continence (Shepard, Poler, & Grabman, 2017). Enuresis can be treated through use of a "urine alarm," a device attached to a child's underwear or pajamas that emits an auditory and/or tactile sensation in response to moisture. The child then develops a conditioned avoidance response that can trigger muscular contractions in the external sphincter of the bladder prior to the leakage of urine. Encopresis treatments supported by empirical studies include enhanced toilet training and biofeedback. In enhanced toilet training, the child is rewarded for continence, given training about appropriate defecation dynamics, and taught breathing techniques and muscle training exercises to gain control over the anal sphincters.

If children have the retentive form of encopresis, they can benefit from behavioral training that rewards them for increasing their intake of fiber and fluid and ensures that they include time on the toilet as part of their daily schedules (Kuhl et al., 2010). Another more psychologically oriented approach focuses on unresolved anger that a child may be expressing in response to family issues. Such issues can include conflict between the parents, the arrival of a newborn sibling, or the behavior of an older sibling who torments the child. Treatment that addresses these family system issues can help to reduce the child's symptoms (Reid & Bahar, 2006).

10.3 Sleep-Wake Disorders

The science of sleep and treatment of sleep-wake disturbances is rapidly gaining attention, so much so that sleep medicine is now a field in its own right. Researchers and clinicians in sleep medicine typically take a biopsychosocial approach, examining genetic and neurophysiological contributions, psychological interactions, and social and cultural factors that impinge on the individual's sleep quality and amount.

DSM-5 organizes the sleep-wake disorders into what the authors believe is a clinically useful system that has a basis in empirical research. This system combines sets of related

Sleep-wake disorders, such as the insomnia this man is experiencing, can be disabling, but new technologies are leading to improved treatments.
©Koldunova Anna/Shutterstock

disorders from the *DSM-IV-TR* in some cases and splits apart others that are best understood as separate entities. Sleep specialists have a more fine-grained diagnostic system than that represented by the *DSM-5* approach, meaning that a client seeking help from a sleep clinic may have a slightly different diagnosis than that provided by *DSM-5*.

The *DSM-5* diagnostic criteria for sleep-wake disorders reflect progress in the availability of technology in assessment and differential diagnosis. Many of these diagnoses now use **polysomnography**, which is a sleep study that records brain waves, blood oxygen levels, heart rate, breathing, eye movements, and leg movements.

We summarize the major categories of sleep-wake disorders in Table 1. As you can see, they fall into the categories of insomnia disorder, narcolepsy, hypersomnolence disorder, breathing sleep-related disorders, circadian rhythm disorders, and parasomnias. To be diagnosable, symptoms must be present for a significant period of time, occur relatively frequently, and cause the individual to experience distress.

Sleeping disorders affect a large number of individuals, with perhaps as many as 30 percent of adults in the general population in the case of insomnia alone (Cole, 2011). If you are like many undergraduates, you most likely have already been affected by one or more of these disorders, given the typical environment of the college dormitory or student-populated apartment building in which noise in the night hours interferes with both sleep quality and quantity.

The availability of wearable technology that records length of time asleep, time awake, and even sleep stages is making it increasingly possible for individuals to gain an understanding of their own sleep patterns. As a result, more individuals may seek sleep therapy than was true in the past, when the only signal people received of a possible sleep disorder was feeling tired.

Treatments for sleep-wake disorders vary considerably depending on the nature of the disorder. Cognitive-behavioral therapy is regarded as highly efficacious for insomnia and, along with relaxation and sleep hygiene training, for improving sleep in college student populations (Friedrich & Schlarb, 2018).

New technologies are making it increasingly possible for individuals not only to detect but also to manage their own treatment in the home. Continuous positive airway pressure (CPAP) machines are mechanical devices used for treating sleep apnea. They are becoming increasingly practical and affordable (Sutherland & Cistulli, 2015).

polysomnography
A sleep study that records brain waves, blood oxygen levels, heart rate, breathing, eye movements, and leg movements.

TABLE 1 **Sleep-Wake Disorders**

Disorder (or Category)	Specific Disorders within Category	Predominant Symptoms
Insomnia disorder		Difficulty initiating or maintaining sleep, along with early-morning awakening.
Narcolepsy		Recurrent periods of an irrepressible need to sleep, lapsing into sleep, or napping within the same day. Diagnosis also requires either episodes of jaw-opening or losing facial muscle tone while laughing or showing abnormal cerebral spinal fluid (CSF) or sleep disturbances on polysomnography.
Hypersomnolence disorder		Recurrent periods of sleep or lapses into sleep during the day, prolonged main sleep episodes, or difficulty being fully awake after abruptly awakening.
Breathing sleep-related disorders	Obstructive sleep apnea separate specific disorder	Frequent episodes of apnea and hypopnea while sleeping as indicated on polysomnography along with either snoring, snorting/gasping, or breathing pauses during sleep and daytime sleepiness, fatigue, or unrefreshing sleep.
	Central sleep apnea	Frequent episodes of apnea while asleep.
	Sleep-related hypoventilation	Episodes of decreased breathing (ventilation) while asleep.
Circadian rhythm sleep-wake disorders		Persistent patterns of sleep disruption due primarily to altered circadian rhythm or misalignment between the individual's internal circadian rhythm and the sleep-wake schedule required by the person's environment, or work or social schedule. Includes delayed sleep phase type (delay in timing of major sleep period), advanced sleep phase type (sleep-wake cycles that are several hours earlier than conventional), irregular sleep-wake type, non-24-hour sleep-wake type, and shift work type.
Parasomnias	Non-rapid eye movement sleep arousal disorder	Recurrent episodes of incomplete awakening from sleep accompanied by either sleepwalking or sleepwalking not associated with rapid eye movements (REMs).
	Nightmare disorder	Repeated occurrences of extended, dysphoric, and well-remembered dreams that typically involve threats to one's life.
	Rapid eye movement sleep behavior disorder	Frequent episodes of arousal during sleep associated with speaking and/or motor behaviors occurring during REM sleep.
	Restless legs syndrome (RLS)	An urge to move the legs along with uncomfortable and unpleasant sensations in the legs, urges that begin or worsen during periods of rest or inactivity that are partially or totally relieved by movement, and are worse or only occur in the evening or night.

MINI CASE

Obstructive Sleep Apnea Hypopnea

Samuel is a 68-year-old married African American heterosexual man. He is seeking marriage counseling because his wife has decided she no longer wants to put up with his snoring and is insisting they sleep in separate bedrooms. In addition, he constantly feels fatigued and sleepy during the day. The counselor sends Samuel to a sleep specialist who conducts a polysomnogram, showing that Samuel goes into periods of not breathing on average every 4 minutes. Samuel is now being evaluated for treatment by the sleep specialist, who is exploring options, including a mechanical device that fits over the nose, to allow Samuel and his wife to resume their previous sleeping patterns in the same bed.

10.4 Disruptive, Impulse-Control, and Conduct Disorders

People with one of the disruptive, impulse-control, or conduct disorders show extreme lack of inhibition ("disinhibition"). They are unable to restrain themselves from expressing what are often high levels of negative emotions. Although people with a variety of other disorders also experience difficulties in self-regulating their behavior, these particular disorders bring the individuals who have them into significant conflict with social norms or authority figures.

Oppositional Defiant Disorder

Most children go through periods of negativism and mild defiance, particularly in adolescence, and most parents complain of occasional hostility or argumentativeness in their children. But what if such behaviors are present most of the time and are not just a phase?

Children and adolescents with **oppositional defiant disorder** display angry or irritable mood, argumentative or defiant behavior, and vindictiveness that results in significant family or school problems. Youths with this disorder repeatedly lose their temper, argue, refuse to do what they are told, and deliberately annoy other people. They are touchy, resentful, belligerent, spiteful, and self-righteous. Rather than seeing themselves as the cause of their problems, they blame other people or insist they are victims of circumstances. To the extent that their behavior interferes with their school performance and friendships, they risk jeopardizing their relationships with teachers and peers. These losses can, in turn, lead them to feel inadequate and depressed and perhaps cause them to act out even more.

Oppositional defiant disorder makes its first appearance during the preteen years between ages 8 and 12, with rates higher in boys. Many children with the disorder, particularly boys, will develop antisocial personality disorder in adulthood; a small percentage will engage in serious criminal behavior (Loeber & Burke, 2011). Girls with oppositional defiant disorder are at higher risk of developing depression, particularly if they show inability to regulate their emotions and a tendency toward defiance (Hipwell et al., 2011).

The goal of treatment for oppositional-defiant disorder is to help the child learn to exhibit appropriate behaviors, such as cooperation and self-control, and to unlearn problem behaviors, such as aggression, stealing, and lying. Therapy focuses on reinforcement, behavioral contracting, modeling, and relaxation training and may take place in the context of peer therapy groups and parent training. One such approach, individualized social competence therapy, uses cognitive-behavioral methods specifically tailored to the situations in which the child has experienced difficulties (Goertz-Dorten et al., 2018).

oppositional defiant disorder
A disorder characterized by angry or irritable mood, argumentative or defiant behavior, and vindictiveness that results in significant family or school problems.

Intermittent Explosive Disorder

People with **intermittent explosive disorder** are unable to hold back their urges to express strong angry feelings and associated violent behaviors. They can have angry outbursts that are either verbal (temper tantrums, tirades, arguments) or physical outbursts in which they

intermittent explosive disorder
An impulse-control disorder involving an inability to hold back urges to express strong angry feelings and associated violent behaviors.

Boys who are diagnosed with oppositional defiant disorder may go on to develop antisocial personality disorder, though many will grow out of the disorder by the time they reach late adolescence.

©Image Source/PunchStock

become assaultive or destructive in ways that are out of proportion to any stress or provocation. These physical outbursts, on at least three occasions in a 12-month period, may cause damage to the individual, other people, or property. However, even if individuals showing verbal or physical aggression do not cause harm, they may still receive this diagnosis.

The rage shown by people with this disorder is out of proportion to any particular provocation or stress, and their actions are not premeditated. Afterward, they feel significantly distressed, suffer interpersonal or occupational consequences, or experience financial or legal consequences.

An estimated 4 to 7 percent of people in the U.S. population have intermittent explosive disorder; of these, 70 percent have at least 3 outbursts per year, with an average of 27 on a yearly basis (Kessler et al., 2006). People with this disorder are more vulnerable to a number of threats to their physical health, including coronary heart disease, hypertension, stroke, diabetes, arthritis, back/neck pain, ulcer, headaches, and other chronic pain (McCloskey et al., 2010). They also are likely to have co-occurring disorders, including bipolar disorder, personality disorders such as antisocial or borderline, substance use disorder (particularly alcohol), and cognitive disorders.

Intermittent explosive disorder appears to have a strong familial component not accounted for by any comorbid conditions associated with it (Coccaro, 2010). Researchers believe the disorder may result from abnormalities in the serotonin system causing a loss of the ability to inhibit movement (Coccaro, Lee, & Kavoussi, 2010).

Faulty cognitions further contribute to the development of intermittent explosive disorder. People with this disorder have a set of negative beliefs that other people wish to harm them, beliefs they may have acquired through harsh punishments they received as children from their parents or caregivers. They feel, therefore, that their violence is justified. In addition, they may have learned through modeling that aggression is the way to cope with conflict or frustration. Adding to these psychological processes is the sanctioning of violence associated with the masculine gender role, a view that may in part explain the greater prevalence of this disorder in men.

Given the possible role of serotonergic abnormalities in this disorder, researchers have investigated the utility of SSRIs in treatment. However, though effective in reducing aggressive behaviors, SSRIs result in full or partial remission in fewer than 50 percent of cases (Coccaro et al., 2009). Mood stabilizers used in the treatment of bipolar disorder (lithium, oxcarbazepine, carbamazepine) also have some effects in reducing aggressive behavior, but there are few well-controlled studies (Jones et al., 2011).

Cognitive-behavioral therapy can also be beneficial for individuals with this disorder. In one approach, a variant of anger management therapy uses relaxation training, cognitive restructuring, hierarchical imaginal exposure, and relapse prevention for a 12-week

MINI CASE

Intermittent Explosive Disorder

Ed is a 28-year-old single Caucasian heterosexual man who works as a high school teacher. He often has unprovoked, violent outbursts of aggressive and assaultive behavior, during which he throws whatever objects he can get his hands on and yells profanities. He soon calms down, though, and feels intense regret for whatever damage he has caused, explaining that he didn't know what came over him. In the most recent episode, Ed threw a coffee pot at another teacher in the faculty lounge, inflicting serious injury. After the ambulance took the injured man to the hospital, Ed's principal called the police. Ed was taken into custody and immediately suspended from his job.

Individuals with intermittent explosive disorder may suffer negative consequences in their interpersonal relationships due to their frequent, and unprovoked, aggressive outbursts.

©Ingram Publishing

period in individual or group modalities. Cognitive-behavioral therapy focuses on reducing anger and aggression as well as improving the individual's social skills (Hudspeth, Wirick, & Matthews, 2015). Particularly important is reducing the individual's misperceptions of social threat, which can, in turn, reduce overt expression of relational aggression (Coccaro, Fanning, Keedy, & Lee, 2016).

Conduct Disorder

Individuals with **conduct disorder** violate the rights of others and society's norms or laws. Their delinquent behaviors include aggression directed toward people and animals such as bullying and acts of animal cruelty, destruction of property, deceitfulness or theft, and serious violations of rules such as being truant from school or running away from home. The *DSM-5* also specifies childhood or adolescent onset (before or after 10 years of age); the presence or absence of remorse, guilt, and empathy; and the severity of the behavior, ranging from lying and truancy to physical cruelty, use of a weapon, and stealing in the presence of the victim.

conduct disorder
An impulse-control disorder that involves repeated violations of the rights of others and society's norms and laws.

Around the world, rates of conduct disorder are estimated at 3.2 percent, with remarkable consistency across countries, although definitions of the disorder do seem to vary from country to country (Canino et al., 2010).

Predisposing conditions to the development of conduct disorder include being raised in harsh environments involving trauma, abuse, and neglect (Wang & Kenny, 2014). Genetic vulnerability may further exacerbate the risk of growing up in such households. In one study, 1,100 pairs of 5-year-old twins and their families were compared on the contributions of genetics and physical maltreatment by parents. Among identical twins whose co-twin had conduct problems (those at high genetic risk), the probability of a conduct disorder diagnosis was nearly 25 percent when parents physically maltreated them. In contrast, those children at low genetic risk who were subject to physical maltreatment had only a 2 percent chance of developing conduct disorder (Jaffee et al., 2005). The specific gene that seems to be active in conduct disorder is not yet known, but genetic researchers are optimistic about the potential of GWAS to identify common variants associated with conduct and other disorders characterized by behavioral dysregulation (Derringer et al., 2015).

Unfortunately, whatever the causes, we know that aggressive and antisocial children are likely to have serious problems as adults. In a classic longitudinal study, only one sixth of the original sample was completely free of psychological disorders in adulthood. More than

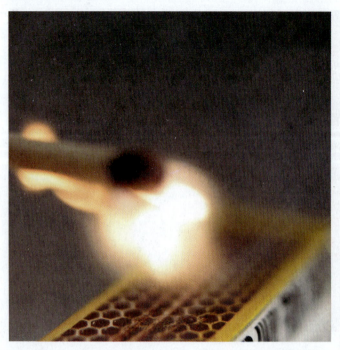

Individuals with pyromania are often fixated on every aspect of firesetting including lighting a match.

©Redfx/Alamy Stock Photo

impulse-control disorders
Psychological disorders in which people repeatedly engage in behaviors that are potentially harmful, feeling unable to stop themselves and experiencing a sense of desperation if their attempts to carry out the behaviors are thwarted.

pyromania
An impulse-control disorder involving the persistent and compelling urge to start fires.

kleptomania
An impulse-control disorder that involves the persistent urge to steal.

A woman with kleptomania feels the irresistible urge to steal even small, inexpensive items while walking through a cosmetics store.

©Ignard ten Have/123RF

one fourth had antisocial personality disorder (Robins, 1966). Subsequent studies have confirmed this pessimistic outlook, with results indicating that at least 50 percent of children with conduct disorder develop antisocial personality disorder (see the chapter "Personality Disorders"). A more recent longitudinal study suggested that callousness, particularly in boys, is a key feature of conduct disorder and predicts continued symptoms into adolescence (Fanti et al., 2018).

Impulse-Control Disorders

People with **impulse-control disorders** engage in repetitive, often harmful, behaviors that they feel are beyond their control. Before they act on their impulses, these individuals experience tension and anxiety that they can relieve only by following through on their impulses. After acting on their impulses, they experience a sense of pleasure or gratification, although later they may regret that they engaged in the behavior.

Pyromania People with **pyromania** deliberately set fires, feeling tension and arousal before they commit the act. They are fascinated with and curious about fire and its situational contexts, and they derive pleasure, gratification, or relief when setting or witnessing fires or participating in their aftermath. For an individual to be diagnosed with pyromania, the firesetting must not be done for monetary reasons, and the individual must not have other medical or psychiatric conditions. Arson, by contrast, is deliberate firesetting intended to produce financial gain, and an arsonist does not experience the relief shown by people with pyromania.

The majority of people with pyromania are male. Pyromania appears to be rare, however, even among arsonists. Among a sample of 90 repeat offenders, Finnish researchers found that only 3 met the *DSM-IV-TR* criteria for pyromania (Lindberg, Holi, Tani, & Virkkunen, 2005). Slightly higher percentages were reported in one study of hospitalized psychiatric patients, in which 3.4 percent had current symptoms and 5.9 percent had lifetime symptoms consistent with a diagnosis of pyromania (Grant, Levine, Kim, & Potenza, 2005).

Pyromania appears to be a chronic condition if the individual does not receive treatment. Some individuals with pyromania may discontinue firesetting and instead switch to another addictive or impulsive behavior such as kleptomania or gambling disorder. An intensive study of 21 participants with a lifetime history of pyromania described the most likely triggers for their behavior as stress, boredom, feelings of inadequacy, and interpersonal conflict (Grant & Kim, 2007).

Like the other impulse-control disorders, pyromania may reflect abnormalities in dopamine functioning in areas of the brain involving behavioral addictions. Nevertheless, treatment for pyromania that follows the cognitive-behavioral model seems to show the most promise (Grant & Odlaug, 2010). The techniques include imaginal exposure and response prevention, cognitive restructuring of response to urges, and relaxation training.

Kleptomania People with the impulse-control disorder **kleptomania** are driven by a persistent urge to steal. Unlike shoplifters or thieves, they are not motivated by monetary gain but instead seek excitement from the act of stealing. Like people with other impulse-control disorders, they would rather not be driven to this behavior, and they feel their urge is unpleasant, unwanted, intrusive, and senseless. They steal in response to an urge or state of craving,

You Be the Judge

Legal Implications of Impulse-Control Disorders

By definition, impulse-control disorders arise from irresistible urges. Individuals with disorders such as kleptomania and pyromania engage in the illegal acts of stealing and firesetting, respectively. Those with intermittent explosive disorder may also commit illegal acts during one of their violent outbursts. When people with these disorders encounter the justice system, then, the question arises whether we should regard them as having a disorder or as practicing a form of illegal and deviant behavior similar to psychopathy.

People with kleptomania commit acts of stealing in response to a failure to resist impulses. The stealing may give them momentary relief from their anxiety-driven urge, but ultimately it leads only to significant distress and dysfunction in their everyday lives. A key difference between kleptomania and antisocial personality disorder is that people with kleptomania feel intense regret; moreover, they do not steal for any particular monetary reason (Aboujaoude, Gamel, & Koran, 2004). Similarly, individuals with pyromania, by definition, do not seek monetary reward from their actions. Those with intermittent explosive disorder do not seek to commit violent acts but are responding to irresistible urges. People with gambling disorder steal or cheat not for the sake of material gain, but in order to support their gambling habit.

According to one view, impulse-control disorders are not "volitional" disorders, which excuse an individual from moral and legal responsibility for his or her actions. A cognitive impairment that prevents knowing or remembering the negative consequences of the person's previous addictive behaviors causes the volitional disorder. Once the behavior begins, it increases the extent of the impairment (Campbell, 2003).

The terminology the mental health profession uses to describe kleptomania and pyromania implies, however, that individuals with these disorders are somehow attracted to the opportunities to steal and start fires. In the case of pyromania, fire fighters, insurance investigators, law enforcement professionals, and even mental health professionals may fail to appreciate fully the diagnostic criteria for the disorder. One erroneous but popular belief is that serial arsonists are pyromaniacs. In fact, clinicians diagnose pyromania in a very small percent of chronic firesetters. We often view people with pyromania as deriving sexual pleasure from their behavior. In reality, this occurs in only a minority of cases. According to Doley (2003), the lack of accurate information about pyromania means that it is not possible to determine whether people with pyromania even exist, let alone are responsible for their behavior.

Q: *You be the judge:* Should we treat people with impulse-control disorders, whose behavior may be illegal and potentially harmful to others, as criminals or as having psychological disorders?

and they experience gratification afterwards. Because their focus is not on the items but on the act of stealing, individuals with kleptomania may give or throw away the stolen goods.

To make a diagnosis of kleptomania, clinicians must be unable to better account for the individual's stealing with another diagnosis of antisocial personality disorder, conduct disorder, or bipolar disorder (in a manic episode). There is overlap among the symptoms of kleptomania and mood, anxiety, and other impulse-control disorders, making it particularly important that clinicians engage in a thorough process of differential diagnosis (Grant, 2006).

Kleptomania has a number of significant effects on the individual's life, not the least of which is the fear of or reality of arrest. In one study of 101 adults (73 percent female), 69 percent were arrested and 21 percent were incarcerated. Over half were arrested on two or more occasions. Their symptoms started when they were 19 years old on average, and they shoplifted at least twice a week. The majority stole items of clothing, household goods, and groceries. To a lesser extent, they also stole from their friends, relatives, and

MINI CASE

Kleptomania

Gloria is a 45-year-old single Caucasian heterosexual woman. She works as an executive for a finance company. For the past few years, she has been under considerable stress and has worked long hours as the result of reorganizations in her company. As a teenager, Gloria occasionally took small, inexpensive items, such as hair barrettes and nail polish, from the drugstore, even though she could afford to pay for them. Lately, she has started shoplifting again. This time, her behavior has an intensity she cannot control. During her lunch hour, she often visits one of the large department stores near her office building, walks around until she finds something that catches her eye, and then slips it into her purse or pocket. Although Gloria has sworn to herself that she will never steal again, every few days she finds the tension so great that she cannot stay out of the stores.

places of employment. This study replicated those of smaller-scale investigations in reporting that people with kleptomania are likely to have high lifetime prevalence rates of co-occurring depressive disorders (43 percent), anxiety disorders (25 percent), other impulse-control disorders (42 percent), and drug abuse or dependence (18 percent). Suicide attempts are common among people with kleptomania (Grant, Odlaug, Davis, & Kim, 2009).

Studies of the neurobiology of kleptomania suggest that, like substance use disorders, this diagnosis is associated with altered dopamine, serotonin, and opioid receptor functions as well as changes in brain structures similar to those in people with cocaine dependence (Grant, Odlaug, & Kim, 2010).

Individuals with kleptomania may struggle with their symptoms for years before seeking treatment (Grant et al., 2015), perhaps because they fear prosecution or because they are ashamed of their illegal yet uncontrollable actions. Naltrexone, a therapeutic medication used to treat individuals with substance dependence, is one approach that appears to have had some effectiveness (Grant et al., 2009). Cognitive-behavioral treatments also are effective, although they may need to be used beyond the typical 12-session structure (Christianini et al., 2015).

10.5 Eating, Elimination, Sleep-Wake, and Impulse-Control Disorder: The Biopsychosocial Perspective

The disorders we have covered in this chapter represent a wide range of symptoms with a combination of biological causes, emotional difficulties, and sociocultural influences. A biopsychosocial approach therefore seems appropriate in understanding each. Moreover, these disorders have a developmental course. Eating and oppositional/conduct disorders appear to originate early in life. Over the course of adulthood, individuals may develop impulse-control disorders, and late in life, physiological changes may predispose older adults to sleep-wake disorders.

In the case of each category of disorder, clients can benefit from a multifaceted approach in which clinicians take into account these developmental and biopsychosocial influences. Some disorders, such as those in the sleep-wake category, may best be diagnosed through physiological tests such as polysomnography, even though treatment may focus on behavioral control of sleep. Individuals with symptoms of eating disorders should also be evaluated medically, but effective treatment requires a multipronged and team approach among mental health and medical professionals. The psychological and sociocultural components of impulse-control disorders tend to be more prominent in both diagnosis and treatment, although there may be biological contributions to each of these as well.

This wide range of disorders provides an excellent example of why a broad-ranging and integrative approach that takes a life-span view can be so important in understanding and treating psychological disorders. As research in these areas progresses, it is likely that clients in the future will benefit increasingly from interventions that take advantage of this multifaceted view.

Return to the Case: Rosa Nomirez

Rosa maintained her attendance at the day treatment program, which consisted of twice-weekly individual psychotherapy and several group therapy sessions every week. She saw a nutritionist who helped teach her the dangers of restricting her diet, and as a condition of the treatment she maintained a diet of at least 1,500 calories per day. At first she struggled with the change in her diet, which caused her much anxiety about becoming overweight. Her work in therapy and group therapy was aimed at maintaining a healthy body image and decreasing her unrealistic beliefs about being overweight.

As the weeks progressed, Rosa continued to gain weight and her distorted body image began to ameliorate. Her husband and family, once a source of tension and anxiety, became an important factor in her recovery from anorexia through their strong support and encouragement. Although Rosa continued to be concerned about becoming overweight, she learned the importance of nutrition and took on a more realistic view of her body. Rosa's depression remitted after the first few weeks of treatment, and she decided to stay in the program for a total of 3 months. After leaving the day treatment program, Rosa continued to see her therapist on a weekly basis.

Dr. Tobin's reflections: It is rare for an individual like Rosa to present for treatment due to actual concern about weight loss, given the typically distorted view these individuals have that they are overweight even when by objective standards they are severely underweight. Indeed, Rosa

ignored her family's encouragement to obtain treatment. Had she been under the age of 18, it would have been acceptable for her family to bring her in for treatment. In this case, however, Rosa's experience of depression motivated her to seek treatment. Some symptoms of depression are typical for individuals suffering from an eating disorder, and her symptoms did not warrant an independent diagnosis of depression. Although Rosa had experienced some eating-disordered behaviors as a teenager, she was able to maintain a normal weight throughout much of her young adulthood. This fluctuating pattern is quite typical in the case of eating disorders. By her report, she continued to maintain a negative body image, although this did not manifest in any symptoms until she became pregnant with her daughter and faced the reality of actual weight gain. This served as a stressor that triggered a pattern of restrictive dieting that led to extreme weight loss.

Finally, the cultural aspect of this case is important to consider. Rosa's family came from a culture much less fixated on body weight and physical appearance. The gap between her experiences growing up in U.S. society, where there is pressure for women to maintain a low body weight, and her family's Colombian culture was a great source of tension for her. Her family was unable to relate to her struggles with weight and body image, which served to increase her feelings of isolation. Emphasis on physical appearance is more prominent in developed countries such as the United States, which leads to higher rates of eating disorders in these countries.

SUMMARY

- People with anorexia nervosa experience three kinds of symptoms: (1) they refuse or are unable to maintain normal weight; (2) they have an intense fear of gaining weight or becoming fat, even though they may be grossly underweight; and (3) they have a distorted perception of the weight or shape of their body. People with bulimia nervosa alternate between eating large amounts of food in a short time (binge eating) and then compensating for the added calories by vomiting or

performing other extreme actions (purging). Binge-eating and avoidant/restrictive food intake disorder are additional forms of eating disorders. Pica and rumination disorder are associated with childhood. Biochemical abnormalities in the norepinephrine and serotonin neurotransmitter systems, perhaps with a genetic basis, are thought to be involved in eating disorders. The psychological perspective views eating disorders as developing in people who suffer a great deal of inner turmoil and pain, and who become obsessed with body issues, often turning to food for comfort and nurturance. According to cognitive theories, over time, people with eating disorders become trapped in their pathological patterns because of resistance to change. Within the sociocultural perspective, eating disorders have been explained in terms of family systems theories. Treatment of eating disorders requires a combination of approaches. While medications, particularly those affecting serotonin, are sometimes prescribed, it is also clear that psychotherapy is necessary, particularly that using cognitive-behavioral and interpersonal techniques. Family therapy, particularly when the client is a teen, can also be an important component of an intervention plan.

- Elimination disorders are most common in children younger than age 15, but they can be diagnosed in individuals of any age. Enuresis involves incontinence of urine, and encopresis involves incontinence of feces.

- Sleep-wake disorders include insomnia, narcolepsy, hypersomnolence, breathing sleep-related disorders, circadian rhythm sleep-wake disorders, and parasomnias. Each of these disorders is characterized by a severe disturbance in sleeping patterns. Insomnia can be identified by an inability to fall asleep or to remain sleeping, while narcolepsy and hypersomnolence involve sleeping too frequently and at inappropriate times. Breathing sleep-related disorders and circadian rhythm sleep-wake disorders, as well as parasomnias, can be characterized by abnormal bodily movements or behaviors, which can disrupt sleep or waking cycles.

- People with disruptive, impulse-control, and conduct disorders repeatedly engage in behaviors that are potentially harmful, feeling unable to stop themselves and experiencing a sense of desperation if they are thwarted from carrying out their impulsive behavior. Oppositional defiant disorder is characterized by angry or irritable mood, argumentative or defiant behavior, and vindictiveness that results in significant family or school problems.

- People with intermittent explosive disorder feel a recurrent inability to resist assaultive or destructive acts of aggression. Theorists propose that an interaction of biological and environmental factors leads to this condition. In terms of biology, serotonin seems to be implicated. In terms of psychological and sociocultural factors, theorists focus on the reinforcing qualities of emotional outbursts, as well as the effects of such behaviors on family systems and intimate relationships. Treatment may involve the prescription of medication, although psychotherapeutic methods would also be included in the intervention.

- People with pyromania are driven by the intense desire to prepare, set, and watch fires. This disorder seems to be rooted in childhood problems and firesetting behavior. In adulthood, people with pyromania typically have various dysfunctional characteristics, such as problems with substance abuse as well as relationship difficulties. Some treatment programs focus on children showing early signs of developing this disorder. With adults, various approaches are used, with the aim of focusing on the client's broader psychological problems, such as low self-esteem, depression, communication problems, and inability to control anger.

- People with kleptomania are driven by a persistent urge to steal, not because they wish to have the stolen objects but because they experience a thrill while engaging in the act of stealing. In addition to recommending medication, clinicians commonly treat people with kleptomania with behavioral treatments to help them control the urge to steal.

KEY TERMS

Anorexia nervosa (AN)
Avoidant/restrictive food intake
  disorder
Binge eating
Binge-eating disorder
Bulimia nervosa
Conduct disorder

Eating disorders
Elimination disorders
Encopresis
Enuresis
Impulse-control disorders
Intermittent explosive disorder
Kleptomania

Oppositional defiant disorder
Pica
Polysomnography
Purging
Pyromania
Rumination disorder

Paraphilic Disorders, Sexual Dysfunctions, and Gender Dysphoria

Learning Objectives

11.1 Identify the patterns of sexual behaviors that represent psychological disorders.

11.2 Compare and contrast paraphilic disorders and theories of their development.

11.3 Recognize symptoms of sexual dysfunction and understand treatment methods for these dysfunctions.

11.4 Comprehend theories and symptoms of gender dysphoria.

11.5 Explain the biopsychosocial perspective of paraphilic disorders, sexual dysfunctions, and gender dysphoria.

©iofoto/123 RF

Case Report: Shaun Boyden

Demographic information: 24-year-old single Caucasian transgender male, who identifies as asexual

Presenting problem: Shaun is seeking psychotherapy for anxiety and history of gender dysphoria. At the time of intake, he reported that he was looking into options to start hormone replacement therapy (HRT) in order to start medically transitioning from female to male. He was experiencing a significant increase in anxiety in the context of making that decision. Shaun added that he has limited social support in the way of people in his life who are affirming and supportive of his gender identity. He comes from a very conservative, religious upbringing, and his family has distanced themselves from him ever since he legally changed his name and started using male pronouns. Since graduating from college, Shaun has struggled to keep close friendships; a few friends stopped talking to him altogether after he came out to them as transgender. He reports that although he has always had a high baseline of anxiety in his life, he has noticed it is more challenging than ever to manage his anxious thoughts. He constantly feels tense and nervous, especially when people misgender him as female, address him by his legal name, or use female pronouns.

Shaun recalls that he was always a tomboy growing up, more interested in playing with boys than with girls. This was not a source of stress for him until he went through puberty and developed secondary sex characteristics, at which point he first started to feel what he now describes as gender dysphoria, or a sense that his identity did not match his biological characteristics. Shaun realized that he felt like a male and experienced distress around the notion that he appeared female to outside observers.

Given that he grew up in a small, conservative town with no visible queer or gender nonconforming people, Shaun felt ashamed and embarrassed for having these feelings, and very confused. After he started to do some research on the Internet, he realized he was not the only person who experienced these feelings, which was both relieving and terrifying to him. At one point, he ordered a breast binder online and wore it whenever he was alone in his room. At these times he noticed his gender dysphoria decreased dramatically, and he reveled in being able to imagine himself appearing as a young man instead of a young woman. In fact, the more he did to appear male or take on male characteristics, the more he felt affirmed in his own identity.

Shaun was never interested in dating while he was a teenager and recalls that he never had any feelings of sexual attraction to other people. He learned about the term *asexual* online and joined several online support groups that connected him to others who identified similarly. He was also able to find online trans communities to connect with. The support Shaun received through his online community was a stark comparison to that in his everyday life, in which he was expected to dress in feminine attire while with his family, who disapproved of his tomboy-style clothes.

While in college, Shaun continued to struggle with gender dysphoria and found it difficult to get support from the people in his life. Over time, he started doing more research on steps to transition medically, such as hormone therapy or "top" surgery (surgically removing breast tissue and creating a male-appearing chest), though he knew that his parents would never support any procedures so he would have to wait until he had his own health insurance. Shaun enjoyed having more freedom in college than he did at home, and so he felt more able to dress in stereotypically masculine attire and keep his hair short. However, much as in his hometown, there were few people on campus with whom he could relate, so he kept his thoughts about transitioning to himself.

After graduating from college, Shaun moved to a new city where he knew there was a thriving LGBTQ community, in hopes of being able to get more social support and pursue a medical transition in earnest. He started to go through the relevant steps, such as legally changing his name and changing his pronouns, and eventually he was able to get a job at a company where he felt he could be accepted for who he was. However, he experienced so much anxiety around meeting new people that he ended up isolated in his apartment except for going to work. Even at work he was withdrawn and kept mostly to himself.

Although there were medical providers he could consult about starting his transition, Shaun felt unable to make an appointment, because he thought that perhaps it was the wrong choice for him even though he knew he wanted to change his body to be more consistent with his gender identity. It was at this point that he came to psychotherapy for the first time.

Relevant history: Shaun has a history of mild anxiety that has never been clinically significant or impairing. He reports a history of gender dysphoria starting around the time of puberty and experiences significant distress related to it.

Case formulation: Shaun meets the relevant criteria for Gender Dysphoria in an Adult as defined by the *DSM-5*, given he has experienced dysphoria for more than 6 months and it is associated with clinically significant distress. Although he is currently experiencing some anxiety and social withdrawal, these symptoms are likely more related to his long-standing gender dysphoria and do not meet criteria for an additional diagnosis of anxiety disorder. Given that his anxiety also decreases with his dysphoria, and that he has never experienced anxiety apart from dysphoria, this further supports ruling out an additional diagnosis.

Treatment plan: Shaun agreed to start meeting for weekly psychotherapy, in order to get support for and process his feelings of gender dysphoria. Getting support in an affirmative environment such as therapy can help Shaun to think through his feelings about medically transitioning more fully. Therapy can also focus on identifying ways for Shaun to start building more social support for himself in his local community and work through some of the anxiety that keeps him from connecting more with others.

Sarah Tobin, PhD

11.1 What Patterns of Sexual Behavior Represent Psychological Disorders?

When it comes to sexuality, deciding which patterns of behavior represent psychological disorders becomes a complicated process, perhaps more so than in other areas of human behavior. When we are evaluating the "normality" of a given sexual behavior, the context is extremely important, as are customs and mores, which change across cultures and over time. Attitudes and behaviors related to sexuality are continually evolving.

As an example of the cultural relativity of deciding what is sexually normative, consider the relatively recent emergence of addiction to sex over the Internet. A survey of more than 1,500 mental health professionals revealed 11 categories of problematic behavior among their clients, with the second most prevalent involving Internet pornography (Figure 1).

Perhaps because the topic has so many taboos, there was little scientific research on sexual disorders until relatively recently. In 1886, the Austro-German psychiatrist Richard Freiherr von Krafft-Ebing wrote a comprehensive treatise called *Psychopathia Sexualis*

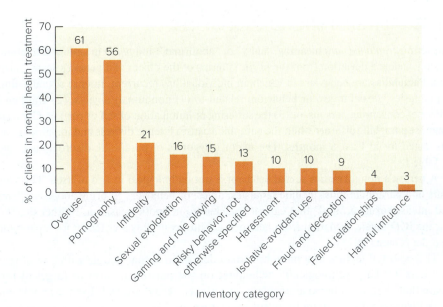

FIGURE 1 Percentage of Clinicians Reporting Client-Related Problematic Internet Experiences

SOURCE: Mitchell, K. J., Becker-Blease, K. A., & Finkelhor, D. (2005). Inventory of problematic internet experiences encountered in clinical practice. *Professional Psychology: Research and Practice,* 36, 489–509. American Psychological Association.

(1886/1950), in which he documented a variety of forms of what he called "sexual perversity," which also linked sexual fantasy with the compulsion to kill.

The three individuals credited with paving the way for contemporary research on human sexuality are Alfred Kinsey, William Masters, and Virginia Johnson. Kinsey was the first to conduct a large-scale survey of sexual behavior in the United States (Kinsey, Pomeroy, & Martin, 1948; Kinsey, Pomeroy, Martin, & Gebhard, 1953). Masters and Johnson (1966, 1970) were the first investigators to study sexual behavior in the laboratory. The Kinsey Institute at Indiana University continues to support research on human sexuality, and the field of sexual medicine has become a specialty in its own right.

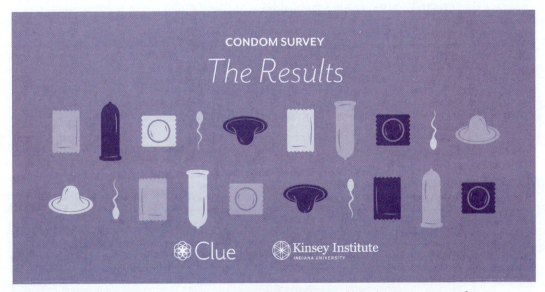

The Kinsey Institute at Indiana University, founded in 1947, continues to be an important source of research on critical issues in sexuality, gender, and reproduction, as in the case shown here of surveys on condom use.

©Hello Clue

11.2 Paraphilic Disorders

The term *paraphilia* (*para* meaning "faulty" or "abnormal," and *philia* meaning "attraction") literally means a deviation from the norm in terms of the object of a person's sexual attraction. **Paraphilias** are behaviors in which an individual has recurrent, intense sexually arousing fantasies, sexual urges, or behaviors related to (1) nonhuman objects, (2) children or other nonconsenting persons, or (3) the suffering or humiliation of self or partner. Clinicians diagnose **paraphilic disorder** when the paraphilia causes intense distress and impairment and has lasted for at least 6 months. The major categories of paraphilic disorders are listed in Table 1.

A person's nonnormative sexual behavior is not pathological in and of itself. The symptoms of a paraphilia must include fantasies, urges, or behaviors to bring about "recurrent and intense sexual arousal" that cannot be achieved in another fashion. Neither the *DSM* nor the ICD regard deviation from heterosexual intercourse as a criterion for a paraphilic disorder (Giami, 2015).

The essential feature of a paraphilic disorder, then, is that people with one of these disorders are so psychologically dependent on the particular form or target of their desire that they are otherwise unable to experience sexual arousal. Even if people with these disorders do not actually fulfill their urges or fantasies, they are obsessed with thoughts about acting upon them. Their attraction can become so strong and compelling that they lose sight of any goals other than achieving sexual fulfillment in this specific way. During periods in which the individual feels especially stressed, the symptoms may become more intense.

The life course of paraphilic disorders is that they begin in adolescence and tend to be chronic; however, the urge to commit acts that others consider sexually deviant may decline in later life (Barbaree & Blanchard, 2008). Paraphilic disorders also are more prevalent in men than women (Långström & Seto, 2006).

Having a paraphilic disorder is not illegal, but acting on paraphilic urges may be. As a result, the person who reports having such a disorder runs the risk of being arrested, convicted, and then required to register as a sex offender. Because people do not voluntarily report paraphilias to mental health care professionals, these disorders can be difficult to

paraphilias

Behaviors in which an individual has recurrent, intense sexually arousing fantasies, sexual urges, or behaviors involving (1) nonhuman objects, (2) children or other nonconsenting persons, or (3) the suffering or humiliation of self or partner.

paraphilic disorder

Diagnosis in which a paraphilia causes distress and impairment.

TABLE 1 **Paraphilic Disorders**

Disorder	Characteristics
Pedophilic disorder	Sexual arousal from the presence of children or adolescents
Exhibitionistic disorder	Sexual arousal from exposing the genitals to unsuspecting stranger
Voyeuristic disorder	Sexual pleasure from observing nudity or sexual activity of others
Fetishistic disorder and partialism	Sexual arousal from an object (fetishism) or from a part of the body (partialism)
Frotteuristic disorder	Sexual urges about and sexually arousing fantasies of rubbing against or fondling a nonconsenting person
Sexual masochism and sexual sadism	Sexual arousal from being made to suffer (masochism) or from inflicting suffering on another person (sadism)
Transvestic disorder	Cross-dressing associated with intense distress or impairment

MINI CASE

Pedophilic Disorder Nonexclusive Type

Kirk is a 38-year-old married heterosexual Caucasian male. Shortly following his marriage, Kirk began developing an inappropriately close relationship with Amy, his 8-year-old stepdaughter. It seemed to start out innocently, when he took extra time to give her bubble baths and back rubs. But after only 2 months of their living in the same house, Kirk's behavior went outside the boundary of common parental physical affection. After his wife left for work early each morning, Kirk invited Amy into his bed on the pretext that she could watch cartoons on the television in his bedroom. Kirk would begin stroking Amy's hair and gradually proceed to more sexually explicit behavior, encouraging her to touch his genitals, saying that it would be "good" for her to learn about what "daddies" are like. Confused and frightened, Amy did as she was told. Kirk reinforced compliance to his demands by threatening that, if Amy told anyone about their secret, he would deny everything and severely beat her. This behavior continued for more than 2 years, until one day Kirk's wife returned home unexpectedly and caught him engaging in this behavior.

diagnose, and self-reports in surveys may actually prove to be more informative (Wilpert, 2018). Online reporting of paraphilias, in turn, produces more self-reports than do telephone surveys (Joyal & Carpentier, 2017).

Pedophilic Disorder

People diagnosed with **pedophilic disorder** are sexually aroused by children or adolescents. Clinicians use this diagnosis for adults who are at least 18 years of age and at least 5 years older than the children to whom they are attracted. The key feature of this disorder is that the individual experiences an intensity of sexual arousal when with children that may be equal to, if not greater than, that which he or she experiences with individuals who are physically mature. This diagnosis includes people who have acted upon their urges with children as well as those whose attraction is represented by viewing Internet pornography involving children but who do not act on those urges (Berlin, 2014).

As mentioned, it is difficult to obtain prevalence data on paraphilic disorders, and particularly on pedophilic disorder given the illegality of the behavior. Perhaps the best estimate comes from a study in which researchers examined its prevalence through an online survey. If they could be assured of not getting caught, 6 percent of men and 2 percent of women stated that they would have sex with a child. The likelihood of these same individuals viewing Internet sex with children was somewhat higher, with 9 percent of men and 3 percent of women stating they would view child pornography. For both men and women, interest in sex with children was associated with higher rates of antisocial or criminal behavior, as well as higher rates of abuse in childhood (Wurtele, Simons, & Moreno, 2014).

The data on the prevalence of child sexual abuse cases in the United States provide another potential source of prevalence data on pedophilic disorder. Based on estimates of cases of sexual abuse, the number of children per year in the United States alone numbers slightly over 135,000 (Sedlak et al., 2010).

Another way to approximate the prevalence of pedophilia is to use reports of sexual assault of children. This measure yields an estimate of nearly two thirds of children under the age of 18. The

pedophilic disorder
A paraphilic disorder in which an adult is sexually aroused by children or adolescents.

Individuals with pedophilic disorder suffer from uncontrollable urges to engage in sexual activity with young children.

©Roman Märzinger/Media Bakery

MINI CASE

Exhibitionistic Disorder, Sexually Aroused by Exposing Genitals to Physically Mature Individuals

Ernie is a 28-year-old single African American heterosexual male. He is in jail for the fourth time in the past 2 years for public exposure. As Ernie explained to the court psychologist who interviewed him, he has "flashed" much more often than he has been apprehended. In each case, he has chosen as his victim an unsuspecting college-age woman, and he jumps out at her from behind a doorway, a tree, or a car parked at the sidewalk. He has never touched any of these girls, instead fleeing the scene after having exposed himself. On some occasions, he masturbates immediately after the exposure, fantasizing that his victim was swept off her feet by his sexual prowess and pleaded with him to make love to her. This time, his latest victim responded by calling the police to track him down. Ernie felt crushed and humiliated by an overwhelming sense of his sexual inadequacy.

most frequent form of sexual assault is forcible fondling (45 percent) followed in frequency by forcible rape (42 percent). Compared to older victims, those who are 18 and under are more likely to be victimized in a residence, and most cases of sexual assault against children occur in the afternoon. Nearly all offenders reported to the law (96 percent) are male; their most frequently reported ages range from 15 to 20 years (Snyder, 2000).

Exhibitionistic Disorder

exhibitionistic disorder
A paraphilic disorder in which a person has intense sexual urges and arousing fantasies involving the exposure of genitals to a stranger.

People who engage in exhibitionism have fantasies, urges, and behaviors suggesting that they derive sexual arousal from exposing their genitals to an unsuspecting stranger. In **exhibitionistic disorder**, these fantasies, urges, and behaviors cause significant distress or impairment.

Exhibitionistic disorder begins early in adulthood and persists throughout life. In one study of a small sample of male outpatients with this disorder (Grant, 2005), researchers found that almost all also had another psychiatric disorder including major depressive disorder and substance abuse. Over half experienced suicidal thoughts. This was one of the few studies in a clinical setting of people with the disorder who were not criminal offenders. In another investigation of men from a sample of police cases, approximately one quarter also suffered from another psychological disorder (Bader, Schoeneman-Morris, Scalora, & Casady, 2008). The data from these samples are consistent with the findings from the Swedish national sample of nonclinical, noncriminal offenders, whose exhibitionism was also related to the presence of other psychological disorders (Långström & Seto, 2006).

The existence of comorbid conditions such as major depressive disorder and substance abuse, along with the reluctance of people with the disorder to come forward, present numerous challenges both for developing an understanding of the causes of the disorder and for planning its treatment (Murphy & Page, 2008). The most important step in treatment is accurately assessing both the disorder itself and these comorbid conditions (Morin & Levenson, 2008).

Voyeuristic Disorder

voyeuristic disorder
A paraphilic disorder in which the individual has a compulsion to derive sexual gratification from observing the nudity or sexual activity of others.

People who engage in voyeurism derive sexual pleasure from observing the nudity or sexual activity of others who are unaware of being watched. Correspondingly, people with **voyeuristic disorder** are sexually aroused by observing an unsuspecting person who is naked, in the process of disrobing, or engaging in sexual activity. Voyeurism is related to exhibitionism and is the most common of the paraphilic disorders. People with either of these disorders are also likely to engage in sadomasochistic behaviors and cross-dressing (Långström, 2010; Långström & Seto, 2006).

Some people obtain sexual excitement by engaging in voyeuristic activities, such as looking at unsuspecting victims with binoculars.

©ColorBlind Images/Blend Images LLC

Fetishistic Disorder

People with **fetishistic disorder** are aroused by an object not specifically intended to be used in a sexual context. There is a wide range of objects to which people with fetishistic disorder can develop attachments. However, they do not include articles of clothing associated with cross-dressing or objects such as vibrators that people use in tactile genital stimulation. In a related disorder, **partialism**, the individual is sexually aroused by the presence of a specific body part. Again, as with all paraphilic disorders, the attraction to objects or body parts must be recurrent, intense, and have lasted at least 6 months.

Fetishistic behavior is often conceptualized as action by a solitary individual who practices it without a partner. However, taking advantage of an online survey approach that, as noted earlier, allows for more accurate and widespread estimates of paraphilic behavior, researchers have established that partnered activity is indeed more common. In fact, partnered fetishistic activity was rated by those reporting in this format as more sexually satisfying than solitary fetishistic activity (Rees & Garcia, 2017a). Furthermore, although having the fetishistic object may be preferred, individuals reporting this activity do not necessarily require its actual presence (Rees & Garcia, 2017b).

fetishistic disorder
A paraphilic disorder in which the individual is preoccupied with an object and depends on this object rather than sexual intimacy with a partner for achieving sexual gratification.

partialism
A paraphilic disorder in which the person is interested solely in sexual gratification from a specific body part, such as feet.

Frotteuristic Disorder

The term *frotteurism* derives from the French word *frotter* (meaning "to rub") and *frotteur* (the person who does the rubbing). The person with **frotteuristic disorder** has recurrent, intense sexual urges and sexually arousing fantasies of rubbing against or fondling a

frotteuristic disorder
A paraphilic disorder in which the individual has intense sexual urges and sexually arousing fantasies of rubbing against or fondling an unsuspecting stranger.

MINI CASE

Fetishistic Disorder, Nonliving Objects

Johann is a 45-year-old single Caucasian heterosexual male. For several years, Johann has been breaking into cars and stealing boots or shoes, and he has come close to being caught on several occasions. Johann takes great pleasure in the excitement he experiences each time he engages in the ritualistic behavior of procuring a shoe or boot and going to a secret place to fondle it and masturbate. In his home, he has a closet filled with dozens of women's shoes, and he chooses from this selection the particular shoe with which he will masturbate. Sometimes he sits in a shoe store and keeps watch for women trying on shoes. After a woman tries on and rejects a particular pair, Johann scoops the shoes from the floor and takes them to the register, explaining to the clerk that the shoes are a gift for his wife. With great eagerness and anticipation, he rushes home to engage once again in his masturbatory ritual.

Individuals with a fetish gain sexual excitement from everyday, nonsexual objects such as feet.

©Image Source/Getty Images

sexual masochism disorder
A paraphilic disorder marked by an attraction to achieving sexual gratification by having painful stimulation applied to one's own body.

sexual sadism disorder
A paraphilic disorder in which sexual gratification is derived from activities that harm, or from urges to harm, another person.

transvestic disorder
Diagnosis applied to individuals who engage in transvestic behavior and have the symptoms of a paraphilic disorder.

nonconsenting person. Among men diagnosed with paraphilic disorders, approximately 10 to 14 percent have committed acts of frotteurism (Långström, 2010).

Men with frotteuristic disorder seek out crowded places, such as a rush-hour subway train, where they can safely rub up against their unsuspecting victims, and public transportation does seem to be a major site at which this behavior takes place. Victims report feeling violated and may go out of their way to avoid crowds, yet few if any file police reports (Clark, Jeglic, Calkins, & Tatar, 2016).

Sexual Masochism and Sexual Sadism Disorders

The term *masochism* describes the act of seeking pleasure from being in pain. People with **sexual masochism disorder** are sexually aroused by being beaten, bound, or otherwise made to suffer. Conversely, people with **sexual sadism disorder** become sexually aroused by the physical or psychological suffering of another person. *DSM-5* does not classify the use of bondage, domination, and sadomasochism (BDSM) as a disorder in and of itself.

As is true for several of the paraphilic disorders, there is very little in the way of scientific research on sexual masochism and sexual sadism disorders. People with these disorders tend not to seek treatment because they feel no need to change, and because their behaviors often occur in the context of a consensual relationship. Even among consenting adults, acts of sexual masochism and sadism are shrouded in secrecy. Yet preference for BDSM activities remains relatively common, with 46.8 percent of respondents in an online Belgian sample reporting that they had performed at least one BDSM-related activity and an additional 22 percent indicating they have or have had fantasies about it. A smaller but significant 12.5 percent of the online sample indicated performing at least one BDSM-related activity on a regular basis (Holvoet et al., 2017).

Transvestic Disorder

Transvestism, also called "cross-dressing," refers to the behavior of dressing in the clothing of the other sex. Men make up the large majority of individuals who show this behavior. A clinician would diagnose an individual with **transvestic disorder** only if he showed the symptoms of a paraphilic disorder, namely distress or impairment. Psychologists would consider a man who frequently cross-dresses and derives sexual pleasure from this behavior as a transvestite, but they would not diagnose him with a disorder (Blanchard, 2010). *DSM-IV-TR* limited this behavior to heterosexual males, but *DSM-5* opened the diagnosis to women or gay men who have this sexual interest.

MINI CASE

Frotteuristic Disorder

Bruce is a 40-year-old married Caucasian heterosexual male. As a delivery messenger in a large city, he rides crowded subways throughout the day. He thrives on this opportunity to become sexually stimulated by rubbing up against unsuspecting women. Having developed some cagey techniques, Bruce is often able to take advantage of women without their realizing what he is doing. As the day proceeds, his level of sexual excitation grows, so that by the evening rush hour he targets a particularly attractive woman and only at that point allows himself to reach orgasm.

MINI CASE

Sexual Sadism and Sexual Masochism Disorders

Jalen is a 55-year-old married biracial heterosexual male. For a number of years, he has insisted that his wife Camille subject him to demeaning and abusive sexual behavior. In the early years of their relationship, Jalen's requests were relatively innocent pleas that Camille pinch him and bite his chest while they were sexually intimate. Over time, however, his desire for pain increased and the nature of the pain changed. At present, the two engage in what they call "special sessions," during which Camille handcuffs Jalen to the bed and inflicts various forms of torture. Camille goes along with Jalen's requests that she surprise him with new ways of inflicting pain, and she has developed a repertoire of behaviors ranging from burning his skin with matches to cutting him with razor blades. Camille and Jalen have no interest in sexual intimacy other than that involving pain.

Theories and Treatment of Paraphilic Disorders

As we mentioned at the outset, deciding what is normal in the area of sexuality is an issue fraught with difficulty and controversy. Critics argued against including several of the paraphilic disorders in *DSM-5* because they felt that to do so pathologizes a sexual behavior that happens to be infrequent. Moreover, they maintained that breaking the law is not a sufficient basis for determining that an individual engaging in a paraphilic behavior has a psychological disorder. This criticism is particularly leveled at the diagnoses of exhibitionistic, voyeuristic, and frotteuristic disorder, which don't have victims in the same sense as do the other paraphilic disorders (Hinderliter, 2010).

Researchers and advocates within the field of sexual sadism and sexual masochism were critical of including these disorders in *DSM-5* at all, arguing that they do not share the qualities of the other paraphilic disorders because they are engaged in by consenting adults (Wright, 2010). The *DSM* authors, they believe, should base their decisions about psychiatric diagnoses on empirical evidence rather than on political or moral considerations (Shindel & Moser, 2011). The present system, though imperfect, nevertheless satisfies some of its critics in that behaviors such as BDSM in and of themselves are not regarded as disorders (Wright, 2014).

To be sure, many challenges face researchers who attempt to understand the causes of a disorder that leads to so much damage and has so many legal ramifications. Apart from the difficulty of identifying people with the disorder, even those who are available for scrutiny by researchers may not represent the population from which they are drawn. For example, most of the people we can study for disorders involving criminal acts such as pedophilic disorder are likely to have been arrested. Even in paraphilic disorders that do not involve a criminal offense, self-selection can determine who decides to participate in research. The problem of unrepresentative samples means that prevalence estimate data are likely to be biased and unreliable.

The main point to keep in mind is that by defining the disorders in this area as accompanying intense distress or impairment, authors of the *DSM-5* hoped to avoid judging a behavior's normality and instead to base the criteria for a disorder on an individual's subjective experience of distress or degree of impairment in everyday life.

Transvestism is considered a psychological disorder only when it causes the individual to feel distress as a result of the cross-dressing behaviors. Transvestism is also distinct from transgenderism in that individuals who engage in cross-dressing typically identify with their biological gender.

©ValaGrenier/Getty Images

MINI CASE

Transvestic Disorder, with Autogynephilia

Phil is a 48-year-old married Caucasian heterosexual male. In the evenings, when his wife leaves the house for her part-time job, Phil often goes to a secret hiding place in his workshop. In a locked cabinet, Phil keeps a small wardrobe of women's underwear, stockings, high heels, and dresses, and makeup and a wig. Closing all the blinds in the house and shutting off his phone, Phil dresses in these clothes and fantasizes that he is being pursued by several men. After about 2 hours, he usually masturbates to the point of orgasm as he imagines that a sexual partner is pursuing him. Then he packs up the women's clothes and puts them away. Though primarily limiting his cross-dressing activity to the evenings, Phil thinks about it frequently during the day, which causes him to become sexually excited and to wish he could get away from work, go home, and put on his special clothes. Knowing that he cannot, he wears women's underwear under his work clothes, and he sneaks off to the men's room to masturbate in response to the sexual stimulation he derives from feeling the silky sensation against his body.

Biological Perspectives Although it recognizes the role of psychological and sociocultural factors, the biological perspective emphasizes altered genetic, hormonal, and sensory factors in paraphilic disorders (Guay, 2009). For men, the male sex hormone testosterone is the focus of theories and treatment, but dopamine and serotonin also play roles in male sexuality. Consequently, the World Federation of Societies of Biological Psychiatry advocates treatment of paraphilic disorders in men that includes SSRIs, antiandrogens, and luteinizing hormone-release hormone (LHRH), which acts as a suppressor in men for the production of testosterone (Thibaut et al., 2010).

Medications that stimulate LHRH receive support as effective treatments in reducing paraphilic symptoms in men. However, they carry the drawback that by reducing testosterone below the level achieved even by castration, they also decrease conventional nonparaphilic sexual activity and desire. Medications that target LHRH also result in a number of side effects such as loss of bone mineral content, cardiovascular disease, fatigue, sleep disorders, and hot flashes and therefore are not recommended for lifelong treatment (Turner & Briken, 2018).

Psychological Perspectives Freud's psychoanalytic understanding of the paraphilic disorders was the dominant psychological perspective throughout the twentieth century. According to Freud, these disorders were "perversions" representing both biological

The World Federation of Societies of Biological Psychiatry has proposed guidelines for the medical treatment of people with paraphilic disorder that are staged according to the severity of the individual's symptoms.

©Paul Bradbury/AGE Fotostock

and psychological factors in early development (Thibaut et al., 2010). The influential theorist John Money (Money & Ehrhardt, 1973/1996), in contrast, regarded paraphilias as the expressions of **lovemaps**—internal representations of an individual's sexual fantasies and preferred practices. People form lovemaps in the late childhood years, when they first begin to discover and test ideas regarding sexuality. "Misprints" in this process can result in the establishment of sexual habits and practices that deviate from the norm. A paraphilia, according to this view, is due to a lovemap gone awry. The individual is, in a sense, programmed to act out fantasies that are socially unacceptable and potentially harmful.

The majority of the psychological literature on paraphilic disorders focuses on pedophilic disorder. A common theme in this literature is the idea of a "victim-to-abuser cycle" or "abused-abusers phenomena," meaning that abusers were themselves abused at some point in their lives, probably when they were young. Arguing against these explanations is the fact that most abuse victims do not go on to abuse or molest children. On the other hand, some people with pedophilic disorder who were abused as children show an age preference that matches their age when they were abused, suggesting that they are replicating behaviors that were directed toward them as children.

Treatments within the psychological perspective seem most effective when combining individual with group therapy. In the group context, in particular, empathy training can help these individuals understand how their victims are feeling. Clinicians may also help clients learn how to control their sexual impulses. Relapse prevention, much as in treatment of

lovemap
The representations of an individual's sexual fantasies and preferred practices.

You Be the Judge

Treatment for Sex Offenders

The paraphilic disorders present an ethical challenge to psychologists because of their potential link to the harming of others, particularly children and young teenagers. Treatment must balance the rights of the clients, including the right to confidentiality, informed consent, and self-determination, against the clinician's duty to prevent harm, both to others and to the client. Since treatment is often court-mandated, another question is whether it represents punishment rather than therapy.

Social workers David Prescott and Jill Levenson (2010), both of whom have an extensive background in treating sex offenders, suggest that clinicians can conduct mandated treatment in a manner consistent with the clinician's code of ethics. Mandated treatment, they argue, rather than representing punishment, is intended to assist offenders to correct the behaviors that were of harm to others and themselves. Moreover, the ethical standards that clinicians abide by regarding confidentiality are consistent with the "duty to warn" component of sex offender therapy: "Mandatory reporting trumps privilege" (Prescott & Levenson, 2010, p. 278). Second, regarding the client's right to self-determination, sex offenders are not the only individuals for whom the law mandates therapy. Child abusers and drivers arrested for operating a vehicle while intoxicated are two examples, but there are other cases in which the justice system gives family members, for example, an ultimatum to receive treatment for such behaviors as compulsive gambling.

Individuals who choose to work with sex offenders, according to Prescott and Levenson (2010), do so out of compassion and a desire to rehabilitate their clients so that they can become functioning members of society. They have found a way to empathize with clients who have committed sexually violent acts without judging the offenders, and to overcome the "natural human reaction" of "disdain" (p. 282) for these individuals.

Q: *You be the judge:* Do you agree that the principles of human rights and the ethical guidelines presented by professional associations serve to protect sex offenders when they enter into therapy? Should the justice system even offer sex offender therapy, or should these individuals simply be incarcerated? On the other hand, is rehabilitation a realistic goal, as Prescott and Levenson claim, or are sex offenders beyond help?

addictive disorders, helps clients accept that even if they slip, this does not mean that they cannot overcome their disorder. Clinicians no longer recommend a method used in the past known as aversion training, in which they teach clients to associate negative outcomes with sexual attraction toward children and use masturbatory reconditioning to change their orientation away from children (Hall, 2007).

Psychotherapy is the recommended treatment at the first level, particularly CBT (Assumpção et al., 2014). At increasing levels of severity, defined according to whether treatment is effective or not, clinicians add hormonal treatment starting with antiandrogens, progressing to progesterone, and finally neurohormones that act on the areas in the pituitary gland that control the release of sex hormones. At this point in treatment, appropriate only for the most severe cases, the goal is complete suppression of sexual desire and activity (Thibaut et al., 2010).

Another focus of treatment may be clinicians themselves. Due to stigmatization of people with these disorders, particularly pedophilic disorder, clinicians may be less willing to offer them treatment. In one intervention, researchers presented therapists in training with a 10-minute video that effectively challenged typical myths about pedophilia, such as the idea that it is a choice and that people with this disorder act upon their urges (Jahnke, Philipp, & Hoyer, 2015).

11.3 Sexual Dysfunctions

sexual dysfunction
An abnormality in an individual's sexual responsiveness and reactions.

Sexual arousal leads to a set of physiological changes throughout the body, often culminating in orgasm. A **sexual dysfunction** is a marked divergence in an individual's response in the sexual response cycle, along with feelings of significant distress or impairment. To consider it a sexual dysfunction, clinicians must not be able to attribute this divergence to a psychological disorder, effects of a substance such as a drug of abuse or medication, or a general medical condition.

The *DSM-5* differentiates between sexual dysfunctions that are lifelong and those that are acquired, as well as whether they are generalized or situational. People with a lifelong sexual dysfunction experienced its symptoms continually since the time at which they became sexually active. By contrast, people with acquired sexual dysfunctions were asymptomatic prior to developing the symptoms. Those dysfunctions that are situational occur with only certain types of sexual stimulation, situations, or partners. Generalized dysfunctions affect the individual in all sexual situations.

Legendary researchers Masters and Johnson (1966, 1970) were the first scientists to systematically observe the sexual responses of men and women under controlled laboratory conditions. They identified four phases of the sexual response cycle—excitement (arousal), plateau, orgasm, and resolution.

During the excitement (or arousal) stage, the individual's sexual interest heightens, and the body prepares for sexual intercourse (vaginal lubrication in the female, penile erection in the male). Sexual excitement continues to build during the plateau phase, and during the orgasm phase the individual experiences muscular contractions in the genital area that bring intense sensations of pleasure. The resolution phase is a period of return to a physiologically normal state. People differ in their typical patterns of sexual activity; some progress more readily through the phases and others at a slower pace. Not every sexual encounter necessarily includes all phases, however, and arousal and desire may occur simultaneously with the processing of sexual stimuli (Basson, 2001).

Physiological factors and chronic health conditions are strongly related to the risk of developing sexual dysfunctions. These conditions can include diabetes, cardiovascular disease, other genitourinary diseases, psychological disorders, other chronic diseases, and smoking. In the case of some of these medical conditions, it is the medication and not the condition itself that places the individual at risk. For example, medications that treat high blood pressure can have the side effect of lowering sexual responsiveness in men (Lewis et al., 2010).

Not surprisingly, perhaps, reliable prevalence data on these disorders are few. Definitions of many disorders have changed periodically, leading to differing estimates (McCabe &

Connaughton, 2014), and people are reluctant to report they are experiencing symptoms. Only recently have researchers begun to arrive at measurable criteria based on the unique assessment methods these disorders require. Fortunately, work toward the *DSM-5* led to improved and more rigorous diagnostic procedures that eventually will lead to more reliable data sources.

In a research context, the Female Sexual Function Index (Rosen et al., 2000) is an empirical measure used in a number of studies to investigate the prevalence of sexual dysfunctions in women and to gauge the efficacy of treatment. The FSFI is a 19-item multidimensional self-report scale that asks questions related to sexual functioning within the past month, with subscales related to specific domains of lubrication, desire, subjective arousal, orgasm, satisfaction, and pain associated with intercourse. Another, more behaviorally oriented approach asks individuals to record sexual events on a daily basis in the form of a self-report diary (van Nes et al., 2017).

Arousal Disorders

People whose sexual disorders occur during the initial phases of the sexual response cycle have low or no sexual desire or are unable to achieve physiological arousal. As a result, they may avoid having or be unable to have sexual intercourse.

The man with **male hypoactive sexual desire disorder** has an abnormally low level of sexual activity or may have no interest in sexual activity. In addition, a man with this disorder either has relatively few or no sexual fantasies. A woman with **female sexual interest/arousal disorder** is interested in having intercourse, but her body does not physiologically respond during the arousal phase. The *DSM-5* merged female hypoactive desire dysfunction and female arousal dysfunction into a single syndrome called female sexual interest/arousal disorder because the two dysfunctions could not reliably be distinguished.

Some reports indicate that low sexual desire is relatively prevalent among women, with estimates in some samples ranging as high as 55 percent, although the majority of studies from around the world place the prevalence at closer to 40 percent (Clayton & Valladares Juarez, 2017). In general, the percent of women who are distressed about having low sexual desire is far lower than is true for men. Therefore, if a sexual dysfunction were defined for women that was characterized by low levels of desire, it would apply to a large percentage of women, and not necessarily those who were truly distressed.

Because low sexual desire seems to be relatively common, the issue for diagnosing women is that loss of desire might not be the best or only criterion to use in deciding who has a sexual dysfunction. *DSM-5* therefore defines this disorder as including loss of sexual interest across a range of behaviors instead of only loss of interest. The behaviors that suggest low sexual interest include lower levels of arousal, fewer erotic thoughts, less enjoyment of sexual activity, and less intense sensations during sexual activity (Brotto, 2010).

male hypoactive sexual desire disorder
A sexual dysfunction in which the individual has an abnormally low level of interest in sexual activity.

female sexual interest/arousal disorder
A sexual dysfunction characterized by a persistent or recurrent inability to attain or maintain normal physiological and psychological arousal responses during sexual activity.

MINI CASE

Female Interest/Arousal Disorder, Acquired

With the pressures of managing a full-time advertising job and raising 3-year-old twins, Carol says that she has "no time or energy" for sexual relations with her husband, Bob. In fact, they have not been sexually intimate since the birth of their children. Initially, Bob tried to be understanding and to respect the fact that Carol was recovering from a very difficult pregnancy and delivery. As the months went by, however, he became increasingly impatient and critical. The more he pressured Carol for sexual closeness, the more angry and depressed she became. Carol feels that she loves Bob, but she does not think about sex and can't imagine ever being sexual again. She is saddened by the effect this change has had on her marriage but feels little motivation to try to change.

Advertisements for male erectile enhancement drugs such as this are widely found on the Internet.

©Photo Mere Technology/Alamy Stock Photo

erectile disorder

Sexual dysfunction in which a man cannot attain or maintain an erection during sexual activity that is sufficient to allow him to initiate or maintain sexual activity.

Men with **erectile disorder** cannot attain or maintain an erection during sexual activity that is sufficient to allow them to initiate or maintain sexual activity. Even if they are able to achieve an erection, they are unable to penetrate or to experience pleasure during a sexual encounter. Although once thought of as either physiologically or psychologically caused, erectile disorder is now understood as having multiple causes that cannot be clearly separated into these two categories (Segraves, 2010). A very rough estimate of the prevalence of erectile disorder is 26 to 28 per 1,000 man-years, with higher rates among older men (Lewis et al., 2010).

Disorders Involving Orgasm

female orgasmic disorder

A sexual dysfunction in which a woman experiences problems having an orgasm during sexual activity.

Inability to achieve orgasm, a distressing delay in achieving orgasm, or reduced intensity of orgasm constitutes **female orgasmic disorder**. Although previous versions of the *DSM* regarded orgasm resulting from clitoral stimulation as distinct from that resulting from intercourse, the *DSM-IV-TR* removed this criterion, recognizing that women can experience orgasm through a wide variety of types of stimulation. The *DSM-5* similarly does not distinguish between sources of orgasm in defining the criteria for this disorder. These changes reflect the recognition that not all women similarly experience the sexual response cycle described by Masters and Johnson (1966).

The factors relating to a woman's reporting of female orgasmic disorder include stress, anxiety, depression, relationship satisfaction, and age-related changes in the genital area that can lead to pain, discomfort, irritation, or bleeding (Laumann & Waite, 2008). Size and location of the clitoris may also relate to a woman's ability to achieve orgasm (Oakley et al., 2014).

MINI CASE

Erectile Disorder, Acquired

Kai is 34 years old and has been dating the same woman for more than a year. This is his first serious relationship, and the woman is the first person with whom he has been sexually intimate. During the past 6 months, they have frequently tried to have intercourse, but each time they have become frustrated by Kai's inability to maintain an erection for more than a few minutes. Every time this happens, Kai becomes very upset, despite his girlfriend's reassurance that things will work out better next time. His anxiety level heightens every time he thinks about the fact that he is in his midthirties, sexually active for the first time in his life, and encountering such frustrating difficulties. He fears he is "impotent" and will never have a normal sex life.

MINI CASE

Female Orgasmic Disorder, Lifelong

Like many of her friends, Margaret often wondered as a teenager what intercourse and orgasm would feel like. When she later became sexually active in college, she realized that she was probably still missing something, since she did not feel "rockets going off" as she had imagined. In fact, she never could experience orgasm when she was with a man in any kind of sexual activity. When Margaret fell in love with Howard, she fervently hoped that things would improve. However, even though he made her feel more sensual pleasure than anyone else, her response to him always stopped just short of climax. She approached every sexual encounter with anxiety and tended to feel depressed and inadequate afterward. To avoid making Howard worry, however, Margaret decided it would be better to fake orgasm than to be honest with him. After 5 years together, she still has not told him that she is not experiencing orgasms, and she feels too embarrassed to seek professional help, despite her ongoing distress.

In general, women are more likely than men to report sexual difficulties involving the subjective quality of the experience. Men are more likely to report physical problems in achieving or maintaining an erection.

Men who have a marked delay in ejaculation or who rarely if ever experience ejaculations have **delayed ejaculation**. Men with **premature (early) ejaculation** reach orgasm in a sexual encounter with minimal sexual stimulation before, on, or shortly after penetration and before wishing to do so (within 1 minute). Clinicians prefer to apply a psychiatric diagnosis only when the individual is distressed about the condition. The prevalence rate for premature ejaculation varies widely, from 8 to 30 percent, and seems to depend on age group and country (Lewis et al., 2010).

The distinction between the nature of orgasmic difficulties for men and women led a group of clinicians and social scientists called the Working Group for a New View of Women's Sexual Problems to criticize the *DSM* for failing to take into account the greater focus in women on relational aspects of sexuality and individual variations in women's sexual experiences. They proposed that the profession define sexual problems as difficulties in any aspect of sexuality—emotional, physical, or relational. Researchers also believe that more work is needed to understand the experiences of women from a variety of cultures, across different age groups, and of differing sexual orientations (Graham, 2010).

Other critics argue that the term *distress* does not accurately capture the subjective experience of women's difficulties in having orgasm. Using the focus group method, researchers found that *frustration* more aptly characterized the feelings of women who experienced problems with orgasm (Kingsberg et al., 2013).

delayed ejaculation
A sexual dysfunction in which a man experiences problems having an orgasm during sexual activity; also known as inhibited male orgasm.

premature (early) ejaculation
A sexual dysfunction in which a man reaches orgasm well before he wishes to, perhaps even prior to penetration.

MINI CASE

Premature (Early) Ejaculation, Lifelong

Jeremy is a 45-year-old investment broker who has struggled with the problem of premature ejaculation for as long as he can remember. Since his first experience with sexual intercourse as a college student, he has been unable to control his orgasms and customarily ejaculates seconds after penetration. Because of this problem, his relationships over the years have been strained and difficult. In each instance, the person he was dating at the time became frustrated, and Jeremy felt too embarrassed to continue the relationship. For a period lasting several years, he avoided sexual relations completely, knowing that each experience of failure would leave him feeling depressed and furious.

What's in the *DSM-5*

The Reorganization of Sexual Disorders

The sexual disorders underwent major rethinking in the *DSM-5*. The most significant was the declaration that clinicians do not consider paraphilias disorders unless they are accompanied by distress or impairment. This change recognizes the continuum along which sexual behavior falls and removes the stigma attached to sexual behaviors that do not cause distress or impairment or harm to others.

The sexual dysfunctions also became redefined in *DSM-5*. Hypoactive sexual desire disorder is diagnosed only in men; women receive a diagnosis of hypoactive sexual interest/arousal. The previously separate disorders of vaginismus (inability to allow penetration) and dyspareunia (pain with intercourse) were combined into one disorder called genito-pelvic pain/penetration disorder, because they are difficult to distinguish from one another.

In other changes, the term "early" was added in parentheses after "premature" ejaculation, and male orgasmic disorder was relabeled "delayed" ejaculation. Both these changes reflect a desire, once again, to destigmatize a variant of human sexuality.

Finally, the relabeling of "gender identity disorder" in *DSM-IV-TR* to the new term "gender dysphoria," along with other changes within this category, provide a revamped view of these disorders that not only is more consistent with the research evidence but also brings a greater understanding of people who experience the emotional distress of a mismatch between their biological sex and their own sense of identity.

Though based on empirical evidence, the *DSM-5* changes in the area of sexual disorders also clarify in important ways the many varieties of normal human sexuality. As these changes take hold in the psychological and psychiatric communities, they will provide directions for successful approaches to the treatment of people whose sexuality causes them to experience distress.

Disorders Involving Pain

Clinicians diagnose sexual pain disorders characterized by the experience of difficulty in a sexual relationship due to painful sensations in the genitals from intercourse, **genito-pelvic pain/penetration disorder**. Genito-pelvic pain/penetration disorder can affect both males and females. The individual experiences recurrent or persistent genital pain before, during, or after sexual intercourse.

Prior to *DSM-5*, clinicians had to choose between disorders that produced vaginismus, or involuntary spasms of the muscles outside the vagina, and dyspareunia, or pain associated with intercourse. Although clinically these were considered difficult to differentiate, some researchers now believe that the two conditions differ significantly on the dimension of fear. Women with vaginismus have greater fear of and avoidance of penetration, even for a gynecological exam (Lahaie et al., 2015). This could be an important distinction in terms of treatment implications, but for now the two conditions remain within the same diagnostic category.

genito-pelvic pain/penetration disorder
A sexual dysfunction affecting both males and females that involves recurrent or persistent genital pain before, during, or after sexual intercourse.

Theories and Treatment of Sexual Dysfunctions

Sexual dysfunctions represent an interaction of complex physiological, psychological, and sociocultural factors, and thus the biopsychosocial perspective is well suited to understand them. To help a client with a sexual dysfunction, the clinician must first conduct a comprehensive assessment that includes a physical examination and psychological testing, including of the client's partner if appropriate. In addition, the clinician must assess the individual's use of substances including not only drugs and alcohol, but also all medications, including psychotherapeutic ones.

Biological Perspectives   Perhaps one of the best-researched sexual dysfunctions is erectile disorder. In 1970, Masters and Johnson claimed that virtually all men (95 percent) with erectile disorder (ED) had psychological difficulties such as anxiety and job stress, boredom with long-term sexual partners, and other relationship issues. Since that time, researchers have arrived at very different conclusions as a result of new and more sophisticated assessment devices sensitive to the presence of physiological abnormalities.

Health care professionals now view more than half the cases of erectile disorder as attributable to physical problems of a vascular, neurological, or hormonal nature, or to impaired functioning caused by drugs, alcohol, and smoking. Thus, clinicians treating men with erectile disorder may first consider physiological contributions to the individual's symptoms before concluding that psychological factors are the cause.

Medications to treat erectile disorder include the prescription drugs Viagra, Levitra, and Cialis. These are all in the category of phosphodiesterase (PDE) inhibitors, which work by increasing blood flow to the penis during sexual stimulation. What makes such medications appealing is the fact that they are so much less invasive than previous treatments for erectile

MINI CASE

Genito-Pelvic Pain/Penetration Disorder, Lifelong

Shirley is a 31-year-old single woman who has attempted to have sex with many different men over the past 10 years. Despite her ability to achieve orgasm through masturbation, she has found herself unable to tolerate penetration during intercourse. In her own mind, she feels a sense of readiness, but her vaginal muscles inevitably tighten up and her partner is unable to penetrate. It is clear to Shirley that this problem has its roots in a traumatic childhood experience when she was sexually abused by an older cousin. Although she recognizes that she should seek professional help, she is too embarrassed to do so and has convinced herself that the problem will go away if she can find the right man who will understand her problems.

disorder, such as surgery and implants, and so much less awkward than vacuum pumps or penile injections. These medications work when accompanied by the experience of sexual excitement, unlike other treatments in which the man achieves an erection artificially and independent of what is going on sexually with the man or his partner.

Hormonal changes that can influence sexuality take place with the climacteric, the gradual loss of reproductive potential that occurs in men and women. For women, these changes occur during the years before and after menopause, when the monthly menstrual cycle ceases and estrogen production declines. For men, the corresponding changes are due to decreasing production of testosterone across middle and later adulthood.

The lowering of estrogen levels throughout the period of menopause can lead women to experience a number of physical symptoms that affect their sexuality, including vaginal dryness and gradual shrinking of vaginal size and muscle tone. These changes themselves do not affect the woman's ability for arousal during sexual activity, however. Women also experience a decline in free testosterone, the male sex hormone, but it is not clear whether this decline is related to changes in sexual desire and satisfaction. A variety of chronic diseases can also interfere with a woman's sexual desire and response, including diabetes, spinal cord injury, multiple sclerosis, hypothyroidism (low thyroid levels), and the aftermath of cancer surgery involving the uterus. Medications that act on the serotonin and dopamine systems can also interfere with sexual responsiveness in women (Both, Laan, & Schultz, 2010).

Treatment of female sexual interest/arousal disorder that follows from the biological perspective incorporates hormonal replacement therapy (estrogen and progesterone), estrogen cream applied directly to the vagina, and testosterone therapy (Traish, Feeley, & Guay, 2009). Doctors may also give women a PDE inhibitor ("female Viagra"), but its efficacy remains undemonstrated (Both et al., 2010). This drug is not to be confused with flibanserin, approved by the FDA in 2015 under the trade name Addyi. Though also dubbed the "female Viagra," Addyi actually works by a different mechanism than PDE inhibitors and is meant to increase a woman's interest in sexual activity. Data on its efficacy suggest that flibanserin may have beneficial effects, though more research is needed (Portman et al., 2017).

Genito-pelvic pain/penetration disorder presents a different set of challenges. From a biological perspective, the physical symptoms can come from a variety of sources, including disturbances in the muscle fibers in the pelvic area (called the "pelvic floor"). When treating these disorders, however, the clinician may be unable to trace the

Sexual dysfunctions can be disruptive and frustrating for intimate couples.

©John Dowland/Getty Images

The prescription drug Addyi, dubbed the "female Viagra," is intended to increase a woman's interest in sexual activity.

©Allen G. Breed/AP Images

exact cause of the individual's pain. The best approach appears to be multifaceted, including application of corticosteroids and physical therapy to promote muscle relaxation and improved blood circulation. The clinician may also use electrical nerve stimulation to relieve the individual's pain and prescribe pharmacological agents such as amitriptyline and pregabalin (Lyrica®) (Bergeron, Morin, & Lord, 2010).

Psychological Perspectives

While recognizing the role of physiological factors, the psychological perspective emphasizes the further contributing effects, if not the causal role, of cognitions, emotions, and attitudes toward sexuality.

Learned associations between sexual stimuli and pleasurable feelings can play an important role in sexual excitability. In the case of erectile disorder, one team of researchers identified as a predisposing factor a man's belief in the "macho myth" of sexual infallibility. Belief in this myth makes males more prone to developing dysfunctional thoughts (such as, "I'm incompetent") when they have an unsuccessful sexual experience. Once the man activates these thoughts, they impair his ability to process erotic stimuli and have sexual thoughts and images. By turning his attentional focus away from the encounter and toward his feelings of incompetence and sadness, they make him less able to achieve and maintain an erection during future sexual encounters (Nobre, 2010).

Researchers have also identified a man's self-image about the size of his genitals as a factor in erectile dysfunction. Among a sample of military men aged 40 and under, those with lower genital self-image had higher rates of sexual anxiety, which in turn was related to higher rates of erectile dysfunction (Wilcox, Redmond, & Davis, 2015).

For women, preoccupation with body image is known to interfere with sexual functioning, perhaps interacting with attitudes toward sexuality in general (Lemer, Salafia, & Benson, 2013).

In addition to discomfort with their bodies, individuals may hold negative "sexual self-schemas" such as feeling unloved, inadequate, and unworthy. They then transfer these self-schemas onto sexual situations, causing them to become anxious when they feel that an inability to achieve an orgasm will make their partner become tired. This belief in their own incompetence in sexual situations understandably inhibits their enjoyment (Nobre & Pinto-Gouveia, 2009). The Questionnaire of Cognitive Schema Activation in Sexual Context: Male Version is a brief test that presents the respondent with four different scenarios illustrating common sexual dysfunctions. For instance, one of the items presents a scenario in which the individual experiences premature ejaculation during intercourse. Respondents are instructed to rate how often they have experienced each of the scenarios and then to select from a list those emotions that represent their primary feelings while experiencing their most frequent sexual dysfunction. The test can identify a number of different self-schemas related to sexual functioning.

The quality of the relationship may also contribute to sexual dysfunction, particularly for women, whose sexual desire is sensitive to interpersonal factors including the frequency of positive interactions (Both et al., 2010). Researchers have also identified the cognitive factors relevant in genito-pelvic pain/penetration disorder that compound the physical causes, making women with this disorder highly sensitized even to words related to sex (Thaler, Meana, & Lanti, 2009).

The core treatment of sexual dysfunctions involving disturbances of arousal and orgasm follows from the principles that Masters and Johnson (1970) established, namely treating both partners in a couple, reducing anxiety about sexual performance, and developing specific skills such as **sensate focus**, in which the interaction is intended to lead not to orgasm but to the experience of pleasurable sensations during the phases prior to orgasm. This procedure reduces the couple's anxiety levels until eventually they are able to focus not on

sensate focus

Method of treating sexual dysfunction in which the interaction is not intended to lead to orgasm but to experience pleasurable sensations during the phases prior to orgasm.

REAL STORIES

Sue William Silverman: Sex Addiction

In *Love Sick: One Woman's Journey Through Sexual Addiction,* author Sue William Silverman tells the story of her battle with sexual addiction and documents the intensive, 28-day inpatient hospital treatment program where she begins to battle her addiction for the first time. Sue joined the treatment program only at the urging of her therapist, Ted, who recognized that her addiction had slowly been destroying every aspect of her life.

The hospital unit Sue attended was populated with other women struggling with sexual addiction. She writes, "The only other time I was surrounded by women (girls, really) was when I lived in a college dorm. Except I didn't feel surrounded by girls then, either. For my attention was always drawn outside my bay window, to men disturbing the nights of Boston." Sue's interactions with the other women helped her gain a different perspective on her addiction by showing how other women were affected by sexual addiction from a more objective point of view.

In the hospital, Sue was required to maintain a rigid daily schedule that included group therapy with other patients, individual therapy with Ted, regular meal times, and time for personal reflection. Much like Alcoholics Anonymous, the treatment followed 12 steps toward recovery. As Sue made her way through the workbook she used throughout treatment, she reflected on her many past sexual encounters with men and the way she repeatedly sought sexual affection in the hope of feeling a sense of genuine fulfillment, though the encounters only left her needing more.

Sue realized that as a result of her constant need for sexual fulfillment and a propensity to shift her identity based on which man's attention she was seeking, she never took the time to understand her own identity. Rather than her true self who had sought out all those men, it was a different version of herself—an addict persona. She writes, "When I'm fully in the power of that addict-woman, when I am *most* sick, I am, ironically, totally capable of swimming, going to parties, socializing: *being what appears to be normal.* Yes, all these years I've convinced not only myself,

Author Sue William Silverman chronicles her struggle with sexual addiction in *Love Sick: One Woman's Journey Through Sexual Addiction.*
Courtesy of Sue William Silverman/www.SueWilliamSilverman.com

but also others, that my behavior is normal because, in the strength of the addiction, I can *seem* normal. . . . Now, however, when the addiction is receding, when I'm in withdrawal, even though I'm getting better, everything scares me and I appear to be a wreck. Except I'm not; I'm in the process of becoming normal." She was in the process not only of recovering from her addiction, but of becoming herself.

In the book, Sue describes how therapy helped her recognize the danger of her addiction and the consequences of her behaviors. "For months, like a mantra, my therapist has told me, 'These men are killing you.' I don't know if he means emotionally, spiritually, or physically. I don't ask. He explains that I confuse sex with love, compulsively repeating this destructive pattern with one man after another. I do this because as a girl I learned that sex is love from my father, the first dangerous man who sexually misloved me." Sue explains that her father sexually abused her from the time she was a young girl until she left home to go to college in Boston. Once she was in college, Sue found herself spending the

majority of her time thinking about and seeking out men for sex. She began a string of sexual affairs that continued until the time she entered the hospital. Each affair began soon after meeting each man, and she would attain an intense feeling of satisfaction during each sexual encounter, followed by feelings of emptiness and then the immediate desire to seek out another sexual encounter.

'The intensity is an addict's "high,"' my therapist says. 'Not love.' To numb the shame and fear associated both with the past and with my current sexual behavior, I medicate, paradoxically, by using sex, he explains. 'But sometimes that "high" stops working. Usually after a scary binge.'

Sue also suffered from eating-disordered behavior and was dangerously thin when she entered the treatment program. Some of the therapy groups in the treatment program focused on the connection between her body image and her addiction, and she reflects on her thoughts about her body: ". . . But *it* is not *me*—although my body is part of me—the thinner, the better. Less body, less trouble. No body. *No* trouble. If no man is able to see my body, then I won't have to keep having sex."

Throughout the book Sue talks about her marriage, which at the time of her entering treatment had dissolved to the point where she and her husband, Andrew, slept in separate bedrooms and barely spoke. She writes that she married him as a way to seek normalcy and stability. Andrew was not aware of her battles with sexual addiction, and when she went to the inpatient program she told him only that she was seeking treatment for depression. Andrew visited briefly while she was in the

hospital, and their relationship offered her a sense of security that helps her through the difficulty of becoming, and staying, sober. In the program Sue found that she longed to achieve a sense of balance and stability in her life. She calls it "a state of nothingness: I won't be drunk; nor will I have to struggle so hard to be sober." With her therapist's help, she came to realize that stability meant more than not giving into her addictive behaviors. It meant finding out who she is and genuinely being that person.

After she left the hospital, Sue continued to attend individual therapy and a

weekly Sex Addicts Anonymous group. With the strength and insight she attained in the hospital, she began the slow process of recovery. The book ends by describing Sue's first day at home from the hospital. Although she finds herself missing the safety of the unit and the women she came to know, she takes comfort in doing ordinary things like making dinner with her husband and begins to plan for her future. "Now I must learn that love is where I carve out my own life," she writes.

SOURCE: *Love Sick: One Woman's Journey Through Sexual Addiction* by Sue William Silverman.

---

their feelings of inadequacy but instead on the sexual encounter itself. Clinicians may also teach the partners to masturbate or to incorporate methods of sexual stimulation other than intercourse, such as clitoral stimulation alone.

Expanding on these methods, therapists rely upon principles derived from cognitive-behavioral therapy that focus on the individual's thoughts that can inhibit sexual arousal and desire. As we saw earlier, distorted body image and negative sexual self-concept can interfere with sexual satisfaction. Restructuring those cognitions could therefore help alleviate sexual dysfunction symptoms. Furthermore, helping clients understand that each sexual encounter does not need to be perfect but can be "good enough" can help couples focus on sexual pleasure rather than on performance (Metz, Epstein & McCarthy, 2018).

Clinicians often involve the client's partner, encouraging both people to communicate more effectively and to have more positive intimate experiences (Both et al., 2010). For sexual pain disorders, cognitive-behavioral therapy alone does not seem to be effective, but it is most beneficial when integrated with muscle relaxation, biofeedback, and education (Bergeron et al., 2010). Women can learn to train or retrain their pelvic muscles to reduce painful muscle contractions during intercourse as well as to decrease their anxiety levels and self-consciousness.

11.4 Gender Dysphoria

biological sex
The sex determined by a person's chromosomes.

gender identity
A person's inner sense of ones' own gender.

gender dysphoria
Distress that may accompany the incongruence between a person's experienced or expressed gender and that person's assigned gender.

transsexualism
A term sometimes used to refer to gender dysphoria, specifically pertaining to individuals choosing to undergo sex reassignment surgery.

transgender
Referring to the identity of a person whose assigned gender does not correspond with their gender identity.

We turn now to disorders in which individuals experience distress from perceiving a mismatch between their **biological sex**, the sex determined by their chromosomes, and their inner sense of gender, called **gender identity**. In the *DSM-5*, the term **gender dysphoria** refers to distress that may accompany the incongruence between a person's experienced or expressed gender and that person's assigned gender.

Not everyone experiences distress as the result of this incongruence, but many are distressed if they are unable to receive treatment through hormones and/or surgery. In the current criteria for disorder, the individual experiences identification with the other sex. The feeling of being "in the wrong body" causes feelings of discomfort and a sense of inappropriateness about the person's assigned gender. Both these conditions must be present for a clinician to assign the diagnosis. Thus, the clinical problem is the dysphoria, not the individual's gender identity.

Another term that relates to cross-gender identification is **transsexualism**, which also describes the inner feeling of belonging to the other sex (individuals who experience this may be referred to as "trans"). The term is generally considered equivalent to **transgender** identity.

Some people with gender dysphoria wish to live as members of the other sex, and they act and dress accordingly. Unlike individuals with transvestic disorder, these people do not derive sexual gratification from cross-dressing. Further, many other identities fall in the category of transgender, including gender nonconforming, nonbinary, and agender. These terms correspond with the notion that not all transgender people see themselves as the opposite gender. Instead they might not feel they belong to any particular gender.

The *DSM-5* authors presented a strong case for using the term *gender dysphoria* to replace *gender identity disorder*, with the specification whether the individual is a child or post-adolescent. One reason for this proposed change was to take away the stigma attached to the label of cross-gender identification as a "disorder." Thus, having cross-gender identification does not necessarily imply that an individual is distressed or has a disorder (Cohen-Kettenis & Pfafflin, 2010). Only if that person feels dysphoria about having the sexual makeup with which he or she was born can a diagnosis be applied. Moreover, although some groups would advocate for the notion of removing gender dysphoria entirely from the diagnostic nomenclature, to do so could preclude individuals who wish to seek gender-affirming surgery from insurance coverage because there would be no diagnosis for the clinician to give (Corneil, Eisfeld, & Botzer, 2010).

Some individuals with gender dysphoria may choose to pursue gender-affirming medical procedures. These range from taking hormones to a variety of surgical procedures such as facial feminization surgery, chest reconstructive surgery ("top" surgery), and genital reconstructive surgery ("bottom" surgery). Each of these procedures requires psychological and other evaluations to ensure that the individual does not have any mental health conditions that might affect judgment or decision making and does have documented and persistent gender dysphoria (Coleman et al., 2012).

Theories and Treatment of Gender Dysphoria

Clinicians who work with transgender individuals experiencing gender dysphoria can provide support through psychotherapy and help clients decide whether they want to seek out other options such as hormone therapy or gender-affirming surgery. The American Psychological Association's Guidelines for Psychological Practice with Transgender and Gender Nonconforming People (TGNP) (APA, 2015a) suggest that clients achieve the most positive outcomes when they receive social support or trans-affirmative care and are seen from an interdisciplinary perspective, and seek to prepare their trainees in psychology to work with clients who identify as TGNP.

According to the World Professional Association for Transgender Health (WPATH), clinicians ideally provide an assessment of a client's well-being, without regard to diagnostic criteria, in determining whether a particular client is able to exercise good judgment and decision making around pursuing medical treatments. In this way, clinicians can be seen in a gatekeeper role, in which their determination can affect a client's ability to pursue gender-affirming treatments.

Given that clinicians will continue to treat individuals with gender dysphoria, new approaches are emerging based on transgender theory that emphasize a more fluid view of gender than the binary male-female dichotomy (Nagoshi & Brzuzy, 2010) a perspective also articulated in the APA TGNP Guidelines. Clinicians can begin by using the gender terminology the client prefers. Rather than assume that people's motivations, behaviors, and attitudes are based on their socially defined identities, clinicians can also recognize that these categories are conditional. For example, they can avoid using terms like *real* or *biological* gender. Through this approach, often referred to as affirmative psychotherapy, clinicians can provide education about medical options and help transgender

After initially coming out as a lesbian and then as transgender, Chaz Bono underwent the process of female-to-male gender conversion between 2008 and 2010.

©buzzfuss/123RF

clients safely explore their gender identity and connect with sources of social support (Austin & Craig, 2015).

Even though transgender identity itself is depathologized in *DSM-5*, clients will nevertheless continue to face **transphobia**, the negative stereotyping and fear of transgender individuals. Providing transgender individuals with social support may also improve their feelings of well-being (Davey, Bouman, Arcelus, & Meyer, 2014).

Rather than recommending gender reassignment surgery to help clients cope with social pressures to conform to one gender or another, clinicians can instead let their clients define their own gender identities. Through this process, transgender individuals can explore more openly and without bias their multiple, intersecting identities.

transphobia
The negative stereotyping and fear of transgender individuals.

11.5 Paraphilic Disorders, Sexual Dysfunctions, and Gender Dysphoria: The Biopsychosocial Perspective

The sexual disorders constitute three discrete sets of difficulties in aspects of sexual functioning and behavior. Although many unanswered questions remain about their causes, we need a biopsychosocial perspective to understand how individuals acquire and maintain these diverse problems over time. Moreover, researchers and clinicians are increasingly developing models that incorporate integrated treatment. The growing research base the *DSM-5* authors used reflects not only expansion of the empirical approaches to sexual disorders but also the adoption of a broader, more inclusive, and socioculturally sensitive approach to understanding and treatment.

Return to the Case: Shaun Boyden

For Shaun, being in psychotherapy was the first opportunity to talk with another person openly about his gender identity in a supportive and affirming environment. Given he had very little support in his relationships, it seems that much of Shaun's anxiety came from a sense of internalized transphobia; that is, it was difficult for him to truly accept himself, since he had not been accepted by others. The anxiety he experienced hindered him from venturing out into his community where he could find more sources of support, so in therapy he worked on setting goals for himself that included going to events and introducing himself to new people, and then building up those relationships over time. Having additional support in therapy helped him feel more affirmed in his identity, although he continued to struggle with dysphoria.

Eventually, Shaun decided he was ready to start HRT, and with the support of his therapist, he was referred to a specialist who prescribed low-dose testosterone. After starting HRT, Shaun noticed an immediate decrease in his gender dysphoria and found that taking this important step toward transitioning gave him a sense of hope. He began to feel more confident about taking additional steps, such as top surgery.

Dr. Tobin's reflections: There is never one particular path or narrative that transgender people follow, so it is critical as a clinician to keep an open mind and focus on supporting transgender clients and helping them feel safe in therapy. Providing affirmative care in this way is crucial so that transgender clients can explore their feelings openly. In some cases, therapy may be one of their few sources of support. Therapists should also help connect transgender clients with resources such as medical clinics or community support services, particularly if clients have struggled to connect with these resources on their own.

Sarah Tobin, PhD

SUMMARY

- When it comes to sexual behavior, the distinction between normal and abnormal becomes even more complicated, perhaps, than in other areas of human behavior. When evaluating the normality of a given sexual behavior, the context is extremely important, as are customs and mores, which change over time.

- Paraphilias are behaviors in which an individual has recurrent, intense sexually arousing fantasies, sexual urges, or behaviors involving (1) nonhuman objects, (2) children or other nonconsenting persons, or (3) the suffering or humiliation of self or partner.

- When a paraphilia causes intense distress and impairment, clinicians may diagnose paraphilic disorder. Paraphilic disorders include pedophilic disorder, exhibitionistic disorder, fetishistic disorder, frotteuristic disorder, sexual masochism disorder, sexual sadism disorder, and transvestic disorder.

- Critics of the *DSM* argued against including several of the paraphilic disorders in *DSM-5* because to do so pathologizes nonnormative sexual behavior. By defining these disorders as resulting in intense distress or impairment, the authors of the *DSM-5* hope to avoid judging a behavior's normality and instead base the criteria for a disorder on an individual's subjective experience of distress or degree of impairment in everyday life.

- From a biological perspective, paraphilic disorders involve a combination of influences including genetic, hormonal, and sensory factors in interaction with cognitive, cultural, and contextual influences. However, these changes could also be the result of early physical abuse or sexual victimization. Researchers have also identified altered serotonin levels in people with this disorder; however, these alterations may also be related to the presence of other psychological disorders in these individuals. Clinicians treating paraphilic disorders based on the biological perspective may use psychotherapeutic medications intended to alter the individual's neurotransmitter levels.

- The majority of studies on paraphilic disorders focus on pedophilic disorder. A common theme in the psychological literature is the idea of a "victim-to-abuser cycle" or "abused-abusers phenomena," meaning that abusers were themselves abused at some point in their lives, probably when they were young. Treatments within the psychological perspective seem most effective when combining individual with group therapy. The cognitive-behavioral perspective is particularly useful in helping clients recognize their distortions and denial. At the same time, these clients benefit from training in empathy, so that they can understand how their victims are feeling. Adding to the equation within the psychological perspective, clinicians may also train clients in learning to control their sexual impulses. Researchers believe that the most effective

- treatment involves a combination of hormonal drugs intended to reduce androgen (male sex hormone) levels and psychotherapy.

- Sexual arousal leads to a set of physiological changes throughout the body, often culminating in orgasm. A sexual dysfunction involves a marked divergence of an individual's response in the sexual response cycle along with feelings of significant distress or impairment.

- Arousal disorders may be diagnosed in individuals who have low or no sexual desire, or who are unable to achieve physiological arousal during the initial phases of the sexual response cycle. As a result, they may avoid or be unable to have sexual intercourse. These disorders include male hypoactive sexual desire disorder, female sexual interest/arousal disorder, and erectile disorder.

- There are also disorders involving orgasm. Inability to achieve orgasm, a distressing delay in achieving orgasm, or reduced intensity of orgasm constitutes female orgasmic disorder. Men with a marked delay in ejaculation or who rarely, if at all, experience ejaculations may have delayed ejaculation.

- Clinicians diagnose sexual pain disorders, which involve difficulties in sexual relationships due to painful sensations in the genitals from intercourse, as genito-pelvic pain/penetration disorder. This disorder can affect both males and females.

- We can best view sexual dysfunctions through a biopsychosocial lens as an interaction of complex physiological, psychological, and sociocultural factors. To help a client with a sexual dysfunction, the clinician must first conduct a comprehensive assessment that includes a physical exam and psychological testing, including the client's partner, if appropriate. In addition, the clinician must assess the individual's use of substances, including not only drugs and alcohol, but also all medications, including psychotherapeutic ones.

- The *DSM-5* authors use the term *gender dysphoria* instead of *gender identity disorder*, specifying whether the individual is a child or post-adolescent. In the current criteria for gender dysphoria, the individual experiences identification with the other sex. The feeling that they are "in the wrong body" causes feelings of discomfort and a sense of inappropriateness about their assigned gender. Both of these conditions must be present for a clinician to assign the diagnosis. Another term that relates to the feeling of cross-gender identification is *transsexualism*, which also refers to this phenomenon in which a person has an inner feeling of belonging to the other sex.

- Theoretical perspectives on the transgendered experience are undergoing radical shifts in the field of psychology. Whereas in the past, the profession equated transgenderism with a "disorder," the new terminology does not focus specifically on what is "wrong" with people whose self-identification differs from their biological characteristics or social roles.

- Paraphilic disorders, sexual dysfunctions, and gender dysphoria constitute three discrete sets of difficulties involving varying aspects of sexual functioning and behavior. Although there are many unanswered questions concerning their causes, we need a biopsychosocial perspective to understand how individuals acquire and maintain these diverse problems over time.

KEY TERMS

Biological sex
Delayed ejaculation
Erectile disorder
Exhibitionistic disorder
Female orgasmic disorder
Female sexual interest/arousal
  disorder
Fetishistic disorder
Frotteuristic disorder
Gender dysphoria

Gender identity
Genito-pelvic pain/penetration
  disorder
Lovemap
Male hypoactive sexual desire
  disorder
Paraphilias
Paraphilic disorder
Partialism
Pedophilic disorder

Premature (early) ejaculation
Sensate focus
Sexual dysfunction
Sexual masochism disorder
Sexual sadism disorder
Transgender
Transphobia
Transsexualism
Transvestic disorder
Voyeuristic disorder

Substance-Related and Addictive Disorders

Learning Objectives

12.1 Explain key features of substance disorders.

12.2 Differentiate among disorders related to specific substances.

12.3 Explain theories and treatment of substance use disorders.

12.4 Identify symptoms of non-substance-related disorders.

12.5 Analyze the biopsychosocial perspective on the development of substance disorders.

©TokenPhoto/Getty Images

Case Report: Carl Wadsworth

Demographic information: 32-year-old single African American heterosexual male

Presenting problem: Carl's sister Sharon made an appointment for Carl to see a therapist at a local outpatient therapy clinic due to concerns about his alcohol use. Sharon stated that their family was "sick of being worried" about him. She reported that Carl had been drinking more frequently and heavily over the past few years than ever before, which culminated in a recent arrest for public intoxication. Sharon explained that Carl has bipolar disorder, although he is not on medication currently, which is also very concerning to his family.

During the intake session, the therapist noticed that Carl appeared intoxicated, though he denied this when she asked whether he had been drinking recently. Consistent with clinic policy, she was forced to end the session prematurely and ensure that he received safe transportation home. When Carl presented for the next appointment intoxicated again, the therapist asked him directly whether he had been drinking prior to the session, because she was concerned that his alcohol use would interfere with therapy. Carl's reply was, "Maybe . . . just a little." The therapist asked Carl to refrain from drinking before their next appointment, to which he agreed.

When Carl showed up for the third appointment intoxicated yet again, it was clear to the therapist that treatment was necessary but could not proceed unless she was able to more directly address Carl's alcohol use with him. Carl had said he was ashamed of his alcohol use but found himself unable to cut down on his drinking, although he was slowly realizing that his years of drinking were taking a toll on him. For instance, he shared that he had been recently fired form his job after the arrest for public intoxication and was forced to live with Sharon as he could not make ends meet.

After that appointment, Carl told Sharon what had happened, and she removed all alcohol from her home and forbade Carl to go out unaccompanied. At first, Carl struggled with severe withdrawal symptoms. He then began to frequently pace around the house and was unable to sleep for three days due to racing thoughts and an abundance of energy. After convincing Sharon that he needed to borrow her car to go to the grocery store, Carl drove to a nearby liquor store, purchased a bottle of whiskey, and drank the entire bottle within a matter of minutes. On his way back to Sharon's home, he drove into a lamppost and was subsequently arrested for driving under the influence. He was then court-ordered to go to therapy, and his therapist allowed him to return to treatment on the condition that he attend his sessions sober.

Over the next few sessions, Carl began telling his therapist his story. He explained that he was diagnosed with bipolar disorder when he was 18 following a manic episode and treated with lithium, a medication that is often prescribed to treat the disorder. He said he preferred drinking to taking medication because he did not experience side effects, and he found weekly blood testing while on lithium "annoying." While he had not been a heavy drinker in his early adult life, his parents are both former alcoholics and he worried that he might be susceptible to alcoholism.

When Carl was 28, the telecom company for which he worked downsized and he lost his job. Carl became so depressed that he attempted suicide at his parents' home, where his mother discovered him. He was hospitalized for about 1 month and enrolled for disability status, which allowed him to receive medication and therapy. He then took up a job at a liquor store to supplement his disability, which helped him to afford his own apartment.

At the time, Carl was stable on medication and had not experienced any significant psychological impairment for several months. "I wasn't planning on drinking at work ever, but my boss sure liked to, so we started getting drunk together after closing up for the night," Carl reported. Since he found it difficult to drink heavily while on lithium, he decided to stop taking his medication so he could drink with his boss, who would taunt Carl if he declined his offer.

Since Carl was drinking mostly at night and lived by himself, no one in his family noticed he was drinking. After a few months of drinking every day at work, he started to experience withdrawal symptoms when he woke in the morning, so he began drinking immediately on awakening as well as while he was at work. He continued this routine for the next 2 years and soon was essentially unable to perform any activities outside work. His family grew increasingly worried, especially when he repeatedly showed up intoxicated at his parents' house. Family members urged him to try Alcoholics Anonymous (AA) and warned him of the dangers of his drinking, although Carl denied that he was having any problems. To prove this to his family, Carl would stop drinking for 1 or 2 weeks, although his desire to drink was too intense to allow him to go any longer than that. He grew increasingly depressed as he went without medication and his drinking grew more severe; however, instead of seeking treatment, Carl only drank more when he was feeling particularly depressed.

Occasionally Carl would get into an argument at work, although his boss typically did not take much notice. One day, however, Carl threatened violence against a customer, and his boss had no choice but to fire him and report him to the police, who arrested Carl for public intoxication. The police held him overnight and released him the next day when the customer chose not to press charges. Without an income, Carl was forced to move out of his apartment and move in with Sharon, who lived nearby. At that point, Sharon became more worried that Carl had spun out of control and unsure how she could help him, at which point she referred him to the therapist. Carl explained that he likely would not have sought help if it were not for Sharon.

Relevant history: Carl was diagnosed with bipolar disorder at the age of 18, following a manic episode. He managed his symptoms with medication for 10 years, at which point he lost his job and attempted suicide. Following starting his job at the liquor store, he started a pattern of daily heavy drinking. He has no prior history of treatment for substance use.

Case formulation: An important distinction to make in Carl's case is whether his alcohol use occurred secondarily as a result of his bipolar disorder, or whether it arose independently, which would qualify him for a dual diagnosis. As Carl stated regarding the episode of drinking that occurred while he lived at his sister's, he began drinking heavily while he was manic, believing he could handle a large quantity of alcohol and still drive safely. However, this was the only instance in which he reported drinking while experiencing mood symptoms.

After careful consideration of his case, it appears that Carl's initial problems with alcohol began in the absence of mood symptoms. Nor did his alcohol consumption appear to cause his mood symptoms. Because of these two distinctions, Carl qualifies for a dual diagnosis of Alcohol use disorder, severe, and Bipolar disorder. Further, he meets the criteria for Bipolar I disorder due to the presence of manic, rather than hypomanic, episodes, which required hospitalization and severely affected his functioning.

Treatment plan: Carl agreed to attend a local AA meeting on a daily basis in conjunction with weekly psychotherapy. He also agreed to see a psychiatrist for a medication evaluation.

Sarah Tobin, PhD

12.1 Key Features of Substance Disorders

A **substance** is a chemical that alters a person's mood or behavior when the person smokes, injects, drinks, inhales, snorts, or swallows it. Substance-related disorders reflect patterns of abuse of these substances, the resulting intoxication, and the consequences of discontinuing use of the substance. A person in a state of substance **withdrawal** shows physiological and psychological changes that vary according to the actual substance involved. **Tolerance** occurs when an individual requires increasingly greater amounts of the substance in order to achieve its desired effects, or when the person feels less of an effect after using the same amount of the substance.

A **substance use disorder** is a cluster of cognitive, behavioral, and physiological symptoms indicating that the individual continues using a substance even though it causes significant problems in his or her life. Clinicians diagnose substance use disorders by assessing the individual on four categories of symptoms: loss of control, social impairment, risky use, and pharmacological changes. Based on the number of symptoms the individual demonstrates, clinicians assign a severity rating from mild to severe.

Although many people refer to these disorders as representing an "addiction," the *DSM-5* authors prefer the term *substance use disorder*, believing it is more precise and has fewer negative connotations. Similarly, people with these disorders are referred to not as "addicts" but as "individuals with substance use disorders." People still use *addict* and *addiction* in ordinary conversation, of course, but these terms are not included in the *DSM-5*'s official diagnostic terminology. The term *addictive* appears in the chapter name as a descriptive term only.

People with substance use disorders suffer a range of significant effects on their daily life. They neglect obligations at work, and their commitments to home and family erode. They may begin to take risks that are personally dangerous and put others in jeopardy, such as driving or operating machinery while intoxicated.

It stands to reason that legal problems can arise for people who abuse substances. In addition to being arrested for driving while under the influence of a substance, they may face charges of disorderly conduct or assaultive behavior. The substance use disorders also frequently instigate interpersonal problems as well, due to the fact that excessive use of drugs or alcohol creates strains on relationships with family, friends, and co-workers. In extreme cases, these disorders can also lead to health problems and even premature death.

Substance-related disorders also include substance-induced disorders, which are disorders arising from the effects of the substance itself.

People receive a diagnosis of **substance intoxication** when they experience a drug's effects on their physiological functioning and show signs of significant impairment. The extent of substance intoxication depends on the specific drug, the speed with which it acts, and the duration of its effects. Efficient absorption of intravenous or smokable drugs into the bloodstream can lead to a more intense kind of intoxication than occurs with drugs taken in pill form.

The second category of substance-induced disorders includes those that reflect the effects of withdrawal, in which individuals develop

substance
A chemical that alters a person's mood or behavior when it is smoked, injected, drunk, inhaled, snorted, or swallowed.

withdrawal
Physiological and psychological changes that occur when an individual stops taking a substance.

tolerance
The extent to which the individual requires larger and larger amounts of a substance in order to achieve its desired effects, or the extent to which the individual feels less of its effects after using the same amount of the substance.

substance use disorder
A cluster of cognitive, behavioral, and physiological symptoms indicating that the individual uses a substance despite significant substance-related problems.

substance intoxication
The temporary maladaptive experience of behavioral or psychological changes that are due to the accumulation of a substance in the body.

What's in the *DSM-5*

Combining Abuse and Dependence

DSM-5's authors combined abuse and dependence into what is now termed "substance use disorder." Individuals receive a diagnosis based on meeting only two criteria but are rated according to the degree of severity of their symptoms. Critics believe the revised system may diagnose substance-related disorder in too many individuals with mild symptoms who do not have an "addiction" (Martin, Steinley, Vergés, & Sher, 2011). However, the dimensional rating theoretically allows clinicians to allow for gradations from mild to severe levels of the disorder.

A second major change in *DSM-5* was the transition of caffeine withdrawal from a research-only category to a clinical diagnosis. The *DSM-5* authors argued that there is sufficient evidence from large enough populations to warrant recognition of this condition as a psychiatric diagnosis. They believe, furthermore, that by their placing a diagnosis on the condition, clinicians will be more likely to recognize, and then correctly treat, individuals who have its symptoms. Many caffeine users who suffer from caffeine withdrawal attribute their symptoms to other disorders, leading to unnecessary health care utilization and associated costs. The inclusion of this diagnosis may help them receive needed interventions.

behavioral changes specific to the particular substance. These changes include physiological and cognitive alterations associated with the discontinuation of the substance in question. Other disorders can also occur as a function of substance use, including psychotic disorder, mood disorder, anxiety disorder, sexual dysfunction, and sleep disorder. People may also show comorbidity of the substance-related disorder with another condition, such as an anxiety disorder or a mood disorder.

12.2 Disorders Associated with Specific Substances

The rising rate of opioid dependence in the United States is attracting widespread attention, while the legalization of marijuana raises different but equally pressing concerns. As public health experts and politicians look for ways to minimize the effects of substance use on at-risk populations, the *DSM-5*'s diagnostic criteria provide a taxonomy for evaluating the scope of the problems associated with psychoactive substances, including alcohol.

According to the U.S. government's Substance Abuse and Mental Health Service (SAMHSA) National Survey on Drug Use and Health (NSDUH), in 2016 an estimated 11 percent of the population used illicit drugs at least once in the preceding 30 days (that is, they were current users) (SAMHSA, 2018). Marijuana is the most commonly used substance, with 28.6 million people 12 and older reporting use of any illicit drug in the United States within the past month. The numbers of users of all illicit drugs appear in Figure 1.

Rates of current illicit drug use by individuals 12 years of age and older vary considerably by demographic group. According to the NSDUH, the three most significant grouping characteristics are race/ethnicity, age, and gender. The rate of past-month illicit drug use is 15.7 percent for American Indians or Alaska Natives, followed by 12.5 percent among people who identify as Black or African American, 10.8 percent for Whites, 9.2 percent for Hispanic or Latino, and 4.1 percent for Asian. The rates generally decline with age from the peak of 22.3 percent at ages 18 to 25 to 1.9 percent at ages 65 and older. Males have a higher rate of drug use (12.8 percent) than females (8.5 percent). Illicit drug use tends to be lower among college graduates, the employed, and Midwesterners and highest among people living in cities (SAMHSA, 2018).

Most drugs of abuse directly or indirectly target the reward center of the brain by flooding its circuits with dopamine, as you can see in Figure 2. Overstimulation of the reward system produces the euphoric effects abusers seek and leads them to engage in the behavior that will allow them to repeat the experience. Drugs are more addictive than the natural

FIGURE 1 Past Month Illicit Drug Use Among Persons Aged 12 or Older: United States, 2016

SOURCE: Substance Abuse and Mental Health Services Administration. (2018). Retrieved from https://www.samhsa.gov/data/sites/default/files/NSDUH-DetTabs-2016/NSDUH-DetTabs-2016.htm#tab1-29A 4/9/2018

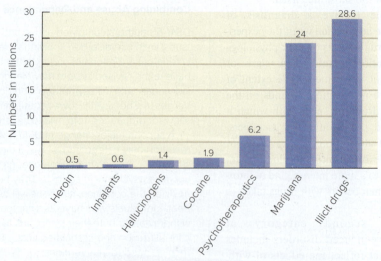

¹Illicit drugs include marijuana/hashish, cocaine (including crack), heroin, hallucinogens, inhalants, or prescription-type psychotherapeutics used nonmedically.

All drugs of abuse target the brain's pleasure center

Brain reward (dopamine) pathways

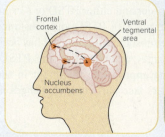

All drugs of abuse increase dopamine

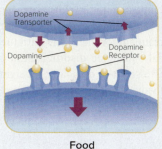

Food

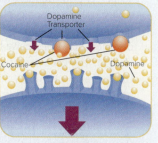

Cocaine

These brain circuits are important for natural rewards such as food, music, and art.

Typically, dopamine increases in response to natural rewards such as food.
When cocaine is taken, dopamine increases are exaggerated, and communication is altered.

FIGURE 2 Effects of Drugs of Abuse on Dopamine Pathways (Using Cocaine as an Example)

"highs" produced by such activities as eating and sex because they release far more dopamine (2 to 10 times as much) than do natural rewards, and the effects last much longer. Over time, the neurons in these dopamine pathways "down-regulate" in response to these surges in dopamine, meaning they produce less dopamine themselves or reduce the number of dopamine receptors. Users then need to take the drugs to raise their dopamine levels back to normal. In order to experience the effects they experienced initially from the drugs, they also need to take higher and higher levels; in other words, they develop tolerance.

In addition to dopamine, some drugs of abuse also influence glutamate, a neurotransmitter active in memory and learning. Long-term drug abuse can lower the individual's level of glutamate and lead to memory impairments.

Because users learn to associate the pleasurable feelings of using the drug with the cues in the environment that were there when they took the drug, they develop classically conditioned responses that maintain their addiction.

Individuals with mood and anxiety disorders are more likely to abuse substances. In 2016, 3.7 million individuals in the United States with a psychological disorder used illicit drugs; of these, 1.3 million used opioids and 1.7 million used marijuana (SAMHSA, 2018). The most common comorbid conditions are mood disorders, anxiety disorders, borderline personality disorder, and antisocial personality disorder. People with schizophrenia are more likely to use alcohol and tobacco and to have drug use disorders. Estimates are that as many as 43 percent of people treated for substance use of prescription painkillers have a diagnosis or symptoms of psychological disorders, particularly major depressive and anxiety disorders (NIDA, 2018a).

There are three possible routes to the development of comorbid substance use and other psychological disorders (NIDA, 2018a). The first is the similarity of risk factors in substance use and other psychological disorders. Second, individuals with psychological disorders or symptoms may use drugs as a form of self-medication. Third, people who use substances may subsequently develop a psychological disorder, due either to changes in brain activity produced by the substances or to changes in lifestyle that precipitate stress, which, in turn, leads to symptoms of depression and anxiety.

Drug use typically begins in adolescence, which is also the time of heightened vulnerability to other psychological disorders. Early drug use is also a risk factor for later substance use disorder and possibly for the subsequent development of other disorders as well. The risks are particularly likely to occur in individuals who have a high genetic vulnerability. In one study following adolescents into early adulthood, only those heavy marijuana users with a particular gene variant had significantly higher risk of developing schizophreniform disorder (Caspi et al., 2005).

Higher rates of substance use disorders also occur in physically or emotionally traumatized individuals. This is a matter of particular concern for the veterans returning from the

Iraq and Afghanistan wars (NIDA, 2013). As many as half of veterans who have a diagnosis of PTSD also have a comorbid substance use disorder. In addition, researchers estimate that 45 percent of offenders in state and local prisons have a comorbid mental health and substance use disorder. People with a comorbid substance disorder and either PTSD or a criminal history may have difficulty receiving treatment. Veterans with PTSD and substance disorders may not receive treatment for the PTSD until the substance use disorder has been treated; however, traditional substance disorder clinics may defer treating the PTSD. Incarcerated criminals may also have difficulty receiving appropriate treatment in the prison system. Clearly, individuals with comorbid disorders face particular challenges in treating their substance use disorders.

Alcohol

Alcohol use is associated with several categories of disorders including use disorders, intoxication, and withdrawal. According to the World Health Organization (WHO), worldwide there are 3.3 million deaths every year due to alcohol, representing nearly 6 percent of all deaths; 5 percent of the global costs of disease and injury is attributable to alcohol use (WHO, 2015).

Patterns of alcohol use are associated with age (Figure 3). Young adults 21 to 25 have the highest rates of binge drinking and the highest rates of heavy drinking. The rates of binge and heavy drinking decline sharply through adulthood; among people 65 and older, 9.7 percent engage in binge drinking and 2.3 percent in heavy drinking (SAMHSA, 2018).

Although the rates of alcohol use by age are lower in those 65 years of age and older, longitudinal studies provide a different picture. People are less likely to start drinking after the young adult years, but many persist in their previously established patterns of alcohol use disorder throughout adulthood. Adults going through certain life transitions may alter their alcohol use patterns, however. For men, parenthood is associated with lower rates of alcohol use after the age of 38; women show the opposite pattern. Men who lose their jobs have the highest rates of alcohol use after age 38; for women, there is no relationship between job status and alcohol-use persistence. These findings suggest that the relationships among alcohol use, life transitions, and gender are complex and that aging alone is not sufficient for understanding age-related changes in alcohol use disorders (Vergés et al., 2011).

To understand how alcohol affects behavior, consider that from a physiological standpoint alcohol is a nervous system **depressant**, and the way it affects the individual depends on how much the drinker ingests. In small amounts, alcohol has sedating effects, and the

depressant
A psychoactive substance that causes the depression of central nervous system activity.

FIGURE 3 Current, Binge, and Heavy Alcohol Use Among Persons Aged 12 or Older, by Age: 2018

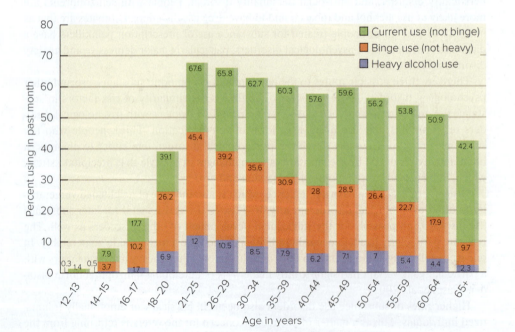

drinker therefore feels more relaxed. With larger amounts, drinkers may begin to feel more outgoing, self-confident, and uninhibited. Beyond that point, the depressant effects become apparent, leading users to experience sleepiness, lack of physical coordination, dysphoria, and irritability. In even larger amounts, alcohol can be fatal, leading the individual's vital functions to shut down. More severe effects also occur when the individual mixes alcohol with other drugs; **potentiation** makes the effects of two drugs taken together greater than the effect of either substance alone. Combining alcohol with another depressant can have a fatal outcome, for example.

The rate at which alcohol absorption occurs in the bloodstream depends on a number of factors, including how much a person consumes and over what time period, and whether food is present in the digestive system. Another factor is the drinker's metabolic rate (the rate at which the body converts food substances to energy). The average person metabolizes alcohol at a rate of one third of an ounce of 100 percent alcohol per hour, which is equivalent to an ounce of whiskey per hour. Following a bout of extensive intake of alcohol, a person is likely to experience an abstinence syndrome, or the phenomenon commonly called a "hangover." The symptoms of abstinence syndrome include a range of phenomena including nausea and vomiting, tremors, extreme thirst, headache, tiredness, irritability, depression, and dizziness. As with alcohol absorption, the extent of abstinence syndrome the person experiences reflects the amount and rate of alcohol consumption and the individual's metabolic rate.

Directly or indirectly, alcohol affects almost every organ system in the body. Long-term use can lead to permanent brain damage, with symptoms of dementia, blackouts, seizures, hallucinations, and damage to the peripheral parts of the nervous system. Two forms of dementia are associated with long-term heavy alcohol use.

Wernicke's disease is an acute and potentially reversible condition characterized by delirium, eye-movement disturbances, difficulties in movement and balance, and deterioration of the peripheral nerves to the hands and feet. It is not alcohol itself but the associated deficiency of thiamine (vitamin B_1) that causes Wernicke's disease. Long-term heavy use of alcohol damages the body's ability to metabolize nutrients, and alcohol users often have an overall pattern of poor nutrition. Adequate thiamine intake can reverse Wernicke's disease.

Korsakoff's syndrome is a permanent form of dementia in which the individual develops **retrograde amnesia**, the inability to remember past events, and **anterograde amnesia**, the inability to remember new information. The chances of recovering from Korsakoff's syndrome are fewer than one in four, and about another one in four people who have this disorder require permanent institutionalization.

Chronic heavy alcohol consumption also causes a number of harmful changes in the rest of the body outside the nervous system, including to the liver, gastrointestinal system, bones,

potentiation
The combination of the effects of two or more psychoactive substances such that the total effect is greater than the effect of either substance alone.

Wernicke's disease
A reversible form of neurocognitive disorder associated with long-term alcohol use.

Korsakoff's syndrome
A permanent form of neurocognitive disorder associated with long-term alcohol use in which the individual develops retrograde and anterograde amnesia, leading to an inability to remember recent events or learn new information.

retrograde amnesia
Amnesia involving loss of memory for past events.

anterograde amnesia
Amnesia involving the inability to remember new information.

MINI CASE

Alcohol Use Disorder

Mala is a 55-year-old married heterosexual Israeli American woman. She has been a stay-at-home parent since the birth of her and her husband's first child. Every afternoon, Mala makes herself the first in a series of daiquiris. On many evenings, she passes out on the couch by the time her husband arrives home from work. Mala lost her driver's license a year ago after being arrested three times on charges of driving while intoxicated. Although her family has urged her to obtain treatment for her disorder, she denies that she has a problem because she

can "control" her drinking. The mother of three grown children, Mala began to drink around age 45, when her youngest child left for college. Before that, she kept herself extremely busy through her children's extracurricular activities. When she found herself alone every afternoon, she took solace in having an early cocktail. Over a period of several years, the daily cocktail developed into a series of five or six strong mixed drinks. Mala's oldest daughter has lately begun to insist that something be done for her mother. She does not want to see Mala develop the fatal alcohol-related illness that caused the premature death of her grandmother.

muscles, and immune system. When people abruptly stop ingesting alcohol after periods of chronic usage, they can experience sleep disturbances, profound anxiety, tremors, hyperactivity of the sympathetic nervous system, psychosis, seizures, or death.

Theories and Treatment of Alcohol Use Disorders

Biological Perspectives

Twin, family, and adoption studies consistently point to the importance of genetic factors as contributors to alcohol-related disorders, with an estimated heritability of 50 to 60 percent. Pinpointing the genes responsible for alcohol-related disorders is a great challenge to researchers, however, because it is likely that multiple genes are active in their transmission (Salvatore et al., 2018). The greatest success has come from studies examining associations between genes that govern alcohol metabolism and neural transmission. Researchers are attempting to connect variations in some of these genes not only with patterns of alcohol use but also with comorbid disorders such as social anxiety disorder, personality traits, and early childhood predictors (Rambau et al., 2018).

Sociocultural influences also appear to interact with genetic vulnerability. In a large nationwide study of midlife adults, researchers found differences between twins in the level of alcohol use, based on socioeconomic status. In families from lower socioeconomic levels, genetic factors seemed to play a larger role than the environment. In higher social status families, the amount of alcohol individuals use is affected by such factors as familial habits and traditions (Hamdi, Krueger, & South, 2015). These findings support the diathesis-stress model that relates genetic predisposition to environmental stressors.

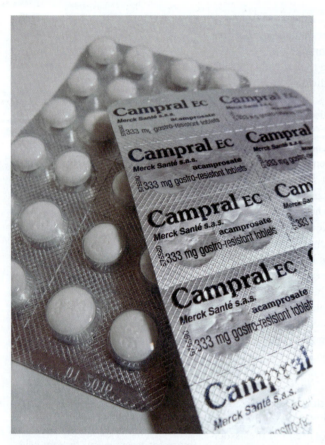

Medications such as acamprosate, sold under the brand name Campral, can help treat individuals with alcohol use disorders.
©Stuart Aylmer/Alamy Stock Photo

In the biological perspective, treatment of individuals with alcohol use disorders relies on prescription medications, alone or in conjunction with psychologically based therapies. A large number of well-controlled studies support the use of naltrexone as an aid in preventing relapse. As an opioid receptor antagonist, it blocks the effects of the body's production of alcohol-induced opioids, perhaps through involving dopamine (Hillemacher et al., 2011). The individual who takes naltrexone is less likely to experience pleasurable effects of alcohol and even less likely to feel pleasure thinking about it. As a result, he or she will feel less of an urge to drink and therefore will be less likely to suffer a relapse of heavy drinking. A large number of studies provide supportive evidence about naltrexone's effect on drinking, including its ability to lower the individual's cravings and, hence, consumption (Hendershot, Wardell, Samokhvalov, & Rehm, 2017).

disulfiram

Known popularly as Antabuse, a medication used in the treatment of alcoholism that inhibits aldehyde dehydrogenase (ALDH) and causes severe physical reactions when combined with alcohol.

Disulfiram is a medication that operates by the principles of aversion therapy. An individual taking disulfiram who consumes alcohol within a 2-week period will experience a variety of unpleasant physical reactions, including flushing, palpitations, increased heart rate, lowered blood pressure, nausea and vomiting, sweating, and dizziness. Disulfiram works primarily by inhibiting the action of an enzyme that normally breaks down acetaldehyde, a toxic product of ethanol metabolism. Although not as effective as naltrexone, it does work for highly motivated individuals, particularly those treated in supervised settings who are also older, have a longer drinking history, and participate in Alcoholics Anonymous meetings (Arias & Kranzler, 2008).

The third medication shown to be effective in treating alcohol use disorders is acamprosate, an amino acid derivative that appears to moderate glutamate receptors. Acamprosate reduces the risk of relapse by reducing the individual's urge to drink and thereby reducing the drive to use alcohol as a way of reducing anxiety and other negative psychological states.

The evidence on acamprosate is generally positive, though individuals who seem to benefit from it the most are those who are older when they become dependent on alcohol, have physiological signs of higher dependence, and have higher levels of anxiety (Arias & Kranzler, 2008). People who are more highly motivated to become fully abstinent at the start of treatment are more likely to remain on the medication and therefore more likely to improve (Koeter, van den Brink, & Lehert, 2010). Individuals who have only recently stopped drinking and are of normal or close to normal body weight appear to derive greater benefit (Gueorguieva et al., 2015).

Psychological Perspectives   Current psychological approaches to alcohol use disorders focus on the cognitive systems that guide people's drinking behavior. According to **dual-process theory**, one cognitive system generates fast, automatic processes that trigger an impulse to drink alcohol. These automatic processes are based on the conditioned positive associations with alcohol that people have formed. The second, and slower, system consists of the controlled, laborious processing that would allow individuals to regulate and inhibit acting on those positive associations. The dual-process theory posits that the more the individual can inhibit the automatic impulse, the less likely he or she is to consume excessive amounts of alcohol (Bechara, Noel, & Crone, 2006). Personality may play a role in this process, because individuals who are lower in emotional control seem to find it more difficult to engage in the deliberate process of inhibiting their urges to drink (Stevenson et al., 2015).

> **dual-process theory**
> A theory regarding alcohol use proposing there are automatic processes that generate an impulse to drink alcohol and controlled, effortful processing that regulates these automatic impulses.

Alcohol consumption is also guided by individuals' expectations about what will happen to them after they consume alcohol. Individuals develop alcohol expectancies early in life, even before they first taste alcohol. These can include the potential for alcohol to reduce tension or help them cope with social challenges, feel better or sexier, or become more mentally alert. Expectancies about alcohol can also include people's beliefs in their self-efficacy, or their ability to resist or control their drinking (Young, Connor, & Feeney, 2011).

Cognitive factors also can influence what happens when a person consumes alcohol. According to **alcohol myopia theory**, individuals narrow their attentional focus the more alcohol they consume (Bayless & Harvey, 2017). This theory also predicts that when people drink alcohol, they also become more likely to engage in impulsive and potentially harmful behaviors, such as high-risk sexual activities. The high prevalence of binge drinking on college campuses presents a particular concern for this reason. As individuals consume greater amounts of alcohol, they are more likely to make risky choices because the immediate temptation of the moment (such as engaging in risky sex) overcomes the long-term consequences of the behavior (such as developing a sexually transmitted disease) (Griffin, Umstattd, & Usdan, 2010).

> **alcohol myopia theory**
> Proposes that as individuals consume greater amounts of alcohol, they are more likely to make risky choices because the immediate temptation of the moment overcomes the long-term consequences of the behavior.

Even individuals who engage in healthy lifestyle behaviors can be at risk for alcohol use disorders. In one large study examining alcohol use (beer) and engagement in physical activity, people who engaged in more activity were also more likely to drink beer the same day (Conroy et al., 2015). College students who believe they are engaging in healthy activity may feel they have "earned" the right to drink, placing themselves at potential risk for developing regular habits in which they overuse alcohol.

Clinicians who design interventions targeting individuals with alcohol use disorders begin by conducting an assessment of the alcohol use patterns of their clients. The AUDIT, or Alcohol Use Disorders Identification Test, summarized in Table 1, is one such instrument (National Institute on Alcohol Abuse and Alcoholism, 2007).

There are several well-tested psychological approaches to treating alcohol use disorders. The most successful rely on cognitive-behavioral interventions, motivational approaches, and expectancy manipulation (Arias & Kranzler, 2008). Part of effective treatment is **relapse prevention**, in which the clinician essentially builds "failure" into treatment. If the client recognizes that occasional slips from abstinence are bound to occur, then he or she will be less likely to give up on therapy altogether after suffering a temporary setback. Mindfulness training may also be added to relapse prevention to help individuals gain greater insight into the factors that trigger their relapses as well as to recognize that substance use may be a way of avoiding the present moment (Penberthy et al., 2015).

> **relapse prevention**
> A treatment method in which individuals are encouraged not to view lapses from abstinence as signs of certain failure.

The **COMBINE** project (Combining Medications and Behavioral Interventions) developed the most comprehensive protocol for psychological treatment as part of a project

TABLE 1 The Alcohol Use Disorders Identification Test ("AUDIT")

The Alcohol Use Disorders Identification Test (AUDIT) provides a self-guided test that individuals can take to assess their alcohol consumption, drinking behaviors, and alcohol-related problems. Below is a summary of the questions found on the AUDIT, each of which is rated with a frequency scale:

1. How often do you drink alcohol?
2. How many alcoholic drinks do you typically have on a day you are drinking?
3. How often do you have 6 or more alcoholic drinks at one time?
4. How often have you found that you were not able to stop drinking daily once you had started?
5. How often during the past year has drinking alcohol kept you from doing something you were normally expected to do?
6. How often in the past year have you needed a first drink in the morning to get yourself going after a night of heavy drinking?
7. How often during the last year have you felt guilty or remorseful after drinking?
8. How often during the last year have you been unable to remember what happened the day before because of drinking too much alcohol?
9. Have you or someone else been hurt or harmed because of your drinking?
10. Has someone close to you or a health care professional spoken to you about your drinking or suggested that you cut down?

SOURCE: Adapted from https://www.drugabuse.gov/sites/default/files/files/AUDIT.pdf

funded by the National Institute on Alcohol Abuse and Alcoholism (NIAAA). In this treatment, known as Combined Behavioral Intervention (CBI) (Miller, 2002), participants receive up to 20 sessions, according to their needs, beginning semiweekly and then eventually biweekly or less, for up to 16 weeks. The primary emphasis of CBI is on enhancing reinforcement and social support for abstinence. Clinicians assign motivational enhancement therapy at the outset, meaning they attempt to draw out the client's own motivation to change. The clinical style used in CBI follows from the motivational interviewing perspective (Table 2), in which the clinician uses a client-centered but directive style.

Clinicians expect and encourage families and significant others to participate throughout treatment, and they also encourage mutual help and involvement among clients, including participation in Alcoholics Anonymous (AA). CBI includes content modules focusing on coping skills (for coping with cravings and urges), ways to refuse drinks and avoid social pressure to drink, communication skills, assertiveness skills, management of moods, social and recreational counseling, social support for sobriety, and job-seeking skills. As needed, clinicians may also monitor sobriety, provide telephone consultation, and provide crisis intervention. They also put procedures in place to work with clients who resume drinking during treatment. Toward the end of the treatment period, clients enter a maintenance phase and then complete treatment in a termination session.

The COMBINE study continues to evaluate the efficacy of naltrexone and acamprosate alone and in combination with CBI, using placebos and medical management as control conditions. Initially, researchers reported that although CBI alone was not as effective in producing abstinent days as was CBI plus medication and management immediately after treatment, 1 year after treatment ended, the CBI-only group did not differ significantly from those receiving medication (Anton et al., 2006). Subsequent studies continue to investigate the mechanisms promoting change in alcohol patterns through medication alone or combined with CBI. One promising avenue investigates the role of cravings as a common factor influenced both by naltrexone and by exposure to CBI (Subbaraman et al., 2013).

TABLE 2 Comparisons Among Reflective Listening and Other Therapist Responses to Client Statements

CLIENT: I guess I do drink too much sometimes, but I don't think I have a *problem* with alcohol.
CONFRONTATION: Yes you do! How can you sit there and tell me you don't have a problem when . . .
QUESTION: Why do you think you don't have a problem?
REFLECTION: So on the one hand you can see some reasons for concern, *and* you really don't want to be labeled as "having a problem."
CLIENT: My wife is always telling me that I'm an alcoholic.
JUDGING: What's wrong with that? She probably has some good reasons for thinking so.
QUESTION: Why does she think that?
REFLECTION: And that really annoys you.
CLIENT: If I quit drinking, what am I supposed to do for friends?
ADVICE: I guess you'll have to get some new ones.
SUGGESTION: Well, you could just tell your friends that you don't drink anymore, but you still want to see them.
REFLECTION: It's hard for you to imagine how life would be without alcohol.

SOURCE: Miller, W. R. (2002). *Combined Behavioral Intervention Manual: A Clinical Research Guide for Therapists Treating People With Alcohol Abuse and Dependence*, Bethesda, MD: National Institute on Alcohol Use and Alcoholism.

Sociocultural Perspective Researchers and theorists working within the sociocultural perspective regard stressors in the family, community, and culture as factors that, when combined with genetic vulnerability, lead the individual to develop alcohol use disorder. As indicated earlier, socioeconomic status seems to interact with genetic vulnerability as an influence on how much alcohol individuals consume. Those in higher-status families seem more likely to have drinking patterns influenced by familial patterns and preferences rather than by genetics.

Support of the sociocultural perspective first became apparent in a landmark longitudinal study in the early 1980s. Researchers followed individuals from childhood or adolescence to adulthood, the time when most individuals who become alcohol-dependent make the transition from social or occasional alcohol use to an alcohol use disorder (Zucker & Gomberg, 1986). Those most likely to develop alcohol use disorder in adulthood had a history of childhood antisocial behavior, including aggressive and sadistic behavior, trouble with the law, rebelliousness, lower achievement in school, completion of fewer years of school, and a higher truancy rate. These individuals also showed a variety of behaviors possibly indicative of early neural dysfunction, including nervousness and fretfulness as infants, hyperactivity as children, and poor physical coordination while growing up through the normal motor development milestones. Researchers concluded that these characteristics reflected a genetically based vulnerability, which, when combined with environmental stresses, led to the development of alcohol use disorder.

Families can also provide social support in other ways that affect alcohol use by teenagers. In a 2-year study of more than 800 suburban adolescents, those who received high levels of social support from their families were less likely to consume alcohol. The effect seemed to be due primarily to the fact that these families were also more likely to strongly emphasize religion in the home. Further, teens earning good grades in school were more likely to be receiving higher levels of social support from their families, which in turn was associated with lower rates of alcohol use. The teens who used alcohol were more likely to show poorer school performance over the course of the study (Mason & Windle, 2001).

Peer pressure and poor grades in school contribute to high rates of alcohol consumption in teenagers.
©*WILL & DENI MCINTYRE/Getty Images*

Another approach within the sociocultural perspective takes into account the impact of socialization on patterns of alcohol use disorders. Researchers have demonstrated the benefits of cognitive-behavioral therapy designed specifically for women (Epstein et al., 2018). Female-specific cognitive-behavioral therapy emphasizes the themes of self-care and self-confidence as well as addressing friendships, social support, and levels of assertiveness, using female models in relevant training vignettes and worksheets.

Stimulants

stimulant
A psychoactive substance that has an activating effect on the central nervous system.

The category of drugs called **stimulants** includes substances that have an activating effect on the nervous system. These differ in their chemical structure, their specific physical and psychological effects, and their potential danger to the user. Stimulants are associated with disorders related to use, intoxication, and withdrawal.

amphetamine
A stimulant that affects both the central nervous and the autonomic nervous systems.

Amphetamines   **Amphetamine** is a stimulant that affects both the central nervous and the autonomic nervous systems. In addition to waking or speeding up the central nervous system, it also causes elevated blood pressure and heart rate, and decreased appetite and physical activity. It may be used for medical purposes, such as to treat ADHD or as a diet pill. Even when used for medical purposes, however, amphetamine can cause dependence and have unpleasant or dangerous side effects. Increasingly large doses can make users hostile, violent, and paranoid. Users may also experience a range of physiological effects including fever, sweating, headache, blurred vision, dizziness, chest pain, nausea, vomiting, and diarrhea.

Methamphetamine is an addictive stimulant drug that is related to amphetamine but one that provokes more intense central nervous system effects. Whether taken orally, through the nose, intravenously, or by smoking, methamphetamine causes a rush or feeling of euphoria and becomes addictive very quickly. Methamphetamine overdose can cause overheating of the body and convulsions, and if not treated immediately, it can result in death. Long-term use of methamphetamine can lead users to develop mood disturbances, violent behavior, anxiety, confusion, insomnia, severe dental problems ("meth mouth"), and a heightened risk of infectious diseases including hepatitis and HIV/AIDS. The long-term effects of methamphetamines also include severe brain damage, as Figure 4 shows.

In 2016, 667,000 people ages 12 and older in the United States (0.2 percent) were current users of methamphetamines, nearly double the numbers from 353,000 (0.1 percent) in 2010. There is a large increase in numbers of users between the age range of 12 to 17 (an estimated 9,000) and further increases in the age group of 18- to 25-year-olds (65,000). Those between the ages of 35 and 39 represent the peak percentage of monthly users (0.5 percent) (SAMHSA, 2018).

Use of the stimulants Adderall and Ritalin by high school students concerns parents and educators, because these potentially abused substances can be obtained from friends with prescriptions or directly from a student's own physician. In 2017, approximately 5.5 percent of high school seniors said they used Adderall, and 1.3 percent said they used Ritalin for nonmedical purposes. The lifetime prevalence of methamphetamine among high school seniors was 1.1 percent, down from 1.9 percent in 2014; lifetime amphetamine prevalence was 9.2 percent, down from the peak in 2013 of 13.8 percent (Monitoring the Future Study, 2017).

Cocaine   **Cocaine** is a highly addictive central nervous system stimulant that an individual snorts, injects, or smokes. Users can snort the powdered hydrochloride salt of cocaine or dissolve it in water and then inject it. Crack is the street name given to the form of cocaine that is processed to form a rock crystal which, when heated, produces vapors that the individual smokes. The effects of cocaine include feelings of euphoria, heightened mental alertness, reduced fatigue, and heightened energy. The faster the bloodstream absorbs the cocaine and delivers it to the brain, the more intense the user's high. Because this intense high is relatively short (5 to 10 minutes), the user may administer the drug again in a binge-like pattern.

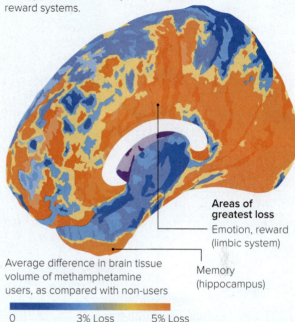

Eroding the Mind
Researchers have mapped brain decay caused by methamphetamine use. The damage affected memory, emotion, and reward systems.

Areas of greatest loss
Emotion, reward (limbic system)

Average difference in brain tissue volume of methamphetamine users, as compared with non-users

Memory (hippocampus)

0   3% Loss   5% Loss

FIGURE 4 Long-Term Effects of Methamphetamine on the Brain

methamphetamine
An addictive stimulant drug that is related to amphetamine but provokes more intense central nervous system effects.

cocaine
A highly addictive central nervous system stimulant that an individual snorts, injects, or smokes.

MINI CASE

Stimulant Use Disorder, Amphetamine-Type Substance

Kaya is a 23-year-old single bisexual African American woman. She has struggled with obesity for many years, and for the past 3 years she has tried many different strategies to lose weight. Her physician prescribed amphetamines but cautioned her about the possibility that she might become dependent on them. Kaya did begin to lose weight, but she also discovered that she liked the extra energy and good feelings the diet pills caused. When she returned to her doctor after having lost the desired weight, she asked him for a refill of her prescription to help her maintain her new figure. When he refused, Kaya asked among her friends until she found the name of a physician willing to accommodate her wish for ongoing refills of the prescription. Over the course of 1 year, Kaya developed a number of psychological problems, including depression, paranoid thinking, and irritability. Despite the fact that she realizes something is wrong, she feels driven to continue using the drug.

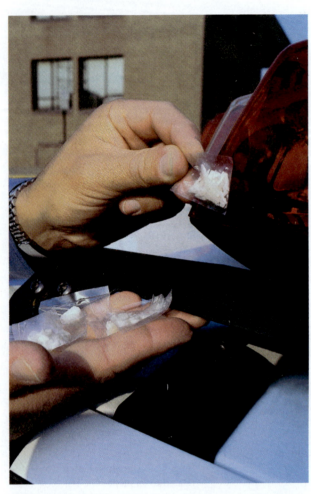

A police officer holds a sample of crack cocaine that has been confiscated from a user. Crack is highly addictive because it produces a very intense but brief high.

©Larry Mulvehill/Corbis

Like amphetamines, cocaine increases body temperature, blood pressure, and heart rate. Cocaine's risks include heart attack, respiratory failure, stroke, seizures, abdominal pain, and nausea. In rare cases, the user can experience sudden death on the first use of cocaine or unexpectedly afterwards. Other adverse effects on the body develop over time and include changes within the nose (loss of sense of smell, chronically runny nose, and nosebleeds), as well as problems with swallowing and hoarseness. Users may experience severe bowel gangrene due to a reduction of blood flow to the digestive system. Cocaine users may also have severe allergic reactions and increased risk of developing HIV/AIDS and other blood-borne diseases. When people use cocaine in binges, they may develop chronic restlessness, irritability, and anxiety. Chronic users may experience severe paranoia in which they have auditory hallucinations and lose touch with reality (NIDA, 2016a).

As Figure 1 illustrated, 1.9 percent of people 12 and older used cocaine in the past month in the year 2016. The rates of cocaine use are about double for men compared to women. The average age of first use is 20.4 years; approximately 1,600 people per day are initiated into the use of cocaine. An estimated 4.2 percent of high school seniors have used it (Monitoring the Future Study, 2017).

Figure 5 shows the impact of cocaine at the synapse. Like other drugs of abuse, cocaine has its effects by stimulating dopamine receptors. Researchers believe it specifically targets an area in the midbrain called the ventral tegmental area (VTA). Pathways from the VTA extend to the nucleus accumbens, a key area of the brain involved in reward. Cocaine's effects appear to be due to its blocking the removal of dopamine from the synapse, which results in an accumulation of dopamine that amplifies the signal to the receiving neurons. The euphoria that users report appears to correspond to this pattern of dopamine activity (NIDA, 2016a). In addition to dopamine, serotonin appears to play a role in the motivational and reinforcing effects of the drug and may also mediate cocaine's aversive effects, at least to some extent (Nonkes, van Bussel, Verheij, & Homberg, 2011).

Cannabis

marijuana
A psychoactive substance derived from the hemp plant whose primary active ingredient is delta-9-tetrahydrocannabinol (THC).

Cannabis is associated with disorders related to use, intoxication, and withdrawal. **Marijuana** is a mix of flowers, stems, and leaves from the hemp plant *Cannabis sativa*, a tall, leafy, green plant that thrives in warm climates. Although the plant contains more than 400 chemical constituents, the primary active ingredient in marijuana is delta-9-tetrahydrocannabinol (THC). Hashish, containing a more concentrated form of THC, comes from the resins of the plant's flowers. The marijuana and hashish that reach the street are never pure THC; other substances, such as tobacco, are always mixed in, too. Synthetic forms of THC serve some medicinal purposes, such as treating asthma and glaucoma and reducing nausea in cancer patients undergoing chemotherapy.

Most people who use marijuana smoke it as a cigarette or in a pipe. Users can also mix the drug in food or serve it as a tea. When smoked, marijuana reaches its peak blood level in about 10 minutes, but the subjective effect of intoxication does not become apparent for another 20 to 30 minutes. This effect may last 2 to 3 hours, but the metabolites of THC can remain in the body for 8 or more days.

People take marijuana in order to alter their bodily sensations and perceptions of their environment. The effects they seek include euphoria, a heightened sense of sensuality and sexuality, and an increased awareness of internal and external stimuli. However, marijuana use also carries a number of unpleasant effects including impaired short-term memory, slowed reaction time, impaired physical coordination, altered judgment, and poor decision making. Instead of feeling euphoric and relaxed, users may experience paranoia and anxiety, particularly when they ingest high doses.

As mentioned earlier in the chapter, marijuana is the most commonly used illicit drug in the United States. However, current prevalence statistics do not take into account the fact that both recreational and medical use of marijuana are now legal in a number of states, and federal regulation has eased in these states as well. The states in which marijuana use is legal (as of 2018) are California, Colorado, Washington, Oregon, Alaska, Nevada, Massachusetts, Vermont, and Maine, as well as the District of Columbia. An additional 21 states allow medical use of marijuana. With these changes in legislation, the definition of an "illicit" drug will need to change in estimates of prevalence statistics. Furthermore, as marijuana use becomes decriminalized, it will be possible to examine the effects of its use on an individual's daily life. A study of Colorado workers showed that marijuana use is most prevalent among workers in the food preparation industry, leading to concerns about occupational safety and the health of the populations these individuals serve (Smith, Hall, Etkind, & Van Dyke, 2018).

THC produces its effects by acting upon specific sites in the brain, called cannabinoid receptors. The brain regions with the highest density of cannabinoid receptors are the areas that influence pleasure but also are active in memory, thinking and concentration, perception of time, sensory responses, and ability to carry out coordinated movement. Many of marijuana's acute effects on cognitive functioning are reversible as long as the individual does not engage in chronic use.

Heavy and continued use of marijuana can produce a number of deleterious effects on bodily functioning, including higher risk of heart attack and impaired respiratory functioning. In addition to developing psychological dependence on marijuana, long-term users may experience lower educational and occupational achievement, psychosis, and persistent cognitive impairment. Table 3 summarizes the research findings on the effects of cannabis use on the cognitive processes that make up executive functioning. Particularly

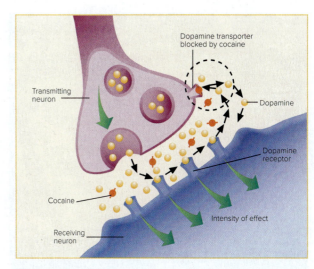

FIGURE 5 Cocaine in the Brain

In the normal communication process, dopamine is released by a neuron into the synapse, where it can bind to dopamine receptors on neighboring neurons. Normally, dopamine is then recycled back into the transmitting neuron by a specialized protein called the dopamine transporter. If cocaine is present, it attaches to the dopamine transporter and blocks the normal recycling process, resulting in a buildup of dopamine in the synapse, which contributes to the pleasurable effects of cocaine.

MINI CASE

Cannabis Use Disorder

Gary is a 22-year-old single heterosexual Caucasian male. He has lived with his parents since dropping out of college midway through his first year 3 years ago. Gary was an average student in high school and, although popular, was not involved in many extracurricular activities. When he entered college, he became interested in the enticing opportunities for new experiences, and he began to smoke marijuana casually with his roommates. However, unlike his roommates, who limited their smoking to parties, Gary found that a nightly hit helped him relax. He started to rationalize that it also helped him study, because it made his thinking more creative.

As his first semester went by, Gary gradually lost interest in his studies, preferring to stay in his room and listen to music while getting high. He realized that it was easy to support his habit by selling marijuana to other people in the dorm. Although he convinced himself that he was not really a dealer, Gary became one of the primary suppliers of marijuana on campus. When he received his first-semester grades, he did not feel particularly discouraged about the fact that he had flunked out. Rather, he felt that he could benefit from having more time to himself. He moved back home and became friendly with some local teenagers who frequented a nearby park and shared drugs there. Gary's parents have all but given up on him, having become deeply discouraged by his laziness and lack of productivity. They know he is using drugs, but they feel helpless to get him to seek professional help. They have learned that it is better to avoid discussing the matter with Gary, because violent arguments always ensue.

Marijuana, shown here in its plant form, is the most frequently used illicit drug in the United States.
©travelib prime/Alamy Stock Photo

hallucinogens

Psychoactive substances that cause abnormal perceptual experiences in the form of illusions or hallucinations, usually visual in nature.

lysergic acid diethylamide (LSD)

A form of a hallucinogenic drug that users ingest in tablets, capsules, and liquid form.

at risk are individuals who begin using marijuana at an early age and continue to use it throughout their lives (Pope & Yurgelun-Todd, 2004).

Hallucinogens

Included in hallucinogen-related disorders are use and intoxication, but not withdrawal. **Hallucinogens** are drugs that cause people to experience profound distortions in their perception of reality. Under the influence of hallucinogens, people see images, hear sounds, and feel sensations that they believe to be real but are not. In some cases, users experience rapid, intense mood swings. Some develop a condition called hallucinogen persisting perception disorder, in which they experience flashbacks or spontaneous hallucinations, delusions, or disturbances in mood similar to the changes that took place while they were intoxicated with the drug. The specific effects and risks of each hallucinogen vary according to the particular substance, as outlined below (NIDA, 2016b).

People take **lysergic acid diethylamide (LSD)** in tablets, capsules, and occasionally liquid form. Users show dramatic changes in their sensations and emotions. They may feel several emotions at once or swing rapidly from one emotion to another. With larger doses, users can experience delusions and visual hallucinations. In addition, they may feel an altered sense of time and self. They may also experience synesthesia, in which they "hear" colors and "see" sounds. These perceptual and mood alterations may be accompanied by severe, terrifying thoughts and feelings of despair, panic, and fear of losing control, going insane, or dying. Even after they stop taking LSD, users may experience flashbacks, leading them to be significantly distressed and impaired in their social and occupational functioning.

Unlike other substances, LSD does not seem to produce compulsive drug-seeking behavior, and most users choose to decrease or stop using it without withdrawal. However, it does produce tolerance, so users may need to take larger doses to achieve the effects they desire. Given the unpredictable nature of the drug's effects, such increases in doses can be dangerous. LSD can also affect other bodily functions, with effects including sweating, loss

TABLE 3 **Summary of Effects of Cannabis on Executive Functions**

Executive Function Measured	Acute Effects	Residual Effects	Long-Term Effects
Attention/concentration	Impaired (light users) Normal (heavy users)	Mixed findings	Largely normal
Decision making and risk taking	Mixed findings	Impaired	Impaired
Inhibition/impulsivity	Impaired	Mixed findings	Mixed findings
Working memory	Impaired	Normal	Normal
Verbal fluency	Normal	Mixed findings	Mixed findings

Acute effects denote 0–6 hours after last cannabis use; residual effects denote 7 hours to 20 days after last cannabis use; and long-term effects denote 3 weeks or longer after last cannabis use.

SOURCE: Crean, R. D., Crane, N. A., & Mason, B. J. (2011). An evidence-based review of acute and long-term effects of cannabis use on executive cognitive functions. *Journal of Addiction Medicine, 5*, 1–8.

MINI CASE

Other Hallucinogen Use Disorder

Candace is a 45-year-old Caucasian married gay woman. An artist, she has used LSD for a number of years because she feels that doing so enhances her paintings and makes them more visually exciting. Although she claims to know how much LSD she can handle, she is occasionally caught off guard and experiences disturbing side effects. She begins sweating, has blurred vision, is uncoordinated, and shakes all over. She commonly becomes paranoid and anxious, and she may act in strange ways, such as running out of her studio and into the street, ranting incoherently. On more than one occasion, the police have picked her up and taken her to the emergency room, where doctors prescribed antipsychotic medication.

of appetite, dry mouth, sleeplessness, tremors, and increased body temperature, blood pressure, and heart rate.

Peyote is a small, spineless cactus whose principal active ingredient, mescaline, can also be produced artificially. Users chew the mescaline-containing crown of the cactus or soak it in water to produce a liquid; some prepare a tea by boiling the cactus in water to rid the drug of its bitter taste. Used as part of religious ceremonies by native peoples in northern Mexico and the southwestern United States, mescaline has long-term effects on these and recreational users that are not known. However, its effects on the body are similar to those of LSD, including increases in body temperature and heart rate, uncoordinated movements, extreme sweating, and flushing. In addition, mescaline may cause flashbacks, much like those associated with LSD.

peyote
A form of a hallucinogenic drug whose primary ingredient is mescaline.

Psilocybin (4-phosphoryloxy-N,N-dimethyltryptamine) and its biologically active form, psilocin (4-hydroxy-N,N-dimethyltryptamine), are substances found in certain mushrooms. Users brew the mushrooms or add them to other foods to disguise their bitter taste. The active compounds in psilocybin-containing mushrooms, like LSD, alter the individual's autonomic functions, motor reflexes, behavior, and perception. Individuals may experience hallucinations, an altered sense of time, and an inability to differentiate between fantasy and reality. Large doses may cause flashbacks, memory impairments, and greater vulnerability to psychological disorders. In addition to the risk of poisoning if the individual incorrectly identifies the mushroom, the bodily effects can include muscle weakness, loss of motor control, nausea, vomiting, and drowsiness.

psilocybin
A form of a hallucinogenic drug found in certain mushrooms.

Researchers developed **phencyclidine (PCP)** in the 1950s as an intravenous anesthetic, but it is no longer used medically because patients became agitated, delusional, and irrational while recovering from its effects. Users can easily mix the white crystalline powder with alcohol, water, or colored dye. PCP may also be available on the illegal drug market in pill, capsule, or colored powder forms that users can smoke, snort, or take orally. When individuals smoke PCP, they may apply the drug to mint, parsley, oregano, or marijuana.

phencyclidine (PCP)
A form of a hallucinogenic drug originally developed as an intravenous anesthetic.

PCP causes users to experience a sense of dissociation from their surroundings and their own sense of self. It has many adverse effects including symptoms that mimic schizophrenia, mood disturbance, memory loss, difficulties with speech and thinking, weight loss, and depression. Although these negative effects led to its diminished popularity as a street drug, PCP appeals to those who still use it because they feel that it makes them stronger, more powerful, and invulnerable. Despite its adverse effects, users can develop strong cravings and compulsive PCP-seeking behavior.

The physiological effects of PCP are extensive. Low to moderate doses produce increases in breathing rate, a rise in blood pressure and pulse, general numbness of the extremities, and loss of muscular coordination, as well as flushing and profuse sweating. At high doses, users experience a drop in blood pressure, pulse rate, and respiration, which may be accompanied by nausea, vomiting, blurred vision, abnormal eye movements, drooling, loss of balance, and dizziness. They may become violent or suicidal. In addition, at high doses users may experience seizures, coma, and death. Those who combine PCP with other central nervous system depressants (such as alcohol) may become comatose.

MDMA, also known as ecstasy, is a purely chemical drug that is often combined with other chemicals to produce long-lasting euphoria for users.

©Fotoman/Alamy Stock Photo

ecstasy (MDMA)
A hallucinogenic drug made from a synthetic substance chemically similar to methamphetamine and mescaline.

The chemical named **MDMA** (3,4-methylenedioxymethamphetamine) and known on the street as **ecstasy** is a synthetic substance chemically similar to methamphetamine and mescaline. Users experience feelings of increased energy, euphoria, emotional warmth, distorted perceptions and sense of time, and unusual tactile experiences. Taken as a capsule or tablet, MDMA was once most popular among white teens and young adults at weekend-long dances known as "raves." Some users combine MDMA with other drugs including marijuana, cocaine, methamphetamine, ketamine, and sildenafil (Viagra), among other substances.

In 2013, 1.4 million individuals in the United States ages 12 and older (0.5 percent of the population) reported they had used hallucinogens (SAMHSA, 2018). Among U.S. high school seniors, 4.9 percent reported using MDMA at least once in their lives, and 5 percent had used LSD at least once (Monitoring the Future Study, 2017).

Users of MDMA may experience a range of unpleasant psychological effects, including confusion, depression, sleep problems, cravings for the drug, and severe anxiety. The drug may be neurotoxic, which means that over time users may experience greater difficulty carrying out cognitive tasks. Like stimulants, MDMA can affect the sympathetic nervous system, leading to increased heart rate and blood pressure, muscle tension, nausea, blurred vision, fainting, chills or sweating, and involuntary teeth clenching. Individuals also risk severe spikes in body temperature, which in turn can lead to liver, kidney, or cardiovascular system failure. Repeated dosages over short periods of time may also interfere with MDMA metabolism, leading to significant and harmful buildup within the body (NIDA, 2016e).

The main neurotransmitter involved with MDMA is serotonin. As shown in Figure 6, in which serotonin is represented by orange-colored triangles, MDMA (labeled "ecstasy") binds to the serotonin transporter responsible for removing serotonin from the synapse. As a result, MDMA extends the effects of serotonin. In addition, MDMA enters the neuron, where it stimulates excessive release of serotonin. MDMA has similar effects on norepinephrine, which leads to increases in autonomic nervous system activity. The drug also releases dopamine, but to a lesser extent.

Researchers find it difficult to investigate the long-term effects of MDMA use on cognitive functioning because users typically take it with other substances. However, significant negative effects on verbal memory do occur with MDMA use alone (Thomasius et al., 2006). MDMA's effects on cognition appear to relate at least in part to the impact of the drug on the availability of an individual's cognitive resources (Roberts, Quednow, Montgomery, & Parrott, 2018). Moreover, when combined with alcohol, MDMA produces a number of long-term adverse psychological effects including paranoia, poor physical health, irritability, confusion, and moodiness.

Opioids

Opioid-related disorders are connected to opioid use, intoxication, and withdrawal. An **opioid** is a substance that relieves pain. Many legally prescribed medications fall within this category, including hydrocodone (Vicodin), oxycodone (OxyContin, Percocet), morphine (Kadian, Avinza), codeine, and related drugs. Clinicians prescribe hydrocodone products most commonly for a variety of painful conditions, including dental procedures and injuries. Physicians often administer morphine before and after surgical procedures to alleviate severe pain. Codeine, on the other hand, is prescribed for mild pain. Some opioid drugs—codeine and diphenoxylate (Lomotil), for example—are used to relieve coughs and severe diarrhea, respectively.

When people take them as prescribed, these medications are effective for managing pain safely. However, because of their potential to produce euphoria as well as physical dependence, they are among the most frequently abused prescription drugs. People who abuse OxyContin may snort or inject it and suffer a serious overdose reaction as a result.

The opioids of abuse include prescription pain relievers, heroin, and synthetic opioids such as fentanyl. The so-called opioid crisis, the rise in the number of individuals addicted to prescription painkillers and resulting deaths, is now seen as a major public health crisis in the United States. It is estimated that 115 U.S. adults a day die after overdosing on opioids. Furthermore, the Centers for Disease Control and Prevention estimates that the total economic burden of prescription opioid misuse alone in the United States has reached $78.5 billion a year, including the costs of health care, lost productivity, addiction treatment, and involvement of the criminal justice system (National Institute on Drug Abuse, 2018b). Figure 7 shows the rates of increase in suspected opioid overdose in the United States by region. The greatest increases have occurred in the Midwest.

Heroin is a form of opioid. It is a painkilling drug synthesized from morphine, a naturally occurring substance extracted from the seed pod of the Asian opium poppy plant. Users inject, snort, sniff, or smoke heroin. The body then converts it to morphine, which binds to the opioid receptors throughout the brain and body, particularly those active in reward and pain perception. Opioid receptors are also located in the brain stem, which contains structures that control breathing, blood pressure, and arousal.

Users experience a surge of euphoric feelings, along with dry mouth, warm flushing of the skin, heaviness in the arms and legs, and compromised mental functioning. Shortly afterward, they alternate between feeling wakeful and drowsy. If users do not inject the drug, they may not feel euphoria at all. With continued use of heroin, users develop tolerance, meaning they need larger amounts of the drug to feel the same effect. Heroin has a high

FIGURE 6 The Impact of Ecstasy (MDMA) on Serotonergic Neurons

opioid
A psychoactive substance that relieves pain.

heroin
A psychoactive substance that is a form of opioid, synthesized from morphine.

MINI CASE

Opioid Use Disorder

Jimmy is a 38-year-old single biracial heterosexual male. He is homeless and has been addicted to heroin for the past 10 years. He began to use the drug at the suggestion of a friend who told him it would help relieve the pressure Jimmy was feeling from his unhappy marriage and financial problems. In a short period of time, he became dependent on the drug and got involved in a theft ring to support his habit. Ultimately, he lost his home and moved to a shelter, where workers assigned Jimmy to a methadone treatment program.

FIGURE 7 Quarterly Rate of Suspected Opioid Overdose by U.S. Region, 2018

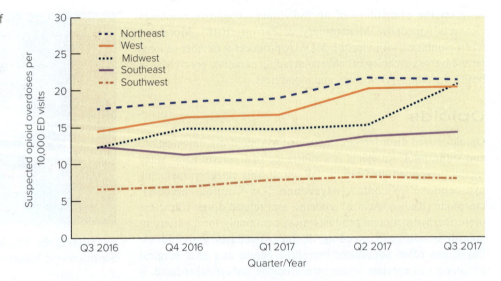

potential for addiction; it is estimated that as many as 23 percent of all users develop dependence (NIDA, 2016c).

There are many serious health consequences of heroin use, including fatal overdoses, infectious diseases (related to needle sharing), damage to the cardiovascular system, abscesses, and liver and kidney disease. Users are often in poor general health and therefore are more susceptible to pneumonia and other pulmonary complications, as well as damage to the brain, liver, and kidneys resulting from the toxic contaminants often added to the drug.

You Be the Judge

Prescribing Prescription Drugs

Patients who suffer from chronic pain present a tremendous challenge to health care professionals. Long-term treatment of chronic pain through prescription medications carries the risk that patients will develop dependence. Moreover, because patients need escalating doses to achieve the same degree of relief, their pain sensitivity and levels of pain might actually increase. At the same time, patients may fear taking an opioid medication that could benefit them due to the risk of developing an addiction and thus may suffer unduly, especially if they are terminally ill. Ironically, some health care professionals as well as patients worry about the risks of addiction among patients who are in their last few months of life.

Addressing the national crisis in overuse of prescription pain medication, the National Institute of Health (2018) launched a campaign known as HEAL (Helping to End Addiction Long-Term Initiative), doubling the federal funding to accelerate scientific solutions to stemming the national epidemic.

Clearly, the development of effective, nonaddicting pain medications is a public health priority. A growing population of older adults and an increasing number of injured military men and women only add to the urgency of this issue. Researchers need to explore alternate medications that can alleviate pain but have less potential for abuse. At the same time, researchers and practitioners in psychology can provide a greater understanding of effective chronic pain management, including identifying factors that predispose some patients to addiction and developing measures to prevent abuse.

Q: *You be the judge*: What is the best way to balance the patient's need for pain relief with the growing national and international crisis in abuse of prescription pain medications?

Chronic heroin users experience severe withdrawal should they discontinue its use. Severe cravings can begin within 2 to 3 days and last for as long as a week, and they can recur years later if the individual experiences certain triggers or stress. There are also dangers to sudden withdrawal, particularly in long-term users who are in poor health. Withdrawal symptoms can include restlessness, muscle and bone pain, insomnia, diarrhea, vomiting, cold flashes, and kicking movements.

Sedatives, Hypnotics, and Anxiolytics

The category of sedatives, hypnotics, and anxiolytics (antianxiety medications) includes prescription medications that act as central nervous system depressants. A **sedative** has a soothing or calming effect, a **hypnotic** induces sleep, and an **anxiolytic** is used to treat anxiety symptoms. The sedating effects of these central nervous system depressants are due to the fact that they increase the levels of the neurotransmitter GABA, which inhibits brain activity and therefore produces a calming effect. Disorders within this category include use disorder, intoxication, and withdrawal.

These medications are among the most commonly abused drugs in the United States. They include benzodiazepines, barbiturates, nonbenzodiazepine sleep medications such as zolpidem (Ambien), eszopiclone (Lunesta), and zaleplon (Sonata). In 2016, 500,000 people ages 12 and older in the United States used sedatives nonmedically, and 2 million misused tranquilizers (SAMHSA, 2017). Although safe when taken as prescribed, these medications have high potential for abuse and dependence. The longer a person uses them, the greater the amount needed to produce the sedating effects. In addition to the risk of dependence, these medications can also have harmful effects on individuals taking other prescription and over-the-counter drugs.

For older adults, the risk of abuse is also high, particularly given the potential for drug interactions with alcohol and other medications. Moreover, older adults with cognitive decline may take their medication incorrectly, which in turn can lead to further cognitive decline (Whitbourne & Meeks, 2011).

Caffeine

Caffeine is a stimulant found in coffee, tea, chocolate, energy drinks, diet pills, and headache remedies. By activating the sympathetic nervous system through increasing the production of adrenaline, caffeine increases an individual's perceived level of energy and alertness. It also increases blood pressure and may lead to increases in the body's production of cortisol, the stress hormone.

Because caffeine is such a common feature of everyday life, people tend not to be aware of its dangers. When consumed in large quantities, caffeine can lead to many adverse reactions, including the development of other forms of substance dependence (Arria et al., 2017). In the United States, at least 130 energy drinks exceed the FDA-recommended limit of 0.02 percent of caffeine. The latest entries are caffeinated flavors of the liquids used in e-cigarettes, which are being marketed as energy enhancers (Lisko et al., 2017).

Disorders included in the caffeine-related category are intoxication and withdrawal, but not caffeine use disorder. Support is growing for adding caffeine use disorder as a diagnosis similar to other substance use disorders (Harstad et al., 2016).

DSM-5 was the first psychiatric manual in the United States to include caffeine withdrawal as a diagnosis (it was already a diagnosis in *ICD-10).* The symptoms of caffeine withdrawal include headache, tiredness and fatigue, sleepiness and drowsiness, dysphoric mood, difficulty concentrating, depression, irritability, nausea,

sedative
A psychoactive substance that has a calming effect on the central nervous system.

hypnotic
A substance that induces sedation.

anxiolytic
An antianxiety medication.

caffeine
A stimulant found in coffee, tea, chocolate, energy drinks, diet pills, and headache remedies.

Energy drinks such as Red Bull contain high amounts of caffeine and other additives such as taurine to boost energy. These drinks put consumers at risk for consuming excess amounts of caffeine, which can lead to major health problems.
©Jill Braaten/McGraw-Hill Education

MINI CASE

Caffeine Intoxication

Carla is a 19-year-old single heterosexual Caucasian woman. She is a sophomore in college who has felt compelled to excel at every endeavor and to become involved in as many activities as time and energy permit. As her commitments increased and her studies became more burdensome, Carla became more and more reliant on coffee, soda, and over-the-counter stimulants to reduce her need for sleep. During final examination week, Carla overdid it. For 3 days straight, she consumed approximately 10 cups of coffee a day, along with a few bottles of energy shots. In addition to her bodily symptoms of restlessness, twitching muscles, flushed face, stomach disturbance, and heart irregularities, Carla began to ramble when she spoke. Her roommate became distressed after seeing Carla's condition and insisted on taking her to the emergency room, where the intake worker recognized her condition as caffeine intoxication.

vomiting, muscle aches, and stiffness. Caffeine withdrawal is estimated to cause significant distress and impairment in daily functioning among 13 percent of people in experimental studies (Juliano & Griffiths, 2004).

Particularly dangerous is the combination of caffeine and alcohol, a problem that is most severe on college campuses where as many as 75 percent report lifetime prevalence of using a caffeinated beverage (Berger, Fendrich, & Fuhrmann, 2013). When users combine alcohol and caffeine, they may not realize how intoxicated they are and as a result may have a higher prevalence of alcohol-related consequences. In one daily-diary study of undergraduates asked to record their daily consumption of caffeine and alcohol, those who consumed caffeine in energy drinks had more alcohol-related problems (Linden-Carmichael & Lau-Barraco, 2017).

Tobacco

nicotine
The psychoactive substance found in cigarettes.

Individuals can be diagnosed with tobacco use disorder or tobacco withdrawal, but not tobacco intoxication. **Nicotine** is the psychoactive substance found in cigarettes. The health risks of tobacco are well known; these risks are primarily associated with smoking cigarettes which, in addition to nicotine, contain tar, carbon monoxide, and other additives. Readily absorbed into the bloodstream, nicotine is also present in chewing tobacco, pipe tobacco, and cigars.

When nicotine enters the bloodstream, it stimulates the release of adrenaline (norepinephrine), which activates the autonomic nervous system and increases blood pressure, heart rate, and respiration. Like other psychoactive substances, nicotine increases the level of dopamine, affecting the brain's reward and pleasure centers. Substances found in tobacco smoke, such as acetaldehyde, may further enhance nicotine's effects on the central nervous system. The withdrawal symptoms associated with quitting tobacco use include irritability, difficulties with concentration, and strong cravings for nicotine.

Although rates of cigarette smoking are decreasing in the United States, from the 2002 high of 26 percent of the population ages 12 and older to the 2016 rate of 19.1 percent, as of 2016 there remained a rate of 23.5 percent among young adults 18 to 25 years old. The rate among youths ages 12 to 17 in 2016 was 3.4 percent (SAMHSA, 2018). Taking the place of tobacco cigarettes, though, are e-cigarettes. In 2016, 3.2 percent of adults were current e-cigarette users, and more than 2 million U.S. middle and high school students had used e-cigarettes in the past 30 days, including 4.3 percent of middle school students and 11.3 percent of high school students (Jamal et al., 2017).

Inhalants

inhalants
A diverse group of substances that cause psychoactive effects by producing chemical vapors.

Inhalants are a diverse group of substances that cause psychoactive effects by producing chemical vapors. These products are not in and of themselves harmful; in fact, they are all products commonly found in the home and workplace. There are four categories of inhalants: volatile solvents (paint thinners or removers, dry-cleaning fluids, gasoline, glue, and lighter fluid), aerosols (sprays that contain propellants and solvents), gases (butane lighters and propane tanks, ether, and nitrous oxide), and nitrites (a special category of products that individuals use as sexual enhancers). Young teens (ages 12 to 15) tend to inhale glue, shoe polish, spray paint, gasoline, and lighter fluid. Older teens (ages 16 to 17) inhale nitrous oxide, and adults (ages 18 and older) are most likely to inhale nitrites. Within the category of inhalant disorders, individuals can be diagnosed as having inhalant use disorder or intoxication, but not inhalant withdrawal.

The effects of an inhalant tend to be short-lived; consequently, users try to extend their high by inhaling repeatedly over a period of several hours. Inhalants have effects similar to those of alcohol, including slurring of speech, loss of coordination, euphoria, dizziness, and, over time, loss of inhibition and control. Users may experience drowsiness and headaches, but depending on the substance, they may also feel confused and nauseated. The vapors displace the air in the lungs, causing hypoxia (oxygen deprivation), which is particularly lethal to neurons in the central nervous system. Long-term use may also cause the myelin sheath around the axon to deteriorate, leading to tremors, muscle spasms, and perhaps permanent muscle damage. The chemicals in inhalants can also cause heart failure and sudden death (NIDA, 2016d).

As Figure 1 shows, 0.6 million persons aged 12 and older in the United States were current inhalant users in 2013. An estimated 3.6 percent of high school seniors reported lifetime inhalant use in 2010 (Johnston, O'Malley, Bachman, & Schulenberg, 2011).

Theories and Treatment of Substance Use Disorders

Since all psychoactive substances operate on the reward and pleasure systems in the brain, similarities exist in the mechanisms through which individuals develop dependence on them. However, important differences exist between alcohol and other substances in the receptor pathways for the substance, the psychosocial factors associated with the users' dependence, and, ultimately, the best treatment methods.

Biological Perspectives Research evidence clearly supports the idea that genetics plays a role in the development of serious substance problems. Extensive studies on humans and laboratory mice suggest possible genetic abnormalities in the opioid receptor on chromosome 1 *(OPRM1)* that may be involved in susceptibility to alcohol and other substances, as well as in sensitivity to pain. A second genetic abnormality appears on chromosome 15 in a cluster of nicotinic receptor subunits *(CHRNA-3, -5,* and *-4)* active in nicotine dependence. The third is a widely studied abnormality affecting catechol-*O*-methyltransferase *(COMT),* which is associated with pain sensitivity, anxiety, and substance abuse (Palmer & de Wit, 2011). Researchers have linked alterations in the gene that codes the adenosine A2A receptor on chromosome 22 to individual differences in the consumption of caffeine and caffeine's effects on sleep, EEGs, and anxiety (Urry & Landolt, 2015).

Except in the case of alcohol dependence, weak evidence exists for the efficacy of pharmacotherapies (Arias & Kranzler, 2008). There are no FDA-approved treatments for dependence on cocaine, methamphetamines, marijuana, hallucinogens, ecstasy, or prescription opioids. There are, however, several treatments for heroin dependence that are particularly effective when combined with behavioral interventions.

Medically assisted detoxification is the first step in treatment of heroin dependence. During detoxification, individuals may receive medications to minimize withdrawal symptoms. To prevent relapse, clinicians may use one or more of three different medications. Developed more than 30 years ago, **methadone** is a synthetic opioid that blocks the effects of heroin by binding to the same receptor sites in the central nervous system. Proper use requires specialized treatment including group and/or individual counseling along with referrals for other medical, psychological, or social services. Methadone is not considered an ideal treatment because of its potential for dependence, even when combined with

methadone
A synthetic opioid that produces a safer and more controlled reaction than heroin and that is used in treating heroin addiction.

REAL STORIES

Robert Downey Jr.: Substance Use Disorder

Set against a Hollywood backdrop, Robert Downey Jr.'s story resembles that of many other individuals struggling with substance use disorder. As a child, Robert was raised by his father, Robert Downey Sr., an actor, producer, and film director, in an environment rich in drug and alcohol use due to his own struggles with substance abuse. Robert himself began using substances at the age of 6 when his father gave him marijuana. Regarding this time in his life, Robert has said, "When my dad and I would do drugs together, it was like him trying to express his love for me in the only way he knew how."

As a teenager, Robert started acting in small roles in his father's films and on Broadway until he began acting in feature films. During the 1980s he gained considerable attention for his roles in several of the "Brat Pack" movies, including *Weird Science* and *The Pick-up Artist* with Molly Ringwald. His major break came in 1987 with a role in *Less than Zero*, in which he played a wealthy young man whose life became consumed by drug use. Robert received considerable praise for his portrayal. "The role was like the ghost of Christmas future," he said later, reflecting on the steady increase in drug use that was to cause him years of turmoil.

As Robert started landing bigger roles in films, substance use problems began to take over his life and impede his professional career. Between 1996 and 2001, he was repeatedly arrested for drug offenses including heroin, cocaine, and marijuana use. He was drinking daily and spending large amounts of time obtaining and doing drugs. In one instance in April 1996, he was pulled over for speeding on Sunset Boulevard in Los Angeles and arrested for possession of heroin and cocaine as well as for having a gun in his car. One month

later, while on parole, he trespassed in a neighbor's home while under the influence and passed out on one of the beds. He was subsequently placed on 3 years' probation with mandatory drug testing. When he missed one of his court-appointed drug tests, he was imprisoned for 4 months.

Like many attempting to break free of the cycle of addiction, Robert had many unsuccessful stays in rehab. He often cited his early drug use and bonding with his father over drugs as a reason it was difficult for him to quit, though he did realize the enormity of his problems. In 1999 he told a judge, "It's like I've got a shotgun in my mouth with my finger on the trigger, and I like the taste of gun metal."

In 2000, Robert spent a year in a California substance abuse treatment facility. Upon his release he joined the cast of the hit television show *Ally McBeal*. Though his role was a huge success that led to a boost in ratings, he was written out of the show after he was again arrested for drug possession.

In an interview with Oprah Winfrey in 2004, Robert said, "When someone says, 'I really wonder if maybe I should go to rehab?' Well, uh, you're a wreck, you just lost your job, and your wife left you. Uh, you might want to give it a shot. . . . I finally said 'you know what? I don't think I can continue doing this.' And I reached out for help, and I ran with it . . . you can reach out for help in kind of a half-assed way and you'll get it

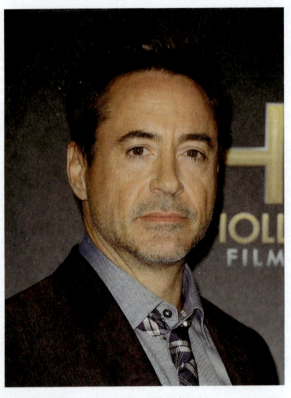

©Jason LaVeris/Getty Images

and you won't take advantage of it. It's not that difficult to overcome these seeming ghastly problems . . . what's hard is to decide to actually do it."

Though he was court-ordered to go to rehab, his changed attitude helped Robert successfully abstain from drug use. After attaining sobriety he came back to Hollywood, and after he had played smaller roles in independent films for several years, his career skyrocketed following his star turn in the blockbuster film *Iron Man* (2008). Since then he has gone on to enjoy lead roles in several major Hollywood films, a feat that had seemed unimaginable at the lowest points in his life.

buprenorphine
A medication used in the treatment of heroin addiction.

naltrexone
A medication used in the treatment of heroin addiction.

psychosocial interventions. **Buprenorphine**, approved by the FDA in 2002, produces less physical dependence, a lower risk of overdose, and fewer withdrawal effects. Originally developed as a pain medication, it is also approved for treatment of opiate dependence. The FDA has also approved **naltrexone** for heroin dependence, but it is not widely used because patients are less likely to comply with treatment due to such side effects as nausea and headaches (NIAAA, 2018).

For nicotine dependence, clinicians may use biologically based treatments. Nicotine replacement therapies (NRTs), including nicotine gum and the nicotine patch, were the first FDA-approved pharmacological treatments. These deliver controlled doses of nicotine to the individual to relieve symptoms of withdrawal. Other FDA-approved products include nasal sprays, inhalers, and lozenges. However, the ability of the nicotine patch to treat nicotine dependence has come under question. In a follow-up study of almost 800 smokers, there were no differences in relapse rates among those who did and did not use the patch (Alpert, Connolly, & Biener, 2012). Other biological approaches to nicotine dependence are medications that do not deliver nicotine, including bupropion (Wellbutrin), an antidepressant, and varenicline tartrate (Chantix), which targets nicotine receptors in the brain.

Psychological Perspectives Whether or not individuals with dependence on substances other than alcohol receive biologically based treatment, cognitive-behavioral therapy (CBT) is now widely understood to be a crucial component of successful treatment (Arias & Kranzler, 2008) and an important counterpart to biological theories and treatments.

The principles applied in treating substance use disorders other than alcohol through CBT are similar to those in treating alcohol dependence. Well-controlled studies support the efficacy of CBT for populations dependent on a wide range of substances. Clinicians may combine CBT with motivational therapies, as well as with behavioral interventions that focus on contingency management. In addition, clinicians can readily adapt CBT to a range of clinical modalities, settings, and age groups. Given the limitations of medication-only treatment, CBT also provides an effective adjunct in both inpatient and outpatient clinics. The ability to help clients develop coping skills is useful in fostering compliance with pharmacotherapies such as methadone and naltrexone as well. Because these interventions are relatively brief and highly focused, they are adaptable to clients treated within managed care who may not have access to longer-term treatment (Carroll, 2011).

12.3 Non-Substance-Related Disorders

Gambling Disorder

People who have **gambling disorder** are unable to resist recurrent urges to gamble despite knowing that it will bring negative consequences to themselves or others. The diagnosis in *DSM-IV-TR* included gambling disorder as an impulse-control disorder. In *DSM-5*, it is included with substance use disorders because it is now conceptualized as showing many of the same behaviors, such as cravings, increasing needs to engage in the behavior, and negative social consequences. The unique features of gambling disorder include behaviors such as chasing a bad bet, lying about how much has been lost, searching for financial bailouts, and committing crimes to support gambling.

As venues for gambling continue to become available on a more widespread basis, including online gambling and such formats as fantasy leagues, the incidence of gambling disorder appears to be on the increase. Among countries with legalized gambling, lifetime prevalence estimates range from about 0.5 to as high as 3.5 percent of the adult population (Stucki & Rihs-Middel, 2007). In the United States, although the large majority of adults have gambled at some point in their lives, gambling disorder was estimated to be diagnosable in 0.6 percent. Moreover, the greater the number of occasions on which people gambled, the higher their chances of developing gambling disorder—with the highest prevalence occurring after people had gambled 1,000 times.

Gambling disorder often co-occurs with other psychological disorders (Rodriguez-Monguio, Brand, & Volberg, 2018). The highest risk of developing gambling disorder occurs among people who engage in gambling on games involving mental skill (such as cards), followed by sports betting, use of gambling machines, and betting on horse races or cock and dog fights (Kessler et al., 2008). People with gambling disorder who bet on sports tend

gambling disorder
A non-substance-related disorder involving the persistent urge to gamble.

Individuals with gambling disorder often experience severe financial problems due to their inability to stop betting money no matter how much they try.

©Glowimages/Getty Images

to be young men who have substance use disorders. Those who bet on slot machines are more likely to be older women who have higher rates of other psychological disorders and begin gambling at a later age (Petry, 2003). For these older women, using bus tours to travel to casinos also presents a risk for problem gambling (Maas et al., 2017). In general, women are less likely than men to engage in the type of gambling that depends on strategy, such as poker (Odlaug, Marsh, Kim, & Grant, 2011).

People with gambling disorder also have high rates of other disorders, particularly nicotine dependence (60 percent), dependence on other substances (58 percent), mood disorder (38 percent), and anxiety disorder (37 percent). Mood and anxiety disorders are more likely to precede, rather than follow, the onset of gambling disorder (Lorains, Cowlishaw, & Thomas, 2011). Older adults are less likely than younger adults to have gambling disorder, but they are nevertheless at risk because of limited incomes and lack of access to more physically engaging activities (Subramaniam et al., 2015).

The repetitive behaviors characteristic of gambling disorder may be viewed as resulting from an imbalance between two competing and relatively separate neurobiological mechanisms—those responsible for urges and those responsible for cognitive control (Grant et al., 2010). There may also be genetic contributions, perhaps including abnormalities in dopamine receptor genes (Uhl et al., 2017).

From a behavioral perspective, gambling disorder may develop in part because gambling follows a variable-ratio reinforcement schedule in which rewards occur, on average, every X number of times. This pattern of reinforcement produces behaviors that are highly resistant to extinction. Slot machines, in particular, produce payoffs on this type of schedule, maintaining high rates of response by gamblers. Classical conditioning also operates to maintain this behavior, because gamblers learn to associate certain cues with gambling, including their internal states or moods and external stimuli such as advertisements for gambling.

Cognitive factors too play an important role in gambling disorder. People with this disorder seem to engage in a phenomenon known as discounting of probabilistic rewards, in which they discount or devalue rewards they could obtain in the future compared to rewards they can obtain right away (Petry, 2011). They also engage in other cognitive distortions, many of which spring from poor judgment of the probabilities that their gambling will lead to successful outcomes, as shown in Table 4.

The **pathways model** approaches gambling disorder from a developmental perspective, proposing that three main paths lead to three distinct subtypes of people with gambling disorder (Valleur et al., 2016). The person with the behaviorally conditioned subtype had few symptoms prior to developing the disorder but, through frequent exposure to gambling, develops positive associations, distorted cognitions, and poor decision making about gambling. The individual in the emotionally vulnerable subtype had preexisting depression, anxiety, and perhaps a history of trauma; gambling helps this individual feel better. The

pathways model
Approach to gambling disorder which predicts that there are three main developmental paths leading to three distinct subtypes.

TABLE 4 **Common Cognitive Distortions in People with Gambling Disorder**

Type of Distortion	Examples of Cognitive Distortions	Example
Representativeness	Gambler's fallacy	When events generated by a random process have deviated from the population average in a short run, such as a roulette ball falling on red four times in a row, individuals may erroneously believe that the opposite deviation (e.g., ball falls on black) becomes more likely.
	Overconfidence	Individuals express a degree of confidence in their knowledge or ability that is not warranted by objective reality.
	Trends in number picking	Lottery players commonly try to apply long-run random patterns to short strings in their picks such as avoiding duplicate numbers and adjacent digits in number strings.
Availability	Illusory correlations	Individuals believe events that they expect to be correlated, due to previous experience or perceptions, have been correlated in previous experience even when they have not been, such as wearing a "lucky hat" they wore when they won previously.
	Availability of others' wins	When individuals see and hear other gamblers winning, they start to believe that winning is a regular occurrence, which reinforces their belief that they will win if they continue to play.
	Inherent memory bias	Individuals are biased to recollect wins with greater ease than losses. They then reframe their memories regarding gambling experiences in a way that focuses on positive experiences (wins) and disregards negative experiences (losses). This causes them to rationalize their decision to continue gambling.
Additional cognitive distortions	Illusion of control	Individuals have a higher expectancy for success than objective probability would warrant.
	Switching and double switching	Individuals recognize errors and process gambling-related situations in a rational way when they are not actively participating but abandon rational thought when they personally take part in gambling.

SOURCE: Fortune, E. E., & Goodie, A. S. (2011). Cognitive distortions as a component and treatment focus of pathological gambling: A review. *Psychology of Addictive Behaviors, 26*(2), 298–310.

third type of person with pathological gambling has preexisting impulsivity, attentional difficulties, and antisocial characteristics. For this individual, the risk of gambling provides thrills and excitement.

The pathways model suggests that differing therapeutic approaches may work for each of the three subtypes of gambling disorder, but cognitive-behavioral therapy has the greatest empirical support. The clinician begins teaching clients to understand the triggers for their gambling by having them describe their pattern of gambling behaviors. For example, common triggers include unstructured or free time, negative emotional states, reminders such as sports broadcasts or advertisements, and available money. Using this information to help clients analyze when they gamble and when they do not, the clinician then helps them increase pleasant activities, think of ways to handle cravings or urges, become more assertive, and correct their irrational cognitions. At the end of treatment, the clinician helps prepare clients for setbacks using relapse-prevention methods in which the goal is not complete abstinence but a reduction to a point below pretreatment levels. The individual who shows positive effects may also show personality changes that will serve to protect against relapse (Müller et al., 2017).

Brief motivational interviewing may also be a beneficial treatment for individuals with problem gambling. The individual may choose to pursue complete abstinence or moderation as a goal of this treatment; both can be equally effective in reducing the amount of money gambled, the number of days the individual gambles, as well as the individual's perception of having achieved treatment-related goals (Stea, Hodgins, & Fung, 2015).

Other Non-Substance-Related Disorders

In addition to classifying gambling disorder as a non-substance-related disorder, the *DSM-5* authors considered adding Internet gaming disorder to the category. For now, however, they have included it in Section 3 as a disorder requiring further study. Although there is ample evidence to indicate that Internet gaming is becoming a problematic behavior in its own right, the available research was not considered sufficiently well developed yet to justify inclusion in the diagnostic system. Much of the data in support of this condition was produced by studies conducted in Asia that used inconsistent definitions of the phenomenon. Therefore, the *DSM-5* work group believed further investigations are required to produce reliable prevalence estimates. Other disorders the work group considered adding were "sex addiction," "exercise addiction," and "shopping addiction," to name a few. However, the group believed there were even fewer empirical studies in peer-reviewed articles to justify their inclusion even in Section 3.

12.4 Substance Disorders: The Biopsychosocial Perspective

The biopsychosocial model provides an extremely useful approach for understanding substance use disorders and approaches to treatment. Genetics clearly plays a role in the development of these disorders, and the action of substances on the central nervous system also operates to maintain dependence. Developmental issues in particular are critical for understanding the nature of these disorders, which often have their origins during late childhood and early adolescence. Moreover, because alcohol, drugs, and medications with high abuse potential continue to be widely available, sociocultural factors play a strong role in maintaining dependence among users. Addictions have characterized human behavior throughout the millennia; however, with more widespread public education and advances in both genetics and psychotherapeutic interventions, it is possible that we will see advances in prevention as well.

Carl initially had some difficulties in finding an AA meeting in which he felt comfortable, although once he found the right group for him, he looked forward to attending on a daily basis and remained highly motivated to refrain from drinking. He connected with many members of the group and felt, for the first time in his life, that he had a supportive group of friends. He also began a course of mood-stabilizing medication that did not require weekly blood tests and that resulted in significantly lower side effects than lithium, which was helpful in encouraging him to continue taking his medication regularly. In psychotherapy, Carl and his therapist focused on processing what he was learning in AA as well as on mood-monitoring skills for bipolar disorder. Carl will continue to live with Sharon until he feels stable enough to look for a job and begin to support himself again.

Dr. Tobin's reflections: Carl's case is somewhat unusual in that many individuals who experience substance abuse and/or dependence begin abusing substances earlier in life. Carl, on the other hand, had been able to refrain from drinking for many years until he was tempted by his boss.

Until that point, he showed good insight in his awareness that he may be genetically predisposed to alcohol use disorder, based on his parents' history. In therapy, he can explore the reasons he began drinking in order to gain approval from his boss.

Carl's case is also a good example of the destructive combination of alcohol use disorder and a psychological disorder. Such comorbidity is not rare, especially among those suffering from mood disorders, due to the self-medicating effects that alcohol sometimes offers. Fortunately, alcohol use disorders typically have a good prognosis after appropriate intervention, and they are not incurable.

Carl will have to work hard at staying sober and monitoring his bipolar disorder. Much of the focus of his treatment will be on keeping his mood stable in order to prevent relapsing into alcohol abuse in the future. Fortunately, he appears highly motivated to remain abstinent from alcohol and get his life back in order. Finding a supportive AA group in which he feels he can trust the other members is a crucial aspect of his treatment and will be a wonderful source of support that will help him through his recovery.

SUMMARY

- A substance is a chemical that alters a person's mood or behavior when smoked, injected, drunk, inhaled, or ingested. Substance intoxication is the temporary maladaptive experience of behavioral or psychological changes that are due to the accumulation of a substance in the body. When some substances are discontinued, people may experience symptoms of substance withdrawal that involve a set of physical and psychological disturbances. Tolerance occurs when an individual requires increasingly greater amounts of the substance in order to achieve its desired effects or when the person feels less of an effect after using the same amount of the substance. Substance use disorder is a cluster of cognitive, behavioral, and physiological symptoms indicating that the individual uses a substance despite significant substance-related problems.

- Approximately one in seven people in the United States have a history of alcohol abuse or dependence. The short-term effects of alcohol use are appealing to many people because

of the sedating qualities of this substance, although side effects such as hangovers cause distress. The long-term effects of heavy use are worrisome and involve serious harm to many organs of the body, resulting in medical problems and possibly dementia. Researchers in the field of alcohol dependence were among the first to propose the biopsychosocial model to explain the development of a psychological disorder. In the realm of biological contributors, researchers have focused on the role of genetics in light of the fact that dependence runs in families. This line of research has focused on markers and genetic mapping. Psychological theories focus on concepts derived from behavioral theory, as well as cognitive-behavioral and social learning perspectives. For example, according to the widely accepted expectancy model, people with alcohol use disorder develop problematic beliefs about alcohol early in life through reinforcement and observational learning. Researchers and theorists working within the sociocultural perspective regard stressors within the family, community, and culture as factors that lead the person to develop alcohol use disorder.

- Clinicians may derive treatment for alcohol problems in varying degrees from each of the three perspectives. In biological terms, medications may be used to control symptoms of withdrawal, to control symptoms associated with coexisting conditions, or to provoke nausea following alcohol ingestion. Clinicians use various psychological interventions, some of which are based on behavioral and cognitive-behavioral techniques.

- Stimulants have an activating effect on the nervous system. Amphetamines in moderate amounts cause euphoria, increased confidence, talkativeness, and energy. In higher doses, the user has more intense reactions and, over time, can become addicted and develop psychotic symptoms. Cocaine users experience stimulating effects for a shorter period of time that are nevertheless quite intense. In moderate doses, cocaine leads to euphoria, sexual excitement, potency, energy, and talkativeness. At higher doses, psychotic symptoms may develop. In addition to disturbing psychological symptoms, serious medical problems can arise from the use of cocaine. Cannabis, or marijuana, causes altered perception and bodily sensations, as well as maladaptive behavioral and psychological reactions. Most of the acute effects of cannabis intoxication are reversible, but a long period of abuse is likely to lead to dependence and adverse psychological and physical effects. Hallucinogens cause abnormal perceptual experiences in the form of illusions and hallucinations.

Opioids include naturally occurring substances (morphine and opium) as well as semisynthetic drugs (heroin) and synthetic drugs (methadone). Opioid users experience a rush characterized by a range of psychological reactions as well as intense bodily sensations, some of which reflect life-threatening symptoms, particularly during episodes of withdrawal. Sedatives, hypnotics, and anxiolytics are substances that induce relaxation, sleep, tranquility, and reduced awareness. Although not typically regarded as an abused substance, caffeine in high doses can cause a number of psychological and physical problems. Nicotine, the psychoactive chemical found in tobacco, is highly addictive. Withdrawal from nicotine can result in mood and behavior disturbances.

- Various treatment programs for people with substance-related disorders have emerged within the biopsychosocial perspective. Biological treatment may include the prescription of substances that block or reduce cravings. Behavioral treatment relies on techniques such as contingency management, while clinicians utilize cognitive-behavioral techniques to help clients modify their thoughts, expectancies, and behaviors associated with drug use. Detailed relapse-prevention plans are an important part of alcohol treatment programs.

- Gambling disorder is characterized by the persistent urge to gamble. Individuals with this disorder may feel unable to stop themselves from participating in gambling events or games, even after they have experienced significant financial and material losses.

KEY TERMS

Alcohol myopia theory	Heroin	Phencyclidine (PCP)
Amphetamine	Hypnotic	Potentiation
Anterograde amnesia	Inhalants	Psilocybin
Anxiolytic	Korsakoff's syndrome	Relapse prevention
Buprenorphine	Lysergic acid diethylamide (LSD)	Retrograde amnesia
Caffeine	Marijuana	Sedative
Cocaine	Methadone	Stimulant
Depressant	Methamphetamine	Substance
Disulfiram	Naltrexone	Substance intoxication
Dual-process theory	Nicotine	Substance use disorder
Ecstasy (MDMA)	Opioid	Tolerance
Gambling disorder	Pathways model	Wernicke's disease
Hallucinogens	Peyote	Withdrawal

Neurocognitive Disorders

Learning Objectives

13.1 Describe characteristics of neurocognitive disorders.

13.2 Identify the symptoms of delirium.

13.3 Understand the symptoms, theories, and treatment of neurocognitive disorder due to Alzheimer's disease.

13.4 Explain the differences among neurocognitive disorders that are unrelated to Alzheimer's disease.

13.5 Identify neurocognitive disorders due to traumatic brain injury (TBI).

13.6 Describe neurocognitive disorders due to substances/medications and HIV infection.

13.7 Explain neurocognitive disorders due to another general medical condition.

13.8 Analyze neurocognitive disorders through the biopsychosocial perspective.

©Imagesbybarbara/Getty Images

Case Report: Irene Heller

Demographic information: 76-year-old married Caucasian heterosexual female

Presenting problem: Irene was referred to a private specialty practice for neuropsychological testing by her primary care physician, who noted a significant decline in Irene's memory and motor functioning from the previous year.

During the initial interview before neuropsychological testing was conducted, Irene was asked about her cognitive functioning. She had difficulty answering some of the questions, and her daughter Jillian, who had accompanied her, provided most of the information. Jillian reported that her mother's visit to the doctor was not the first sign of abnormalities in her recent behavior, and that over the past month she and her brother Steve had noticed their mother was acting strangely. Irene currently lives by herself in the town where her two grown children live. On two separate occasions neighbors have reported finding her in the parking lot of her apartment complex late at night, wearing her nightgown and looking "totally out of it." The neighbors brought her home, though Irene did not recall these incidents.

When asked about any physical changes she had noticed recently, Irene stated that she was having difficulty writing because she was unable to grasp pens or other writing instruments. As a result she hadn't been able to pay her bills and sometimes had trouble preparing food for herself. In fact, she noted that she had lost about 10 pounds over the past 2 months because of this. Jillian also reported that she had noticed her mother was having significant walking difficulties recently. Irene preferred to stay at home as a result and had begun to miss out on many activities she had previously enjoyed, including spending time with her family and going to weekly bridge games.

Jillian added that Irene typically called either her or her brother at least once per day, and that they had family meals together once or twice every week. During the past 2 months when she or her brother called their mother on the phone, Jillian said, Irene's speech was sometimes difficult to understand, and she would forget to whom she was speaking. All this was very troubling to Jillian, though Irene wasn't able to acknowledge much of what Jillian was reporting. "I guess I sometimes have a hard time paying my bills or calling my children. I guess I just don't feel like it these days."

Jillian stated that she and her brother thought Irene's behavior might be due to medical reasons. Irene has been diagnosed with type II diabetes and according to Jillian had forgotten to check her blood sugar and take insulin for 2 consecutive days. When they didn't hear from her, Jillian and Steve went to Irene's house to check on her and found her nearly unconscious in her living room. After giving her insulin, the siblings made an appointment with Irene's primary care physician for the next day.

After the clinical interview, Irene completed neuropsychological testing, which consisted of a battery of cognitive tests aimed at measuring her overall cognitive functioning.

Relevant history: Irene reported that she has remained relatively healthy throughout her life and that she has never experienced any major medical, emotional, or cognitive problems. Jillian stated that her mother was diagnosed with type II diabetes 2 years ago and has been taking insulin to regulate her blood sugar. Jillian also reported that until her recent decline, Irene had remained quite active and participated in many social activities, carrying out all her activities of daily living without difficulty.

Case formulation: The sudden onset of Irene's symptoms is typical of neurocognitive disorder due to vascular disease. Since Irene had stopped taking her medication, she was putting herself at significant medical risk. Further, consistent with diagnostic criteria, Irene's functioning was significantly impaired—she had ceased her previous activities and had even stopped paying her bills due to her motor difficulties.

The results of the neuropsychological testing indicated that Irene indeed was experiencing a significant impairment in her short-term memory and her ability to speak fluently and coherently. She also evidenced difficulties in her executive functioning, including organizing and sequencing information presented to her. Taking this together with the physical examination by her doctor, Irene is given a diagnosis of major vascular neurocognitive disorder with behavioral disturbance, although until she has an MRI to confirm the existence of brain lesions, the diagnosis will be tentative.

Treatment plan: Irene will be referred for an MRI to confirm her diagnosis, upon which she will be given a referral for medication and follow-up home care, if needed.

Sarah Tobin, PhD

13.1 Characteristics of Neurocognitive Disorders

neurocognitive disorder
Disorders involving decline acquired in life in one or more domains of cognition associated with alterations in the brain.

Many sources of insult or injury can affect an individual's brain, such as trauma, disease, and exposure to toxic substances including drugs. People can develop delusions, hallucinations, mood disturbances, and extreme personality changes as a result of these influences on the brain. The **neurocognitive disorders** specifically describe decline acquired in one or more domains of cognition associated with alterations in the brain.

Clinicians use neuropsychological testing and neuroimaging techniques, as well as an individual's medical history, to decide whether an individual's symptoms fall into the category of a neurocognitive disorder. Neuropsychological testing helps clinicians identify specific patterns of responses that appear to fit known disease profiles. They combine this knowledge with their client's medical history to see whether a specific event triggered the symptoms. In addition, neuroimaging provides clinicians with an inside look at the brain to help them connect symptoms with specific illnesses or injuries. Both forms of assessment are required for an individual to receive a diagnosis of one of these disorders.

Table 1 shows the domains covered in the neurocognitive disorders and types of abilities included in each. Clinicians incorporate additional tests from neuropsychological batteries as needed to help assess the client's level of functioning in each of these domains. Using interviews with the client and family members or significant others, they also rate the client as showing major or mild neurocognitive disorder based on criteria indicated within each domain. For example, a mild level of memory impairment indicates the individual relies on notes or reminders in everyday tasks. Major impairment is diagnosed if the individual is unable to keep track of short lists or complete a task in a single sitting.

In *DSM-5*, the term *neurocognitive disorder* replaces *dementia*, used in *DSM-IV-TR* to refer to a form of cognitive impairment in which individuals undergo progressive loss of cognitive functions severe enough to interfere with their normal daily activities and social relationships. The *DSM-5* work group considered the term *dementia* to be acceptable for use in medical settings, but there is hope that this overly general term will eventually be replaced altogether.

major neurocognitive disorders
Disorders involving significant cognitive decline from a previous level of performance.

Major neurocognitive disorders are diagnosed when individuals show significant cognitive decline from a previous level of performance in the six domains of Table 1 based on a standardized neuropsychological or other quantified clinical assessment. These cognitive deficits must interfere with the individual's ability to perform necessary tasks in everyday living, not occur exclusively with delirium, and lack a better explanation as another

TABLE 1 Neurocognitive Domains in *DSM-5*

Domain	Examples of Relevant Abilities	Assessment Task Examples
Complex attention	Sustained attention	Maintaining attention over time
	Selective attention	Separating signals from distractors
	Divided attention	Attending to two or more tasks at once
Executive function	Planning	Deciding on a sequence of actions
	Decision making	Performing tasks that require choosing between alternatives
	Working memory	Being able to hold information in memory while manipulating stimuli
	Mental/cognitive flexibility	Switching between two concepts, tasks, or response rules (e.g., picking odd numbers, then picking even numbers)
Learning and memory	Immediate memory span	Remembering a series of digits or words
	Recent memory	Encoding new information such as word lists or a short story
Language	Expressive language	Being able to name objects
	Grammar and syntax	Speaking without errors while performing other tasks
	Receptive language	Being able to understand word definitions and instructions
Perceptual-motor	Visual perception	Assessing whether a figure can be "real" based on its depiction in two-dimensional space
	Visuoconstructional	Assembling items requiring hand-eye coordination
	Praxis	Being able to engage in common motor skills, use common tools, imitate the use of tools, and imitate gestures
	Gnosis	Recognizing faces and colors
Social cognition	Recognition of emotions	Identifying emotions in images of faces
	Theory of mind	Being able to consider another person's mental state based on pictures or stories

psychological disorder. The diagnosis of **mild neurocognitive disorder** is applied when the individual shows modest levels of cognitive decline. These declines are not severe enough to interfere with the individual's capacity for living independently.

After diagnosing the level of cognitive impairment, the clinician next must take on the sometimes challenging process of specifying which disease appears to be responsible for the cognitive symptoms. When one specific disease cannot be diagnosed, the clinician can indicate this or indicate multiple diseases that contribute to the symptoms.

mild neurocognitive disorders
Disorders involving modest cognitive decline from a previous level of performance.

13.2 Delirium

People diagnosed with **delirium** temporarily experience disturbances in their attention and awareness. The symptoms tend to appear abruptly and fluctuate over the duration of the disorder. The core of delirium is an acute state of confusion or impairment in cognitive processing that affects memory, orientation, executive functioning, ability to use language, visual perception, and learning.

To receive a diagnosis of delirium, the individual must show these changes in consciousness or awareness over a very short period of time, on the order of hours or days. The diagnosis also requires that a general medical condition must cause the disturbance. Clinicians therefore specify whether the delirium results from substance intoxication, substance withdrawal, a medication, or other medical condition(s). The clinician also rates the delirium as acute (occurring a few hours or days) or persistent (occurring over weeks or months).

delirium
A neurocognitive disorder that is temporary in nature involving disturbances in attention and awareness.

MINI CASE

Delirium Due to Another Medical Condition, Acute

Jack is a 23-year-old single heterosexual African American male. He works as a contractor, and one day toward the end of his shift he collapsed with a high fever accompanied by chills. Luckily, his co-workers saw him. When they told him he would be rushed to the hospital, Jack repeatedly responded with the nonsensical answer, "The hammer's no good." Jack's co-workers were then startled by his suggestions that they were trying to steal his tools. Grabbing at things in the air, he also insisted that people were throwing objects at him. He couldn't remember the name of anyone at the site; in fact, he was unsure where he was. Initially, he resisted his co-workers' attempts to take him to the hospital because of his concern that they had formed a plot to harm him.

Delirium is a temporary condition that can have a wide range of physiological causes. Individuals who experience this condition suffer from several sensory disturbances simultaneously.

©Marie Docher/Media Bakery

Delirium can develop for a variety of reasons, including substance intoxication or withdrawal, head injury, high fever, and vitamin deficiency. People of any age can experience delirium, but it is more common among older adults who have been hospitalized for medical or psychiatric reasons. In addition to age, the risk factors for delirium include a previous history of stroke, neurocognitive disorder, sensory impairment, and use of multiple prescription medications ("polypharmacy"). People at risk may develop delirium following infections, urinary retention or use of catheters, dehydration, loss of mobility, and disorders affecting heart rate. Increases in immune system inflammatory responses may also contribute to delirium (Dillon et al., 2017).

Infection is another precipitating factor in at-risk individuals. In a survey of nearly 1.3 million patients studied over the years 1998 to 2005, researchers found that the most frequent causes of delirium were infections, including respiratory infections, cellulitis, and urinary tract and kidney infections. The next largest cause was some type of central nervous system disorder, including cancer, neurocognitive disorder, stroke, and seizure. The third most frequent cause of delirium included metabolic disorders, cardiovascular disease, and orthopedic procedures. However, over the course of the study, drug-induced delirium increased in prevalence among older adults, suggesting that either hospital workers became more attuned to this diagnosis or that people in this age group are becoming increasingly likely to receive delirium-inducing medications. Making health professionals aware of adverse drug effects may ultimately help to reduce the prevalence of delirium in high-risk individuals (Lin, Heacock, & Fogel, 2010).

Apart from the cognitive symptoms of inattention and memory loss, individuals experiencing delirium may also have hallucinations, delusions, abnormalities in sleep/wake cycles, changes in mood, and movement abnormalities (Jain, Chakrabarti, & Kulhara, 2011). Once they experience this condition, people who have delirium are more likely to experience medical complications that can cause rehospitalization and a higher risk of mortality (Marcantonio et al., 2005). Alzheimer's disease is another potential outcome due to the effects on the brain of inflammation of the immune system following a surgical procedure or injury (Cortese & Burger, 2017).

There are several specialized tests to assess delirium. The Delirium Rating Scale–Revised (DRS-R-98) (Trzepacz et al., 2001) is a widely used measure that has been translated into several languages (Table 2) and has well-established validity and reliability (Grover, Chakrabarti, Shah, & Kumar, 2011). The advantage of this

TABLE 2 Delirium Rating Scale Items

The following items are used to rate the presence of delirium using rating scales developed within each area of functioning:

1. Presence of sleep-wake cycle disturbance
2. Perceptual disturbances and hallucinations
3. Delusions
4. Outward presentation of emotions reflecting instability, lack of self-control, or inappropriate responses to a situation
5. Language impairment
6. Abnormalities in thought processes such as loose associations
7. Motor agitation such as pacing, fidgeting, or restlessness
8. Slowing or loss of spontaneity of motor movements
9. Lack of orientation to person, place, and time
10. Loss of attentional focus and ability to sustain attention
11. Loss of short-term memory
12. Loss of long-term memory
13. Difficulty in navigating one's living area or environment

SOURCE: Trzepacz, P. T., Mittal, D., Torres, R., Kanary, K., Norton, J., & Jimerson, N. (2001). Validation of the Delirium Rating Scale-Revised–98: Comparison with the Delirium Rating Scale and the Cognitive Test for Delirium. *The Journal of Neuropsychiatry and Clinical Neurosciences, 13,* 229–242.

scale is that although it was designed for psychiatrists, other professionals (physicians, nurses, psychologists) and researchers can also use it. When completing the instrument, the clinician can use information gathered from family members, visitors, hospital staff, physicians, medical charts, and even hospital roommates.

Treatment of delirium includes a pharmacological approach that relies on antipsychotics including haloperidol and risperidone. In one study, this combination was found to resolve symptoms of delirium in as many as 84 percent of cases over a period of 4 to 7 days (Boettger, Breitbart, & Passik, 2011). Although haloperidol is considered potentially useful in reducing delirium in high-risk patients, research does not support its efficacy as a preventive (van den Boogaard et al., 2018).

Instead of using medications as a prevention for the development of delirium, clinicians can provide high-risk patients with cognitively stimulating activities such as discussions of current events or word games. In this approach, multidisciplinary staff addresses the risk factors of delirium as soon as a patient is admitted to an acute care facility for rehabilitation (after, for example, a hip fracture) rather than wait for delirium to develop (Oberai et al., 2018).

13.3 Neurocognitive Disorder Due to Alzheimer's Disease

Neurocognitive disorder due to Alzheimer's disease is a disorder associated with progressive, gradual declines in memory, learning, and at least one other cognitive domain (see Table 3). The first symptoms of memory loss precede a cascade of changes that eventually ends in death due to the development of medical illness resulting from infection or failure of vital bodily organs.

Alzheimer's disease was first reported in 1907 by a German psychiatrist and neuropathologist, Alois Alzheimer (1864–1915), who documented the case of "Auguste D.," a 51-year-old woman complaining of poor memory and disorientation regarding time and place (Alzheimer, 1907/1987). Eventually, Auguste D. became depressed and began to hallucinate. She showed the classic cognitive symptoms now understood as part of the diagnostic criteria for the disorder. Alzheimer was unable to explain this process of deterioration

neurocognitive disorder due to Alzheimer's disease
A neurocognitive disorder associated with progressive, gradual declines in memory, learning, and at least one other cognitive domain.

TABLE 3 Diagnostic Criteria for Neurocognitive Disorder Due to Alzheimer's Disease

The diagnostic criteria for neurocognitive disorder due to Alzheimer's disease include the diagnostic criteria for major or mild neurocognitive disorder as well as the following:

For major neurocognitive disorder, because Alzheimer's disease cannot be definitively diagnosed until autopsy, clinicians can assign the diagnosis as either "probable" (when both 1 and 2 are met) or "possible" (when only one of the two is met):

1. Evidence of a genetic mutation known to be associated with Alzheimer's disease from family history or genetic testing

2. All three of these symptoms:

   A. Clear evidence of decline in memory and learning and at least one other cognitive domain

   B. Steadily progressive, gradual decline in cognitive functions

   C. No evidence of another neurodegenerative disease or other disease that can contribute to cognitive decline

For minor neurocognitive disorder, "probable" is diagnosed if either genetic testing or family history provide evidence of a genetic mutation, and "possible" if there is no genetic indication, but all three of the above symptoms in criterion 2 are present.

until after the patient had died, when an autopsy revealed that most of the tissue in her cerebral cortex had undergone severe degeneration. Upon examining the brain tissue under a microscope, Alzheimer also found that individual neurons had degenerated and formed abnormal clumps of neural tissue. Ninety years later, a discovery of brain slides from this famous case confirmed that the changes seen in Auguste D.'s brain were those of what now is known as Alzheimer's disease (Enserink, 1998) (Figure 1).

Prevalence of Alzheimer's Disease

The popular press widely but inaccurately reports the prevalence of Alzheimer's disease as 5 to 5.7 million in the United States, which would constitute 12 percent of the population over age 65 and 50 percent of those over age 85. The World Health Organization (2001) provides a far lower prevalence estimate of 5 percent of men and 6 percent of women worldwide. The incidence rate of new cases is less than 1 percent a year in those ages 60 to 65, or possibly as high as 6.5 percent in those 85 and older (Kawas et al., 2000). Indeed, a study based on Canadian health insurance data reported a decline in the number of new cases reported in 2015, noting in addition that "since 60 to 80% of all major dementias have a vascular component, the falling incidence of stroke may have further contributed to the decline in dementia incidence" (Sposato et al., 2015, p. 1530).

Autopsy studies support the lower estimate. In one rural Pennsylvania community, researchers found Alzheimer's disease to be the cause of death in 4.9 percent of people age 65 and older (Ganguli et al., 2005). Of course, this estimate includes only those whose deaths were confirmed to have resulted from Alzheimer's disease. In many cases, another disease, such as pneumonia, is actually the immediate cause of death in people with advanced Alzheimer's disease. Nevertheless, this percentage is substantially lower than what we would expect on the basis of figures published in the media. Amazingly, among the 100-year-old and older participants in the New England Centenarian Study, approximately 90 percent were symptom-free until age 92 (Perls, 2004).

The common overestimation of the incidence of Alzheimer's disease reinforces the false notion that any cognitive changes experienced by people in later life (or earlier) reflect the disease's onset. Loss of working memory occurs normally in later life for most individuals. Once people become self-conscious about their memory, however, they tend to exaggerate even small losses, thinking they have Alzheimer's disease. Unfortunately, this self-consciousness only worsens their memory, which further perpetuates the cycle. Rather than taking preventive steps, such as engaging in memory exercises or other cognitively challenging activities, people in this situation are likely to give in to despair (Jones, Whitbourne, Whitbourne, & Skultety, 2009).

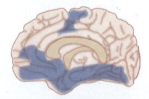

Very early Alzheimer's

Mild to moderate Alzheimer's

Severe Alzheimer's

FIGURE 1 Changes in the Brain Associated with Alzheimer's Disease

As Alzheimer's disease progresses, neurofibrillary tangles (shown in blue) spread throughout the brain. Plaques also spread throughout the brain, starting in the neocortex. By the final stage, damage is widespread and brain tissue has shrunk significantly.

Why do these overestimates occur? Most importantly, report authors tend to include other forms of neurocognitive disorder due to Alzheimer's disease in their estimates. As many as 55 percent of neurocognitive disorders can be caused by disease processes other than Alzheimer's (Jellinger & Attems, 2010), including 20 percent caused solely by cardiovascular disease (Knopman, 2007). Consequently, the "5.5 million" actually includes perhaps as many as 2 to 3 million people who have some form of vascular disease or other neurological disorder. Because cardiovascular disease is related to hypertension (Sharp et al., 2011) and diabetes (Knopman & Roberts, 2010), both of which people can control or prevent through diet and exercise, it is particularly important for older adults and their families to receive accurate diagnoses of any neurocognitive symptoms they experience.

The Alzheimer's Association also uses the term "Alzheimer's dementia" in its estimates, including to describe "those with mild cognitive impairment due to Alzheimer's and asymptomatic individuals who have verified biomarkers of Alzheimer's" (Alzheimer's Association, 2018). This expanded terminology is not consistent with *DSM-5* (which does not use the term *dementia* in the diagnosis) and also expands the definition beyond individuals who meet the actual diagnostic criteria.

Other reasons for the potentially misleading public information about Alzheimer's disease in the United States include failure to take into account the education level of individuals who participate in epidemiological surveys, variations in the measurement of symptoms, and failure to account adequately for health status or other possible forms of neurocognitive disorder (Whitbourne & Whitbourne, 2017).

What's in the *DSM-5*

Recategorization of Neurocognitive Disorders

Revisions in the *DSM-5* resulted in major categorization changes in the set of disorders that formerly included delirium and dementia. The revisions divided the disorders into two broad groups consisting of major and mild neurocognitive disorders. Among the many controversial diagnoses added in *DSM-5,* mild neurocognitive disorder due to Alzheimer's disease was one of the most heavily criticized. Mild neurocognitive disorder includes minor cognitive changes from previous functioning that do not interfere with an individual's ability to live independently but that may require compensatory strategies in response.

Critics of this new category argue that it applies a diagnostic label to behaviors that clinicians would not otherwise consider diagnosable. Moreover, if the deficits do not affect an individual's ability to live independently in the community, the benefits of assigning a diagnosis are not all that clear. Although eliminating the term *dementia* helps reduce the stigma we associate with memory deficits, labeling as a mental disorder what may be minor normal age-related changes cancels this advantage, according to critics.

In addition, the *DSM-5* now allows for the term *probable* to be applied in the absence of any abnormalities in memory and learning, but only some loss of abilities and a family history of Alzheimer's disease. The distinction between *probable* and *possible* may be a difficult one for the general public, if not professionals, to grasp. Although the *DSM-5* authors clearly wish to indicate that probable is less serious than possible, individuals hearing the terms out of context may not discern the nuance and come to the wrong conclusion about their own, or a relative's, condition.

Stages of Alzheimer's Disease

By definition, the symptoms of Alzheimer's disease become progressively worse over time. However, not all people who show early symptoms of Alzheimer's disease actually have this disease. As you can see from Figure 2, some individuals remain healthy until death. Some experience memory problems (referred to here as "amnestic mild neurocognitive disorder") but are able to compensate for them and never develop Alzheimer's disease. In those individuals who develop Alzheimer's disease, however, the loss of independent function continues in a progressive manner until death. Factors related to more rapid decline in the early stages of the disease include being younger at the age of onset, having higher education, and having poorer cognitive status when symptoms of the disease are first recognized (Lopez et al., 2010).

Diagnosis of Alzheimer's Disease

Because of the need for early diagnosis to rule out treatable neurocognitive disorders, researchers and clinicians devote significant energy and attention to the development of behavioral tests for diagnosing Alzheimer's disease in its initial stages. An incorrect diagnosis would be a fatal mistake if the person had a neurocognitive disorder that would have been reversible if the clinician had applied proper treatment when the symptoms first became evident. Similarly, if the individual had a disorder with a strictly psychological basis,

FIGURE 2 Charting the Course of Healthy Aging, Mild Neurocognitive Disorder, and Alzheimer's Disease (AD)

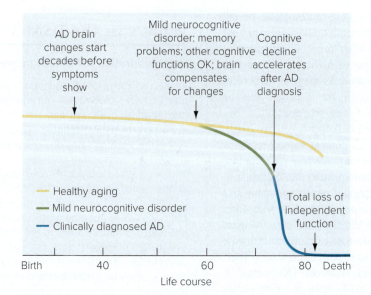

AD brain changes start decades before symptoms show

Mild neurocognitive disorder: memory problems; other cognitive functions OK; brain compensates for changes

Cognitive decline accelerates after AD diagnosis

— Healthy aging
— Mild neurocognitive disorder
— Clinically diagnosed AD

Total loss of independent function

Birth   40   60   80   Death

Life course

the clinician would have missed a crucial opportunity to intervene. Unfortunately, the early symptoms of Alzheimer's do not provide a sufficient basis for diagnosis.

Only an autopsy can produce a definitive diagnosis of Alzheimer's disease by allowing pathologists to observe the characteristic changes in brain tissue. Assessments of individuals suspected of having the disease, particularly early in its progress, therefore depend on clinicians making a diagnosis by exclusion. In the later stages of the disease, the clinician can apply diagnostic guidelines that have 85 to 90 percent accuracy. A joint commission of the National Institute of Neurological and Communicative Disorders and Stroke and the Alzheimer's Disease and Related Diseases Association developed these in 1984, and they are referred to as the NINCDS/ADRDA Guidelines (McKhann et al., 1984). The diagnosis of Alzheimer's disease, which at present is based on the NINCDS/ADRDA criteria, requires thorough medical and neuropsychological screenings. Even with these very stringent and complete guidelines, the diagnoses to which they lead is at best one of "probable" Alzheimer's disease, again reflecting the fact that only through an autopsy can clinicians obtain a certain diagnosis.

In 2011, a group of researchers and clinicians convened to revise the 1984 NINCDS/ADRDA Guidelines, taking into account improved knowledge of the clinical manifestations

In order to be diagnosed with Alzheimer's disease, individuals who show symptoms must undergo a series of neurocognitive assessments including memory tests.

©Blend Images/Alamy Stock Photo

of and biological changes in Alzheimer's disease (McKhann et al., 2011). They also believed it important to acknowledge that memory changes may or may not occur in individuals whose brains show signs of the disease. Their goal was to develop diagnostic criteria not dependent on the expensive and potentially invasive brain scans used in research. The group recognized that there is still no infallible way of diagnosing the disorder in a living person, proposing that clinicians diagnose an individual as having "probable" or "possible" Alzheimer's disease. They also suggested a third diagnostic category, "probable or possible," with evidence of brain pathology. This would not be a clinical diagnosis but would be intended for research purposes only. However, the authors of *DSM-5* adopted this terminology, which is now used to indicate a level of certainty of the diagnosis.

The clinical tool clinicians most commonly use for providing a quick screening for Alzheimer's disease is a specialized form of the mental status examination, known as the MiniMental State Examination (MMSE) (Folstein, Folstein, & McHugh, 1975) (Table 4). People with Alzheimer's disease respond in certain ways to several items on this instrument. They tend to be circumstantial, repeat themselves, and lack richness of detail when describing objects, people, and events. As a screening tool, the MMSE can provide preliminary indications that an individual may have neurocognitive disorder, but it should not be used as the sole basis for a diagnosis.

Adding to the complexity of separating the causes of neurocognitive disorder in disorders other than Alzheimer's is the fact that depression can lead to symptoms similar to those apparent in the early stages of Alzheimer's disease. The condition known as **pseudodementia**, or false neurocognitive disorder, is a severe form of depression that has primarily cognitive symptoms.

Several indicators can help the clinician differentiate depression from neurocognitive disorder. For example, depressed individuals are more keenly aware of their impaired cognition and frequently complain about their faulty memory. In contrast, individuals with Alzheimer's usually try to hide or minimize the extent of impairment or explain it away when they cannot conceal the loss. As the disorder progresses, people with Alzheimer's disease lose awareness of the extent of their cognitive deficits and may even report improvement as they lose their capacity for critical self-awareness.

In a 40-year longitudinal study of nearly 1,400 older adults, men who were depressed had twice the risk of developing Alzheimer's disease as men who were not depressed (Dal Forno et al., 2005). Interestingly, the brain autopsies of 90 of the participants who died during the course of the study did not show the characteristic brain changes that occur with Alzheimer's disease (Wilson, Grilo, & Vitousek, 2007). A study linking loneliness to the development of Alzheimer's disease in both men and women showed similar findings. Such findings strengthen the idea that loneliness can trigger depression, which in time may lead to harmful changes in the brain and symptoms of neurocognitive disorder similar to those in people with diagnosable Alzheimer's disease.

pseudodementia
Literally, false neurocognitive disorder, or a set of symptoms caused by depression that mimic those apparent in the early stages of Alzheimer's disease.

TABLE 4 MiniMental State Examination

Orientation to time
"What is the date?"
Registration
Listen carefully. I am going to say three words. You say them back after I stop. Ready? Here they are . . .
APPLE (pause), PENNY (pause), TABLE (pause). Now repeat those words back to me." [Repeat up to 5 times, but score only the first trial.]
Naming
"What is this?" [Point to a pencil or pen.]
Reading
"Please read this and do what it says." [Show examinee the words on the stimulus form.]
CLOSE YOUR EYES

SOURCE: Psychological Assessment Resources, Inc., 16204 North Florida Avenue, Lutz, Florida 33549, from the MiniMental State Examination, by Marshal Folstein and Susan Folstein.

Theories and Treatment of Alzheimer's Disease

All theories regarding the cause of Alzheimer's disease focus on biological abnormalities of the nervous system. However, approaches to treatment incorporate other perspectives, recognizing that at present no biological treatments have more than temporary effects on reducing symptom severity.

Theories   The biological theories of Alzheimer's disease attempt to explain the development of two characteristic abnormalities in the brain: neurofibrillary tangles and amyloid plaques. **Neurofibrillary tangles** are made up of a protein called **tau** (Figure 3), a protein which seems to play a role in maintaining the stability of microtubules, supporting the axon's internal structure. The microtubules are like train tracks that guide nutrients from the cell body down to the axon's ends. The tau proteins are like the railroad ties or crosspieces of the microtubule train tracks. In Alzheimer's disease, the tau changes chemically and loses its ability to separate and support the microtubules. With their support gone, the tubules begin to wind around each other and can no longer perform their function. This collapse of the transport system within the neuron may first result in malfunctions in communication between neurons and may eventually lead to the neuron's death. The development of neurofibrillary tangles appears to occur early in the disease process and may progress quite substantially before the individual shows any behavioral symptoms.

Amyloid plaques are collections of clusters outside the neuron made up of abnormal protein fragments called beta amyloid. Amyloid is a generic name for protein fragments that collect together in a specific way to form insoluble deposits (meaning that they do not dissolve). Amyloid plaques (also called beta-amyloid plaques) are formed when a substance found in the brain known as amyloid precursor protein (APP) embeds itself in the neuron's membrane. A small piece of APP lodges inside the neuron, and a larger part of it remains outside. In healthy aging, enzymes called **secretases** harmlessly trim away the extra length of the APP. In Alzheimer's disease, something goes wrong with this process so that the APP does not snip neatly at the cell membrane. The cut-off fragments of beta amyloid eventually clump together into beta-amyloid plaques that the body cannot dispose of or recycle (Figure 4).

Although researchers are testing various theories to identify the causes of Alzheimer's disease, the most probable is that an underlying defect in the genetic programming of neural activity triggers the formation of tangles and plaques. The genetic theory was given impetus with the discovery that a form of the disease called early-onset familial Alzheimer's disease, which begins at the unusually young ages of 40 to 50, occurs with higher than expected prevalence in certain

neurofibrillary tangles
A characteristic of Alzheimer's disease in which the material within the cell bodies of neurons becomes filled with densely packed, twisted protein microfibrils, or tiny strands.

tau
A protein that normally helps maintain the internal support structure of the axons.

amyloid plaques
A characteristic of Alzheimer's disease in which clusters of dead or dying neurons become mixed together with fragments of protein molecules.

secretases
Enzymes that trim part of the APP remaining outside the neuron so that it is flush with the neuron's outer membrane.

FIGURE 3 Neurofibrillary Tangle Develops over Time

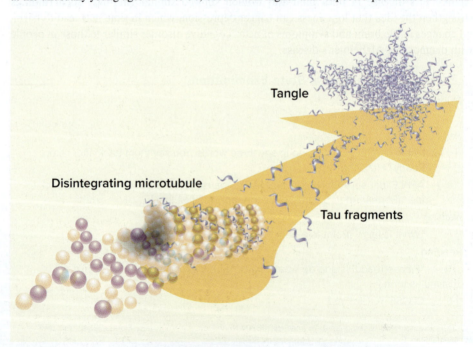

families. Other genes appear to be involved in a form of late-onset familial Alzheimer's disease that starts at the more expected ages of 60 to 65. Researchers postulate that these genes lead to the formation of excessive amounts of beta-amyloid protein.

With the discovery of familial patterns of early-onset Alzheimer's disease along with advances in genetic engineering, researchers have identified several genes that may hold the key to understanding the cause of the disease. The apoE gene on chromosome 19 has three common forms: e2, e3, and e4. Each produces a corresponding form of apolipoprotein E (apoE) called E2, E3, and E4. The presence of the e4 allele sets up the mechanism for production of the E4 form of apoE, which researchers believe damages the microtubules within the neuron, which in turn likely play an essential role in the cell's activity. Ordinarily, apoE2 and apoE3 protect the tau protein, which helps stabilize the microtubules. The theory is that if the tau protein is unprotected by apoE2 and apoE3, the microtubules will degenerate, eventually leading to the neuron's destruction.

Most early-onset familial Alzheimer's disease cases occur with defects in the so-called presenilin genes (PS1 and PS2), which, as the name implies, are most likely involved in causing the brain

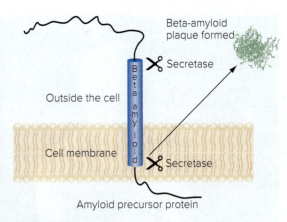

FIGURE 4 Development of Amyloid Plaques

Early Diagnosis of Alzheimer's Disease

As you've learned in the chapter, there are no treatments of Alzheimer's disease for anything other than its symptoms, and even these treatments can stave off decline for only a matter of months. These problems raise the question whether early diagnosis of Alzheimer's disease through potentially invasive methods such as spinal taps and brain scans would be worth the expense and effort.

On one hand, early diagnosis that rules out Alzheimer's disease is beneficial to individuals who have a treatable form of a neurocognitive disorder. By identifying one of the many other conditions that can lead to severe cognitive changes, clinicians can diagnose surgical, medical, or other rehabilitative procedures to allow these individuals to resume their previous levels of activity and engagement in work, family, and social roles. On the other hand, because the methods of diagnosis are not 100 percent accurate, clinicians might incorrectly tell people who do not have Alzheimer's disease that their condition is untreatable.

Genetic testing can also identify those at risk of developing Alzheimer's disease. But if a person is asymptomatic, what might be the benefits of informing him or her of a genetic risk for which there are no treatments? The individual could try interventions that seem to have some benefits, such as physical exercise, mentally challenging activities, or avoidance of potentially harmful environmental toxins. There is no harm in engaging in these behaviors, as they benefit most older individuals, not just those with a genetic marker for Alzheimer's disease.

Advocates of early diagnosis argue that knowledge gained from genetic testing can allow individuals and their families to make plans for the future. But if the information were available to insurance companies and programs, including those administered by the government, at-risk individuals could face increases in their premiums or restrictions on how they could spend their assets. For example, if you knew you were going to develop Alzheimer's disease and would therefore require expensive private care, you might divest yourself of your assets by putting money into a trust fund for your children in order to qualify for government assistance with your medical bills.

These are only a few of the practical and ethical dilemmas raised by the question of whether individuals should receive a diagnosis that can only be "probable" at best for a disease that has no known treatment at worst.

Q: *You be the judge:* Under these conditions, would you want to know whether you were at risk for developing Alzheimer's disease?

Older adults who exercise regularly can prevent the onset of many age-related physical problems.

©Jupiterimages/Getty Images

to age prematurely. The mean age of onset in families with mutations in the PS1 gene is 45 years (ranging from 32 to 56 years) and age 52 years for people with PS2 gene mutations (ranging from 40 to 85 years). The pattern of inheritance for the presenilin genes is autosomal dominant, meaning that if one parent carries the allele that occurs with the disease, the offspring has a 50 percent chance of developing the disorder. Researchers are attempting to determine how presenilin genes 1 and 2 interact with APP, beta-amyloid plaques, and tangles. Researchers estimate that the four genes, presenilin 1 and 2, APP, and apoE, account for approximately half the genetic risk for Alzheimer's disease (St. George-Hyslop & Petit, 2005).

While the genetic theory is compelling, it accounts for at most 50 percent of cases of people who develop Alzheimer's disease but have no known genetic risk, so behavioral factors would appear to be implicated. These include cigarette smoking (Gons et al., 2011) and a sedentary lifestyle. Conversely, people who eat healthy diets have a lower risk of Alzheimer's disease. The Mediterranean diet includes foods that are high in tomatoes and olive oil, with low amounts of red meat and an occasional glass of red wine. Individuals who follow this diet have a lower risk of developing Alzheimer's disease (Gu, Luchsinger, Stern, & Scarmeas, 2010).

There are two main implications of research documenting the behavioral risk factors for Alzheimer's disease. First, people can reduce their risk of Alzheimer's disease by avoiding behaviors that contribute to its development. Second, these risk factors also increase the likelihood of an individual's developing cerebrovascular disease, depression, and other causes of neurocognitive disorder. This finding supports the contention that estimates of Alzheimer's prevalence statistics are inflated by the existence of other preventable neurocognitive disorders related to risk factors within the aging population. Advances in public health efforts intended to reduce obesity, diabetes, and smoking should lead to a decrease in the estimates of Alzheimer's disease, if not actual reductions in the number of people who truly have the disorder.

TABLE 5 Mechanism of Action and Side Effects of Alzheimer's Medications

Drug Name	Drug Type and Use	How It Works	Side Effects
Namenda® **(memantine)**	N-methyl D-aspartate (NMDA) antagonist prescribed to treat symptoms of moderate to severe AD	Blocks the toxic effects associated with excess glutamate and regulates glutamate activation	Dizziness, headache, constipation, confusion
Razadyne® **(galantamine)**	Cholinesterase inhibitor prescribed to treat symptoms of mild to moderate AD	Prevents the breakdown of acetylcholine and stimulates nicotinic receptors to release more acetylcholine in the brain	Nausea, vomiting, diarrhea, weight loss, loss of appetite
Exelon® **(rivastigmine)**	Cholinesterase inhibitor prescribed to treat symptoms of mild to moderate AD	Prevents the breakdown of acetylcholine and butyrylcholine (a brain chemical similar to acetylcholine) in the brain	Nausea, vomiting, diarrhea, weight loss, loss of appetite, muscle weakness
Aricept® **(donepezil)**	Cholinesterase inhibitor prescribed to treat symptoms of mild to moderate, and moderate to severe AD	Prevents the breakdown of acetylcholine in the brain	Nausea, vomiting, diarrhea

SOURCE: "Evaluating Prescription Drugs Used to Treat: Alzheimer's Disease," *Consumer Reports Best Buy Drugs,* updated May 2012.

Treatment   Clearly, the ultimate goal of the intense research on Alzheimer's disease is to find effective treatment, if not a prevention or cure. There is a great deal of optimism in the scientific community that this treatment, when discovered, will also benefit those with other degenerative brain diseases. As the search for the cause of Alzheimer's disease proceeds, researchers are attempting to find medications that will alleviate its symptoms.

The U.S. Food and Drug Administration–approved medications for treating mild to moderate Alzheimer's disease symptoms include galantamine (Razadyne), rivastigmine (Exelon), and donepezil (Aricept) (Table 5). Clinicians only rarely prescribe another medication, tacrine (Cognex), due to concerns about its safety.

Current medications inhibit the action of acetylcholinesterase, the enzyme that normally destroys acetylcholine after its release into the synaptic cleft and which is implicated as a contributor to memory loss (Sultzer, 2018). Because these slow the breakdown of acetylcholine, they allow higher levels to remain in the brain, thus facilitating memory. All have significant side effects. Memantine falls into a separate category of FDA-approved medications for treatment of Alzheimer's disease in the moderate to severe stages. An NMDA antagonist, memantine regulates glutamate, which, in excessive amounts, may destroy neurons.

The side effects listed in Table 5 include those that clinicians consider mild and therefore tolerable. However, the anticholinesterases can have serious side effects that include fainting, depression, anxiety, severe allergic reactions, seizures, slow or irregular heartbeat, fever, and tremor. Memantine's side effects can include hallucinations, seizures, speech changes, sudden and severe headache, aggressiveness, depression, and anxiety. Clinicians must weigh benefits against side effects when prescribing these medications, which themselves may interact with those the individual is receiving for other health conditions, such as aspirin and nonsteroidal anti-inflammatory drugs (NSAIDs), Tagamet (used to treat heartburn), certain antibiotics, antidepressants, and medications that improve breathing.

The benefits of the current medications to treat Alzheimer's disease symptoms are short-lived (see Figure 5). Administering higher levels of anticholinesterases may slow the progression somewhat but does not prevent deterioration in cognitive functioning over the long term (Wattmo, Wallin, Londos, & Minthon, 2011). Donepezil may reduce the perception by caregivers of their burden and of the other symptoms shown by the patients they care for, but these effects have not been studied past 12 weeks of treatment (Carrasco et al., 2011). Another medication, galantamine (Razadyne), acts as an anticholinesterase and may have positive effects for up to 3 years, but it also has a higher associated death rate (Scarpini et al., 2011). Medications that address the deleterious changes in tau are being developed but at present are not suitable for use in humans (Navarrete, Pérez, Morales, & Maccioni, 2011).

Other approaches to treating neurocognitive disorder due to Alzheimer's disease target the free radicals, which are molecules that form when beta amyloid breaks into fragments. Free radicals can damage neurons in the surrounding brain tissue (Wani et al., 2017). Antioxidants can disarm free radicals and therefore may be another treatment for Alzheimer's disease. Bioflavonoid, a substance that occurs naturally in wine, tea, fruits, and vegetables, is one such antioxidant. Researchers view naturally occurring bioflavonoids (in, for example, blueberries) as having important preventive roles in reducing the extent of memory loss in later adulthood (Joseph, Shukitt-Hale, & Casadesus, 2005). A longitudinal study of over 1,300 French people found that bioflavonoids were beneficial in reducing the risk of Alzheimer's disease (Commenges et al., 2000).

One of the reasons current medical treatments for Alzheimer's disease are not proving effective is that changes other than the development of amyloid plaques and neurofibrillary tangles may occur in its development and progression. Changes in cardiovascular functioning and diabetes must also be accounted for as possible contributors (Fessel, 2018).

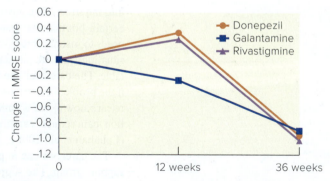

FIGURE 5 Comparison of Alzheimer's Disease Medications

Each of the FDA-approved treatments for Alzheimer's disease has effects that are relatively short-lived, with all benefits disappearing after 36 weeks (note: MMSE refers to MiniMental State Examination).

SOURCE: Lopez et al., 2013

MINI CASE

Major Neurocognitive Disorder Due to Alzheimer's Disease, Probable

Ellen is a married, Caucasian, heterosexual 69-year-old woman. Her husband took her to her family physician after becoming increasingly concerned by Ellen's failing memory and strange behavior, such as her not being able to remember the names of basic household items like *spoon* and *dishwasher*. Her day-to-day forgetfulness had become so problematic that she would repeatedly forget to feed or walk the dog. As the weeks went by, Ellen seemed to get worse. She would leave food burning on the stove and water overflowing the bathtub. However, she had no family history of relatives diagnosed with early-onset Alzheimer's disease. Ellen's physician sought consultation from a neuropsychologist, who determined that Ellen showed significant impairments in memory, learning, and language. In addition, a complete medical examination identified no other possible causes for her cognitive symptoms, and she did not meet the criteria for major depressive disorder.

Given that no medical treatments exist to cure the disease, behavioral psychologists are developing strategies to maximize the daily functioning of people with Alzheimer's disease. They often target these efforts at the caregivers, who are the people (usually family members) primarily responsible for caring for the person with the disease. Caregivers often suffer adverse effects from the constant demands placed on them, effects that we call "caregiver burden". However, caregivers can learn behavioral strategies that promote the independence of their loved ones while also reducing the frequency of their distressing behaviors. Support groups can also provide a forum in which caregivers learn ways to manage the emotional stress that occurs with their role.

Behavioral strategies aimed at increasing the patient's independence include giving prompts, cues, and guidance for self-maintenance. For example, the clinician can encourage the patient to relearn the steps in getting dressed and then positively reward him or her with praise and attention for having completed them. Through modeling, the patient relearns old skills through imitation. The caregiver can also learn time management, which encourages following a strict daily schedule. As a result, the patient is more likely to fall into a regular routine of everyday activities. All these methods benefit both the patient and the caregiver. The patient regains some measure of independence, which reduces the caregiver's burden to the extent that the patient can engage in self-care tasks.

Behavioral strategies can also eliminate, or at least reduce the frequency of, wandering and aggression in an Alzheimer's patient. One possible approach, which is not always practical, is extinction. The caregiver ignores certain disruptive behaviors, with the intention of eliminating the reinforcement that has helped maintain them. Extinction is not practical for behaviors that may lead to patient harm, however, such as leaving the house and wandering into the street. One possibility is to give the patient positive reinforcement for staying within certain boundaries; however, this may not be sufficient, and at that point the caregiver needs to install protective barriers. Another possible approach is for the caregiver to identify situations that are particularly problematic for the patient, such as the bathtub or the dining table. The caretaker can then use behavioral methods in these circumstances. For example, if the problem occurs while eating, it may be that the caretaker can encourage the patient to relearn how to use a knife and fork, rather than feeding him or her. Again, such an intervention can reduce caregiver burden as well as increasing the patient's functional skills (Callahan et al., 2006).

The caregiver can implement behavioral interventions through individual therapy or in a support group. The support group facilitator can teach these methods to participants, and caregivers can share strategies among themselves based on their experiences. The emotional support caregivers can provide for each other can be just as valuable as the actual instruction they receive. Ultimately, the Alzheimer's patient receives better-quality care when caregiver burden is minimized.

You can see, then, that although the prospect of Alzheimer's is frightening and painful for all those concerned about the individual, a number of interventions are available. Until

REAL STORIES

Ronald Reagan: Alzheimer's Disease

Born in 1911, Ronald Reagan was at the time the oldest U.S. president to take the oath of office, at almost 70 years of age. He served two terms between 1981 and 1989 and is remembered as one of the most popular presidents in recent history. His political and economic policies changed the face of the nation, and as president he helped end the cold war between the United States and the former Soviet Union. In 1994, just 4 years after leaving office, Reagan publicly disclosed that he had been diagnosed with Alzheimer's disease. He passed away in 2004, after spending the final 3 years of his life confined to a hospital bed in his California home.

A native of Illinois, Reagan attended college in Eureka before moving to Iowa to begin his career in radio broadcasting. He soon moved to Los Angeles and launched his acting career, starring in many popular films and television shows. Following a turn as a spokesperson for General Electric, Reagan became involved in politics. He served as governor of California for 10 years before he was elected president in 1980, having run unsuccessfully twice before and then beating out the incumbent President Jimmy Carter.

A *New York Times* article from 1997 described Reagan's life just a few short years after he came forward with his diagnosis. At the time, Reagan appeared unchanged, although he was on the verge of showing some of the more severe signs of Alzheimer's. The article stated, "If, at the age of 86, the old movie actor still looks the image of vigorous good health, the truth is that the man behind the firm handshake and barely gray hair is steadily, surely ebbing away." Reagan was still able to perform activities of daily living such as dressing himself, and he continued his regular routine, which included playing golf, exercising, and making occasional public appearances. But despite his healthy exterior and extensive support network, at this point Reagan's condition began to deteriorate.

During his presidency, Ronald Reagan notoriously struggled with his memory, particularly when it came to remembering people's names. By 1997, this difficulty was much more pronounced, and the only person he was able to remember on a consistent basis was his wife, Nancy. Following the revelation of his diagnosis, there was much controversy as to whether he had had symptoms of Alzheimer's disease during his presidency. The *New York Times* article cited Reagan's doctor, who confirmed that he did not actually start showing any symptoms until at least 3 years following the end of his final term.

"Alzheimer's is often said to involve a family of victims," the article states. "As it inexorably shuts off communication, the disease breeds loneliness, frustration and confusion not just for the patient, but for the spouse, relatives and friends. Many longtime friends and aides say they find it too painful to compare the Ronald Reagan afflicted with Alzheimer's with his former self."

In 2001, 4 years after the article appeared, Reagan suffered a fall in his home and broke his hip. Although the fracture healed, he became homebound because his condition had greatly deteriorated. In her book *The Long Goodbye*, Reagan's daughter Patti Davis recalls that doctors had given him just months to live. In the end, he lived another 4 years. Her book poignantly depicts the heartache and struggle that haunts not only the patients but also the families of those dying from Alzheimer's disease. Patti highlights that the most painful aspect of the process of watching a loved one suffer from Alzheimer's is the length of the process of physical and mental deterioration and the psychological effect this has on the family.

"I am a daughter who lived her life missing her father." Patti describes her father as a man who had little time to be involved in the lives of his children because he spent 8 years as leader of a powerful nation. The turmoil of watching their father's long and slow death was made all the more excruciating due to Reagan's guarded personal disposition. As Patti describes in the book, "Even my mother has admitted there was a part of him—a core—that she could never touch."

The book started as a collection of diary entries Patti had written about her experiences watching her father succumb to his disease. The second-youngest of five children, Patti was often at odds with her father's social and political views. In the book she writes about how their relationship changed as the years went on and as she stuck by his side throughout the progression of his illness. Not only did her father's relationship with her change with the course of his disease, but the entire family dynamic shifted as the differences between them drifted away in light of their desire to be together through this difficult time. This is not uncommon as families come together to cope with the slow loss of a loved one to Alzheimer's.

"Alzheimer's disease locks all the doors and exits. There is no reprieve, no escape.

Ronald Reagan began to show pronounced signs of Alzheimer's disease only a few years after completing two consecutive terms as U.S. president.

SOURCE: Library of Congress Prints and Photographs Division [LC-DIG-highsm-15747]

Time becomes the enemy, and it seemed to stretch out in front of us like miles of fallow land." Patti goes on to describe the insidious nature of the disease and its slow progression throughout the years as she witnessed in her father. Alongside observations of her father as he grew older and as Alzheimer's increasingly took its toll, Patti recalls the memories of him throughout her life–giving a speech on her wedding day, swimming with her in the ocean, singing together in church. These memories were important in helping the family cope with the pain of slowly losing their father. "You breathe life into your own memories because right there, in front of you, sitting in the chair he always goes to, or walking down the hall, or gazing out the window, is a reminder of the hollowness that's left when memories are erased. So you welcome it when images come back, or bits of conversations. You seize them, dust them off, and pray they'll stay as bright."

In her book, Patti describes the process that her mother endured as she slowly lost her husband of over 40 years. "My mother speaks of the loneliness of her life now. He's here, but in so many ways he's not. She feels the loneliness in small ways–he used to put lotion on her back; now he doesn't. And in the huge, overwhelming ways–a future that will be spent missing him."

Patti also addresses the issue of Nancy Reagan's decision to keep the details of her husband's suffering private from the watchful eye of the media. "My mother has called it a long goodbye–the way Alzheimer's slowly steals a person away. It's been one of her only public comments; upon agreement, we have chosen the cloak of respectful silence when it comes to the subject of my father's condition. It's a heartbreaking phrase, and she's told me she won't say it again because it ushers in tears." Even on the day that her father passed away on June 5, 2004, Patti recalls a reporter hovering

around the home as rumors that he was nearing the end of his life surfaced. As the family gathered around Reagan's bed during his final moments of life, Patti remembers hearing news reports in the next room that his condition was grave, and more reporters began calling and coming to the house. In the end, the family was prepared for their father to pass away, although this did not erase the pain they shared when his battle with Alzheimer's finally ended.

"There will be times," Patti writes of their reaction to his death, "when we are lifted up on the back of memories, and other times when sorrow drives us to our knees. Especially my mother, who will have moments of wondering why he had to leave first. We will wait for him to enter our dreams. We will look for him in every breeze that drifts through every open window. We will breathe deep and wait for his whisper to stream into us–tell us secrets and make us smile."

---

researchers find a cure for the disorder, however, clinicians must be content to measure their gains less as progress toward a cure and more as success in prolonging the period of maximum functioning for the individual and the family.

13.4 Neurocognitive Disorders Due to Neurological Disorders Other than Alzheimer's Disease

The symptoms of neurocognitive disorder can have a number of causes that include degenerative neurological conditions other than Alzheimer's disease. Each of these disorders has a separate diagnosis associated with it. Figure 6 shows the overlap among symptoms of these neurological disorders. Rather than manifesting as a decline in memory, as we see in Alzheimer's disease, **frontotemporal neurocognitive disorder** is reflected in personality changes, such as apathy, lack of inhibition, obsessiveness, and loss of judgment. Eventually, the individual becomes neglectful of personal habits and loses the ability to communicate. The onset of the disorder is slow and insidious. On autopsy, the brain shows atrophy in the frontal and temporal cortex, but there are no amyloid plaques or arterial damage.

Neurocognitive disorder with Lewy bodies is characterized by progressive loss of memory, language, calculation, and reasoning, as well as other higher mental functions. The disorder gets its name from the presence in the brain of Lewy bodies, abnormal deposits of a protein called alpha-synuclein. These deposits affect dopamine and norepinephrine, which in turn affect motor functioning and memory. Individuals with neurocognitive disorder with Lewy bodies experience alterations in mood and movement in addition to cognitive changes.

Another possible cause of neurocognitive disorder is cardiovascular disease affecting the supply of blood to the brain. This condition, called **vascular neurocognitive disorder**, is highly prevalent, and researchers link it to a variety of cardiovascular risk factors. The most common form is **multi-infarct dementia (MID)**, caused by transient attacks in which blood flow to the brain is interrupted by a clogged or burst artery. The damage to the artery deprives the surrounding neurons of blood and oxygen, which causes the neurons to die. Although each infarct is too small to be noticed at first, over time the progressive damage caused by the infarcts leads the individual to lose cognitive abilities. Memory impairment appears to be similar to that observed in Alzheimer's disease; however, there are some significant differences between

frontotemporal neurocognitive disorder
Neurocognitive disorder that involves the frontotemporal area of the brain.

neurocognitive disorder with Lewy bodies
A form of neurocognitive disorder with progressive loss of memory, language, calculation, and reasoning, as well as other higher mental functions resulting from the accumulation of abnormalities called Lewy bodies throughout the brain.

vascular neurocognitive disorder
A form of neurocognitive disorder resulting from a vascular disease that causes deprivation of the blood supply to the brain.

multi-infarct dementia (MID)
A form of neurocognitive disorder caused by transient attacks in which blood flow to the brain is interrupted by a clogged or burst artery.

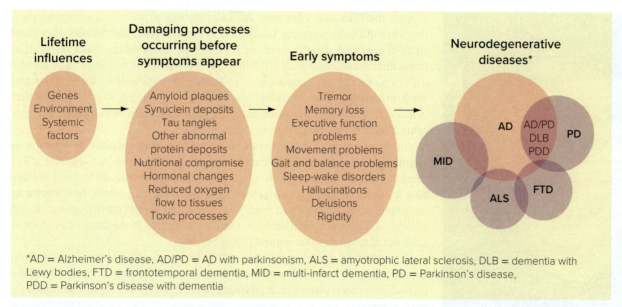

*AD = Alzheimer's disease, AD/PD = AD with parkinsonism, ALS = amyotrophic lateral sclerosis, DLB = dementia with Lewy bodies, FTD = frontotemporal dementia, MID = multi-infarct dementia, PD = Parkinson's disease, PDD = Parkinson's disease with dementia

FIGURE 6 Other Diseases That Can Cause Deterioration in Cognitive Function

As shown here, a variety of lifetime influences and damaging processes ranging from nutritional influences to toxins can lead to symptoms that appear to mimic Alzheimer's disease. These disorders may occur along with Alzheimer's disease (shown in the overlapping circles) or may occur independently of it.

SOURCE: Progress Report on Alzheimer's Disease 2004–2005, U.S. Department of Health and Human Services.

these two disorders. People with vascular neurocognitive disorder show a particular set of physical abnormalities, such as walking difficulties and weakness in the arms and legs, and a pattern of cognitive functioning distinctly different from that in people with Alzheimer's.

In the typical clinical picture of vascular neurocognitive disorder, certain cognitive functions remain intact and others show significant loss, a pattern neuropsychologists call patchy deterioration. Another unique feature of vascular neurocognitive disorder is that it shows a step-wise deterioration in cognitive functioning: a function that was relatively unimpaired is suddenly lost or severely deteriorates. This is in contrast to the gradual pattern of deterioration in Alzheimer's disease.

As is true for Alzheimer's disease, there is no treatment to reverse the cognitive losses in vascular neurocognitive disorder. However, individuals can take preventive actions throughout adulthood to protect themselves from the subsequent onset of this disease. Reducing the risk of hypertension and diabetes is one important way to lower the chances of developing cognitive disorders in later life (Papademetriou, 2005).

Pick's disease is a relatively rare, progressive degenerative disease that affects the frontal and temporal lobes of the cerebral cortex. It is caused by the accumulation in neurons of unusual protein deposits called Pick bodies. In addition to having memory problems, people with this disorder become socially disinhibited, either acting inappropriately and impulsively or appearing apathetic and unmotivated. In contrast to the sequence of changes people with Alzheimer's disease show, those with Pick's disease undergo personality alterations before they begin to have memory problems. For example, they may experience deterioration in social skills, language abnormalities, flat emotionality, and a loss of inhibition.

Neurocognitive disorder due to Parkinson's disease brings about neuronal degeneration of the basal ganglia, the subcortical structures that control motor movements. Deterioration of diffuse areas of the cerebral cortex may occur. Cognitive changes do not occur in all people with Parkinson's disease, but researchers estimate rates as high as 60 percent, mostly among those who are older and at a more advanced stage of the disease. Parkinson's disease is usually progressive, with various motor disturbances being the most striking feature of the disorder. For example, at rest, the person's hands, legs, or head may shake involuntarily. The muscles become rigid, and it is difficult for the person to initiate movement, a symptom called **akinesia**. A general slowing of motor activity, known as **bradykinesia**, also occurs, as does a loss of fine motor coordination. Some people with Parkinson's disease walk with a

Pick's disease
A relatively rare degenerative disease that affects the frontal and temporal lobes of the cerebral cortex and that can cause neurocognitive disorders.

neurocognitive disorder due to Parkinson's disease
A neurocognitive disorder that involves degeneration of neurons in the subcortical structures that control motor movements.

akinesia
A motor disturbance in which a person's muscles become rigid and movement is difficult to initiate.

bradykinesia
A motor disturbance involving a general slowing of motor activity.

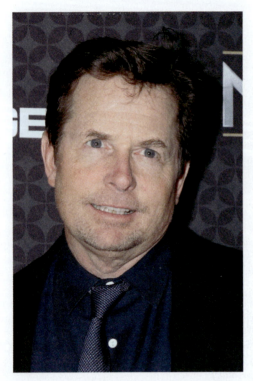

As one of the best-known individuals to suffer from neurocognitive disorder due to Parkinson's disease, Michael J. Fox has brought public attention to the reality of this disabling condition.

©Kathy Hutchins/Shutterstock

neurocognitive disorder due to Huntington's disease

A hereditary condition causing neurocognitive disorder that involves a widespread deterioration of the subcortical brain structures and parts of the frontal cortex that control motor movements.

neurocognitive disorder due to prion disease (Creutzfeldt-Jakob disease)

A neurological disease transmitted from animals to humans that leads to neurocognitive disorder and death resulting from abnormal protein accumulations in the brain.

prion disease

A disease caused by an abnormal protein particle that infects brain tissue.

traumatic brain injury (TBI)

Damage to the brain caused by exposure to trauma.

neurocognitive disorder due to traumatic brain injury

A disorder in which there is evidence of impact to the head along with cognitive and neurological symptoms that persist past the acute postinjury period.

slowed, shuffling gait. They have difficulty starting to walk, and once they start, they have difficulty stopping. In addition to these motor abnormalities, they show signs of cognitive deterioration, such as slowed scanning on visual recognition tasks, diminished conceptual flexibility, and slowed motor responses. The individual's face also appears expressionless and speech becomes stilted, losing its normal rhythmic quality. The individual has difficulty producing words on tests that demand verbal fluency. However, many cognitive functions, such as attention, concentration, and immediate memory, remain intact.

Although it is primarily a loss of motor control, **neurocognitive disorder due to Huntington's disease** is a degenerative neurological disorder that can also affect personality and cognitive functioning. Researchers have traced Huntington's disease to an abnormality on chromosome 4 that causes a protein, now known as huntingtin, to accumulate and reach toxic levels. The symptoms first appear during adulthood, between ages 30 and 50. The disease results in the death of neurons in subcortical structures that control motor behavior.

A number of disturbances occur with Huntington's disease, ranging from altered cognitive functioning to social and personality changes. We associate the disease with mood disturbances, changes in personality, irritability and explosiveness, suicidality, changes in sexuality, and a range of specific cognitive deficits. Because of these symptoms, clinicians may incorrectly diagnose the disorder as schizophrenia or a mood disorder, even if the individual has no history suggestive of these disorders. People with Huntington's disease can also appear apathetic because of their decreased ability to plan, initiate, or carry out complex activities. Their uncontrolled motor movement interferes with sustained performance of any behavior, even maintaining an upright posture, and eventually most people with Huntington's disease become bedridden.

Neurocognitive disorder due to prion disease, also known as **Creutzfeldt-Jakob disease**, is a rare neurological disorder known as a **prion disease**, which researchers believe is caused by an infectious agent and that results in abnormal protein accumulations in the brain. Initial symptoms include fatigue, appetite disturbance, sleep problems, and concentration difficulties. As the disease progresses, the individual shows increasing signs of neurocognitive loss and eventually dies. Underlying these symptoms is widespread damage known as spongiform encephalopathy, meaning that large holes develop in brain tissue. The disease appears to be transmitted to humans from cattle that have eaten the body parts of dead farm animals infected with the disease (particularly sheep, in which the disease is known as scrapie). In 1996, an epidemic in England of "mad cow disease," along with reported cases of the disease in humans, led to a ban on importation of British beef. Concerns about this disease continue to exist in European countries, as well as in the United States.

13.5 Neurocognitive Disorder Due to Traumatic Brain Injury

Trauma to the head that results in an alteration or loss of consciousness, or post-traumatic amnesia, is called **traumatic brain injury (TBI)**. The diagnostic criteria for **neurocognitive disorder due to traumatic brain injury** require evidence of impact to the head along with loss of consciousness, amnesia following the trauma, disorientation and confusion, and neurological abnormalities such as seizures. The symptoms must occur immediately after the trauma or after recovery of consciousness, and past the acute postinjury period.

In 2013, there were an estimated 2.8 million TBI-related hospitalizations, emergency department visits, and deaths (Taylor, Bell, Breiding, & Xu, 2017). (Figure 7). Children aged 0 to 4 years, adolescents and young adults aged 15 to 24 years, and adults 75 years and older have the greatest risk of TBI. The highest rates of hospitalization and death due to TBI occur in adults 75 years of age and older. People within these age groups sustain accidental TBIs for different reasons. Children and adolescents are most likely to suffer TBIs through falls, sports injuries, and accidents. In older adults, falls are the most common cause of TBIs; falls are also the most deadly for this age group because they are generally associated with other severe injuries and complications.

As many as 12 to 20 percent of the U.S. veterans of the Iraq and Afghanistan wars may have experienced TBIs resulting from injuries from improvised explosive devices (IEDs). Most of these cases are relatively mild in severity, meaning they involved loss of consciousness for 30 minutes or less, or post-traumatic amnesia of 24 hours or less. Most victims recover within 6 months of their injury, but a subgroup of veterans do not. Another group may have undetectable symptoms lasting until after their deployment. Not only does TBI carry significant health risks, but veterans who experienced it are at higher risk of developing PTSD, anxiety, and adjustment disorders (Carlson et al., 2010). Unlike previous combat veterans, those who fought in the Iraq and Afghanistan wars are more likely to have had head injuries because their modern helmets offered better protection than those worn by soldiers in previous wars. Thus they will survive a blast only to suffer serious head (and other) injuries.

People undergoing mild TBI may experience a related condition known as **postconcussion syndrome (PCS)** in which they continue to have symptoms such as fatigue, dizziness, poor concentration, memory problems, headache, insomnia, and irritability. Individuals most at risk of developing PCS are those who had an anxiety or depressive disorder prior to their injury and acute post-traumatic stress for approximately 5 days after their injury. However, PCS may also develop in traumatized individuals with these characteristics who do not actually suffer a mild TBI (Meares et al., 2011).

Professional athletes may also suffer mild TBIs, particularly those who play contact sports such as football and hockey. Their injuries may not be properly assessed when they occur, leading them to return to play before they are fully ready to do so. Although they may appear to have recovered enough to go back onto the field, they may nevertheless suffer mental impairments that are only evident later. In one study of male and female college athletes engaged in high-contact sports, researchers found memory impairments even in players who did not appear to have suffered a concussion (Killam, Cautin, & Santucci, 2005). Unlike trauma victims, athletes are more likely to return to pre-injury functioning within 2 to 14 days (Iverson, 2005).

Repeated injuries over time, such as those experienced by college and professional football players, may lead to chronic traumatic encephalography (CTE), which causes a form of neurocognitive disorder and can lead to premature death. Football players are particularly likely to experience deficits in executive functioning associated with the damage to their frontal lobes (Seichepine et al., 2013). CTE's effects appear to be

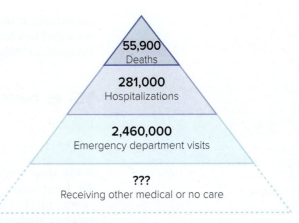

FIGURE 7   U.S. Prevalence Estimates and Associated Risks of Traumatic Brain Injury, 2013

SOURCE: Taylor, Bell, Breiding, & Xu, 2017

postconcussion syndrome (PCS)
A disorder in which a constellation of physical, emotional, and cognitive symptoms persists from weeks to years.

MINI CASE

Neurocognitive Disorder Due to Traumatic Brain Injury

Stephen is a married 28-year-old biracial heterosexual male and has been a running back in the National Football League since graduating college 6 years ago. During a game, he suffered a particularly hard hit when another player tackled him. Stephen's helmet came off, and he suffered a traumatic brain injury as a result. He was taken off the field and assessed by the team's medical staff. During the assessment, he was unable to remember how old he was, where he was born, whether he was married, or anything that had happened during the preceding 2 weeks. This inability to remember his personal past was a source of great distress to Stephen. In contrast, he had no trouble remembering the ambulance ride to the hospital or the name of the team physician who first examined him. Following a 3-day hospital stay, Stephen was transferred to a rehabilitation facility for 3 months, where memory therapy helped him learn mnemonic strategies for recalling important information.

attributable, at least in part, to alterations in tau proteins, leading to the development of neurofibrillary tangles in areas of the brain active in both motor control and cognitive functioning (Mufson et al., 2016).

13.6 Neurocognitive Disorders Due to Substances/Medications and HIV Infection

A wide range of infectious diseases can cause the changes that occur with neurocognitive disorder. These include neurosyphilis, encephalitis, tuberculosis, meningitis, human immunodeficiency virus (HIV), and localized infections in the brain. People who experience kidney failure may have symptoms of neurocognitive disorder as a result of the toxic accumulation of substances that the kidneys cannot cleanse from the blood. People with certain kinds of brain tumors also experience cognitive impairments and other symptoms of neurocognitive disorder.

The individual's cognitive functioning can also be negatively affected by anoxia (oxygen deprivation to the brain), which may occur during surgery under general anesthesia or as a result of carbon monoxide poisoning. Anoxia can have severe effects on many brain functions because neurons die quickly if they are deprived of oxygen. Because brain neurons do not replace themselves, significant neuron loss can lead to impairments in concrete thinking and functions such as new learning ability, attention, concentration, and tracking. The emotional effects of brain damage due to anoxia can include affective dulling and disinhibition, as well as depression. These changes can drastically reduce the person's ability to plan, initiate, and carry out activities.

Exposure to certain drugs and environmental toxins can cause brain damage and result in a condition called substance/medication-induced neurocognitive disorder. Such toxins can come from intense fumes from house paint, styrene used in plastics manufacturing, and fuels distilled from petroleum.

Nutritional deficiencies can also cause cognitive decline. People who are severely undernourished are prone to develop a deficiency of folate, a critical nutrient, leading to progressive cerebral atrophy. If the deficiency is not corrected by dietary improvements, the individual can become depressed and show various cognitive impairments, such as poor memory and impaired abstract reasoning.

The cognitive losses that occur with physical disorders and toxic reactions may be reversible if the person receives prompt and appropriate medical treatment. However, if intervention for a treatable neurocognitive disorder is not introduced in the early stages, the brain damage becomes irreversible. The more widespread the structural damage to the brain, the lower the chance that the person will ever regain lost functions.

Prior to the introduction of antiretroviral therapies for acquired immune deficiency syndrome (AIDS), the disease that can result from HIV, neurocognitive disorder in the late stages of the disease was a common and devastating complication (Gisslen et al., 2007). With improvements in treatment, this condition, known as AIDS dementia complex, has become less prevalent; however, cases continue to rise among people who go undiagnosed and untreated, a situation particularly common in developing countries (Wu et al., 2007; Zhao et al., 2015).

13.7 Neurocognitive Disorders Due to Another General Medical Condition

Amnesia is the inability to recall information that was previously learned or to register new memories. In *DSM-5,* people with amnesia receive a diagnosis of **major neurocognitive disorder due to another general medical condition**. Their memory loss can result from a wide variety of medical problems, including head trauma, loss of oxygen, and herpes simplex.

Substance-induced persisting amnestic disorder occurs when drugs or medications cause serious memory impairment. An array of substances may cause this condition, including prescribed medications, illicit drugs, industrial solvents, and environmental toxins such as

amnesia
Inability to recall information that was previously learned or to register new memories.

major neurocognitive disorder due to another medical condition
Cognitive disorders involving the inability to recall previously learned information or to register new memories.

lead, mercury, and insecticides. The most common cause of this form of neurocognitive disorder is chronic alcohol use. The memory loss must persist over time for the clinician to assign the diagnosis of neurocognitive disorder due to another general medical condition. For some people, especially chronic abusers of alcohol, the neurocognitive disorder due to another general medical condition persists for life, causing such severe impairment that the individual may require custodial care. For others, such as those whose condition results from medications, full recovery is possible.

13.8 Neurocognitive Disorders: The Biopsychosocial Perspective

We can best understand the cognitive impairments that occur with the disorders discussed in this chapter from a biological perspective. However, the biological perspective has not yet produced a viable treatment for one of the most devastating of these disorders, Alzheimer's disease. Until researchers find a cure, individuals and their families whose lives are touched by the disease must be willing to try a variety of approaches to alleviate the suffering. Many research programs are currently underway to explore strategies for reducing the stress placed on caregivers. Some of these strategies make use of innovative, high-tech methods such as computer networks. Others take the more traditional approach of providing emotional support to individuals with Alzheimer's disease and their families. The application of cognitive-behavioral and other methods of therapy to help people cope with Alzheimer's is another useful approach. It seems that the bottom line in all this research on understanding and treating those affected by Alzheimer's disease is that it is not necessary for psychologists to wait until biomedical researchers discover a cure. They can do quite a bit to improve the quality of life for people with Alzheimer's and to help them maintain their functioning and dignity for as long as possible.

Return to the Case: Irene Heller

Irene's MRI showed multiple vascular legions on her cerebral cortex and the subcortical structures of her brain, confirming her diagnosis of neurocognitive disorder due to vascular disease. The qualifier of "with behavioral disturbance" was added to her diagnosis due to her history of wandering spells that had occurred with the onset of her symptoms.

Following her diagnosis, Irene was immediately started on medication, and after a few weeks she and her family began noticing that she had returned to her "premorbid" (previous) level of functioning. Upon a recommendation made by the neuropsychologist she saw for testing, Irene began to attend a support group for those who have been diagnosed with neurocognitive disorder due to vascular disease, offered in a community center in her town. Irene avidly attends every week and has reported benefiting from the social support of the group as well as learning more about the disease and how it affects each person differently. The support group has also educated Irene to be mindful of any changes in her cognition or motor movements, and to immediately seek consultation with her physician should any new difficulties arise. Due to her improved memory, Irene's health remained stable because she was now remembering to take her insulin as prescribed. Irene enjoyed taking part in her regular activities again and spending time with her family, no longer burdened by motor difficulties. Irene will undergo a brief battery of neuropsychological testing every 6 months to monitor for any further deterioration in her cognition and to assess the efficacy of her treatment regimen.

Dr. Tobin's reflections: Neurocognitive disorder due to vascular disease can result from a stroke. Due to the patchy and irregular deterioration of Irene's symptoms, it is more likely that her symptoms resulted from a more gradual process of cerebrovascular disease. In many cases, adults live for some time with mild symptoms of neurocognitive disorder. Irene was fortunate to have attentive children who noticed her symptoms relatively soon after they arose, and she was able to seek treatment that I hope will slow the development of this disorder. She was also fortunate that her diagnosis was based on careful consideration of multiple sources of testing, because many older adults with neurocognitive disorder due to vascular disease are incorrectly diagnosed with Alzheimer's disease, which is irreversible and requires a different course of treatment and case planning.

SUMMARY

- Neurocognitive disorders (former called "delirium, dementia, amnestic, and other cognitive disorders") are those in which the central characteristic is cognitive impairment that results from causes such as brain trauma, disease, or exposure to toxic substances.

- Delirium is a temporary state in which individuals experience a clouding of consciousness in which they are unaware of what is happening and are unable to focus or pay attention. They experience cognitive changes in which their memory is foggy and they are disoriented, and they may have various other symptoms, such as rambling speech, delusions, hallucinations, and emotional disturbances. Delirium, which is caused by a change in the brain's metabolism, can result from various factors, including substance intoxication or withdrawal, head injury, high fever, and vitamin deficiency. The onset is generally rapid and the duration brief.

- The best-known of these disorders is neurocognitive disorder due to Alzheimer's disease. Symptoms are characterized by progressive cognitive impairment involving a person's memory, communication abilities, judgment skills, motor coordination, and ability to learn new information. In addition to experiencing cognitive changes, individuals with this condition undergo changes in their personality and emotional state. It is challenging to make this diagnosis due to the fact that some conditions, such as vascular neurocognitive disorder and major depressive disorder, mimic the symptoms of Alzheimer's disease.

- The biological perspective is predominant among theories regarding the cause of Alzheimer's. Current research focuses on abnormalities in the nervous system—specifically, two types of structure changes in the brain. The first is the formation of neurofibrillary tangles, in which the cellular material within the cell bodies of neurons becomes replaced by densely packed, twisted microfibrils, or tiny strands, of protein. The second change is the development of amyloid plaques, which are clusters of dead or dying neurons mixed with fragments of protein molecules. Although there is no cure for this disease, medications such as anticholinesterase agents can slow the progress of cognitive decline. In the absence of a biological cure, psychological perspectives have led to the use of psychopharmacological medication to alleviate secondary symptoms such as depression. Researchers are exploring social contributors, such as the role of certain behaviors in preventing the development of the disease. Additionally, experts are refining behavioral techniques for managing symptoms and developing strategies for alleviating caregiver burden.

- Neurocognitive disorders can also occur as the result of other disease processes as well as substances or medication. They may also be associated with infectious diseases, including AIDS, which is a disease that can result from HIV infection.

- Researchers are increasingly recognizing traumatic brain injury (TBI) as an important cause of mental and physical dysfunction.

- Major neurocognitive disorder due to another medical condition is a disorder in which people are unable to recall previously learned information or to register new memories. This disorder is due either to the use of substances or to medical conditions such as head trauma, loss of oxygen, and herpes simplex.

KEY TERMS

Akinesia

Amnesia

Amyloid plaques

Bradykinesia

Delirium

Frontotemporal neurocognitive disorder

Major neurocognitive disorder due to another medical condition

Major neurocognitive disorders

Mild neurocognitive disorders

Multi-infarct dementia (MID)

Neurocognitive disorder

Neurocognitive disorder due to Alzheimer's disease

Neurocognitive disorder due to Huntington's disease

Neurocognitive disorder due to Parkinson's disease

Neurocognitive disorder due to prion disease (Creutzfeld-Jakob disease)

Neurocognitive disorder due to traumatic brain injury

Neurocognitive disorder with Lewy bodies

Neurofibrillary tangles

Pick's disease

Postconcussion syndrome (PCS)

Prion disease

Pseudodementia

Secretases

Tau

Traumatic brain injury (TBI)

Vascular neurocognitive disorder

Personality Disorders

Learning Objectives

14.1 Describe the nature of personality disorders and the alternative diagnostic system in the *DSM-5*.

14.2 Identify the characteristics, theories, and treatments of Cluster A personality disorders.

14.3 Identify the characteristics, theories, and treatments of Cluster B personality disorders.

14.4 Identify the characteristics, theories, and treatments of Cluster C personality disorders.

14.5 Analyze the biopsychosocial perspective on personality disorders.

©Thinkstock Images/Getty Images

Case Report: Harold Morrill

Demographic information: 21-year-old single heterosexual Caucasian male

Presenting problem: Harold presented for an emergency intake evaluation at his university's counseling center due to self-reported suicidal ideation, in the form of a strong, pervasive desire to kill himself. He presented as angry and emotionally distraught, and he easily grew frustrated with the counselor several times throughout the interview. Harold reported that this was not the first time he had wanted to kill himself, and without being prompted he showed the counselor a large, vertical scar down his left forearm indicating a previous suicide attempt. He said he was 17 at the time he slit his wrist, that he had been under the influence of alcohol and cocaine at the time, and that he barely remembered the incident. Following this suicide attempt, Harold had been admitted to an inpatient psychiatric unit and was stabilized on medication, though he discontinued the medication on his own once he was discharged, against the recommendations of his doctors.

During the evaluation Harold became highly agitated when asked questions about his past, at one point yelling at the counselor and threatening to storm out of the room. Once the counselor was able to calm him down, Harold said tearfully, "I'm just so sick of feeling this way," and agreed to continue with the evaluation.

Harold reported having few close interpersonal relationships. He said he didn't have any close friends at school and had switched dormitories four times during his freshman year alone. He was vague in describing the reason, remarking only that "all my roommates have been total jerks." Harold went on to discuss his history of romantic relationships throughout the past 4 years. Each relationship lasted a few weeks,

the longest for 2 months, and they usually ended due to "blow out" arguments. When asked about the nature of the arguments, Harold said in each case he had accused the woman of infidelity and immediately ended the relationship. He described feeling that "no one could ever make me happy. I don't know why I even try. Nothing that I ever do makes me feel better, so I keep trying new things and looking for new people. But none of it works." He related this to his recurrent thoughts of suicide and past suicide attempts. When asked about his family, Harold reported that he was "disgusted" with them and the way they treated him as a child (see "Relevant history").

Harold reported that he frequently abuses alcohol—as many as 7 days per week—and that he typically drinks to the point of blacking out. He described that he mostly enjoys going to bars and did so with a fake ID before he turned 21. He explained that he enjoys meeting new people and that drinking "helps me to not be so bored all the time." Harold also reported a history of drug abuse including marijuana, cocaine, and ecstasy since the age of 13. He had been caught with substances by the police on campus, though he had avoided being arrested. He was arrested for DUI during his freshman year and had attended alcohol education classes, which he called "a complete waste of my time." Following the arrest, Harold lost his driver's license, which greatly upset him because he typically enjoyed driving to bars in other towns when he was feeling tired of his own town. He regained his license and had been frequenting bars and drinking heavily until 3 weeks prior to the current intake evaluation.

Harold explained that for the past 3 weeks he had been spending most of his time alone in his room, saying, "Why would anyone want to spend time with such a lousy person? That's why I wanted to die." He had also quit his part-time job at a grocery store and was attending only a few classes per week. He was unable to recall a specific event that had brought on his current depression, and when asked about it, he burst into tears and pleaded with the clinician for help. "I just know I'm going to kill myself." He revealed burn marks on his legs that appeared to be recently inflicted. The clinician asked Harold about his current suicidal ideation, and he was able to contract for safety, meaning he agreed not to hurt himself and affirmed that if his thoughts about death grew stronger he would call the emergency room or the counseling center. Then Harold asked the clinician whether she could be his therapist. She described the counseling center's policy, that as the intake clinician she could not see clients being evaluated for psychotherapy. "Just like a typical woman," he retorted. "You don't want to be with me. I think you're terrible at your job, anyway."

Relevant history: Harold stated that he had attended psychotherapy sessions in the past but had "hated every single one of them," referring to his therapists, when describing why he never stayed in therapy long. He had seen about five different therapists since the age of 14 but described the experiences as "uncomfortable and just weird. They didn't get me." When the clinician asked Harold why he had gone to therapy as an adolescent, he stated, "I think my mom thought I was messed up. I didn't think I needed it." He described his childhood as "a disaster" and his father as a severe alcoholic who was

often emotionally and sometimes physically abusive. He reported that his mother worked two jobs to support the family, and so as a child he spent much of his time alone.

Case formulation: Harold's behaviors and reported history during the evaluation match the criteria for a personality disorder as defined by the *DSM-5,* and his symptoms meet criteria for borderline personality disorder. Although he often abused substances, Harold's personality disorder was not a result of substance use and instead is a reflection of the impulsivity and inability to cope with strong emotions that is typical of borderline individuals.

His symptoms of depression for the past 3 weeks meet criteria for a major depressive episode, though it is unknown whether these have been recurrent or whether this was a discrete, severe episode. Given his prior suicide attempts, it is possible that he has had recurrent depressive episodes, though these may be more closely related to the instability that is a feature of his borderline personality disorder. Thus, major depressive disorder was ruled out as a diagnosis.

Treatment plan: Dialectical behavior therapy (DBT) is currently the preferred treatment for borderline personality disorder. It consists of a combination of intensive individual psychotherapy and group therapy. Once Harold had made a safety plan with the counselor, he was referred to a private DBT outpatient program 2 miles from his college campus. Harold was also referred to the psychiatrist on campus for a medication consultation.

Sarah Tobin, PhD

In this chapter, our focus shifts to the set of disorders that represent long-standing patterns of impairments in an individual's self-understanding, ways of relating to others, and personality traits. As we discussed in the chapter "Theoretical Perspectives," a personality trait is an enduring pattern of perceiving, relating to, and thinking about the environment and others, a pattern that characterizes the majority of a person's interactions and experiences. Most people are able to draw upon their personality traits in a flexible manner, adjusting their responses to the needs of the situation. When people become rigidly fixed on one particular trait or set of traits, however, they may place themselves at risk for developing a personality disorder.

14.1 The Nature of Personality Disorders

When does a personality trait become a disorder? What may be a characteristic way of responding can develop into a fixed pattern that impairs a person's ability to function satisfactorily. Perhaps you're the type of person who likes to have your room look "just so." If someone moves your books around or changes the arrangement of your clothes on the hanger, you may feel a little bothered. At what point does your unhappiness with a change in the order of your possessions become so problematic that you have crossed over from a being a little finicky to having a personality disorder characterized by extreme rigidity? Should this behavioral pattern place you in a diagnostic category with a distinct set of criteria that separates you from people with other personality traits and related behaviors? These are the questions raised in the diagnosis of the disorders you will read about in this chapter.

Personality Disorders in *DSM-5*

A **personality disorder** is an ingrained way of relating to other people, situations, and events, characterized by a rigid and maladaptive pattern of inner experience and behavior, dating back to adolescence or early adulthood. As conceptualized in the *DSM-5,* the personality disorders represent a collection of distinguishable sets of behavior falling into 10 distinct categories (plus one additional "not otherwise specified" diagnosis). Fitting the general

> ### What's in the *DSM-5*
>
> #### Dimensionalizing the Personality Disorders
>
> The history of personality disorders, which are not so much illnesses as characteristics of an individual's core ways of relating to others and experiencing the self, reflects the tension between those who support categorical diagnoses and those who prefer a system of personality trait ratings. Proponents of the dimensional approach argue that we cannot summarize the many complex facets of personality into a discrete set of units. However, clinicians are used to thinking of these disorders in terms of categories. It is more convenient to describe clients as fitting into the "borderline" diagnostic category rather than to list all the personality traits that particular individuals display. Therefore, proponents of the categorical system argue that these diagnoses are a more legitimate way to capture the essence of a personality disorder.
>
> Reflecting these debates, the area of personality disorders received perhaps the greatest attention from clinicians and researchers as they awaited the unveiling of the final revisions to the *DSM-5*. To satisfy proponents of both approaches, the *DSM-5* authors had initially proposed a compromise that would have included categorical diagnoses for six of the personality disorders as well as a dimensional rating system of pathological personality traits. However, these changes were not implemented. When the American Psychiatric Association's Board of Directors took the final vote on approving *DSM-5*'s changes, they rejected any changes to the *DSM-IV-TR* system.
>
> Although the dimensional system for the personality disorders was rejected, the APA Board decided it could be included in Section 3 of the *DSM-5*, where it could receive continued testing. It is possible that, should this be favorably received, a future *DSM-5.1* will adopt dimensions in lieu of categorical diagnoses.

definition of a psychological disorder, a personality disorder deviates markedly from the individual's culture and leads to distress or impairment. The types of behavior that personality disorders represent can be, for example, excessive dependency, overwhelming fear of intimacy, intense worry, exploitive behavior, or uncontrollable rage. To fit the current diagnostic criteria, these behaviors must manifest themselves in at least two of four areas: (1) cognition, (2) affectivity, (3) interpersonal functioning, and (4) impulse control. As a result of these behaviors, the individual experiences distress or impairment.

personality disorder
Ingrained patterns of relating to other people, situations, and events involving a rigid and maladaptive pattern of inner experience and behavior, dating back to adolescence or early adulthood.

The *DSM-5* groups the 10 diagnoses into three clusters based on the fundamental characteristics they share. Cluster A includes paranoid, schizoid, and schizotypal personality disorders, all of which share features of odd and eccentric behavior. Cluster B includes antisocial, borderline, histrionic, and narcissistic personality disorders, marked by overdramatic, emotional, and erratic or unpredictable attitudes and behaviors. Cluster C includes avoidant, dependent, and obsessive-compulsive personality disorders, which have anxious and fearful behaviors in common. The 11th personality disorder is reserved for individuals who do not clearly meet one of the other 10 diagnostic criteria, which is why it receives the label "not otherwise specified."

Because each personality disorder is defined as a distinct entity, clinicians evaluating individuals for a possible diagnosis must decide how many of the criteria a client meets within each category and assign a diagnosis on that basis. The clinician may start by trying to match the individual's most prominent symptoms with the diagnostic criteria. If the client does not fit the criteria for that disorder, the clinician may either move to another disorder or decide that the client has a personality disorder "not otherwise specified" because it is not uniquely identifiable.

Currently, studies in both the United States and the United Kingdom yield an overall prevalence among nationally representative samples of 9 to 10 percent. Personality disorders are highly comorbid with drug dependence. For example, among people with antisocial personality disorder, the lifetime prevalence rate of alcohol dependence is 27 percent and 59 percent for nicotine dependence (Trull et al., 2010).

Alternative Personality Disorder Diagnostic System in Section 3 of the *DSM-5*

As you can see, personality disorders represent distinct diagnostic entities. Whereas people can be high or low on a given personality trait, such as introversion or conscientiousness, they either have or do not have a given personality disorder.

Those who are critical of the *DSM-5* maintain that the 10 diagnoses there require too many fine distinctions to be made about behaviors and qualities that, in reality, occur as a continuum (see the "What's in the *DSM-5*" box above). Indeed, because of the forced-choice categories the system requires, clinicians found that they were most often using the less-than-precise diagnosis of "personality disorder not otherwise specified" (Widiger & Trull, 2007).

In response to these criticisms and questions, although they retained the categorical diagnostic system, the *DSM-5* authors decided to include dimensional ratings of pathological personality traits on a trial basis. Clinicians can use these dimensional ratings of the six most readily differentiated personality disorders to evaluate the corresponding personality and interpersonal functioning of each (Livesley, 2011). This dimensional system is shown in Table 1. It remains in Section 3 of *DSM-5*, allowing clinicians and researchers to test the new system and work to help decide whether it should replace the categorical diagnostic system.

TABLE 1 Dimensional Ratings of DSM-5 Personality Disorders from Section 3

Personality Disorder	Personality Functioning		Interpersonal Functioning		Personality Traits
	Identity	Self-direction	Empathy	Intimacy	
Antisocial	Egocentrism with self-esteem based on being able to get power	Sets goals based on personal needs; fails to comply with laws or ethical standards	Lacks ability to understand feelings and needs of others	Unable to engage in mutually intimate relationships	Antagonism Disinhibition
Avoidant	Low self-esteem and sees self as socially inferior	Unable to take risks or engage in new activities involving contact with others.	Preoccupied with being criticized or rejected	Difficulty forming close relationships unless sure of being liked	Negative Affectivity Detachment
Borderline	Poorly developed and unstable self-image; chronic feelings of emptiness	Unstable goals, aspirations, and plans	Unable to understand how others may be feeling	Intense, conflicted, and unstable relationships	Negative Affectivity Disinhibition Antagonism
Narcissistic	Excessively dependent on being appreciated by others	Sets either unrealistically high or low standards	Unable to gauge how others are feeling due to extreme self-preoccupation	Superficial relationships; sees others as relevant only in terms of own self-esteem	Antagonism
Obsessive-compulsive	Identity derived primarily from work or being productive	Difficulty completing tasks due to excessively high standards	Difficulty understanding feelings of others	Work seen as more important than relationships	Extreme Conscientiousness Negative Affectivity Detachment
Schizotypal	Unable to distinguish boundaries between self and others	No clear set of goals	Misunderstands how others are feeling	Mistrustful and anxious about close relationships	Psychoticism Detachment

TABLE 2 General Criteria for a Personality Disorder in Section 3

This description summarizes the Section 3 personality trait criteria from *DSM-5*.

- Moderate or greater impairment in personality as reflected in self and interpersonal functioning (Table 1)
- One or more pathological personality traits (Table 3)
- These impairments are relatively inflexible, pervasive across a range of situations, stable across time, and can be traced back at least to adolescence or early adulthood.
- Another psychological disorder does not better explain these impairments, nor are they attributable to the physiological effects of a substance or another medical condition.
- The impairments are not better understood as normal for an individual's developmental level or social and cultural context.

TABLE 3 Personality Domains in the *DSM-5* Section 3 Rating System

Negative Affectivity: Experiencing negative emotions frequently and intensely.

Detachment: Withdrawal from other people and from social interactions.

Antagonism: Behaviors that put the person at odds with other people.

Disinhibition: Engaging in behaviors on impulse, without reflecting on potential future consequences.

Psychoticism: Having unusual and bizarre experiences.

SOURCE: Few, L. R., et al. (2013). Examination of the Section III DSM-5 diagnostic system for personality disorders in an outpatient clinical sample. *Journal of Abnormal Psychology, 122*, 1057–1069.

To use the Section 3 dimensional ratings, clinicians assign one of six personality disorder diagnoses to their clients and then evaluate them on the above five dimensions (divided into three groups). The first group of dimensions reflects "personality functioning," defined as the individual's sense of identity and self-direction. The second group includes two ratings of "interpersonal functioning" that tap the client's ability to understand other people's perspectives (empathy) and form close relationships (intimacy). Clinicians rate individuals from mild to extreme in these domains. The third group is actually a single rating of the client on traits related to each of the six personality disorders.

Table 2 summarizes in brief how personality disorders would be diagnosed using the dimensional criteria, and Table 3 defines each of the personality traits listed in Table 1. Keep in mind that this system is not yet in place but is being actively investigated as an alternative to the categorization system in *DSM-5* currently in use (Bach, Markon, Simonsen, & Krueger, 2015; Skodol, Morey, Bender, & Oldham, 2015). To date, the evidence generally supports the Section 3 dimensional rating system, but it also suggests that further refinement is needed before this system can replace the categorical system entirely (Yam & Simms, 2014).

As you read about the personality disorders in *DSM-5* as currently structured, think about this alternative system and consider whether you believe the dimensional ratings would help or hinder the accurate diagnosis of individuals with these long-standing maladaptive qualities.

14.2 Cluster A Personality Disorders

Cluster A of the personality disorders in *DSM-5* include those disorders characterized by odd and eccentric behavior. People with these disorders have qualities suggesting they feel different, unlikable, and unable to fit into the social world of their friends, families, fellow students, and co-workers, leaving them with a preference for avoiding interpersonal relationships (Renton & Mankiewicz, 2015).

MINI CASE

Paranoid Personality Disorder

Anita is a single 34-year-old African American female who identifies as gay. She is a computer programmer who constantly worries that other people will exploit her knowledge. She regards as "top secret" the new database management program she is writing and even fears that, when she leaves the office at night, someone will sneak into her desk and steal her notes. Her distrust of others pervades all her interpersonal dealings, with suspicions that she is being cheated tainting even routine transactions in banks and stores. Anita likes to think of herself as rational and able to make objective decisions; she regards her inability to trust other people as a natural reaction to a world filled with what she calls "opportunistic and insincere corporate ladder climbers."

Paranoid Personality Disorder

paranoid personality disorder

A personality disorder whose outstanding feature is that the individual is unduly suspicious of others and is always on guard against potential danger or harm.

People with **paranoid personality disorder** are extremely suspicious of others and are always on guard against potential danger or harm. Their view of the world is narrowly focused, in that they seek to confirm their expectations that other people will take advantage of them, making it virtually impossible for them to trust even their friends and associates.

As an example, consider an individual with this disorder who believes a spouse or partner to be unfaithful, even if no substantiating evidence exists. Seeing an unexplained text on a partner's phone, such an individual will regard this as proof that the partner is having an affair. Indeed, with their guarded behavior and suspiciousness, those with paranoid personality disorder are known to have difficulty establishing the type of interpersonal closeness that helps maintain the quality of a long-term intimate relationship (Disney, Weinstein & Oltmanns, 2012).

Another manifestation of paranoid personality disorder is the inability to take blame for mistakes, seeing others as being at fault instead. The disorder also shows up as the perception that there is hidden meaning in innocent comments or glances. A real or imagined slight leads to years of resentment.

On the positive side, individuals with this disorder may be relatively successful in certain kinds of jobs requiring that they be on the lookout for threats to themselves, co-workers, or the public. In dangerous political climates in which people must be on guard just to stay alive, these traits can be adaptive. However, in ordinary circumstances, individuals' excessive caution and high level of suspicion means they find it difficult to place trust in other people, even those who love and care about them.

Unfortunately, because people with paranoid personality disorder do not see themselves as the source of their problems, they refuse to seek professional help. In the unlikely event they do seek therapy, their rigidity and defensiveness make it difficult for the clinician to form the kind of working relationship needed to make progress and work toward any kind of lasting change.

Schizoid Personality Disorder

schizoid personality disorder

A personality disorder primarily characterized by an indifference to social relationships, as well as a limited range of emotional experience and expression.

An indifference to social and sexual relationships characterizes **schizoid personality disorder**. With a limited range of emotional experience and expression, individuals with this disorder prefer to be by themselves rather than with others, and they appear to lack any desire for acceptance or love, even by their families. They are not even interested in becoming sexually involved with others. In turn, others perceive them as cold, reserved, withdrawn, and seclusive.

Throughout their lives, people with schizoid personality disorder seek out situations that require only minimal interaction with others. Those who are able to tolerate work are drawn to jobs in which they spend all their work hours alone. They choose to live alone, guarding their privacy and avoiding any but the most superficial dealings with neighbors.

MINI CASE

Schizoid Personality Disorder

Demetrios is a single 45-year-old heterosexual Greek American male. He works as a night security guard at a bank and likes his job because he can enter the private world of his thoughts without interruptions from other people. Even though his long years of service make him eligible for a daytime security position, Dmitri has repeatedly turned down these opportunities because daytime work would require him to deal with bank employees and customers. Dmitri has resided for more than 20 years in a small room at a boarding house. He has no television or radio, and he has resisted any attempts by other house residents to include him in social activities. He has made it clear he is not interested in small talk and prefers to be left alone. Neighbors, co-workers, and even his family members (whom he also avoids) perceive him as a peculiar person who seems strikingly cold and detached. When his brother died, Dmitri decided not to attend the funeral because he did not want to be bothered by all the carrying on and sympathetic wishes of relatives and others.

Both paranoid and schizoid personality disorders would have been eliminated in the new *DSM-5* system. Researchers believe that existing research does not support their continued inclusion in the psychiatric nomenclature because they cannot be uniquely identified (Hopwood & Thomas, 2012; Hummelen, Pedersen, Wilberg, & Karterud, 2015). Their names are also somewhat misleading in that they sound as if they refer to a variant of schizophrenia, when in fact individuals with these qualities have not lost touch with reality.

Schizotypal Personality Disorder

Individuals with **schizotypal personality disorder** have odd if not eccentric beliefs, behavior, appearance, and interpersonal style. Unlike the term *schizoid*, the term *schizotypal* implies a connection with schizophrenia, and people who fit this diagnosis are vulnerable to developing a full-blown psychosis if exposed to difficult life circumstances that challenge their coping ability.

The pathological personality traits of people with schizotypal personality disorder fall along the extremely maladaptive end of the psychoticism dimension (Balaratnasingam & Janca, 2015). Thus, individuals with this disorder may hold eccentric ideas, have unusual beliefs and experiences, and have difficulty forming accurate perceptions and cognitions about their world, leading to more negative views about themselves than are warranted by objective data (Cohen, Auster, MacAulay, & McGovern, 2014). They also show a tendency to be high on the personality trait of openness to experience, specifically, openness to unusual ideas (Chmielewski et al., 2014). As we show in Table 1, people with schizotypal personality disorder also have restricted affect and withdrawal tendencies, which reflect the pathological personality trait of detachment.

schizotypal personality disorder
A personality disorder that primarily involves odd beliefs, behavior, appearance, and interpersonal style. People with this disorder may have bizarre ideas or preoccupations, such as magical thinking and beliefs in psychic phenomena.

MINI CASE

Schizotypal Personality Disorder

Ronan is a single 21-year-old Caucasian male who identifies as asexual. He is a college junior who has devised an elaborate system for deciding which courses to take, depending on the course number. He will not take a course with the number 5 in it because he believes that if he does so, he might have to "plead the Fifth Amendment." Rarely does he talk to people in his dormitory, believing that others are intent on stealing his term paper ideas. He has acquired a reputation for being somewhat of a "flake" because of his odd manner of dress, his reclusive tendencies, and the ominous drawings of sinister animals displayed on the door of his room. The sound of the nearby elevator, he claims, is actually a set of voices singing a monastic chant.

14.3 Cluster B Personality Disorders

People with Cluster B personality disorders behave in ways that are best described as dramatic, emotional, or erratic. These individuals act impulsively, seem to have an inflated view of their own importance or self-esteem, and are high in the desire to seek stimulation.

Antisocial Personality Disorder

antisocial personality disorder

A personality disorder characterized by a lack of regard for society's moral or legal standards and an impulsive and risky lifestyle.

psychopathy

A cluster of traits that form the core of the antisocial personality.

Synonymous in the past with "psychopath" or "sociopath," the *DSM-5* term **antisocial personality disorder** describes a personality disorder characterized by a lack of regard for society's moral or legal standards and an impulsive and risky lifestyle. People with this disorder are high in the quality of **psychopathy** and thus defined as being able to exploit others, extremely egocentric and incapable of love, unreliable and deceptive, charming but insincere, and unable to feel remorse. They engage in impulsive and aggressive acts, take risks despite experiencing negative consequences, and fail to conform to social or ethical norms. Their antisocial lifestyle may also include a history of early behavioral problems or juvenile delinquency.

People with antisocial personality disorder do not actually experience feelings of remorse, but they may feign their regret for harming others in order to get themselves out of a difficult situation when they get caught. These individuals also try hard to present themselves in as favorable a light as possible. You might think of them as the "smooth talkers" who can con anyone out of anything, such as asking for money or favors they have no intention of repaying.

dark triad

Personality traits that include psychopathy, extreme self-centeredness, and a tendency to regard other people as objects to be used.

Personality researchers also believe that related to psychopathy is the trait of fearless dominance, a tendency toward boldness that includes a desire to dominate social situations, charm, willingness to take physical risks, and an immunity to feelings of anxiety (Few et al., 2015; Lilienfeld et al., 2012). Personality researchers coined the fitting term **dark triad** to reflect the makeup of individuals high in psychopathy who are also highly self-centered and regard other people as objects to be exploited (Jonason et al., 2015).

The accepted wisdom for many years in the field of abnormal psychology was that people with antisocial personality disorder are untreatable, and current therapy effectiveness studies unfortunately continue to support the difficulty of working with this population (Wilson, 2014). Because they seem unable to experience empathy and do not learn from the negative consequences of their behaviors, they are resistant to approaches using either insight or behavioral interventions. Indeed, the problems of working with these individuals include the

Typical antisocial behaviors include lying, cheating, and stealing.
©D-Keine/Getty Images

MINI CASE

Antisocial Personality Disorder

Tommy is a single 38-year-old Caucasian heterosexual male. He grew up in a chaotic home atmosphere, his mother having lived with a series of violent men who were heavily involved in drug dealing and prostitution. At age 18, Tommy was jailed for brutally mugging and stabbing an older woman. This was the first in a long series of arrests for offenses ranging from drug trafficking to car thefts to counterfeiting. At one point, between jail terms, he met a woman at a bar and married her the next day. Two weeks later, he beat her when she complained about his incessant drinking and involvement with shady characters. Tommy left her when she became pregnant, and he refused to pay child support. From his vantage point now as a drug trafficker and leader of a child prostitution ring, Tommy shows no regret for what he has done, claiming that life has "sure given me a bum steer."

You Be the Judge

Antisocial Personality Disorder and Moral Culpability

If antisocial personality disorder is a psychological disorder, should people who meet the diagnosis be held responsible for criminal acts they may commit? What about people who have the personality trait of psychopathy? Are they somehow more or less culpable than others? The question of criminal responsibility permeates the ethical literature on antisocial personality disorder and the related personality trait of psychopathy. According to Robert Hare (1997), when the judicial system applies the term *psychopathy* rather than *antisocial personality disorder* to an offender, that offender is likely to receive a harsher sentence because the court perceives the person (usually a male) as lacking any redeeming qualities. Canadian philosopher Ishtiyaque Haji (2010) challenges the idea that people high in psychopathy are mentally healthy and thus responsible for their crimes. He suggests that these individuals have less moral responsibility for their crimes than do people who are not high in the psychopathy trait. According to Haji, the emotional insensitivity that is a hallmark of psychopathy makes an individual less able to appreciate the moral consequences of his or her actions.

Carrying this argument further, consider the factors that may lead individuals to develop high levels of the psychopathy trait. Perhaps their lack of emotional sensitivity relates to an abnormality of brain development, as some researchers suggest. If they truly cannot experience empathy, how can they relate to the harm they may be causing a victim? Similarly, if they lack the neurological basis for learning fear and thus are less likely to avoid the negative consequences of criminal activity, does this flaw of brain development make them similar to people who have a physical illness? Without the ability to appreciate the punishment that may follow a crime, people high in psychopathy cannot learn from their experiences and seem doomed to continue being "emotionally depraved" (in Haji's words).

The question whether people high in psychopathy have a true impairment that prevents them from recognizing the moral implications of their actions will, no doubt, continue to be debated. Each serial murderer with antisocial personality disorder or psychopathy seems to raise the issue all over again. With increasingly sophisticated evidence on the neurodevelopmental factors that predispose individuals to developing this disorder, we may eventually understand the issue with greater clarity.

Q: *You be the judge*: Should people with antisocial personality disorder be considered responsible for their illegal behaviors? Why or why not?

REAL STORIES

Ted Bundy: Antisocial Personality Disorder

Infamous serial killer Ted Bundy was born in 1946 in Burlington, Vermont. Although the identity of his father is unknown, various sources have suspected that it may have been his grandfather, who was abusive and violent toward Ted's mother. It is thought that Ted harbored a lifelong resentment toward his mother for never revealing the identity of his father. He looked up to his grandfather, however, who was known for his bigotry and propensity toward violence. As a child, Ted's mother recalls, he engaged in strange behaviors, including placing knives around her bed while she slept, when she would wake to find him standing over her and smiling.

When Ted was 4 years old, his mother moved the family to Washington State, where she later met and married Johnny Bundy, who formally adopted Ted. Johnny and Ted's mother had four children of their own, and although they made it a point to include Ted in all their activities, he preferred to stay out of the family's affairs and kept mostly to himself. Ted gave varying accounts of his early life to biographers, although in general it appears that he presented himself in those years as a charming, outgoing young man. On the inside, however, he felt no desire to make any connection with others and had difficulty keeping friends and romantic partners.

After dropping out of college, Ted began working at a suicide hotline and enrolled in a community college where he studied psychology. Eventually he went to law school at the University of Utah, although by the end of his first year he had stopped attending classes. He moved back to the Pacific Northwest and worked on political campaigns, and around this time, young women began disappearing. Profilers on the cases of the murdered women had Ted on their suspect list, although they had difficulty believing that such an engaging and motivated young man could be capable of such crimes. Between the years 1974 and 1978, Ted was responsible for the grisly murders of at least 30 women in Utah, Washington, Oregon, Idaho, and Florida. In his book *The*

Bundy Murders, Kevin M. Sullivan describes the murders: "The planning, hunting, taking, and subsequent killing of his victims (not to mention his penchant for necrophilia) would prove to be a time-consuming process." Ted would reportedly approach his young female victims in public places, often in broad daylight, and pretend either to be an authority figure or to be injured before taking them to a more secluded area where he would molest, assault, and eventually murder them.

Ted escaped from prison following his first arrest but was finally convicted for the murder of Kimberly Leach. Sullivan describes this murder: "He was intoxicated, but not with alcohol. His intoxication was the deep and vicious craving to which he had surrendered himself long ago. This craving, which had so utterly taken control and superseded every other aspect of his life, would never stop seeking victims as long as he was alive."

During the trial, Ted attempted to use his law school experience to argue his way out of a guilty conviction. Dr. Emmanuel Tanay, a professor of psychiatry at Wayne State University, conducted a clinical interview with Ted with an aim of finding him not guilty by reason of insanity. Consider this excerpt from the interview:

"In the nearly three hours which I spent with Mr. Bundy, I found him to be in a cheerful even jovial mood; he was witty but not flippant, he spoke freely; however, meaningful communication was never established. He was asked about his apparent lack of concern so out of keeping with the charges facing him. He acknowledged that he is facing a possible death sentence, however, 'I will cross that bridge when I get to it.' Mr. Bundy has an incapacity to recognize the significance of evidence held against him. It would be simplistic to

Executed in 1989 for murder, Ted Bundy admitted to being responsible for the deaths of at least 30 people.
©Anonymous/AP Images

characterize this as merely lying inasmuch as he acts as if his perception of the significance of evidence was real. . . . In his decision-making process, Mr. Bundy is guided by his emotional needs, sometimes to the detriment of his legal interests. The pathological need of Mr. Bundy to defy authority, to manipulate his associates and adversaries, supplies him with 'thrills' to the detriment of his ability to cooperate with his counsel."

In the end, Ted decided not to plead insanity. As Sullivan writes, Ted did not believe his behavior was consistent with the legal definition of insanity. "The removal and sequestering of his victims' heads and having sex with the dead did not, in his mind, constitute mental aberration. He would refer to this sort of thing only as 'my problem.'"

After the court rejected his final appeal, Ted Bundy was executed by electric chair on the morning of January 24, 1989. Of his execution, Sullivan described Ted as having a "conciliatory" and accepting attitude, as well as an apparent lack of negative feelings toward the legal process that eventually brought an end to his life. "When it came to his last statement," Sullivan writes, "he spoke only of giving his 'love to my family and friends.'"

SOURCE: *The Bundy Murders: A Comprehensive History* by Kevin M. Sullivan.

very characteristics of the disorder itself: a seeming lack of motivation to change, a tendency toward deception and manipulation, inability to see the world from the perspective of other people, and a lack of deep or lasting emotion (Newbury-Helps, Feigenbaum, & Fonagy, 2017).

What, then, are reasonable treatment goals? Should researchers measure the effectiveness of therapy in terms of rearrest or recidivism (return of symptoms), or should they focus instead on changes in job performance, relationships with others, and engagement in noncriminal activities (such as sports or hobbies) (Salekin, Worley, & Grimes, 2010)?

Reflecting the many difficulties in both working with the population and defining reasonable goals of therapy, at present no one accepted method of treatment has been shown to be effective in reducing the core features of the disorder (Hatchett, 2015). Nevertheless, therapists can take a pragmatic approach to helping clients satisfy their needs through prosocial ways, such as cooperation rather than exploitation and manipulation. Motivational interviewing, focused on providing clients with opportunities to connect to core values and the need for fulfillment, can also be of value as a means to help these clients make better life decisions (Mitchell, Tafrate, & Freeman, 2015).

Individuals with antisocial personality disorder may engage in manipulative behaviors due to a lack of remorse about hurting other people.
©James Lauritz/Digital Vision/Getty Images

Borderline Personality Disorder

The central quality of instability of self and relationships forms the key diagnostic feature of **borderline personality disorder (BPD)**. Diagnosis of BPD rests on the individual's demonstration of at least five of nine possible behaviors: frantic efforts to avoid abandonment; unstable and intense relationships; identity disturbance; impulsivity in areas such as sexuality, spending, or driving; recurrent suicidal behavior; unstable affect; chronic feelings of emptiness; difficulty controlling anger; and occasional feelings of paranoia or dissociative symptoms.

The symptoms of BPD influence the lives of people with the disorder in a number of significant ways. Their insecurity reaches such an extreme that they rely on other people to help them feel "whole." Even after they have passed through the customary time of identity questioning that most people experience in adolescence, these individuals remain unsure and conflicted about their life's goals. Their chronic feelings of emptiness also lead them to almost merge their identities into those of the people to whom they are close. Unfortunately for them, the more they seek the reassurance and closeness of others, the more they drive these people away. As a result, their disturbed feelings only become more intense, and they

borderline personality disorder (BPD)
A personality disorder characterized by a pervasive pattern of poor impulse control and instability in mood, interpersonal relationships, and sense of self.

MINI CASE

Borderline Personality Disorder

Anastasia is a single 28-year-old Caucasian heterosexual woman. She works as an account executive, and at the office her co-workers view her as intensely moody and unpredictable. On some days she is pleasant and high spirited, but on other days she exhibits uncontrollable anger. People are often struck by her inconsistent attitudes toward her supervisors. She may boast about the brilliance of a supervisor one day, only to deliver a burning criticism the next. Her co-workers keep their distance from her because they have become annoyed with her constant demands for attention. Anastasia has also gained a reputation in the office for her promiscuous relationships with a variety of people, male and female. On several occasions, colleagues have reprimanded her for becoming inappropriately entangled in the personal lives of her clients. One day, after losing one of her accounts, she became so distraught that she slashed her wrists. This incident prompted her supervisor to insist that Anastasia obtain professional help.

Individuals with borderline personality may experience chronic feelings of emptiness.
©Corbis

splitting
A defense, common in people with borderline personality disorder, in which individuals perceive others, or themselves, as being all good or all bad, usually resulting in disturbed interpersonal relationships.

parasuicide
Attempted suicide, often a call for help.

become more and more demanding, moody, and reckless. In this way, the symptoms of the disorder become cyclical and self-perpetuating, often escalating to the point at which the individual requires hospitalization.

A term that aptly describes the way that people with BPD often relate to others is **splitting**. This means their preoccupation with feelings of love for the object of their desire and attention can readily turn to extreme rage and hatred when that love object rejects them. They may apply this all-good versus all-bad dichotomy to other experiences and people as well. The intense despair into which they can be thrust may also lead them to perform suicidal gestures, as a way to either gain attention or derive feelings of reality from the physical pain the action causes. These so-called **parasuicides** may lead to hospitalization, where clinicians detect that the act was, in fact, a gesture and not a true desire to end their lives.

At one time, researchers believed that women were more likely to have BPD than were men, but they now consider the prevalence equal between the genders. However, there are gender differences in specific symptoms and in other disorders that occur in conjunction with a diagnosis of BPD. Men with BPD are more likely to have substance use disorder and antisocial personality characteristics. Women have higher rates of mood and anxiety disorders, eating disorders, and post-traumatic stress disorder. These differences may account for the previous estimates of higher rates of the disorder in women, whom clinicians more likely encountered in mental health settings. In contrast, clinicians are more likely to see men in substance use disorder programs (Sansone, Dittoe, Hahn, & Wiederman, 2011).

A diagnosis of BPD prior to the age of 19 may signify that the individual will face a difficult life ahead. In a review of 18 studies on long-term outcomes of BPD among children and adolescents, researchers found evidence that diagnosis prior to adulthood predicted significant social, educational, work, and financial impairment in the years to come (Winsper et al., 2015).

Overall, however, there is a trend for individuals who have BPD to improve over the course of their lives in that their symptoms become less severe. Among a sample of 175 adults with BPD studied over the course of 10 years, 85 percent no longer had symptoms by the end of the period, although they improved at slower rates than did people with either major depressive disorder or other personality disorders. Furthermore, they remained less well adapted socially over time than did people with other personality disorders. Thus, although people with BPD may experience improved functioning in terms of their psychiatric disorder, they continue to face challenges in such areas as work and interpersonal relationships (Gunderson et al., 2011).

Disturbances in emotional functioning form an important component of the diagnosis of BPD, and researchers have thus focused their efforts on identifying the specific psychological processes that contribute to these disturbances. People with BPD seem to have an inability to regulate emotions, known as **emotional dysregulation**, limitations in the ability to withstand distress (distress tolerance), and avoidance of emotionally uncomfortable situations and feelings (experiential avoidance).

You might be able to imagine how these difficulties can translate into the symptoms of BPD in everyday life when individuals with BPD encounter stressful situations. More than other people, they dislike emotionally tense situations, feel uncomfortable when distressed, and have great difficulty handling their anger when something does go wrong. Researchers investigating the relationships among these three types of emotional disturbance in a sample of young adult outpatients found that, after controlling for depressive symptoms, it was experiential avoidance that had the highest relationship to BPD symptoms (Iverson, Follette, Pistorello, & Fruzzetti, 2011).

Early childhood experiences play an important role in the development of BPD. These include childhood neglect, traumatic experiences, and marital or psychiatric difficulties in the home. Children who were insecurely attached are also more likely to develop into adults with BPD (Gunderson et al., 2011).

The treatment with the greatest demonstrated effectiveness is dialectical behavior therapy (DBT), a form of behavioral therapy. Psychologist Marsha Linehan developed DBT specifically to treat individuals with BPD who might otherwise not respond to conventional psychotherapy (Linehan, Cochran, & Kehrer, 2001). In DBT, the clinician integrates supportive and cognitive-behavioral treatments with the goal of reducing the frequency of the client's self-destructive acts and increasing his or her ability to handle emotional distress.

Using a process called core mindfulness, DBT clinicians teach their clients to balance their emotions, reason, and intuition as they approach life's problems. Although important for any type of psychotherapy, the building of the therapeutic alliance seems particularly crucial in DBT, and specifically in reducing the likelihood of suicide attempts (Bedics, Atkins, Harned, & Linehan, 2015).

Mentalization therapy, in which clients are helped to identify their feelings, can also assist these individuals in gaining control over their dysfunctional thoughts and corresponding emotions (Caligor, Levy, & Yeomans, 2015). In the early steps, the therapist provides support and empathy, an essential ingredient of much psychotherapy. Therapists then help clients clarify and elaborate on what they're feeling by putting their feelings at the moment into words. Now they can start to identify their own feelings and where they originate. Finally, clients learn how to use what they gained in their relationships with people in their lives outside therapy (Daubney & Bateman, 2015).

Another evidence-based treatment for BPD, **transference-focused psychotherapy**, uses the client–clinician relationship as the framework for helping clients achieve greater understanding of their unconscious feelings and motives (Levy et al., 2006). Psychiatrically based management incorporates psychodynamic therapy as developed for BPD treatment, along with family interventions and pharmacologic treatment (Gunderson & Links, 2008).

Regardless of the specific treatment approach they use, clinicians have the greatest success if they follow a set of basic principles (Table 4). These principles set the stage for the clinician to help the client because they focus on providing key features that can be therapeutic for people with this specific disorder. Although many of these principles could generalize beyond clients with BPD, the need to establish clear boundaries, expectations, structure, and support are particularly important for individuals with this diagnosis.

The last principle encourages clinicians to seek support themselves when the client's symptoms lead to difficulties within therapy. For example, the symptom of splitting shown by individuals with BPD may lead them alternatively to devalue and idealize the clinician. In these cases, the clinician may experience complicated reactions and may benefit from the outside perspective of a supervisor or consultant.

emotional dysregulation
Lack of awareness, understanding, or acceptance of emotions; inability to control the intensity or duration of emotions; unwillingness to experience emotional distress as an aspect of pursuing goals; and inability to engage in goal-directed behaviors when experiencing distress.

mentalization therapy
A form of therapy in which clients are helped to identify their feelings by gaining control over their dysfunctional thoughts.

transference-focused psychotherapy
A treatment for borderline personality disorder that uses the client–clinician relationship as the framework for helping clients achieve greater understanding of their unconscious feelings and motives.

TABLE 4 **Needs Involved in Basic Principles of Effective Treatment for Clients with BPD**

Need for Clinicians to:	Explanation
Take over a primary role in treatment	One clinician discusses diagnosis, assesses progress, monitors safety, and oversees communication with other practitioners and family.
Provide a therapeutic structure	The clinician establishes and maintains goals and roles, particularly outlining limits on his or her availability and a plan to manage the client's possible suicidal impulses or other emergencies.
Support the client	The clinician validates the client's emotions of distress and desperation, providing hopeful statements that change is possible.
Involve the client in the therapeutic process	The clinician recognizes that progress depends on the client's active efforts to take control over his or her behavior.
Take an active role in treatment	The clinician is active in therapy, focuses on situations in the here-and-now, and helps the client connect his or her feelings to events in the past.
Deal with the client's suicidal threats or self-harming acts	The clinician expresses concern about and listens patiently to threats, but behaves judiciously (i.e., not always recommending hospitalization).
Be self-aware and ready to consult with colleagues	The clinician may require consultation when the client–clinician relationship becomes problematic.

SOURCE: Gunderson, J. G. (2011). Clinical practice. Borderline personality disorder. *New England Journal of Medicine, 364,* 2037–2042.

Histrionic Personality Disorder

histrionic personality disorder

A personality disorder characterized by exaggerated emotional reactions, approaching theatricality, in everyday behavior.

Clinicians diagnose **histrionic personality disorder** in people who show extreme pleasure at being the center of attention and who behave in whatever way necessary to ensure that this happens. The criteria for this disorder include excessive concern with physical appearance and constant and extreme efforts to draw attention to self. Flirtatious and seductive, people with this disorder become furious if they don't get the attention they seek. They want immediate gratification of their wishes and overreact to even minor provocations, usually in an exaggerated way such as by weeping or fainting.

Although their relationships are superficial, people with histrionic personality disorder interpret them as being close and intimate. Even their casual acquaintances are "good friends" in their eyes. Their cognitive style is vague and impressionistic, making them easily influenced by others and unable to solve problems on their own. To some extent, individuals with these traits may be successful because of their outward self-confidence and attention-grabbing behavior, but in the long run their flightiness, tendency to flirt, and

MINI CASE

Histrionic Personality Disorder

Lynnette is a married 44-year-old African American heterosexual female. She works as an administrator at a local college and has gained a reputation for outlandish behavior and inappropriate flirtatiousness. She often greets students with overwhelming warmth and apparent concern over their welfare, which leads some to find her appealing and engaging at first; however, they invariably become disenchanted when they realize her shallowness. To her colleagues, she brags about her minor accomplishments as if they were major victories, yet if she fails to achieve a desired objective, she sulks and breaks down into tears. She is so desperate for the approval of others that she will change her story to suit whomever she is talking to at the time. Because she is always creating crises and never reciprocates the concern of others, people have become immune and unresponsive to her frequent pleas for help and attention.

shallowness lead to instability in close relationships, including higher divorce rates (Disney et al., 2012).

This disorder was at one time regarded as synonymous with Freud's characterization of the "hysteric" individual (typically a woman), and with the decline in psychoanalytic thinking, it has fallen out of use (Blashfield, Reynolds, & Stennett, 2012). It is rarely diagnosed and difficult to distinguish reliably from other personality disorders. In fact, it was almost eliminated in the proposed reworking of *DSM-5,* but it was retained as part of the decision to leave the personality disorder categories from *DSM-IV-TR* as is.

Despite questions about its validity as a diagnosis, researchers continue to investigate personality traits associated with this disorder. For example, the "colorful" personality includes people who would not receive the diagnosis but who enjoy expressing themselves in a dramatic fashion, have difficulty listening to others, tend to interrupt, and enjoy being the focus of attention (Furnham, 2014).

Narcissistic Personality Disorder

People who meet the criteria for the diagnosis of **narcissistic personality disorder (NPD)** have as their core characteristic an extreme form of egocentrism in which they see themselves as the center of the universe. A term now in widespread popular use, "narcissism" refers to the excessive self-love and grandiosity (Krizan & Herlache, 2018) believed to be a predominant feature of NPD. Anyone in a relationship with a person truly having NPD (versus being highly narcissistic) knows how difficult such a person can be to tolerate. Entitled, haughty, and unable to see the world from anyone's perspective but their own, people with NPD seem to show little regard for the people who care about them. Ironically, however, they are highly dependent on the way they believe others perceive them, and as a result they need constant flattery, attention, and reassurance.

The sense of entitlement is one of NPD's most prominent symptoms, but it is a sword that can cut both ways. Because individuals with this disorder see themselves as exceptional, they may set their personal standards unrealistically high, being satisfied with nothing less than perfection. Conversely, they may regard themselves as deserving of whatever they want and therefore not push themselves as hard as they could, setting their personal standards far too low while believing they merit the best others can offer them.

The greatest paradox in NPD is the combination of grandiosity and vulnerability in the sense of self. Some individuals with NPD seem to think of themselves entirely in an inflated and self-aggrandizing way. These are the NPD individuals clinicians refer to as high in **grandiose narcissism**. Those high in **vulnerable narcissism**, in contrast, have an internally weak sense of self and so become despondent when they feel someone important to them is humiliating or betraying them (Besser & Priel, 2010). The *DSM-5* does not explicitly make

narcissistic personality disorder (NPD)
A personality disorder primarily characterized by an unrealistic, inflated sense of self-importance and a lack of sensitivity to the needs of other people.

grandiose narcissism
The form of narcissistic personality disorder in which individuals think of themselves entirely in an inflated and self-aggrandizing way.

vulnerable narcissism
The form of narcissistic personality disorder in which individuals have an internally weak sense of self and so become despondent when they feel that someone who is important to them is humiliating or betraying them.

MINI CASE

Narcissistic Personality Disorder

Chad is a single 26-year-old Caucasian male who identifies as gay. For the past few years, he has been desperately trying to find success as an actor. However, he has had only minor acting jobs and has been forced to support himself by working as a waiter. Despite his lack of success, he brags to others about all the roles he rejects because they aren't good enough for him. Trying to break into acting, he has been selfishly exploitative of any person he sees as a possible connection. He intensely resents acquaintances who have obtained acting roles and devalues their achievements by

commenting that they are just lucky. Yet if anyone tries to give him constructive criticism, Chad reacts with outrage, refusing to talk to the person for weeks. Because of what he regards as his terrific looks, he thinks he deserves special treatment from everyone. At the restaurant, he has recurrent arguments with his supervisor because he insists he is a "professional" who should not have to demean himself by clearing dirty dishes from the tables. He annoys others because he always seeks compliments on his clothes, hair, intelligence, and wit. He is so caught up in himself that he barely notices other people and is grossly insensitive to their needs and problems.

this distinction, but clinicians and researchers maintain that it is an important differentiation (Caligor et al., 2015).

Some researchers believe the increasing presence of social media has in effect created a population of narcissists. Whatever position we may take in a debate about this (and it is a debatable point), a narcissist is not the same as a person with NPD. Further, there can be a healthy form of narcissism associated with having a positive sense of self-esteem (Akehurst & Thatcher, 2010).

The traditional Freudian psychoanalytic approach regards narcissism as the individual's failure to progress beyond the early, highly self-focused stages of psychosexual development when we derive gratification solely from within ourselves. The disorder is no longer seen from this viewpoint. Theorists operating within the object relations approach regard the narcissistic individual as having failed to form a cohesive, integrated sense of self. The narcissistic individual expresses insecurity, paradoxically, in an inflated sense of self-importance as he or she tries to make up for early parental support (Kohut, 1966, 1971). Lacking the firm foundation of a healthy self, such a person develops a false self precariously based on grandiose and unrealistic notions about his or her competence and desirability (Masterson, 1981).

The current psychodynamic perspective incorporates the object relations view in seeing narcissistic personality disorder as the adult's expression of childhood insecurity and need for attention. Following this logic, clinicians attempt to provide a corrective developmental experience, using empathy to support the client's search for recognition and admiration. At the same time, they attempt to guide the client toward a more realistic appreciation that no one is flawless. As clients feel their therapists increasingly support them, they become less grandiose and self-centered (Kohut, 1971). Part of this process may be a form of reparenting in which the therapist works with the client to foster early, unmet needs (Behary & Dieckmann, 2013).

Cognitive-behavioral theorists focus on the maladaptive ideas their clients hold, particularly the view held by people with the grandiose variety of the disorder in which they regard themselves as exceptional people who deserve far better treatment than ordinary humans. These beliefs hamper their ability to perceive their experiences realistically, and as a result they encounter problems when their inflated ideas about themselves clash with their experiences of failure in the real world.

Rather than simply confronting them with their erroneous beliefs, clinicians working in the cognitive-behavioral perspective structure interventions that work with, rather than against, the client's self-aggrandizing and egocentric tendencies (Freeman & Fox, 2013). This allows the individual to accept the therapist's help because the intervention seems less threatening. For example, rather than try to convince the client to act less selfishly, the therapist might try to show that there are better ways to reach important personal goals. At the

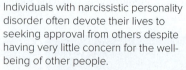

Individuals with narcissistic personality disorder often devote their lives to seeking approval from others despite having very little concern for the well-being of other people.

©CSP_karelnoppe/AGE Fotostock

same time, the therapist avoids capitulating to the client's demands for special favors and attention. Interestingly, this approach is not all that different from the contemporary psychodynamic perspective, which supports the individual's need to feel recognized and accepted while still helping him or her develop a more realistic sense of self.

Unfortunately, people with NPD are difficult to treat because they tend not to have insight into their disorder. Moreover, the therapists who treat them may experience strong negative reactions to them due to the very nature of their symptoms of grandiosity and entitlement, making them critical and demeaning of their therapists (Dhawan, Kunik, Oldham, & Coverdale, 2010). Their extreme perfectionism can also obstruct treatment. Clients with NPD have filled their lives with success and accomplishments that preserve their self-esteem and ward off their insecurities. As a result, it is particularly difficult for them to confront their anxieties and insecurities (Ronningstam, 2011).

14.4 Cluster C Personality Disorders

People within the Cluster C personality disorders tend to be extremely restrained and may draw little attention to themselves, in contrast to those individuals with personality disorders in Cluster B. Each disorder in Cluster C has its own unique qualities that distinguish it, but as a group they share this inner directedness.

Avoidant Personality Disorder

As the term implies, people with **avoidant personality disorder** stay away from others, believing they lack social skills and have no desirable qualities that would make others want to be with them. Their symptoms go beyond shyness to feelings of shame and inadequacy so strong that they prefer not to be around others. They stay away almost entirely from social encounters and are especially likely to avoid any situation that could embarrass them. They may set unrealistically high standards for themselves, which in turn lead them to avoid situations in which they feel doomed to fail. Intimate relationships present a severe threat to them because they fear shame or ridicule should they expose their flaws to a partner.

Researchers believe avoidant personality disorder exists along a continuum extending from the normal personality trait of shyness to social anxiety disorder (Reich, 2010). According to this view, avoidant personality disorder is a more severe form of social anxiety disorder (Rettew, 2000). Data from a longitudinal study of more than 34,000 adults found people with avoidant personality disorder were more likely to continue to experience symptoms of social anxiety disorder even after adjusting for a number of demographic factors (Cox et al., 2011). It is possible that the link between social anxiety disorder and avoidant personality disorder is that both are characterized by excessive self-criticism, which in turn leads people with these disorders to expect the same level of criticism from others.

The contemporary psychodynamic approach to this disorder regards it as the expression of fear of attachment in close relationships. People with this disorder avoid getting close to

avoidant personality disorder
A personality disorder in which people have low estimation of their social skills and are fearful of disapproval, rejection, and criticism or being ashamed or embarrassed.

MINI CASE

Avoidant Personality Disorder

Eduard is a single 53-year-old African American male who identifies as gay. He works as delivery person for a large equipment corporation. Eduard's co-workers describe him as a loner because he does not spend time in casual conversation and avoids going out to lunch with others. Little do they know that every day he struggles with the desire to interact with them but is too intimidated to follow through. Recently, Eduard turned down a promotion to a manager's job because he realized it would require a considerable amount of day-to-day contact with others. What bothered him most about the prospect was that he might make mistakes others would notice. Eduard has hardly dated, and every time he feels interested in a man, he becomes paralyzed with anxiety over the prospect of talking to him, much less asking him for a date. When co-workers talk to him, he blushes and nervously tries to end the conversation as soon as possible.

People with avoidant personality disorder stay away from social contact of any kind for a significant portion of the time due to excessive fears of embarrassment or rejection by others.

©Juta/Shutterstock

others because they fear being abandoned or neglected in the same way they were by their caregiver in early childhood (Levy et al., 2015).

From a cognitive-behavioral perspective, avoidant personality disorder may reflect the individuals' hypersensitivity to shame (Currie, Katz, & Yovel, 2017). This hypersensitivity causes them to misinterpret seemingly neutral and even positive remarks. Hurt by perceived rejection, they retreat inward, placing further distance between themselves and others.

The main goal of therapists working in the cognitive-behavioral framework is to break the client's negative cycle of avoidance. Clients learn to articulate the automatic thoughts and dysfunctional attitudes that interfere with their ability to establish relationships with others. Although clinicians point out the irrationality of these beliefs, they do so in a supportive atmosphere. In order for these interventions to be successful, however, clients must learn to trust the therapist rather than see him or her as yet another person who may ridicule or reject them.

Cognitive-behavioral therapists may also use graduated exposure to present the client with social situations that are increasingly more difficult to confront. They may train the client in specific skills intended to improve his or her intimate relationships. Consistent with the theory that dysfunctional cognitions are an important factor in this disorder, a pilot study of brief cognitive therapy showed that it produced improvements in negative affect and quality of life among individuals with avoidant personality disorder symptoms (Rees & Pritchard, 2015).

Dependent Personality Disorder

dependent personality disorder

A personality disorder whose main characteristic is that the individual is extremely passive and tends to cling to other people, to the point of being unable to make any decisions or to take independent action.

Individuals with **dependent personality disorder** are strongly drawn to others. However, they are so clinging and passive that they may achieve the opposite of their desires as others become impatient with their lack of autonomy. Convinced of their inadequacy, they cannot make even the most trivial decisions on their own.

Others may characterize individuals with dependent personality disorder as "clingy," and indeed, when alone these clients feel despondent and abandoned. They are likely to throw themselves wholeheartedly into relationships and are therefore devastated when relationships end. Their extreme dependence causes them to urgently seek another relationship to fill the void. Even when with others, they become preoccupied with the fear of being left. They cannot comfortably initiate new activities on their own because they are hampered by worries that they will make mistakes unless others guide their actions.

MINI CASE

Dependent Personality Disorder

Betty is a married 52-year-old Caucasian heterosexual woman. She has never lived on her own; even while a college student 30 years ago, she commuted from home. Betty was known by her classmates as someone who was dependent on others. Relying on others to make choices for her, she did whatever her friends advised, whether it choosing courses or selecting the clothes she should wear each day. The week after graduation, she married Ken, whom she had dated all senior year. She was particularly attracted to Ken because his domineering style relieved her of the responsibility to make decisions. As she has customarily done with all the close people in her life, Betty goes along with whatever Ken suggests, even if she does not fully agree. She fears that he will become angry with her and leave her if she rocks the boat. Although she wants to get a job outside the home, Ken has insisted that she remain a full-time homemaker, and she has complied with his wishes. However, when she is home alone, she calls friends and desperately pleads with them to come over for coffee. The slightest criticism from Ken, her friends, or anyone else can leave her feeling depressed and upset for the whole day.

As you might imagine, people with this disorder go to extremes to avoid having people dislike them—for example, by stating that they agree with others even when they do not. Such individuals may also seek approval by taking on responsibilities no one else wants, but if anyone criticizes them, they feel shattered.

Research on the personality traits of individuals with dependent personality disorder suggests that they have unusually high levels of agreeableness. Although we tend to think of agreeableness as an adaptive trait, at high levels it can become a tendency to be overly docile, self-sacrificing, and clinging (Samuel & Gore, 2012). Anxiousness, submissiveness, and an insecure attachment style are the pathological traits associated with dependent personality disorder (McClintock & McCarrick, 2017).

Cognitive-behavioral treatment for people with dependent personality disorder appears to be effective, particularly if the clinician alternates as needed between changing behaviors and challenging the client's faulty beliefs (Brauer & Reinecke, 2015). Mindfulness training can also be useful in helping individuals with this disorder identify and manage their interpersonal anxiety (McClintock & Anderson, 2015).

Obsessive-Compulsive Personality Disorder

People with **obsessive-compulsive personality disorder (OCPD)** have a set of symptoms that revolve around defining their sense of self and self-worth in terms of their work productivity. Perfectionistic to a fault, people with OCPD find it difficult to complete a task because they can always see a flaw in what they have done. Their work products are never good enough to meet their unrealistic standards. They can also be overly moralistic because they stick to overly conscientious standards that almost anyone would find difficult to meet.

The interpersonal relationships of people with OCPD also suffer due to their difficulty understanding how others feel, particularly when those feelings differ from their own. Because they have such high standards for themselves, people with OCPD are critical of other people who they see as not matching their own expectations. Others, in turn, perceive those with OCPD as rigid and stubborn.

The words *obsessive* and *compulsive* as applied to the OCPD personality disorder have a different meaning than in the context of obsessive compulsive disorder (OCD). Unlike those with OCD, people with OCPD do not experience obsessions and compulsions but instead are rigidly compulsive (such as being fixated on certain routines) and obsessed with the need to be perfect. This is an important clarification even though, at a future point, OCPD may someday be reclassified within this group of disorders (Fineberg et al., 2015).

obsessive-compulsive personality disorder (OCPD)
A personality disorder involving intense perfectionism and inflexibility manifested in worrying, indecisiveness, and behavioral rigidity.

A woman with obsessive-compulsive personality disorder is so highly driven for order and perfection that she is unable to tolerate having disorganized objects in her environment.

©Anthony Lee/Getty Images

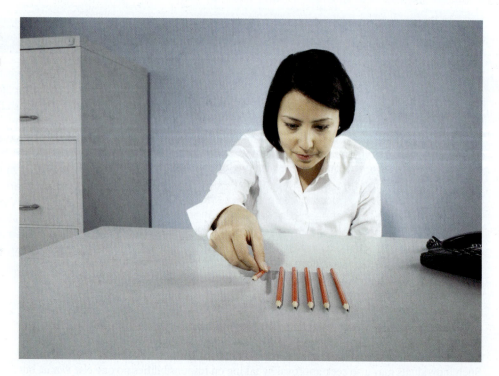

In exploring the causes of OCPD from a historical psychodynamic standpoint, Freud believed people with an obsessive-compulsive style have not progressed from, or are constantly returning to, the anal stage of psychosexual development. Contemporary psychodynamic theorists no longer focus entirely on psychosexual stages but instead give more attention to cognitive factors and prior learning experiences as central to the development of OCPD.

As a maladaptive personality disposition, OCPD can also be looked at from the perspective of trait theory. Rather than scoring high in overall conscientiousness, individuals with OCPD are particularly likely to be high in achievement striving and the need for order (Mike, King, Oltmanns, & Jackson, 2018). From the standpoint of cognitive-behavioral theory, people with this disorder have unrealistic expectations about being perfect and avoiding mistakes (Beck, Freeman, & Davis, 2004). Their feelings of self-worth depend on their behaving in ways that conform to an abstract ideal of perfectionism. If they fail to

MINI CASE

Obsessive-Compulsive Personality Disorder

Trevor is a married 42-year-old Latino heterosexual male. For as long as he can remember, Trevor has been preoccupied with neatness and order. As a child, he kept his room meticulously clean. Friends and relatives chided him for excessive organization. For example, he insisted on arranging the toys in his toy closet according to color and category. In college, his rigid housekeeping regimen both amazed and annoyed his roommates. He was tyrannical in his insistence on keeping the room orderly and free of clutter. Trevor has continued this pattern into his adult life. Employed as a file clerk, he prides

himself on never having missed a day of work, regardless of health problems and family crises. However, his boss will not offer Trevor a promotion because she feels he is overly attentive to details of the filing process, thus slowing the work of the office as he checks and rechecks everything he does. Trevor enhances his sense of self-importance in the office by looking for opportunities to take control. For example, when his co-workers are planning a party, he tends to slow matters because of his concerns about every detail of the event, such as the time it will start, how much food to order, and decorations. More often than not, his co-workers try to avoid letting him get involved because they object to his rigidity in such trivial matters.

achieve that ideal (which, inevitably, they must), they regard themselves as worthless. In this framework, obsessive-compulsive personality disorder is based on a problematic way of viewing the self.

Clinicians using cognitive-behavioral treatment for clients with OCPD face challenges due to the characteristic features of this personality disorder. The person with OCPD tends to intellectualize, to ruminate over past actions, and to worry about making mistakes. Cognitive-behavioral therapy, with its focus on examining the client's thought processes, may reinforce this ruminative tendency. Instead, metacognitive interpersonal therapy can help individuals with OCPD "think about their thinking." In this procedure, clinicians help their clients take a step back and learn to identify their problematic ruminative thinking patterns in the context of building a supportive therapeutic alliance (Dimaggio et al., 2011).

14.5 Personality Disorders: The Biopsychosocial Perspective

The personality disorders represent a fascinating mix of long-standing personal dispositions and behavior patterns and disturbances in identity and interpersonal relationships.

Although we tend to focus on these disorders as they appear at one point in time, clearly they evolve over an individual's life. The *DSM* authors will likely continue to refine and elaborate on their scientific base if not their classification. We may hope that mental health professionals will develop not only a better understanding of this form of disturbance but also, perhaps, a richer appreciation of the factors that contribute to normal personality growth and change through life.

Return to the Case: Harold Morrill

Harold was enrolled in a year-long contract at a local DBT clinic where he attended twice-weekly psychotherapy and three therapy groups per week. The program focused on teaching emotion regulation skills, mindfulness, interpersonal effectiveness, and distress tolerance. By fostering a supportive relationship with Harold, his therapist was able to model correct emotional regulation and validation of a wide range of emotions, so that Harold would not feel the need to resort to extreme measures in order to gain attention from others.

Dr. Tobin's reflections: Like many individuals with borderline personality disorder, Harold grew up in what is known as an invalidating environment—with parents who were more or less absent in his upbringing. He found that acting in an extreme manner was the only way he was able to get attention from them, so this became the only way for him to connect with others. He even displayed this in the intake evaluation by showing the clinician the marks of his self-mutilation, threatening to storm out of the room, and spontaneously bursting into tears. Further, he showed interpersonal instability in his request of the clinician to be his therapist and then immediately turning on her (or "devaluing" her) when told she could not see him for therapy. Unlike females with borderline personality disorder, who often present with largely depressed affect, males tend to present with an angry affect and are more likely to engage in substance abuse as a coping mechanism. Females are more likely to be sexually promiscuous or to engage in eating-disordered behaviors in order to cope with their extreme emotions.

It is typical for an individual with borderline personality disorder to present for treatment only after making a suicide attempt or having strong suicidal ideation, because the disorder is ego-syntonic—meaning the individual rarely understands that the behavior is abnormal. With the appropriate treatment, Harold's chance of continuing to experience highly unstable and shifting mood and relational patterns greatly decreases.

You may be wondering why Harold was not referred for substance abuse treatment. It was the opinion of the intake clinician that his substance abuse, especially his alcohol use, was secondary to Harold's personality disorder. It is typical for DBT treatment programs to require clients to abstain from abusing substances during the course of treatment. Further, with more appropriate mood regulation skills, Harold's substance abuse may remit. Should he continue to abuse substances throughout his treatment, he will then be referred for a specific substance use disorder treatment program.

SUMMARY

- A personality disorder is an ingrained pattern of relating to other people, situations, and events with a rigid and maladaptive pattern of inner experience and behavior, dating back to adolescence or early adulthood. In the *DSM-5*, personality disorders represent a collection of distinguishable sets of behavior, falling into 10 distinct categories. These 10 diagnoses are grouped into three clusters based on shared characteristics. Cluster A includes paranoid, schizoid, and schizotypal personality disorders, which share the features of odd and eccentric behavior. Cluster B includes antisocial, borderline, histrionic, and narcissistic personality disorders, which share overdramatic, emotional, and erratic or unpredictable attitudes and behaviors. Cluster C includes avoidant, dependent, and obsessive-compulsive personality disorders, which share anxious and fearful behaviors.

- Because the personality disorders are grouped into discrete categories, clinicians evaluating individuals for a possible diagnosis must decide how many of the criteria a client meets within each category and assign a diagnosis on that basis. Either the client has the disorder or not. The clinician may start by trying to match the most prominent symptoms that the individual shows with the diagnostic criteria. If the client does not fit the criteria for that disorder, the clinician may either move to another disorder or decide that the client has a personality disorder "not otherwise specified."

- Canadian psychologist Robert D. Hare (1997) developed the Psychopathy Checklist–Revised (PCL-R), an assessment instrument whose two factors are the core psychopathic personality traits and an antisocial lifestyle. The core personality traits include glibness and superficial charm, a grandiose sense of self-worth, pathological lying, a lack of empathy for others, lack of remorse or guilt, and an unwillingness to accept responsibility for one's actions.

- Borderline personality disorder involves extreme instability in the individual's sense of self and relationships. Theories focus on disturbances in emotional regulation, and effective treatments include dialectical behavioral therapy and mentalization therapy.

- Narcissistic personality disorder is divided into two types, grandiose and vulnerable, but both involve unrealistically high self-focus and preoccupation.

- The personality disorders are historically regarded as very difficult to treat, but they are proving to respond to cognitive-behavioral therapy in which clients are helped to question their long-standing assumptions and change their disturbed behaviors. Understanding of these disorders will likely change as *DSM* increasingly moves to a dimensional diagnostic approach.

KEY TERMS

Antisocial personality disorder
Avoidant personality disorder
Borderline personality disorder
  (BPD)
Dark triad
Dependent personality disorder
Emotional dysregulation
Grandiose narcissism

Histrionic personality disorder
Mentalization therapy
Narcissistic personality disorder
  (NPD)
Obsessive-compulsive personality
  disorder (OCPD)
Paranoid personality disorder
Parasuicide

Personality disorder
Psychopathy
Schizoid personality disorder
Schizotypal personality disorder
Splitting
Transference-focused
  psychotherapy
Vulnerable narcissism

Ethical and Legal Issues

Learning Objectives

15.1 Explain ethical standards including competence, informed consent, confidentiality, relationships with clients/students/research collaborators, and record keeping.

15.2 Explain ethical and legal issues in providing services, including commitment of clients, right to treatment, and refusal of treatment and least restrictive alternatives.

15.3 Understand forensic issues in psychological treatment, such as the insanity defense, competency to stand trial, and the purpose of punishment.

©alexsl/Getty Images

Case Report: Allison Yang

Demographic information: 19-year-old heterosexual Asian American female

Presenting problem: Allison has been attending individual psychotherapy at a private outpatient clinic on a weekly basis for 8 months after initially presenting to treatment following a major depressive episode. Allison had never before received psychiatric treatment, and after she confided to the resident director of her dormitory that she had been having a difficult time with her transition to college, the director gave her information about nearby therapy clinics because the small college had no counseling center of its own. Shortly after Allison began therapy, the clinician referred her to a psychiatrist who prescribed an SSRI. Allison responded well to both therapy and the antidepressant, and her symptoms remitted within about 4 weeks, although she still experienced a persistently low mood. She continued to come for weekly psychotherapy sessions to work on the issues underlying her depression. Her mood has been relatively stable, and she has had few complaints about depressive symptoms for the majority of the time since starting therapy. Allison started to become more engaged in extracurricular activities at school and began attending more social events.

Over the past three sessions, however, she has been presenting with increased depressive symptoms. She reported sleeping about 10 to 12 hours per night and still does not feel rested. She is eating only once per day, has difficulty concentrating, and experiences frequent, unprovoked crying episodes. These symptoms are similar to those she reported when she initially presented for therapy. Allison also admitted that she had not left her dorm room except to come to her therapy session. During her most recent session, her affect was markedly depressed and despondent. She

was tearful as she reported that she was feeling increasingly hopeless and was having recurrent thoughts about ending her life. She was unable to identify a particular stressor for this current episode, remarking that "all of a sudden things just feel so . . . pointless." She stated that she had been having thoughts about suicide for about 2 weeks, but that the thoughts had become much more pervasive over the past few days.

During the session, Allison's therapist responded to her report of suicidality by performing a safety evaluation. He asked whether Allison had thought about how she would commit suicide, to which Allison responded that she was in possession of a rope at home and planned on hanging herself from a ceiling beam in her dorm room. The therapist then asked how strong her intention was to commit suicide, to which Allison responded that she had planned on hanging herself that morning but decided to come in for one last therapy session and to "say goodbye."

Recently in therapy Allison had been discussing how she felt significant pressure from her family to achieve high grades in college. As a double major in economics and political science, she had been finding it difficult to keep up with all her coursework and attain "acceptable" grades. Much of her work in therapy had focused on her low self-image and propensity to undervalue not only her achievements but also her abilities to perform well in school and in other areas. Allison had been working with her therapist to learn strategies to help generate feelings of self-worth and to take pride in her accomplishments so far. She attributed her patterns of low self-worth to her parents and how, as she explained, "They never think I'm good enough, no matter what I do. I always have to be doing better. They're never satisfied." Allison has no siblings, which she believes adds to her parents' "excessive nagging." Although Allison recognized that this was a source of distress, she found it difficult to "fight back" and value herself because she had never learned to do this on her own. Throughout therapy, Allison and her clinician discussed ways to improve her relationship with her family. Allison found this difficult given that she and her parents got into arguments when they spoke on the phone. Several times she had thought about cutting off contact with them altogether; however, this presented a challenge, given that her parents supported her financially. Due to her intensive focus on schoolwork, Allison had little time in college to make friends and was often by herself in her dorm room. She reported that even when she had down time, she was constantly worrying about schoolwork and found it quite difficult to relax.

Relevant history: Allison experienced three depressive episodes prior to starting therapy. The first lasted approximately 8 months and remitted without intervention. The other two lasted approximately 2 to 3 months each and also remitted on their own. Although these episodes were much shorter than the first, the time between them was very short. The period between Allison's starting therapy and her current depressive episode was the longest gap between episodes to date. Although she

had reported thoughts of suicide during her prior depressive episodes, she had never had a plan or clear intent to commit suicide. Allison reported that she wasn't sure whether her family had any history of depression or mood disorders.

Case formulation: Due to her prior depressive episodes and absence of a manic episode, Allison carries a diagnosis of major depressive disorder, recurrent. In addition, she currently meets criteria for a major depressive episode. We add the qualifier of "severe" to the diagnosis, due to her intent and plan to commit suicide.

Treatment plan: Allison's clinician determined that she posed a significant threat to herself, based on her report that she had a plan and intent to commit suicide. The clinician asked Allison whether she could agree to make a contract to protect her safety. He would allow Allison to leave the session only if she agreed to call 911 should she feel an increase in intent to commit suicide. Allison was unable to state that she would be safe should she go home, and the clinician informed Allison that she would have to go to the hospital immediately. The clinician called 911, and an ambulance transported Allison to a nearby psychiatric hospital for stabilization.

Sarah Tobin, PhD

Psychologists are guided in both their clinical and research work by the professional guidelines established by the major professional organization, the American Psychological Association (APA). These guidelines do not hold legal power, but individual states and territories in the United States establish strict codes required for psychologists and other mental health professionals to obtain and keep their licenses. Not only are health professionals required to follow these standards, but they must regularly recertify their ability to provide services by obtaining continuing education to ensure that they are able to practice according to the highest standards.

15.1 Ethical Standards

Many states require that to be considered a psychologist, an individual must pass a rigid set of licensing requirements. All states in the United States have a board of psychologists that oversees the legal requirements for obtaining and retaining a psychology license. These requirements typically include passing an examination, obtaining a certain number of hours of supervised training, receiving recommendations from other licensed psychologists, and, to remain licensed, participating in a certain number of hours of continuing education.

As discussed in the chapter "Diagnosis and Treatment," psychologists follow the APA Ethical Principles of Psychologists and Code of Conduct (Ethics Code) (2010). The general principles are not enforceable rules but are intended for psychologists to consider in arriving at an ethical course of action. In contrast, the ethical standards are enforceable rules. Failure to follow them can result in sanctions, including loss of membership in the APA and of a state professional license. In making decisions about their professional behavior, psychologists must consider the Ethics Code as well as any applicable laws and regulations of their state psychology boards.

There are 10 standards contained within the Ethics Code (see Table 1). Since writing the first version in 1953, the APA has rewritten the Ethics Code to keep up with changes in electronic communication and, most recently, to set forth codes that psychologists in the military should follow that prohibit their participation in interrogation of suspected terrorists. The APA is also active in developing codes of conduct for the provision of Internet-based psychotherapy (Fisher & Fried, 2008).

TABLE 1 Summary of APA Ethics Code

Standard	Summary
1: Resolving Ethical Issues	Establishes the way psychologists should resolve ethical conflicts, report ethical violations, and cooperate with professional ethics committees.
2: Competence	Establishes the fact that psychologists must work within their boundaries of competence based on their training, experience, consultation, and supervision; describes what psychologists should do in emergencies; sets forth criteria for delegating work to others; describes how to resolve personal problems and conflicts that might interfere with their ability to provide services.
3: Human Relations	Provides criteria that psychologists must follow when they relate to employees, clients, and trainees; describes how psychologists should avoid conflicts of interest; regulates the nature of informed consent in research, clinical practice, or consulting, including administering psychological services through corporations.
4: Privacy and Confidentiality	Sets forth the principles for protecting research participants and clients; mandates that any public information (such as published research) includes reasonable steps to disguise the person or organization.
5: Advertising and Other Public Statements	Instructs psychologists not to provide false statements through advertising or other public outlets, in media presentations, and in testimonials; sets forth limits to in-person solicitation of potential clients or people in need of care.
6: Record Keeping and Fees	Provides conditions that psychologists must follow in maintaining their records, charging clients for services, and providing reports to payors of service or sources of research funding.
7: Education and Training	Regulates the activities of psychologists in the classroom, as supervisors or trainers, and as developers of education and training programs.
8: Research and Publication	Offers specific guidelines for psychologists who conduct research, including informing participants about their rights, offering inducements for research participation, using deception in research, debriefing participants, providing humane care for animals, reporting research results, avoiding plagiarism, and taking precautions in publishing of research articles.
9: Assessment	Describes the code for psychologists in conducting assessments, including how assessment data should be collected, use of informed consent, release of test data, principles of test construction, scoring and interpretation of test results, and maintenance of test security.
10: Therapy	Sets forth code for psychologists who provide therapy, including obtaining informed consent; conducting therapy with individuals, couples, families, and groups; interrupting and terminating therapy; and avoiding sexual intimacies with clients, relatives of clients, and former clients.

What's in the *DSM-5*

Ethical Implications of the New Diagnostic System

Following release of the *DSM-5* draft in late 2011, a number of mental health professional organizations composed a joint response to what they perceived as the potentially disastrous consequences of adding some diagnoses and removing others. For example, critics contend that eliminating the category of Asperger's syndrome could leave many thousands of individuals who suffer from its symptoms untreated. In the chapter "Neurocognitive Disorders," we discussed the potential problems in broadening the dementia diagnosis to include individuals with mild cognitive impairments. Such changes would create the opposite problem, mislabeling individuals who are experiencing normal age-related changes in memory.

The *DSM-5* was written in a manner intended to reflect the latest scientific evidence in the most objective manner possible. Inevitably, however, there will be room for debate as researchers and clinicians examine the available research studies and the evidence they infer from working with their clients. There are also social and political implications of changes in the diagnostic system. If individuals do not receive a diagnosis, as may happen with children formerly diagnosed with autistic disorder, then they cannot qualify for certain types of insurance to cover the costs of their education, treatment, and medications. Politicians then are faced with making decisions about how to allocate public funding for treatment, education, and research.

Another significant change in the *DSM-5* that has widespread implications is the shift to diagnosing major depressive disorder in the cases of people who are suffering bereavement after the loss of a loved one. In the *DSM-IV-TR*, people who suffered the symptoms of bereavement were excluded from the diagnosis of major depressive disorder, a situation called the bereavement exclusion. The elimination of the bereavement exclusion could mean that a clinician would diagnose an individual experiencing depressive symptoms following the death of someone close to him or her with major depressive disorder. That person will now have a psychiatric diagnosis that could interfere with his or her ability to find employment in certain sectors.

However, if practitioners don't assign a diagnosis to a client with clinically significant symptoms, does this mean the clients will be unable to obtain medication to treat their symptoms? Conversely, in order to continue to provide services to their clients who may no longer qualify for a diagnosis, should clinicians find ways around the changing guidelines to ensure their clients do receive the diagnosis?

Unfortunately, because in many cases psychological symptoms are more difficult to identify than are physical symptoms, the debate about appropriate diagnostic categories and criteria will no doubt continue throughout each subsequent edition of the *DSM*. Maintaining your awareness of these continued debates can ultimately help you and the people you know receive the best care possible. If you continue in a professional career in mental health, it will be vital for you to stay on top of both the latest literature and the latest diagnostic issues to provide the best treatment possible for your own clients.

Competence

As you can see from Standard 2, psychologists are expected to have appropriate competence to carry out therapy, consulting, teaching, and research. They achieve this competence, first of all, in their post-baccalaureate training. The APA provides accreditation to clinical doctoral training programs in the United States to ensure that these programs provide future psychologists with sufficient breadth and depth to form the basis for their career in providing mental health services. As mentioned briefly in the chapter "Diagnosis and Treatment," upon completing their coursework, PhD and PsyD (Doctor of Psychology) graduates must obtain intensive supervision as interns and postdoctoral trainees. They must then pass a nationally administered licensing exam and complete any additional requirements of their particular state. To maintain their license, they must take and complete a required number of continuing education courses within each year or two after licensure and be able to document this participation.

The result of this intensive training is that psychologists have the competence to assess, conceptualize, and provide interventions for clients whom they accept into treatment. On a related note, Standard 5 also instructs psychologists to be truthful about their areas of expertise. Clinicians who claim to be, for example, sports psychologists should have received training in this field, preferably with supervision under a professional with appropriate training credentials. When clinicians advertise their specialty, they should have suitable expertise, including current familiarity with a field, in order to be able to offer those services.

Turning to other requirements of professional training, clinicians should also have the **emotional competence** to be able to provide services to their clients. This means that, within a range of acceptable variations, they should be free of a diagnosable psychological disorder. Should they develop such a disorder, they should receive treatment and consider suspending their practice until their symptoms are in remission or at least under control. To ensure that mental health professionals meet these standards of competence, they are expected to conduct regular self-scrutiny, in which they objectively evaluate their competence to carry out their work. They can also benefit from seeking supervision or consultation from another professional, perhaps one with more experience or expertise.

emotional competence
A quality desired in clinicians in which they are free of a diagnosable psychological disorder.

A witness testifies in a court hearing to protect a relative with a psychological disorder.
©Heide Benser/Corbis

In a court of law, counsel often asks psychologists to give expert testimony, such as outlining the limits of eyewitness memory or explaining the nature of a psychiatric diagnosis. If they do, they must make clear the limits of their areas of expertise. If they do not have expertise in a particular area, they must obtain consultation from an expert who does.

Even more complicated than the role of expert witness is the task of conducting evaluations in child protection cases. Such evaluations are necessary in situations in which there are concerns about the child's welfare. For example, if there has been evidence of or charges of abuse, a court might call a mental health professional to make recommendations about the child's care. A judge might appoint a clinician as an agent of the court or a child protection agency, or one of the parents might hire the clinician. In some instances, the clinician is a **guardian** *ad litem*, a person whom the court appoints to represent or make decisions for a minor or incapacitated adult who is legally incapable of doing so in a civil legal proceeding.

Other challenges present themselves when clients seeking the services of clinicians have needs beyond the clinician's area of competence. In these cases, the clinician should either make a referral or obtain appropriate supervision. For example, a clinician who does not treat older adults with neurocognitive disorder may receive a referral from a middle-aged client seeking help with her mother who is experiencing memory problems. Unless the clinician is qualified to provide psychological assessments of older adults, he or she should recommend that someone else evaluate the mother.

To assist psychologists in evaluating their competencies in areas that may be outside their areas of expertise, the APA has developed guidelines in specific areas of treatment. The APA has approved a variety of practice guidelines and related criteria as policy in such areas as treatment of gay, lesbian, and bisexual clients (Table 2); child protection evaluations (Table 3); psychological practice with older adults (Table 4); psychological practice with girls and women (Table 5); and assessment of and intervention with people with disabilities (Table 6). These guidelines are intended to educate practitioners and provide recommendations about professional conduct. They are useful tools for psychologists in practice to develop and maintain competencies and/or learn about new practice areas.

Increasingly, psychologists who specialize in a particular field are seeking board certification with "diplomate status." The American Board of Professional Psychology (ABPP) sets forth criteria for certification of potential diplomates and arranges for their testing by experts in each particular specialty. If you see "ABPP" after a psychologist's signature, this

guardian *ad litem*
A person appointed by the court to represent or make decisions for a minor or an incapacitated adult who is legally incapable of doing so in a civil legal proceeding.

TABLE 2 Guidelines for Psychotherapy with Lesbian, Gay, and Bisexual Clients

1. Psychologists understand that homosexuality and bisexuality are not indicative of mental illness.
2. Psychologists are encouraged to recognize how their attitudes and knowledge about lesbian, gay, and bisexual issues may be relevant to assessment and treatment and seek consultation or make appropriate referrals when indicated.
3. Psychologists strive to understand the ways in which social stigmatization (i.e., prejudice, discrimination, and violence) poses risks to the mental health and well-being of lesbian, gay, and bisexual clients.
4. Psychologists strive to understand how inaccurate or prejudicial views of homosexuality or bisexuality may affect the client's presentation in treatment and the therapeutic process.
5. Psychologists strive to be knowledgeable about and respect the importance of lesbian, gay, and bisexual relationships.
6. Psychologists strive to understand the particular circumstances and challenges faced by lesbian, gay, and bisexual clients.
7. Psychologists recognize that the families of lesbian, gay, and bisexual people may include people who are not legally or biologically related.
8. Psychologists strive to understand how a person's homosexual or bisexual orientation may have an impact on his or her family of origin and the relationship to that family of origin.
9. Psychologists are encouraged to recognize the particular life issues or challenges that are related to multiple and often conflicting cultural norms, values, and beliefs that lesbian, gay, and bisexual members of racial and ethnic minorities face.
10. Psychologists are encouraged to recognize the particular challenges that bisexual individuals experience.
11. Psychologists strive to understand the special problems and risks that exist for lesbian, gay, and bisexual youth.
12. Psychologists consider generational differences within lesbian, gay, and bisexual populations and the particular challenges that lesbian, gay, and bisexual older adults may experience.
13. Psychologists are encouraged to recognize the particular challenges that lesbian, gay, and bisexual individuals experience with physical, sensory, and cognitive-emotional difficulties.
14. Psychologists support the provision of professional education and training on lesbian, gay, and bisexual issues.
15. Psychologists are encouraged to increase their knowledge and understanding of homosexuality and bisexuality through continuing education, training, supervision, and consultation.
16. Psychologists make reasonable efforts to familiarize themselves with relevant mental health, educational, and community resources for lesbian, gay, and bisexual people.

Ethical Issues

Even though a person may be in extreme distress, on his or her admission to a psychiatric hospital, the clinician must obtain informed consent.

SOURCE: American Psychological Association. (2012b). Guidelines for psychological practice with lesbian, gay, and bisexual clients. *American Psychologist, 67*, 10–42.

means the individual has received this official certification. Doctoral students in clinical psychology are being advised to track their training so they can qualify for this status early in their careers.

The APA also serves a more general credentialing role in the profession, providing accreditation of clinical training programs, approval of specialty fields (such as neuropsychology or geropsychology), and curriculum standards for programs ranging from high school to postgraduate training in psychology.

Informed Consent

Although you may think only of research when you hear the term "informed consent," this criterion for ethical behavior applies to other contexts, including therapy. The reason is that clinical psychologists are expected to provide their clients with knowledge ahead of time about what they can expect to occur in treatment. At the outset of therapy, clinicians should provide clients with a written statement that outlines the goals of treatment, the process of therapy, the client's rights, the therapist's responsibilities, the treatment risks, the techniques he or she will use, what the client should pay, and the limits of confidentiality. If the treatment includes medication, the clinician should make the client aware of possible short-term and long-term side effects. The clinician has a responsibility to ensure that the client is

TABLE 3 Guidelines for Psychological Evaluations in Child Protection Matters

1. The primary purpose of the evaluation is to provide relevant, professionally sound results or opinions in matters where a child's health and welfare may have been and/or may in the future be harmed.

2. In child protection cases, the child's interest and well-being are paramount.

3. The evaluation addresses the particular psychological and developmental needs of the child and/or parent(s) that are relevant to child protection issues, such as physical abuse, sexual abuse, neglect, and/or serious emotional harm.

4. The role of the psychologist conducting evaluations is that of a professional expert who strives to maintain an unbiased, objective stance.

5. The serious consequences of psychological assessment in child protection matters place a heavy burden on psychologists.

6. Psychologists gain specialized competence.

7. Psychologists are aware of personal and societal biases and engage in nondiscriminatory practice.

8. Psychologists avoid multiple relationships.

9. Based on the nature of the referral questions, the scope of the evaluation is determined by the evaluator.

10. Psychologists performing psychological evaluations in child protection matters obtain appropriate informed consent from all adult participants and, as appropriate, inform the child participant. Psychologists need to be particularly sensitive to consent issues.

11. Psychologists inform participants about the disclosure of information and the limits of confidentiality.

12. Psychologists use multiple methods of data gathering.

13. Psychologists neither overinterpret nor inappropriately interpret clinical or assessment data.

14. Psychologists conducting a psychological evaluation in child protection matters provide an opinion regarding the psychological functioning of an individual only after conducting an evaluation of the individual adequate to support their statements or conclusions.

15. Recommendations, if offered, are based on whether the child's health and welfare have been and/or may be seriously harmed.

16. Psychologists clarify financial arrangements.

17. Psychologists maintain appropriate records.

SOURCE: Committee on Professional Practice and Standards Board of Professional Affairs. (1998). *Guidelines for psychological evaluations in child protection matters* (published report). American Psychological Association.

aware of these issues, receives answers to any questions, and has the opportunity to refuse treatment. The client is then prepared to decide whether to continue in treatment.

There are possible complications. Psychotherapy is an imprecise procedure, and it is not always possible to predict its course, risks, or benefits. The clinician's job, however, is to give a best estimate at the onset of therapy and to provide further information as therapy proceeds. Most people are able to discuss these matters with the clinician and to make an informed choice. There are special cases, however, when prospective clients are unable to understand the issues in order to make informed consent. These cases include children and people who are unable to understand the full nature of the treatment into which they might enter due to cognitive or other psychological disabilities. In these cases, the clinician must work with the individual's family or other legally appointed guardians.

Confidentiality

Several of the standards in the APA Ethics Code cover the issue of confidentiality. This means that the client can expect that what takes place in therapy is private. Confidentiality has long been regarded as a sacred part of the clinician–client relationship and is strictly maintained by licensed psychologists (Fisher & Vacanti-Shova, 2012). Safeguards against the disclosure of confidential information exist within the laws of most states. In order to adhere to the highest standards of professional practice, clinicians should have a clearly

TABLE 4 Guidelines for Psychological Practice with Older Adults

Attitudes

Guideline 1.   Psychologists are encouraged to work with older adults within their scope of competence.

Guideline 2.   Psychologists are encouraged to recognize how their attitudes and beliefs about aging and about older individuals may be relevant to their assessment and treatment of older adults, and to seek consultation or further education about these issues when indicated.

General Knowledge about Adult Development, Aging, and Older Adults

Guideline 3.   Psychologists strive to gain knowledge about theory and research in aging.

Guideline 4.   Psychologists strive to be aware of the social/psychological dynamics of the aging process.

Guideline 5.   Psychologists strive to understand diversity in the aging process, particularly how sociocultural factors such as gender, ethnicity, socioeconomic status, sexual orientation, disability status, and urban/rural residence may influence the experience and expression of health and of psychological problems in later life.

Guideline 6.   Psychologists strive to be familiar with current information about biological and health-related aspects of aging.

Clinical Issues

Guideline 7.   Psychologists strive to be familiar with current knowledge about cognitive changes in older adults.

Guideline 8.   Psychologists strive to understand problems in daily living among older adults.

Guideline 9.   Psychologists strive to be knowledgeable about psychopathology within the aging population and cognizant of the prevalence and nature of that psychopathology when providing services to older adults.

Assessment

Guideline 10.   Psychologists strive to be familiar with the theory, research, and practice of various methods of assessment with older adults, and knowledgeable of assessment instruments that are psychometrically suitable for use with them.

Guideline 11.   Psychologists strive to understand the problems of using assessment instruments created for younger individuals when assessing older adults, and to develop skill in tailoring assessments to accommodate older adults' specific characteristics and contexts.

Guideline 12.   Psychologists strive to develop skill at recognizing cognitive changes in older adults, and in conducting and interpreting cognitive screening and functional ability evaluations.

Intervention, Consultation, and Other Service Provision

Guideline 13.   Psychologists strive to be familiar with the theory, research, and practice of various methods of intervention with older adults, particularly with current research evidence about their efficacy with this age group.

Guideline 14.   Psychologists strive to be familiar with and develop skill in applying specific psychotherapeutic interventions and environmental modifications with older adults and their families, including adapting interventions for use with this age group.

Guideline 15.   Psychologists strive to understand the issues pertaining to the provision of services in the specific settings in which older adults are typically located or encountered.

Guideline 16.   Psychologists strive to recognize issues related to the provision of prevention and health promotion services with older adults.

Guideline 17.   Psychologists strive to understand issues pertaining to the provision of consultation services in assisting older adults.

Guideline 18.   In working with older adults, psychologists are encouraged to understand the importance of interfacing with other disciplines, and to make referrals to other disciplines and/or to work with them in collaborative teams and across a range of sites, as appropriate.

Guideline 19.   Psychologists strive to understand the special ethical and/or legal issues entailed in providing services to older adults.

Education

Guideline 20.   Psychologists are encouraged to increase their knowledge, understanding, and skills with respect to working with older adults through continuing education, training, supervision, and consultation.

SOURCE: American Psychological Association. (2018). *Guidelines for psychological practice with older adults* (published report). Retrieved from http://www.apa.org/practice/guidelines/older-adults.aspx.

TABLE 5 Guidelines for Psychological Practice with Girls and Women

Guideline 1.	Psychologists strive to be aware of the effects of socialization, stereotyping, and unique life events on the development of girls and women across diverse cultural groups.
Guideline 2.	Psychologists are encouraged to recognize and utilize information about oppression, privilege, and identity development as they may affect girls and women.
Guideline 3.	Psychologists strive to understand the impact of bias and discrimination upon the physical and mental health of those with whom they work.
Guideline 4.	Psychologists strive to use gender and culturally sensitive, affirming practices in providing services to girls and women.
Guideline 5.	Psychologists are encouraged to recognize how their socialization, attitudes, and knowledge about gender may affect their practice with girls and women.
Guideline 6.	Psychologists are encouraged to employ interventions and approaches that have been found to be effective in the treatment of issues of concern to girls and women.
Guideline 7.	Psychologists strive to foster therapeutic relationships and practices that promote initiative, empowerment, and expanded alternatives and choices for girls and women.
Guideline 8.	Psychologists strive to provide appropriate, unbiased assessments and diagnoses in their work with girls and women.
Guideline 9.	Psychologists strive to consider the problems of girls and women in their sociopolitical context.
Guideline 10.	Psychologists strive to acquaint themselves with and utilize relevant mental health, education, and community resources for girls and women.
Guideline 11.	Psychologists are encouraged to understand and work to change institutional and systemic bias that may impact girls and women.

SOURCE: American Psychological Association. (February 2007). *Guidelines for psychological practice with girls and women*. Retrieved from https://www.apa.org/practice/guidelines/girls-and-women.aspx

articulated protocol regarding the way in which they will inform clients about the nature, extent, and limits of confidentiality.

The content of therapy is privileged communication. In other words, the clinician may not disclose any information about the client in a court of law without the client's express permission. The protection offered by confidentiality allows clients in therapy to freely discuss their symptoms, problems in relationships with others, and early childhood history, all of which may contain extremely personal and delicate information. Confidentiality also protects research subjects from having the information they disclose to an investigator revealed to the public without their express consent.

There are, however, exceptions to confidentiality. Legally, there are instances in which the court is entitled to receive information that emerges within the context of the case (Barsky & Gould, 2002). These include child custody cases, trials in which a defendant is using mental disability as a defense in a criminal trial, and instances when a court appoints a psychologist to establish whether the defendant is competent to stand trial. Court-ordered assessments are an exception to the confidentiality standard. Defendants must be informed of this limitation in writing and acknowledge their understanding.

The principle of confidentiality also has limits in cases involving abuse. Every state requires some form of mandated reporting by professionals when they learn firsthand of cases of child abuse or neglect. Abuse, which can be physical or sexual, is an act by a caretaker that causes serious physical or emotional injury. Neglect is the intentional withholding of food, clothing, shelter, or medical care. The purposes of mandated reporting are to protect victims from continued abuse and neglect, to initiate steps toward clinical intervention with the abused individual, and to deter, punish, and rehabilitate abusers. Victims can include vulnerable people, such as those with physical or intellectual handicaps and impaired elders who cannot otherwise protect themselves. Some states require that psychologists report not only financial, emotional, physical, or sexual abuse but also

TABLE 6 Guidelines for Assessment of and Intervention with Persons with Disabilities

Disability Awareness, Training, Accessibility, and Diversity

Guideline 1.   Psychologists strive to gain awareness of models of disability and an understanding of how these can impact they way they provide services.

Guideline 2.   Psychologists try to examine their own beliefs and reactions toward disabilities and understand how these can affect their work.

Guideline 3.   Psychologists gain education and consultation to improve their knowledge and skills for working with people who have disabilities.

Guideline 4.   Psychologists try to use the language and behavior that will be appropriate and communicate respect for people who have disabilities.

Guideline 5.   To ensure that clients with disabilities can access their services, psychologists work to provide barrier-free environments.

Guideline 6.   Psychologists try to understand both the common and individual experiences that affect their clients with disabilities.

Guideline 7.   Psychologists strive to recognize and learn the diversity of experiences of people with disabilities, including how disability affects the individual's development over the life course.

Guideline 8.   Psychologists gain understanding of the strengths and challenges that face families of people with disabilities.

Guideline 9.   Psychologists strive to recognize the increased risk of abuse that can affect people with disabilities.

Guideline 10. Psychologists try to learn how assistive technology can be used to benefit individuals with disabilities.

Testing and Assessment

Guideline 11. In their assessment of clients with disabilities, psychologists strive to see disability as one among other forms of diversity, and strive to provide appropriate assessment instruments in order to yield valid test scores.

Guideline 12. Psychologists strive to assess their clients with disabilities through a range of methods in order to understand their strengths and limitations.

Interventions

Guideline 13. Psychologists strive to collaborate with their clients, as well as families when appropriate, to plan, develop, and implement psychological interventions.

Guideline 14. Psychologists strive to be aware of how the environment in which therapy takes place can affect their work with clients who have disabilities.

Guideline 15. Psychologists strive to provide interventions for clients with disabilities that enhance their well-being as well as reduce distress and help to ameliorate any skill deficits.

Guideline 16. Maintaining the perspectives of their clients when working with larger treatment or educational systems can allow psychologists to help them achieve self-determination, integration, choice, and availability of the least restrictive alternatives.

Guideline 17. Psychologists strive to promote the health of individuals with disabilities.

SOURCE: American Psychological Association. (2012a). Guidelines for assessment of and intervention with persons with disabilities. *American Psychologist, 67*, 43–62.

self-neglect by persons age 60 or older who do not attend to their needs for food, clothing, safe and secure shelter, personal care, and medical treatment.

Another exception to the principle of confidentiality occurs when the clinician learns that a client is planning to hurt another person. These cases face the psychologist with a **duty to warn (or otherwise protect)**. The duty-to-warn mandate requires that the clinician inform the intended victim about possible dangers posed by the client's behavior.

duty to warn (or otherwise protect)
The clinician's responsibility to notify a potential victim of a client's harmful intent toward that individual.

Duty-to-warn laws have their origins in a famous case, *Tarasoff v. Regents of the University of California* (Tarasoff v. The Regents of the University of California, 551 P 2d 334 [California 1976]), in which a community college student named Tatiana Tarasoff was shot and fatally stabbed by Prosenjit Poddar, a graduate student who came from India in 1967 to study electronics and naval architecture at the University of California, Berkeley. Poddar met and began to pursue Tarasoff romantically, but she was not interested in him and in March 1969 rejected his marriage proposal. Poddar became despondent and told his roommate that he wanted to

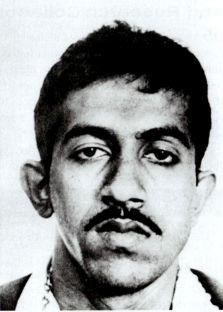

Tatiana Tarasoff (left), a junior at the University of California, was shot and stabbed to death on the doorstep of her home by Prosenjit Poddar (right), who had told his therapist that he intended to kill her.
©AP Images

blow up Tarasoff's house. The roommate advised Poddar to seek treatment, and in June 1969 Poddar saw a psychiatrist at the university health services who prescribed antipsychotic medications and referred him to a psychologist for therapy. In August, Poddar repeatedly announced his homicidal thoughts about Tarasoff to the psychologist. After the psychologist warned Poddar that he would restrain him if he continued to express these thoughts, Poddar abruptly discontinued therapy. Although the psychologist and psychiatrist told the police about Poddar's intentions and the police then confronted him, he denied this intention, and the law took no further action. Poddar began to stalk Tarasoff, and in October 1969 he found her home alone and killed her. He then turned himself over to the police. Her parents sued the university and the police for not warning Tarasoff, and finally, in December 1976, the California Supreme Court ruled in favor of the parents. The essential question was "whether a psychotherapist must, on pain of a civil suit for damages, recognize that a patient poses a risk of serious harm or death to an identified third party and then must warn or otherwise protect that third party" (Herbert, 2002, p. 419).

The ramifications of this landmark decision continue to be felt by psychologists, who struggle to differentiate between their clients' serious threats and random fantasies, weighing the client's right of confidentiality against the rights of others. In April 2007, a student at Virginia Polytechnic Institute and State University named Seung-Hui Cho killed 32 people and wounded 25 others. He had received treatment from a mental health facility after having demonstrated threatening and harassing behavior on campus. In Virginia's version of the Tarasoff duty-to-warn statute, mental health caregivers must prevent the client from using physical violence or other means of harm to others until the appropriate law enforcement agency can be summoned and takes custody of the client. Although Cho named no specific victims, the case once again raised questions about the legal responsibilities of mental health professionals when their clients express homicidal or suicidal intentions.

James E. Holmes appears in Arapahoe County District Court, Monday, July 23, 2012, in Centennial, Colorado following his arrest for the Aurora movie theater massacre that killed 12 and wounded 70.
©Pool/Getty Images News/Getty Images

Relationships with Clients, Students, and Research Collaborators

The APA's Ethics Code makes it clear that psychologists must take steps to ensure that they conduct all dealings with other individuals, including other psychologists, with the utmost professionalism. In therapy, clear roles and boundaries are essential in order for the client to feel safe and trusting and for the clinician to maintain objectivity and effectiveness. When a clinician violates boundaries within a therapeutic relationship, clients can experience a variety of nontherapeutic outcomes that only make their symptoms worse.

An extreme form of violation of the therapeutic relationship is sexual intimacy with clients, which is explicitly forbidden in the ethical codes of the mental health professions. In

You Be the Judge

Multiple Relationships Between Clients and Psychologists

The APA Ethics Code explicitly prohibits most multiple relationships between psychologists and their clients. However, given the nature of the therapist–client relationship, it is almost inevitable that potential multiple relationships can develop. In evaluating the ethics of a multiple relationship, we should distinguish between sexual and nonsexual. Sexual relationships are prohibited for at least 2 years after the ending of a therapeutic relationship. The boundaries around nonsexual relationships can be much murkier, however. In rural communities or small towns, for example, psychologists may find it almost impossible to avoid such dilemmas in situations ranging from retail sales to education to provision of other professional services. Social interactions between therapists and their clients may also prove difficult, even in larger communities with multiple intersecting social circles. In the chapter "Assessment," we discussed the ethics facing psychologists in the legal system. Here we will look more generally at multiple relationships as they affect psychologists in their clinical practice.

According to research on multiple relationships (Lamb, Catanzaro, & Moorman, 2004), social interactions are in fact the largest group of situations in which psychologists find themselves facing potential complications from client encounters. Psychologists also reported relationships in the spheres of business, financial dealings, and religious affiliations. These were more likely to occur between psychologists and their former clients than their current clients. In the area of sexual intimacy, the researchers asked psychologists to indicate whether the potential had ever existed for them to have relationships with their clients. However, even though they may have been tempted, these psychologists did not follow through on their interest due to their personal ethics, values, and morals. They also were highly unlikely to pursue a sexual relationship with a former client. At least half the psychologists also indicated that they wished to avoid dual relationships and/or did not want to take advantage of the unequal power dynamics between themselves and clients. Relatively few respondents mentioned that they refrained from these relationships due to possible legal repercussions or to their peers or professional associations sanctioning them.

The results of this survey suggest that psychologists adhere to high ethical standards in their relationships with current and former clients. As the study's authors acknowledge, however, it is possible that the participants who were the guiltiest of multiple relationships were the least likely to respond.

Q: *You be the judge:* Turning back to the ethical issue, consider the pros and cons of multiple relationships. Once a professional relationship is over, is it absolutely necessary for the psychologist not to become involved with a former client, particularly if they had a close connection during the course of treatment? Or is the very nature of the client–therapist relationship such that each party should respect the boundaries, even for years after treatment has ended? Should ethics codes be as stringent as they are in the area of multiple relationships?

fact, psychologists are prohibited from becoming sexually involved with a client for at least 2 years after treatment ends (or longer in many cases).

Psychologists must also refrain from **multiple relationships**, particularly with their clients in a therapy context. The APA Ethics Code defines multiple relationships as occurring when a psychologist is in a professional role with a person and has another role with that person that could impair the psychologist's "objectivity, competence, or effectiveness in performing his or her functions as a psychologist" or otherwise risks exploiting or harming the other person. However, multiple relationships that we would reasonably not believe to cause impairment or risk exploitation or harm are not unethical. For instance, therapists commonly provide individual psychotherapy to their patients while also facilitating a therapy group that the patient participates in.

Other ethical guidelines affect the way psychologists relate to others. In August 2015 at the APA's Annual Convention, its governance body, the Council of Representatives, voted to amend the Ethics Code explicitly to prohibit any of its members from participating in enhanced interrogation methods. The resolution states that psychologists "shall not conduct, supervise, be in the presence of, or otherwise assist any national security interrogations for any military or intelligence entities, including private contractors working on their behalf, nor advise on conditions of confinement insofar as these might facilitate such an interrogation" (American Psychological Association, 2015b). Critics had argued for a decade that this explicit prohibition must be included in the organization's ethical codes.

Other ethical safeguards stipulate that psychologists avoid harming others, refrain from engaging in relationships with any conflict of interest, and not exploit other people with whom they have a professional relationship. When psychologists collaborate on research, for example, they should give or take credit only for work they have actually performed. They must also disclose their source of funding for research they publish based on funding from that source.

Record Keeping

With increasing use of electronic health care records (including maintenance of files on portable tablets), the need to protect clients becomes even more critical. This need led to passage by the U.S. Congress of a complex series of rules governing patient records in the **Health Insurance Portability and Accountability Act of 1996 (HIPAA)**. HIPAA went into effect in several stages beginning in 2003 and ending in 2008. To enforce the new rules, civil monetary penalties can be levied for failure on the part of the employer, health care provider, or insurance company.

Title I of HIPAA protects workers and their families from loss of health care insurance when they change or lose their jobs. Prior to HIPAA's passage, people moving from one job to another were vulnerable to losing their health insurance if they had a history of serious illness. For example, someone who was treated for a cancerous condition and took a new job might have encountered the disturbing fact that he or she could not receive insurance coverage from the new employer because of this "pre-existing" illness.

Title II is intended to regulate the ways in which providers and insurance companies maintain and transmit medical records, called protected health information. Now that organizations send health records, prescriptions, and billing information via the Internet, health care professionals must take special care to protect confidential medical records.

The Ethics Code also governs the way in which psychologists charge fees for their services. They must inform clients about their fees prior to beginning any interventions and should reach an agreement with clients about arrangements for billing. Fee practices must also be consistent with the law. Surprisingly, psychologists can barter with their clients for services—that is, accept goods, services, or other nonmonetary remuneration in return for psychological services. They cannot do so, however, if this arrangement is clinically counterindicated or exploits their clients.

multiple relationships
Unethical relationships occurring when a psychologist is in a professional role with a person and has another role with that person that could impair the psychologist's "objectivity, competence, or effectiveness in performing his or her functions as a psychologist" or otherwise risks exploiting or harming the other person.

Health Insurance Portability and Accountability Act of 1996 (HIPAA)
U.S. legislation intended to ensure adequate coverage and protect consumers from loss of insurance coverage when they change or lose their jobs.

15.2 Ethical and Legal Issues in Providing Services

Psychologists and other mental health professionals face a number of issues in ensuring that clients receive the best possible treatment. At the same time, clinicians must balance the rights of clients with those of the community, issues that create ethical and legal dilemmas.

Commitment of Clients

In the best of all possible situations, clients who are in need of psychological treatment seek it themselves; however, clients are not always in a position to judge when they need the care of a psychologist. In these cases, the mental health professional may consider recommending **commitment**, an emergency procedure for involuntary hospitalization. Clinicians begin commitment proceedings in the cases of people who, if not hospitalized, are likely to create harm for self or other people as a result of mental illness.

The concept of commitment stems from the legal principle that the state has the authority to protect those who are unable to protect themselves. The law refers to this authority as *parens patriae*, Latin for "the parent of his or her country." It is vested in various professionals, such as psychologists, physicians, and nurse specialists, who are authorized to sign an application for a time-limited commitment (usually 10 days). If a health professional is not accessible, a police officer may file commitment papers. In the application, the professional states why failure to hospitalize the individual would result in the likelihood of serious harm due to mental illness.

In some instances, the application for commitment goes to a district court judge, perhaps instigated by the concerns of a family member (though a family member cannot directly apply for commitment). After hearing the reasons for commitment, the judge may issue a warrant to apprehend the mentally ill person in order for that individual to receive a qualified professional assessment. Once the individual has been hospitalized, subsequent applications and hearings may be necessary to extend the period of commitment.

More than two dozen states now give courts, police officers, psychiatrists, mental health professionals, and families the option to coerce mentally ill individuals who have broken the law into treatment rather than to arrest them. Those supporting legislation that permits outpatient commitment assert that the benefits to society, in addition to the therapeutic benefits for the individual, outweigh the risks. In 1999, New York State enacted "Kendra's Law," which provides for the state's court-ordered involuntary outpatient commitment program, termed assisted outpatient treatment (AOT). The law is named after the tragic death of Kendra Webdale, who was pushed in front of a subway train in Manhattan by a stranger who had untreated schizophrenia. Recent evidence shows that the program has resulted in decreased hospitalization and improved service engagement and medication adherence (Swartz et al., 2010).

In May 2018, a decision by the Massachusetts Supreme Judicial Court (SJC) set a precedent for guidance to colleges and universities in their duty to take reasonable measures to prevent student suicides. The decision came as part of the final ruling in a case involving a student's suicide in 2009 at the Massachusetts Institute of Technology (MIT). The family of graduate student Han Nyugen sued MIT for failure to protect the student despite allegedly having knowledge about his mental health struggles. The lawsuit was originally filed in 2011 and eventually moved up to the SJC, who dismissed all claims against MIT and found that the school was not responsible for Nyugen's death. Part of the ruling stated that a school has the duty to intervene when the school has actual knowledge of either a student's attempted suicide or plan to commit suicide while enrolled or recently prior to enrollment. If this duty is triggered, the SJC ruled that the reasonable measures include either initiating a suicide prevention protocol (if the school has developed such a protocol), or otherwise assisting the student in obtaining clinical care. If the student refuses to seek care, notification of the student's emergency contact is permissible.

It is important to note that the SJC ruling applies to employees and staff who are not licensed mental health clinicians, as clinicians are to abide by their own professional ethical

commitment
An emergency procedure for involuntary psychiatric hospitalization.

parens patriae
The state's authority to protect those who are unable to protect themselves.

A court hearing is held to determine whether a client should receive involuntary psychological treatment. These hearings include expert testimony from psychologists who have evaluated the client.

©David R. Frazier Photolibrary, Inc./Alamy Stock Photo

codes when working with suicidal students. It is likely that this ruling will greatly impact the ways in which colleges and universities manage the care of their students, and although they are not responsible for monitoring all aspects of the lives of their students, the school has a special duty to protect students from harm they may do to themselves.

Right to Treatment

Admission to a psychiatric hospital, whether voluntary or involuntary, is only the beginning of the story. Once admitted, the client enters a world unfamiliar to most people, which can frighten and confuse them. If hospitalized against their will, they may feel outraged. To minimize these reactions, health professionals try to ensure that they give clients appropriate care, including an understanding of their legal rights immediately upon entry to a facility. We have already discussed the importance of obtaining informed consent, when possible, prior to beginning treatment to ensure that clients understand the nature of treatment, the options available, and the client's rights.

Perhaps the most important legal right of the person entering a psychiatric hospital is the **right to treatment**. It may seem odd that we need laws to ensure that patients in hospitals receive treatment, but as you read the legal history of these statutes, you will understand why they are necessary. The right to treatment emerged as the outcome of a landmark legal case, *Wyatt v. Stickney* (Wyatt v. Stickney, 325 F. Supp. 781 [M.D. Ala. 1971]; 344 F. Supp. [M.D. Ala. 1972]). In this case, a patient named Ricky Wyatt instituted a class-action suit against the commissioner of mental health for the state of Alabama, Dr. Stickney, in response to the horrifying conditions in psychiatric and mental retardation facilities. These institutions failed to provide even a minimum of treatment and were so inhumane that they were actually detrimental to the patients' mental health. In ruling against the state of Alabama, the court relied on a principle put forth by a legal scholar invoking the constitutional right to due process. In other words, the court ruled that mental health professionals cannot commit people to an institution that is supposed to help them unless they can guarantee that institutionalization *will* help them. Otherwise, their commitment constitutes the equivalent of imprisonment without a trial. Similarly, people with psychiatric disorders are entitled to treatment in the community rather than relegation to institutions.

Patients also have the right to a humane environment, including privacy, appropriate clothing, opportunities for social interaction, comfortable furnishings, physical exercise, adequate diet, and mail, telephone, and visitation privileges. A related right is that of liberty

right to treatment
Legal right of person entering psychiatric hospital to receive appropriate care.

and safety (Youngberg v. Romeo, 457 U.S. 307 [1982]), which includes the right to move about the ward and receive protection from violent patients. Seclusion and mechanical restraints are forbidden unless medically indicated and, when clinicians use them, they can do so only for a limited amount of time and only for appropriate purposes (La Fond, 1994).

Refusal of Treatment and Least Restrictive Alternative

It is accepted in our society that competent adults have the right to either accept or decline medical treatment. In view of the serious side effects of certain psychotherapeutic medications, some U.S. states have enacted laws that give the client the right to refuse unwanted medications. If the client is involuntarily committed, the clinician must obtain a written order from a court of law documenting the need for medication.

Similarly, clients may regard as harsh or even punitive treatments such as the application of aversive noise or unpleasant shock. They may therefore refuse such treatment if they are capable of giving or withholding informed consent. However, cognitively compromised clients incapable of making informed decisions about such interventions may require protection by the law. A court can, in these cases, apply a doctrine called **substituted judgment** for people deemed incompetent of making such treatment decisions themselves. In substituted judgment, health professionals and family members try to make the decision the patient would have made if he or she were able to make decisions (Torke, Alexander, & Lantos, 2008). For example, a judge would attempt to determine whether the client would willingly approve the administration of aversive shock as a treatment designed to stop from engaging in life-threatening head-banging behavior.

Clients also have the right to placement in what we call the **least restrictive alternative** to treatment in an institution, meaning adult protective services provided in a manner no more restrictive of a vulnerable adult's liberty and no more intrusive than necessary to achieve and ensure essential services. This right was established in 1975 by a landmark ruling in the U.S. Supreme Court (O'Connor v. Donaldson [1975] 95 S. Ct. 2486). In 1943, Kenneth Donaldson was a 34-year-old father of three working in a General Electric defense plant when he showed what appeared to be symptoms of paranoid schizophrenia. Sent to a state hospital, he was given 23 electroshock treatments and resumed normal life. In the mid-1950s, he developed paranoid delusions that he was being poisoned. At the instigation of his father, Donaldson was committed to Florida's Chattahoochee State Hospital in 1956,

substituted judgment
A doctrine that allows health professionals and family members to try to make the decision that the patient would have made if he or she were able to make decisions.

least restrictive alternative
A treatment setting that provides the fewest constraints on the client's freedom.

This woman is a patient in an eating-disorder day-treatment facility, where part of her treatment is ingesting a certain amount of calories per day. Since she has decision-making capacity, she reserves the right to refuse this treatment, even if her care providers do not think this is in her best interest.

©Katarzyna Białasiewicz/123RF

where he remained for 15 years. Steadfastly denying he was ill, he refused all treatment and never exhibited signs of threatening behavior. His disorder, which clinicians diagnosed as paranoid schizophrenia, went into remission soon after his commitment. Nevertheless, Donaldson was kept in the hospital for nearly 2 decades, during which time he was denied many fundamental privileges.

The evidence showed that Donaldson's confinement was a simple regime of enforced custodial care, not a program designed to alleviate or cure his supposed illness. Numerous witnesses had testified that Donaldson had received nothing but custodial care while at the hospital. For substantial periods, he was simply kept in a large room that housed 60 patients, many of whom were under criminal commitment. Donaldson's requests for ground privileges, occupational training, and an opportunity to discuss his case with the hospital superintendent, D. J. B. O'Connor, or other staff members were repeatedly denied.

The Supreme Court's ruling in Donaldson's favor, along with several less-known cases, paved the way for major changes in the mental health system. This case established the legal principle that the presence of mental illness in a person is not sufficient reason for confinement to a mental hospital.

15.3 Forensic Issues in Psychological Treatment

At the interface between psychology and the law, forensic psychologists provide advice to the judicial system in many ways. We have already seen that psychologists may serve as expert witnesses. More generally, they may also help assess whether an individual who commits a crime should be incarcerated or be treated in a mental health facility.

The Insanity Defense

Insanity is a legal term that describes an individual's lack of moral responsibility for committing criminal acts. The **insanity defense** is the argument a lawyer presents on behalf of a client who, because of the existence of a mental disorder, should not be held legally responsible for criminal actions. Criminal law is based on the principle that people have free choice in their actions and that, if they break the law, they must therefore be held responsible. We judge people determined to be insane to lack the freedom to choose their behavior, as well as the mental competence to distinguish right from wrong. The insanity defense originated as an attempt to protect people with mental disorders from being punished for harmful behavior that resulted from their disturbed psychological state.

The insanity defense emerged from various legal precedents and the legal profession's attempts at clarification. In 1843, the British court handed down the **M'Naghten Rule** in the landmark case of a Scottish woodcutter named Daniel M'Naghten. Under the delusional belief that God was commanding him, M'Naghten killed an English government official. When he went to trial, the defense argued that he should not be held responsible for the murder because his mental disorder prevented him from knowing the difference between right and wrong. He believed he was following the commands of a higher power and, therefore, saw nothing wrong in his behavior. This is why the M'Naghten Rule is referred to as the "right-wrong test."

Most jurisdictions in the United States adopted the M'Naghten Rule. U.S. legislatures and courts eventually modified and expanded the definition of insanity, adding the **irresistible impulse** test to take into account the possibility that some disturbed behaviors may result from people's inability to inhibit actions they feel compelled to carry out. Although they may know an act is wrong, they are unable to stop themselves from acting on their impulses.

The **Durham Rule** later expanded the insanity defense after a court decision in 1954 asserted that a person is not criminally responsible if the "unlawful act was the product of mental disease or defect." The intent was to protect individuals with disturbed psychological functioning due to any of a variety of conditions, including personality disorders. This expansion of the insanity defense put the burden on mental health experts to prove a defendant was mentally disturbed, even when there was no evidence of overt psychosis.

insanity
A legal term that refers to the individual's lack of moral responsibility for committing criminal acts.

insanity defense
The argument, presented by a lawyer acting on behalf of the client, that, because of the existence of a mental disorder, the client should not be held legally responsible for criminal actions.

M'Naghten Rule
The "right-wrong test" used in cases of the insanity defense to determine whether a defendant should be held responsible for a crime.

irresistible impulse
The legal argument that although clients in a forensic setting knew an act was wrong, they were unable to stop themselves from acting on their impulses.

Durham Rule
An expansion of the insanity defense based on determining that the individual was not criminally responsible if the unlawful act was due to the presence of a psychological disorder.

REAL STORIES

Susanna Kaysen: Involuntary Commitment

"Don't you think you need a rest?"

"Yes," I said.

He strode off to the adjacent room, where I could hear him talking on the phone.

I have thought often of the next 10 minutes–my last 10 minutes. I had the impulse, once, to get up and leave through the door I'd entered, to walk the several blocks to the trolley stop and wait for the train that would take me back to my troublesome boyfriend, my job at the kitchen store. But I was too tired.

He strutted back into the room, busy, pleased with himself.

"I've got a bed for you," he said. "It'll be a rest. Just for a couple of weeks, okay?" He sounded conciliatory, or pleading, and I was afraid.

"I'll go Friday," I said. It was Tuesday, maybe by Friday I wouldn't want to go.

He bore down on me with his belly. "No. You go now."

I thought this was unreasonable. "I have a lunch date," I said.

"Forget it," he said. "You aren't going to lunch. You're going to the hospital." He looked triumphant.*

In 1967, Susanna Kaysen, then 19 years old, was committed to McLean Hospital in Belmont, Massachusetts, following a suicide attempt in which she consumed 50 aspirin pills along with vodka. In her book, *Girl, Interrupted*, Susanna provides her own insight into her experience contrasted with actual documents from her commitment that she later obtained. Throughout the book, Susanna questions the judgment of her psychiatrist who decided to commit her, a decision that resulted in a hospitalization lasting nearly 2 years. Susanna discusses mental illness from a philosophical standpoint and uses her experience, as well as the experiences of her fellow patients, as a way of questioning whether she was really in need of inpatient treatment, whether she was really "crazy." As you can note from the passage above, the book also underscores the changes that have taken place over the past 50 years in procedures and laws regarding involuntary psychiatric hospitalizations. Although perhaps her doctor at the time felt that Susanna was a threat to herself, given her suicide attempt as well as a history of some self-harming behaviors (cutting and wrist-banging), his process of commitment did not include a thorough risk assessment and was solely based on his clinical judgment.

When Susanna was admitted to McLean, clinicians diagnosed her with borderline personality disorder. Looking back at her case now as described in the book, it could be argued that her symptoms point more to a diagnosis of major depressive episode. In *Girl, Interrupted*, Susanna contemplates the meaning of her diagnosis at the time and whether her symptoms as described in the *DSM* matched up with her true experience.

In her time at McLean, Susanna thought at length about the implications of her hospitalization for her own mental health. At times throughout the book it appears that she is trying to reason with herself and make a case for committing herself. We could argue that this reasoning was actually harmful to her, that she had to make herself believe she needed to be there. By today's standards, we would deem lack of clarity about her need to be hospitalized unethical, given that it was more than likely causing her more harm than good. In other words, she was not being treated appropriately. Further, by current ethical standards, mental health professionals would consider her length of stay almost unimaginable, given that the average length of stay is now closer to about one week for most inpatient hospitalizations. At the time the book was written, however, a patient's stay was dictated by the family's ability to pay for hospitalization. Currently, clinicians focus on stabilizing the patient as efficiently as possible so that he or she may safely return to the community. In the end, the hospital allowed Susanna to sign herself out, and she moved into her own apartment.

In the book, Susanna discusses her difficult transition back to living independently following her hospitalization. She details the agonizing experience of trying to explain the gaps in her resume to potential employers. She had to list the address of the hospital, which was well known to belong to McLean, adding to the stigma she faced when applying for jobs, leases, or even a driver's license following her discharge.

In reflecting on her experience of being hospitalized, Susanna speaks to the lasting memories of that time, as well as the long-term impact of the diagnosis on her sense of identity.

"Maybe I was just flirting with madness the way I flirted with my teachers and my classmates. I wasn't convinced I was crazy, though I feared I was. Some people say that having any conscious opinion on the matter is a mark of sanity, but I'm not sure that's true. I still think about it. I'll always have to think about it. . . . It's a common phrase, I know. But it means something particular to me: the tunnels, the security screens, the plastic forks, the shimmering, ever-shifting borderline that like all boundaries beckons and asks to be crossed. I do not want to cross it again."

*SOURCE: Susanna Kaysen. *Girl, Interrupted*, Vintage, 1994.

Susanna Kaysen wrote about her experience in an inpatient psychiatric facility in *Girl, Interrupted*. In the book, she questions the validity of her diagnosis and whether she should have been hospitalized for her symptoms.

©Boston Globe/Getty Images

In an attempt to develop uniform standards for the insanity defense, the **American Law Institute's (ALI) guidelines** in 1962 (Sec. 4.01) took a middle position between the pre-Durham Rule codes and the liberal standing the Durham Rule takes. According to ALI, people are not responsible for criminal behavior if their mental disorder prevents them from appreciating the wrongfulness of their behavior or from exerting the necessary willpower to control their acts (the irresistible impulse rule). The important term here is "appreciating." In other words, knowing what is right and wrong is not equivalent to understanding that your behavior is wrong.

The ALI code allows for the introduction of medical and psychiatric evidence and thus provides a modern test for the insanity defense. Another important feature of the ALI code is the exclusion from the insanity defense of people whose only maladaptive behavior is repeated criminal or otherwise antisocial conduct. The ALI guideline is a more viable standard of insanity than the Durham Rule, because it takes the question of guilt or innocence away from mental health experts and places it in the hands of the jury, who can then make a determination based on the evidence related to the crime itself.

In the years following the publication of the ALI standards, the courts applied the insanity defense much more widely. However, the situation changed once again after John Hinckley Jr. attempted to assassinate President Ronald Reagan in 1981. Hinckley was obsessed with actor Jodie Foster and believed that if he killed the president she would be so impressed that she would fall in love with him and marry him. When the case went to trial, the jury determined that Hinckley's actions justified the insanity defense. He was sent to St. Elizabeth's Hospital in Washington, D.C., where he remained until 2016. This case brought to the nation's attention the rarely used but controversial insanity plea as it had been broadened through the Durham and ALI standards. The public was particularly outraged about the possibility that an assassin could get away with murder on the grounds of having a mental disorder.

In response to the Hinckley case, Congress passed the Insanity Defense Reform Act of 1984, which added the criterion of "severe disturbance" to the insanity defense. This meant that people with personality disorders would no longer be able to plead insanity. The law also moved the burden of proof. Previously, the defense needed to provide reasonable doubt regarding the prosecution's argument that the defendant was sane. The Reform Act meant that the defense must now prove that the defendant fits the legal definition of insanity, which is a more difficult argument to make.

The nature of the insanity defense varies somewhat by state. Some states separate the matter of guilt from that of mental disorder by allowing the plea of "guilty but mentally ill." The court does not exonerate defendants who use this plea but does give them special consideration in sentencing.

Partly because of the storm of criticism following the Hinckley case, however, the court took a very different route in 1992. This time, a 31-year-old man, Jeffrey Dahmer, had confessed to murdering and dismembering 17 boys and young men in Wisconsin, explaining that he was driven to kill out of a compulsion to have sex with dead bodies. His defense attorney argued that the crimes could have been committed only by someone who fit the legal definition of insanity. The jury rejected the guilty but mentally ill plea because they believed Dahmer to be responsible for his crimes and able to appreciate the wrongfulness of his conduct. Dahmer was sentenced to consecutive life terms for the murders of each of his victims. In 1994, he was killed in prison by another inmate.

Other highly publicized cases since Dahmer's have brought out subtleties in the insanity defense as we currently construe it. In California, Lyle and Erik Menendez admitted to the premeditated murder of their parents in response, they claimed, to years of abuse. Their defense attorneys presented the argument of "imperfect self-defense," asserting that the brothers, in their twenties at the time, acted in the mistaken belief that their parents were about to kill them,

American Law Institute's (ALI) guidelines
Guidelines proposing that people are not responsible for criminal behavior if their mental disorder prevents them from appreciating the wrongfulness of their behavior or exerting the willpower to control it.

The case of John Hinckley Jr., who in 1981 tried to assassinate President Ronald Reagan, raised public concern over possible misuse of the insanity defense. Hinckley, who was declared insane by the courts, was not imprisoned; instead he was committed for treatment at St. Elizabeth's Hospital in Washington, D.C., until his release in 2016.
©RON EDMONDS/AP Images

Lyle and Erik Menendez continue to serve life sentences in prison for murdering their parents in 1989.
©Nick Ut/AP Images

a belief stemming from a lifelong history of physical, emotional, and sexual abuse. The defense argued that on the night of the killings one of the brothers, in an altered mental state, retrieved his shotgun, loaded it, and burst in on his parents. The prosecution, which proved its case, claimed the brothers were instead motivated by the $14 million they stood to inherit.

The irresistible impulse defense came to light in the highly publicized case of Lorena Bobbitt, a Virginia woman who claimed to be temporarily insane as a result of years of physical and psychological abuse by her husband, leading her to cut off his penis. Bobbitt claimed that she had been overcome by what she called "pictures," or mental images, of his abusive actions toward her. The jury concluded that she was temporarily insane and acquitted her of all charges of malicious and unlawful wounding. As mandated by Virginia law, the judge in the case ordered Bobbitt to be evaluated at a state psychiatric hospital to determine whether she posed a danger to herself or others. After the required 45-day period, she was released.

Yet another variant of the insanity defense occurred in the case of Andrea Yates, who in June 2001 drowned her five children in the bathtub of her Texas home. Yates had a history of profound postpartum depression following the births of her fourth and fifth children. Although her case seemed to merit the insanity plea, the court convicted her of capital murder in March 2002. In 2006, however, an appeals court overturned the verdict on the basis that one of the expert witnesses in the trial had presented false testimony relevant to Yates's mental state at the time of the killings. In July 2006, the court moved Yates from a high-security mental health facility to a low-security state mental hospital.

The homicide trial of Lee Boyd Malvo and John Allen Muhammad presented the case of two individuals who had committed a crime together, but only one qualified for the insanity defense. The pair were arrested in October 2002 after conducting sniper attacks in which they murdered 10 people in the Washington, D.C., area. The prosecution asserted that Muhammad, a man in his forties, had undertaken the shooting spree and ordered 17-year-old Malvo to help him. Malvo's defense attorneys pleaded the insanity defense on the grounds that he was indoctrinated and therefore had a form of mental illness. Because he was a teenager under the power of a much older man, they said, Malvo did not know right from wrong. However, the jury rejected this version of the insanity defense. Ultimately, Muhammad was executed by lethal injection in Virginia in 2009, and Malvo was sentenced in 2006 to six consecutive life sentences without the possibility of parole.

The opposite situation occurred in the case of Theodore Kaczynski, known as the Unabomber. From his cabin in Montana, Kaczynski mounted an 18-year campaign against the "industrial-technological system." He admitted that he had killed three people and maimed many others by sending package bombs to government addresses. His history and

Following a psychiatric evaluation, Anders Behring Breivik, a right-wing extremist, was declared sane and guilty of murdering 77 people in Norway in 2011.

©Jeff Gilbert/Alamy Stock Photo

extensive clinical evaluation offered compelling evidence that he had schizophrenia, paranoid type. However, he refused to use the insanity defense because he did not consider himself to have a psychological disorder. A federal grand jury indicted Kaczynski in April 1996 on 10 counts of illegally transporting, mailing, and using bombs, and three counts of murder; he remains in a federal penitentiary in Colorado.

Competency to Stand Trial

Based on the principle that people should be able to participate in their own defense, the finding of **competency to stand trial** asserts that defendants are aware of and able to participate in criminal proceedings against them. To assess competency, a forensic expert evaluates the defendant's cognitive capacity, emotional stamina, and ongoing symptoms at the time of the trial. The court may postpone trial until the defendant's symptoms subside, if necessary mandating that the individual receive medication. Although structured instruments are available for establishing competency, the majority of forensic experts rely on their clinical judgment (Bartol & Bartol, 2012).

competency to stand trial
A prediction by a mental health expert of the defendant's cognitive and emotional stability during the period of the trial.

Understanding the Purpose of Punishment

Separate from the issue of competency to stand trial is the question whether a mentally ill person who is convicted of a capital offense is able to understand the nature and purpose of a death sentence. The case of Scott Louis Panetti, which the U.S. Supreme Court heard in 2007, highlights some of the complexities here.

In 1992, Panetti killed his in-laws while holding hostage his estranged wife and their 3-year-old daughter. Even though Panetti had a lengthy history of mental illness and psychiatric hospitalizations, the Texas court sentenced him to death. In 2003, Panetti petitioned the Texas state appeals court to determine his competency for execution, asserting his belief that satanic forces had sought his execution to prevent him from preaching the Gospel. His defense lawyers claimed that since Panetti could not understand why the jury had sentenced him to death, the death penalty would constitute cruel and unusual punishment and therefore violate the Eighth Amendment of the Constitution. The Texas Department of Criminal Justice objected to this argument, contending that capital punishment in such cases should rest not on whether a convict has rational understanding of the reasons for execution, but on the convict's moral culpability at the time he or she committed the crime.

For almost 2 decades the case of Scott Louis Panetti has been the focus of legal debate and controversy. Panetti's death sentence in Texas was overturned by the U.S. Supreme Court on the grounds that Panetti lacked understanding of why he was to be put to death.
©BRETT COOMER/Tribune News Service/HUNTSVILLE/TX/USA/Newscom

In 2007, the U.S. Supreme Court blocked Panetti's execution and returned the case to the U.S. District Court in Austin, Texas, returning him to prison in Texas, where he remains on death row. The court based this decision in part on arguments that the American Psychological Association, the American Psychiatric Association, and the National Alliance on Mental Illness put forward. These organizations had jointly submitted a brief stating that individuals with psychotic conditions, such as Panetti, may experience delusions and a disrupted understanding of reality. They may also be unable to connect events or understand cause and effect—namely, the connection between the murder and the punishment.

Concluding Perspectives on Forensic Issues

As you can see from our discussion of forensic issues, there is an entire body of knowledge forming on the border between psychology and the law. Mental health professionals are playing an increasingly important role in the legal system and at the same time finding that they must familiarize themselves with an array of forensic issues. Clearly, the areas of intersection between psychology and the law will continue to grow as society looks for interventions that are humane, ethical, and effective.

Return to the Case: Allison Yang

Allison was hospitalized for 5 days while health care professionals thoroughly assessed her, focusing on her suicidality and depressive symptoms. She attended group therapy and worked with a psychiatrist to change her medication regimen. Once she had stabilized and was no longer suicidal, she was released. Her parents picked her up, and she decided to stay with them for the rest of the semester and return to school the following year.

Before her hospitalization, Allison's parents had not been aware that she was experiencing psychological difficulties. Much to her surprise, they said they understood her need to stay home to recuperate. Since her parents lived several hours away from her school, Allison and her therapist decided to have weekly telephone sessions in order to continue their work together. They focused on the relationship between Allison and her parents, and Allison used the time at home to learn to discuss with her parents how she felt about the pressure they had placed on her and why that been a source of much stress.

Dr. Tobin's reflections: Clinicians are sometimes faced with the difficult decision to hospitalize their therapy clients. Allison's clinician performed the appropriate steps to assess her level of safety and found her in great need of hospitalization because she appeared to be an immediate threat to her own life. Thus he was ethically bound to break confidentiality and send Allison to the hospital for further evaluation. Luckily, the two had a strong enough alliance

that Allison felt she should come in for "one last session" rather than ending her life. This may have been a cry for help because Allison knew her clinician would be able to help her.

Allison's first depressive episode was severe, lasting around 8 months. Usually, the more severe the initial episode, the more persistent and severe subsequent episodes will become. Considering that the current work with her clinician is the first time Allison has received psychological help, part of her treatment will be to help her gain a sense of insight into her psychological struggles. For instance, should she begin to notice the same pattern of symptoms in the future that led to her current depressive episode, she may then recognize that her symptoms could turn more severe if she does not bring them to the attention of her therapist or psychiatrist.

Finally, psychotherapy conducted over the phone, called teletherapy, is an increasingly common protocol and is covered by the APA's Ethics Code. If both parties agree it is the best way to maintain the therapeutic alliance over a certain period of time, as in Allison's case, it may be a suitable alternative to stopping therapy altogether. Because Allison did plan on returning to school and continuing to work with her therapist in person, it appears that teletherapy was an appropriate way to continue until then and avoid a break in her progress.

SUMMARY

- Clinicians have various roles and responsibilities. We expect them to have the intellectual competence to assess, conceptualize, and treat clients whom they accept into treatment, in addition to having the emotional capability of managing the clinical issues that emerge. When beginning work with clients, they should obtain the client's informed consent to ensure that the client understands the goals of treatment, the therapy process, the client's rights, the therapist's responsibilities, the treatment risks, the techniques that the clinician will use, financial issues, and the limits of confidentiality.

- Confidentiality is the principle that the therapist must safeguard disclosures in therapy as private. With only a few exceptions, the content of therapy is privileged communication; that is, the clinician may not disclose any information about the client in a court without the client's express permission. Exceptions to confidentiality include instances involving mandated reporting and duty to warn (or otherwise protect). Mental health professionals are mandated by law to report information involving the abuse or neglect of children or other people who are unable to protect themselves. The duty to warn involves the clinician's responsibility to take action to inform a possible victim of a client's intention to do harm to that person.

- In their relationships with clients, we expect clinicians to adhere to the highest standards of ethical and professional conduct. They are to avoid inappropriate relationships, such as sexual intimacy with clients, and must maintain neutrality and distance in their dealings with clients. In overseeing the business aspects of psychotherapy practice, mental health professionals face various challenges, particularly when operating within managed health care delivery systems. Sometimes clinicians must serve in roles that present unique ethical challenges (e.g., expert witness, child custody evaluations, and evaluations of people with dementia).

- Clinicians are sometimes involved in the process of commitment, an emergency procedure for the involuntary hospitalization of a person who, if not hospitalized, is likely to create harm for self or others as a result of mental illness. Hospitalized clients have the right to treatment—the right to a humane environment with appropriate amenities, in addition to liberty and safety. Clients also have the right to refuse unwanted treatment, unless a court deems that the client is at risk of harming self or others without needed intervention. Clients also have the right for placement in the least restrictive alternative to treatment in an institution.

- The major forensic issues that pertain to the field of mental health involve the insanity defense and competency to stand trial. The insanity defense is the argument that the lawyer acting on behalf of the client presents, which states that, because of the existence of a mental disorder, the law should not hold the client legally responsible for criminal actions. Various controversies have emerged during the past 2 decades regarding the insanity defense as courts have struggled with issues of assessing a defendant's responsibility in well-publicized cases involving violent assault and murder. The determination of competency to stand trial pertains to the question of whether defendants are aware of and able to participate in criminal proceedings against them.

KEY TERMS

American Law Institute's (ALI) guidelines
Commitment
Competency to stand trial
Durham Rule
Duty to warn (or otherwise protect)
Emotional competence

Guardian *ad litem*
Health Insurance Portability and Accountability Act of 1996 (HIPAA)
Insanity
Insanity defense
Irresistible impulse
Least restrictive alternative

M'Naghten Rule
Multiple relationships
Parens patriae
Right to treatment
Substituted judgment

GLOSSARY

A

acceptance and commitment therapy (ACT) A therapeutic approach that aims to indirectly reduce symptoms by focusing on improving psychological flexibility.

acceptance-based approaches A group of psychotherapy approaches that use behavioral strategies as well as cognitive framework to improve overall effectiveness.

active phase A period in the course of schizophrenia in which psychotic symptoms are present.

acute stress disorder An anxiety disorder that develops after a traumatic event, and lasts for up to 1 month with symptoms such as depersonalization, numbing, dissociative amnesia, intense anxiety, hypervigilance, and impairment of everyday functioning.

adaptive testing Testing in which the client's responses to earlier questions determine the subsequent questions presented to him or her.

agoraphobia Intense anxiety triggered by the real or anticipated exposure to situations in which individuals may be unable to get help should they become incapacitated.

akinesia A motor disturbance in which a person's muscles become rigid and movement is difficult to initiate.

alcohol myopia theory Proposes that as individuals consume greater amounts of alcohol, they are more likely to make risky choices because the immediate temptation of the moment overcomes the long-term consequences of the behavior.

allele One of two or more different variations of a gene.

American Law Institute's (ALI) guidelines Guidelines proposing that people are not responsible for criminal behavior if their mental disorder prevents them from appreciating the wrongfulness of their behavior or exerting the willpower to control it.

amnesia Inability to recall information that was previously learned or to register new memories.

amphetamine A stimulant that affects both the central nervous and the autonomic nervous systems.

amyloid plaques A characteristic of Alzheimer's disease in which clusters of dead or dying neurons become mixed together with fragments of protein molecules.

analog observations Assessments that take place in a setting or context such as a clinician's office or a laboratory specifically designed for observing the target behavior.

anorexia nervosa (AN) An eating disorder characterized by severely restricted eating, an intense fear of gaining weight, and distorted body perception.

anterograde amnesia Amnesia involving the inability to remember new information.

antisocial personality disorder A personality disorder characterized by a lack of regard for society's moral or legal standards and an impulsive and risky lifestyle.

anxiety A future-oriented and global response, involving both cognitive and emotional components, in which an individual is inordinately apprehensive, tense, and uneasy about the prospect of something terrible happening.

anxiety disorders Disorders characterized by excessive fear and anxiety, and related disturbances in behavior.

anxiety sensitivity theory The belief that panic disorder is caused in part by the tendency to interpret cognitive and somatic manifestations of stress and anxiety in a catastrophic manner.

anxiolytic An antianxiety medication.

archetypes In Jung's theory, a set of images common to all human experience.

asociality Lack of interest in social relationships.

Asperger's disorder A term once used to describe individuals with high-functioning autism spectrum disorder.

assertive community treatment (ACT) Treatment modality in which a team of professionals from psychiatry, psychology, nursing, and social work reach out to clients in their homes and workplaces.

attachment figures Caregivers or adults to whom the individual is attached.

attachment style The way a person relates to a caregiver figure.

attention-deficit/hyperactivity disorder (ADHD) A neurodevelopmental disorder involving a persistent pattern of inattention and/or hyperactivity.

autism spectrum disorder A neurodevelopmental disorder involving impairments in the domains of social communication and the performance of restricted, repetitive behaviors.

automatic thoughts Ideas that are the product of dysfunctional attitudes so deeply entrenched the individual is not even aware they exist.

aversive conditioning Classical conditioning in which the individual associates a maladaptive response with a stimulus that could not itself cause harm.

avoidant personality disorder A personality disorder in which people have low estimation of their social skills and are fearful of disapproval, rejection, and criticism or being ashamed or embarrassed.

avoidant/restrictive food intake disorder A disorder in which individuals avoid eating out of concern about aversive consequences or restrict intake of food with specific sensory characteristics.

avolition A lack of initiative, either not wanting to take any action or lacking the energy and will to take action.

axis A class of information in previous *DSM*s regarding one dimension of an individual's functioning.

B

Barnum effect The tendency for clinicians to unintentionally make generic and vague statements about their clients that do not specifically characterize the client.

behavioral activation Behavioral therapy for depression in which the clinician helps the client identify activities associated with positive mood.

behavioral assessment A form of measurement based on objective recording of the individual's behavior.

behavioral genetics Research area focused on identifying the role of hereditary factors in psychological disorders.

behavioral interviewing Assessment process in which clinicians ask questions about the target behavior's frequency, antecedents, and consequences.

behavioral medicine An interdisciplinary approach to medical conditions affected by psychological factors that is rooted in learning theory.

behavioral perspective A theoretical perspective in which it is assumed that abnormality is caused by faulty learning experiences.

behavioral self-report A method of behavioral assessment in which the individual provides information about the frequency of particular behaviors.

binge eating The ingestion of large amounts of food during a short period of time, even after reaching a point of feeling full, and a lack of control over what or how much is eaten.

binge-eating disorder An eating disorder in which individuals lack control over their eating and engage in binges for at least twice a week for 6 months.

biological perspective A theoretical perspective in which it is assumed that disturbances in emotions, behavior, and cognitive processes are caused by abnormalities in the functioning of the body.

biological sex The sex determined by a person's chromosomes.

biopsychosocial perspective A model in which the interaction of biological, psychological, and sociocultural factors is seen as influencing the development of the individual over time.

bipolar disorder A mood disorder involving manic episodes—intense and disruptive experiences of heightened mood, possibly alternating with major depressive episodes.

bipolar disorder, rapid cycling A form of bipolar disorder involving four or more episodes within the previous year that meet the criteria for manic, hypomanic, or major depressive disorder.

body dysmorphic disorder A disorder in which individuals are preoccupied with the idea that a part of their body is ugly or defective.

borderline personality disorder (BPD) A personality disorder characterized by a pervasive pattern of poor impulse control and instability in mood, interpersonal relationships, and sense of self.

bradykinesia A motor disturbance involving a general slowing of motor activity.

brief psychotic disorder A diagnosis clinicians use when an individual develops symptoms of psychosis for more than a day but less than a month.

bulimia nervosa An eating disorder involving alternation between the extremes of eating large amounts of food in a short time, and then compensating for the added calories either by vomiting or other extreme actions to avoid gaining weight.

buprenorphine A medication used in the treatment of heroin addiction.

C

caffeine A stimulant found in coffee, tea, chocolate, energy drinks, diet pills, and headache remedies.

case formulation A clinician's analysis of the client's development and the factors that might have influenced his or her current psychological status.

case study An intensive study of a single person described in detail.

catatonia A condition in which the individual shows marked psychomotor disturbances.

childhood-onset fluency disorder (stuttering) A communication disorder that involves a disturbance in the normal fluency and patterning of speech characterized by such verbalizations as sound repetitions or prolongations, broken words, the blocking out of sounds, word substitutions to avoid problematic words, or words expressed with an excess of tension.

circadian rhythms Biological clocks that set patterns of sleepfulness and wakefulness on approximately a 24-hour basis.

classical conditioning The process in the behavioral perspective that accounts for the learning of emotional, automatic responses.

client A person seeking psychological treatment.

client-centered An approach based on the belief held by Rogers that people are innately good and that the potential for self-improvement lies within the individual.

clinical interview A series of questions that clinicians administer in face-to-face interaction with the client.

clinical psychologist A mental health professional with training in the behavioral sciences who provides direct service to clients.

clinical significance The criterion for a psychological disorder in which the behavior being evaluated includes a measurable degree of impairment that the clinician can observe.

clinician The person providing treatment.

cocaine A highly addictive central nervous system stimulant that an individual snorts, injects, or smokes.

cognitive-behavioral therapy (CBT) Treatment method in which clinicians focus on changing both maladaptive thoughts and maladaptive behaviors.

cognitive-behavioral therapy for psychosis (CBTp) Method of treating symptoms of psychosis in which clinicians do not try to change clients' delusions or eliminate their hallucinations but instead try to reduce their distress and preoccupation with these symptoms.

cognitive perspective A theoretical perspective in which it is assumed that abnormality is caused by maladaptive thought processes that result in dysfunctional behavior.

cognitive restructuring One of the fundamental techniques of cognitive-behavioral therapy in which the clinician attempts to change the client's thoughts by questioning and challenging the client's dysfunctional attitudes and irrational beliefs.

cognitive triad According to the cognitive theory of depression, the view that a depressed person's dysphoria results from a negative view of the self, the world, and the future.

commitment An emergency procedure for involuntary psychiatric hospitalization.

communication disorders Neurodevelopmental disorders involving impairment in language, speech, and communication.

community mental health center (CMHC) Outpatient clinic that provides psychological services on a sliding fee scale for individuals who live within a certain geographic area.

comorbidity Two (or more) disorders that co-occur within the same individual.

competency to stand trial A prediction by a mental health expert of the defendant's cognitive and emotional stability during the period of the trial.

compulsion A repetitive and seemingly purposeful behavior performed in response to uncontrollable urges or according to a ritualistic or stereotyped set of rules.

computed axial tomography (CAT or CT) scan A series of X-rays taken from various angles around the brain that are integrated by computer to produce a composite picture.

concordance rate Agreement ratios between people diagnosed as having a particular disorder and their relatives.

conditioned fear reactions Acquired associations between an internal or external cue and feelings of intense anxiety.

conduct disorder An impulse-control disorder that involves repeated violations of the rights of others and society's norms and laws.

contingency management A form of behavioral therapy in which clinicians provide clients with positive reinforcement for performing desired behaviors.

conversion disorder (functional neurological symptom disorder) A somatic symptom disorder involving the translation of unacceptable drives or troubling conflicts into physical symptoms.

coping The process through which people reduce stress.

correlational design Study in which researchers test the relationships between variables that they cannot experimentally manipulate.

counterconditioning The process of replacing an undesired response to a stimulus with an acceptable response.

cross-fostering A type of adoption study in which researchers examine the frequency of the disorder in children whose biological parents had no disorder, but whose adoptive parents do.

cultural concepts of distress Ways that individuals in specific cultural groups experience, understand, and communicate their suffering, behavioral problems, or troubling thoughts and emotions.

cultural formulation A tool that includes the clinician's assessment of the client's degree of identification with the culture of origin, the culture's beliefs about psychological disorders, the ways in which the culture interprets particular events, and the cultural supports available to the client.

Cultural Formulation Interview A set of questions that assess the impact of culture on key aspects of the client's clinical presentation and care.

culture-bound syndromes Recurrent patterns of abnormal behavior or experience that are limited to specific societies or cultural areas.

cyclothymic disorder A mood disorder with symptoms that are more chronic and less severe than those of bipolar disorder.

D

dark triad Personality traits that include psychopathy, extreme self-centeredness, and a tendency to regard other people as objects to be used.

day treatment program A structured program in a community treatment facility that provides activities similar to those provided in a psychiatric hospital.

deep brain stimulation (DBS) A treatment in which a neurosurgeon implants a microelectrode that delivers a constant low electrical stimulation to a small region of the brain, powered by an implanted battery; also called *neuromodulation*.

defense mechanisms Tactics that keep unacceptable thoughts, instincts, and feelings out of conscious awareness and thus protect the ego against anxiety.

deinstitutionalization movement The release of hundreds of thousands of patients from mental hospitals starting in the 1960s.

delayed ejaculation A sexual dysfunction in which a man experiences problems having an orgasm during sexual activity; also known as inhibited male orgasm.

delirium A neurocognitive disorder that is temporary in nature involving disturbances in attention and awareness.

delusion Deeply entrenched false belief not consistent with the client's intelligence or cultural background.

delusional disorder Disorder in which the only symptoms are delusions that have lasted for at least 1 month.

dependent personality disorder A personality disorder whose main characteristic is that the individual is extremely passive and tends to cling to other people, to the point of being unable to make any decisions or to take independent action.

dependent variable The variable whose value is the outcome of the experimenter's manipulation of the independent variable.

depersonalization Condition in which people feel detached from their own body.

depersonalization/derealization disorder A dissociative disorder in which the individual experiences recurrent and persistent episodes of depersonalization, derealization, or both.

depressant A psychoactive substance that causes the depression of central nervous system activity.

depressive disorder A disorder characterized by periods in which, among other symptoms, an individual experiences an unusually intense sad mood.

derealization Condition in which people feel a sense of unreality or detachment from their surroundings.

developmental cascade hypothesis A proposal for the cause of schizophrenia that integrates genetic vulnerabilities, damage occurring in the prenatal and early childhood periods, adversity, and drug abuse as causes of changes in dopamine expressed in psychosis.

developmental coordination disorder A motor disorder characterized by marked impairment in the development of motor coordination.

deviation intelligence (IQ) An index of intelligence derived from comparing the individual's score on an intelligence test with the mean score for that individual's reference group.

Diagnostic and Statistical Manual of Mental Disorders (DSM) A book published by the American Psychiatric Association that contains standard terms and definitions of psychological disorders.

dialectical behavior therapy (DBT) Treatment approach for people with borderline personality disorder that integrates supportive and cognitive-behavioral treatments to reduce the frequency of self-destructive acts and to improve the client's ability to handle disturbing emotions, such as anger and dependency.

diathesis-stress model The proposal that people are born with a predisposition (or "diathesis") that places them at risk for developing a psychological disorder if exposed to certain extremely stressful life experiences.

differential diagnosis The process of systematically ruling out alternative diagnoses.

diffusion tensor imaging (DTI) A method to investigate abnormalities in the white matter of the brain.

disinhibited social engagement disorder Diagnosis given to children who engage in culturally inappropriate, overly familiar behavior with people who are relative strangers.

disorganized speech Language that is incomprehensible and incoherent.

disruptive mood dysregulation disorder A depressive disorder in children who exhibit chronic and severe irritability and have frequent temper outbursts.

dissociative amnesia An inability to remember important personal details and experiences; usually associated with traumatic or very stressful events.

dissociative identity disorder (DID) A dissociative disorder in which an individual develops more than one self or personality.

disulfiram Known popularly as Antabuse, a medication used in the treatment of alcoholism that inhibits aldehyde dehydrogenase (ALDH) and causes severe physical reactions when combined with alcohol.

DNA methylation The process that can turn off a gene when a chemical group, methyl, attaches itself to the gene.

double-blind An experimental procedure in which neither the person giving the treatment nor the person receiving the treatment knows whether the participant is in the experimental or control group.

Down syndrome A form of intellectual disability caused most commonly when individuals inherit an extra copy of chromosome 21 and therefore have 47 chromosomes instead of the typical 46.

downward drift A progression observed in people with schizophrenia in which their disorder drives them into poverty, which interferes with their ability to work and earn a living.

dual-process theory A theory regarding alcohol use proposing there are automatic processes that generate an impulse to drink alcohol and controlled, effortful processing that regulates these automatic impulses.

Durham Rule An expansion of the insanity defense based on determining that the individual was not criminally responsible if the unlawful act was due to the presence of a psychological disorder.

duty to warn (or otherwise protect) The clinician's responsibility to notify a potential victim of a client's harmful intent toward that individual.

dyscalculia A pattern of difficulties in number sense, ability to learn arithmetic facts, and calculations.

dysfunctional attitudes Negative beliefs about the self that are deeply ingrained.

dysphoria An unusually elevated sad mood.

E

eating disorders Diagnosis for people who experience persistent disturbances of eating or eating-related behavior that result in the person's altering the consumption or absorption of food.

echolalia Repetition of the same sounds over and over.

ecstasy (MDMA) A hallucinogenic drug made from a synthetic substance chemically similar to methamphetamine and mescaline.

ego In psychoanalytic theory, the structure of personality that gives the individual the mental powers of judgment, memory, perception, and decision making.

ego psychology Theoretical perspective based on psychodynamic theory emphasizing the ego as the main force in personality.

electroconvulsive therapy (ECT) The application of electrical shock to the head for the purpose of inducing therapeutically beneficial seizures.

electroencephalogram (EEG) A measure of changes in the electrical activity of the brain.

elimination disorders Disorders characterized by age-inappropriate incontinence, beginning in childhood.

emotional competence A quality desired in clinicians in which they are free of a diagnosable psychological disorder.

emotional dysregulation Lack of awareness, understanding, or acceptance of emotions; inability to control the intensity or duration of emotions; unwillingness to experience emotional distress as an aspect of pursuing goals; and inability to engage in goal-directed behaviors when experiencing distress.

emotion-focused coping A type of coping in which a person does not change anything about the situation itself but instead tries to improve feelings about the situation.

encopresis An elimination disorder in which the child is incontinent of feces and has bowel movements either in clothes or in another inappropriate place.

endophenotypes Biobehavioral abnormalities that are linked to genetic and neurobiological causes of psychological disorders.

enuresis An elimination disorder in which the child is incontinent of urine and urinates in clothes or in bed after the age when the child is expected to be continent.

epigenesis The process of inheriting alterations in gene regulation and expression.

epigenetics The science that attempts to identify the ways that the environment influences genes to produce phenotypes.

erectile disorder Sexual dysfunction in which a man cannot attain or maintain an erection during sexual activity that is sufficient to allow him to initiate or maintain sexual activity.

erotomanic type of delusional disorder Delusional disorder in which individuals falsely believe that another person is in love with them.

euphoria A feeling state that is more cheerful and elated than average, possibly even ecstatic.

evidence-based assessment Assessment characterized by the clinician's (1) relying on research findings and scientifically viable theories, (2) using psychometrically strong measures, and (3) empirically evaluating the assessment process.

evidence-based practice in psychology Clinical decision making that integrates the best available research evidence and clinical expertise in the context of the cultural background, preferences, and characteristics of clients.

evidence-based treatment Treatment in which clients receive interventions based on the findings of controlled clinical studies.

excoriation (skin-picking) disorder Recurrent picking at one's own skin.

executive functioning The ability to formulate goals, make plans, carry out those plans, and then complete the plans in an effective way.

exhibitionistic disorder A paraphilic disorder in which a person has intense sexual urges and arousing fantasies involving the exposure of genitals to a stranger.

exorcism A ritual believed to cure psychological disturbance by ritually driving away evil spirits.

expressed emotion (EE) Family interactions with the individual that reflect criticism, hostile feelings, and emotional overinvolvement or overconcern.

extrapyramidal symptoms (EPS) Motor disorders involving rigid muscles, tremors, shuffling movement, restlessness, and muscle spasms affecting posture.

F

factitious disorder imposed on another A condition in which a person induces physical symptoms in another person who is under that person's care.

factitious disorder imposed on self A disorder in which people fake symptoms or disorders not for the purpose of any particular gain but because of an inner need to maintain a sick role.

family perspective A theoretical perspective in which it is assumed that abnormality is caused by disturbances in the pattern of interactions and relationships within the family.

family therapy Psychological treatment in which the therapist works with several or all members of the family.

fear The emotional response to real or perceived imminent threat.

female orgasmic disorder A sexual dysfunction in which a woman experiences problems having an orgasm during sexual activity.

female sexual interest/arousal disorder A sexual dysfunction characterized by a persistent or recurrent inability to attain or maintain normal physiological and psychological arousal responses during sexual activity.

fetal alcohol spectrum disorder (FASD) A lesser form of fetal alcohol syndrome developed in children who have some exposure to alcohol prenatally.

fetal alcohol syndrome (FAS) A condition associated with intellectual disability in a child whose mother consumed large amounts of alcohol on a regular basis while pregnant.

fetishistic disorder A paraphilic disorder in which the individual is preoccupied with an object and depends on this object rather than sexual intimacy with a partner for achieving sexual gratification.

first-rank symptom (FRS) Symptom that is truly defining, or key, in the diagnosis of schizophrenia.

Five Factor Model (or "Big Five") Trait theory proposing that there are five basic dispositions in personality, each of which has six facets.

flooding A behavioral technique in which the client is immersed in the sensation of anxiety by being exposed to the feared situation in its entirety.

fragile X syndrome A genetic disorder caused by a change in the gene FMRI.

free association A method used in psychoanalysis in which the client speaks freely, saying whatever comes to mind.

frontotemporal neurocognitive disorder Neurocognitive disorder that involves the frontotemporal area of the brain.

frotteuristic disorder A paraphilic disorder in which the individual has intense sexual urges and sexually arousing fantasies of rubbing against or fondling an unsuspecting stranger.

fugue An episode of amnesia involving inability to recall some or all of one's past and the loss of identity, with either bewildered wandering or travel that seems focused on a particular purpose.

functional magnetic resonance imaging (fMRI) Provides a picture of how areas of the brain react to stimuli in real time.

G

gambling disorder A non-substance-related disorder involving the persistent urge to gamble.

gender dysphoria Distress that may accompany the incongruence between a person's experienced or expressed gender and that person's assigned gender.

gender identity A person's inner sense of ones' own gender.

gene mapping The approach used by biological researchers in which they examine variations in chromosomes and connect them to performance on psychological tests or diagnosis of specific disorders.

generalized anxiety disorder An anxiety disorder characterized by anxiety and worry that is not associated with a particular object, situation, or event but seems to be a constant feature of a person's day-to-day existence.

genes The instructions for forming proteins contained within each of the body's cells.

genito-pelvic pain/penetration disorder A sexual dysfunction affecting both males and females that involves recurrent or persistent genital pain before, during, or after sexual intercourse.

genome-wide association studies (GWAS) Genetic method in which researchers scan the entire genome of individuals who are not related to find the associated genetic variations with a particular disease.

genome-wide linkage study Genetic method in which researchers study the families of people with specific psychological traits or disorders.

genotype The genetic makeup of an organism.

graded *in vivo* A procedure in which clients gradually expose themselves to increasingly challenging anxiety-provoking situations.

grandiose narcissism The form of narcissistic personality disorder in which individuals think of themselves entirely in an inflated and self-aggrandizing way.

grandiose type of delusional disorder An exaggerated view of oneself as possessing special and extremely favorable personal qualities and abilities.

group therapy Psychological treatment in which the therapist facilitates discussion among several clients who talk together about their problems.

guardian *ad litem* A person appointed by the court to represent or make decisions for a minor or an incapacitated adult who is legally incapable of doing so in a civil legal proceeding.

H

halfway house A community treatment facility designed for deinstitutionalized clients leaving a hospital who are not yet ready for independent living.

hallucination A false perception not corresponding to the objective stimuli present in the environment.

hallucinogens Psychoactive substances that cause abnormal perceptual experiences in the form of illusions or hallucinations, usually visual in nature.

hassle A relatively minor event that can cause stress.

health anxiety Undue concern about physical symptoms and illness.

Health Insurance Portability and Accountability Act of 1996 (HIPAA) U.S. legislation intended to ensure adequate coverage and protect consumers from loss of insurance coverage when they change or lose their jobs.

heroin A psychoactive substance that is a form of opioid, synthesized from morphine.

histrionic personality disorder A personality disorder characterized by exaggerated emotional reactions, approaching theatricality, in everyday behavior.

hoarding A compulsion in which people have persistent difficulties discarding things, even if they have little value.

humanistic perspective A theoretical view of personality and psychological disorder proposing that people are motivated to strive for self-fulfillment and meaning in life.

humanitarian explanations Explanations that regard psychological disorders as the result of cruelty, stress, or poor living conditions.

hypnotic A substance that induces sedation.

hypomanic episode A period of elated mood not as long as a manic episode.

I

id In psychoanalytic theory, the structure of personality hidden in the unconscious that contains instincts oriented toward fulfilling basic biological drives, including sexual and aggressive needs.

illness anxiety disorder A somatic symptom disorder characterized by the misinterpretation of normal bodily functions as signs of serious illness.

imaginal flooding A behavioral technique in which the client is immersed through imagination into the feared situation.

impulse-control disorders Psychological disorders in which people repeatedly engage in behaviors that are potentially harmful, feeling unable to stop themselves and experiencing a sense of desperation if their attempts to carry out the behaviors are thwarted.

inappropriate affect The extent to which a person's emotional expressiveness fails to correspond either to the social cues present in a situation or to the content of what is being discussed.

incidence The frequency of new cases within a given time period.

independent variable The variable whose level is adjusted or controlled by the experimenter.

individual psychotherapy Psychological treatment in which the therapist works on a one-to-one basis with the client.

inhalants A diverse group of substances that cause psychoactive effects by producing chemical vapors.

insanity A legal term that refers to the individual's lack of moral responsibility for committing criminal acts.

insanity defense The argument, presented by a lawyer acting on behalf of the client, that, because of the existence of a mental disorder, the client should not be held legally responsible for criminal actions.

intellectual disability (intellectual developmental disorder) Diagnosis used to characterize individuals who have intellectual and adaptive deficits that first became evident when they were children.

intermittent explosive disorder An impulse-control disorder involving an inability to hold back urges to express strong angry feelings and associated violent behaviors.

International Classification of Diseases (ICD) The diagnostic system of the World Health Organization (WHO).

interpersonal therapy (IPT) A time-limited form of psychotherapy for treating people with major depressive disorder, based on the assumption that interpersonal stress induces an episode of depression in a person who is genetically vulnerable to this disorder.

***in vivo* flooding** A behavioral technique in which the client is immersed in the actual feared situation.

***in vivo* observation** Process of recording behavior in its natural context, such as the classroom or the home.

irresistible impulse The legal argument that although clients in a forensic setting knew an act was wrong, they were unable to stop themselves from acting on their impulses.

J

jealous type of delusional disorder Delusional disorder in which individuals falsely believe that their romantic partner is unfaithful to them.

K

kleptomania An impulse-control disorder that involves the persistent urge to steal.

Korsakoff's syndrome A permanent form of neurocognitive disorder associated with long-term alcohol use in which the individual develops retrograde and anterograde amnesia, leading to an inability to remember recent events or learn new information.

L

language disorder A communication disorder characterized by having a limited and faulty vocabulary, speaking in short sentences with simplified grammatical structures, omitting critical words or phrases, and putting words together in peculiar order.

least restrictive alternative A treatment setting that provides the fewest constraints on the client's freedom.

libido An instinctual pressure that strives for gratification of sexual and aggressive desires.

loosening of associations Flow of thoughts that is vague, unfocused, and illogical.

lovemap The representations of an individual's sexual fantasies and preferred practices.

lysergic acid diethylamide (LSD) A form of a hallucinogenic drug that users ingest in tablets, capsules, and liquid form.

M

magnetic resonance imaging (MRI) The use of radio waves rather than X-rays to construct a static picture of the living brain based on the water content of various tissues.

mainstreaming A governmental policy to integrate fully into society people with cognitive disabilities.

major depressive disorder A disorder in which the individual experiences acute but time-limited episodes of depressive symptoms.

major depressive episode A period in which the individual experiences intense psychological and physical symptoms accompanying feelings of overwhelming sadness (dysphoria).

major neurocognitive disorder due to another medical condition Cognitive disorders involving the inability to recall previously learned information or to register new memories.

major neurocognitive disorders Disorders involving significant cognitive decline from a previous level of performance.

male hypoactive sexual desire disorder A sexual dysfunction in which the individual has an abnormally low level of interest in sexual activity.

malingering The fabrication of physical or psychological symptoms for some ulterior motive.

manic episode Acute but time-limited period of intense and unusual elation.

marijuana A psychoactive substance derived from the hemp plant whose primary active ingredient is delta-9-tetrahydrocannabinol (THC).

mental hygiene The focus within psychiatry on helping individuals maintain mental health and prevent the development of psychological disorders.

mentalization therapy A form of therapy in which clients are helped to identify their feelings by gaining control over their dysfunctional thoughts.

mental status examination A method of objectively assessing a client's behavior and functioning in a number of spheres, with particular attention to the symptoms associated with psychological disturbance.

methadone A synthetic opioid that produces a safer and more controlled reaction than heroin and that is used in treating heroin addiction.

methamphetamine An addictive stimulant drug that is related to amphetamine but provokes more intense central nervous system effects.

mild neurocognitive disorders Disorders involving modest cognitive decline from a previous level of performance.

milieu therapy A treatment approach, used in an inpatient psychiatric facility, in which all facets of the milieu, or environment, are components of the treatment.

mindfulness A mental state achieved by intentionally bringing one's awareness to the present moment without judgment of internal or external observations.

Mindfulness-based cognitive therapy (MBCT) Treatment that combines cognitive therapy with mindfulness skills.

Mini-Mental State Examination (MMSE) A structured tool that clinicians use as a brief screening device to assess neurocognitive disorders.

Minnesota Multiphasic Personality Inventory (MMPI) Self-report personality inventory containing 567 true-false items, all in the form of statements that describe the individual's thoughts, behaviors, feelings, and attitudes.

M'Naghten Rule The "right-wrong test" used in cases of the insanity defense to determine whether a defendant should be held responsible for a crime.

modality Form in which the clinician offers psychotherapy.

molecular genetics The study of how genes translate hereditary information.

moral treatment The belief that people could develop self-control over their behaviors if they had a quiet and restful environment.

motivational interviewing (MI) A technique that uses empathic understanding as a means of promoting behavioral change in clients.

multiaxial system A multidimensional classification and diagnostic system in previous *DSM*s summarizing relevant information about an individual's physical and psychological functioning.

multicultural approach Therapy that relies on awareness, knowledge, and skills of the client's sociocultural context.

multicultural assessment Assessment process in which clinicians take into account the person's cultural, ethnic, and racial background.

multi-infarct dementia (MID) A form of neurocognitive disorder caused by transient attacks in which blood flow to the brain is interrupted by a clogged or burst artery.

multiple relationships Unethical relationships occurring when a psychologist is in a professional role with a person and has another role with that person that could impair the psychologist's "objectivity, competence, or effectiveness in performing his or her functions as a psychologist" or otherwise risks exploiting or harming the other person.

N

naltrexone A medication used in the treatment of heroin addiction.

narcissistic personality disorder (NPD) A personality disorder primarily characterized by an unrealistic, inflated sense of self-importance and a lack of sensitivity to the needs of other people.

negative symptoms The symptoms of schizophrenia that involve functioning below the level of normal behavior.

neologisms Invented ("new") words.

neurocognitive disorder Disorders involving decline acquired in life in one or more domains of cognition associated with alterations in the brain.

neurocognitive disorder due to Alzheimer's disease A neurocognitive disorder associated with progressive, gradual declines in memory, learning, and at least one other cognitive domain.

neurocognitive disorder due to Huntington's disease A hereditary condition causing neurocognitive disorder that involves a widespread deterioration of the subcortical brain structures and parts of the frontal cortex that control motor movements.

neurocognitive disorder due to Parkinson's disease A neurocognitive disorder that involves degeneration of neurons in the subcortical structures that control motor movements.

neurocognitive disorder due to prion disease (Creutzfeldt-Jakob disease) A neurological disease transmitted from animals to humans that leads to neurocognitive disorder and death resulting from abnormal protein accumulations in the brain.

neurocognitive disorder due to traumatic brain injury A disorder in which there is evidence of impact to the head along with cognitive and neurological symptoms that persist past the acute postinjury period.

neurocognitive disorder with Lewy bodies A form of neurocognitive disorder with progressive loss of memory, language, calculation, and reasoning, as well as other higher mental functions resulting from the accumulation of abnormalities called Lewy bodies throughout the brain.

neurodevelopmental disorders Conditions that begin in childhood and have a major impact on social and cognitive functioning.

neurodevelopmental hypothesis Theory proposing that schizophrenia is a disorder of development that arises during adolescence or early adulthood due to alterations in the genetic control of brain maturation.

neurofibrillary tangles A characteristic of Alzheimer's disease in which the material within the cell bodies of neurons becomes filled with densely packed, twisted protein microfibrils, or tiny strands.

neuroimaging Assessment method that provides a picture of the brain's structures or level of activity and therefore is a useful tool for "looking" at the brain.

neuroleptics A term used to refer to antipsychotic medications.

neuroplasticity Adaptive changes in the brain in response to experience.

neuropsychological assessment A performance-based method assessing cognitive functioning used to examine the cognitive consequences of brain damage, brain disease, and severe mental illness.

neurotransmitter A chemical substance released from a neuron into the synaptic cleft, where it drifts across the synapse and is absorbed by the receiving neuron.

nicotine The psychoactive substance found in cigarettes.

O

object relations A psychodynamically oriented theory that focuses on the relationships people have with the others ("objects") in their lives.

obsession An unwanted thought, word, phrase, or image that persistently and repeatedly comes into a person's mind and causes distress.

obsessive-compulsive disorder (OCD) An anxiety disorder characterized by recurrent obsessions or compulsions that are inordinately time-consuming or that cause significant distress or impairment.

obsessive-compulsive personality disorder (OCPD) A personality disorder involving intense perfectionism and inflexibility manifested in worrying, indecisiveness, and behavioral rigidity.

Oedipus complex According to Freud, the child's feelings toward the opposite-sex parent peak in early childhood.

operant conditioning A learning process in which an individual acquires a response by learning to pair a behavior with its consequences.

opioid A psychoactive substance that relieves pain.

oppositional defiant disorder A disorder characterized by angry or irritable mood, argumentative or defiant behavior, and vindictiveness that results in significant family or school problems.

P

panic attack A period of intense fear and physical discomfort accompanied by the feeling that one is being overwhelmed and is about to lose control.

panic-control therapy (PCT) Treatment that consists of cognitive restructuring, exposure to bodily cues associated with panic attacks, and breathing retraining.

panic disorder An anxiety disorder in which an individual has panic attacks on a recurrent basis or has constant apprehension and worry about the possibility of recurring attacks.

paranoia The irrational belief or perception that others wish to cause you harm.

paranoid personality disorder A personality disorder whose outstanding feature is that the individual is unduly suspicious of others and is always on guard against potential danger or harm.

paraphilias Behaviors in which an individual has recurrent, intense sexually arousing fantasies, sexual urges, or behaviors involving (1) nonhuman objects, (2) children or other nonconsenting persons, or (3) the suffering or humiliation of self or partner.

paraphilic disorder Diagnosis in which a paraphilia causes distress and impairment.

parasuicide Attempted suicide, often a call for help.

parens patriae The state's authority to protect those who are unable to protect themselves.

partialism A paraphilic disorder in which the person is interested solely in sexual gratification from a specific body part, such as feet.

participant modeling A form of therapy in which the therapist first shows the client a desired behavior and then guides the client through the behavioral change.

pathways model Approach to gambling disorder which predicts that there are three main developmental paths leading to three distinct subtypes.

patient In the medical model, a person who receives treatment.

pedophilic disorder A paraphilic disorder in which an adult is sexually aroused by children or adolescents.

persecutory type of delusional disorder Delusional disorder in which individuals falsely believe that someone close to them is treating them in a malevolent manner.

persistent depressive disorder (dysthymia) Chronic but less severe mood disturbance in which the individual does not experience a major depressive episode.

personality disorder Ingrained patterns of relating to other people, situations, and events involving a rigid and maladaptive pattern of inner experience and behavior, dating back to adolescence or early adulthood.

personality trait An enduring pattern of perceiving, relating to, and thinking about the environment and others.

person-centered theory The humanistic theory that focuses on the uniqueness of each individual, the importance of allowing each individual to achieve maximum fulfillment of potential, and the need for the individual to honestly confront the reality of his or her experiences in the world.

peyote A form of a hallucinogenic drug whose primary ingredient is mescaline.

pharmacogenetics The use of genetic testing to identify who will and will not improve with a particular medication.

phencyclidine (PCP) A form of a hallucinogenic drug originally developed as an intravenous anesthetic.

phenotype The expression of the genetic program in the individual's physical and psychological attributes.

phenylketonuria (PKU) Condition in which children are born missing an enzyme called phenylalanine hydroxase.

phobia An irrational fear associated with a particular object or situation.

pica A condition in which a person eats inedible substances, such as dirt or feces; commonly associated with intellectual developmental disabilities.

Pick's disease A relatively rare degenerative disease that affects the frontal and temporal lobes of the cerebral cortex and that can cause neurocognitive disorders.

placebo condition Condition in an experiment in which participants receive a treatment similar to the experimental treatment, but lacking the key feature of the treatment of interest.

placebo-controlled randomized clinical trial Experimental method in which participants are randomly assigned to a placebo versus treatment group.

pleasure principle In psychoanalytic theory, a motivating force that seeks the immediate and total gratification of sensual needs and desires.

polygenic A model of inheritance in which more than one gene participates in the process of determining a given characteristic.

polysomnography A sleep study that records brain waves, blood oxygen levels, heart rate, breathing, eye movements, and leg movements.

positive psychology Perspective that emphasizes the potential for growth and change throughout life.

positive symptoms The symptoms of schizophrenia that represent exaggerations or distortions of normal thoughts, emotions, and behavior.

positron emission tomography (PET) scan A measure of brain activity in which a small amount of radioactive compounds is injected into an individual's bloodstream, following which a computer measures the varying levels of radiation in different parts of the brain and yields a multicolored image.

postconcussion syndrome (PCS) A disorder in which a constellation of physical, emotional, and cognitive symptoms persists from weeks to years.

post-traumatic growth The personal growth that can occur following exposure to a traumatic experience.

post-traumatic stress disorder (PTSD) An anxiety disorder in which the individual experiences several distressing symptoms for more than a month following a traumatic event, such as a reexperiencing of the traumatic event, an avoidance of reminders of the trauma, a numbing of general responsiveness, and increased arousal.

potentiation The combination of the effects of two or more psychoactive substances such that the total effect is greater than the effect of either substance alone.

premature (early) ejaculation A sexual dysfunction in which a man reaches orgasm well before he wishes to, perhaps even prior to penetration.

premenstrual dysphoric disorder (PMDD) Changes in mood, irritability, dysphoria, and anxiety that occur during the premenstrual phase of the monthly menstrual cycle and subside after the menstrual period begins for most of the cycles of the preceding year.

prevalence The number of people who have ever had a disorder at a given time or over a specified period.

primary gain The relief from anxiety or responsibility due to the development of physical or psychological symptoms.

principal diagnosis The disorder most closely aligned with the primary reason the individual is seeking professional help.

prion disease A disease caused by an abnormal protein particle that infects brain tissue.

problem-focused coping Coping in which the individual takes action to reduce stress by changing whatever it is about the situation that makes it stressful.

projective test A technique in which the test-taker is presented with an ambiguous item or task and is asked to respond by providing his or her own meaning or perception.

proton magnetic resonance spectroscopy (MRS) A scanning method that measures metabolic activity of neurons and therefore may indicate areas of brain damage.

pseudodementia Literally, false neurocognitive disorder, or a set of symptoms caused by depression that mimic those apparent in the early stages of Alzheimer's disease.

psilocybin A form of a hallucinogenic drug found in certain mushrooms.

psychiatrist Person with a degree in medicine (MD) who receives specialized advanced training in diagnosing and treating people with psychological disorders.

psychodynamic perspective The theoretical orientation in psychology that emphasizes unconscious determinants of behavior.

psychoeducation Professionally delivered treatment that integrates psychotherapeutic with educational interventions.

psychological assessment A broad range of measurement techniques, all of which involve having people provide scorable information about their psychological functioning.

psychological factors affecting other medical conditions Disorder in which clients have a medical disease or symptom that appears to be exacerbated by psychological or behavioral factors.

psychologist Licensed health care professional offering psychological services.

psychopathy A cluster of traits that form the core of the antisocial personality.

psychosexual stages According to psychoanalytic theory, the normal sequence of development through which each individual passes between infancy and adulthood.

psychosurgery A form of brain surgery, the purpose of which is to reduce psychological disturbance.

purging Eliminating food through unnatural methods, such as vomiting or the excessive use of laxatives.

pyromania An impulse-control disorder involving the persistent and compelling urge to start fires.

Q

qualitative research A method of analyzing data in which researchers use rigorous methods to code the data and summarize information in a way that reflects an objectively applied set of standards.

R

randomized controlled trial (RCT) Experimental method in which participants are randomly assigned to intervention groups.

reactive attachment disorder A disorder involving a severe disturbance in the ability to relate to others in which the individual is unresponsive to people, is apathetic, and prefers to be alone rather than to interact with friends or family.

reality principle In psychoanalyic theory, the motivational force that leads the individual to confront the constraints of the external world.

reinforcement In operant conditioning, the outcome that makes the individual more likely to repeat the behavior in the future.

relapse prevention A treatment method in which individuals are encouraged not to view lapses from abstinence as signs of certain failure.

relaxation training A behavioral technique used in the treatment of anxiety disorders that involves progressive and systematic patterns of muscle tensing and relaxing.

reliability When used with regard to diagnosis, the degree to which clinicians provide diagnoses consistently across individuals who have a particular set of symptoms.

remission Situation in which the individual's symptoms no longer interfere with his or her behavior and are below those required for a *DSM* diagnosis.

restricted affect Narrowing of the range of outward expressions of emotions.

retrograde amnesia Amnesia involving loss of memory for past events.

Rett syndrome A condition in which the child develops normally early in life (up to age 4) and then begins to show neurological and cognitive impairments including deceleration of head growth and some of the symptoms of autism spectrum disorder.

right to treatment Legal right of person entering psychiatric hospital to receive appropriate care.

Rorschach Inkblot Test Projective assessment method in which individuals describe their perceptions of each of a set of symmetrical inkblots.

rumination disorder An eating disorder in which the infant or child regurgitates food after it has been swallowed and then either spits it out or reswallows it.

S

schizoaffective disorder A disorder involving the experience of a major depressive episode, a manic episode, or a mixed episode while also meeting the diagnostic criteria for schizophrenia.

schizoid personality disorder A personality disorder primarily characterized by an indifference to social relationships, as well as a limited range of emotional experience and expression.

schizophrenia A disorder with a range of symptoms involving disturbances in content of thought, form of thought, perception, affect, sense of self, motivation, behavior, and interpersonal functioning.

schizophrenia spectrum Range of disorders that reflect a similar underlying disease process as that involved in schizophrenia.

schizophreniform disorder A disorder characterized by psychotic symptoms that are essentially the same as those found in schizophrenia, except for their duration; specifically, symptoms usually last from 1 to 6 months.

schizotypal personality disorder A personality disorder that primarily involves odd beliefs, behavior, appearance, and interpersonal style. People with this disorder may have bizarre ideas or preoccupations, such as magical thinking and beliefs in psychic phenomena.

scientific explanations Explanations that regard psychological disorders as the result of causes that we can objectively measure, such as biological alterations, faulty learning processes, or emotional stressors.

scientific method The process of testing ideas about the nature of psychological phenomena without bias before accepting these ideas as adequate explanations.

secondary gain The sympathy and attention that a sick person receives from other people.

secondary process thinking In psychoanalytic theory, the kind of thinking involved in logical and rational problem solving.

secretases Enzymes that trim part of the APP remaining outside the neuron so that it is flush with the neuron's outer membrane.

sedative A psychoactive substance that has a calming effect on the central nervous system.

selective mutism A disorder originating in childhood in which the individual consciously refuses to talk.

self-actualization In humanistic theory, the maximum realization of the individual's potential for psychological growth.

self-efficacy The individual's perception of competence in various life situations.

self-monitoring A self-report technique in which the client keeps a record of the frequency of specified behaviors.

self-report clinical inventory A psychological test with standardized questions having fixed response categories that the test-taker completes independently, self-reporting the extent to which the responses are accurate characterizations.

sensate focus Method of treating sexual dysfunction in which the interaction is not intended to lead to orgasm but to experience pleasurable sensations during the phases prior to orgasm.

separation anxiety disorder A childhood disorder characterized by intense and inappropriate anxiety, lasting at least 4 weeks, concerning separation from home or caregivers.

sexual dysfunction An abnormality in an individual's sexual responsiveness and reactions.

sexual masochism disorder A paraphilic disorder marked by an attraction to achieving sexual gratification by having painful stimulation applied to one's own body.

sexual sadism disorder A paraphilic disorder in which sexual gratification is derived from activities that harm, or from urges to harm, another person.

shared psychotic disorder Delusional disorder in which one or more people develop a delusional system as a result of a close relationship with a psychotic person who is delusional.

single case experimental design (SCED) Design in which the same person serves as the subject in both the experimental and control conditions.

single nucleotide polymorphism (SNP) A small genetic variation that can occur in a person's DNA sequence.

single photon emission computed tomography (SPECT) scan A variant of the PET scan that allows a longer and more detailed imaging analysis to be performed.

social (pragmatic) communication disorder Disorder involving deficits in the ability to use verbal and nonverbal communication in relating to others.

social anxiety disorder An anxiety disorder characterized by marked, or intense, fear or anxiety in social situations in which the individual may be scrutinized by others.

social discrimination Prejudicial treatment of a class of individuals, seen in the sociocultural perspective as a cause of psychological problems.

social learning theory Perspective that focuses on understanding how people develop psychological disorders through their relationships with others and through observation of other people.

sociocultural perspective The theoretical perspective that emphasizes the ways that individuals are influenced by people, social institutions, and social forces in the world around them.

somatic symptom disorder A disorder involving physical symptoms that may or may not be accounted for a medical condition and accompanied by maladaptive thoughts, feelings, and behaviors.

somatic symptoms Symptoms involving physical problems and/or concerns about medical symptoms.

somatic type of delusional disorder Delusional disorder in which individuals falsely believe that they have a medical condition.

specific learning disorder A delay or deficit in an academic skill that is evident when an individual's achievement and skills are substantially below what would be expected for others of comparable age, education, and level of intelligence.

specific learning disorder with impairment in mathematics A learning disorder in which the individual has difficulty with tasks and concepts involving numbers and numerical reasoning.

specific learning disorder with impairment in reading (dyslexia) A learning disorder in which the individual omits, distorts, or substitutes words when reading and reads in a slow, halting fashion.

specific learning disorder with impairment in written expression A learning disorder in which the individual's writing is characterized by poor spelling, grammatical or punctuation errors, and disorganization of paragraphs.

specific phobia An irrational and unabating fear of a particular object, activity, or situation.

speech sound disorder A communication disorder in which the individual substitutes, omits, or misarticulates speech sounds.

spiritual explanations Explanations that regard psychological disorders as the product of possession by evil or demonic spirits.

splitting A defense, common in people with borderline personality disorder, in which individuals perceive others, or themselves, as being all good or all bad, usually resulting in disturbed interpersonal relationships.

standardization A psychometric criterion that clearly specifies a test's instructions for administration and scoring.

stereotypic movement disorder A disorder in which the individual engages in repetitive, seemingly driven nonfunctional behaviors.

stigma A negative label that causes certain people to be regarded as different, defective, and set apart from mainstream members of society.

stimulant A psychoactive substance that has an activating effect on the central nervous system.

stress The unpleasant emotional reaction that a person has when an event is perceived as threatening.

stressful life event An event that disrupts the individual's life.

Structured Clinical Interview for *DSM-5* Disorders (SCID-5) A structured clinical interview developed to assess *DSM-5* symptoms.

structured interview A standardized series of assessment questions, with a predetermined wording and order.

substance A chemical that alters a person's mood or behavior when it is smoked, injected, drunk, inhaled, snorted, or swallowed.

substance intoxication The temporary maladaptive experience of behavioral or psychological changes that are due to the accumulation of a substance in the body.

substance use disorder A cluster of cognitive, behavioral, and physiological symptoms indicating that the individual uses a substance despite significant substance-related problems.

substituted judgment A doctrine that allows health professionals and family members to try to make the decision that the patient would have made if he or she were able to make decisions.

superego In psychoanalytic theory, the structure of personality that includes the conscience and the ego ideal.

survey A research tool used to gather information from a sample of people considered representative of a particular population, in which participants are asked to answer questions about the topic of concern.

systematic desensitization A variant of counterconditioning that involves presenting the client with progressively more anxiety-provoking images while in a relaxed state.

T

tardive dyskinesia Motor disorder that consists of involuntary movements of the mouth, arms, and trunk of the body.

target behavior A behavior of interest or concern in an assessment.

tau A protein that normally helps maintain the internal support structure of the axons.

Tay-Sachs disease An inherited disease that produces deficits in intellectual functioning due to a lack of hexosaminidase A, an enzyme that helps break down an otherwise toxic chemical in nervous tissue called ganglioside.

teratogens Environmental hazards mothers experience while pregnant that affect the developing child.

Thematic Apperception Test (TAT) A projective test in which individuals invent a story to explain what is happening in a set of ambiguous pictures.

theoretical perspective An orientation to understanding the causes of human behavior and the treatment of psychological disorders.

tic A rapid, recurring, involuntary movement or vocalization.

token economy A form of contingency management in which a client who performs desired activities earns tokens that can later be exchanged for tangible benefits.

tolerance The extent to which the individual requires larger and larger amounts of a substance in order to achieve its desired effects, or the extent to which the individual feels less of its effects after using the same amount of the substance.

Tourette's disorder A disorder involving a combination of chronic motor and vocal tics.

transference The carrying over of feelings that clients have from their parents to their therapists.

transference-focused psychotherapy A treatment for borderline personality disorder that uses the client–clinician relationship as the framework for helping clients achieve greater understanding of their unconscious feelings and motives.

transgender Referring to the identity of a person whose assigned gender does not correspond with their gender identity.

transphobia The negative stereotyping and fear of transgender individuals.

transsexualism A term sometimes used to refer to gender dysphoria, specifically pertaining to individuals choosing to undergo sex reassignment surgery.

transvestic disorder Diagnosis applied to individuals who engage in transvestic behavior and have the symptoms of a paraphilic disorder.

trauma A condition that results from circumstances experienced by an individual as harmful or life threatening and that has lasting adverse effects on the individual's functioning and mental health.

trauma informed care An approach to treatment that acknowledges the role that trauma can have on the mental health of individuals.

traumatic brain injury (TBI) Damage to the brain caused by exposure to trauma.

treatment plan The outline for how therapy should take place.

trephining The process of cutting a hole in the skull to allow so-called "evil spirits" to escape.

trichotillomania (hair-pulling disorder) An impulse-control disorder involving the compulsive, persistent urge to pull out one's own hair.

type A behavior pattern Set of behaviors that include being hard driving, competitive, impatient, cynical, suspicious of and hostile toward others, and easily irritated.

type D personality A personality type seen in those who experience emotions that include anxiety, irritation, and depressed mood.

U

unconditional positive regard A method in client-centered therapy in which the clinician gives total acceptance of what the client says, does, and feels.

unstructured interview A series of open-ended questions aimed at determining the client's reasons for being in treatment, symptoms, health status, family background, and life history.

uplifts Events that boost your feelings of well-being.

V

validity The extent to which a test, diagnosis, or rating accurately and distinctly characterizes a person's psychological status.

vascular neurocognitive disorder A form of neurocognitive disorder resulting from a vascular disease that causes deprivation of the blood supply to the brain.

vicarious reinforcement A form of learning in which a new behavior is acquired through the process of watching someone else receive reinforcement for the same behavior.

virtual reality exposure therapy (VRET) A method of exposure therapy that uses virtual reality, in which clients become immersed in computer-generated environments that resemble the situations they fear.

voyeuristic disorder A paraphilic disorder in which the individual has a compulsion to derive sexual gratification from observing the nudity or sexual activity of others.

vulnerability The idea that individuals have a biologically determined predisposition to developing schizophrenia but that the disorder develops only when certain environmental conditions are in place.

vulnerable narcissism The form of narcissistic personality disorder in which individuals have an internally weak sense of self and so become despondent when they feel that someone who is important to them is humiliating or betraying them.

W

Wechsler Adult Intelligence Scale (WAIS) The first comprehensive individual test that researchers specifically designed to measure adult intelligence.

Wernicke's disease A reversible form of neurocognitive disorder associated with long-term alcohol use.

withdrawal Physiological and psychological changes that occur when an individual stops taking a substance.

Z

Z codes Codes in the *ICD* that indicate the presence of psychosocial and environmental problems.

REFERENCES

A

Abé, C., Ekman, C., Sellgren, C., Petrovic, P., Ingvar, M., & Landén, M. (2015). Manic episodes are related to changes in frontal cortex: A longitudinal neuroimaging study of bipolar disorder 1. *Brain: A Journal of Neurology, 138*(11), 3440-3448. doi:10.1093/brain/awv266

Abelson, J. F., Kwan, K. Y., O'Roak, B. J., Baek, D. Y., Stillman, A. A., Morgan, T. M., . . . State, M. (2005). Sequence variants in SLITRK1 are associated with Tourette's syndrome. *Science, 310,* 317-320.

Aboujaoude, E., Gamel, N., & Koran, L. M. (2004). Overview of kleptomania and phenomenological description of 40 patients. *Primary Care Companion Journal of Clinical Psychiatry, 6,* 244-247.

Abraham, K. (1911/1968). Notes on the psychoanalytic investigation and treatment of manic-depressive insanity and allied conditions. In K. Abraham (Ed.), *Selected papers of Karl Abraham.* New York: Basic Books.

Abram, S. V., Wisner, K. M., Fox, J. M., Barch, D. M., Wang, L., Csernansky, J. G., . . . Smith, M. J. (2017). Fronto-temporal connectivity predicts cognitive empathy deficits and experiential negative symptoms in schizophrenia. *Human Brain Mapping, 38*(3), 1111-1124. doi:10.1002/hbm.23439

Achterhof, R., Dorahy, M. J., Rowlands, A., Renouf, C., Britt, E., & Carter, J. D. (2018). Predictors of posttraumatic growth 10-11 months after a fatal earthquake. *Psychological Trauma: Theory, Research, Practice, and Policy, 10*(2), 208-215. doi:10.1037/tra0000286

Adler, L. A., Barkley, R. A., Wilens, T. E., & Ginsberg, D. L. (2006). Differential diagnosis of attention-deficit/hyperactivity disorder and comorbid conditions. *Primary Psychiatry, 13,* 1-14.

Ahrberg, M., Trojca, D., Nasrawi, N., & Vocks, S. (2011). Body image disturbance in binge eating disorder: A review. *European Eating Disorders Review, 19,* 375-381.

Ainsworth, M. D. S., Blehar, M. C., Waters, E., & Wall, S. (1978). *Patterns of attachment: A psychological study of the strange situation.* Oxford, England: Lawrence Erlbaum.

Akehurst, S., & Thatcher, J. (2010). Narcissism, social anxiety, and self-presentation in exercise. *Personality and Individual Differences, 49,* 130-135.

Aliane, V., Pérez, S., Bohren, Y., Deniau, J.-M., & Kemel, M.-L. (2011). Key role of striatal cholinergic interneurons in processes leading to arrest of motor stereotypes. *Brain: A Journal of Neurology, 134,* 110-118.

Alpert, H. R., Connolly, G. N., & Biener, L. (2012). A prospective cohort study challenging the effectiveness of population-based medical intervention for smoking cessation. *Tobacco Control 22*(1):32-7. doi: 10.1136/tobaccocontrol-2011-050129. Epub 2012 Jan 10.

Altarac, M., & Saroha, E. (2007). Lifetime prevalence of learning disability among US children. *Pediatrics, 119,* S77-S83.

Altunoz, U., Kokurcan, A., Kirici, S., Bastug, G., & Ozel-Kizil, E. T. (2018). Clinical characteristics of generalized anxiety disorder: Older vs. young adults. *Nordic Journal of Psychiatry, 72*(2), 97-102. doi:10.1080/08039488.2017.1390607

Alzheimer, A. (1907/1987). About a peculiar disease of the cerebral cortex. *Alzheimer's Disease and Associated Disorders, 1,* 7-8.

Alzheimer's Association. (2018). 2018 Alzheimer's disease facts and figures. https://www.alz.org/media/HomeOffice/Facts%20and%20Figures/facts-and-figures.pdf (accessed 4/19/2018)

American Psychological Association. (2010). Ethical principles of psychologists and code of conduct. Retrieved from http://www.apa.org/ethics/code/index.aspx

American Psychiatric Association. (2013). *DSM-5: Diagnostic and statistical manual of mental disorders.* Washington, D.C: American Psychiatric Association.

American Psychological Association. (2015a). Guidelines for psychological practice with transgender and gender nonconforming people. *American Psychologist, 70* (9), 832-864. doi:10.1037/a0039906

American Psychological Association. (2015b). Retrieved from http://www.apa.org/news/press/releases/2015/08/psychologist-interrogations.aspx

American Psychological Association Presidential Task Force on Evidence-Based Practice. (2006). Evidence-based practice in psychology. *American Psychologist, 61,* 271-285.

Anderson, M. L., Ziedonis, D. M., & Najavits, L. M. (2014). Posttraumatic stress disorder and substance use disorder comorbidity among individuals with physical disabilities: Findings from the National Comorbidity Study Replication. *Journal of Traumatic Stress, 27*(2), 182-191. doi:10.1002/jts.21894

Andreasen, N. C. (2010). The lifetime trajectory of schizophrenia and the concept of neurodevelopment. *Dialogues in Clinical Neuroscience, 12,* 409-415.

Anton, R. F., O'Malley, S. S., Ciraulo, D. A., Cisler, R. A., Couper, D., Donovan, D. M., . . . Zweben, A. (2006). Combined pharmacotherapies and behavioral interventions for alcohol dependence: The COMBINE study: A randomized controlled trial. *Journal of the American Medical Association, 295,* 2003-2017.

Arch, J. J., Eifert, G. H., Davies, C., Vilardaga, J. C. P., Rose, R. D., & Craske, M. G. (2012). Randomized clinical trial of cognitive behavioral therapy (CBT) versus acceptance and commitment therapy (ACT) for mixed anxiety disorders. *Journal of Consulting and Clinical Psychology, 80*(5), 750.

Arias, A. J., & Kranzler, H. R. (2008). Treatment of co-occurring alcohol and other drug use disorders. *Alcohol Research & Health, 31,* 155-167.

Arria, A. M., Caldeira, K. M., Bugbee, B. A., Vincent, K. B., & O'Grady, K. E. (2017). Trajectories of energy drink consumption and subsequent drug use during young adulthood. *Drug and Alcohol Dependence, 179,* 424-432. doi:10.1016/j.drugalcdep.2017.06.008

Assumpção, A. A., Garcia, F. D., Garcia, H. D., Bradford, J. W., & Thibaut, F. (2014). Pharmacologic treatment of paraphilias. *Psychiatric Clinics of North America, 37,* 173-181. doi:10.1016/j.psc.2014.03.002

Austin, A., & Craig, S. L. (2015). Transgender affirmative cognitive behavioral therapy: Clinical considerations and applications. *Professional Psychology: Research and Practice, 46*(1), 21.

Ayers, C. R., Najmi, S., Mayes, T. L., & Dozier, M. E. (2015). Hoarding disorder in older adulthood. *The American Journal of Geriatric Psychiatry, 23,* 416-422. doi:10.1016/j.jagp.2014.05.009

B

Bach, B., Markon, K., Simonsen, E., & Krueger, R. F. (2015). Clinical utility of the *DSM-5* alternative model of personality disorders: Six cases from practice. *Journal of Psychiatric Practice, 21,* 3-25. doi:10.1097/01.pra.0000460618.02805.ef

Bader, S. M., Schoeneman-Morris, K. A., Scalora, M. J., & Casady, T. K. (2008). Exhibitionism: Findings from a Midwestern police contact sample. *International Journal of Offender Therapy and Comparative Criminology, 52,* 270-279.

Baer, R. A., & Huss, D. B. (2008). Mindfulness- and acceptance-based therapy. In J. L. Lebow (Ed.), *Twenty-first century psychotherapies: Contemporary approaches to theory and practice,* (pp. 123-166). Hoboken, NJ: John Wiley & Sons Inc.

Balaratnasingam, S., & Janca, A. (2015). Normal personality, personality disorder and psychosis: Current views and future perspectives. *Current Opinion in Psychiatry, 28,* 30-34. doi:10.1097/YCO.0000000000000124

Bandura, A. (1971). Psychotherapy based upon modeling principles. In A. E. Bergin &

S. L. Garfield (Eds.), *Handbook of psychotherapy and behavior change* (pp. 653-708). New York: Wiley.

Banerjee, P., Grange, D. K., Steiner, R. D., & White, D. A. (2011). Executive strategic processing during verbal fluency performance in children with phenylketonuria. *Child Neuropsychology, 17,* 105-117.

Barbaree, H. E., & Blanchard, R. (2008). Sexual deviance over the lifespan: Reductions in deviant sexual behavior in the aging sex offender. In D. R. Laws & W. T. O'Donohue (Eds.), *Sexual deviance: Theory, assessment, and treatment* (2nd ed., pp. 37-60). New York: Guilford Press.

Barkley, R. A. (1997). *ADHD and the nature of self-control.* New York, NY: Guilford Press.

Barkley, R. A. (2017). What are the consequences of untreated ADHD? In R. A. Barkley (Ed.), *When an adult you love has ADHD: Professional advice for parents, partners, and siblings* (pp. 71-103). Washington, DC: American Psychological Association. doi:10.1037/15963-005

Barkley, R. A., & Murphy, K. R. (2011). The nature of executive function (EF) deficits in daily life activities in adults with ADHD and their relationship to performance on EF tests. *Journal of Psychopathology and Behavioral Assessment, 33,* 137-158.

Barsky, A. E., & Gould, J. W. (2002). *Clinicians in court: A guide to subpoenas, depositions, testifying, and everything else you need to know.* New York: Guilford Press.

Bartol, C. R., & Bartol, A. M. (2012). *Introduction to forensic psychology: Research and application.* Los Angeles, CA: Sage Publications.

Basson, R. (2001). Using a different model for female sexual response to address women's problematic low sexual desire. *Journal of Sex and Marital Therapy, 27,* 395-403.

Bastiaansen, L., Rossi, G., Schotte, C., & De Fruyt, F. (2011). The structure of personality disorders: Comparing the *DSM-IV-TR* axis II classification with the five-factor model framework using structural equation modeling. *Journal of Personality Disorders, 25,* 378-396.

Bayless, S. J., & Harvey, A. J. (2017). Testing Alcohol Myopia Theory: Examining the effects of alcohol intoxication on simultaneous central and peripheral attention. *Perception, 46*(1), 90-99. doi:10.1177/0301006616672221

Bearman, S. K., Wadkins, M., Bailin, A., & Doctoroff, G. (2015). Pre-practicum training in professional psychology to close the research-practice gap: Changing attitudes toward evidence-based practice. *Training and Education in Professional Psychology, 9*(1), 13-20. doi:10.1037/tep0000052

Bechara, A., Noel, X., & Crone, E. A. (2006). Loss of willpower: Abnormal neural mechanisms of impulse control and decision making in addiction. In R. W. Wiers & A. W. Stacy (Eds.), *Handbook of implicit cognition and addiction* (pp. 215-232). Thousand Oaks, CA: Sage Publications, Inc.

Beck, A. T. (1967). *Depression: Clinical, experimental, and theoretical aspects.* New York: Harper & Row.

Beck, A. T., Freeman, A., & Davis, D. D. (2004). *Cognitive therapy of personality disorders* (2nd ed.). New York: Guilford Press.

Beck, A. T., Rush, A. J., Shaw, B. F., & Emery, G. (1979). *Cognitive therapy of depression: A treatment manual.* New York: Guilford Press.

Beck, A. T., & Weishaar, M. (1989). Cognitive therapy. In A. Freeman, K. M. Simon, L. E. Beutler, & H. Arkowitz (Eds.), *Comprehensive handbook of cognitive therapy* (pp. 21-36). New York: Plenum Press.

Bedics, J. D., Atkins, D. C., Harned, M. S., & Linehan, M. M. (2015). The therapeutic alliance as a predictor of outcome in dialectical behavior therapy versus nonbehavioral psychotherapy by experts for borderline personality disorder. *Psychotherapy, 52,* 67-77. doi:10.1037/a0038457

Behary, W. T., & Dieckmann, E. (2013). Schema therapy for pathological narcissism: The art of adaptive reparenting. In J. S. Ogrodniczuk (Ed.), *Understanding and treating pathological narcissism* (pp. 285-300). Washington, DC: American Psychological Association. doi:10.1037/14041-017

Bemporad, J. R. (1985). Long-term analytic treatment of depression. In E. E. Beckham & W. R. Leber (Eds.), *Handbook of depression: Treatment, assessment, and research* (pp. 82-89). Homewood, IL: Dorsey Press.

Berger, L., Fendrich, M., & Fuhrmann, D. (2013). Alcohol mixed with energy drinks: Are there associated negative consequences beyond hazardous drinking in college students? *Addictive Behaviors, 38,* 2428-2432. http://dx.doi.org/10.1016/j.addbeh.2013.04.003

Berger, W., Mendlowicz, M. V., Marques-Portella, C., Kinrys, G., Fontenelle, L. F., Marmar, C. R., & Figuera, I. (2009). Pharmacologic alternatives to antidepressants in posttraumatic stress disorder: A systematic review. *Progress in Neuro-Psychopharmacology & Biological Psychiatry, 33,* 169-180.

Bergeron, S., Morin, M., & Lord, M.-J. (2010). Integrating pelvic floor rehabilitation and cognitive-behavioural therapy for sexual pain: What have we learned and were do we go from here? *Sexual and Relationship Therapy, 25,* 289-298.

Berlin, F. S. (2014). Pedophilia and *DSM-5*: The importance of clearly defining the nature of a pedophilic disorder. *Journal of the American Academy of Psychiatry and the Law, 42,* 404-407.

Berrettini, W., & Lohoff, F. W. (2017). Genetics of bipolar and unipolar disorders. In R. J. DeRubeis & D. R. Strunk (Eds.), *The Oxford handbook of mood disorders* (pp. 111-119). New York: Oxford University Press.

Bertrand, J., Floyd, R. L., Weber, M. K., O'Connor, M., Riley, E. P., Johnson, K. A., & Cohen, D. E. (2004). *Fetal alcohol syndrome: Guidelines for referral and diagnosis.* Atlanta: National Task Force on FAS/FAE.

Besser, A., & Priel, B. (2010). Grandiose narcissism versus vulnerable narcissism in threatening situations: Emotional reactions to achievement failure and interpersonal rejection. *Journal of Social and Clinical Psychology, 29,* 874-902.

Beyer, K. M., Szabo, A., Hoormann, K., & Stolley, M. (2018). Time spent outdoors, activity levels, and chronic disease among American adults. *Journal of Behavioral Medicine, 1*(4), 494-503. doi:10.1007/s10865-018-9911-1

Biederman, J., Mick, E., Faraone, S. V., & Burback, M. (2001). Patterns of remission and symptom decline in conduct disorder: A four-year prospective study of an ADHD sample. *Journal of the American Academy of Child & Adolescent Psychiatry, 40,* 290-298.

Bjornsson, A. S., Didie, E. R., & Phillips, K. A. (2010). Body dysmorphic disorder. *Dialogues in Clinical Neuroscience, 12,* 221-232.

Blanchard, R. (2010). The *DSM* diagnostic criteria for transvestic fetishism. *Archives of Sexual Behavior, 39,* 363-372.

Blashfield, R. K., Reynolds, S. M., & Stennett, B. (2012). The death of histrionic personality disorder. In T. A. Widiger (Ed.), *The Oxford handbook of personality disorders* (pp. 603-627). New York: Oxford University Press. doi:10.1093/oxfordhb/9780199735013.013.0028

Boe, H. J., Holgersen, K. H., & Holen, A. (2011). Mental health outcomes and predictors of chronic disorders after the North Sea oil rig disaster: 27-year longitudinal follow-up study. *Journal of Nervous and Mental Disease, 199,* 49-54.

Boeckle, M., Liegl, G., Jank, R., & Pieh, C. (2016). Neural correlates of conversion disorder: Overview and meta-analysis of neuroimaging studies on motor conversion disorder. *BMC Psychiatry, 16,* 195.

Boettger, S., Breitbart, W., & Passik, S. (2011). Haloperidol and risperidone in the treatment of delirium and its subtypes. *The European Journal of Psychiatry, 25,* 59-67.

Bomyea, J., Ramsawh, H., Ball, T. M., Taylor, C. T., Paulus, M. P., Lang, A. J., & Stein, M. B. (2015). Intolerance of uncertainty as a mediator of reductions in worry in a cognitive behavioral treatment program for generalized anxiety disorder. *Journal of Anxiety Disorders, 3390-3394.* doi:10.1016/j.janxdis.2015.05.004

Bond, K., & Anderson, I. M. (2015). Psychoeducation for relapse prevention in bipolar disorder: A systematic review of efficacy in randomized controlled trials. *Bipolar Disorders, 17,* 349-362. doi:10.1111/bdi.12287

Bonifacci, P., Storti, M., Tobia, V., & Suardi, A. (2016). Specific learning disorders: A look inside children's and parents' psychological well-being and relationships. *Journal of Learning Disabilities, 49*(5), 532-545. doi:10.1177/0022219414566681

Borkovec, T. D., & Ruscio, A. M. (2001). Psychotherapy for generalized anxiety disorder. *Journal of Clinical Psychiatry, 62,* S37-S42.

Both, S., Laan, E., & Schultz, W. W. (2010). Disorders in sexual desire and sexual arousal in women, a 2010 state of the art. *Journal of Psychosomatic Obstetrics & Gynecology, 31,* 207-218.

Bowden, C. L. (2005). Treatment options for bipolar depression. *Journal of Clinical Psychiatry, 66,* S3-S6.

Bowlby, J. (1980). *Attachment and loss: Vol. III. Loss: Sadness and depression.* New York: Basic Books.

Brauer, L., & Reinecke, M. A. (2015). Dependent personality disorder. In A. T. Beck, D. D. Davis, & A. Freeman (Eds.), *Cognitive therapy of personality disorders* (3rd ed., pp. 155-173). New York: Guilford Press.

Breggin, P. R., & Barkley, R. A. (2005). Issue 11: Is Ritalin overprescribed? In R. P. Halgin (Ed.), *Taking sides: Clashing views on controversial issues in abnormal psychology* (3rd ed., pp. 176-195). New York: McGraw-Hill.

Brotto, L. A. (2010). The *DSM* diagnostic criteria for hypoactive sexual desire disorder in women. *Archives of Sexual Behavior, 39,* 221-239.

Brown, K. W., & Ryan, R. M. (2003). The benefits of being present: Mindfulness and its role in psychological well-being. *Journal of Personality and Social Psychology, 84*(4), 822.

Brown, L. A., Fernandez, C. A., Kohn, R., Saldivia, S., & Vicente, B. (2018). Pre-disaster PTSD as a moderator of the relationship between natural disaster and suicidal ideation over time. *Journal of Affective Disorders, 230,* 7-14. doi:10.1016/j.jad.2017.12.096

Brown, M. L., Pope, A. W., & Brown, E. J. (2011). Treatment of primary nocturnal enuresis in children: A review. *Child: Care, Health and Development, 37,* 153-160.

Brown, T. A., & Rosellini, A. J. (2011). The direct and interactive effects of neuroticism and life stress on the severity and longitudinal course of depressive symptoms. *Journal of Abnormal Psychology, 120,* 844-856.

Bryant-Waugh, R., Markham, L., Kreipe, R. E., & Walsh, B. T. (2010). Feeding and eating disorders in childhood. *International Journal of Eating Disorders, 43,* 98-111.

Budman, E., Deeb, W., Martinez-Ramirez, D., Pilitsis, J. G., Peng-Chen, Z., Okun, M. S., & Ramirez-Zamora, A. (2018). Potential indications for deep brain stimulation in neurological disorders: An evolving field. *European Journal of Neurology, 25*(3), 434-e30. doi:10.1111/ene.13548

Büttner, G., & Shamir, A. (2011). Learning disabilities: Causes, consequences, and responses. *International Journal of Disability, Development and Education, 58,* 1-4.

C

Caligor, E., Levy, K. N., & Yeomans, F. E. (2015). Narcissistic personality disorder: Diagnostic and clinical challenges. *The American Journal of Psychiatry, 172,* 415-422. doi:10.1176/appi.ajp.2014.14060723

Callahan, C. M., Boustani, M. A., Unverzagt, F. W., Austrom, M. G., Damush, T. M., Perkins, A. J., . . . Hendrie, H. C. (2006). Effectiveness of collaborative care for older adults with Alzheimer disease in primary care: A randomized controlled trial. *Journal of the American Medical Association, 295,* 2148-2157.

Campbell, W. G. (2003). Addiction: A disease of volition caused by a cognitive impairment. *Canadian Journal of Psychiatry, 48,* 669-674.

Canino, G., Polanczyk, G., Bauermeister, J. J., Rohde, L. A., & Frick, P. J. (2010). Does the prevalence of CD and ODD vary across cultures? *Social Psychiatry and Psychiatric Epidemiology, 45,* 695-704.

Carlson, K. F., Nelson, D., Orazem, R. J., Nugent, S., Cifu, D. X., & Sayer, N. A. (2010). Psychiatric diagnoses among Iraq and Afghanistan war veterans screened for deployment-related traumatic brain injury. *Journal of Traumatic Stress, 23,* 17-24.

Carmody, J., Reed, G., Kristeller, J., & Merriam, P. (2008). Mindfulness, spirituality, and health-related symptoms. *Journal of Psychosomatic Research, 64,* 393-403.

Carpenter, J. K., Andrews, L. A., Witcraft, S. M., Powers, M. B., Smits, J. J., & Hofmann, S. G. (2018). Cognitive behavioral therapy for anxiety and related disorders: A meta-analysis of randomized placebo-controlled trials. *Depression and Anxiety, 35*(6), 502-514. doi:10.1002/da.22728

Carrasco, M. M., Aguera, L., Gil, P., Morinigo, A., & Leon, T. (2011). Safety and effectiveness of donepezil on behavioral symptoms in patients with Alzheimer disease. *Alzheimer Disease and Associated Disorders, 25,* 333-340.

Carroll, K. M. (2011). Cognitive-behavioral therapies. In M. Galanter & H. D. Kleber (Eds.), *Psychotherapy for the treatment of substance abuse* (pp. 175-192). Arlington, VA: American Psychiatric Publishing, Inc.

Caselli, I., Poloni, N., Ielmini, M., Diurni, M., & Callegari, C. (2017). Epidemiology and evolution of the diagnostic classification of factitious disorders in *DSM-5. Psychology Research and Behavior Management, 10,* 387-394. doi:10.2147/PRBM.S153377

Caspi, A., Moffitt, T. E., Cannon, M., McClay, J., Murray, R., Harrington, H., . . . Craig, I. W. (2005). Moderation of the effect of adolescent-onset cannabis use on adult psychosis by a functional polymorphism in the catechol-O-methyltransferase gene: Longitudinal evidence of a gene X environment interaction. *Biological Psychiatry, 57,* 1117-1127.

Centers for Disease Control and Prevention. (2011a). Fetal alcohol spectrum disorders. Retrieved from http://www.cdc.gov/ncbddd/fasd/data.html

Centers for Disease Control and Prevention. (2011b). Suicide: Definitions, from http://www.cdc.gov/violenceprevention/suicide/definitions.html

Centers for Disease Control and Prevention. (2015a). Autism spectrum disorder (ASD). Retrieved from http://www.cdc.gov/ncbddd/autism/data.html

Centers for Disease Control and Prevention. (2015b). Developmental disabilities. Retrieved from http://www.cdc.gov/ncbddd/developmentaldisabilities/features/birthdefects-dd-keyfindings.html

Centers for Disease Control and Prevention. (2018). ICD-10-CM Official Guidelines for Coding and Reporting. https://www.cdc.gov/nchs/icd/icd10cm.htm (accessed 1/2/2018)

Chapel, J. M., Ritchey, M. D., Zhang, D., & Wang, G. (2017). Prevalence and medical costs of chronic diseases among adult Medicaid beneficiaries. *American Journal of Preventive Medicine, 53*(6, Suppl 2), S143-S154. doi:10.1016/j.amepre.2017.07.019

Chmielewski, M., Bagby, R. M., Markon, K., Ring, A. J., & Ryder, A. G. (2014). Openness to experience, intellect, schizotypal personality disorder, and psychoticism: Resolving the controversy. *Journal of Personality Disorders, 28,* 483-499. doi:10.1521/pedi_2014_28_128

Choy, Y., Fyer, A. J., & Lipsitz, J. D. (2007). Treatment of specific phobia in adults. *Clinical Psychology Review, 27,* 266-286.

Christianini, A. R., Conti, M. A., Hearst, N., Cordás, T. A., de Abreu, C. N., & Tavares, H. (2015). Treating kleptomania: Cross-cultural adaptation of the Kleptomania Symptom Assessment Scale and assessment of an outpatient program. *Comprehensive Psychiatry, 56,* 289-294. doi:10.1016/j.comppsych.2014.09.013

Ciao, A. C., Accurso, E. C., Fitzsimmons-Craft, E. E., & Le Grange, D. (2015). Predictors and moderators of psychological changes during the treatment of adolescent bulimia nervosa. *Behaviour Research and Therapy, 69,* 48-53. doi:10.1016/j.brat.2015.04.002

Clark, M. L., Waters, F., Vatskalis, T. M., & Jablensky, A. (2017). On the interconnectedness and prognostic value of visual and auditory hallucinations in first-episode psychosis. *European Psychiatry, 41,* 122-128. doi:10.1016/j.eurpsy.2016.10.011

Clark, S. K., Jeglic, E. L., Calkins, C., & Tatar, J. R. (2016). More than a nuisance: The prevalence and consequences of frotteurism and exhibitionism. *Sexual Abuse: Journal of Research and Treatment, 28*(1), 3–19. doi:10.1177/1079063214525643

Clayton, A. H., & Valladares Juarez, E. M. (2017). Female sexual dysfunction. *Psychiatric Clinics of North America, 40*(2), 267–284. doi:10.1016/j.psc.2017.01.004

Clement, S., Schauman, O., Graham, T., Maggioni, F., Evans-Lacko, S., Bezborodovs, N., . . . Thornicroft, G. (2015). What is the impact of mental health-related stigma on help-seeking? A systematic review of quantitative and qualitative studies. *Psychological Medicine, 45*, 11–27. doi:10.1017/S0033291714000129

Coccaro, E. F. (2010). A family history study of intermittent explosive disorder. *Journal of Psychiatric Research, 44*, 1101–1105.

Coccaro, E. F., Fanning, J. R., Keedy, S. K., & Lee, R. J. (2016). Social cognition in intermittent explosive disorder and aggression. *Journal of Psychiatric Research, 83*, 140–150. doi:10.1016/j.jpsychires.2016.07.010

Coccaro, E. F., Lee, R. J., & Kavoussi, R. J. (2009). A double-blind, randomized, placebo-controlled trial of fluoxetine in patients with intermittent explosive disorder. *Journal of Clinical Psychiatry, 70*, 653–662.

Coccaro, E. F., Lee, R., & Kavoussi, R. J. (2010). Inverse relationship between numbers of 5-HT transporter binding sites and life history of aggression and intermittent explosive disorder. *Journal of Psychiatric Research, 44*, 137–142.

Cocchi, L., Harrison, B. J., Pujol, J., Harding, I. H., Fornito, A., Pantelis, C., et al. (2012). Functional alterations of large-scale brain networks related to cognitive control in obsessive-compulsive disorder. *Human Brain Mapping, 33*(5), 1089–1106.

Coelho, C. M., Goncalves, D. C., Purkis, H., Pocinho, M., Pachana, N. A., & Byrne, G. J. (2010). Specific phobias in older adults: Characteristics and differential diagnosis. *International Psychogeriatrics, 22*, 702–711.

Cohen, A. S., Auster, T. L., MacAulay, R. K., & McGovern, J. E. (2014). Illusory superiority and schizotypal personality: Explaining the discrepancy between subjective/objective psychopathology. *Personality Disorders: Theory, Research, and Treatment, 5*, 413–418. doi:10.1037/per0000080

Cohen-Kettenis, P. T., & Pfafflin, F. (2010). The *DSM* diagnostic criteria for gender identity disorder in adolescents and adults. *Archives of Sexual Behavior, 39*, 499–513.

Cole, C. S. (2011). Sleep and primary care of adults and older adults. In N. S. Redeker & G. McEnany (Eds.), *Sleep disorders and sleep promotion in nursing practice* (pp. 291–308). New York: Springer Publishing Co.

Coleman, E., Bockting, W., Botzer, M., Cohen-Kettenis, P., DeCuypere, G., Feldman, J., . . . Monstrey, S. (2012). Standards of care for the health of transsexual, transgender, and gender-nonconforming people, version 7. *International Journal of Transgenderism, 13*(4), 165–232.

Commenges, D., Scotet, V., Renaud, S., Jacqmin-Gadda, H., Barberger-Gateau, P., & Dartigues, J. F. (2000). Intake of flavonoids and risk of dementia. *European Journal of Epidemiology, 16*, 357–363.

Conroy, D. E., Ram, N., Pincus, A. L., Coffman, D. L., Lorek, A. E., Rebar, A. L., & Roche, M. J. (2015). Daily physical activity and alcohol use across the adult lifespan. *Health Psychology, 34*, 653–660. doi:10.1037/hea0000157

Cook, R., Pan, P., Silverman, R., & Soltys, S. M. (2010). Do-not-resuscitate orders in suicidal patients: Clinical, ethical, and legal dilemmas. *Psychosomatics: Journal of Consultation Liaison Psychiatry, 51*, 277–282.

Corneil, T. A., Eisfeld, J. H., & Botzer, M. (2010). Proposed changes to diagnoses related to gender identity in the *DSM*: A World Professional Association for Transgender Health consensus paper regarding the potential impact on access to health care for transgender persons. *International Journal of Transgenderism, 12*, 107–114.

Cortese, G. P., & Burger, C. (2017). Neuroinflammatory challenges compromise neuronal function in the aging brain: Postoperative cognitive delirium and Alzheimer's disease. *Behavioural Brain Research, 322*(Part B), 269–279. doi:10.1016/j.bbr.2016.08.027

Costa, P. T., Jr., & McCrae, R. R. (1992). *NEO-PI-R manual.* Odessa, FL: Psychological Assessment Resources.

Cox, B. J., Turnbull, D. L., Robinson, J. A., Grant, B. F., & Stein, M. B. (2011). The effect of avoidant personality disorder on the persistence of generalized social anxiety disorder in the general population: Results from a longitudinal, nationally representative mental health survey. *Depression and Anxiety, 28*, 250–255.

Cox, D. J., Cox, B. S., & Cox, J. C. (2011). Self-reported incidences of moving vehicle collisions and citations among drivers with ADHD: A cross-sectional survey across the lifespan. *The American Journal of Psychiatry, 168*(3), 329–330.

Craske, M. G., Kircanski, K., Epstein, A., Wittchen, H. U., Pine, D. S., Lewis-Fernandez, R., et al. (2010). Panic disorder: A review of *DSM-IV* panic disorder and proposals for *DSM-V. Depression and Anxiety, 27*, 93–112.

Crisafulli, C., Drago, A., Calabrò, M., Spina, E., & Serretti, A. (2015). A molecular pathway analysis informs the genetic background at risk for schizophrenia. *Progress in Neuro-Psychopharmacology & Biological Psychiatry, 5921*–5930. doi:10.1016/j.pnpbp.2014.12.009

Crisafulli, C., Fabbri, C., Porcelli, S., Drago, A., Spina, E., De Ronchi, D., & Serretti, A. (2011). Pharmacogenetics of antidepressants. *Frontiers in Pharmacology, 2*, 6. doi: 10.3389/fphar.2011.00006

Crowther, J. H., Armey, M., Luce, K. H., Dalton, G. R., & Leahey, T. (2008). The point prevalence of bulimic disorders from 1990 to 2004. *International Journal of Eating Disorders, 41*, 491–497.

Crump, F. M., Arndt, L., Grivel, M., Horga, G., Corcoran, C. M., Brucato, G., & Girgis, R. R. (2017). Attenuated first-rank symptoms and conversion to psychosis in a clinical high-risk cohort. *Early Intervention in Psychiatry.* doi:10.1111/eip.12529

Cserjési, R., Vermeulen, N., Luminet, O., Marechal, C., Nef, F., Simon, Y., & Lénárd, L. (2010). Explicit vs. implicit body image evaluation in restrictive anorexia nervosa. *Psychiatry Research, 175*, 148–153.

Currie, C. J., Katz, B. A., & Yovel, I. (2017). Explicit and implicit shame aversion predict symptoms of avoidant and borderline personality disorders. *Journal of Research in Personality, 71*, 13–16. doi:10.1016/j.jrp.2017.08.006

D

Dahlgren, C. L., Wisting, L., & Rø, Ø. (2017). Feeding and eating disorders in the *DSM-5* era: A systematic review of prevalence rates in non-clinical male and female samples. *Journal of Eating Disorders, 5*, 56.

Dal Forno, G., Palermo, M. T., Donohue, J. E., Karagiozis, H., Zonderman, A. B., & Kawas, C. H. (2005). Depressive symptoms, sex, and risk for Alzheimer's disease. *Annals of Neurology, 57*, 381–387.

Dana, R. H. (2002). Multicultural assessment: Teaching methods and competence evaluations. *Journal of Personality Assessment, 79*, 195–199.

D'Aniello, C., Marek, L. I., & Moore, L. (2017). A systemic perspective on military service members' and their partners' perception of PTSD and reintegration stress: A dyadic analysis. *Journal of Systemic Therapies, 36*(2), 39–53. doi:10.1521/jsyt.2017.36.2.39

Das, S., & Chatterjee, S. S. (2017). Say no to evil: Predatory journals, what we should know. *Asian Journal of Psychiatry, 28*, 161–162. doi:10.1016/j.ajp.2017.05.011

Daubney, M., & Bateman, A. (2015). Mentalization-based therapy (MBT): An overview. *Australasian Psychiatry, 23*, 132–135. doi:10.1177/1039856214566830

Davey, A., Bouman, W. P., Arcelus, J., & Meyer, C. (2014). Social support and psychological well-being in gender dysphoria: A comparison of patients with matched controls. *Journal of Sexual Medicine, 11,* 2976–2985. doi:10.1111/jsm.12681

Davis, T. E., III, & Ollendick, T. H. (2011). Specific phobias. In D. McKay & E. A. Storch (Eds.), *Handbook of child and adolescent anxiety disorders* (pp. 231–244). New York: Springer Science + Business Media.

Dean, O. M., Gliddon, E., Van Rheenen, T. E., Giorlando, F., Davidson, S. K., Kaur, M., . . . Williams, L. J. (2018). An update on adjunctive treatment options for bipolar disorder. *Bipolar Disorders, 20*(2), 87–96. doi:10.1111/bdi.12601

de Graaf, G., Engelen, J. M., Gijsbers, A. J., Hochstenbach, R., Hoffer, M. V., Kooper, A. A., . . . Voorhoeve, E. (2017). Estimates of live birth prevalence of children with Down syndrome in the period 1991–2015 in the Netherlands. *Journal of Intellectual Disability Research, 61*(5), 461–470. doi:10.1111/jir.12371

de Guise, E., Leblanc, J., Gosselin, N., Marcoux, J., Champoux, M. C., Couturier, C., et al. (2010). Neuroanatomical correlates of the clock drawing test in patients with traumatic brain injury. *Brain Injury, 24,* 1568–1574.

de Jong, P. J., & Merckelbach, H. (2000). Phobia-relevant illusory correlations: The role of phobic responsivity. *Journal of Abnormal Psychology, 109,* 597–601.

de Jong, P. J., & Peters, M. L. (2007). Blood-injection-injury fears: Harm- vs. disgust-relevant selective outcome associations. *Journal of Behavior Therapy and Experimental Psychiatry, 38,* 263–274.

de Lijster, J. M., Dierckx, B., Utens, E. J., Verhulst, F. C., Zieldorff, C., Dieleman, G. C., & Legerstee, J. S. (2017). The age of onset of anxiety disorders: A meta-analysis. *The Canadian Journal of Psychiatry / La Revue Canadienne De Psychiatrie, 62*(4), 237–246. doi:10.1177/0706743716640757

Delinsky, S. S. (2011). Body image and anorexia nervosa. In T. F. Cash & L. Smolak (Eds.), *Body image: A handbook of science, practice, and prevention* (2nd ed., pp. 279–287). New York: Guilford Press.

Demazeux, S. (2013). *Qu'est ce que le DSM? Genèse et transformations de la bible Américaine de la psychiatrie* [What is DSM? Genesis and transformations of the psychiatric American bible]. Paris: Ithaque.

Denollet, J., & Pedersen, S. S. (2011). Type D personality in patients with cardiovascular disorders. In R. Allan & J. Fisher (Eds.), *Heart and mind: The practice of cardiac psychology* (2nd ed., pp. 219–247). Washington, DC: American Psychological Association.

Derogatis, L. R. (1994). *Manual for the symptom check list-90 revised (SCL-90-R).* San Antonio, TX: Pearson Publishers.

Derringer, J., Corley, R. P., Haberstick, B. C., Young, S. E., Demmitt, B. A., Howrigan, D. P., . . . McQueen, M. B. (2015). Genome-wide association study of behavioral disinhibition in a selected adolescent sample. *Behavior Genetics, 45,* 375–381. doi:10.1007/s10519-015-9705-y

Deutsch, A. (1949). *The mentally ill in America* (2nd ed.). New York: Columbia University Press.

Dhawan, N., Kunik, M. E., Oldham, J., & Coverdale, J. (2010). Prevalence and treatment of narcissistic personality disorder in the community: A systematic review. *Comprehensive Psychiatry, 51,* 333–339.

Dickerson, F. B., Tenhula, W. N., & Green-Paden, L. D. (2005). The token economy for schizophrenia: Review of the literature and recommendations for future research. *Schizophrenia Research, 75,* 405–416.

Dillon, S. T., Vasunilashorn, S. M., Ngo, L., Otu, H. H., Inouye, S. K., Jones, R. N., . . . Libermann, T. A. (2017). Higher c-reactive protein levels predict postoperative delirium in older patients undergoing major elective surgery: A longitudinal nested case-control study. *Biological Psychiatry, 81*(2), 145–153. doi:10.1016/j.biopsych.2016.03.2098

Dimaggio, G., Carcione, A., Salvatore, G., Nicolò, G., Sisto, A., & Semerari, A. (2011). Progressively promoting metacognition in a case of obsessive-compulsive personality disorder treated with metacognitive interpersonal therapy. *Psychology and Psychotherapy: Theory, Research and Practice, 84,* 70–83.

Disney, K. L., Weinstein, Y., & Oltmanns, T. F. (2012). Personality disorder symptoms are differentially related to divorce frequency. *Journal of Family Psychology, 26,* 959–965. doi:10.1037/a0030446

Dittrich, L. (2016). *Patient H.M.: A story of memory, madness, and family secrets.* New York: Random House.

Dodson, W. W. (2005). Pharmacotherapy of adult ADHD. *Journal of Clinical Psychology, 61,* 589–606.

Doley, R. (2003). Pyromania: Fact or fiction? *British Journal of Criminology, 43,* 797–807.

Driessen, E., & Hollon, S. D. (2010). Cognitive behavioral therapy for mood disorders: Efficacy, moderators and mediators. *Psychiatric Clinics of North America, 33,* 537–555.

Ducharme, E. L. (2017). Best practices in working with complex trauma and dissociative identity disorder. *Practice Innovations, 2*(3), 150–161. doi:10.1037/pri0000050

Dudley, M., Goldney, R., & Hadzi-Pavlovic, D. (2010). Are adolescents dying by suicide taking SSRI antidepressants? A review of observational studies. *Australasian Psychiatry, 18,* 242–245.

Duke, D. C., Bodzin, D. K., Tavares, P., Geffken, G. R., & Storch, E. A. (2009). The phenomenology of hairpulling in a community sample. *Journal of Anxiety Disorders, 23,* 1118–1125.

Duke, D. C., Keeley, M. L., Geffken, G. R., & Storch, E. A. (2010). Trichotillomania: A current review. *Clinical Psychology Review, 30,* 181–193.

E

Eddy, K. T., Thomas, J. J., Hastings, E., Edkins, K., Lamont, E., Nevins, C. M., . . . Becker, A. E. (2015). Prevalence of *DSM-5* avoidant/restrictive food intake disorder in a pediatric gastroenterology healthcare network. *International Journal of Eating Disorders, 48*(5), 464–470. doi:10.1002/eat.22350

Eddy, P., Wertheim, E. H., Kingsley, M., & Wright, B. J. (2017). Associations between the effort-reward imbalance model of workplace stress and indices of cardiovascular health: A systematic review and meta-analysis. *Neuroscience and Biobehavioral Reviews, 83,* 252–266. doi:10.1016/j.neubiorev.2017.10.025

Edelstein, B., Martin, R. R., & McKee, D. R. (2000). Assessment of older adult psychopathology. In S. K. Whitbourne (Ed.), *Psychopathology in later life* (pp. 61–88). New York: Wiley.

Edwards, L. M., Burkard, A. W., Adams, H. A., & Newcomb, S. A. (2017). A mixed-method study of psychologists' use of multicultural assessment. *Professional Psychology: Research and Practice, 48*(2), 131–138. doi:10.1037/pro0000095

Eilenberg, T., Fink, P., Jensen, J. S., Rief, W., & Frostholm, L. (2016). Acceptance and commitment group therapy (ACT-G) for health anxiety: A randomized controlled trial. *Psychological Medicine, 46*(1), 103–115. doi:10.1017/S0033291715001579

Eisendrath, S. J., Gillung, E., Delucchi, K., Mathalon, D. H., Yang, T. T., Satre, D. D., . . . Wolkowitz, O. M. (2015). A preliminary study: Efficacy of mindfulness-based cognitive therapy versus sertraline as first-line treatments for major depressive disorder. *Mindfulness, 6,* 475–482. doi:10.1007/s12671-014-0280-8

Eley, T. C., McAdams, T. A., Rijsdijk, F. V., Lichtenstein, P., Narusyte, J., Reiss, D., . . . Neiderhiser, J. M. (2015). The intergenerational transmission of anxiety: A children-of-twins study. *The American Journal of Psychiatry, 172,* 630–637. doi:10.1176/appi.ajp.2015.14070818

Ellis, A. (2005). *The myth of self-esteem.* Buffalo, NY: Prometheus.

Elran-Barak, R., Fitzsimmons-Craft, E. E., Benyamini, Y., Crow, S. J., Peterson, C. B., Hill, L. L., . . . Grange, D. L. (2015). Anorexia nervosa, bulimia nervosa, and binge eating disorder in midlife and beyond. *Journal of Nervous and Mental Disease, 203,* 583–590. doi:10.1097/NMD.0000000000000333

Enserink, M. (1998). First Alzheimer's disease confirmed. *Science, 279,* 2037.

Epstein, E. E., McCrady, B. S., Hallgren, K. A., Cook, S., Jensen, N. K., & Hildebrandt, T. (2018). A randomized trial of female-specific cognitive behavior therapy for alcohol dependent women. *Psychology of*

Addictive Behaviors, 32(1), 1–15. doi:10.1037/adb0000330

Esposito, R., Cieri, F., di Giannantonio, M., & Tartaro, A. (2018). The role of body image and self-perception in anorexia nervosa: The neuroimaging perspective. *Journal of Neuropsychology, 12*(1), 41–52. doi:10.1111/jnp.12106

F

Falkenburg, J., & Tracy, D. K. (2014). Sex and schizophrenia: A review of gender differences. *Psychosis: Psychological, Social and Integrative Approaches, 6,* 61–69. doi:10.1080/17522439.2012.733405

Fang, A., & Hofmann, S. G. (2010). Relationship between social anxiety disorder and body dysmorphic disorder. *Clinical Psychology Review, 30,* 1040–1048.

Fang, A., & Wilhelm, S. (2015). Clinical features, cognitive biases, and treatment of body dysmorphic disorder. *Annual Review of Clinical Psychology, 11,* 187–212. doi:10.1146/annurev-clinpsy-032814-112849

Fanti, K. A., Kyranides, M. N., Lordos, A., Colins, O. F., & Andershed, H. (2018). Unique and interactive associations of callous-unemotional traits, impulsivity and grandiosity with child and adolescent conduct disorder symptoms. *Journal of Psychopathology and Behavioral Assessment, 40*(1), 40–49. doi:10.1007/s10862-018-9655-9

Farabaugh, A., Fisher, L., Nyer, M., Holt, D., Cohen, M., Baer, L., . . . Alpert, J. E. (2015). Similar changes in cognitions following cognitive-behavioral therapy or escitalopram for major depressive disorder: Implications for mechanisms of change. *Annals of Clinical Psychiatry, 27,* 118–125.

Faraone, S. V., Perlis, R. H., Doyle, A. E., Smoller, J. W., Goralnick, J. J., Holmgren, M. A., & Sklar, P. (2005). Molecular genetics of attention-deficit/hyperactivity disorder. *Biological Psychiatry, 57,* 1313–1323.

Farrell, H. M. (2010). Dissociative identity disorder: No excuse for criminal activity. *Current Psychiatry, 10,* 33–40.

Farrell, H. M. (2011). Dissociative identity disorder: Medicolegal challenges. *Journal of the American Academy of Psychiatry and the Law, 39,* 402–406.

Federal Drug Administration (2018). *MedWatch: The FDA Safety Information and Adverse Event Reporting Program.* Silver Spring, MD: Food and Drug Safety Administration.

Ferentinos, P., Koukounari, A., Power, R., Rivera, M., Uher, R., Craddock, N., . . . Lewis, C. M. (2015). Familiality and SNP heritability of age at onset and episodicity in major depressive disorder. *Psychological Medicine, 45,* 2215–2225. doi:10.1017/S0033291715000215

Fessel, J. (2018). Alzheimer's disease combination treatment. *Neurobiology of*

Aging, 63, 165. doi:10.1016/j.neurobiolaging.2017.10.022

Few, L. R., Lynam, D. R., Maples, J. L., MacKillop, J., & Miller, J. D. (2015). Comparing the utility of *DSM-5* Section II and III antisocial personality disorder diagnostic approaches for capturing psychopathic traits. *Personality Disorders: Theory, Research, and Treatment, 6,* 64–74. doi:10.1037/per0000096

Fineberg, N. A., Kaur, S., Kolli, S., Mpavaenda, D., & Reghunandanan, S. (2015). Obsessive-compulsive personality disorder. In K. A. Phillips & D. J. Stein (Eds.), *Handbook on obsessive-compulsive and related disorders* (pp. 247–272). Arlington, VA: American Psychiatric Publishing, Inc.

Firmin, R. L., Lysaker, P. H., McGrew, J. H., Minor, K. S., Luther, L., & Salyers, M. P. (2017). The Stigma Resistance Scale: A multi-sample validation of a new instrument to assess mental illness stigma resistance. *Psychiatry Research, 258,* 37–43. doi:10.1016/j.psychres.2017.09.063

Fisher, C. B., & Fried, A. L. (2008). Internet-mediated psychological services and the American Psychological Association Ethics Code. In D. N. Bersoff (Ed.), *Ethical conflicts in psychology* (4th ed., pp. 376–383). Washington, DC: American Psychological Association.

Fisher, C. B., & Vacanti-Shova, K. (2012). The responsible conduct of psychological research: An overview of ethical principles, APA Ethics Code standards, and federal regulations. In S. J. Knapp, M. C. Gottlieb, M. M. Handelsman, & L. D. VandeCreek (Eds.), *APA handbook of ethics in psychology* (Vol. 2, pp. 335–369). Washington, DC: American Psychological Association.

Fisher, M., Loewy, R., Carter, C., Lee, A., Ragland, D., Niendam, T., . . . Vinogradov, S. (2015). Neuroplasticity-based auditory training via laptop computer improves cognition in young individuals with recent onset schizophrenia. *Schizophrenia Bulletin, 41,* 250–258. doi:10.1093/schbul/sbt232

Fiske, K. E., Isenhower, R. W., Bamond, M. J., Delmolino, L., Sloman, K. N., & LaRue, R. H. (2015). Assessing the value of token reinforcement for individuals with autism. *Journal of Applied Behavior Analysis, 48,* 448–453. doi:10.1002/jaba.207

Flessner, C. A., Woods, D. W., Franklin, M. E., Keuthen, N. J., & Piacentini, J. (2009). Cross-sectional study of women with trichotillomania: A preliminary examination of pulling styles, severity, phenomenology, and functional impact. *Child Psychiatry and Human Development, 40,* 153–167.

Flint, J., & Kendler, K. S. (2014). The genetics of major depression. *Neuron, 81*(3), 484–503.

Folstein, M. F., Folstein, S. E., & McHugh, P. R. (1975). Mini-Mental State: A practical method for grading the cognitive state of patients for the clinician. *Journal of Psychiatric Research, 12,* 189–198.

Foote, B., Smolin, Y., Kaplan, M., Legatt, M. E., & Lipschitz, D. (2006). Prevalence of dissociative disorders in psychiatric outpatients. *The American Journal of Psychiatry, 163,* 623–629.

Forcano, L., Ýlvarez, E., Santamaría, J. J., Jimenez-Murcia, S., Granero, R., Penelo, E., . . . Fernández-Arand, F. (2011). Suicide attempts in anorexia nervosa subtypes. *Comprehensive Psychiatry, 52,* 352–358.

Forsyth, K., Maciver, D., Howden, S., Owen, C., & Shepherd, C. (2008). Developmental coordination disorder: A synthesis of evidence to underpin an allied health professions' framework. *International Journal of Disability, Development and Education, 55,* 153–172.

Fortinsky, R. H., Tennen, H., & Steffens, D. C. (2013). Resilience in the face of chronic illness and family caregiving in middle and later life. *Psychiatric Annals, 43,* 549–554. doi:10.3928/00485713-20131206-07

Frank, E. (2007). Interpersonal and social rhythm therapy: A means of improving depression and preventing relapse in bipolar disorder. *Journal of Clinical Psychology, 63,* 463–473.

Frankl, V. (1963). *Man's search for meaning.* New York: Simon & Schuster.

Franklin, M. E., Zagrabbe, K., & Benavides, K. L. (2011). Trichotillomania and its treatment: A review and recommendations. *Expert Review of Neurotherapeutics, 11,* 1165–1174.

Franklin, T. B., & Mansuy, I. M. (2011). The involvement of epigenetic defects in mental retardation. *Neurobiology of Learning and Memory, 96,* 61–67.

Franko, D. L., Keshaviah, A., Eddy, K. T., Krishna, M., Davis, M. C., Keel, P. K., & Herzog, D. B. (2013). A longitudinal investigation of mortality in anorexia nervosa and bulimia nervosa. *The American Journal of Psychiatry, 170,* 917–925. doi:10.1176/appi.ajp.2013.12070868

Frattaroli, J. (2006). Experimental disclosure and its moderators: A meta-analysis. *Psychological Bulletin, 132,* 823–865.

Freeman, A., & Fox, S. (2013). Cognitive behavioral perspectives on the theory and treatment of the narcissistic character. In J. S. Ogrodniczuk (Ed.), *Understanding and treating pathological narcissism* (pp. 301–320). Washington, DC: American Psychological Association. doi:10.1037/14041-018

Freud, D., Kichin-Brin, M., Ezrati-Vinacour, R., Roziner, I., & Amir, O. (2017). The relationship between the experience of stuttering and demographic characteristics of adults who stutter. *Journal of Fluency Disorders, 52,* 53–63. doi:10.1016/j.jfludis.2017.03.008

Freud, S. (1911). *Formulations of the two principles of mental functioning* (J. Strachey, Trans.). In J. Strachey (Ed.), *The standard edition of the complete psychological works of Sigmund Freud* (Vol. 12). London: Hogarth.

Freud, S. (1923). *The ego and the id* (J. Strachey, Trans.). In J. Strachey (Ed.), *The standard edition of the complete psychological works of Sigmund Freud* (Vol. 19). London: Hogarth.

Friedrich, A., & Schlarb, A. A. (2018). Let's talk about sleep: A systematic review of psychological interventions to improve sleep in college students. *Journal of Sleep Research, 27*(1), 4-22. doi:10.1111/jsr.12568

Furness, D. L., Dekker, G. A., & Roberts, C. T. (2011). DNA damage and health in pregnancy. *Journal of Reproductive Immunology, 89*, 153-162.

Furnham, A. (2014). A bright side, facet analysis of histrionic personality disorder: The relationship between the HDS colourful factor and the NEO-PI-R facets in a large adult sample. *The Journal of Social Psychology, 154*, 527-536. doi:10.1080 /00224545.2014.953026

G

Ganguli, M., Dodge, H. H., Shen, C., Pandav, R. S., & DeKosky, S. T. (2005). Alzheimer disease and mortality: A 15-year epidemiological study. *Archives of Neurology, 62*, 779-784.

Garcia, R. (2017). Neurobiology of fear and specific phobias. *Learning and Memory, 24*(9), 462-471. doi:10.1101/lm.044115.116

Garner, D. M., Anderson, M. L., Keiper, C. D., Whynott, R., & Parker, L. (2016). Psychotropic medications in adult and adolescent eating disorders: Clinical practice versus evidence-based recommendations. *Eating and Weight Disorders, 21*(3), 395-402. doi:10.1007/s40519-016-0253-0

Gatov, E., Rosella, L., Chiu, M., & Kurdyak, P. A. (2017). Trends in standardized mortality among individuals with schizophrenia, 1993-2012: A population-based, repeated cross-sectional study. *Canadian Medical Association Journal, 189*(37), E1177-E1187. doi:10.1503/cmaj.161351

Geary, D. C. (2011). Consequences, characteristics, and causes of mathematical learning disabilities and persistent low achievement in mathematics. *Journal of Developmental and Behavioral Pediatrics, 32*, 250-263.

Giami, A. (2015). Between *DSM* and ICD: Paraphilias and the transformation of sexual norms. *Archives of Sexual Behavior, 44*, 1127-1138. doi:10.1007/s10508-015-0549-6

Gigante, A. D., Barenboim, I. Y., Dias, R. da S., Toniolo, R. A., Mendonça, T., Miranda-Scippa, Â., . . . Lafer, B. (2016). Psychiatric and clinical correlates of rapid cycling bipolar disorder: A cross-sectional study. *Revista Brasileira de Psiquiatria, 38*(4), 270-274. doi-org.silk.library.umass. edu/10.1590/1516-4446-2015-1789

Gillett, G. (2011). The gold-plated leucotomy standard and deep brain stimulation. *Journal of Bioethical Inquiry, 8*, 35-44.

Gisslen, M., Hagberg, L., Brew, B. J., Cinque, P., Price, R. W., & Rosengren, L. (2007). Elevated cerebrospinal fluid neurofilament light protein concentrations predict the development of AIDS dementia complex. *Journal of Infectious Diseases, 195*, 1774-1778.

Gleason, M. M., Fox, N. A., Drury, S., Smyke, A., Egger, H. L., Nelson, C. A., III, . . . Zeanah, C. H. (2011). Validity of evidence-derived criteria for reactive attachment disorder: Indiscriminately social/disinhibited and emotionally withdrawn/inhibited types. Journal of the American Academy of Child & Adolescent Psychiatry, 50(3), 216-231. doi:10.1016/j. jaac.2010.12.012

Goertz-Dorten, A., Benesch, C., Berk-Pawlitzek, E., Faber, M., Hautmann, C., Hellmich, M., . . . Doepfner, M. (2018). Efficacy of individualized social competence training for children with oppositional defiant disorders/conduct disorders: A randomized controlled trial with an active control group. *European Child & Adolescent Psychiatry.* doi:10.1007/ s00787-018-1144-x

Goldsmith, S. K., Pellman, R. C., Kleinman, A. M., & Bunney, W. E. (Eds.). (2002). *Reducing suicide: A national imperative.* Washington, DC: The National Academies Press.

Gómez-de-Regil, L., Kwapil, T. R., Blanqué, J. M., Vainer, E., Montoro, M., & Barrantes-Vidal, N. (2010). Predictors of outcome in the early course of first-episode psychosis. *The European Journal of Psychiatry, 24*, 87-97.

Gonidakis, F., Kravvariti, V., & Varsou, E. (2015). Sexual function of women suffering from anorexia nervosa and bulimia nervosa. *Journal of Sex & Marital Therapy, 41*, 368-378. doi:10.1080/0092623X .2014.915904

Gons, R. A., van Norden, A. G., de Laat, K. F., van Oudheusden, L. J., van Uden, I. W., Zwiers, M. P., . . . de Leeuw, F. E. (2011). Cigarette smoking is associated with reduced microstructural integrity of cerebral white matter (part 7). *Brain, 134*, 2116-2124.

Gottesman, I. I., & Gould, T. D. (2003). The endophenotype concept in psychiatry: Etymology and strategic intentions. *American Journal of Psychiatry, 160*, 636-645.

Gottesman, I. I., & Shields, J. (1972). *Schizophrenia and genetics: A twin study vantage point.* New York: Academic Press.

Gottesman, I. I., & Shields, J. (1973). Genetic theorizing and schizophrenia. *British Journal of Psychiatry, 122*, 15-30.

Govind, V., Gold, S., Kaliannan, K., Saigal, G., Falcone, S., Arheart, K. L., . . . Maudsley, A. A. (2010). Whole-brain proton MR spectroscopic imaging of mild-to-moderate traumatic brain injury and correlation with neuropsychological deficits. *Journal of Neurotrauma, 27*, 483-496.

Graham, C. A. (2010). The *DSM* diagnostic criteria for female orgasmic disorder. *Archives of Sexual Behavior, 39*, 256-270.

Grant, J. E. (2005). Clinical characteristics and psychiatric comorbidity in males with exhibitionism. *Journal of Clinical Psychiatry, 66*, 1367-1371.

Grant, J. E. (2006). Kleptomania. In E. Hollander & D. J. Stein (Eds.), *Clinical manual of impulse-control disorders* (pp. 175-201). Arlington, VA: American Psychiatric Publishing, Inc.

Grant, J. E., Chamberlain, S. R., Odlaug, B. L., Potenza, M. N., & Kim, S. W. (2010). Memantine shows promise in reducing gambling severity and cognitive inflexibility in pathological gambling: A pilot study. *Psychopharmacology, 212*, 603-612.

Grant, J. E., & Kim, S. W. (2007). Clinical characteristics and psychiatric comorbidity of pyromania. *Journal of Clinical Psychiatry, 68*, 1717-1722.

Grant, J. E., Levine, L., Kim, D., & Potenza, M. N. (2005). Impulse control disorders in adult psychiatric inpatients. *American Journal of Psychiatry, 162*, 2184-2188.

Grant, J. E., & Odlaug, B. L. (2008). Clinical characteristics of trichotillomania with trichophagia. *Comprehensive Psychiatry, 49*, 579-584. doi:10.1016/j. comppsych.2008.05.002

Grant, J. E., & Odlaug, B. L. (2010). Impulse control disorders. In D. McKay, J. S. Abramowitz & S. Taylor (Eds.), *Cognitive-behavioral therapy for refractory cases: Turning failure into success* (pp. 231-254). Washington, DC: American Psychological Association. doi:10.1037/12070-011

Grant, J. E., Odlaug, B. L., Davis, A., & Kim, S. W. (2009). Legal consequences of kleptomania. *Psychiatric Quarterly, 80*, 251-259.

Grant, J. E., Odlaug, B. L., & Kim, S. W. (2010). Kleptomania: Clinical characteristics and relationship to substance use disorders. *The American Journal of Drug and Alcohol Abuse, 36*, 291-295.

Grant, J. E., Odlaug, B. L., Medeiros, G., Christianine, A. R., & Tavares, H. (2015). Cross-cultural comparison of compulsive stealing (kleptomania). *Annals of Clinical Psychiatry, 27*, 150-151.

Griffin, J. A., Umstattd, M. R., & Usdan, S. L. (2010). Alcohol use and high-risk sexual behavior among collegiate women: A review of research on alcohol myopia theory. *Journal of American College Health, 58*, 523-532.

Grinshpun-Cohen, J., Miron-Shatz, T., Ries-Levavi, L., & Pras, E. (2015). Factors that affect the decision to undergo amniocentesis in women with normal Down syndrome screening results: It is all about the age. *Health Expectations: An International Journal of Public Participation in Health Care & Health Policy, 18*(6), 2306-2317. doi:10.1111/hex.12200

Gross, C. G. (1999). "Psychosurgery" in renaissance art. *Trends in Neurosciences, 22,* 429-431.

Grover, S., Chakrabarti, S., Shah, R., & Kumar, V. (2011). A factor analytic study of the Delirium Rating Scale-Revised-98 in untreated patients with delirium. *Journal of Psychosomatic Research, 70,* 473-478.

Gu, Y., Luchsinger, J. A., Stern, Y., & Scarmeas, N. (2010). Mediterranean diet, inflammatory and metabolic biomarkers, and risk of Alzheimer's disease. *Journal of Alzheimer's Disease, 22,* 483-492.

Guay, D. R. P. (2009). Drug treatment of paraphilic and nonparaphilic sexual disorders. *Clinical Therapeutics: The International Peer-Reviewed Journal of Drug Therapy, 31,* 1-31.

Gueorguieva, R., Wu, R., Tsai, W., O'Connor, P. G., Fucito, L., Zhang, H., & O'Malley, S. S. (2015). An analysis of moderators in the COMBINE study: Identifying subgroups of patients who benefit from acamprosate. *European Neuropsychopharmacology, 25,* 1586-1599. doi:10.1016/j.euroneuro.2015.06.006

Gunderson, J. G., & Links, P. S. (2008). *Borderline personality disorder: A clinical guide* (2nd ed.). Washington, DC: American Psychiatric Press, Inc.

Gunderson, J. G., Stout, R. L., McGlashan, T. H., Shea, M. T., Morey, L. C., Grilo, C. M., . . . Skodol, A. E. (2011). Ten-year course of borderline personality disorder: Psychopathology and function from the Collaborative Longitudinal Personality Disorders study. *Archives of General Psychiatry, 68,* 827-837.

Guo, W., Liu, F., Xiao, C., Zhang, Z., Liu, J., Yu, M., . . . Zhao, J. (2015). Decreased insular connectivity in drug-naive major depressive disorder at rest. *Journal of Affective Disorders, 179,* 31-37. doi:10.1016/j.jad.2015.03.028

H

Haaland, Å. T., Eskeland, S. O., Moen, E. M., Vogel, P. A., Haseth, S., Mellingen, K., . . . Hummelen, B. (2017). ACT-enhanced behavior therapy in group format for trichotillomania: An effectiveness study. *Journal of Obsessive-Compulsive and Related Disorders, 12,* 109-116. doi:10.1016/j.jocrd.2017.01.005

Haji, I. (2010). Psychopathy, ethical perception, and moral culpability. *Neuroethics, 3,* 135-150.

Hall, B. J., Tolin, D. F., Frost, R. O., & Steketee, G. (2013). An exploration of comorbid symptoms and clinical correlates of clinically significant hoarding symptoms. *Depression and Anxiety, 30,* 67-76. doi:10.1002/da.22015

Hall, R. C. (2007). A profile of pedophilia: Definition, characteristics of offenders, recidivism, treatment outcomes, and forensic issues. *Mayo Clinic Proceedings, 82,* 457-471.

Hamdi, N. R., Krueger, R. F., & South, S. C. (2015). Socioeconomic status moderates genetic and environmental effects on the amount of alcohol use. *Alcoholism: Clinical and Experimental Research, 39,* 603-610. doi:10.1111/acer.12673

Hammen, C. (2005). Stress and depression. *Annual Review in Clinical Psychology, 1,* 293-319.

Hansen, S. N., Schendel, D. E., & Parner, E. T. (2015). Explaining the increase in the prevalence of autism spectrum disorders: The proportion attributable to changes in reporting practices. *JAMA Pediatrics, 169,* 56-62. doi:10.1001/jamapediatrics.2014.1893

Hare, R. D. (1997). *Hare psychopathy checklist–Revised (PCL-R).* Odessa, FL: Personality Assessment Resources.

Harstad, E., Sideridis, G., Sherritt, L., Shrier, L. A., Ziemnik, R., & Levy, S. (2016). Concurrent validity of caffeine problems and diagnostic criteria for substance use disorders. *Journal of Caffeine Research, 6*(4), 141-147. doi:10.1089/jcr.2016.0006

Hatchett, G. T. (2015). Treatment guidelines for clients with antisocial personality disorder. *Journal of Mental Health Counseling, 37,* 15-27.

Hauck, T. S., Lau, C., Wing, L. F., Kurdyak, P., & Tu, K. (2017). ADHD treatment in primary care: Demographic factors, medication trends, and treatment predictors. *The Canadian Journal of Psychiatry / La Revue Canadienne De Psychiatrie, 62*(6), 393-402. doi:10.1177/0706743716689055

Hayes, J. F., Marston, L., Walters, K., King, M. B., & Osborn, D. J. (2017). Mortality gap for people with bipolar disorder and schizophrenia: UK-based cohort study 2000-2014. *The British Journal of Psychiatry, 211*(3), 175-181. doi:10.1192/bjp.bp.117.202606

Hayes, J. F., Miles, J., Walters, K., King, M., & Osborn, D. J. (2015). A systematic review and meta-analysis of premature mortality in bipolar affective disorder. *Acta Psychiatrica Scandinavica, 131,* 417-425. doi:10.1111/acps.12408

Hayes, J. P., LaBar, K. S., McCarthy, G., Selgrade, E., Nasser, J., Dolcos, F., . . . Morey, R.A. (2011). Reduced hippocampal and amygdala activity predicts memory distortions for trauma reminders in combat-related PTSD. *Journal of Psychiatric Research, 45,* 660-669.

Hayes, S. C. (2016). Acceptance and commitment therapy, relational frame theory, and the third wave of behavioral and cognitive therapies–republished article. *Behavior Therapy, 47*(6), 869-885.

Hayes, S. C., Strosahl, K., & Wilson, K. G. (1999). *Acceptance and commitment therapy: Understanding and treating human suffering.* New York: Guilford.

Heeren, A., & McNally, R. J. (2018). Social anxiety disorder as a densely interconnected network of fear and avoidance for social situations. *Cognitive Therapy and Research, 42*(1), 103-113. doi:10.1007/s10608-017-9876-3

Hendershot, C. S., Wardell, J. D., Samokhvalov, A. V., & Rehm, J. (2017). Effects of naltrexone on alcohol self-administration and craving: Meta-analysis of human laboratory studies. *Addiction Biology, 22*(6), 1515-1527. doi:10.1111/adb.12425

Herbert, P. B. (2002). The duty to warn: A reconsideration and critique. *Journal of the American Academy of Psychiatry and the Law, 30,* 417-424.

Hettema, J. M., Prescott, C. A., & Kendler, K. S. (2004). Genetic and environmental sources of covariation between generalized anxiety disorder and neuroticism. *American Journal of Psychiatry, 161,* 1581-1587.

Hewitt, P. L., Caelian, C. F., Chen, C., & Flett, G. L. (2014). Perfectionism, stress, daily hassles, hopelessness, and suicide potential in depressed psychiatric adolescents. *Journal of Psychopathology and Behavioral Assessment, 36,* 663-674. doi:10.1007/s10862-014-9427-0

Hillemacher, T., Heberlein, A., Muschler, M. A., Bleich, S., & Frieling, H. (2011). Opioid modulators for alcohol dependence. *Expert Opinion on Investigational Drugs, 20,* 1073-1086.

Hinderliter, A. C. (2010). Disregarding science, clinical utility, and the *DSM*'s definition of mental disorder: The case of exhibitionism, voyeurism, and frotteurism. *Archives of Sexual Behavior, 39,* 1235-1237.

Hipwell, A. E., Stepp, S., Feng, X., Burke, J., Battista, D. R., Loeber, R., & Keenan, K. (2011). Impact of oppositional defiant disorder dimensions on the temporal ordering of conduct problems and depression across childhood and adolescence in girls. *Journal of Child Psychology and Psychiatry, 52*(10), 1099-1108. doi:10.1111/.1469-7610.2011.02448.x

Hoffman, E. J., & State, M. W. (2010). Progress in cytogenetics: Implications for child psychopathology. *Journal of the American Academy of Child and Adolescent Psychiatry, 49,* 736-751.

Hofmann, S. G., Rief, W., & Spiegel, D. A. (2010). Psychotherapy for panic disorder. In D. J. Stein, E. Hollander, & B. O. Rothbaum (Eds.), *Textbook of anxiety disorders* (2nd ed., pp. 417-433). Arlington, VA: American Psychiatric Publishing, Inc.

Hogan, M. F. (2003). The President's New Freedom Commission: Recommendations to transform mental health care in America. *Psychiatric Services, 54,* 1467-1474.

Hoge, C. W., Castro, C. A., Messer, S. C., McGurk, D., Cotting, D. I., & Koffman, R. L. (2004). Combat duty in Iraq and

Afghanistan, mental health problems, and barriers to care. *New England Journal of Medicine, 351,* 13–22.

Hoge, C. W., Terhakopian, A., Castro, C. A., Messer, S. C., & Engel, C. C. (2007). Association of posttraumatic stress disorder with somatic symptoms, health care visits, and absenteeism among Iraq war veterans. *Americal Journal of Psychiatry, 164,* 150–153.

Hollingshead, A. B., & Redlich, F. C. (1958). *Social class and mental illness: A community study.* New York: Wiley.

Hollon, S. D. (2016). The efficacy and acceptability of psychological interventions for depression: Where we are now and where we are going. *Epidemiology and Psychiatric Sciences, 25*(4), 295–300. doi:10.1017 /S2045796015000748

Hollon, S. D., & Ponniah, K. (2010). A review of empirically supported psychological therapies for mood disorders in adults. *Depression and Anxiety, 27,* 891–932.

Holmes, T. H., & Rahe, R. H. (1967). The social readjustment rating scale. *Journal of Psychosomatic Research, 11,* 213–218.

Holvoet, L., Huys, W., Coppens, V., Seeuws, J., Goethals, K., & Morrens, M. (2017). Fifty shades of Belgian gray: The prevalence of BDSM-related fantasies and activities in the general population. *Journal of Sexual Medicine, 14*(9), 1152–1159. doi:10.1016 /j.jsxm.2017.07.003

Hopper, K., Harrison, G., Janca, A., & Sartorius, N. (2007). *Recovery from schizophrenia: An international perspective: A report from the WHO Collaborative Project, the international study of schizophrenia.* New York: Oxford University Press.

Hopwood, C. J., & Thomas, K. M. (2012). Paranoid and schizoid personality disorders. In T. A. Widiger (Ed.), *The Oxford handbook of personality disorders* (pp. 582–602). New York: Oxford University Press. doi:10.1093/oxfor dhb/9780199735013.013.0027.

Hoven, C. W., Duarte, C. S., Lucas, C. P., Wu, P., Mandell, D. J., Goodwin, R. D., . . . Susser, E. (2005). Psychopathology among New York city public school children 6 months after September 11. *Archives of General Psychiatry, 62,* 545–552.

Howe, E. (2008). Ethical considerations when treating patients with schizophrenia. *Psychiatry (Edgmont), 5,* 59–64.

Howland, M., Hunger, J. M., & Mann, T. (2012). Friends don't let friends eat cookies: Effects of restrictive eating norms on consumption among friends. *Appetite, 59,* 505–509. doi:10.1016/j.appet.2012.06.020

Hrabosky, J. I. (2011). Body image and binge-eating disorder. In T. F. Cash & L. Smolak (Eds.), *Body image: A handbook of science, practice, and prevention* (2nd ed., pp. 296–304). New York: Guilford Press.

Hudson, C. G. (2012). Patterns of residential mobility of people with schizophrenia:

Multi-level tests of downward geographic drift. *Journal of Sociology and Social Welfare, 39*(3), 149–179.

Hudson, J. I., Hiripi, E., Pope, H. G., Jr., & Kessler, R. C. (2007). The prevalence and correlates of eating disorders in the National Comorbidity Survey Replication. *Biological Psychiatry, 61,* 348–358.

Hudspeth, E. F., Wirick, D., & Matthews, K. M. (2015). Intermittent explosive disorder. In G. M. Kapalka (Ed.), *Treating disruptive disorders: A guide to psychological, pharmacological, and combined therapies* (pp. 161–179). New York: Routledge/ Taylor & Francis Group.

Hummelen, B., Pedersen, G., Wilberg, T., & Karterud, S. (2015). Poor validity of the *DSM-IV* schizoid personality disorder construct as a diagnostic category. *Journal of Personality Disorders, 29,* 334–346. doi:10.1521/pedi_2014_28_159

Humphreys, K. L., Nelson, C. A., Fox, N. A., & Zeanah, C. H. (2017). Signs of reactive attachment disorder and disinhibited social engagement disorder at age 12 years: Effects of institutional care history and high-quality foster care. *Development and Psychopathology, 29*(2), 675–684. doi:10.1017/S0954579417000256

Hunsley, J., & Mash, E. J. (2007). Evidence-based assessment. *Annual Review of Clinical Psychology, 3,* 29–51.

Huppert, J. D., Foa, E. B., McNally, R. J., & Cahill, S. P. (2009). Role of cognition in stress-induced and fear circuitry disorders. In G. Andrews, D. S. Charney, P. J. Sirovatka, & D. A. Regier (Eds.), *Stress-induced and fear circuitry disorders: Advancing the research agenda for DSM-V* (pp. 175–193). Arlington, VA: American Psychiatric Publishing, Inc.

Hyman, S. E. (2011). Diagnosis of mental disorders in light of modern genetics. In D. A. Regier, W. E. Narrow, E. A. Kuhl, & D. J. Kupfer (Eds.), *The conceptual evolution of DSM-5* (pp. 3–17). Washington, DC: American Psychiatric Publishers.

I

Inder, M. L., Crowe, M. T., Luty, S. E., Carter, J. D., Moor, S., Frampton, C. M., & Joyce, P. R. (2015). Randomized, controlled trial of interpersonal and social rhythm therapy for young people with bipolar disorder. *Bipolar Disorders, 17,* 128–138. doi:10.1111/bdi.12273

Ip, H. S., Wong, S. L., Chan, D. Y., Byrne, J., Li, C., Yuan, V. N., & . . . Wong, J. W. (2018). Enhance emotional and social adaptation skills for children with autism spectrum disorder: A virtual reality enabled approach. *Computers & Education, 117,* 1–15. doi:10.1016/j.compedu.2017.09.0

Iverson, G. L. (2005). Outcome from mild traumatic brain injury. *Current Opinion in Psychiatry, 18,* 301–317.

Iverson, K. M., Follette, V. M., Pistorello, J., & Fruzzetti, A. E. (2012). An investigation of experiential avoidance, emotion dysregulation, and distress tolerance in young adult outpatients with borderline personality disorder symptoms. *Personality Disorders: Theory, Research, and Treatment, 3*(4), 415–422. doi:10.1037/a0023703.

Iwase, S., Berube, N. G., Zhou, Z., Kasri, N. N., Battaglioli, E., Scandaglia, M., & Barco, A. (2017). Epigenetic etiology of intellectual disability. *Journal of Neuroscience, 37*(45), 10773–10782.

J

Jaffee, S. R., Caspi, A., Moffitt, T. E., Dodge, K. A., Rutter, M., Taylor, A., & Tully, L. A. (2005). Nature × nurture: Genetic vulnerabilities interact with physical maltreatment to promote conduct problems. *Development and Psychopathology, 17,* 67–84.

Jahnke, S., Philipp, K., & Hoyer, J. (2015). Stigmatizing attitudes towards people with pedophilia and their malleability among psychotherapists in training. *Child Abuse & Neglect, 40,* 93–102. doi:10.1016/j. chiabu.2014.07.008

Jain, G., Chakrabarti, S., & Kulhara, P. (2011). Symptoms of delirium: An exploratory factor analytic study among referred patients. *General Hospital Psychiatry, 33,* 377–385.

Jamal, A., et al. (2017). Tobacco use among middle and high school students—United States, 2011–2016. *MMWR Morbidity and Mortality Weekly Report, 66,* 597–603.

Jarry, J. L. (2010). Core conflictual relationship theme-guided psychotherapy: Initial effectiveness study of a 16-session manualized approach in a sample of six patients. *Psychology and Psychotherapy: Theory, Research and Practice, 83,* 385–394.

Jeffers, A. J., Benotsch, E. G., Green, B. A., Bannerman, D., Darby, M., Kelley, T., & Martin, A. M. (2015). Health anxiety and the non-medical use of prescription drugs in young adults: A cross-sectional study. *Addictive Behaviors, 5074–5077.* doi:10.1016 /j.addbeh.2015.06.012

Jellinger, K. A., & Attems, J. (2010). Prevalence and pathology of vascular dementia in the oldest-old. *Journal of Alzheimer's Disease, 21,* 1283–1293.

Jenkins, S. R. (2017). Not your same old story: New rules for thematic apperceptive techniques (TATs). *Journal of Personality Assessment, 99*(3), 238–253. doi:10.1080 /00223891.2016.1248972

Jobe, T. H., & Harrow, M. (2010). Schizophrenia course, long-term outcome, recovery, and prognosis. *Current Directions in Psychological Science, 19,* 220–225.

Johnson, J., Wood, A. M., Gooding, P., Taylor, P. J., & Tarrier, N. (2011). Resilience to suicidality: The buffering hypothesis. *Clinical Psychology Review, 31,* 563-591.

Johnson, J. G., Cohen, P., Kasen, S., Smailes, E., & Brook, J. S. (2001). Association of maladaptive parental behavior with psychiatric disorder among parents and their offspring. *Archives of General Psychiatry, 58,* 453-460.

Johnston, L. D., O'Malley, P. M., Bachman, J. G., & Schulenberg, J. E. (2011). Monitoring the Future national survey results on drug use, 1975-2010. Volume I: Secondary school students (p. 744). Ann Arbor, MI: Institute for Social Research, The University of Michigan.

Jonason, P. K., Strosser, G. L., Kroll, C. H., Duineveld, J. J., & Baruffi, S. A. (2015). Valuing myself over others: The dark triad traits and moral and social values. *Personality and Individual Differences, 81,* 102-106. doi:10.1016/j.paid.2014.10.045

Jones, K. M., Whitbourne, S. K., Whitbourne, S. B., & Skultety, K. M. (2009). Identity processes and memory controllability in middle and later adulthood. *Journal of Applied Gerontology, 28,* 582-599.

Jones, R. M., Arlidge, J., Gillham, R., Reagu, S., van den Bree, M., & Taylor, P. J. (2011). Efficacy of mood stabilisers in the treatment of impulsive or repetitive aggression: Systematic review and meta-analysis. *British Journal of Psychiatry, 198*(2), 93-98.

Jonsbu, E., Dammen, T., Morken, G., Lied, A., Vik-Mo, H., & Martinsen, E. W. (2009). Cardiac and psychiatric diagnoses among patients referred for chest pain and palpitations. *Scandinavian Cardiovascular Journal, 43,* 256-259.

Jonsbu, E., Dammen, T., Morken, G., Moum, T., & Martinsen, E. W. (2011). Short-term cognitive behavioral therapy for non-cardiac chest pain and benign palpitations: A randomized controlled trial. *Journal of Psychosomatic Research, 70,* 117-123.

Jorstad-Stein, E. C., & Heimberg, R. G. (2009). Social phobia: An update on treatment. *Psychiatric Clinics of North America, 32,* 641-663.

Joseph, J. A., Shukitt-Hale, B., & Casadesus, G. (2005). Reversing the deleterious effects of aging on neuronal communication and behavior: Beneficial properties of fruit polyphenolic compounds. *American Journal of Clinical Nutrition, 81,* 313S-316S.

Joyal, C. C., & Carpentier, J. (2017). The prevalence of paraphilic interests and behaviors in the general population: A provincial survey. *Journal of Sex Research, 54*(2), 161-171. doi:10.1080/00224499.2016.1139034

Juliano, L. M., & Griffiths, R. R. (2004). A critical review of caffeine withdrawal: Empirical validation of symptoms and signs, incidence, severity, and associated features. *Psychopharmacology (Berlin), 176,* 1-29.

Jung, C. G. (1961). *Memories, dreams, reflections.* New York: Pantheon.

K

Kabat-Zinn, J. (2003). Mindfulness-based interventions in context: Past, present, and future. *Clinical Psychology: Science and Practice, 10*(2), 144-156.

Kahl, K. G., Winter, L., & Schweiger, U. (2012). The third wave of cognitive behavioural therapies: What is new and what is effective? *Current Opinion in Psychiatry, 25*(6), 522-528.

Kaiser, R. H., Andrews-Hanna, J. R., Wager, T. D., & Pizzagalli, D. A. (2015). Large-scale network dysfunction in major depressive disorder: A meta-analysis of resting-state functional connectivity. *JAMA Psychiatry, 72,* 603-611. doi:10.1001/jamapsychiatry.2015.0071

Kalk, N. J., Nutt, D. J., & Lingford-Hughes, A. R. (2011). The role of central noradrenergic dysregulation in anxiety disorders: Evidence from clinical studies. *Journal of Psychopharmacology, 25,* 3-16.

Kanaan, R. A., & Wessely, S. C. (2010). The origins of factitious disorder. *History of the Human Sciences, 23,* 68-85.

Kane, J. M., & Correll, C. U. (2010). Pharmacologic treatment of schizophrenia. *Dialogues in Clinical Neuroscience, 12,* 345-357.

Karow, A., Reimer, J., König, H., Heider, D., Bock, T., Huber, C., . . . Lambert, M. (2012). Cost-effectiveness of 12-month assertive community treatment as part of integrated care versus standard care in patients with schizophrenia treated with quetiapine immediate release (ACCESS Trial). *Journal of Clinical Psychiatry, 73,* e402-e408. doi:10.4088/JCP.11m06875

Kawas, C., Gray, S., Brookmeyer, R., Fozard, J., & Zonderman, A. (2000). Age-specific incidence rates of Alzheimer's disease: The Baltimore Longitudinal Study of Aging. *Neurology, 54,* 2072-2077.

Kearney, C. A., & Vecchio, J. L. (2007). When a child won't speak. *The Journal of Family Practice, 56,* 917-921.

Keel, P. K., Gravener, J. A., Joiner, T. E., Jr., & Haedt, A. A. (2010). Twenty-year follow-up of bulimia nervosa and related eating disorders not otherwise specified. *International Journal of Eating Disorders, 43,* 492-497.

Kellas, J. K., Horstman, H. K., Willer, E. K., & Carr, K. (2015). The benefits and risks of telling and listening to stories of difficulty over time: Experimentally testing the expressive writing paradigm in the context of interpersonal communication between friends. *Health Communication, 30,* 843-858. doi:10.1080/10410236.2013.850017

Kelley, M. E., Wan, C. R., Broussard, B., Crisafio, A., Cristofaro, S., Johnson, S., . . . Compton, M. T. (2016). Marijuana use in the immediate 5-year premorbid period is associated with increased risk of onset of schizophrenia and related psychotic disorders. *Schizophrenia Research, 171*(1-3), 62-67. doi:10.1016/j.schres.2016.01.015

Kellner, M. (2010). Drug treatment of obsessive-compulsive disorder. *Dialogues in Clinical Neuroscience, 12,* 187-197.

Kessing, L. V., Hellmund, G., Geddes, J. R., Goodwin, G. M., & Andersen, P. K. (2011). Valproate v. lithium in the treatment of bipolar disorder in clinical practice: Observational nationwide register-based cohort study. *British Journal of Psychiatry, 199,* 57-63.

Kessing, L. V., Vradi, E., McIntyre, R. S., & Andersen, P. K. (2015). Causes of decreased life expectancy over the life span in bipolar disorder. *Journal of Affective Disorders, 180,* 142-147. doi:10.1016/j.jad.2015.03.027

Kessler, R. C., Adler, L., Barkley, R., Biederman, J., Conners, C. K., Demler, O., . . . Zaslavsky, A. M. (2006). The prevalence and correlates of adult ADHD in the United States: Results from the National Comorbidity Survey Replication. *The American Journal of Psychiatry, 163,* 716-723.

Kessler, R. C., Berglund, P., Demler, O., Jin, R., Merikangas, K. R., & Walters, E. E. (2005). Lifetime prevalence and age-of-onset distributions of *DSM-IV* disorders in the National Comorbidity Survey Replication. *Archives of General Psychiatry, 62,* 593-602.

Kessler, R. C., Chiu, W. T., Demler, O., Merikangas, K. R., & Walters, E. E. (2005). Prevalence, severity, and comorbidity of 12-month *DSM-IV* disorders in the National Comorbidity Survey Replication. *Archives of General Psychiatry, 62*(6), 617-627.

Kessler, R. C., Green, J. G., Adler, L. A., Barkley, R. A., Chatterji, S., Faraone, S. V., . . . Van Brunt, D. L. (2010). Structure and diagnosis of adult attention-deficit/hyperactivity disorder: Analysis of expanded symptom criteria from the Adult ADHD Clinical Diagnostic Scale. *Archives of General Psychiatry, 67,* 1168-1178.

Kessler, R. C., Hwang, I., LaBrie, R., Petukhova, M., Sampson, N. A., Winters, K. C., & Schaffer, H. J. (2008). *DSM-IV* pathological gambling in the National Comorbidity Survey Replication. *Psychological Medicine: A Journal of Research in Psychiatry and the Allied Sciences, 38,* 1351-1360.

Kessler, R. C., Petukhova, M., Sampson, N. A., Zaslavsky, A. M., & Wittchen, H. (2012). Twelve-month and lifetime prevalence and lifetime morbid risk of anxiety and mood disorders in the United States. *International Journal of Methods in Psychiatric Research, 21,* 169-184. doi:10.1002/mpr.1359

Kihlstrom, J. R. (2005). Dissociative disorders. *Annual Review of Clinical Psychology, 1,* 227-253.

Killam, C., Cautin, R. L., & Santucci, A. C. (2005). Assessing the enduring residual neuropsychological effects of head trauma in college athletes who participate in contact sports. *Archives of Clinical Neuropsychology, 20,* 599-611.

Kimmel, R. J., Roy-Byrne, P. P., & Cowley, D. S. (2015). Pharmacological treatments for panic disorder, generalized anxiety disorder, specific phobia, and social anxiety disorder. In P. E. Nathan & J. M. Gorman (Eds.), *A guide to treatments that work* (pp. 463-505). New York: Oxford University Press.

Kingsberg, S. A., Tkachenko, N., Lucas, J., Burbrink, A., Kreppner, W., & Dickstein, J. B. (2013). Characterization of orgasmic difficulties by women: Focus group evaluation. *Journal of Sexual Medicine, 10,* 2242-2250. doi:10.1111/jsm.12224

Kinsey, A. C., Pomeroy, W. B., & Martin, C. E. (1948). *Sexual behavior in the human male.* Philadelphia: Saunders.

Kinsey, A. C., Pomeroy, W. B., Martin, C. E., & Gebhard, P. H. (1953). *Sexual behavior in the human female.* Philadelphia: Saunders.

Kirsch, I., Deacon, B. J., Huedo-Medina, T. B., Scoboria, A., Moore, T. J., & Johnson, B. T. (2008). Initial severity and antidepressant benefits: A meta-analysis of data submitted to the Food and Drug Administration. *PLoS Medicine, 5,* e45.

Knapp, S., & VandeCreek, L. (2001). Ethical issues in personality assessment in forensic psychology. *Journal of Personality Assessment, 77,* 242-254.

Knopman, D. S. (2007). Cerebrovascular disease and dementia. *British Journal of Radiology, 80,* S121-S127.

Knopman, D. S., & Roberts, R. (2010). Vascular risk factors: Imaging and neuropathologic correlates. *Journal of Alzheimer's Disease, 20,* 699-709.

Ko, H.-C., & Kuo, F.-Y. (2009). Can blogging enhance subjective well-being through self-disclosure? *CyberPsychology & Behavior, 12,* 75-79.

Kocovski, N. L., Fleming, J. E., Hawley, L. L., Ho, M. R., & Antony, M. M. (2015). Mindfulness and acceptance-based group therapy and traditional cognitive behavioral group therapy for social anxiety disorder: Mechanisms of change. *Behaviour Research and Therapy, 7011-7022.* doi:10.1016/j.brat.2015.04.005

Kodituwakku, P. W. (2009). Neurocognitive profile in children with fetal alcohol spectrum disorders. *Developmental Disabilities Research Reviews, 15,* 218-224.

Kodituwakku, P. W., & Kodituwakku, E. L. (2011). From research to practice: An integrative framework for the development of interventions for children with fetal alcohol spectrum disorders. *Neuropsychology Review, 21*(2), 204-223.

Koegel, R. L., Koegel, L. K., & McNerney, E. K. (2001). Pivotal areas in intervention for autism. *Journal of Clinical Child Psychology, 30,* 19-32.

Koeter, M. W. J., van den Brink, W., & Lehert, P. (2010). Effect of early and late compliance on the effectiveness of acamprosate in the treatment of alcohol dependence. *Journal of Substance Abuse Treatment, 39,* 218-226.

Kohut, H. (1966). Forms and transformations of narcissism. *Journal of the American Psychoanalytic Association, 14,* 243-272.

Kohut, H. (1971). *The analysis of the self.* New York: International Universities Press.

Krafft-Ebing, R. V. (1886/1950). *Psychopathia sexualis.* New York: Pioneer Publications.

Krizan, Z., & Herlache, A. D. (2018). The narcissism spectrum model: A synthetic view of narcissistic personality. *Personality and Social Psychology Review, 22*(1), 3-31. doi:10.1177/1088868316685018

Krystal, J. H., Rosenheck, R. A., Cramer, J. A., Vessicchio, J. C., Jones, K. M., Vertrees, J. E., et al. (2011). Adjunctive risperidone treatment for antidepressant-resistant symptoms of chronic military service–related PTSD: A randomized trial. *JAMA: Journal of the American Medical Association, 306,* 493-502.

Kuhl, E. S., Hoodin, F., Rice, J., Felt, B. T., Rausch, J. R., & Patton, S. R. (2010). Increasing daily water intake and fluid adherence in children receiving treatment for retentive encopresis. *Journal of Pediatric Psychology, 35,* 1144-1151.

Kuhn, J. (2015). Developmental dyscalculia: Causes, characteristics, and interventions. *Zeitschrift Für Psychologie, 223*(2), 67-68. doi:10.1027/2151-2604/a000204

Kushnir, J., Kushnir, B., & Sadeh, A. (2013). Children treated for nocturnal enuresis: Characteristics and trends over a 15-year period. *Child & Youth Care Forum, 42,* 119-129. doi:10.1007/s10566-013-9195-0

Kyrios, M., Mogan, C., Moulding, R., Frost, R. O., Yap, K., & Fassnacht, D. B. (2017). The cognitive–behavioural model of hoarding disorder: Evidence from clinical and non-clinical cohorts. *Clinical Psychology & Psychotherapy, 25*(2), 311-321. doi:10.1002/cpp.2164

L

La Fond, J. Q. (1994). Law and the delivery of involuntary mental health services. *American Journal of Orthopsychiatry, 64,* 209-222.

Lahaie, M., Amsel, R., Khalifé, S., Boyer, S., Faaborg-Andersen, M., & Binik, Y. M. (2015). Can fear, pain, and muscle tension discriminate vaginismus from dyspareunia/provoked vestibulodynia? Implications for the new *DSM-5* diagnosis of genito-pelvic pain/penetration disorder. *Archives of Sexual Behavior, 44,* 1537-1550. doi:10.1007/s10508-014-0430-z

Laing, R. D. (1959). *The divided self.* New York: Penguin.

LaLonde, K. B., MacNeill, B. R., Eversole, L. W., Ragotzy, S. P., & Poling, A. (2014). Increasing physical activity in young adults with autism spectrum disorders. *Research in Autism Spectrum Disorders, 8,* 1679-1684. doi:10.1016/j.rasd.2014.09.001

Lamb, D. H., Catanzaro, S. J., & Moorman, A. S. (2004). A preliminary look at how psychologists identify, evaluate, and proceed when faced with possible multiple relationship dilemmas. *Professional Psychology: Research and Practice, 35,* 248-254.

Långström, N. (2010). The *DSM* diagnostic criteria for exhibitionism, voyeurism, and frotteurism. *Archives of Sexual Behavior, 39,* 317-324.

Långström, N., & Seto, M. C. (2006). Exhibitionistic and voyeuristic behavior in a Swedish national population survey. *Archives of Sexual Behavior, 35,* 427-435.

Lau, J. Y. F., & Eley, T. C. (2010). The genetics of mood disorders. *Annual Review of Clinical Psychology, 6,* 313-337.

Laumann, E. O., & Waite, L. J. (2008). Sexual dysfunction among older adults: Prevalence and risk factors from a nationally representative U.S. probability sample of men and women 57-85 years of age. *Journal of Sexual Medicine, 5,* 2300-2311.

Lazarus, A. A. (1968). Learning theory and the treatment of depression. *Behaviour Research and Therapy, 6,* 83-89.

Lazarus, R. S., & Folkman, S. (1984). *Stress, appraisal, and coping.* New York: Springer.

Leaf, J. B., Leaf, R., McEachin, J., Cihon, J. H., & Ferguson, J. L. (2017). Advantages and challenges of a home- and clinic-based model of behavioral intervention for individuals diagnosed with autism spectrum disorder. *Journal of Autism and Developmental Disorders, 48*(6), 2258-2266. doi:10.1007/s10803-017-3443-3

LeBeau, R. T., Glenn, D., Liao, B., Wittchen, H. U., Beesdo-Baum, K., Ollendick, T., et al. (2010). Specific phobia: A review of *DSM-IV* specific phobia and preliminary recommendations for *DSM-V. Depression and Anxiety, 27,* 148-167.

Lebel, C., Roussotte, F., & Sowell, E. R. (2011). Imaging the impact of prenatal alcohol exposure on the structure of the developing human brain. *Neuropsychology Review, 21,* 102-118.

Leckman, J. F., Denys, D., Simpson, H. B., Mataix-Cols, D., Hollander, E., Saxena, S., et al. (2010). Obsessive-compulsive disorder: A review of the diagnostic criteria and possible subtypes and dimensional specifiers for *DSM-V. Depression and Anxiety, 27,* 507-527.

Lee, D. J., Schnitzlein, C. W., Wolf, J. P., Vythilingam, M., Rasmusson, A. M., & Hoge, C. W. (2016). Psychotherapy versus pharmacotherapy for posttraumatic stress disorder: Systemic review and meta-analyses to determine first-line treatments. *Depression and Anxiety, 33*(9), 792-806. doi:10.1002/da.22511

Lehmann, S., Breivik, K., Heiervang, E. R., Havik, T., & Havik, O. E. (2015). Reactive attachment disorder and disinhibited social engagement disorder in school-aged foster children—a confirmatory approach to dimensional measures. *Journal of Abnormal Child Psychology, 44*(3), 445–457. doi:10.1007/s10802-015-0045-4

Leichsenring, F., & Steinert, C. (2017). Short-term psychodynamic therapy for obsessive-compulsive disorder: A manual-guided approach to treating the "inhibited rebel." *Bulletin of the Menninger Clinic, 81*(4), 341–389. doi:10.1521/bumc_2017_81_07

Le Jeune, F., Vérin, M., N'Diaye, K., Drapier, D., Leray, E., Du Montcel, S. T., et al. (2010). Decrease of prefrontal metabolism after subthalamic stimulation in obsessive-compulsive disorder: A positron emission tomography study. *Biological Psychiatry, 68,* 1016–1022.

Lemer, J. L., Salafia, E. B., & Benson, K. E. (2013). The relationship between college women's sexual attitudes and sexual activity: The mediating role of body image. *International Journal of Sexual Health, 25,* 104–114. doi:10.1080/19317611.2012.722593

Lemmens, L., Arntz, A., Peeters, F., Hollon, S., Roefs, A., & Huibers, M. (2015). Clinical effectiveness of cognitive therapy v. interpersonal psychotherapy for depression: Results of a randomized controlled trial. *Psychological Medicine* [serial online], *45,* 2095–2110. Ipswich, MA: PsycINFO.

LePage, J. P., DelBen, K., Pollard, S., McGhee, M., VanHorn, L., Murphy, J., . . . Mogge, N. (2003). Reducing assaults on an acute psychiatric unit using a token economy: A 2-year follow-up. *Behavioral Interventions, 18,* 179–190.

Levy, K. N., Clarkin, J. F., Yeomans, F. E., Scott, L. N., Wasserman, R. H., & Kernberg, O. F. (2006). The mechanisms of change in the treatment of borderline personality disorder with transference focused psychotherapy. *Journal of Clinical Psychology, 62,* 481–501.

Levy, K. N., Ellison, W. D., Scott, L. N., & Bernecker, S. L. (2011). Attachment style. *Journal of Clinical Psychology, 67,* 193–201.

Levy, K. N., Johnson, B. N., Clouthier, T. L., Scala, J. W., & Temes, C. M. (2015). An attachment theoretical framework for personality disorders. *Canadian Psychology/Psychologie Canadienne, 56,* 197–207. doi:10.1037/cap0000025

Lewinsohn, P. M. (1974). A behavioral approach to depression. In R. J. Friedman & M. M. Katz (Eds.), *The psychology of depression: Contemporary theory and research,* 157–174. Oxford, England: John Wiley & Sons.

Lewis, A. J., Dennerstein, M., & Gibbs, P. M. (2008). Short-term psychodynamic psychotherapy: Review of recent process and outcome studies. *Australian and New Zealand Journal of Psychiatry, 42,* 445–455.

Lewis, R. W., Fugl-Meyer, K. S., Corona, G., Hayes, R. D., Laumann, E. O., Moreira, E. D., Jr., . . . Segraves, T. (2010). Definitions/epidemiology/risk factors for sexual dysfunction. *Journal of Sexual Medicine, 7,* 1598–1607.

Li, X., Tang, Y., Wang, C., & de Leon, J. (2015). Clozapine for treatment-resistant bipolar disorder: A systematic review. *Bipolar Disorders, 17,* 235–247. doi:10.1111/bdi.12272

Li, Z., Guo, Z., Wang, N., Xu, Z., Qu, Y., Wang, X., . . . Kingdon, D. (2015). Cognitive-behavioural therapy for patients with schizophrenia: A multicentre randomized controlled trial in Beijing, China. *Psychological Medicine, 45,* 1893–1905. doi:10.1017/S0033291714002992

Lilienfeld, S. O., & Lynn, S. J. (2015). Dissociative identity disorder: A contemporary scientific perspective. In S. O. Lilienfeld, S. J. Lynn, & J. M. Lohr (Eds.), *Science and pseudoscience in clinical psychology* (2nd ed., pp. 113–152). New York: Guilford Press.

Lilienfeld, S. O., Patrick, C. J., Benning, S. D., Berg, J., Sellbom, M., & Edens, J. F. (2012). The role of fearless dominance in psychopathy: Confusions, controversies, and clarifications. *Personality Disorders: Theory, Research, and Treatment, 3,* 327–340. doi:10.1037/a0026987

Lin, R. Y., Heacock, L. C., & Fogel, J. F. (2010). Drug-induced, dementia-associated and non-dementia, non-drug delirium hospitalizations in the United States, 1998–2005: An analysis of the National Inpatient Sample. *Drugs & Aging, 27,* 51–61.

Linardon, J., Fairburn, C. G., Fitzsimmons-Craft, E. E., Wilfley, D. E., & Brennan, L. (2017). The empirical status of the third-wave behaviour therapies for the treatment of eating disorders: A systematic review. *Clinical Psychology Review, 58,* 125–140. doi:10.1016/j.cpr.2017.10.005

Lindberg, N., Holi, M. M., Tani, P., & Virkkunen, M. (2005). Looking for pyromania: Characteristics of a consecutive sample of Finnish male criminals with histories of recidivist fire-setting between 1973 and 1993. *BMC Psychiatry, 5,* 47.

Linden-Carmichael, A. N., & Lau-Barraco, C. (2017). A daily diary examination of caffeine mixed with alcohol among college students. *Health Psychology, 36*(9), 881–889. doi:10.1037/hea0000506

Linehan, M. (1993). *Cognitive-behavioral treatment of borderline personality disorder.* New York City: Guilford Press.

Linehan, M. (2014). *DBT® skills training manual.* New York City: Guilford Publications.

Linehan, M. M., Cochran, B. N., & Kehrer, C. A. (2001). Dialectical behavior therapy for borderline personality disorder. In D. H. Barlow (Ed.), *Clinical handbook of psychological disorders: A step-by-step treatment manual* (3rd ed., pp. 470–522). New York: Guilford Press.

Lippert, T., Gelineau, L., Napoli, E., & Borlongan, C. V. (2018). Harnessing neural stem cells for treating psychiatric symptoms associated with fetal alcohol spectrum disorder and epilepsy. *Progress in Neuro-Psychopharmacology & Biological Psychiatry, 80* (Part A), 10–22. doi:10.1016/j.pnpbp.2017.03.021

Lisanby, S. H. (2007). Electroconvulsive therapy for depression. *New England Journal of Medicine, 357,* 1939–1945.

Lisko, J. G., Lee, G. E., Kimbrell, J. B., Rybak, M. E., Valentin-Blasini, L., & Watson, C. H. (2017). Caffeine concentrations in coffee, tea, chocolate, and energy drink flavored e-liquids. *Nicotine & Tobacco Research, 19*(4), 484–492.

Livesley, W. J. (2011). An empirically-based classification of personality disorder. *Journal of Personality Disorders, 25,* 397–420.

Lochner, C., Grant, J. E., Odlaug, B. L., & Stein, D. J. (2012). DSM-5 field survey: Skin picking disorder. *Annals of Clinical Psychiatry, 24,* 300–304.

Loeber, R., & Burke, J. D. (2011). Developmental pathways in juvenile externalizing and internalizing problems. *Journal of Research on Adolescence, 21,* 34–46.

Lopez, O. L., Becker, J. T., Chang, Y. F., Sweet, R. A., Aizenstein, H., Snitz, B., . . . Klunk, W. E. (2013). The long-term effects of conventional and atypical antipsychotics in patients with probable Alzheimer's disease. *American Journal of Psychiatry, 170,* 1051–1058. doi:10.1176/appi.ajp.2013.12081046

Lopez, O. L., Schwam, E., Cummings, J., Gauthier, S., Jones, R., Wilkinson, D., . . . Schindler, R. (2010). Predicting cognitive decline in Alzheimer's disease: An integrated analysis. *Alzheimer's and Dementia, 6,* 431–439.

Lorains, F. K., Cowlishaw, S., & Thomas, S. A. (2011). Prevalence of comorbid disorders in problem and pathological gambling: Systematic review and meta-analysis of population surveys. *Addiction, 106,* 490–498.

Lovaas, O. I. (1987). Behavioral treatment and normal educational and intellectual functioning in young autistic children. *Journal of Consulting and Clinical Psychology, 55,* 3–9.

Lubeiro, A., de Luis-García, R., Rodríguez, M., Álvarez, A., de la Red, H., & Molina, V. (2017). Biological and cognitive correlates of cortical curvature in schizophrenia. *Psychiatry Research: Neuroimaging, 270,* 68, 75. doi:10.1016/j.pscychresns.2017.10.011

M

Maas, M., Mann, R. E., Matheson, F. I., Turner, N. E., Hamilton, H. A., & McCready, J. (2017). A free ride? An analysis of the association of casino bus tours and problem gambling among older adults. *Addiction, 112*(12), 2217-2224. doi:10.1111/add.13914

Machado, M., & Einarson, T. R. (2010). Comparison of SSRIs and SNRIs in major depressive disorder: A meta-analysis of head-to-head randomized clinical trials. *Journal of Clinical Pharmacy and Therapeutics, 35,* 177-188.

Magill, M., Apodaca, T. R., Borsari, B., Gaume, J., Hoadley, A., Gordon, R. F., . . . Moyers, T. (2018). A meta-analysis of motivational interviewing process: Technical, relational, and conditional process models of change. *Journal of Consulting and Clinical Psychology, 86*(2), 140-157. doi:10.1037/ccp0000250

Maher, W. B., & Maher, B. A. (1985). Psychopathology: I. From ancient times to the eighteenth century. In G. A. Kimble & K. Schlesinger (Eds.), *Topics in the history of psychology* (Vol. 2, pp. 251-294). Hillsdale, NJ: Lawrence Erlbaum.

Mainous, A. G., III, Everett, C. J., Diaz, V. A., Player, M. S., Gebregziabher, M., & Smith, D. W. (2010). Life stress and atherosclerosis: A pathway through unhealthy lifestyle. *International Journal of Psychiatry in Medicine, 40,* 147-161.

Majuri, J., Joutsa, J., Johansson, J., Voon, V., Parkkola, R., Alho, H., . . . Kaasinen, V. (2017). Serotonin transporter density in binge eating disorder and pathological gambling: A PET study with [¹¹C]MADAM. *European Neuropsychopharmacology, 27*(12), 1281-1288. doi:10.1016/j.euroneuro.2017.09.007

Makrygianni, M. K., & Reed, P. (2010). A meta-analytic review of the effectiveness of behavioural early intervention programs for children with autistic spectrum disorders. *Research in Autism Spectrum Disorders, 4,* 577, 593. doi:10.1016/j.rasd.2010.01.014

Mao, A. R., Babcock, T., & Brams, M. (2011). ADHD in adults: Current treatment trends with consideration of abuse potential of medications. *Journal of Psychiatric Practice, 17,* 241-250.

Marcantonio, E. R., Kiely, D. K., Simon, S. E., John Orav, E., Jones, R. N., Murphy, K. M., & Bergmann, M. A. (2005). Outcomes of older people admitted to postacute facilities with delirium. *Journal of the American Geriatrics Society, 53,* 963-969.

Marco, E. M., Adriani, W., Ruocco, L. A., Canese, R., Sadile, A. G., & Laviola, G. (2011). Neurobehavioral adaptations to methylphenidate: The issue of early adolescent exposure. *Neuroscience and Biobehavioral Reviews, 35,* 1722-1739.

Marom, S., Munitz, H., Jones, P. B., Weizman, A., & Hermesh, H. (2005). Expressed emotion: Relevance to rehospitalization in schizophrenia over 7 years. *Schizophrenia Bulletin, 31,* 751-758.

Martel, M. M., Nikolas, M., Jernigan, K., Friderici, K., Waldman, I., & Nigg, J. T. (2011). The dopamine receptor D4 gene (DRD4) moderates family environmental effects on ADHD. *Journal of Abnormal Child Psychology: An Official Publication of the International Society for Research in Child and Adolescent Psychopathology, 39,* 1-10.

Martin, C. A., Drasgow, E., Halle, J. W., & Brucker, J. M. (2005). Teaching a child with autism and severe language delays to reject: Direct and indirect effects of functional communication training. *Educational Psychology, 25,* 287-304.

Martin, C. S., Steinley, D. L., Vergés, A., & Sher, K. J. (2011). The proposed 2/11 symptom algorithm for *DSM-5* substance use disorders is too lenient. *Psychological Medicine: A Journal of Research in Psychiatry and the Allied Sciences, 41,* 2008-2010.

Martino, D., & Pringsheim, T. M. (2018). Tourette syndrome and other chronic tic disorders: An update on clinical management. *Expert Review of Neurotherapeutics, 18*(2), 125-137. doi:10.1080/14737175.2018.1413938

Maslow, A. H. (1962). *Toward a psychology of being.* Princeton, NJ: Van Nostrand.

Mason, W. A., & Windle, M. (2001). Family, religious, school and peer influences on adolescent alcohol use: A longitudinal study. *Journal of Studies on Alcohol, 62,* 44-53.

Masters, W. H., & Johnson, V. E. (1966). *Human sexual response.* Boston: Little Brown.

Masters, W. H., & Johnson, V. E. (1970). *Human sexual inadequacy.* Boston: Little Brown.

Masterson, J. F. (1981). *The narcissistic and borderline disorders: An integrated developmental approach.* New York: Brunner/Mazel.

Mataix-Cols, D., Rosario-Campos, M. C., & Leckman, J. F. (2005). A multidimensional model of obsessive-compulsive disorder. *American Journal of Psychiatry, 162,* 228-238.

Maulik, P. K., Mascarenhas, M. N., Mathers, C. D., Dua, T., & Saxena, S. (2011). Prevalence of intellectual disability: A meta-analysis of population-based studies. *Research in Developmental Disabilities, 32,* 419-436.

May, R. (1983). *The discovery of being: Writings in existential psychology.* New York: Norton.

McCabe, M. P., & Connaughton, C. (2014). How the prevalence rates of male sexual dysfunction vary using different criteria. *International Journal of Sexual Health, 26,* 229-237. doi:10.1080/19317611.2013.873104

McCarthy, M. J., Leckband, S. G., & Kelsoe, J. R. (2010). Pharmacogenetics of lithium response in bipolar disorder. *Pharmacogenomics, 11,* 1439-1465.

McClintock, A. S., & Anderson, T. (2015). The application of mindfulness for interpersonal dependency: Effects of a brief intervention. *Mindfulness, 6,* 243-252. doi:10.1007/s12671-013-0253-3

McClintock, A. S., & McCarrick, S. M. (2017). An examination of dependent personality disorder in the alternative *DSM-5* model for personality disorders. *Journal of Psychopathology and Behavioral Assessment, 39*(4), 635-641. doi:10.1007/s10862-017-9621-y

McCloskey, M. S., Kleabir, K., Berman, M. E., Chen, E. Y., & Coccaro, E. F. (2010). Unhealthy aggression: Intermittent explosive disorder and adverse physical health outcomes. *Health Psychology, 29,* 324-332.

McClung, C. A. (2007). Circadian genes, rhythms and the biology of mood disorders. *Pharmacology & Therapeutics, 114,* 222-232.

McCrae, R. R., & Costa, P. T., Jr. (1987). Validation of the five-factor model of personality across instruments and observers. *Journal of Personality and Social Psychology, 52,* 81-90.

McCullumsmith, R. E. (2015). Evidence for schizophrenia as a disorder of neuroplasticity. *The American Journal of Psychiatry, 172,* 312-313. doi:10.1176/appi.ajp.2015.15010069

McEwen, B. S., & Gianaros, P. J. (2010). Central role of the brain in stress and adaptation: Links to socioeconomic status, health, and disease. *Annals of the New York Academy of Science, 1186,* 190-222.

McGrath, J., Saha, S., Chant, D., & Welham, J. (2008). Schizophrenia: A concise overview of incidence, prevalence, and mortality. *Epidemiological Review, 30,* 67-76.

McHugh, R. K., Whitton, S. W., Peckham, A. D., Welge, J. A., & Otto, M. W. (2013). Patient preference for psychological vs. pharmacological treatment of psychiatric disorders: A meta-analytic review. *Journal of Clinical Psychiatry, 74,* 595-602. doi:10.4088/JCP.12r07757

McKhann, G., Drachman, D., Folstein, M., Katzman, R., Price, D., & Stadlan, E. M. (1984). Clinical diagnosis of Alzheimer's disease: Report of the NINCDS-ADRDA Work Group under the auspices of Department of Health and Human Services Task Force on Alzheimer's Disease. *Neurology, 34,* 939-944.

McKhann, G. M., Knopman, D. S., Chertkow, H., Hyman, B. T., Jack, C. R., Jr., Kawas, C. H., . . . Phelps, C. H. (2011). The diagnosis of dementia due to Alzheimer's disease: Recommendations from the National Institute on Aging-Alzheimer's Association workgroups on diagnostic guidelines for Alzheimer's disease. *Alzheimer's and Dementia, 7,* 263-269.

Meares, S., Shores, E. A., Taylor, A. J., Batchelor, J., Bryant, R. A., Baguley, I. J., . . . Marosszeky, J. E. (2011). The prospective course of postconcussion syndrome: The role of mild traumatic brain injury. *Neuropsychology, 25,* 454-465.

Menzel, J. (2018). Avoidant/restrictive food intake disorder: Assessment and treatment. In L. K. Anderson, S. B. Murray, & W. H. Kaye (Eds.), *Clinical handbook of complex and atypical eating disorders* (pp. 149-168). New York: Oxford University Press.

Metz, M. E., Epstein, N. B., & McCarthy, B. (2018). *Cognitive-behavioral therapy for sexual dysfunction.* New York: Routledge/ Taylor & Francis Group.

Meyers, J. E., & Rohling, M. L. (2009). CT and MRI correlations with neuropsychological tests. *Applied Neuropsychology, 16,* 237-253.

Michaels, T. I., Long, L. L., Stevenson, I. H., Chrobak, J. J., & Chen, C. A. (2018). Effects of chronic ketamine on hippocampal cross-frequency coupling: Implications for schizophrenia pathophysiology. *European Journal of Neuroscience.* doi:10.1111/ ejn.13822

Michel, E., Molitor, S., & Schneider, W. (2018). Differential changes in the development of motor coordination and executive functions in children with motor coordination impairments. *Child Neuropsychology, 24*(1), 20-45. doi:10.1080/09297049.2016 .1223282

Mike, A., King, H., Oltmanns, T. F., & Jackson, J. J. (2018). Obsessive, compulsive, and conscientious? The relationship between OCPD and personality traits. *Journal of Personality.* doi:10.1111/jopy.12368

Miller, L., Wickramaratne, P., Gameroff, M. J., Sage, M., Tenke, C. E., & Weissman, M. M. (2011). Religiosity and major depression in adults at high risk: A ten-year prospective study. *American Journal of Psychiatry, 169,* 89-94. doi:appi.ajp.2011.10121823

Miller, W. R. (2002). Project COMBINE, Combined Behavioral Intervention Therapist Manual. https://pubs.niaaa.nih.gov/ publications/COMBINE.htm (accessed 6/5/2018)

Mitchell, D., Tafrate, R. C., & Freeman, A. (2015). Antisocial personality disorder. In A. T. Beck, D. D. Davis, & A. Freeman (Eds.), *Cognitive therapy of personality disorders* (3rd ed., pp. 346-365). New York: Guilford Press.

Mitchell, K. J., Becker, K. A., & Finkelhor, D. (2005). Inventory of problematic Internet experiences encountered in clinical practice. *Professional Psychology: Research and Practice, 36,* 498-509. doi:10.1037/0735 -7028.36.5.498.

Mitteer, D. R., Romani, P. W., Greer, B. D., & Fisher, W. W. (2015). Assessment and treatment of pica and destruction of holiday decorations. *Journal of Applied Behavior Analysis.* doi:10.1002/jaba.255

Molina, V., Sanz, J., Sarramea, F., Benito, C., & Palomo, T. (2005). Prefrontal atrophy in first episodes of schizophrenia associated with limbic metabolic hyperactivity. *Journal of Psychiatric Research, 39,* 117-127.

Mond, J., Mitchison, D., Latner, J., Hay, P., Owen, C., & Rodgers, B. (2013). Quality of life impairment associated with body dissatisfaction in a general population sample of women. *BMC Public Health, 13,* 920. doi:10.1186/1471-2458-13-920

Money, J., & Ehrhardt, A. (1973/1996). *Man and woman, boy and girl.* Northvale, NJ: Jason Aronson.

Monitoring the Future Study. (2017). http:// www.monitoringthefuture.org/data/17data. html#2017data-drugs (accessed 4/12/2018)

Morey, L. C. (1991). *Personality Assessment Inventory professional manual.* Lutz, FL: Psychological Assessment Resources.

Morey, L. C. (2007). *Personality Assessment Inventory professional manual* (2nd ed.). Lutz, FL: Psychological Assessment Resources.

Morin, J. W., & Levenson, J. S. (2008). Exhibitionism: Assessment and treatment. In D. R. Laws & W. T. O'Donohue (Eds.), *Sexual deviance: Theory, assessment, and treatment* (2nd ed., pp. 76-107). New York: Guilford Press.

Morina, N., Ijntema, H., Meyerbröker, K., & Emmelkamp, P. M. (2015). Can virtual reality exposure therapy gains be generalized to real-life? A meta-analysis of studies applying behavioral assessments. *Behaviour Research and Therapy,* 7418-7424. doi:10.1016/j.brat.2015.08.010

Mueller, A. S., Abrutyn, S., & Stockton, C. (2015). Can social ties be harmful? Examining the spread of suicide in early adulthood. *Sociological Perspectives, 58,* 204-222.

Mufson, E. J., Perez, S. E., Nadeem, M., Mahady, L., Kanaan, N. M., Abrahamson, E. E., . . . McKee, A. C. (2016). Progression of tau pathology within cholinergic nucleus basalis neurons in chronic traumatic encephalopathy: A chronic effects of neurotrauma consortium study. *Brain Injury, 30*(12), 1399-1413. doi:10.1080/02699052. 2016.1219058

Mukherjee, N., Kang, C., Wolfe, H. M., Hertzberg, B. S., Smith, J. K., Lin, W., . . . Gilmore, J. H. (2009). Discordance of prenatal and neonatal brain development in twins. *Early Human Development, 85,* 171-175.

Müller, E., & VanGilder, R. (2014). The relationship between participation in Project SEARCH and job readiness and employment for young adults with disabilities. *Journal of Vocational Rehabilitation, 40*(1), 15-26.

Müller, K. W., Wölfling, K., Dickenhorst, U., Beutel, M. E., Medenwaldt, J., & Koch, A. (2017). Recovery, relapse, or else? Treatment outcomes in gambling disorder from a multicenter follow-up study. *European Psychiatry, 43,* 28-34. doi:10.1016 /j.eurpsy.2017.01.326

Murphy, K. (2005). Psychosocial treatments for ADHD in teens and adults: A practice-friendly review. *Journal of Clinical Psychology, 61*(5), 607-619. doi:10.1002/ jclp.20123

Murphy, S. L., Xu, J. Q., Kochanek, K. D., Curtin, S. C., & Arias, E. (2017). Deaths: Final data for 2015. *National Vital Statistics Reports 66*(6). Hyattsville, MD: National Center for Health Statistics.

Murphy, W. D., & Page, I. J. (2008). Exhibitionism: Psychopathology and theory. In D. R. Laws & W. T. O'Donohue (Eds.), *Sexual deviance: Theory, assessment, and treatment* (2nd ed., pp. 61-75). New York: Guilford Press.

Mychasiuk, R., Ilnytskyy, S., Kovalchuk, O., Kolb, B., & Gibb, R. (2011). Intensity matters: Brain, behaviour and the epigenome of prenatally stressed rats. *Neuroscience, 180,* 105-110.

Mynatt, B. S., Gibbons, M. M., & Hughes, A. (2014). Career development for college students with Asperger's syndrome. *Journal of Career Development, 41*(3), 185-198. doi:10.1177/0894845313507774

N

Nagahama, Y., Okina, T., Suzuki, N., Nabatame, H., & Matsuda, M. (2005). The cerebral correlates of different types of perseveration in the Wisconsin Card Sorting Test. *Journal of Neurology, Neurosurgery & Psychiatry, 76,* 169-175.

Nagoshi, J. L., & Brzuzy, S. I. (2010). Transgender theory: Embodying research and practice. *Affilia: Journal of Women & Social Work, 25,* 431-443.

Naoi, M., Maruyama, W., & Shamoto-Nagai, M. (2018). Type A monoamine oxidase and serotonin are coordinately involved in depressive disorders: From neurotransmitter imbalance to impaired neurogenesis. *Journal of Neural Transmission, 125*(1), 53-66. doi:10.1007/s00702-017-1709-8

Naragon-Gainey, K., & Watson, D. (2018). What lies beyond neuroticism? An examination of the unique contributions of social-cognitive vulnerabilities to internalizing disorders. *Assessment, 25*(2), 143-158. doi:10.1177/1073191116659741

Nass, R., & Ross, G. (2008). Developmental disabilities. In W. G. Bradley, R. B. Daroff, G. M. Fenichel, & J. Jankovic (Eds.), *Neurology in clinical practice.* Philadelphia, PA: Butterworth-Heinemann.

National Institute of Alcohol Abuse and Alcoholism (2018). Answers to frequently asked medication questions. https://pubs. niaaa.nih.gov/publications/combine/faqs. htm (accessed 5/18/2018)

National Institute of Mental Health. (2015). Schizophrenia. Retrieved from http://www .nimh.nih.gov/health/statistics/prevalence /schizophrenia.shtml

National Institute of Mental Health. (2018). Major depression. https://www.nimh.nih.gov/health/statistics/major-depression.shtml (accessed 4/23/2018)

National Institute on Alcohol Abuse and Alcoholism. (2007). Helping patients who drink too much: A clinician's guide. https://pubs.niaaa.nih.gov/publications/practitioner/cliniciansguide2005/guide.pdf (accessed 6/5/2018)

National Institute on Drug Abuse (2013). Substance abuse in the military. https://www.drugabuse.gov/publications/drugfacts/substance-abuse-in-military (accessed 4/12/2018)

National Institute on Drug Abuse. (2016a). NIDA InfoFacts: Cocaine. https://www.drugabuse.gov/publications/research-reports/cocaine/what-cocaine (accessed 10/24/2018)

National Institute on Drug Abuse. (2016b). NIDA InfoFacts: Hallucinogens-LSD, peyote, psilocybin, and PCP. https://www.drugabuse.gov/publications/drugfacts/hallucinogens (accessed 10/24/2018)

National Institute on Drug Abuse. (2016c). NIDA InfoFacts: Heroin. Retrieved from https://www.drugabuse.gov/publications/drugfacts/heroin (accessed 10/24/2018)

National Institute on Drug Abuse. (2016d). NIDA InfoFacts: Inhalants. https://www.drugabuse.gov/publications/drugfacts/inhalants (accessed 10/24/2018)

National Institute on Drug Abuse. (2016e). NIDA InfoFacts: MDMA (Ecstasy). Retrieved from https://www.drugabuse.gov/publications/drugfacts/mdma-ecstasymolly (accessed 10/24/2018)

National Institute on Drug Abuse (2018a). Common physical and mental health comorbidities with substance use disorders. https://www.drugabuse.gov/publications/research-reports/common-physical-mental-health-comorbidities-substance-use-disorders/part-1-connection-between-substance-use-disorders-mental-illness (accessed 4/12/2018)

National Institute on Drug Abuse. (2018b). Opioid overdose crisis. https://www.drugabuse.gov/drugs-abuse/opioids/opioid-overdose-crisis (accessed 4/12/2018)

Navarrete, L. P., Pérez, P., Morales, I., & Maccioni, R. B. (2011). Novel drugs affecting tau behavior in the treatment of Alzheimer's disease and tauopathies. *Current Alzheimer Research, 8,* 678–685.

Neumann, N., Dubischar-Krivec, A. M., Braun, C., Löw, A., Poustka, F., Bölte, S., & Birbaumer, N. (2010). The mind of the mnemonists: An MEG and neuropsychological study of autistic memory savants. *Behavioural Brain Research, 215,* 114–121.

Newbury-Helps, J., Feigenbaum, J., & Fonagy, P. (2017). Offenders with antisocial personality disorder display more impairments in mentalizing. *Journal of Personality Disorders, 31*(2), 232–255. doi:10.1521/pedi_2016_30_246

Newby, J. M., Hobbs, M. J., Mahoney, A. J., Wong, S. K., & Andrews, G. (2017). *DSM-5* illness anxiety disorder and somatic symptom disorder: Comorbidity, correlates, and overlap with *DSM-IV* hypochondriasis. *Journal of Psychosomatic Research, 101,* 31–37. doi:10.1016/j.jpsychores.2017.07.010

Nishimura, A., Aritomi, Y., Sasai, K., Kitagawa, T., & Mahableshwarkar, A. R. (2018). Randomized, double-blind, placebo-controlled 8-week trial of the efficacy, safety, and tolerability of 5, 10, and 20 mg/day vortioxetine in adults with major depressive disorder. *Psychiatry and Clinical Neurosciences, 72*(2), 64–72. doi:10.1111/pcn.12565

Nobre, P. J. (2010). Psychological determinants of erectile dysfunction: Testing a cognitive-emotional model. *Journal of Sexual Medicine, 7,* 1429–1437.

Nobre, P. J., & Pinto-Gouveia, J. (2009). Cognitive schemas associated with negative sexual events: A comparison of men and women with and without sexual dysfunction. *Archives of Sexual Behavior, 38,* 842–851.

Nonkes, L. J. P., van Bussel, I. P. G., Verheij, M. M. M., & Homberg, J. R. (2011). The interplay between brain 5-hydroxytryptamine levels and cocaine addiction. *Behavioural Pharmacology, 22,* 723–738.

Novak, C. E., Keuthen, N. J., Stewart, S. E., & Pauls, D. L. (2009). A twin concordance study of trichotillomania. *American Journal of Medical Genetics Series B: Neuropsychiatry of Genetics, 150B,* 944–949.

Nutt, D. J., & Malizia, A. L. (2001). New insights into the role of the GABA(A)-benzodiazepine receptor in psychiatric disorder. *British Journal of Psychiatry, 179,* 390–396.

O

Oakley, S. H., Vaccaro, C. M., Crisp, C. C., Estanol, M. V., Fellner, A. N., Kleeman, S. D., & Pauls, R. N. (2014). Clitoral size and location in relation to sexual function using pelvic MRI. *Journal of Sexual Medicine, 11,* 1013–1022. doi:10.1111/jsm.12450

Oberai, T., Laver, K., Crotty, M., Killington, M., & Jaarsma, R. (2018). Effectiveness of multicomponent interventions on incidence of delirium in hospitalized older patients with hip fracture: A systematic review. *International Psychogeriatrics, 30*(4), 481–492. doi:10.1017/S1041610217002782

O'Brian, S., Jones, M., Packman, A., Menzies, R., & Onslow, M. (2011). Stuttering severity and educational attainment. *Journal of Fluency Disorders, 36,* 86–92.

O'Connor, M. J., Frankel, F., Paley, B., Schonfeld, A. M., Carpenter, E., Laugeson, E. A., & Marquardt, R. (2006). A controlled social skills training for children with fetal alcohol spectrum disorders. *Journal of Consulting and Clinical Psychology, 74,* 639–648.

O'Connor v. Donaldson. (1975). 95 S. Ct. 2486.

Odlaug, B. L., Marsh, P. J., Kim, S. W., & Grant, J. E. (2011). Strategic vs nonstrategic gambling: Characteristics of pathological gamblers based on gambling preference. *Annals of Clinical Psychiatry, 23,* 105–112.

Oerbeck, B., Overgaard, K. R., Stein, M. B., Pripp, A. H., & Kristensen, H. (2018). Treatment of selective mutism: A 5-year follow-up study. *European Child & Adolescent Psychiatry, 27,* 997–1009. doi:10.1007/s00787-018-1110-7

Oerbeck, B., Stein, M. B., Pripp, A. H., & Kristensen, H. (2015). Selective mutism: Follow-up study 1 year after end of treatment. *European Child & Adolescent Psychiatry, 24,* 757–766. doi:10.1007/s00787-014-0620-1

Oliveira, E. B., Leppink, E. W., Derbyshire, K. L., & Grant, J. E. (2015). Excoriation disorder: Impulsivity and its clinical associations. *Journal of Anxiety Disorders, 3019*–3022. doi:10.1016/j.janxdis.2014.12.010

Ollendick, T. H., Öst, L., Ryan, S. M., Capriola, N. N., & Reuterskiöld, L. (2017). Harm beliefs and coping expectancies in youth with specific phobias. *Behaviour Research and Therapy, 91,* 51–57. doi:10.1016/j.brat.2017.01.007

Ollikainen, M., Smith, K. R., Joo, E. J., Ng, H. K., Andronikos, R., Novakovic, B., . . . Craig, J. M. (2010). DNA methylation analysis of multiple tissues from newborn twins reveals both genetic and intrauterine components to variation in the human neonatal epigenome. *Human Molecular Genetics, 19,* 4176–4188.

Öst, L., Havnen, A., Hansen, B., & Kvale, G. (2015). Cognitive behavioral treatments of obsessive-compulsive disorder. A systematic review and meta-analysis of studies published 1993–2014. *Clinical Psychology Review, 40,* 156–169. doi:10.1016/j.cpr.2015.06.003

Ougrin, D., Tranah, T., Stahl, D., Moran, P., & Asarnow, J. R. (2015). Therapeutic interventions for suicide attempts and self-harm in adolescents: Systematic review and meta-analysis. *Journal of the American Academy of Child & Adolescent Psychiatry, 54,* 97–107. doi:10.1016/j.jaac.2014.10.009

Ouyang, L., Grosse, S., Raspa, M., & Bailey, D. (2010). Employment impact and financial burden for families of children with fragile X syndrome: Findings from the National Fragile X Survey. *Journal of Intellectual Disability Research, 54,* 918–928.

Ovenden, E. S., McGregor, N. W., Emsley, R. A., & Warnich, L. (2018). DNA methylation and antipsychotic treatment mechanisms in schizophrenia: Progress and future directions. *Progress in Neuro-Psychopharmacology & Biological Psychiatry, 81,* 38, 49. doi:10.1016/j.pnpbp.2017.10.004

Owens, M. E., & Beidel, D. C. (2015). Can virtual reality effectively elicit distress associated with social anxiety disorder? *Journal of Psychopathology and Behavioral Assessment, 37,* 296-305. doi:10.1007/s10862-014-9454-x

Oxman, T. E., Barrett, J. E., Sengupta, A., & Williams, J. W., Jr. (2000). The relationship of aging and dysthymia in primary care. *The American Journal of Geriatric Psychiatry, 8,* 318-326.

P

Pail, G., Huf, W., Pjrek, E., Winkler, D., Willeit, M., Praschak-Rieder, N., & Kasper, S. (2011). Bright-light therapy in the treatment of mood disorders. *Neuropsychobiology, 64,* 152-162.

Pallaskorpi, S., Suominen, K., Ketokivi, M., Mantere, O., Arvilommi, P., Valtonen, H., . . . Isometsä, E. (2015). Five-year outcome of bipolar I and II disorders: Findings of the Jorvi Bipolar Study. *Bipolar Disorders, 17,* 363-374. doi:10.1111/bdi.12291

Palmer, A. A., & de Wit, H. (2011). Translational genetic approaches to substance use disorders: Bridging the gap between mice and humans. *Human Genetics, 131*(6):931-939. doi: 10.1007/s00439-011-1123-5

Papademetriou, V. (2005). Hypertension and cognitive function. Blood pressure regulation and cognitive function: A review of the literature. *Geriatrics, 60,* 20-22, 24.

Papadimitriou, G. N., Calabrese, J. R., Dikeos, D. G., & Christodoulou, G. N. (2005). Rapid cycling bipolar disorder: Biology and pathogenesis. *International Journal of Neuropsychopharmacology, 8,* 281-292.

Parker, G. F. (2014). *DSM-5 and psychotic and mood disorders. Journal of the American Academy of Psychiatry and the Law, 42,* 182-190.

Penberthy, J. K., Konig, A., Gioia, C. J., Rodríguez, V. M., Starr, J. A., Meese, W., . . . Natanya, E. (2015). Mindfulness-based relapse prevention: History, mechanisms of action, and effects. *Mindfulness, 6,* 151-158. doi:10.1007/s12671-013-0239-1

Pennebaker, J. W., Colder, M., & Sharp, L. K. (1990). Accelerating the coping process. *Journal of Personality and Social Psychology, 58,* 528-537.

Pérez Benítez, C. I., Shea, M. T., Raffa, S., Rende, R., Dyck, I. R., Ramsawh, H. J., et al. (2009). Anxiety sensitivity as a predictor of the clinical course of panic disorder: A 1-year follow-up study. *Depression and Anxiety, 26,* 335-342.

Perlis, R. H., Ostacher, M. J., Patel, J. K., Marangell, L. B., Zhang, H., Wisniewski, S. R., . . . Thase, M. E. (2006). Predictors of recurrence in bipolar disorder: Primary outcomes from the Systematic Treatment Enhancement Program for Bipolar Disorder (STEP-BD). *American Journal of Psychiatry, 163,* 217-224.

Perls, T. (2004). Centenarians who avoid dementia. *Trends in Neuroscience, 27,* 633-636.

Petry, N. M. (2003). A comparison of treatment-seeking pathological gamblers based on preferred gambling activity. *Addiction, 98,* 645-655.

Petry, N. M. (2011). Discounting of probabilistic rewards is associated with gambling abstinence in treatment-seeking pathological gamblers. *Journal of Abnormal Psychology, 121,* 151-159.

Pfaffenseller, B., Kapczinski, F., Gallitano, A. L., & Klamt, F. (2018). EGR3 immediate early gene and the brain-derived neurotrophic factor in bipolar disorder. *Frontiers in Behavioral Neuroscience, 12.* doi:10.3389/fnbeh.2018.00015

Phillips, K. A., Menard, W., Fay, C., & Pagano, M. E. (2005). Psychosocial functioning and quality of life in body dysmorphic disorder. *Comprehensive Psychiatry, 46,* 254-260.

Polanczyk, G., de Lima, M. S., Horta, B. L., Biederman, J., & Rohde, L. A. (2007). The worldwide prevalence of ADHD: A systematic review and metaregression analysis. *The American Journal of Psychiatry, 164,* 942-948.

Pollack, M. H., & Simon, N. M. (2009). Pharmacotherapy for panic disorder and agoraphobia. In M. M. Antony & M. B. Stein (Eds.), *Oxford handbook of anxiety and related disorders* (pp. 295-307). New York: Oxford University Press.

Pope, H. G., Jr., & Yurgelun-Todd, D. (2004). Residual cognitive effects of long-term cannabis use. In D. Castle & R. Murray (Eds.), *Marijuana and madness: Psychiatry and neurobiology* (pp. 198-210). New York: Cambridge University Press.

Portman, D. J., Brown, L., Yuan, J., Kissling, R., & Kingsberg, S. A. (2017). Flibanserin in postmenopausal women with hypoactive sexual desire disorder: Results of the PLUMERIA study. *Journal of Sexual Medicine, 14*(6), 834-842. doi:10.1016/j.jsxm.2017.03.258

Prescott, D. S., & Levenson, J. S. (2010). Sex offender treatment is not punishment. *Journal of Sexual Aggression, 16,* 275-285.

Q

Qiu, M.-G., Ye, Z., Li, Q.-Y., Liu, G.-J., Xie, B., & Wang, J. (2011). Changes of brain structure and function in ADHD children. *Brain Topography, 24*(3-4), 243-252.

Quick, V. M., & Byrd-Bredbenner, C. (2012). Weight regulation practices of young adults. Predictors of restrictive eating. *Appetite, 59,* 425-430. doi:10.1016/j.appet.2012.06.004

Quinn, P. O. (2005). Treating adolescent girls and women with ADHD: Gender-specific issues. *Journal of Clinical Psychology, 61,* 579-587.

R

Rabin, L. A., Barr, W. B., & Burton, L. A. (2005). Assessment practices of clinical neuropsychologists in the United States and Canada: A survey of INS, NAN, and APA Division 40 members. *Archives of Clinical Neuropsychology, 20,* 33-65.

Rambau, S., Forstner, A. J., Wegener, I., Mücke, M., Wissussek, C. S., Staufenbiel, S. M., . . . Conrad, R. (2018). Childhood adversities, bonding, and personality in social anxiety disorder with alcohol use disorder. *Psychiatry Research, 262,* 295-302. doi:10.1016/j.psychres.2018.02.006

Rane, P., Cochran, D., Hodge, S. M., Haselgrove, C., Kennedy, D. N., & Frazier, J. A. (2015). Connectivity in autism: A review of MRI connectivity studies. *Harvard Review of Psychiatry, 23,* 223-244. doi:10.1097/hrp.0000000000000072

Reas, D. L., Kjelsas, E., Heggestad, T., Eriksen, L., Nielsen, S., Gjertsen, F., & Gotestam, K. G. (2005). Characteristics of anorexia nervosa-related deaths in Norway (1992-2000): Data from the National Patient Register and the Causes of Death Register. *International Journal of Eating Disorders, 37,* 181-187.

Rees, C. S., & Pritchard, R. (2015). Brief cognitive therapy for avoidant personality disorder. *Psychotherapy, 52,* 45-55. doi:10.1037/a0035158

Rees, G., & Garcia, J. R. (2017a). An investigation into the solitary and interpersonal aspects of sexual object fetishism: A mixed-methods approach. *Psychology & Sexuality, 8*(4), 252-267.

Rees, G., & Garcia, J. R. (2017b). All I need is shoe: An investigation into the obligatory aspect of sexual object fetishism. *International Journal of Sexual Health, 29*(4), 303-312. doi:10.1080/19317611.2017.1309483

Reich, J. (2010). Avoidant personality disorder and its relationship to social phobia. In S. G. Hofmann & P. M. DiBartolo (Eds.), *Social anxiety: Clinical, developmental, and social perspectives* (2nd ed., pp. 207-222). San Diego, CA: Elsevier Academic Press. doi:10.1016/B978-0-12-375096-9.00008-0

Reichenberg, A. (2010). The assessment of neuropsychological functioning in schizophrenia. *Dialogues in Clinical Neuroscience, 12,* 383-392.

Reid, H., & Bahar, R. J. (2006). Treatment of encopresis and chronic constipation in young children: Clinical results from interactive parent-child guidance. *Clinical Pediatrics, 45,* 157-164.

Reme, S. E., Tangen, T., Moe, T., & Eriksen, H. R. (2011). Prevalence of psychiatric disorders in sick listed chronic low back pain patients. *European Journal of Pain, 15,* 1075-1080.

Renner, M. J., & Mackin, R. S. (1998). A life stress instrument for classroom use. *Teaching of Psychology, 25,* 46–48.

Renton, J. C., & Mankiewicz, P. D. (2015). Paranoid, schizotypal, and schizoid personality disorders. In A. T. Beck, D. D. Davis, & A. Freeman (Eds.), *Cognitive therapy of personality disorders* (3rd ed., pp. 244–275). New York: Guilford Press.

Resnick, R. J. (2005). Attention deficit hyperactivity disorder in teens and adults: They don't all outgrow it. *Journal of Clinical Psychology, 61,* 529–533.

Rettew, D. C. (2000). Avoidant personality disorder, generalized social phobia, and shyness: Putting the personality back into personality disorders. *Harvard Review of Psychiatry, 8,* 283–297.

Richings, C., Cook, R., & Roy, A. (2011). Service evaluation of an integrated assessment and treatment service for people with intellectual disability with behavioural and mental health problems. *Journal of Intellectual Disabilities, 15,* 7–19.

Riehm, K. E., Azar, M., & Thombs, B. D. (2015). Transparency of outcome reporting and trial registration of randomized controlled trials in top psychosomatic and behavioral health journals: A 5-year follow-up. *Journal of Psychosomatic Research, 79,* 1–12. doi:10.1016/j.jpsychores.2015 .04.010

Riggs, S. E., & Creed, T. A. (2017). A model to transform psychosis milieu treatment using CBT-informed interventions. *Cognitive and Behavioral Practice, 24*(3), 353–362. doi:10.1016/j.cbpra.2016.08.001

Ringen, P. A., Engh, J. A., Birkenaes, A. B., Dieset, I., & Andreassen, O. A. (2014). Increased mortality in schizophrenia due to cardiovascular disease—A non-systematic review of epidemiology, possible causes, and interventions. *Frontiers in Psychiatry, 5,* 137.

Rizvi, S. L., & Nock, M. K. (2008). Single-case experimental designs for the evaluation of treatments for self-injurious and suicidal behaviors. *Suicide and Life-Threatening Behavior, 38,* 498–510.

Robbins, C. A. (2005). ADHD couple and family relationships: Enhancing communication and understanding through Imago Relationship Therapy. *Journal of Clinical Psychology, 61,* 565–577.

Roberts, C. A., Quednow, B. B., Montgomery, C., & Parrott, A. C. (2018). MDMA and brain activity during neurocognitive performance: An overview of neuroimaging studies with abstinent 'Ecstasy' users. *Neuroscience and Biobehavioral Reviews, 84,* 470–482. doi:10.1016/j.neubiorev.2017 .07.015

Roberts, R. E., Alegría, M., Roberts, C. R., & Chen, I. G. (2005). Mental health problems of adolescents as reported by their caregivers: A comparison of European, African, and Latino Americans. *The Journal of Behavioral Health Services & Research, 32,* 1–13.

Robins, L. N. (1966). *Deviant children grow up: A sociological and psychiatric study of sociopathic personality.* Baltimore: Williams & Wilkins.

Rodriguez-Monguio, R., Brand, E., & Volberg, R. (2018). The economic burden of pathological gambling and co-occurring mental health and substance use disorders. *Journal of Addiction Medicine, 12*(1), 53–60.

Roepke, S. K., & Grant, I. (2011). Toward a more complete understanding of the effects of personal mastery on cardiometabolic health. *Health Psychology, 57,* 539–548.

Rogers, C. R. (1951). *Client-centered therapy: Its current practice implications, and theory.* Boston: Houghton Mifflin.

Ronningstam, E. (2011). Narcissistic personality disorder: A clinical perspective. *Journal of Psychiatric Practice, 17,* 89–99.

Rose, E., Schreiber-Agus, N., Bajaj, K., Klugman, S., & Goldwaser, T. (2016). Challenges of pre- and post-test counseling for Orthodox Jewish individuals in the premarital phase. *Journal of Genetic Counseling, 25*(1), 18–24. doi:10.1007 /s10897-015-9880-2

Rosebush, P. I., & Mazurek, M. F. (2011). Treatment of conversion disorder in the 21st century: Have we moved beyond the couch? *Current Treatment Options in Neurology, 13,* 255–266.

Rosen, R., Brown, C., Heiman, J., Leiblum, S., Meston, C., Shabsigh, R., . . . D'Agostino, R., Jr. (2000). The Female Sexual Function Index (FSFI): A multidimensional self-report instrument for the assessment of female sexual function. *Journal of Sex & Marital Therapy, 26,* 191–208.

Rosso, I. M., Makris, N., Britton, J. C., Price, L. M., Gold, A. L., Zai, D., et al. (2010). Anxiety sensitivity correlates with two indices of right anterior insula structure in specific animal phobia. *Depression and Anxiety, 27,* 1104–1110.

Rowland, A. S., Skipper, B. J., Rabiner, D. L., Qeadan, F., Campbell, R. A., Naftel, A. J., & Umbach, D. M. (2017). Attention-deficit/ hyperactivity disorder (ADHD): Interaction between socioeconomic status and parental history of ADHD determines prevalence. *Journal of Child Psychology and Psychiatry,* doi:10.1111/jcpp.12775

Rudd, M. D., Bryan, C. J., Wertenberger, E. G., Peterson, A. L., Young-McCaughan, S., Mintz, J., . . . Bruce, T. O. (2015). Brief cognitive-behavioral therapy effects on post-treatment suicide attempts in a military sample: Results of a randomized clinical trial with 2-year follow-up. *The American Journal of Psychiatry, 172,* 441–449. doi:10.1176 /appi.ajp.2014.14070843

Rush, A. J., Trivedi, M. H., Wisniewski, S. R., Nierenberg, A. A., Stewart, J. W., Warden, D., . . . Fava, M. (2006). Acute and longer-term outcomes in depressed outpatients requiring one or several treatment steps: A STAR*D report. *American Journal of Psychiatry, 163,* 1905–1917.

Rylands, A. J., McKie, S., Elliott, R., Deakin, J. F., & Tarrier, N. (2011). A functional magnetic resonance imaging paradigm of expressed emotion in schizophrenia. *Journal of Nervous and Mental Disease, 199,* 25–29.

S

Salehi, A., Ashford, J. W., & Mufson, E. J. (2016). Editorial: The link between Alzheimer's disease and Down syndrome. A historical perspective. *Current Alzheimer Research, 13*(1), 2–6. doi:10.2174/15672050 12999151021102914

Salekin, R. T., Worley, C., & Grimes, R. D. (2010). Treatment of psychopathy: A review and brief introduction to the mental model approach for psychopathy. *Behavioral Sciences & the Law, 28,* 235–266.

Salvatore, J. E., Han, S., Farris, S. P., Mignogna, K. M., Miles, M. F., & Agrawal, A. (2018). Beyond genome-wide significance: Integrative approaches to the interpretation and extension of GWAS findings for alcohol use disorder. *Addiction Biology.* doi:10.1111/adb.12591

Salyers, M. P., McGuire, A. B., Rollins, A. L., Bond, G. R., Mueser, K. T., & Macy, V. R. (2010). Integrating assertive community treatment and illness management and recovery for consumers with severe mental illness. *Community Mental Health Journal, 46,* 319–329.

Samuel, D. B., & Gore, W. L. (2012). Maladaptive variants of conscientiousness and agreeableness. *Journal of Personality, 80,* 1669–1696. doi:10.1111/j.1467-6494.2012 .00770.x

Sanders, N., Smeets, P. M., van Elburg, A. A., Danner, U. N., van Meer, F., Hoek, H. W., & Adan, R. H. (2015). Altered food-cue processing in chronically ill and recovered women with anorexia nervosa. *Frontiers in Behavioral Neuroscience, 9,* 46.

Sansone, R. A., Dittoe, N., Hahn, H. S., & Wiederman, M. W. (2011). The prevalence of borderline personality disorder in a consecutive sample of cardiac stress test patients. *The Primary Care Companion for CNS Disorders, 13*(3): PCC.10l01087. doi: [10.4088/PCC.10l01087]

Santucci, L. C., Ehrenreich, J. T., Trosper, S. E., Bennett, S. M., & Pincus, D. B. (2009). Development and preliminary evaluation of a one-week summer treatment program for separation anxiety disorder. *Cognitive and Behavioral Practice, 16,* 317–331.

Sar, V., Akyuz, G., Kundakci, T., Kiziltan, E., & Dogan, O. (2004). Childhood trauma, dissociation, and psychiatric comorbidity in patients with conversion disorder. *American Journal of Psychiatry, 161,* 2271–2276.

Sautter, F. J., Glynn, S. M., Cretu, J. B., Senturk, D., & Vaught, A. S. (2015). Efficacy of structured approach therapy in reducing PTSD in returning veterans: A randomized clinical trial. *Psychological Services, 12,* 199–212. doi:10.1037/ser0000032

Sayal, K., Prasad, V., Daley, D., Ford, T., & Coghill, D. (2017). ADHD in children and young people: Prevalence, care pathways, and service provision. *The Lancet Psychiatry, 5*(2), 175–186. doi:10.1016/S2215-0366(17)30167-0

Scarpini, E., Bruno, G., Zappalà, G., Adami, M., Richarz, U., Gaudig, M., . . . Schäuble, B. (2011). Cessation versus continuation of galantamine treatment after 12 months of therapy in patients with Alzheimer's disease: A randomized, double blind, placebo controlled withdrawal trial. *Journal of Alzheimer's Disease, 26,* 211–220.

Scarr, S., & McCartney, K. (1983). How people make their own environments: A theory of genotype S environment effects. *Child Development, 54,* 424–435.

Schaakxs, R., Comijs, H. C., Lamers, F., Beekman, A. F., & Penninx, B. H. (2017). Age-related variability in the presentation of symptoms of major depressive disorder. *Psychological Medicine, 47*(3), 543–552. doi:10.1017/S0033291716002579

Schieber, K., Kollei, I., de Zwaan, M., & Martin, A. (2015). Classification of body dysmorphic disorder—What is the advantage of the new *DSM-5* criteria? *Journal of Psychosomatic Research, 78,* 223–227. doi:10.1016/j.jpsychores.2015.01.002

Schilpzand, E. J., Sciberras, E., Alisic, E., Efron, D., Hazell, P., Jongeling, B., . . . Nicholson, J. M. (2017). Trauma exposure in children with and without ADHD: Prevalence and functional impairment in a community-based study of 6–8-year-old Australian children. *European Child & Adolescent Psychiatry, 27*(6), 811–819. doi:10.1007/s00787-017-1067-y

Schneck, C. D., Miklowitz, D. J., Miyahara, S., Araga, M., Wisniewski, S., Gyulai, L., . . . Sachs, G. S. (2008). The prospective course of rapid-cycling bipolar disorder: Findings from the STEP-BD. *The American Journal of Psychiatry, 165,* 370–377.

Schneider, S., & Stone, A. A. (2015). Mixed emotions across the adult life span in the United States. *Psychology and Aging, 30,* 369–382. doi:10.1037/pag0000018

Schneiderman, N., Ironson, G., & Siegel, S. D. (2005). Stress and health: Psychological, behavioral, and biological determinants. *Annual Review of Clinical Psychology, 1,* 607–628.

Sedlak, A. J., Mettenburg, J., Basena, M., Petta, I., McPherson, K., Greene, A., & Li, S. (2010). Fourth National Incidence Study of Child Abuse and Neglect (NIS-4): Report to Congress. Washington, DC: U.S. Department of Health and Human Services, Administration for Children and Families.

Segal, D. L., Hook, J. N., & Coolidge, F. L. (2001). Personality dysfunction, coping styles, and clinical symptoms in younger and older adults. *Journal of Clinical Geropsychology, 7,* 201–212.

Segal, Z. V., Williams, J. M. G., & Teasdale, J. D. (2002). *Mindfulness-based cognitive therapy for depression: A new approach to preventing relapse.* New York: Guilford Press.

Segraves, R. T. (2010). Considerations for an evidence-based definition of premature ejaculation in the *DSM-V. Journal of Sexual Medicine, 7,* 672–679.

Seichepine, D. R., Stamm, J. M., Daneshvar, D. H., Riley, D. O., Baugh, C. M., Gavett, B. E., . . . Stern, R. A. (2013). Profile of self-reported problems with executive functioning in college and professional football players. *Journal of Neurotrauma, 30,* 1299–1304.

Seltzer, M. M., Krauss, M. W., Shattuck, P. T., Orsmond, G., Swe, A., & Lord, C. (2003). The symptoms of autism spectrum disorders in adolescence and adulthood. *Journal of Autism and Developmental Disorders, 33,* 565–581.

Shah, D. B., Pesiridou, A., Baltuch, G. H., Malone, D. A., & O'Reardon, J. P. (2008). Functional neurosurgery in the treatment of severe obsessive compulsive disorder and major depression: Overview of disease circuits and therapeutic targeting for the clinician. *Psychiatry (Edgmont), 5,* 24–33.

Shankman, S. A., Funkhouser, C. J., Klein, D. N., Davila, J., Lerner, D., & Hee, D. (2017). Reliability and validity of severity dimensions of psychopathology assessed using the structured clinical interview for *DSM-5* (SCID). *International Journal of Methods in Psychiatric Research.* doi:10.1002/mpr.1590

Sharma, P., & Sinha, U. K. (2010). Defense mechanisms in mania, bipolar depression and unipolar depression. *Psychological Studies, 55,* 239–247.

Sharp, S. I., Aarsland, D., Day, S., Sønnesyn, H., & Ballard, C. (2011). Hypertension is a potential risk factor for vascular dementia: Systematic review. *International Journal of Geriatric Psychiatry, 26,* 661–669.

Shedler, J. (2010). The efficacy of psychodynamic psychotherapy. *American Psychologist, 65,* 98–109.

Shepard, J. A., Poler, J. J., & Grabman, J. H. (2017). Evidence-based psychosocial treatments for pediatric elimination disorders. *Journal of Clinical Child and Adolescent Psychology, 46*(6), 767–797. doi:10.1080/15374416.2016.1247356

Shindel, A. W., & Moser, C. A. (2011). Why are the paraphilias mental disorders? *Journal of Sexual Medicine, 8,* 927–929.

Shipherd, J. C., & Salters-Pedneault, K. (2018). Do acceptance and mindfulness moderate the relationship between maladaptive beliefs and posttraumatic distress? *Psychological Trauma: Theory, Research, Practice, and Policy, 10*(1), 95–102. doi:10.1037/tra0000248

Shriver, M. D., Segool, N., & Gortmaker, V. (2011). Behavior observations for linking assessment to treatment for selective mutism. *Education & Treatment of Children, 34,* 389–411.

Shusterman, A., Feld, L., Baer, L., & Keuthen, N. (2009). Affective regulation in trichotillomania: Evidence from a large-scale Internet survey. *Behaviour Research and Therapy, 47,* 637–644.

Silarova, B., Giltay, E. J., Van Reedt Dortland, A., Van Rossum, E. C., Hoencamp, E., Penninx, B. H., & Spijker, A. T. (2015). Metabolic syndrome in patients with bipolar disorder: Comparison with major depressive disorder and non-psychiatric controls. *Journal of Psychosomatic Research, 78,* 391–398. doi:10.1016/j.jpsychores.2015.02.010

Silove, D., Alonso, J., Bromet, E., Gruber, M., Sampson, N., Scott, K., . . . Kessler, R. C. (2015). Pediatric-onset and adult-onset separation anxiety disorder across countries in the World Mental Health Survey. *The American Journal of Psychiatry, 172,* 647–656. doi:10.1176/appi.ajp.2015.14091185

Skinner, B. F. (1953). *Science and human behavior.* New York: Free Press.

Skodol, A. E., Morey, L. C., Bender, D. S., & Oldham, J. M. (2015). The alternative *DSM-5* model for personality disorders: A clinical application. *The American Journal of Psychiatry, 172,* 606–613. doi:10.1176/appi.ajp.2015.14101220

Slikboer, R., Reser, M. P., Nedeljkovic, M., Castle, D. J., & Rossell, S. L. (2018). Systematic review of published primary studies of neuropsychology and neuroimaging in trichotillomania. *Journal of The International Neuropsychological Society, 24*(2), 188–205. doi:10.1017/S1355617717000819

Smart, D., Youssef, G. J., Sanson, A., Prior, M., Toumbourou, J. W., & Olsson, C. A. (2017). Consequences of childhood reading difficulties and behaviour problems for educational achievement and employment in early adulthood. *British Journal of Educational Psychology, 87*(2), 288–308. doi:10.1111/bjep.12150

Smith, R., Hall, K.E., Etkind, P., & Van Dyke, M. (2018) Current marijuana use by industry and occupation—Colorado, 2014–2015. *MMWR Morbidity and Mortality Weekly Report, 67,* 409–413. doi:http://dx.doi.org/10.15585/mmwr.mm6714a

Smith-Hicks, C. L., Gupta, S., Ewen, J. B., Hong, M., Kratz, L., Kelley, R., . . . Naidu, S. (2017). Randomized open-label trial of dextromethorphan in Rett syndrome. *Neurology, 89*(16), 1684–1690. doi:10.1212/WNL.0000000000004515

Snorrason, I., Belleau, E. L., & Woods, D. W. (2012). How related are hair pulling disorder (trichotillomania) and skin picking disorder? A review of evidence for comorbidity, similarities and shared etiology. *Clinical Psychology Review, 32,* 618-629. doi:10.1016/j.cpr.2012.05.008

Snorrason, I., Berlin, G. S., & Lee, H. (2015). Optimizing psychological interventions for trichotillomania (hair-pulling disorder): An update on current empirical status. *Psychology Research and Behavior Management, 8,* 105-113.

Snyder, H. N. (2000). *Sexual assault of young children as reported to law enforcement: Victim, incident, and offender characteristics.* Washington, DC: U.S. Department of Justice.

Soares-Weiser, K., Maayan, N., Bergman, H., Davenport, C., Kirkham, A. J., Grabowski, S., & Adams, C. E. (2015). First rank symptoms for schizophrenia (Cochrane diagnostic test accuracy review). *Schizophrenia Bulletin, 41,* 792-794. doi:10.1093/schbul/sbv061

Solem, S., Håland, Å. T., Vogel, P. A., Hansen, B., & Wells, A. (2009). Change in metacognitions predicts outcome in obsessive-compulsive disorder patients undergoing treatment with exposure and response prevention. *Behaviour Research and Therapy, 47,* 301-307.

Specht, M. W., Mahone, E. M., Kline, T., Waranch, R., Brabson, L., Thompson, C. B., & Singer, H. S. (2017). Efficacy of parent-delivered behavioral therapy for primary complex motor stereotypies. *Developmental Medicine & Child Neurology, 59*(2), 168-173. doi:10.1111/dmcn.13164

Spetie, L., & Arnold, L. E. (2007). Ethical issues in child psychopharmacology research and practice: Emphasis on preschoolers. *Psychopharmacology, 191,* 15-26.

Spinhoven, P., van Hemert, A. M., & Penninx, B. H. (2017). Experiential avoidance and bordering psychological constructs as predictors of the onset, relapse and maintenance of anxiety disorders: One or many? *Cognitive Therapy and Research, 41*(6), 867-880. doi:10.1007/s10608-017-9856-7

Sposato, L. A., Kapral, M. K., Fang, J., Gill, S. S., Hackam, D. G., Cipriano, L. E., & Hachinski, V. (2015). Declining incidence of stroke and dementia: Coincidence or prevention opportunity? *JAMA Neurology, 72*(12), 1529-1531. doi:10.1001/jamaneurol.2015.2816

Stade, B. C., Bailey, C., Dzendoletas, D., Sgro, M., Dowswell, T., & Bennett, D. (2009). Psychological and/or educational interventions for reducing alcohol consumption in pregnant women and women planning pregnancy. *Cochrane Database of Systematic Reviews,* CD004228.

State v. Darnall. (1980). 161, 614 P. 2d 120 (Or. Ct. App.)

State v. Greene. (1998). 960 P.2d 980 (Wash. Ct. App.)

State v. Jones. (1998). 743 P. 2d 276 P 2d 1183, 1185 (Washington Court Appellate 1987. Affiliated 759.)

State v. Lockhart. (2000). 542 S.E.2d 443 (W. Va.)

State v. Milligan, No. 77-CR-11-2908 (Franklin County, Ohio. Dec. 4, 1978).

Stea, J. N., Hodgins, D. C., & Fung, T. (2015). Abstinence versus moderation goals in brief motivational treatment for pathological gambling. *Journal of Gambling Studies, 31,* 1029-1045. doi:10.1007/s10899-014-9461-6

Steel, C., Macdonald, J., & Schroder, T. (2018). A systematic review of the effect of therapists' internalized models of relationships on the quality of the therapeutic relationship. *Journal of Clinical Psychology, 74*(1), 5-42. doi:10.1002/jclp.22484

Stein, M. B., & Gelernter, J. (2014). Genetic factors in social anxiety disorder. In J. W. Weeks (Ed.), *The Wiley Blackwell handbook of social anxiety disorder* (pp. 53-66). Hoboken, NJ: Wiley-Blackwell. doi:10.1002/9781118653920.ch3

Steinberg, M. (1994). *Structured clinical interview for DSM-IV dissociative disorders–Revised (SCID-D-R).* Washington, DC: American Psychiatric Association.

Stevenson, B. L., Dvorak, R. D., Kuvaas, N. J., Williams, T. J., & Spaeth, D. T. (2015). Cognitive control moderates the association between emotional instability and alcohol dependence symptoms. *Psychology of Addictive Behaviors, 29,* 323-328. doi:10.1037/adb0000045

St. George-Hyslop, P. H., & Petit, A. (2005). Molecular biology and genetics of Alzheimer's disease. *Comptes Rendus Biologies, 328,* 119-130.

Stilo, S. A., & Murray, R. M. (2010). The epidemiology of schizophrenia: Replacing dogma with knowledge. *Dialogues in Clinical Neuroscience, 12,* 305-315.

Striegel-Moore, R. H., Rosselli, F., Perrin, N., DeBar, L., Wilson, G. T., May, A., & Kraemer, H. C. (2009). Gender difference in the prevalence of eating disorder symptoms. *International Journal of Eating Disorders, 42*(5), 471-474.

Stucki, S., & Rihs-Middel, M. (2007). Prevalence of adult problem and pathological gambling between 2000 and 2005: An update. *Journal of Gambling Studies, 23,* 245-257.

Sturmey, P. (2009). Behavioral activation is an evidence-based treatment for depression. *Behavior Modification, 33,* 818-829.

Subbaraman, M. S., Lendle, S., van der Laan, M., Kaskutas, L. A., & Ahern, J. (2013). Cravings as a mediator and moderator of drinking outcomes in the COMBINE study. *Addiction, 108,* 1737-1744. doi:10.1111/add.12238

Subramaniam, M., Wang, P., Soh, P., Vaingankar, J. A., Chong, S. A., Browning, C. J., & Thomas, S. A. (2015). Prevalence and determinants of gambling disorder among older adults: A systematic review. *Addictive Behaviors, 41,* 199-209. doi:10.1016/j.addbeh.2014.10.007

Substance Abuse and Mental Health Services Administration. (2014). SAMHSA's concept of trauma and guidance for a trauma-informed approach. (HHS Publication No. SMA 14-4884). Rockville, MD: Substance Abuse and Mental Health Services Administration.

Substance Abuse and Mental Health Services Administration (SAMHSA). (2017). Key substance use and mental health indicators in the United States: Results from the 2016 National Survey on Drug Use and Health (HHS Publication No. SMA 17-5044, NSDUH Series H-52). Rockville, MD: Center for Behavioral Health Statistics and Quality, Substance Abuse and Mental Health Services Administration. Retrieved from https://www.samhsa.gov/data/(accessed 5/18/2018)

Substance Abuse and Mental Health Services Administration. (2018). Retrieved from https://www.samhsa.gov/data/sites/default/files/NSDUH-DetTabs-2016/NSDUH-DetTabs-2016.htm#tab1-29A 4/9/2018

Sullivan, P. F., Neale, M. C., & Kendler, K. S. (2000). Genetic epidemiology of major depression: Review and meta-analysis. *American Journal of Psychiatry, 157,* 1552-1562.

Sultzer, D. L. (2018). Cognitive ageing and Alzheimer's disease: The cholinergic system redux. *Brain: A Journal of Neurology, 141*(3), 626-628. doi:10.1093/brain/awy040

Sunderland, T., Hill, J. L., Mellow, A. M., Lawlor, B. A., Gundersheimer, J., Newhouse, P. A., & Grafman, J. H. (1989). Clock drawing in Alzheimer's disease: A novel measure of dementia severity. *Journal of the American Geriatrics Society, 37,* 725-729.

Sungur, M. B., Soygür, H., Güner, P., Üstün, B., Çetin, İ., & Falloon, I. R. (2011). Identifying an optimal treatment for schizophrenia: A 2-year randomized controlled trial comparing integrated care to a high-quality routine treatment. *International Journal of Psychiatry in Clinical Practice, 15,* 118-127.

Sutherland, K., & Cistulli, P. A. (2015). Recent advances in obstructive sleep apnea pathophysiology and treatment. *Sleep and Biological Rhythms, 13,* 26-40. doi:10.1111/sbr.12098

Swann, A. C. (2010). The strong relationship between bipolar and substance-use disorder. *Annals of the New York Academy of Sciences, 1187,* 276-293.

Swartz, H. A., Frank, E., O'Toole, K., Newman, N., Kiderman, H., Carlson, S., . . . Ghinassi, F. (2011). Implementing interpersonal and social rhythm therapy for mood disorders across a continuum of care. *Psychiatric Services, 62,* 1377-1380. doi:10.1176/appi.ps.62.11.1377

Swartz, M. S., Wilder, C. M., Swanson, J. W., Van Dorn, R. A., Robbins, P. C., Steadman, H. J., . . . Monahan, J. (2010). Assessing outcomes for consumers in New York's assisted outpatient treatment program. *Psychiatric Services, 61,* 976–981.

T

Tarasoff v. The Regents of the University of California. (1976). 551 P 2d334 (California).

Taylor, C. A., Bell, J. M., Breiding, M. J., & Xu, L. (2017). Traumatic brain injury–related emergency department visits, hospitalizations, and deaths—United States, 2007 and 2013. *Morbidity and Mortality Weekly Reports Surveillance Summary, 66*(No. SS-9), 1–16. doi:http://dx.doi.org/10.15585/mmwr.ss6609a1

Terracciano, A., McCrae, R. R., Brant, L. J., & Costa, P. T. J. (2005). Hierarchical linear modeling analyses of the NEO-PI-R Scales in the Baltimore Longitudinal Study of Aging. *Psychology and Aging, 20,* 493–506.

Thaler, L., Meana, M., & Lanti, A. (2009). Misremembering pain: Memory bias for pain words in women reporting sexual pain. *Journal of Sexual Medicine, 6,* 1369–1377. doi:10.1111/j.1743-6109.2008.01211.x

Thibaut, F., De LaBarra, F., Gordon, H., Cosyns, P., & Bradford, J. W. (2010). The World Federation of Societies of Biological Psychiatry (WFSBP) Guidelines for the biological treatment of paraphilias. *The World Journal of Biological Psychiatry, 11*(3–4), 604–655. doi:10.3109/15622971003671628

Thioux, M., Stark, D. E., Klaiman, C., & Schultz, R. T. (2006). The day of the week when you were born in 700 ms: Calendar computation in an autistic savant. *Journal of Experimental Psychology: Human Perception and Performance, 32,* 1155–1168.

Thomasius, R., Zapletalova, P., Petersen, K., Buchert, R., Andresen, B., Wartberg, L., . . . Schmoldt, A. (2006). Mood, cognition and serotonin transporter availability in current and former ecstasy (MDMA) users: The longitudinal perspective. *Journal of Psychopharmacology, 20,* 211–225.

Tolin, D. F. (2011). Understanding and treating hoarding: A biopsychosocial perspective. *Journal of Clinical Psychology, 67,* 517–526. doi:10.1002/jclp.20795

Tolin, D. F., Franklin, M. E., Diefenbach, G. J., Anderson, E., & Meunier, S. A. (2007). Pediatric trichotillomania: Descriptive psychopathology and an open trial of cognitive behavioral therapy. *Cognitive Behaviour Therapy, 36,* 129–144.

Tolin, D. F., Frost, R. O., Steketee, G., & Muroff, J. (2015). Cognitive behavioral therapy for hoarding disorder: A meta-analysis. *Depression and Anxiety, 32,* 158–166. doi:10.1002/da.22327

Tombaugh, T. N., Stormer, P., Rees, L., Irving, S., & Francis, M. (2006). The effects of mild and severe traumatic brain injury on the auditory and visual versions of the Adjusting-Paced Serial Addition Test (Adjusting-PSAT). *Archives of Clinical Neuropsychology, 21,* 753–761.

Torke, A. M., Alexander, G. C., & Lantos, J. (2008). Substituted judgment: The limitations of autonomy in surrogate decision making. *Journal of General Internal Medicine, 23,* 1514–1517. doi:http://doi.org/10.1007/s11606-008-0688-8

Traish, A. M., Feeley, R. J., & Guay, A. T. (2009). Testosterone therapy in women with gynecological and sexual disorders: A triumph of clinical endocrinology from 1938 to 2008. *Journal of Sexual Medicine, 6,* 334–351.

Trull, T. J., Jahng, S., Tomko, R. L., Wood, P. K., & Sher, K. J. (2010). Revised NESARC personality disorder diagnoses: Gender, prevalence, and comorbidity with substance dependence disorders. *Journal of Personality Disorders, 24,* 412–426.

Trzepacz, P. T., Mittal, D., Torres, R., Kanary, K., Norton, J., & Jimerson, N. (2001). Validation of the Delirium Rating Scale-Revised–98: Comparison with the Delirium Rating Scale and the Cognitive Test for Delirium. *The Journal of Neuropsychiatry and Clinical Neurosciences, 13,* 229–242.

Tsai, J., Armour, C., Southwick, S. M., & Pietrzak, R. H. (2015). Dissociative subtype of *DSM-5* posttraumatic stress disorder in U.S. veterans. *Journal of Psychiatric Research, 66–67,* 67–74. doi:10.1016/j.jpsychires.2015.04.017

Tsuang, M. T., Stone, W. S., Faraone, S. V. (1999). Schizophrenia: A review of genetic studies. *Harvard Rev of Psychiatry, 7*(4), 185–207.

Turner, D., & Briken, P. (2018). Treatment of paraphilic disorders in sexual offenders or men with a risk of sexual offending with luteinizing hormone-releasing hormone agonists: An updated systematic review. *Journal of Sexual Medicine, 15*(1), 77–93. doi:10.1016/j.jsxm.2017.11.013

Turner, E. H., Matthews, A. M., Linardatos, E., Tell, R. A., & Rosenthal, R. (2008). Selective publication of antidepressant trials and its influence on apparent efficacy. *The New England Journal of Medicine, 358,* 252–260.

U

Uhl, G. R., Nautiyal, K. M., Okuda, M., Hen, R., & Blanco, C. (2017). Gambling disorder: An integrative review of animal and human studies. *Annals of the New York Academy of Sciences, 1394*(1), 106. doi:10.1111/nyas.13356

UK ECT Review Group. (2003). Efficacy and safety of electroconvulsive therapy in depressive disorders: A systematic review and meta-analysis. *The Lancet, 361,* 799–808.

Urry, E., & Landolt, H. (2015). Adenosine, caffeine, and performance: From cognitive neuroscience of sleep to sleep pharmacogenetics. In P. Meerlo, R. M. Benca & T. Abel (Eds.), *Sleep, neuronal plasticity and brain function* (pp. 331–366). New York: Springer-Verlag Publishing.

V

Vaidyanathan, U., Patrick, C. J., & Cuthbert, B. N. (2009). Linking dimensional models of internalizing psychopathology to neurobiological systems: Affect-modulated startle as an indicator of fear and distress disorders and affiliated traits. *Psychological Bulletin, 135,* 909–942.

Vaivre-Douret, L., Lalanne, C., Ingster-Moati, I., Boddaert, N., Cabrol, D., Dufier, J.-L., . . . Falissard, B. (2011). Subtypes of developmental coordination disorder: Research on their nature and etiology. *Developmental Neuropsychology, 36,* 614–643.

Valenzuela, F., Lock, J., Le Grange, D., & Bohon, C. (2018). Comorbid depressive symptoms and self-esteem improve after either cognitive-behavioural therapy or family-based treatment for adolescent bulimia nervosa. *European Eating Disorders Review, 26*(3), 253–258. doi:10.1002/erv.2582

Valleur, M., Codina, I., Venisse, J., Romo, L., Magalon, D., Fatseas, M., . . . Challet-Bouju, G. (2016). Towards a validation of the three pathways model of pathological gambling. *Journal of Gambling Studies, 32*(2), 757–771. doi:10.1007/s10899-015-9545-y

van den Boogaard, M., Slooter, A. C., Brüggemann, R. M., Schoonhoven, L., Beishuizen, A., Vermeijden, J. W., . . . Pickkers, P. (2018). Effect of haloperidol on survival among critically ill adults with a high risk of delirium: The REDUCE randomized clinical trial. *JAMA: Journal of the American Medical Association, 319*(7), 680–690. doi:10.1001/jama.2018.0160

van Haren, N. E. M., Schnack, H. G., Cahn, W., van den Heuvel, M. P., Lepage, C., Collins, L., . . . Kahn, R. S. (2011). Changes in cortical thickness during the course of schizophrenia. *Archives of General Psychiatry, 68,* 871–880.

van Hoeken, D., Veling, W., Sinke, S., Mitchell, J. E., & Hoek, H. W. (2009). The validity and utility of subtyping bulimia nervosa. *International Journal of Eating Disorders, 42,* 595–602.

van Nes, Y., Bloemers, J., van der Heijden, P. M., van Rooij, K., Gerritsen, J., Kessels, R., . . . Tuiten, A. (2017). The Sexual Event Diary (SED): Development and validation of a standardized questionnaire for assessing female sexual functioning during discrete sexual events. *Journal of Sexual Medicine, 14*(11), 1438–1450. doi:10.1016/j.jsxm.2017.09.008

van Os, J., Linscott, R. J., Myin-Germeys, I., Delespaul, P., & Krabbendam, L. (2009).

A systematic review and meta-analysis of the psychosis continuum: Evidence for a psychosis proneness-persistence-impairment model of psychotic disorder. *Psychological Medicine, 39,* 179–195.

Veale, D. & Roberts, A. (2014). Obsessive-compulsive disorder. *British Medical Journal,* 348:g2183. doi: 10.1136/bmj.g218

Vecchio, J., & Kearney, C. A. (2009). Treating youths with selective mutism with an alternating design of exposure-based practice and contingency management. *Behavior Therapy, 40,* 380–392.

Veling, W., Selten, J. P., Susser, E., Laan, W., Mackenbach, J. P., & Hoek, H. W. (2007). Discrimination and the incidence of psychotic disorders among ethnic minorities in the Netherlands. *International Journal of Epidemiology, 36,* 761–768.

Vergés, A., Jackson, K. M., Bucholz, K. K., Grant, J. D., Trull, T. J., Wood, P. K., & Sher, K. J. (2011). Deconstructing the age-prevalence curve of alcohol dependence: Why "maturing out" is only a small piece of the puzzle. *Journal of Abnormal Psychology, 121,* 511–523.

Vermeulen, J., van Rooijen, G., Doedens, P., Numminen, E., van Tricht, M., & de Haan, L. (2017). Antipsychotic medication and long-term mortality risk in patients with schizophrenia; a systematic review and meta-analysis. *Psychological Medicine, 47*(13), 2217–2228. doi:10.1017/S0033291717000873

Vissia, E. M., Giesen, M. E., Chalavi, S., Nijenhuis, E. S., Draijer, N., Brand, B. L., & Reinders, A. S. (2016). Is it trauma- or fantasy-based? Comparing dissociative identity disorder, post-traumatic stress disorder, simulators, and controls. *Acta Psychiatrica Scandinavica, 134*(2), 111–128. doi:10.1111/acps.12590

Volkmar, F. R., Klin, A., Schultz, R. T., Rubin, E., & Bronen, R. (2000). Asperger's disorder. *The American Journal of Psychiatry, 157,* 262–267.

Volkow, N. D., Wang, G.-J., Kollins, S. H., Wigal, T. L., Newcorn, J. H., Telang, F., . . . Swanson, J. M. (2009). Evaluating dopamine reward pathway in ADHD: Clinical implications. *JAMA: Journal of the American Medical Association, 302,* 1084–1091.

von Gontard, A. (2011). Elimination disorders: A critical comment on *DSM-5* proposals. *European Child & Adolescent Psychiatry, 20,* 83–88.

von Polier, G. G., Meng, H., Lambert, M., Strauss, M., Zarotti, G., Karle, M., . . . Schimmelmann, B. G. (2014). Patterns and correlates of expressed emotion, perceived criticism, and rearing style in first admitted early-onset schizophrenia spectrum disorders. *Journal of Nervous and Mental Disease, 202,* 783–787. doi:10.1097/NMD.0000000000000209

Vos, T., Flaxman, A. D., Naghavi, M., Lozano, R., Michaud, C., Ezzati, M., Shibuya, K., Salomon, J. A., Abdalla, S., Aboyans, V., et al. (2012). Years lived with disability (YLDs) for 1160 sequelae of 289 diseases and injuries 1990–2010: A systematic analysis for the Global Burden of Disease Study 2010. *Lancet, 380,* 2163–2196.

Vyas, N. S., Buchsbaum, M. S., Lehrer, D. S., Merrill, B. M., DeCastro, A., Doninger, N. A., . . . Mukherjee, J. (2017). D2/D3 dopamine receptor binding with [F-18] fallypride correlates of executive function in medication-naïve patients with schizophrenia. *Schizophrenia Research, 192,* 442–456. doi:10.1016/j.schres.2017.05.017

W

Wagner, G., De la Cruz, F., Schachtzabel, C., Güllmar, D., Schultz, C. C., Schlösser, R. G., & Koch, K. (2015). Structural and functional dysconnectivity of the fronto-thalamic system in schizophrenia: A DCM-DTI study. *Cortex: A Journal Devoted to the Study of the Nervous System and Behavior,* 6635–6645. doi:10.1016/j.cortex.2015.02.004

Wagner, S., Engel, A., Engelmann, J., Herzog, D., Dreimüller, N., Müller, M. B., . . . Lieb, K. (2017). Early improvement as a resilience signal predicting later remission to antidepressant treatment in patients with major depressive disorder: Systematic review and meta-analysis. *Journal of Psychiatric Research, 9496,* 106. doi:10.1016/j.jpsychires.2017.07.003

Walker, R. M., Sussmann, J. E., Whalley, H. C., Ryan, N. M., Porteous, D. J., McIntosh, A. M., & Evans, K. L. (2016). Preliminary assessment of pre-morbid DNA methylation in individuals at high genetic risk of mood disorders. *Bipolar Disorders, 18*(5), 410–422. doi:10.1111/bdi.12415

Walter, H., Ciaramidaro, A., Adenzato, M., Vasic, N., Ardito, R. B., Erk, S., & Bara, B. G. (2009). Dysfunction of the social brain in schizophrenia is modulated by intention type: An fMRI study. *Social Cognitive and Affective Neuroscience, 4,* 166–176. doi:10.1093/scan/nsn047

Walther, S., Stegmayer, K., Sulzbacher, J., Vanbellingen, T., Müri, R., Strik, W., & Bohlhalter, S. (2015). Nonverbal social communication and gesture control in schizophrenia. *Schizophrenia Bulletin, 41,* 338–345. doi:10.1093/schbul/sbu222

Walton, C., & Kerr, M. (2015). Down syndrome: Systematic review of the prevalence and nature of presentation of unipolar depression. *Advances in Mental Health and Intellectual Disabilities, 9*(4), 151–162. doi:10.1108/AMHID-11-2014-0037

Wang, M., & Kenny, S. (2014). Longitudinal links between fathers' and mothers' harsh verbal discipline and adolescents' conduct problems and depressive symptoms. *Child Development, 85,* 908–923. doi:10.1111/cdev.12143

Wang, S., Hsiao, P., Yeh, L., Liu, C., Liu, C., Hwang, T., . . . Chen, W. J. (2018). Polygenic risk for schizophrenia and neurocognitive performance in patients with schizophrenia. *Genes, Brain & Behavior, 17*(1), 49–55. doi:10.1111/gbb.12401

Wani, W. Y., Chatham, J. C., Darley-Usmar, V., McMahon, L. L., & Zhang, J. (2017). O-GlcNAcylation and neurodegeneration. *Brain Research Bulletin, 133,* 80–87. doi:10.1016/j.brainresbull.2016.08.002

Wardenaar, K. J., Lim, C. W., Al-Hamzawi, A. O., Alonso, J., Andrade, L. H., Benjet, C., . . . de Jonge, P. (2017). The cross-national epidemiology of specific phobia in the World Mental Health Surveys. *Psychological Medicine, 47*(10), 1744–1760. doi:10.1017/S0033291717000174

Watanabe, Y., Urakami, T., Hongo, S., & Ohtsubo, T. (2015). Frontal lobe function and social adjustment in patients with schizophrenia: Near-infrared spectroscopy. *Human Psychopharmacology: Clinical and Experimental, 30,* 28–41. doi:10.1002/hup.2448

Wattmo, C., Wallin, A. K., Londos, E., & Minthon, L. (2011). Long-term outcome and prediction models of activities of daily living in Alzheimer disease with cholinesterase inhibitor treatment. *Alzheimer Disease and Associated Disorders, 25,* 63–72.

Wechsler, D. (2002). *Wechsler preschool and primary scale of intelligence (WPPSI-III).* San Antonio, TX: Psychological Corporation.

Wechsler, D. (2003). *Wechsler intelligence scale for children-IV (WISC-IV).* San Antonio, TX: Psychological Corporation.

Wechsler, D. (2008). *Wechsler adult intelligence scale* (4th ed.). San Antonio, TX: Psychological Corporation.

Weiner, I. B., & Greene, R. L. (2008). *Handbook of personality assessment.* Hoboken, NJ: John Wiley & Sons, Inc.

Weiss, K. J., & Van Dell, L. (2017). Liability for diagnosing malingering. *Journal of the American Academy of Psychiatry and the Law, 45*(3), 339–347.

Weiss, M., & Murray, C. (2003). Assessment and management of attention-deficit hyperactivity disorder in adults. *Canadian Medical Association Journal, 168,* 715–722.

Weissman, M. M. (2007). Recent non-medication trials of interpersonal psychotherapy for depression. *International Journal of Neuropsychopharmacology, 10,* 117–122.

West, A. L. (2015). Associations among attachment style, burnout, and compassion fatigue in health and human service workers: A systematic review. *Journal of Human Behavior in the Social Environment, 25,* 571–590. doi:10.1080/10911359.2014.988321

Whitbourne, S. K., & Meeks, S. (2011). Psychopathology, bereavement, and aging. In K. W. Schaie & S. L. Willis (Eds.), *Handbook of the psychology of aging* (7th ed, pp. 311-324). London: Elsevier.

Whitbourne, S. K., & Whitbourne, S. B. (2017). *Adult development and aging: Biopsychosocial perspectives* (6th ed.). Hoboken, NJ: Wiley.

White, K. S., Brown, T. A., Somers, T. J., & Barlow, D. H. (2006). Avoidance behavior in panic disorder: The moderating influence of perceived control. *Behaviour Research and Therapy, 44,* 147-157.

Widiger, T. A., & Trull, T. J. (2007). Plate tectonics in the classification of personality disorder: Shifting to a dimensional model. *American Psychologist, 62,* 71-83.

Wiggins, L., Reynolds, A., Rice, C., Moody, E., Bernal, P., Blaskey, L., . . . Levy, S. (2015). Using standardized diagnostic instruments to classify children with autism in the Study to Explore Early Development. *Journal of Autism and Developmental Disorders, 45,* 1271-1280. doi:10.1007/s10803-014-2287-3

Wilcox, S. L., Redmond, S., & Davis, T. L. (2015). Genital image, sexual anxiety, and erectile dysfunction among young male military personnel. *Journal of Sexual Medicine, 12,* 1389-1397. doi:10.1111/jsm.12880

Wilens, T. E. (2011). A sobering fact: ADHD leads to substance abuse. *Journal of the American Academy of Child & Adolescent Psychiatry, 50,* 6-8. doi:10.1016/j.jaac.2010.10.002

Wilens, T. E., Faraone, S. V., & Biederman, J. (2004). Attention-deficit/hyperactivity disorder in adults. *JAMA: Journal of the American Medical Association, 292,* 619-623.

Wilens, T. E., Martelon, M., Joshi, G., Bateman, C., Fried, R., Petty, C., & Biederman, J. (2011). Does ADHD predict substance-use disorders? A 10-year follow-up study of young adults with ADHD. *Journal of the American Academy of Child & Adolescent Psychiatry, 50,* 543-553.

Wilhelm, S., Buhlmann, U., Hayward, L. C., Greenberg, J. L., & Dimaite, R. (2010). A cognitive-behavioral treatment approach for body dysmorphic disorder. *Cognitive and Behavioral Practice, 17,* 241-247.

Willhite, R. K., Niendam, T. A., Bearden, C. E., Zinberg, J., O'Brien, M. P., & Cannon, T. D. (2008). Gender differences in symptoms, functioning and social support in patients at ultra-high risk for developing a psychotic disorder. *Schizophrenia Research, 104,* 237-245.

Williams, D. E., Kirkpatrick-Sanchez, S., Enzinna, C., Dunn, J., & Borden-Karasack, D. (2009). The clinical management and prevention of pica: A retrospective follow-up of 41 individuals with intellectual disabilities and pica. *Journal of Applied Research in Intellectual Disabilities, 22,* 210-215.

Wilpert, J. (2018). Self-reported versus diagnosed paraphilias in outpatient sexual offenders. *Journal of Forensic Psychiatry & Psychology, 29*(2), 252-264. doi:10.1080/14789949.2017.1365156

Wilson, D. K. (2015). Behavior matters: The relevance, impact, and reach of behavioral medicine. *Annals of Behavioral Medicine, 49,* 40-48. doi:10.1007/s12160-014-9672-1

Wilson, G. T., Grilo, C. M., & Vitousek, K. M. (2007). Psychological treatment of eating disorders. *American Psychologist, 62,* 199-216.

Wilson, H. A. (2014). Can antisocial personality disorder be treated? A meta-analysis examining the effectiveness of treatment in reducing recidivism for individuals diagnosed with ASPD. *The International Journal of Forensic Mental Health, 13,* 36-46. doi:10.1080/14999013.2014.890682

Winsper, C., Marwaha, S., Lereya, S. T., Thompson, A., Eyden, J., & Singh, S. P. (2015). Clinical and psychosocial outcomes of borderline personality disorder in childhood and adolescence: A systematic review. *Psychological Medicine, 45,* 2237-2251. doi:10.1017/S0033291715000318

Wittchen, H. U., Gloster, A. T., Beesdo-Baum, K., Fava, G. A., & Craske, M. G. (2010). Agoraphobia: A review of the diagnostic classificatory position and criteria. *Depression and Anxiety, 27,* 113-133.

Witthoft, M., & Hiller, W. (2010). Psychological approaches to origins and treatments of somatoform disorders. *Annual Review of Clinical Psychology, 6,* 257-283.

Wonderlich, S. A., Gordon, K. H., Mitchell, J. E., Crosby, R. D., & Engel, S. G. (2009). The validity and clinical utility of binge eating disorder. *International Journal of Eating Disorders, 42,* 687-705.

World Health Organization. (2001). The world health report: Some common disorders. Retrieved from http://www.who.int/whr/2001/chapter2/en/index4.html

World Health Organization. (2011). Suicide rates per 100,000 by country, year and sex. Retrieved from http://www.who.int/gho/mental_health/suicide_rates/en/

World Health Organization. (2015). Fact sheet: Alcohol. http://www.who.int/mediacentre/factsheets/fs349/en/ Retrieved 4/12/2018.

World Health Organization. (2018). https://www.who.int/classifications/icd/revision/en/

Wright, S. (2010). Depathologizing consensual sexual sadism, sexual masochism, transvestic fetishism, and fetishism. *Archives of Sexual Behavior, 39,* 1229-1230.

Wright, S. (2014). Kinky parents and child custody: The effect of the *DSM-5* differentiation between the paraphilias and paraphilic disorders. *Archives of Sexual Behavior, 43,* 1257-1258. doi:10.1007/s10508-013-0250-6

Wu, Y. C., Zhao, Y. B., Tang, M. G., Zhang-Nunes, S. X., & McArthur, J. C. (2007). AIDS dementia complex in China. *Journal of Clinical Neuroscience, 14,* 8-11.

Wurtele, S. K., Simons, D. A., & Moreno, T. (2014). Sexual interest in children among an online sample of men and women: Prevalence and correlates. *Sexual Abuse: Journal of Research and Treatment, 26,* 546-568. doi:10.1177/1079063213503688

Wyatt v. Stickney. (1971). 325 F. Supp. 781 (M.D. Ala.); (1972) 344 F. Supp. (M.D. Ala.)

Wykes, T., Steel, C., Everitt, B., & Tarrier, N. (2008). Cognitive behavior therapy for schizophrenia: Effect sizes, clinical models, and methodological rigor. *Schizophr Bulletin, 34,* 523-537.

Y

Yalch, M. M., Hebenstreit, C. L., & Maguen, S. (2018). Influence of military sexual assault and other military stressors on substance use disorder and PTS symptomology in female military veterans. *Addictive Behaviors, 80,* 28-33. doi:10.1016/j.addbeh.2017.12.026

Yam, W. H., & Simms, L. J. (2014). Comparing criterion- and trait-based personality disorder diagnoses in *DSM-5. Journal of Abnormal Psychology, 123,* 802-808. doi:10.1037/a0037633

Young, R. M., Connor, J. P., & Feeney, G. F. X. (2011). Alcohol expectancy changes over a 12-week cognitive-behavioral therapy program are predictive of treatment success. *Journal of Substance Abuse Treatment, 40,* 18-25.

Youngberg v. Romeo. (1982). 457 U.S. 307.

Yovita, M., & Asih, S. R. (2018). The effects of academic stress and optimism on subjective well-being among first-year undergraduates. In A. A. Ariyanto, H. Muluk, P. Newcombe, F. P. Piercy, E. K. Poerwandari & S. R. Suradijono (Eds.), *Diversity in unity: Perspectives from psychology and behavioral sciences* (pp. 559-563). New York: Routledge/Taylor & Francis Group.

Yrondi, A., Péran, P., Sauvaget, A., Schmitt, L., & Arbus, C. (2018). Structural-functional brain changes in depressed patients during and after electroconvulsive therapy. *Acta Neuropsychiatrica, 30*(1), 17-28. doi:10.1017/neu.2016.62

Z

Zhang, J., & Wheeler, J. J. (2011). A meta-analysis of peer-mediated interventions for young children with autism spectrum disorders. *Education and Training in Autism and Developmental Disabilities, 46,* 62-77.

Zhao, T., Wei, B., Long, J., Tang, X., Zhou, M., & Dang, C. (2015). Cognitive disorders in HIV-infected and AIDS patients in Guangxi, China. *Journal of Neurovirology, 21,* 32-42. doi:10.1007/s13365-014-0295-x

Zivanovic, O. (2017). Lithium: A classic drug—frequently discussed, but, sadly, seldom prescribed! *Australian and New Zealand Journal of Psychiatry, 51*(9), 886–896. doi:10.1177/0004867417695889

Zubin, J., & Spring, B. (1977). Vulnerability: A new view of schizophrenia. *Journal of Abnormal Psychology, 86,* 103–126.

Zuchner, S., Wendland, J. R., Ashley-Koch, A. E., Collins, A. L., Tran-Viet, K. N., Quinn, K., . . . Murphy, D. L. (2009). Multiple rare SAPAP3 missense variants in trichotillomania and OCD. *Molecular Psychiatry, 14,* 6–9.

Zucker, R. A., & Gomberg, E. S. (1986). Etiology of alcoholism reconsidered: The case for a biopsychosocial process. *American Psychologist, 41,* 783–793.

Zugliani, M. M., Martin-Santos, R., Nardi, A. E., & Freire, R. C. (2017). Personality traits in panic disorder patients with and without comorbidities. *Journal of Nervous and Mental Disease, 205*(11), 855–858. doi:10.1097/NMD.0000000000000745

Zygouris, S., & Tsolaki, M. (2015). Computerized cognitive testing for older adults: A review. *American Journal of Alzheimer's Disease and Other Dementias, 30*(1), 13–28. doi:10.1177/1533317514522852

NAME INDEX

A

Aarsland, D., 333
Abdalla, S., 173
Abé, C., 180
Abelson, J. F., 214
Aboujaoude, E., 263
Aboyans, V., 173
Abraham, K., 184
Abrahamson, E. E., 346
Abram, S. V., 157
Abrutyn, S., 190
Accurso, E. C., 254
Achterhof, R., 220
Adami, M., 339
Adams, C. E., 151
Adams, H. A., 68
Adan, R. H., 253
Adenzato, M., 157
Adler, Alfred, 91
Adler, L., 133
Adler, L. A., 134
Adriani, W., 137
Agrawal, A., 302
Aguera, L., 339
Ahern, J., 304
Ahrberg, M., 253
Ainsworth, Mary Salter, 92
Aizenstein, H., 339
Akehurst, S., 366
Akyuz, G., 234
Alegría, M., 9
Alexander, G. C., 390
Al-Hamzawi, A. O., 199
Alho, H., 253
Aliane, V., 140
Alisic, E., 136
Alonso, J., 197, 199
Alpert, H. R., 319
Alpert, J. E., 182
Altarac, M., 129
Altunoz, U., 206
Álvarez, A., 70
Alzheimer, A., 331–332
Alzheimer's Association, 333
Alzheimer's Disease and Related
    Diseases Association,
    334–335
American Association of
    Intellectual and
    Developmental Disabilities
    (AAIDD), 115
American Board of Professional
    Psychology (ABPP),
    379–380
American Psychiatric
    Association, 4, 15, 32–33,
    68, 157
American Psychological
    Association, 70, 220, 289,
    376–377, 379–384, 387
American Psychological
    Association Presidential
    Task Force on
    Evidence-Based
    Practice, 44

Amir, O., 131
Amsel, R., 284
Andersen, P. K., 178, 183
Andershed, H., 262
Anderson, E., 216
Anderson, I. M., 186
Anderson, M. L., 37, 253
Anderson, T., 369
Andrade, L. H., 199
Andreasen, N. C., 158
Andreassen, O. A., 161
Andresen, B., 312–313
Andrews, G., 233
Andrews, L. A., 209
Andrews-Hanna, J. R., 180
Andronikos, R., 25
Anton, R. F., 304
Antony, M. M., 203
Apodaca, T. R., 101
Araga, M., 179
Arbus, C., 184
Arcelus, J., 290
Arch, J. J., 206
Ardito, R. B., 157
Arheart, K. L., 73
Arias, A. J., 302–303, 317, 319
Arias, E., 188
Aritomi, Y., 180
Arlidge, J., 260
Armey, M., 252
Armour, C., 231
Arndt, L., 151
Arnold, L. E., 136
Arnold, S. E., 335
Arntz, A., 188
Arria, A. M., 315
Arvilommi, P., 178
Asarnow, J. R., 190
Ashford, J. W., 117
Ashley-Koch, A. E., 214
Asih, S. R., 240
Asperger, Hans, 126
Assumpção, A. A., 280
Atkins, D. C., 363
Attems, J., 333
Auster, T. L., 357
Austin, A., 289–290
Austrom, M. G., 340
Ayers, C. R., 213
Azar, M., 17

B

Babcock, T., 137
Bach, B., 355
Bachman, J. G., 317
Bader, S. M., 274
Baek, D. Y., 214
Baer, L., 182, 215
Baer, R. A., 106, 107
Bagby, R. M., 357
Baguley, I. J., 345
Bahar, R. J., 256
Bailey, C., 120
Bailey, D., 119
Bailin, A., 44

Bajaj, K., 118
Balaratnasingam, S., 357
Ball, T. M., 206
Ballard, C., 333
Baltuch, G. H., 85
Bamond, M. J., 125
Bandura, Albert, 15, 97
Banerjee, P., 117
Bannerman, D., 233
Bara, B. G., 157
Barbaree, H. E., 272
Barberger-Gateau, P., 339
Barch, D. M., 157
Barco, A., 116
Barkley, R. A., 133–134, 135, 138
Barlow, D. H., 204
Barnes, L. L., 335
Barnum, P. T., 53
Barr, W. B., 70
Barram, R. A., 57
Barrantes-Vidal, N., 154
Barrett, J. E., 174
Barsky, A. E., 383
Bartol, A. M., 395
Bartol, C. R., 395
Baruffi, S. A., 358
Basena, M., 273
Basson, R., 280
Bastiaansen, L., 88
Bastug, G., 206
Batchelor, J., 345
Bateman, A., 363
Bateman, C., 132
Battaglioli, E., 116
Battista, D. R., 259
Bauermeister, J. J., 261
Baugh, C. M., 345
Bayless, S. J., 303
Bearden, C. E., 154
Bearman, S. K., 44
Bechara, A., 303
Beck, A. T., 15, 98, 185, 370
Becker, A. E., 256
Becker, J. T., 339
Becker, K. A., 271
Beckman, S., 135
Bedics, J. D., 363
Beekman, A. F., 174
Beesdo-Baum, K., 199, 204
Beethoven, Ludwig van, 66
Behary, W. T., 366
Beidel, D. C., 203
Bell, J., 344, 345
Belleau, E. L., 216
Bemporad, J. R., 184
Benavides, K. L., 215
Bender, D. S., 355
Benesch, C., 259
Benito, C., 157
Benjet, C., 199
Bennett, D., 120
Bennett, D. A., 335
Bennett, S. M., 198
Benning, S. D., 358
Benotsch, E. G., 233
Ben-Porath, Y., 62

Benson, K. E., 286
Benyamini, Y., 252
Berg, J., 358
Berger, L., 316
Berger, W., 219
Bergeron, S., 286, 288
Berglund, P., 174, 178, 202, 206,
    207, 218
Bergman, H., 151
Bergmann, M. A., 330
Berk-Pawlitzek, E., 259
Berlin, F. S., 273
Berlin, G. S., 216
Berman, M. E., 260
Bernal, P., 123
Bernecker, S. L., 93
Berrettini, W., 180
Bertrand, J., 120
Berube, N. G., 116
Besser, A., 365
Beutel, M. E., 322
Beyer, K. M., 242
Bezborodoys, N., 6
Biederman, J., 132, 133, 134
Biener, L., 319
Binet, Alfred, 57
Binik, Y. M., 284
Birbaumer, N., 123
Birkenaes, A. B., 161
Bjornsson, A. S., 212, 213
Blanchard, R., 272, 276
Blanco, C., 320
Blanqué, J. M., 154
Blashfield, R. K., 365
Blaskey, L., 123
Bleich, S., 302
Bleuler, Eugene, 150–151
Bloemers, J., 281
Bobbitt, Lorena, 394
Bock, T., 166
Bockting, W., 289
Boddaert, N., 129, 138
Bodzin, D. K., 214
Boe, H. J., 218
Boeckle, M., 234
Boettger, S., 331
Bohlhalter, S., 162
Bohon, C., 254
Bohren, Y., 140
Bölte, S., 123
Bomyea, J., 206
Bond, K., 186
Bonifacci, P., 129
Bono, Chaz, 289
Borden-Karasack, D., 255
Borkovec, T. D., 206
Borlongan, C. V., 121
Borsari, B., 101
Bosch, Hieronymus, 11
Both, S., 285, 286, 288
Botzer, M., 289
Bouman, W. P., 290
Boustani, M. A., 340
Bowden, C. L., 187
Bowlby, J., 92, 184
Boyer, S., 284

Vermeulen, J., 154
Vermeulen, N., 251
Vertrees, J. E., 219
Vessicchio, J. C., 219
Vicente, B., 218
Vik-Mo, H., 232
Vilardaga, J. C. P., 206
Vincent, K. B., 315
Vinogradov, S., 163, 164
Virkkunen, M., 262
Vissia, E. M., 229
Vocks, S., 253
Vogel, P. A., 209, 216
Volberg, R., 319
Volkmar, F. R., 128
Volkow, N. D., 134
von Gontard, A., 256
von Polier, G. G., 164
Voon, V., 253
Voorhoeve, E., 117
Vos, T., 173
Vradi, E., 178
Vyas, N. S., 158
Vythilingam, M., 220

W

Wadkins, M., 44
Wager, T. D., 180
Wagner, G., 157
Wagner, S., 46
Waite, L. J., 282
Waldman, I., 136
Walker, Herschel, 228–229
Walker, R. M., 179
Wallin, A. K., 339
Walsh, B. T., 256
Walter, H., 157
Walters, E. E., 174, 178, 197, 199, 202, 206, 207, 218
Walters, K., 178
Walther, S., 162
Walton, C., 117
Wan, C. R., 162
Wang, C., 183
Wang, G., 147
Wang, G.-J., 134
Wang, J., 134
Wang, L., 157
Wang, M., 261
Wang, N., 163
Wang, P., 320
Wang, S., 158
Wang, X., 163
Wang, W. Y., 339
Wani, W. Y., 339
Waranch, R., 140
Wardell, J. D., 302
Wardenaar, K. J., 199

Warnich, L., 83
Wartberg, L., 312–313
Wasserman, R. H., 363
Watanabe, Y., 157
Waters, F., 1
Watson, C. H., 315
Watson, D., 209, 220
Watson, John B., 15
Wattmo, C., 339
Webdale, Kendra, 388
Weber, M. K., 120
Wechsler, David, 57
Wegener, I., 302
Wei, B., 346
Weiner, I. B., 67–68
Weinstein, Y., 356, 365
Weishaar, M., 185
Weiss, K. J., 234
Weiss, M., 133
Weissman, M. M., 187, 188
Weizman, A., 164
Welge, J. A., 188
Welham, J., 165
Wells, A., 209
Wendland, J. R., 214
Wertenberger, E. G., 190
Wertheim, E. H., 240
Wessely, S. C., 235
West, A. L., 241
Whalley, H. C., 179
Wheeler, J. J., 125
Whitbourne, S. B., 332, 333
Whitbourne, S. K., 10, 315, 332, 333
White, D. A., 117
White, K. S., 204
Whitton, S. W., 188
Whynott, R., 253
Wickramaratne, P., 188
Widiger, T. A., 354
Wiederman, M. W., 362
Wigal, T. L., 134
Wiggins, L., 123
Wilberg, T., 357
Wilcox, S. L., 286
Wilder, C. M., 388
Wilens, T. E., 132, 134
Wilfley, D. E., 254
Wilhelm, S., 213
Wilkinson, D., 333
Willeit, M., 184
Willer, E. K., 241
Willhite, R. K., 154
Williams, D. E., 255
Williams, J. M. G., 197
Williams, J. W., Jr., 174
Williams, L. J., 186
Williams, T. J., 303

Wilpert, J., 273
Wilson, D. K., 242
Wilson, G. T., 252
Wilson, H. A., 358
Wilson, K. G., 106
Wilson, R. S., 335
Windle, M., 305
Wing, L. F., 137
Winkler, D., 184
Winnicott, D. W., 92
Winsper, C., 362
Winter, L., 106
Winters, K. C., 319
Wirick, D., 261
Wisner, K. M., 157
Wisniewski, S., 179
Wisniewski, S. R., 178
Wissussek, C. S., 302
Wisting, L., 255
Witcraft, S. M., 209
Wittchen, H., 173
Wittchen, H. U., 199, 203, 204
Witthoft, M., 236
Witzel, B., 135
Wolf, J. P., 220
Wolfe, H. M., 25
Wölfling, K., 322
Wolkowitz, O. M., 186
Wolpe, Joseph, 96
Wonderlich, S. A., 255
Wong, J. W., 125
Wong, S., 233
Wong, S. L., 125
Wood, A. M., 190
Wood, P. K., 300, 353
Woods, D. W., 214, 216
World Health Organization, 20, 34, 35, 36, 189, 300, 332
World Professional Association for Transgender Health, 289
Worley, C., 361
Wright, B. J., 240
Wright, S., 277
Wu, P., 198
Wu, R., 303
Wu, Y. C., 346
Wurtele, S. K., 273
Wyatt, Rickey, 389
Wykes, T., 163

X

Xiao, C., 180
Xie, B., 134
Xu, J. Q., 188
Xu, L., 344, 345
Xu, Z., 163

Y

Yalch, M. M., 218
Yalom, Irvin, 103, 104
Yam, W. H., 355
Yang, T. T., 186
Yap, K., 213
Yates, Andrea, 394
Ye, Z., 134
Yeh, L., 158
Yeomans, F. E., 363, 366
Ýlvarez, E., 249
Young, R. M., 303
Young, S. E., 261
Young-McCaughan, S., 190
Youssef, G. J., 129
Yovel, I., 368
Yovita, M., 240
Yrondi, A., 184
Yu, M., 180
Yuan, J., 285
Yuan, V. N., 125
Yurgelun-Todd, D., 310

Z

Zagrabbe, K., 215
Zai, D., 200
Zapletalova, P., 312–313
Zarotti, G., 164
Zaslavsky, A. M., 133, 173
Zeanah, C. H., 217
Zhang, D., 147
Zhang, H., 178, 303
Zhang, J., 125, 339
Zhang, Z., 180
Zhang-Nunes, S. X., 346
Zhao, J., 180
Zhao, T., 346
Zhao, Y. B., 346
Zhou, M., 346
Zhou, Z., 116
Ziedonis, D. M., 37
Zieldorff, C., 197
Ziemnik, R., 315
Zinberg, J., 154
Zivanovic, O., 183
Zonderman, A. B., 332, 335
Zubin, J., 82
Zuchner, S., 214
Zucker, R. A., 305
Zugliani, M. M., 204
Zweben, A., 304
Zwiers, M. P., 338
Zygouris, S., 72
Zyzanski, J., 241

SUBJECT INDEX

Bold locators indicate definitions of terms.

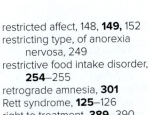